D1539171

r Theological Semin:

PAUL, MINNESOTA

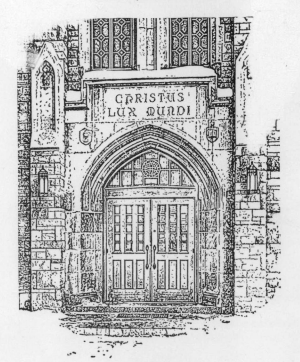

EX LIBRIS

6

Accent and Rhythm

*Prosodic Features of Latin and Greek:
a Study in Theory and Reconstruction*

CAMBRIDGE STUDIES IN LINGUISTICS

General Editors · W. SIDNEY ALLEN · EUGENIE J. A. HENDERSON
FRED W. HOUSEHOLDER · JOHN LYONS · R. B. LE PAGE
F. R. PALMER · J. L. M. TRIM

1   DAVID CRYSTAL: *Prosodic systems and intonation in English*
2   PIETER A. M. SEUREN: *Operators and nucleus*
3   RODNEY D. HUDDLESTON: *The sentence in written English*
4   JOHN M. ANDERSON: *The grammar of case*
5   M. L. SAMUELS: *Linguistic evolution*
6   P. H. MATTHEWS: *Inflectional morphology*
7   GILLIAN BROWN: *Phonological rules and dialect variation*
8   BRIAN NEWTON: *The generative interpretation of dialect*
9   R. M. W. DIXON: *The Dyirbal language of North Queensland*
10 BRUCE L. DERWING: *Transformational grammar as a theory of language acquisition*
11 MELISSA F. BOWERMAN: *Early syntactic development*
12 W. SIDNEY ALLEN: *Accent and rhythm*
13 PETER TRUDGILL: *The social differentiation of English in Norwich*

ACCENT AND RHYTHM

PROSODIC FEATURES OF
LATIN AND GREEK:
A STUDY IN THEORY AND
RECONSTRUCTION

W. SIDNEY ALLEN

Professor of Comparative Philology
University of Cambridge

CAMBRIDGE

at the University Press · 1973

Published by the Syndics of the Cambridge University Press
Bentley House, 200 Euston Road, London NW1 2DB
American Branch: 32 East 57th Street, New York, N.Y.10022

© Cambridge University Press 1973

PA185
A5

Library of Congress Catalogue Card Number: 72–91361

ISBN: 0 521 20098 9

Printed in Great Britain
at the University Printing House, Cambridge
(Brooke Crutchley, University Printer)

Contents

Preface   *page* xi
General symbolic conventions   xiii

PART I: THE GENERAL AND THEORETICAL BACKGROUND

1   'Prosody' and 'prosodies': the historical setting   3

2   Grammatical considerations   17

3   The Syllable; Vowels and Consonants   27
    Phonological approaches   27
        Syllabification   28
            Ancient theories   29
    Phonetic approaches   30
        Segmental vs contextual criteria   35
        Respiratory theory   38
        Acoustic theory   38
        Articulatory theory   39
        Motor theory   40

4   Length and Quantity   46
    Vowel length   46
        Qualitative factors   46
        Time ratios   48
        Non-temporal approaches   49
    Consonant length   49
    Syllabic quantity   50
        $\breve{V}C = \bar{V}$ (vs $\breve{V}$)   51
        Heavy ('long') vs light ('short')   53
        Pre-pausal $\breve{V}C$ 55
        Time ratios   56
    A motor approach   62
        Vowel length in motor terms   62
        Syllabic quantity in motor terms   64
            Summary of motor definitions   65

[v]

97192

Hypercharacterization   *page* 66
Pre-pausal V̆C again   67
Syllabification again   68
Complex elements   69

5   Stress   74

6   Pitch   83

7   Accent   86

8   Rhythm   96

9   Metre   103
    Stylization   103
    Poetic levels   104
    Rules and variations   106
        Tension   110
    Line and colon; caesura and enjambment   113
    The foot   122

PART II: THE PROSODIES OF LATIN

10   Syllable structure; Quantity and Length   129
     ∼VCV∼ and ∼V̆CCV∼ (general)   129
     Quantity of pre-pausal ∼V̆C   130
     Vowel length   131
     Complex pausal releases and arrests   135
     ∼V̆CC(C)V∼ (non-pausal sequences)   135
                  (pre-pausal sequences)   136
                  (post-pausal sequences)   136
        (a) non-junctural: 137
            1. *s*+plosive   137
            2. Plosive (and *f*)+liquid   137
        (b) junctural: 139
            1. *s*+plosive (and /w/)   139
            2. Plosive+liquid   140
            3. *f*+liquid   141
     Hypercharacterization   141

11   Word juncture (∼V+V∼)   142

12   Accent   *page* 151

    (a) Typology   151

    (b) Incidence   155

        Reformulation of rules   161

        Accentual matrices   163

        Disyllabic stress   170

        Iambic shortening   179

        Staccato stress   185

        End-stress   186

        Secondary stress   188

  Excursus A: Iambic shortening and staccato stress
                in English   191

PART III: THE PROSODIES OF GREEK

13   Syllable structure; Quantity and Length   203

    ~ VCV ~ and ~ V̆CCV ~ (general)   203

    Quantity of pre-pausal ~ V̆C   204

    Vowel length   207

    Complex pausal releases and arrests   208

    ~ V̆CC(C)V ~ (non-pausal sequences)   208

                    (pre-pausal sequences)   209

                    (post-pausal sequences)   210

      (a) non-junctural: 210

        1. General   210

        2. Plosive + liquid or nasal   210

        3. Other special sequences   213

      (b) junctural: 216

        1. General   216

        2. Plosive + liquid or nasal   217

        3. Other sequences with liquid or nasal   218

        4. Sequences with semivowel   220

    Hypercharacterization   222

14   Word juncture (~ V + V ~)   224

15   Accent   230

    (a) Typology   230

        Musical evidence   231

        The 'contonation'   234

        The mora   235

(b) Incidence   *page* 236
    Limiting rules   236
    Enclitics   240
    Synenclisis   244
    The grave accent-mark   244
    Intonation; Enclitics (and proclitics) again   248
    Interrogatives   251
    The 'middle' accent   253

Excursus B: The equivalence of one heavy to two light
    syllables in Greek hexameters   255

16 Stress   260
  (a) Accentually related stress   260
    (1) Classical correlations   260
    (2) Post-classical correlations   264
    (3) The dynamic accent   268
  Excursus C: The Anglo-Dutch tradition   271
  (b) Non-accentual stress   274
    Evidence (1) metre (a priori)   275
    Evidence (2) music   278
    Evidence (3) metre (a posteriori)   279
  Previous approaches to the problem   280
  A new approach   283
    (i) Heavy syllables   284
      The hexameter   286
      A tentative conclusion   292
      Final $\sim\breve{V}C$ 295
  Excursus D: The principle of 'indifference'   296
    The iambic trimeter   304
      Porson's Law   304
      The caesura   313
    The trochaic tetrameter   314
    Lyric metres; anapaests   314
    (ii) Light syllables; resolution   316
      Disyllabic stress   318
      First feet   327
      Anapaestic substitution   330
  Summary of stress-rules   333

APPENDIX. THE LATIN HEXAMETER   *page* 335

Editions of ancient western grammatical and technical works   360

List of modern works cited   361

Index   391

Accentus est quasi anima uocis

POMPEIUS, *Comm. Artis Donati*, v, 126 K

Τῇ δὴ τῆς κινήσεως τάξει ῥυθμὸς ὄνομα

PLATO, *Laws* ii 665

Preface

The general field of study to which the title of this book refers has increasingly engaged my attention in the last few years, and has provided the subjects of articles in journals and chapters of books. It was recently suggested to me that a useful purpose might be served by bringing this material together into a single volume of reprints. But the more I considered this proposal, the less desirable did it appear. For one thing, the various items had been written with varying aims and readers in mind, so that the texture of such a collection would be very uneven. For another, my views on several matters had developed and changed over the years, so that, to ensure coherence, it would be necessary to append a number of additional footnotes, preambles, and postscripts to most of the items. And thirdly, the basic trend of development was from specific, 'data-orientated' studies towards more general principles; whilst such a presentation of one's work would no doubt reveal something of the author's thought-processes, it is not to be expected that this would be of any public interest.

It seemed, therefore, that I might perform a more useful service for potential readers by writing a completely new book, incorporating the essence of various previous publications (with consequently rather frequent references to these),[1] but inverting the whole order of treatment – beginning, that is, with discussion of the underlying concepts and general principles (as I envisaged them at the time of writing), which would then be applied to the description and elucidation of the particular language phenomena. At the same time an opportunity would be offered of providing a fuller and more up-to-date survey of the views of other writers, which might be of particular usefulness in the case of the general, theoretical first part, which covers a rather wide range of subjects and publications.

In two recent books devoted to the phonetics of the classical languages (A 1965; 1968a) attention was directed primarily to the phonematic vowel and consonant segments, with mostly incidental and *ad hoc*

---

[1] The author's name is abbreviated throughout to A.

discussion of some of the more extensional, 'suprasegmental' features such as length, quantity, accent, and juncture. The present book is concerned almost exclusively with these latter types of phenomena; its general scope is indicated by the main title, but will be made more precise in the course of the introductory chapters. The term 'rhythm' in particular is liable to a wide variety of interpretations; already in the 4 c. A.D. a writer on music, replying to the question, 'What is Rhythm?', could cite the differing views of half-a-dozen authorities;[1] and in recent times the usages of the term have been estimated at around fifty.[2] Whilst this very breadth of meaning makes it useful as a title, it will (after some discussion in Ch. 8) be discarded in favour of more specific terms. The term 'prosodic', which appears in the sub-title, will form the subject of a special study in Ch. 1.

It is hoped that the application of recent research and of observations on phonetically accessible, living languages will do much to elucidate certain features of the 'dead' languages with which Parts II and III are primarily concerned. But conversely it is possible that abstract models set up to account for ancient phenomena may prove to have some relevance to modern languages, including English, and may even lead to the observation of hitherto unsuspected features in the latter. One particular case of this kind forms the subject of a separate excursus in Part II.

I am grateful to Mr R. G. G. Coleman for his careful reading of a long and often difficult typescript and for thereby saving me from a number of infelicities of statement and expression: for those that remain I alone am culpable.

CAMBRIDGE   W.S.A.

June 1972

---

[1] Baccheius, ap. Jan 1895, 313.
[2] de Groot 1932, 82.

General symbolic conventions

(Special conventions are described in the relevant pages)

$\sim$ = omission of irrelevant items

C = consonant

V ($\breve{V}$, $\bar{V}$) = vowel (short, long)

Σ ($\underset{\smile}{\Sigma}$, $\underline{\Sigma}$) = syllable (light, heavy)

$\underset{\smile}{V}$, $\underline{V}$ = vowel in light, heavy syllable

$\breve{\Sigma}$, $\bar{\Sigma}$ = syllable containing short, long vowel

$(C)V^+(C)$ = syllable with thoracic (chest) arrest

$(C)V^{\circ}(C)$ = syllable without thoracic (chest) arrest

/ / = phonemic statement

[ ] = phonetic statement

{ } = morphemic statement

aa, etc. = long vowel (in phonetic and phonemic statements)

- = grammatical boundary (within word)

. = syllabic boundary

, = word boundary (where not indicated by space)

| = foot boundary

‖ = metron boundary

‖‖ = line boundary

: = colon boundary (caesura or diaeresis)

I ... VI = 1st ... 6th foot

a = first element of foot

b = second element of foot

a_1/b_1, a_2/b_2 = first, second syllable of disyllabic element (e.g. 'word division at IVb_1' of hexameter = after trochaic portion of dactylic 4th foot)

References

Unless otherwise indicated, numerals refer to pages.

Numerals preceded by p. indicate internal cross-references to pages of this book.

Details of works cited are given in the list on pp. 361 ff.

Where two authors have the same surname, one is asterisked in citations and list.

If one work of any author is frequently cited in a chapter, the date is omitted after the first citation and this date is printed in bold-face in the list.

Part I

THE GENERAL AND THEORETICAL
BACKGROUND

I   'Prosody' and 'prosodies': the historical setting

In its earliest linguistic use the Greek term προσῳδία has a clear and limited meaning; as its etymology would indicate, it signifies a 'tune' to which speech is intoned, and more particularly the melodic accent which characterized each full word in ancient Greek. Such accentuation was appropriately so termed 'quia προσᾴδεται ταῖς συλλαβαῖς', as a Latin grammarian was later to observe.[1] In this sense the term was well established by the time of Aristotle; and the Latin *accentus* is clearly a calque based on the specifically accentual meaning of the Greek.

There is no unambiguous evidence for any further innovation of meaning by Aristotle,[2] though he continues to employ the term also in its more generalized sense of the intonation of longer stretches of utterance. At a later date, however, the term came to be extended to certain other features which, like the accent, were not accounted for by the segmental analysis of speech into vowel and consonant phonemes (στοιχεῖα) – in the first instance to aspiration and vowel length. These features had indeed been mentioned by Aristotle alongside accentual categories (*Poet.* 1456b), but clearly set apart from these as they are from the phonematic elements. This extension of meaning is perhaps to be traced to Dionysius Thrax (2 c. B.C.),[3] and was certainly well established by the time of Herodian (2 c. A.D.); indeed already in Varro (1 c. B.C.) we find an eloquent if imaginative rationalization of this grouping of aspiration and length with pitch, as three 'dimensions' of the 'body' of speech:[4]

[1] Diomedes, i, 431 K.
[2] Laum 1928, 21. At *Soph. El.* 177b Aristotle mentions ὅρος as being distinguished by προσῳδία from, according to the texts, ὅρος (with a difference of 'breathing'). But Uhlig (1883, 171) comments, 'dubito an ita corrigendus sit ut ὅρος mutetur in ὁρός', which would involve only an accentual distinction; and in fact at *Schol. in D. Thr.* 171 H this specific contrast is cited ('τὸ ὑδατῶδες τοῦ γάλακτος'); cf. also Margoliouth 1911, 329.
[3] Laum 1928, 25 f.
[4] Ed. Goetz & Schoell, Frag. 76.

Scire oportet uocem sicut omne corpus tris habere distantias: altitudinem ciassitudinem ⟨longitudinem⟩. longitudinem tempore ac syllabis metimur: nam et quantum ⟨m⟩or⟨a⟩e enuntiandis uerbis teratur et quanto numero modoque syllabarum unum quodque si⟨t⟩ uerbum, plurimum refert. ab altitudine discernit accentus, cum pars uerbi aut in graue deprimitur aut sublimatur in acutum. crassitudo autem in spiritu est, unde etiam Graeci aspirationem appellant ⟨δασεῖαν et ψιλήν⟩; nam omnes uoces aut aspirando facimus pinguiores aut sine aspiratu pronuntiando tenuiores.

It is not surprising that Greek grammarians should have taken note of these particular features, since, although they were all potentially distinctive in the language (as e.g. δῆμος vs δημός, εἴην vs εἴην, λῐπαρῶς vs λῑπαρῶς), they were not normally indicated in writing in classical times, apart from the length distinctions inherent in some of the vowel symbols (short ε, o vs long η, ω, ει, ου) and aspiration in combination with plosive consonants (φ, θ, χ vs π, τ, κ). In Alexandrian times, as knowledge of the earlier language declined, and as Greek came to be taught as a foreign language, the need was felt for marking such features in classical texts in cases where ambiguity might otherwise result (πρὸς διαστολὴν τῆς ἀμφιβόλου λέξεως), and the name of Aristophanes of Byzantium is traditionally associated with the introduction of the relevant symbols (the accent signs, the *longum* and *breve*, and the 'rough' and 'smooth' breathings). At the same time symbols were also introduced to remove ambiguity regarding word boundaries in continuously written texts – the apostrophe to indicate elision, the comma to indicate division between words, and the ligature (ὑφέν) to indicate continuity, more particularly in compound words: thus, for example, καθ'ημων (vs καθημαι), ηλθε,νηπιος (vs ηλθεν,ηπιος), μεγαλητορα (vs μεγαλη,τομη).

By about 300 A.D. it seems that the term προσῳδία had come to be applied not only to the original prosody of pitch, and the two other *intra*-word 'prosodies' of aspiration and length, but also (like 'accent' in current usage) to the marks which indicated these features, and thence by extension to the *inter*-word marks of juncture or disjuncture.[1] This later extension was at first recognized as being 'by misuse' (καταχρηστικῶς), but by the time of Theodosius (*c.* 400 A.D.) it was fully inte-

---

[1] Uhlig 1883, 170 f: 'ita ut προσῳδίας notione omnia comprehendantur quae in pronuntiandis vocibus praeter ea quae litteris exprimuntur observanda sunt: tenores, productio aut correptio vocalium ancipitum, spiritus, synaloephe duarum vocum quae prioris vocali finali elisa efficitur, coniunctio syllabarum in unam vocem, disiunctio in plures.'

grated into the meaning of προσῳδία;[1] and the extension could be justified to the extent that even these junctural signs were relevant to the original prosody, in that they served to indicate whether or not a particular sequence was to be spoken with a single word-accent (ἕνωσις τοῦ τόνου).[2]

There was also an extension in the use of the signs of accent and aspiration to all occurrences of these features, and not simply for cases of potential ambiguity;[3] and with this extension came a blurring of the functional distinction between 'prosodic' signs and the marks of punctuation, which served as guides to pause and intonation in reading (πρὸς τὸ βέλτιον παρασκευάσασθαι τὴν ἀνάγνωσιν); even these latter features, however, could be considered as 'prosodies' of the clause or sentence, comparable with the more traditional prosodies of the word.

Such, then, was the situation by Byzantine times; and no further developments are to be observed until the Renaissance. Then (in England beginning in the 15 c.) the word 'prosody' reappears with a characteristically new reference. It denotes a subject rather than a phenomenon (whether phonetic or graphic), a special branch of humane science, of which only part is concerned with the field of the ancient προσῳδία. The character of the new prosody is clearly defined in the once popular *English Grammar* of Lindley Murray:[4]

PROSODY consists of two parts: the former teaches the true PRONUNCIATION of words, comprising ACCENT, QUANTITY, EMPHASIS, PAUSE, and TONE; and the latter, the laws of VERSIFICATION.

The newcomer to the field of meaning is, of course, 'versification'. The principal link between the two subjects lies in syllabic 'quantity', of which the old prosody of vowel-length was a prime constituent. Until quite recent times the study of versification was essentially that of *classical* versification (though often misapplied to later poetry: cf. pp. 351 ff.); and since classical metres have a quantitative basis, it was natural enough to link such study with the discipline concerned with its basic prosody. The boundaries between words, clauses, and sentences

---

[1] Laum 1928, 27 f.
[2] Palmer 1957, 191.
[3] The length-marks, however, though occasionally used in papyri (more particularly of dialect texts, and especially to indicate ᾱ = Attic η), did not become part of the normal orthographic system – presumably because the ambiguous (δίχρονα) vowels, viz. ι, υ, α, were rarely involved in serious contrasts: Ruipérez 1956, 76; Fischer 1961; A 1968a, 86.
[4] 3rd edn (1816), i, 345.

may also be relevant to verse, and these too were prosodies in the extended use of the term.

Emphasis on the metrical aspects of prosody would have been encouraged by the insistence, especially in English schools, on the virtues of Latin verse composition;[1] and finally the newcomer all but usurped the title 'prosody' to its exclusive use.

Meanwhile, however, the old prosodies had continued to form a subject of study, though often under different names. Henry Sweet, for example, having dealt under the heading of 'Analysis' with the segmental consonant and vowel units, proceeds under the heading of 'Synthesis' to discuss 'the different ways in which they are joined together in speech . . . their relative *quantity, stress,* and *intonation*' (1891, 226 ff.);[2] under this heading Sweet also deals with syllables and transitions. With the rapid development of descriptive linguistics in the second quarter of the twentieth century, various such phenomena were again accorded the title of 'prosodic', notably in the work of American linguists and of the 'Prague School'.[3] Thus for Trubetzkoy (1935/1968, 30; 1939/1969, 95) 'prosodic units' or 'prosodemes' are 'rhythmic-melodic' units, closely associated with the syllable, and their 'properties' include duration, intensity, and pitch. For Bloch & Trager (1942, 34) 'prosodic features' comprise '*quantity* (length), *stress* (loudness), and *tone* (pitch)', the last two being 'usually grouped together as features of *accent*',[4] whilst phenomena of 'juncture' constitute a related topic. More recently, in applying the term 'prosodic' to the three features mentioned, Martinet (1960, 77) observes that they utilize characteristics which are essentially present in every utterance.

By American writers the term 'prosodeme' has also been used to refer to *distinctive* prosodic features or 'prosodic phonemes',[5] i.e. features which are paradigmatically *opposed* to one another (as, say, high vs low pitch occurring in identical environments in a tonal language). The difference between such features and those which only *contrast* with one another syntagmatically (as, say, strong vs weak stress in Latin, which are not opposed to one another in comparable environments) is also emphasized: e.g. Rischel 1964, 87 f; Pulgram 1969, 394.

[1] Attridge 1972, 35 ff.
[2] Cf. also Sweet 1906, 44 ff.
[3] Vachek 1966, 63 f.
[4] More specifically (Trager 1941, 132) when characterizing the word or 'the syllable as part of a word', being thereby differentiated from the more extended 'intonational' features.
[5] Hamp 1957, *s.vv.*

A common alternative to 'prosodic' in these uses is 'suprasegmental';[1] by Trager (1941, 135) the term 'exponential' has also been used, with the further observation that 'any secondary phonetic character – such as glottalization, nasalization, labialization, retroflexion, "throatiness" "weight", etc. – may conceivably function as exponential in a given language'.

Partially overlapping with the types of features already mentioned are what Harris has termed 'phonemic long components' (e.g. 1951, 125 ff.). Harris observes that the segmental phoneme 'is not independent of its environment', and seeks to express the implied dependences by abstracting 'long components extending over the length of the dependence'. Whilst this category could clearly include, for example, accentual features extending over the syllable (which are normally treated as separate from the phonematic segments by any analysis),[2] it further extends to such features as, say, voicelessness in the sequence /st/; thus *bust* = /bʌz̄d/ beside *buzzed* = /bʌzd/, thereby eliminating the need for an environmental statement that /d/ does not occur after /s/. The 'domain' of such features may vary, from two segments in the above example to longer stretches of speech; 'vowel harmony' in Turkish, for instance, could well be described in terms of word-length components (cf. p. 8).

In the work of the 'London School'[3] the term 'prosody' came to regain and even extend the range of uses that it had in later antiquity, beginning with Firth's programmatic article 'Sounds and Prosodies' in 1948. This use of the term is based on a type of phonology which emphasizes the rôle of synthesis (in Sweet's sense) by treating it as a distinct dimension of description; the 'horizontal' dimension deals only with the segmental 'phonematic' elements, whereas anything that is relevant to larger units is allocated to the 'vertical' dimension of prosodic categories ('prosodies'). 'Relevance' is here widely interpreted; it is not confined to the mere phonetic continuity of some feature over a more or less extended domain, but may also apply to relations (e.g. of positive or negative mutual implication) between features which need not be continuous. Unlike Harris' long components, prosodies in this sense are generally related to some higher structural unit, most commonly the

[1] Hamp 1957, *s.v*; and now especially Lehiste 1970, 1 ff. *et passim.*
[2] Tonal features characterizing individual vowel units, however, would be excluded, and are separately classified by Harris as 'unit-length components' (1951, 143 ff.).
[3] Langendoen 1968, 49 ff; *Palmer 1970, ix ff.

syllable or word;[1] and any features which delimit such units (cf. the 'boundary signals' of the Prague School)[2] may also be treated as prosodic. Thus, as Firth points out (1948, 146), although the English *h* has phonematic value in such paradigms as *eating, heating*, . . ., it is also a mark of initiality in the syllable (and so a prosody). It is, however, also emphasized by Firth (1948, 152) that the allocation of features to phonematic or prosodic categories depends upon their function in the particular languages, so that 'what is a phonematic constituent in one may be a prosody in another';[3] as Rischel comments (1964, 87) on the choice between segmental and 'suprasegmental' treatment, 'gain in structural simplicity is the ultimate motivation'.

'The elementary pattern underlying any grouping of phonemes is the syllable';[4] and the 'profile' of a word in terms of its syllabic make-up may therefore also be considered prosodic,[5] as indicating the articulation of the structure within which the vowel and consonant elements function: e.g. heavy–light–heavy (or 'cretic') characterizing Latin words of the type *cāritās*, *pontifex*, rather as one characterizes words accentually in Greek as 'paroxytone', 'properispomenon', etc.

It is clear that for certain features a description in Firthian prosodic terms will differ only in idiom from a description in terms of long components;[6] and a prosodic description of 'vowel harmony' in Turkish, for example, may also be taken to typify the latter. The relevant phenomena may be described[7] in terms of the word-prosodies 'back' (vs 'front') and 'rounded' (vs 'unrounded'). When these features are abstracted, the only segmental vowel-elements that need to be stated are describable simply as 'close' (I) or 'open' (A). By such an analysis the vowels of two words like *gözlerimiz* 'our eyes' and *kollarımız* 'our arms' could be stated as identical (A–A–I–I), and would thus incidentally reflect the identical grammatical structure, the phonetic differences being attributable to the presence of the prosody 'front' in the first word vs 'back' in the second.

In the above example the feature 'rounded' applies to both words, but its operation is restricted by certain regular rules; the prosody in such a case is *relevant* to the whole word, but this does not necessarily

---

[1] Robins 1957, 4; 1969, 112 f.   [2] E.g. Trubetzkoy 1935/1968, 43 ff.
[3] Cf. Robins 1957, 5.
[4] Jakobson & Halle 1968, 422
[5] Cf. Firth 1948, 133.
[6] Cf. Langendoen 1968, 54 ff.
[7] As by Waterson (1956); cf. Lyons 1968, 128 ff.

imply its phonetic extension over the whole domain.[1] The principle is particularly clearly illustrated by certain Sanskrit phenomena involving retroflexion of the tongue-tip;[2] this feature may be abstracted as a prosody of the word, but its actual phonetic extension is determined positively by the location of a 'focus' and negatively, as the Indians themselves observed,[3] by the occurrence of certain phonetically classifiable 'interfering' consonants (Skt *vighna-kṛt*). Thus in a word like *pramāṇam* the retroflexion 'focussed' on the *r* is maintained throughout the word, whereas in *pradānam* it is terminated by the interfering articulation of the dental *d*. It will be evident that, by such an analysis, the orthographic distinction between the retroflex consonant *ṇ* and the non-retroflex *n* is redundant, since the difference is an automatic consequence of the realization rules for the word-prosody of retroflexion.

Sanskrit, together with Greek, may also be taken to illustrate a prosody involving a syntagmatic relationship between phonetic features rather than the continuity of a feature. This is the phenomenon in both languages generally referred to as 'Grassmann's Law'. Diachronically it involves a 'dissimilation of aspirates', in the sense that, if aspiration originally occurred in successive syllables, the first occurrence was suppressed: thus the reduplicated form **dha.dhā.mi* → *dadhāmi*, **θι.θη.μι* → τίθημι. The synchronic effects of the process are seen in such alternations as pres. τρέφω (where the second syllable φω contains an aspirated consonant) vs fut. θρέψω (where the second syllable σω contains no aspiration, and the first syllable consequently does). In a prosodic analysis aspiration may be abstracted as a feature (generally of the radical complex)[4] whose location is determined by its environment. Thus the verb in the preceding Greek example could be stated invariably as *H*τρεπ- (vs τρεπ- in τρέπω, τρέψω), the *H* prosody being realized as aspiration of the root-final consonant if a vowel follows (τρέφ-ω) and of the initial if a consonant follows (θρέπ-σω). This particular phenomenon was in fact also seen by Harris (1944, 196) as amenable to a componential form of analysis.[5]

The types of features which function prosodically in this sense tend to recur in various languages. In the case of aspiration, for example, although Sanskrit and Greek are genetically related, it is generally be-

[1] In the shorter (and more common) form for 'our eyes', viz. *gözümüz* (where the plural morpheme of 'eyes' is omitted), the rounding applies throughout.
[2] A 1951, 940 ff.   [3] A 1953, 66 f.
[4] A 1951, 944.
[5] For a transformational-generative treatment see *Anderson 1970.

lieved that the phenomena in the two languages are of quite separate origin;[1] and a comparable but undoubtedly independent development in more recent times has been observed in a modern Indo-Aryan dialect (Hārautī).[2] Thus Prakrit *bhikkhā* 'alms' (< Skt *bhikṣā*) → H. *bhīk* (with suppression of the *second* aspirate) and Pkt *pokkhara* 'lotus pool' (< Skt *pauṣkara*) → H. *phokar* (with transfer of aspiration); a general descriptive rule can then be stated that in aspirated words in this dialect the relevant phonetic feature occurs at, and only at, the first possible location.

It will have been noticed that in its most recent extension the semantic field covered by the various 'prosodies' has come to include that of the extended Greek προσῳδίαι. On the face of it this might seem a remarkable coincidence. For whereas the modern prosodies have been distinguished from the phonematic elements by purely linguistic criteria, the προσῳδίαι of the Greeks, in the wider applications of the term, had a predominantly graphic basis, referring to such relevant features as were not indicated in the segmental orthography of vowels and consonants – in fact anything which necessitated 'marking the text' (στίζειν τὰς γραφάς). The non-indication of aspiration, for example, could be seen as having a purely fortuitous cause. In early Greek the letter H (derived from the Semitic *ḥēt*) had been used to represent the aspirate /h/. But in East Ionic, as a result of psilosis, the character became redundant, and was thus conveniently left free to represent the long half-open vowel /εε/ which had developed in Attic and Ionic from earlier /aa/; and when, at the end of the 5 c. B.C., Attic came to adopt the Ionic alphabet, it employed the character H in its vocalic use and ceased to indicate the aspirate, even though in Attic this was still pronounced.

But the very fact that the features classed as προσῳδίαι were not indicated in the orthography may in some cases reflect an awareness of their dissimilar function from that of the segmental phonemes. On the negative side, it could have involved an intuition that their lexical function (their potentiality for expressing differences of referential meaning) was slight in comparison with that of the vowels and consonants; and, more positively, that their function was generally different in kind, being related to the expression of grammatical rather than lexical meaning, e.g. to the delimitation or characterization of the grammatical unit

---

[1] In Greek it is subsequent to the devoicing of the voiced aspirates and to the change *s→h, neither of which developments occurs in Sanskrit; see, however, Kiparsky 1965, 3–17 ff.

[2] Analysed on a prosodic basis in A 1957.

'word'. The latter function is served by the accent, and the former by phenomena of juncture and disjuncture. In the case of aspiration, on the negative side certainly the lexical distinctions effected by its presence vs absence are relatively few compared with those effected by long /εε/ vs short /e/, and this could have influenced the Attic adoption of H in the latter function to the exclusion of the former.[1] On the positive side, the occurrence of /h/ is a general indication of word-beginning; moreover, unlike in English, the Greek /h/ does not occupy a consonantal 'slot' in syllabic structure – it has no effect on quantity and it does not prevent elision or crasis: the English distribution of the article *an/a* in *an owl/a howl*, *a towel* contrasts with that of the presence vs absence of 'ν ἐφελκυστικόν' in ἔστιν οὐδέν, ἔστιν οὗτος/ἔστι τοῦτο. Such functional criteria for the Greek distinction of προσῳδίαι from στοιχεῖα, as reflected in the writing system, are likely to have been more intuitive than rational, but in part at least may be held to account for the considerable area of overlap between the old prosodies and the new.

Most recently, a further extension of the term 'prosody' is found in Crystal 1969,[2] where this title covers also such features as pause, tempo, and 'rhythmicality' – which, however, still have evident relationships with the more traditional senses of the term.

It has sometimes been remarked, as by Firth (1948, 152), that in the historical development of languages prosodic features tend to be dominant and to survive changes in the segmental, phonematic constituents. For example, the Indo-European consonant sequence $*sk'(h)$ developed in Sanskrit to *cch*, as in $*g^w mske \rightarrow gaccha$ (= Gk βάσκε), which preserves the original quantity of the first syllable; in word-initial position the result is simple *ch*, as $*sk'hid- \rightarrow chid-$ (cf. Gk σχίζω); but when the preceding word ends in a short vowel, the original quantitative pattern of the word-group is maintained by doubling the initial consonant, as *na cchidyate* 'is not cut off'.[3] At a later period, in the change from Skt *kartati* 'cuts' to Pkt *kaṭṭaï* and thence Hindi *kāṭe*, the consonantal changes have also left intact the prosody of retroflexion (originally 'focussed' on the *r*): it is only the mode of realization that is altered.

Certain of the prosodic features tend to be particularly persistent. It has been claimed, for example, that sufferers from subcortical motor

---

[1] Often, however, it continues to appear in its aspirate value to distinguish the word ὅρος 'boundary' from ὄρος 'mountain', where significant ambiguity could arise.

[2] Of which Ch. 2 includes a valuable survey of recent work on prosodic features, whether presented under 'prosodic' or other labels.

[3] A 1962, 47 f., 55 ff.

aphasia continue to make as many chest pulses as there are syllables in the attempted utterance;[1] and Jakobson observes that features characteristic of the sentence as a whole tend to be preserved in aphasic disturbances: 'In contrast to the phoneme, they possess their own constant meaning, as, e.g., the specific intonation at the end of the sentence, which marks the end of a meaningful unit' (1941/1968, 43). Both pathologically and historically the features which tend to persist are the most general, in the sense both of functioning prosodically in the most languages and of utilizing the least specialized, most basic features of phonation. These are, in Martinet's terms (1960, 77), force, pitch, and duration (though we shall later have occasion to reinterpret the last of these in terms of syllable structure). It is, moreover, these features which perform the accentual and rhythmic functions with which this study is primarily concerned.

This delimitation of the field of linguistic 'prosodies' also brings our subject into close relationship with the study of 'prosody' in the sense of versification.

In the words of T. S. Eliot (1942, 17), 'The music of poetry must be a music latent in the common speech of its time'; and the relationship of verse to normal spoken language has been commented upon by numerous writers, particularly in recent years; their views may be typified by the following brief anthology:

Under normal conditions the rhythm of poetry is based upon the rhythm of the spoken language (Miller 1902, 499).

The implementation of the metrical scheme is conditioned by the underlying linguistic system. Thus it is known that no versification system can be based on prosodic elements which are not relevant in the language (Stankiewicz 1960, 77 f.).

The metrical pattern imitates the structure of sound of the language (Thompson 1961, 167).

The formal characteristics of a verse form are dictated by the structural features of the prosody of the language (Watkins 1963, 218).

The rhythm of everyday speech is the foundation of verse, in most languages (Abercrombie 1967, 98).

If a poem is defined as a work of literary art, i.e. 'art of language', it follows that the features stylized are features of the language in which the poem is written (de Groot 1968, 537).

[1] Cf. Stetson 1951, 171.

With special reference to the stylization of Latin poetry, Fraenkel comments that in the rules of its structure it is in no respect different from the ordinary language of the educated Roman; that 'stylization' in this context means simply the selection and enhancement of principles which were already developed in the language of everyday intercourse (1932, 198); nothing is permitted which could never occur in actual life (1928, 343). Vendryes (1936, 105) expresses himself in similar terms, to the effect that poets put into practice – generally without realizing it, but with a surer instinct than other men – the phonological principles of the language they use.

It has been suggested that the origins of at least some metrical patterns may be even more closely linked with the language on which they are based, deriving not so much from abstract principles as from the prosodic patterns of actual phrases which have become traditional in speech.[1] One naturally thinks in this connexion of the formulaic element in Homeric verse, which is generally accepted as characteristic of pre-literate composition. It is, however, in one sense an oversimplification to oppose 'oral' to 'written' composition (as e.g. Parry 1930; 1932). For the 'literate' poet writing is certainly a means of recording and trans-mitting his composition, and a useful aid to amendment. But the act of composition itself can and to a large extent does remain oral, especially in a culture where primarily oral performance is envisaged; the extent to which even the more subtle prosodic patterns of natural language, dependent in part on environments longer than the word, appear to be respected in ancient 'literate' poetry[2] (e.g. of Attic tragedy)[3] suggests that, at the very least, stretches of the order of cola, rather than indi-vidual words, were orally composed before final commitment to writing. Nor, incidentally, is it entirely true that an 'oral' poet necessarily 'always makes his verse out of formulas' (Parry 1932, 6), that 'he cannot, with-out paper, make of his own words a poem of any length' (Parry 1930, 77 f.).[4] In Aryan India writing was slow to make its appearance, and it is unlikely that much literature existed in manuscript form before the 2 c. B.C.;[5] nevertheless, long before this there existed, quite apart from the Vedic hymns, an extensive philosophical, ritual, and scientific (in-cluding grammatical) literature in both verse and prose, with little to

---

[1] Cf. Nagy 1970b, 95 f.
[2] Cf. pp. 283 ff.
[3] On writing in this connexion cf. Greene 1951, 37 ff.
[4] Cf. also Kirk 1966, 134 ff.
[5] Burrow 1955, 65.

indicate its oral character.[1] And even after the introduction of writing the oral tradition survived and has been an important constituent of Indian education and culture right up to the present day. The dichotomy set up by Parry may in fact rest too heavily on 'the composition of oral poetry as it is practiced in our own times in Serbia, among the Tuaregs, in Afghanistan . . .' (Parry 1930, 78); a different picture might have emerged, for example, from a study of the compositional practice of the bards (Chāraṇs) of Rajasthan. To avoid misunderstanding[2] one should distinguish two types of non-literate authorship – one in which the author composes in the presence of his audience (the type clearly envisaged by Parry and widely believed to form the basis of Homeric poetry); and another in which he composes in private, only 'publishing' his work when he has completed it to his satisfaction (the type most probably underlying the Indian tradition). The latter, by its nature, has a definitive form similar to that of literate work, which marks it off from the variability of the former.[3]

But whilst one may accept that a formulaic mode of composition tends to characterize one type of non-literate authorship, and that in a literate culture the verse tends to free itself from the constraints of the traditional phraseology and to 'assume dynamics of its own' (Nagy 1970b, 96),[4] this does not imply that the composition of literate verse is necessarily less regardful of phonetic realities. To take an extreme case, one would be surprised to find, for example, a verse composition in which the vowel lengths required by the metre were quite different from those of the constituent words in speech; the startling assumption of such a possibility by Aelfric[5] rests upon the misleading evidence of his own Anglo-Saxon pronunciation of Latin.

Nevertheless, as later discussion will suggest (pp. 335 ff.), there is some substance in the cautious reservations expressed by Miller and by

---

[1] One such indication may be the extreme compression of the grammatical 'sūtra' style (culminating in the notorious brevity of Pāṇini's last aphorism: see e.g. A 1953, 58), together with the fact that even the most 'algebraic' of grammatical formulae are pronounceable.

[2] Cf. also Lord 1960, 5.

[3] On Celtic and other parallels see especially Young 1967, 295 ff.

[4] Cf. Lord 1960, 130.

[5] *Aelfrics Grammatik und Glossar*, ed. Zupitza, 2: 'Miror valde, quare multi corripiunt sillabas in prosa, quae in metro breues sunt, cum prosa absoluta sit a lege metri; sicut pronuntiant *pater* brittonice (i.e. with the short vowel of *fæder*) et *malus* et similia, quae in metro habentur breues. mihi tamen videtur melius inuocare deum patrem honorifice producta sillaba, quam brittonice corripere, quia nec deus arti grammaticae subiciendus est.' Cf. Campbell 1953, 13 f.

Abercrombie (p. 12) – 'under normal conditions' and 'in most languages'; for, as Vendryes goes on to say (1936, 106), systems of versification may be borrowed by one language from another (or from an earlier stage of the same language); so that, before making use of poetry in establishing the phonology, one must first determine the extent of convention and artifice in the poet's usage.

The relationship between language and metre is two-fold. Firstly, as is now generally accepted, metrical patterns are ultimately founded on phenomena of ordinary speech; and secondly, the manifestation of such patterns is in terms of speech. In fact 'prosody' could be defined (Zirin 1970, 13) as the relationship between such patterns and manifestations. As Halle & Keyser memorably express it,[1] a successful theory of prosody should be capable of characterizing the difference between the line 'Much have I travelled in the realms of gold' and the title 'On first looking into Chapman's Homer', or between 'O wild West Wind, thou breath of Autumn's being' and 'Ode to the West Wind by Percy Bysshe Shelley'.

From this relationship certain consequences follow for the study of such linguistic features as are selected for the characterization of verse. In general, even for a living language, it has been pointed out (Bazell 1953, 63) that 'A metrical text is a perfectly good text, and the fact that such texts may either not be available, or may simply not exist, for many languages is no argument for not regarding metrical criteria as essential where they are available'. And for a 'dead' language in particular the evidence of such texts is invaluable; for by observing how the linguistic forms are projected on to the basically regular metrical grid we may be enabled to deduce information about the former which is not revealed by mere inspection of their orthography, nor happens to be available from other sources. In fact the very practice objected to by Aelfric represented one very simple application of this principle.

Since it is certain of the prosodic phonetic features that tend particularly to characterize the periodicities of verse, the linguist/phonetician studying such features in a dead language will thus inevitably be forced to take note of metrical facts;[2] Gordon (1966, 16) even goes so far as to claim that 'it would be possible from the evidence of poetry to exhibit the stress-system of English prose of every period'.

However, research tends to be a two-way activity. When one seeks to

---

[1] 1966, 189; 1971, 139, 167; Keyser 1969, 380.
[2] Cf. Halle & Keyser 1971, xvi.

increase one's understanding of x by reference to the facts of an already known y, the process not uncommonly suggests some reinterpretation of the latter – which in the present case involves the linguist donning the mantle of the metrist. Indeed the view is being increasingly expressed[1] that only by becoming a linguist can the metrist be adequate to his task; and Lotz (1960, 137) has frankly proclaimed that, 'Since all metric phenomena are language phenomena, it follows that metrics is entirely within the competence of linguistics'.

The field of classical metrics is a highly complex and specialized one, to which generations of scholars have devoted their principal attention; and whilst accepting the theoretical principles that underlie statements like the above, it would be rash for the linguist/phonetician to assume that he is qualified to annex the subject to himself. But it may be that the present study, in its inevitably Janus-like rôle, will be able to throw occasional light on metrical phenomena which traditional methods have left unexplained or have presented in what seem to be inadequate terms. The rôle is not an easy one; for 'take-over bids' as expressed by Lotz tend to be matched by reaction on the metrical side – to the point where one eminent classical metrist rejected without argument a contrary opinion on a certain matter, as 'deriving I think from linguistics'.[2] But one can at least hope to do something towards remedying the situation lamented by Abercrombie (1964a, 5), that 'most phoneticians have paid little attention to verse structure. Most writers on prosody, moreover, have paid little attention to phonetics.'

[1] E.g. Stankiewicz 1960, 81; Pace 1961, 419.
[2] Dale 1964, 20 n.9.

2 *Grammatical considerations*

Our concern in what follows will be primarily with the nature of certain general phonetic phenomena (whether from the phonatory, acoustic, or auditory point of view) and with their functioning in the structures of the particular languages studied – in other words the phonology of those languages. But it is never possible entirely to divorce phonological from grammatical structure; it often happens, for example, that different systems of phonological contrasts are relevant to different grammatical categories (in English the restriction of initial /ð/ to 'deictics' etc. is an obvious case in point); and in the transformational-generative model of grammar which currently predominates the two are particularly closely integrated: to quote Postal (1968, 114), 'The systematic phonemic representation involves not only the phonological matrix specifying properties determined by phonetics but also properties provided by the output of the syntactic part of the grammar, that is, by the Surface Syntactic Structure'. With regard to stress in English, for example, Chomsky & Halle (1968, 59 f.) seek to demonstrate that 'both the placement of main stress and the stress contours within the word and phrase are largely predictable from the syntactic and the non-prosodic phonological structure of an utterance by means of a transformational cycle';[1] in support of their thesis they refer to experimental evidence that even a trained phonetician cannot detect such contours with reliability or precision in a language unknown to him, i.e. 'a language for which he cannot determine the surface structure of utterances' (25). As a corollary, the orthography of a language is designed for readers who know the language, 'who understand sentences and therefore know the surface structures of sentences'; and consequently stress placement and regular vowel or consonant alternations are generally not reflected – indeed it is even claimed by the authors that 'English orthography, despite its often cited inconsistencies, comes remarkably close to being an optimal orthographic system for English' (49).

[1] Cf. Halle & Keyser 1971, xiii f; also (but on the basis of less general rules) Waldo 1968, 1.

The interconnexion of grammar and phonology is clearly seen in the differing rules for main stress placement in nouns and verbs in English.[1] These differences can largely be explained historically;[2] but the synchronic grammatical motivation can be seen, for example, within the noun category, in the different stress levels of the second syllable, and vowel qualities in the first two syllables, of words like *relaxation* vs *devastation* – differences which could be attributed to the fact that the former noun is related to a verb *reláx* (with main-stressed second syllable), whereas the latter has no corresponding verb **devást*.[3]

A generative approach to Greek accentuation has been pioneered by Kiparsky (1967a),[4] who concludes that a more adequate account will thereby be given than by a 'taxonomic' description of the resulting accentual structures. It is certainly true, as was preeminently shown by Pāṇini over two thousand years ago,[5] that by a judicious ordering of rules the facts may be accounted for in a comprehensive, economical, and often elegant manner. But it cannot necessarily be assumed that, simply because the rules 'work', i.e. generate the correct output, one has thereby achieved a satisfying *explanation* of the facts in the common-sense use of the term.[6] Thus, referring to the Latin phenomenon of 'Lachmann's Law' (whereby e.g. *făcio* forms a past participle *făctus*, but *ăgo* forms *āctus*), Kiparsky (1965, 1–29 ff; 1967a, 87 f.) suggests that it can be accounted for by introducing the presumed Latin vowel-lengthening rule V → long/—*g*[7] before, rather than after, the Indo-European consonant-assimilating rule C → voiceless/—*t*.[8] In the rules set up by Chomsky & Halle to account for the phenomena of Eng. *relaxation* etc. the derivation includes reference to an underlying verbal form *reláx*, which is at least motivated by demonstrable facts of the language; but there is no such motivation for a Latin form *āg-* as generated by Kiparsky's first rule; it is simply a matter of internal economy, valid as such, but not in any way advancing our *understanding* of the

---

[1] Chomsky & Halle 1968, 37 n.26, 44, 70.
[2] Kurath 1964, 147; Halle & Keyser 1971, 119 ff.
[3] Chomsky 1967, 116 f; Chomsky & Halle 1968, 38 f; Halle & Keyser 1971, 51 ff. Variations in the (American) pronunciation of a word such as *presentation* are no doubt attributable, as Chomsky & Halle recognize, to differences in derivational 'history' (161, 182 f.); cf. also 38 f. on *condensation* and 112 n.64 on *information*.
[4] Cf. also 1967b, 124 ff; Warburton 1970a; Sommerstein 1971, 162 ff.
[5] A 1962, 24.
[6] Cf. Gardiner 1952, 5 ff.
[7] Cf. already de Saussure 1916/1960, 167 f.
[8] Also Postal 1968, 262; King 1969, 43 f., 114, 126.

phenomenon[1] in the sense of de Saussure's dictum: 'To explain means to relate to known terms' (1916/1960, 189). *Formulation* is not always equivalent to *explanation*.

It is necessary to make these points only to clarify the nature of the particular 'explicandi cacoethes' which motivates the present study, and to emphasize that its primary aim will be the characterization of the prosodic phonological systems in terms of their phonetic exponents, rather than in terms of their (descriptive) derivational histories. Such characterization has two purposes: one, in its own right, as an exercise in performative reconstruction; and the other, as an aid to understanding the phonology by relating it to the framework of material constraints within which it functions. Thus in dealing with the accentuation of, say, (pres.) διδόμενός τε vs (perf.) δεδομένος τε, we should not be concerned with accounting for the grammatically motivated difference in the primary accentuation of the two forms, but with the phonetic motivation that requires a secondary accent in the first and not in the second.

There will indeed be cases where grammatical considerations are relevant to the interpretation of the phonological systems; for example, the grammatical comparability of (participles) βάς and λιπών and of (subjunctives) βῆς and λίπης is one argument in favour of describing the Greek accent in terms of 'morae'.[2] But for the purposes of this study such occasional relevances can be incorporated more economically by *ad hoc* cross-reference to the grammar than by full integration with a grammatical structure which is most of the time irrelevant to the discussion.[3]

In thus emphasizing the performative side one is perhaps running a comparable risk to that recognized by Chomsky & Halle (1968, 111), that ultimately 'we may find that some of the facts we are attempting to explain do not really belong to the grammar but instead fall under the theory of performance, and that certain facts that we neglect, believing

[1] It might of course be claimed, as by some TG grammarians, that such rules are correlates of a speaker's mental processes; but since this is not demonstrable, it fails to provide an explanation: cf. the general criticism by Newton (1971, 53). In fact the particular phenomenon probably has much more complex grammatical motivations than Kiparsky *et al.* realize: see now Kuryłowicz 1968a; Watkins 1970 (who remarks (57) of Kiparsky's proposal that 'This seems merely a displacement of the problem, not a solution'); *Campbell 1971, 195 f; Collinge 1971, 257; cf. also Weinreich, Labov & Herzog 1968, 144; Samuels 1972, 55 n.2.
[2] See pp. 92, 236 ff., and Garde 1968, 146.
[3] Cf. Hall 1971, 30 n.9.

them to be features of performance, should really have been incorporated in the grammatical rules'. But we are running the risk, so to speak, in a reverse direction from that of current trends, and this complementarity of approach may do something to diminish the risk overall. In particular, when we come to considering the syllable, we shall adopt a model that gives primacy to units of performance rather than 'competence'; unlike some linguists at the present day, we believe with Fromkin (1968, 47) that 'the interrelationship between competence and performance is the concern of linguistics' and that, in addition to Jakobson's view that linguistics without meaning is meaningless, 'linguistics without speech is unspeakable'.

The most frequent cases where 'grammatical prerequisites' will be invoked concern the delimitation of the major units – primarily the sentence, word, and morpheme.[1] The relevance of such delimitations to matters of present concern may be summarized in main outline as follows:

$$\left.\begin{array}{l} \text{Sentence:} \\ \text{Word:} \\ \\ \text{Morpheme:} \end{array}\right\} \text{relevant to} \left\{\begin{array}{l} \text{Pause; Intonation.} \\ \text{Accentuation; Syllabification} \\ \qquad\qquad\qquad (\rightarrow \text{Quantity).} \\ \text{Syllabification } (\rightarrow \text{Quantity).} \end{array}\right.$$

The relevance of the Clause is generally comparable with that of the Sentence, and the Phrase may sometimes have similar relevance to that of the Word.[2]

Morphemic division may also be directly relevant to accentuation in Greek, accounting for such differences as in (pres. imper.) ἔπ-ισχε vs (aor. imper.) ἐπί-σχες. But, as was explained above, such variation falls outside the scope of this study, just as does, for instance, the difference between the active compound λιθο-βόλος and the passive λιθό-βολος; we are here concerned only to explain why all these forms, which are taken as 'givens', are possible but e.g. *ἔπισχει or *λίθοβολος is not. With syllabification, on the other hand, the case may be otherwise; the fact, for example, that in early Latin verse a word like *abripi* has the first syllable regularly heavy, whereas that of *fabrica* is regularly light, requires a grammatical explanation in terms of a morphemic division of the former, but not the latter, as *ab-ripi*, motivating a syllabification *ab.ri.pi* vs *fa.bri.ca*.[3] For it is not normally the case in early Latin that

---

[1] Cf. Pike 1947.   [2] Cf. Lyons 1968, 170 ff.
[3] A 1965, 90; Drexler 1967, 12 n.10. Accentuation also could, though very rarely, be thereby affected, as perhaps in *quam-ób-rem* beside e.g. *ténebrae*.

syllabification is freely variable, as is, from a purely phonological stand-point, accentuation in Greek. Apparent variation in the former therefore requires an other than phonetic explanation, whereas in the latter (for our purposes) it does not, provided that it remains within the range of phonetic constraints that is normal in the language.

Grammatically motivated variation involving syllabic transitions is particularly common where, as in the above Latin examples, certain types of consonant sequence are involved.[1] In English, to take an often cited case, there are clearly perceptible differences in the transitions of *night rate* and *dye trade*,[2] where, in Hockett's terminology, the /tr/ sequence constitutes respectively a 'coda' + 'onset' and a complex on-set; and these syllabic differences are reflected in allophonic variation in the segmental phonemes, e.g. in the degree of devoicing and friction in the /r/ and the duration of the diphthong /ai/. Similarly, for those speakers who use 'glottal reinforcement', it may be present in the first /t/ of e.g. *market rate* but not of *arbitrate*.[3]

The underlying principle of such variation is of very widespread application; a recent study of Mandarin Chinese, for example, con-cludes that 'the morphophonemic transformations may rely upon the syntactic component for information as to types of inter-syllabic junc-tures and as to the category to which a syllable belongs' (Cheng 1966, 152).

Syllabic and allophonic differences due to grammatical structure are also often reflected in historical developments.[4] In Greek the difference in the development of **ti̯* between **toti̯os* → Attic-Ionic τόσος and **meliti̯a* → Attic μέλιττα : Ionic μέλισσα may be explained by the fact that the latter was analysable as **melit-i̯a* (cf. μέλιτ-ος etc.), whereas there was no motivation for such an analysis of the former. A near parallel could be cited from English in the different phonetic values of the sequence /tʃ/ in e.g. *hatchet* vs *hat-shop*, where the different mor-phemic structures are reflected in differences of syllabification and duration of consonants.

However, it is also true that 'many examples can be found of regulari-ties which operate both within morphemes and across morpheme boundaries' (Brown 1970, 9); and it would clearly be uneconomical, particularly for our present purposes, to take cognizance of grammatical

[1] Cf. Ebeling 1960, 56.
[2] Hockett 1955, 52, 63 f; Gimson 1970, 207, 301.
[3] Cf. p. 58 and Higginbottom 1964, 135 f., 138.
[4] Cf. Wyatt 1970, 51, 76 n.19.

boundaries where these are phonologically irrelevant. Cheng, for example, couples his conclusion quoted above with the recognition that sections of the phonology can be treated apart from syntactical structure, with special reference to the setting up of a 'syllable grammar'. In the classical languages the possibilities of such an independent treatment of syllabic structure, with grammatical boundaries invoked only where they are relevant to the phonology, is considerably greater than in a language such as English;[1] and this reinforces the general decision to treat grammatical prerequisites on an *ad hoc* basis – which does not conflict with Chomsky's view (1964, 106) that '*some* phonetic processes depend on syntactic and morphological structure'.[2]

Where the explanation does require reference to grammatical units, it must obviously presuppose that these units have themselves been identified. And in the case of the morpheme or the sentence such identification is readily made, at least for the purposes for which we shall here require it – a reservation that is particularly relevant to the morpheme. As the sentence is the maximal unit of conventional grammatical analysis, so morphemes may be described as the minimal units. But it is to be remembered that such units are *abstractions* and that their phonological representation may often raise problems.[3] Thus both *rats* and *mice* contain the morpheme {plural}, and both *bigger* and *worse* contain the morpheme {comparative}; but so far as the phonological representations are concerned, *rats* and *bigger* admit of the morphemic analysis being neatly projected on to the phonology as /ræt-s/ and /big-ə/, with the relevant morphemes represented by the morphs /s/ and /ə/; whereas this is clearly not the case with *mice* and even less so with *worse*, where a morphemic analysis of the type {bad}+{comparative} cannot be matched by a segmentation of the phonological representation /wəəs/ into two successive morphs. In fact 'whether a word can be divided into smaller grammatical segments is a matter of degree' (Lyons 1968, 181). But any cases of morphemic analysis relevant to the matters to be discussed are all of the type which permits a corresponding segmentation into morphs on the phonological plane; and when such analysis needs to be made, no problems will arise regarding the point of segmentation.

The unit most commonly relevant to our prosodic features is the *word*. Word junctions are of course invariably also morph junctions – but the phonological characteristics of word junctions often differ from

---

[1] Cf. Trubetzkoy 1935/1968, 46.   [2] The italics are Chomsky's.
[3] Cf. Fudge 1969, 258.

those of morph junctions within the word. A simple example may be taken from Sanskrit, where the principles of juncture ('*sandhi*') are particularly transparent. In this language the permitted phonological sequences in 'internal' (*intra*-word) sandhi are largely identical with those permitted within individual morphs, and are less restricted than those of 'external' (*inter*-word) sandhi.[1] Thus in the word *mahatas*, gen. sing. of *mahat* 'great', the sequence /ta/ is permitted just as within a single morph (e.g. *śatam* '100'); but at a word junction, as *mahad asti* 'it is great', the voice component inherent in the initial vowel /a/ extends also to the final consonant of the preceding word, with resultant /d/, not /t/. A similar contrast is provided by the behaviour of the morph-initial sequence /s/+plosive in Latin; at morph junctions within the word, where the preceding morph ends in a short vowel, this group invariably implies heavy quantity of the preceding syllable, as e.g. in *re-spiro*, just as within a morph (e.g. *restis*); but at word junctions, in early Latin, the quantity of such syllables is normally light, as e.g. *sator sartorque scelerum* ∼ (Plautus, *Capt.* 661).[2]

It may be generally said that word boundaries are phonologically more clearly marked than intra-word morph boundaries.[3] But compared with the morpheme or sentence the definition of the *word* is notoriously liable to present difficulties. It is the prime unit of traditional grammar; something like it appears to be intuitively recognized by native speakers of all languages, and in literate societies it tends to be institutionalized in writing, e.g. by inter-word spaces. Yet even the Greeks had no unambiguous word for it, until Dionysius Thrax redefined the general term λέξις 'utterance' for grammatical purposes as μέρος ἐλάχιστον τοῦ κατὰ σύνταξιν λόγου (*Ars Gramm.*, 22 U), thereby anticipating one of its most familiar modern definitions as a 'minimal free form'.[4] Part of the difficulty is that at this hierarchical level the semantic, grammatical, and phonological criteria for delimitation of units *tend*, but only tend, to coincide; so that agreement between criteria, more particularly of the last two types, comes to be expected, but the incompleteness of the agreement leads to frequent disappointment of this expectation. The English definite article, for instance, would presumably qualify semantically as a word; but phonologically it behaves unlike a word in that, in its normal usage, it is never stressed; and grammatical criteria are

---

[1] A 1962, 25.
[2] Cf. p. 139 and Hoenigswald 1949a; Drexler 1967, 12 n.10; Collinge 1970, 196 n.1.
[3] Cf. Kuryłowicz 1948/1960, 210 f.
[4] Robins 1967, 33; A 1968a, 113 n.

ambivalent – it cannot occur as a minimal free form (i.e. as a one-word sentence); but by the criterion of 'interruptability' of combinations in which it occurs, as in e.g. *the (big) house*,[1] it is clearly more independent than, say, the morpheme of the present participle (*-ing*),[2] and is so recognized in the orthography.

The existence of such conflicts of criteria has led some linguists to give priority to the grammatical status of the unit (e.g. Lyons 1968, 206) and others to its phonological status (e.g. Fudge 1969, 258), whilst Reichling (1935, 436) concludes that 'We recognize words on account of their meaning'. But in choosing between grammatical and phonological definitions, some status is also generally accorded to units of a comparable level in the non-chosen hierarchy, even though these are denied the title of 'words'; and it is mostly recognized that it is less important to determine which side should receive the title than to separate clearly the two types of criteria. Thus Pulgram (1969, 387 f; cf. 1970, 24 f.) terms the relevant grammatical ('morphological-lexical') unit a 'lexeme',[3] whereas the term 'word' is reserved for 'a phonological unit, that is, an item coextensive with, or longer than, a lexeme, which in an utterance behaves phonologically – as regards boundary signals and accentuation – like a single lexeme in citation'. It has further to be recognized that 'there are great differences with regard to the place of the word in the systems of many of the languages of the world' (Krámský 1969, 78).

So far as this study is concerned, problems of definition at the word level are only sporadically relevant. They will generally arise in cases where a sequence of two (or occasionally more) grammatical 'words' behaves like a single word in regard to its prosodic phonology (in Pulgram's terms, where two or more 'lexemes' constitute a 'nexus': 1970, 25 ff.). These problems are not generally serious; for it is normally the case either that one of the words in the sequence is of a particularly clearly defined category phonologically, in that it regularly attaches itself prosodically to a preceding or following word (i.e. an 'enclitic' or 'proclitic'), and/or that there is a close grammatical connexion between the words.

Anticipating later and more detailed discussions, we may note that in Greek, for example, a sequence such as φιλῶ σε, with enclitic pronoun,

[1] Cf. Lyons 1968, 204.
[2] Or the postposed definite article in a language like Rumanian (e.g. *lupul* 'the wolf') or Icelandic (e.g. *skipið* 'the ship').
[3] The term is used in a different sense by Lyons (1968, 197).

shows the single accent characteristic of a word like φιλοῦσα; and the phonological adherence of proclitics to the following word is seen in the accentuation of such forms as πρόπαλαι, διάπεντε.[1] In Latin, a combination of the word *Caesar* with the enclitic particle *-ne* is accented as *Caesárne*, just as a single word like *lantérna*, although the particle has no special *grammatical* relationship to *Caesar* but rather to the whole sentence of which *Caesar* is the first word.[2] As regards proclitics, Quintilian (i.5.27) observes: 'cum dico *circum lítora*, tamquam unum enuntio dissimulata distinctione, itaque tamquam in una uoce una est acuta', i.e. *circum lítora*. Further evidence for such phonological coherence of word sequences is seen in the patterns of early Latin verse, which suggest accentuations of the type *ád forum, uoluptás mea, (in) malám crucem* (with close idiomatic connexion); this is also supported by historical evidence in forms such as *ílico, sédulo* < **in (s)loco, *se dolo*, which show the weakening of vowels (**o → i, u*) characteristic of the unaccented medial syllables of words.[3]

It is not only accentual features that may be involved in such coherence. We have referred to a word prosody of retroflexion in Sanskrit (p. 9); and in the Vedic hymns this feature is found to extend across the boundaries between closely connected words – as e.g. *agneṣ* 'of fire' + *avena* 'by favour' → *agner aveṇa*, where the retroflexion of the first word, focussed on the *ṣ* (→ *r* in juncture), extends to the grammatically linked following word and so is responsible for the retroflexion of *n → ṇ*.[4]

The degree of cohesion is, however, variable. In Greek a word followed by an enclitic normally retains its own accent unchanged, and the enclitic is accommodated if necessary by means of a secondary accent, as e.g. in ἄνθρωπός τε; whereas in Latin the cohesion is complete, with the accent of *hómines* shifted in the combination *hominésque*. And within Greek, as against the complete cohesion of forms like πρόπαλαι, in the combination of article + noun (as e.g. ἡ πόλις) the noun retains its accent and the article is proclitic only in the sense of being unaccented.

The intermediate status of some such sequences between cohesion and independence can lead to variations in usage. In Slavonic, for example, prepositions may sometimes form an accentual unity with the following word, as Russian *ú morja* 'by the sea' or Czech *ná mostĕ* 'on

---

[1] Vendryes 1929, 93.
[2] Fudge 1969, 258 f.
[3] Harsh 1949, 19; Drexler 1967, 14 f.
[4] A 1962, 49 n.10.

LUTHER SEMINARY LIBRARY
2375 COMO AVENUE WEST
ST. PAUL, MINNESOTA 55108

the bridge';[1] but in the former case Nicholson (1968, 84 f.) notes that this is no longer normative, and that 'prepositions . . . are tending to forfeit stress back to the noun'; and for Czech Vachek observes (1968, 145 f.): 'the orthoepic norm . . . demands the stressing of the syllabic preposition but the actual practice of Czech speakers very often shifts the stress on to the first syllable of the directed word', so as 'to obtain the independent word status for the preposition'.[2] In Polish similarly Kuryłowicz (1958, 379 f.) comments on doubts regarding the accentuation of combinations with the enclitic *-by*, as e.g. *písałby* or *pisáłby* 'he would write', where, since Polish words normally have penultimate stress, the first accentuation would imply two separate words and the latter a single word unit.

Potential variation of this type may also be utilized by poets for metrical purposes. In Greek, Koster (1953, 57; cf. 17 f.) remarks upon the tendency to avoid prepositions before the caesura, or postpositions after the caesura, but only as being *more or less* marked. This is perhaps something of an understatement; but certainly there are cases where, for caesural purposes, such forms are treated as independent words: e.g. Sophocles, *El.* 921 τί δ᾽ ἔστιν; οὐ πρὸς : ἡδονὴν λέγω τάδε;[3] – whereas at Aeschylus, *Supp.* 949 the combination ἐξ ὀμμάτων is treated as a single word for purposes of 'Porson's Bridge' (see p. 304); and whereas at *Prom.* 107 the combination θνητοῖς γὰρ is also thus treated, at e.g. *Supp.* 467 γὰρ seems to be treated as an independent word in as much as it follows a caesura: ξυνῆκας· ὠμμάτωσα : γὰρ σαφέστερον.[4] In such cases, as Fraenkel observes in a similar connexion (1928, 346 f.), it is a matter of the poet exercising an option to use either the syntactic or the isolate rhythmic pattern.

[1] Garde 1968, 73 (the acute accent here indicates stress, not, as in Czech orthography, vowel length).
[2] Cf. also Pulgram 1969, 381 n.
[3] Cf. Descroix 1931, 254.
[4] On the status of γάρ see further Sobolevskij 1964, 55; Parker 1968, 244 f.

LUTHER SEMINARY LIBRARY
2375 COMO AVENUE WEST
ST. PAUL, MINNESOTA 55108

3   The Syllable; Vowels and Consonants

Whilst questions of grammatical theory have only a marginal relevance to the matters to be discussed, it is far otherwise with certain basic problems of phonetics and phonology; and of these the most crucial concerns the *syllable*. This fact has long been recognized by linguists of all schools; already in 1906 Poirot (395) observed that accentual theory was still in a backward state because it was closely linked to that of the syllable, and that this latter field of phonetics was still largely a *terra incognita*; and in 1949 Haugen (280) expressed the view that a valid analysis of prosodic phenomena could not be made without some implicit or explicit definition of the syllable. The relevance of the syllable to metrical 'prosody' was already well realized in antiquity, most specifically in Longinus' Prolegomena to Hephaestion's *Enchiridion* (83 C): 'The material (ὕλη) of metre is the syllable, and without the syllable there could be no metre.' But as Haugen later complained (1956, 213), 'The syllable has become something of a stepchild in linguistic description. While sooner or later everyone finds it convenient to use, no one does much about defining it.'[1] Pulgram similarly (1970, 11) remarks that the syllable has been widely employed without being defined – 'on the assumption, it seems, that everyone knows what it is. Everyone does not know.' It is perhaps symptomatic that in Crystal's discussion of English prosodies the inventory of syllables is taken as 'given' (1968, 5 n.1), and for 'issues of syllable division, etc.' one is referred to O'Connor & Trim 1953 (see below); the latter, however, as Crystal points out, make 'a complementary deliberate omission' by taking no account of prosodic features.

Phonological approaches

A glance at the studies by Rosetti (1959) or Hála (1961) or Laziczius (1961/1966) will give an idea of the multiplicity of views on the subject; but the most basic differentiation of the various approaches is that of

---

[1] Cf. Bell 1970b, 17.

phonetic vs phonological or 'phonotactic'.[1] To take the latter first, the most uncompromising representative of the phonological, structural approach is, characteristically, Hjelmslev: 'If phonetics has not as yet succeeded in giving a consistent definition of the syllable, the vowel and the consonant, the reason is that these units have been conceived as pure sound units' (1938, 272); more positively (266), 'A syllable is a chain of expression including one and only one accent' – a definition carried to its logical conclusion in an 'accentless' language like French, which is consequently said to have no true syllables.[2] A more realistic approach to the question from a phonological angle is that of O'Connor & Trim (1953); first, the phonemes of English are classified into vowel and consonant categories on the basis of their combinatory potentials; then the syllable may be defined as 'a minimal pattern of phoneme combination with a vowel unit as nucleus, preceded and followed by a consonant unit or permitted consonant combination' (122). This method has also been applied to French by Arnold (1956).

SYLLABIFICATION

However, it is one thing to produce a viable definition of the syllable in general, and another to establish criteria for the delimitation of syllables one from another – i.e. for 'syllabification'. Such criteria are generally sought in the permitted initial and final phoneme sequences[3] of words; thus in considering English *anger* /æŋgə/, the syllabic division would be placed between the /ŋ/ and /g/ because the sequence /ŋg/ is permitted neither initially nor (in RP) finally in a word, whereas /ŋ/ is permitted finally and /g/ is permitted initially. But the main difficulty arises from the fact that latitude in the permitted word-initial and word-final sequences often makes either one or another division equally possible by this criterion: the word *extra*, for example, would allow of divisions /ek.strə/ or /eks.trə/ or /ekst.rə/ (cf. *back stroke, sex trial, next row*). In such cases of indeterminacy a preference for one or other syllabification may be stated in terms of statistical probability. Thus, with regard to

[1] Cf. Pulgram 1970, 22.

[2] Hjelmslev concedes, however, that vowel and consonant can be determined in such a language if it possesses words of a single phoneme, as Fr. *à, ou*. Such phonemes are thereby classifiable as vowels, and on this basis a unit including one and only one vowel can be defined as a 'pseudo-syllable'.

[3] The term *sequence* will be used throughout as a general term, with its function specified as necessary, in preference to a series of terms implying function, as 'cluster', 'group', 'series', 'string', etc. (e.g. Pulgram 1970, 57 n.28, 79; Collinge 1970, 194 n.); cf. Huffman 1972, 66.

the choice between VC.V and V.CV, one may take into account the number of types of word-initial V and CV, and of word-final V and VC; these are respectively (for English) 12, 421; 12, 277. The probability of a division VC.V would then be assessed as $277 + 12 = 289$, and that of V.CV as $12 + 421 = 433$, which is clearly in favour of the latter. Similarly, if divisions V.CCV, VCC.V, and VC.CV are all possible, one would also take into account the number of types of word-initial and word-final CC, viz. 26 and 59 respectively; the probability of a division V.CCV would then be assessed as $12 + 26 = 38$, of VCC.V as $59 + 12 = 71$, and of VC.CV as a decisive $277 + 421 = 698$ (O'Connor & Trim 1953, 121).[1]

Ancient theories

The application of this kind of criterion has a long history. It begins with the rules of the Greek grammarians, as e.g. of Herodian (ii, 393 ff. L), that consonant sequences are generally divided between syllables, but that those which may occur initially are taken in combination (ἐν συλλήψει) with the following vowel, as are single consonants: 'thus in κτῆμα the κτ is initial in the word; but even when it occurs medially, as in ἔτικτον, the κ and τ are combined' (i.e. ἔ.τι.κτον). Such rules were primarily formulated for practical, graphical purposes of internal word-division at the ends of lines,[2] and as such were unobjectionable. In typographical practice the main principles of the Greek rules still persist, though sometimes modified on the basis of confused phonetic reasoning.[3] That they were not in origin of purely phonetic or phonological motivation is seen from the exception which permits the normal rules to be overridden by grammatical considerations, as e.g. προσ.ῆκεν (Herodian, ii, 407 L); and in fact the syllabic delimitations which they advocate would often be in conflict with other phonological criteria. But, disregarding their prime motivation, they evidently contain more than a grain of phonological reasoning regarding the distribution of phonemes in relation to word-initial and word-final position;[4] the principle is basically that expressed by Pulgram (1970, 46): 'any syllable boundary in any part of the utterance must obey the constraints that prevail in the language under scrutiny at the word boundary'. The criterion of initial sequences is a case in point; and the

---

[1] Cf. Arnold 1956, 280 f. For criticism see Bell 1970b, 43 ff., 80 f. n.4.
[2] Cf. *Hermann 1923, 123 ff.   [3] For further details see A 1968a, 99 n.2.
[4] Cf. Bell 1971, 44 n.4.

rule which divides a sequence VCV as V.CV rather than VC.V could be based on a realization that the inventory of true word-final single consonants in Greek is exceptionally limited, viz. ν, ρ, ς.[1] Moreover, whereas the Latin grammarians typically repeat the Greek rules, Latin inscriptions tend, to a greater degree than Greek, to disregard these where they conflict with phonetic intuitions.[2]

The much earlier and probably pre-literate Sanskrit rules for sylla-bification can hardly have had an orthographic basis;[3] they are likely to stem from close phonetic observation, and come much nearer to satisfy-ing other phonological criteria. With some slight variation in doctrine, for example, the first consonant of a medial consonant sequence is allotted to the preceding syllable, without any reference to possible word-initial sequences.[4]

Phonetic approaches

Assuming that it is possible to determine unambiguously for a given language the boundaries between, and so the structure of, syllables on the basis of vowel and consonant distribution, the question may then legitimately be raised whether the syllable is a necessary concept in phonology (thus Kohler 1966; cf. A 1956, 170). If, having been estab-lished on the basis of such distribution, it is then used as an explanation of that distribution,[5] and if this is its only use, then, on grounds of circularity and redundancy, the answer seems to be negative. But if syllable structure provides an explanation of other phonological char-acteristics, the situation is quite different; and in the languages with which we are primarily concerned this is certainly the case. But it is also the case that in these languages syllable structure cannot be determined solely on the basis of phoneme distribution. In Latin, for example, we might explain the difference in accentuation between *honéstus* and *tónitrus* on the basis of a syllabification /ho.nes.tus/ vs /to.ni.trus/. But the difference between the sequences *st* and *tr* can hardly be estab-lished on the basis of distributional criteria relating to word initials or

---

[1] ἐκ and οὐκ are proclitic forms; the pre-pausal forms are ἐξ and οὐ.
[2] Cf. A 1965, 90; 1968a, 99 n.2.
[3] Particularly as in the Indian writing systems medial consonant sequences are compounded into a single character regardless of their nature: thus in Devanāgarī script a word *patanti* 'they fall' is written पतन्ति = *pa/ta/nti*, though other con-siderations make it inconceivable that *nt* could begin a syllable in Sanskrit.
[4] A 1953, 81 f.   [5] Cf. Anderson 1969, 140.

finals; for both are equally permissible as word initials, whilst *t* and *r* are also equally possible initially and *s* and *t* finally.[1] The difference in syllabification would then have to be inferred from the difference in accentuation, and the argument would again be circular. Certainly there are distributional differences between *st* and *tr* in Latin[2] which would be congruent with the above syllabifications, but they are not such as to explain them.

Moreover, as Bell (1970b, 21) observes, 'The universality of the distributional regularities and the role of the synchronic process in their preservation[3] argue strongly that their basis is phonetic, and probably ultimately physiological'.

It therefore seems necessary in this context to break out of the phonological circle, and to see whether a phonetic approach to the definition and delimitation of the syllable will provide a more satisfactory explanation of the phenomena. It is hoped that the particular approach to be adopted will be found not only to avoid circularity, but also to account for a number of characteristics which could in any case not be explained simply on the basis of the phonological structure in terms of vowels and consonants.

In any case a clear separation of the phonetic and phonological criteria for syllabification is essential; and the phonetic criteria must moreover be based on an explicitly stated theory and not simply on impressionistic judgements – a principle that is obviously of particular importance in dealing with 'dead' languages. If criteria are not clearly stated, then there is no way of selecting between the often bewildering choice of solutions presented by different approaches, phonetic as well as phonological. A few examples will make this evident.

Hála (1961, 129) records no less than three different opinions on the syllabification of geminate consonants; and the single intervocalic consonants of English provide a wide variety of interpretations. O'Connor & Trim (1953, 121) suggest that their criteria account for the 'often heard dictum' that 'if possible a syllable should begin with a consonant'. But this dictum is subject to considerable modification by other writers. Haugen (1956, 219) refers to a 'traditional rule of English syllable

---

[1] Note also that in the history of both Latin and Greek the syllabification of certain sequences (as shown by other criteria) has varied, although distribution has remained basically unaltered (cf. pp. 138, 211).

[2] E.g. the fact that *tr*, like simple *t*, can follow an initial *s*, whereas *st* cannot be preceded by an initial consonant; or that *st* can occur in final position, whereas *tr* cannot.   [3] Cf. pp. 11, 52.

division that a single intervocalic consonant goes with preceding
"short" vowel, but not with preceding "long" vowel'; such a rule,
however, as others have pointed out, needs to include reference to the
incidence of stress so far as short vowels are concerned.[1] The kind of
dilemma that can arise from the conflict of phonetic and phonological
criteria is highlighted by Sharp (1960, 132 ff., in connexion with the
further problem of morpheme structure): a phonetically intuited division
of *beetroot*, for example, as /bii.truut/, 'though morphemically regret-
table, would not be likely to shock the *phonological* conscience of most
scholars', whereas Sharp's intuited division /be.dru(u)m/ for *bedroom*
'is in danger of being rejected on the ground that a stressed syllable
ending in a short vowel is impossible'.[2] The conflict of views on intervocalic single consonants has been resolved for several writers by the
assumption that they may in some languages, including English, belong
to both preceding and following syllables, being then variously described as 'ambisyllabic' (Eliason 1942, 146), 'interlude' (Hockett 1955,
52), 'intersyllabic' (Higginbottom 1964, 139), 'ambivalent' (Kohler
1966): cf. also Sievers 1901, 209; Sturtevant 1922, 42.[3]

Another and more abstract approach to the problem is to consider all
syllables as beginning with a consonant, i.e. as having a structure CV(C),
where C = one or more consonants and the final C is optional; essential
to this analysis, of course, is the acceptance that the first (syllable-initial)
C may = # (zero).[4]

As a brief historical survey will show, it is not only in modern discussions that we find the syllable recognized as a basic phonetic unit,
and moreover as being composed of what may be termed 'nuclear' and
'marginal' phases, generally corresponding to the vowel and consonant
sounds respectively. The earliest descriptions, however, distinguish
these two categories on a segmental, auditory basis which, for Greek, is
reflected in the titles φωνήεντα and ἄφωνα, referring to their independent
audibility or otherwise: e.g. Plato, *Crat.* 426c; *Phil.* 18B; Aristotle,
Poet. 1456b. This criterion may also be supplemented by equally segmental articulatory factors, notably by the absence or presence of con-

---

[1] E.g. Sturtevant 1922, 42; Trager & Bloch 1941, 234; Vanvik 1961, 40 f; Hoard
1966, 107; similarly, on Welsh, Roberts 1968, 112. Bell (1970b, 42) notes, for
example, the difference in syllabification between *supplánt* and *súpplicate*.
[2] Cf. Pulgram 1970, 49.
[3] Another possible factor underlying such indeterminacy is discussed on p. 44.
[4] Cf. Anderson 1969, 137 ff; Zirin 1970, 62 f., 85 f. (the former suggesting # as
the 'lenis equivalent' of /h/ in English, and the latter as = /h/ in Latin).

tact (προσβολή) between the speech organs: e.g. Aristotle, *Poet.* 1457a; *Hist. An.* 535a. For the ancient Indian phoneticians this latter is the primary criterion for the vowel/consonant dichotomy,[1] e.g. in the phonetic treatise of the Black Yajur-Veda:[2] 'For the vowels the "place of articulation" (*sthānam*) signifies the place to which APPROXIMATION (*upasaṃhāras*) is made, and the 'articulator' (*karaṇam*) refers to the organ which effects the approximation. For the rest the "place of articulation" refers to the place where CONTACT (*sparśanam*) is made, and the "articulator" refers to the organ which effects the contact.' Such a distinction is closely paralleled, in a modern idiom, by Pike's dichotomy (1943, 78) of 'vocoids' vs 'contoids': 'A *vocoid* is a sound during which air leaves the mouth over the center of the tongue and without friction in the mouth. A *contoid* is anything else.'

By Greek writers the auditory and articulatory criteria are combined in order to account for a class of sounds which are 'independently audible' but articulated with some degree of contact; and to this category is given the title of ἡμίφωνα (→ Latin *semiuocales*), comprising the fricative σ, the 'liquids' λ ρ, and the nasals ν μ; the list is extended by the fricative ʒ [z] in later Greek,[3] and by the further fricative *f* in Latin.[4]

In the later Greek writers, as Dionysius Thrax (11 f. U), the criterion of 'nuclear' vs 'marginal' function begins to make its appearance with the retitling of the ἄφωνα as σύμφωνα (→ Latin *consonantes*): 'They are called "consonants" because by themselves they have no speech sound (φωνή), but combined with the vowels they produce sound.'[5] The word 'syllable' (συλλαβή) is not expressly used in these classifications, but its relevance to them is implied in Dionysius' statement (16 U) that 'a syllable is, properly speaking, the combination (σύλληψις) of a consonant with a vowel' (cf. the statement of the phonetic treatise of the Ṛg-Veda:[6] 'A vowel with a consonant, or even by itself, forms a syllable').

It will have been noted that the Greek ἡμίφωνα (and the Latin *semiuocales*) form a class of 'continuant' consonants and have little in

---

[1] A 1953, 24 ff.   [2] *Taittirīya-Prātiśākhya* ii. 31 ff.
[3] Cf. A 1968a, 55 f.
[4] E.g. Aristotle, *Poet.* 1456b; Dionysius Thrax, 11 f. U; Dionysius Hal., *De Comp.*, 49, 52 ff. UR; Donatus, iv, 367 K. In Old Icelandic this category (with the calqued title '*hálft hljóð*') was yet further extended to the Icelandic fricatives ð, þ, and v (e.g. in the 2nd grammatical appendix to *Snorra Edda*, ed. Dahlerup & Jónsson, 65).
[5] Cf. Priscian, ii, 7 K.
[6] *Ṛk-Prātiśākhya* xviii. 32.

common with what are generally termed 'semivowels' in modern phonetics:[1] e.g. Jones 1962, 47 §183, 'a voiced gliding sound in which the speech organs start by producing a weakly articulated vowel of comparatively small inherent sonority and immediately change to another sound of equal or greater prominence. Examples English **j** (as in *yard*), **w**.' Though such sounds did not occur in classical Attic Greek, they were normal features of Latin; the fact is, however, that from an articulatory point of view they were identifiable with the vowel sounds [i] and [u], and in Latin were so written, viz. as I, V (cursive *j*, *u*): thus IVS, VIS, etc., and with ambiguous value in VOLVIT.

The modern definition of this category involves, explicitly or implicitly, consideration of their syllabic function rather than their purely segmental articulation, i.e. as vowel-like sounds which are nevertheless marginal by contrast with a 'more prominent' nuclear vowel. The Indians did indeed recognize such sounds as a special 'intermediate' category (*antaḥsthās*), no doubt on the basis of their marginal syllabic function, but with typical concentration on articulatory criteria they attempted to classify them by reference to their degree of contact, alleging them to have greater stricture even than the fricatives, which is almost certainly mistaken.[2]

The modern approach to the categorization of semivowels in terms of syllabic function is to some extent foreshadowed by Priscian (ii, 13 K): '*i* et *u*, quamuis unum nomen et unam habent figuram tam uocales quam consonantes, tamen, quia diuersum sonum et diuersam uim habent in metris et in pronuntiatione syllabarum, non sunt in eisdem meo iudicio elementis accipiendae.' But no distinction between the vocalic and consonantal values was generally made in the writing of Latin until quite recent times.[3] In the Middle Ages the material basis was laid for such a distinction by the tendency to specialize *v* and *j* as word-initial variants; but the definitive adoption of these for consonantal purposes dates only from Pierre la Ramée's *Scholae Grammaticae* of 1559.[4] In modern times, as Pike comments (1943, 76), 'Syllabic contextual function is reflected in phonetic alphabets. Sounds which are

---

[1] Exceptionally, however, Grammont 1946, 77.

[2] A 1953, 27 f. Since Sanskrit (like some modern Slavonic languages, for example) also had 'nuclear' *ṛ* and *ḷ*, the 'liquid' consonants *r* and *l* are similarly classed as 'intermediate' by the native grammarians.

[3] For some use of the '*i* longa' in a consonantal value, however, see Väänänen 1959, 35.

[4] A 1965, 37 n.2.

described by the same procedure but which are used differently in phonemic systems as syllabics in contrast to non-syllabics are given different symbols' (the **j** and **w** of the International Phonetic Alphabet are an obvious case in point).

SEGMENTAL VS CONTEXTUAL CRITERIA

The semivowels do in fact catalyse the whole matter of the difference between segmental-articulatory and contextual-syllabic criteria, which Pike clearly underlines by creating a terminological distinction between the articulatorily defined 'vocoids' and 'contoids' on the one hand, and on the other hand 'vowels' and 'consonants', which are 'categories of sounds, not as determined by their own phonetic nature, but according to their grouping in specific syllabic contextual functions' (1943, 78), i.e. as 'nuclear' vs 'marginal'. Moreover, as Pike also recognizes, whereas the former classification is universal, the latter is a flexible one, depending on the characteristics of the particular languages. In this sense it might be considered as 'phonological', but it is based on the interrelationship between two phonetic parameters, the oral articulation and the syllabic process, a relationship which different languages may handle in rather different ways. Examples of such differences already encountered would be the consonantal utilization of close 'vocoid' articulations ([i] and [u]) in Latin as against Greek, and the vocalic utilization of 'contoid' liquid articulations ([r] and [l]) in Sanskrit as against Greek or Latin.[1]

It has seemed worth while to devote some attention to the duality of criteria for the consonant/vowel classification even within phonetics; for confusion of these criteria is liable in turn to bedevil any attempt to understand the phonetic nature of the syllable. The dangers have been well stated by Pike (1943, 78 f.): 'No other phonetic dichotomy entails so many difficulties as consonant–vowel division; articulatory and acoustic criteria are there so thoroughly entwined with contextual and strictural function and problems of segmentation that only a rigid descriptive order will separate them . . . lacking it, difficulties initiating at this point carry clear through a system.' Specifically, it is essential to recognize that the most common and intuitive criterion for the dichotomy is the one which relates to syllabic function; and consequently that

[1] In various languages a wide range of 'contoid' articulations may function as syllabic nuclei, including nasals, fricatives, and even stops (cf. Bell 1970a; 1970b, 159 ff.); for the last of these note even in English the syllabic value of [b] in a type of pronunciation of the word *probably* in which the middle vowel is suppressed.

a description of the syllabic process is a prerequisite to this dichotomy rather than vice versa.

Whilst the number of syllables in a given language depends, from a phonological standpoint, upon the criteria applied, which may result in widely differing statements, there is generally less variation in the assessment of the number of phonetic syllables. This may be most clearly exemplified by one or two extreme cases. For some languages Hockett (1955, 57 f.)[1] recognizes the possibility of 'onset-type' syllables, in which the consonantal onset is the only essential feature; such a language is Bella Coola (of British Columbia), in which, on this basis, a word such as *sk'lxlxc* 'I'm getting cold' is syllabified phonologically as /s.k'l.xl.x.c/, i.e. five syllables. A slightly different situation is presented by the Dravidian Kota language (of the Nilgiri Hills), where a word of the form *anžrčgčgvdk* 'because ~ will cause ~ to frighten ~' is similarly syllabifiable as /an.ž.r.č.g.č.g.v.d.k/, i.e. ten syllables; but since in this language every word contains at least one syllable with a distinctive peak (here the vowel /a/), one might choose to define the syllable as containing a peak, in which case the example would be monosyllabic.[2] A similar case is presented by Abaza (of the N.W. Caucasus),[3] where, according to the phonological criteria selected, a word such as *yg'yzdmlrətxd* 'they couldn't make him give it back to her' may be stated as having either eleven syllables or one; whilst yet another analysis, inspired by the remarkable vowel distribution in this language, would completely eliminate the syllable (together with vowel and consonant) as a primary phonological concept.[4] But *phonetically*, in the case of the Kota example (as Hockett points out), any full consonant before another full consonant 'is followed by "loose transition" to the next, producing a murmur vowel, an aspiration, or the like; phonetically, but not phonologically, this may be taken as a syllable peak'. In Abaza the incidence of such 'loose transition' is governed by the number and type of consonants in sequence;[5] phonetically the example cited is [jig̬iizdıml̩'rıtxd], which I have found to be interpreted (by mostly English-speaking hearers) as containing either five or six syllables. All are agreed on the five phonetic

[1] Cf. Bell 1970a, 30.
[2] As in fact implied in Emeneau's description of the language (1944, 16). In contrast with the extensive final consonant-sequences, Emeneau observes that initially there are *no* sequences except in loan words, which in any case are liable to modification: e.g. /krič̆t/ 'Christ' (also /kirič̆t/), /pruup/ 'proof' (also /purp/).
[3] A 1956, 170 ff.
[4] Cf. Kuipers 1960, 50 ff., 104 ff. on the closely related Kabardian.
[5] A 1956, 141 f.

peaks represented by [i], [ii], [ɪ], [ḷ], [ɪ] respectively. But one's interpretation is liable to be influenced also by the distributional characteristics of one's native language; and the variation in response relates to the unfamiliar consonant-sequence [txd], where the untrained English speaker would tend to insert a 'murmur vowel' transition at some point, and so infers its presence even if objectively it does not occur. Similar considerations can apply to more familiar languages; for example, the untrained English hearer's interpretation of Russian *tkat'* 'to weave' or *rta* 'mouth' (gen.) as disyllabic; or the interpretation of e.g. English *skates* /skeits/ by Chinese speakers as trisyllabic and by Japanese speakers as quadrisyllabic.[1] Interpretations of this kind are often reflected in the form in which foreign words are borrowed, as e.g. Japanese /arupensuttoku/ (alpenstock) or Hausa /sukuru-direba/ (screwdriver).[2]

Such variations of interpretation as these last depend not so much on the application of different theoretical criteria as on interference by native speech-habits; for the ear trained to the 'key' of a particular language, especially that of the native speaker, the syllable-count at least tends to be consistent. But it is one thing to agree on the *number* of syllables in an utterance (and even perhaps the identification of their nuclei), and quite another to determine their precise constitution (which also involves their points of delimitation or transition), whether in the rôle of speaker or of hearer. Experimental evidence seems to suggest that 'the perception of syllable structure . . . is based mainly on kinaesthetic memory' (Fry 1964, 218) – that, in other words, the speaker interprets what he hears not on a directly auditory basis, but by referring it to the movements which he would perform as speaker in order to produce the given audible effect. But unlike the articulation of consonants, for example, which involves relatively small and superficially sensitive organs or areas of organs (lips, tongue-tip, etc.), the syllabic process, however clearly felt in its entirety, and in spite of its possibly functioning as the prime 'unit of motor control' (Fry 1964, 219; cf. p. 72), is less accessible to detailed kinaesthetic analysis. For deep-seated processes of this type, introspection may indeed prove as valid as any other approach so long as one is concerned only with relatively simple judgements, involving, for example, binary choices such as yes/no, same/different; but questions of the internal constitution of the process can hardly be answered by

[1] Cf. Pike 1967, 373. Bloch (1950, 92 n.14) even notes, 'In the English word *asks*, pronounced with a long vowel and distinctly released consonants, a Japanese will hear five syllables.'

[2] Firth 1948, 149 f.

such methods. Any detailed theory of the phonetic nature of the syllable, therefore, must look elsewhere for its inspiration. In choosing between rival theories one will of course require that an acceptable theory should not be actually counterintuitive, but apart from this one's choice will depend on the scope of its effectiveness, as judged by such criteria as universality of application, or explanatory power in relation to other phenomena.

RESPIRATORY THEORY

Of the phonetic theories of the syllable proposed in the course of the last hundred years, the principal may be classified as respiratory, articulatory, and acoustic. The earliest of these is one form of respiratory theory, whereby the syllable is defined in such terms as 'a sound-group produced with a single respiratory impulse'.[1] But as stated in this crude form it was easy to disprove even by quite elementary experimentation, which showed that what everyone would acknowledge to be two or more syllables might be spoken during a single expiration; and this failure led some experimentalists, e.g. Scripture and Panconcelli-Calzia,[2] to write a premature obituary of the whole idea of the syllable.

ACOUSTIC THEORY

By other phoneticians a solution was sought in the acoustic concept of 'sonority' (Germ. 'Schallfülle'), such that maxima of sonority represented syllabic nuclei and minima syllabic margins.[3] 'Sonority' in this sense is a portmanteau term for the acoustic resultant of a number of factors, which in its most extended form may include voicing (glottal vibration), degree of aperture/stricture between the articulating organs, expiratory force, pitch, muscular energy (of consonants), duration (of vowels), 'penetration' (of fricative sounds).[4] It is generally conceived of in impressionistic auditory terms, as a measure of the 'audibility' of sounds; and since variations on this scale are maximally discernible in voiced sounds and minimally in voiceless, a prime rôle is attributed to

---

[1] For references see e.g. Vietor 1894, 296 ff; Jespersen 1913, 190. A forerunner of this definition is seen in Marius Victorinus (vi, 26 K): 'syllaba est coniunctio litterarum cum uocali uel uocalibus sub uno accentu (cf. Hjelmslev) et spiritu continuata'; similarly Priscian (ii, 44 K): 'comprehensio litterarum consequens sub uno accentu et uno spiritu prolata'. One suspects a common Greek source, but the references to accent and breath are not found in Dionysius Thrax.

[2] Cf. Malmberg 1955, 81; Rosetti 1959, 12.

[3] For further discussion cf. Bell 1970b, 31 ff.

[4] Vietor 1894, 296.

the factor of voicing.[1] The auditory impressions do in fact tend to corre-late reasonably well with degrees of acoustic energy, which can nowadays be accurately measured by electronic methods.[2] The weakness of the theory is its inability to establish any meaningful order amongst sounds of low sonority; and a particular problem is presented by the fricative [ʃ], which by both auditory and acoustic criteria turns out not only, like other fricatives, to be more 'sonorous' than the plosives, but also than any of the nasals;[3] so that the theory could hardly account for such words as Eng. *Horsham* [hɔɔʃm̩] or *station* [steiʃn̩], where [ʃ] forms a syllabic margin and [m̩] or [n̩] a nucleus.[4] More recently this particular problem is avoided by Hála (1961, 75), who adopts a more restricted definition of 'sonority', viz. as lack of damping of the glottal tone, and so excludes the factor of 'penetration' which tends to exaggerate the status of the fricatives. This approach would, however, involve a denial of the possibility of nuclear function for the fricatives, which is contra-dicted by the existence of such forms as *pst!* [ps̩t].[5]

Some phoneticians have admitted the possibility of both expiratory and sonorant syllables (e.g. Sievers 1901, 203); it is suggested that, for instance, the sonorant syllable formed by the diphthong [ai] may be broken into two expiratory syllables [a.i]; and conversely (Sievers, 209) a word such as Eng. *hammer* [hæmə], containing two sonorant syllables, may form a single expiratory syllable, in which case (225) the intervening consonant belongs equally to both syllables.

ARTICULATORY THEORY

Another and influential approach to the problem was that of de Saussure (1916/1960, 51 ff.), based on the articulatory criterion of aperture alone; a syllable then consists of a sound or sequence of sounds of increasing aperture (constituting an 'explosion') followed by a sound or sequence of decreasing aperture (constituting an 'implosion'). This theory will of course take care of syllables such as [ps̩t], in Saussurean notation p̌s̑t̑, but on the other hand will not explain cases of the type of Greek κτείνω (with initials of equal aperture), nor of e.g. Eng. *steps*, which begins with a decrease in aperture and ends with an increase, i.e. s̑t̑ĕp̂s̑. De Saussure attempts to deal with such cases by various *ad hoc* devices (54 f; cf. 59 ff.) which, however, carry little conviction. In fact the theory can

---

[1] Sweet 1906, 65; Jespersen 1913, 190.   [2] Cf. Heffner 1950, 74.
[3] Cf. Zirin 1970, 20.
[4] For other criticisms see Lebrun 1966a.   [5] Rosetti 1959, 27.

only deal satisfactorily with what de Saussure himself (57) significantly termed the 'normal chain' of explosions and implosions, as e.g. in Eng. *drĭnk*.[1]

Underlying the aperture theory, as Grammont puts it (1946, 99), is the 'notion vulgaire que pour parler il faut ouvrir la bouche; après l'avoir ouverte pour parler, on la referme pour se taire'; and in an attempt to remedy its shortcomings Grammont introduces (100 ff.) the concept of 'tension', with the rule that transition from one syllable to another is implied if a sound of decreasing tension is followed by a sound of increasing tension,[2] but not otherwise. Thus in Grammont's notation *un arbre creux* appears as

ɶnarbrɶkrɶ

and English *steps* would appear as . But unfortunately the term 'tension' remains undefined except in terms of the very phenomena it is intended to explain;[3] the first and second *r* of *arbre*, for example, are said to have decreasing and increasing tension respectively only on account of their positions in the syllables.

MOTOR THEORY

It will be seen later that elements of all the theories discussed above[4] may be connected in various ways with the syllabic process. But this does not mean that the model of description to be followed is simply a synthesis of all the others, as tends to be the case, for example, with that of Hála (1961, esp. 101 f.). We shall instead adopt a unitary theory of the syllable which is essentially that of Stetson (1945; 1951). This theory seems to possess a high degree of 'explanatory' adequacy, in Chomsky's sense (1964, 28), in so far as it enables one to evaluate other theories in relation to one another and to account for their respective inadequacies. But the primary reason for our choice is that Stetson's theory also proves to have a higher degree of 'descriptive' adequacy in relation to the phenomena which we shall be studying, in so far as it 'specifies the

[1] Cf. Fouché's 'perfect' (vs 'imperfect') syllables (1927, 7).
[2] Similarly Sommerfelt 1931, 158.
[3] Cf. Hála 1961, 78 f.
[4] For a fuller account of these and other theories see de Groot 1927; Hála 1961; Laziczius 1961/1966.

observed data in terms of significant generalizations that express underlying regularities in the language'.

As the title of Stetson's main published work (1951) indicates, his
model of the syllabic process rests upon a 'motor' theory; that is to say,
the process is described in terms of a physiological movement, more
specifically of the intercostal muscles of the chest, and is thus in some
way related to respiration. But earlier respiratory approaches to the
syllable had, in Stetson's terms, been concerned with the 'abdominal
breath pulse', effected by the opposed actions of the rectus abdominis
and diaphragm muscles, and characterizing the 'breath-group' and
'foot'[1] rather than the syllable; whereas 'the rapid pulses of the intercostal muscles for individual syllables have been generally overlooked
by experimenters' (1951, 16). The intercostal muscles, external and
internal, which in respiration have the respective functions of raising
and lowering the ribs (in inspiration and expiration), act in mutual
opposition to effect the 'chest pulse', which, according to Stetson, defines the syllable: 'A slight (air) pressure is generally maintained during
the breath group . . . but the chest pulses of the syllable rise from this
level' (3). This movement of the chest muscles is further characterized
as a 'ballistic' type of movement, as opposed to 'controlled' or 'tense'.[2]
In the latter type, the 'opposing groups of muscles work together in
producing the movement . . . The direction of the movement can be
changed after it is under way; such a movement is relatively slow' (28);
as an example Stetson mentions the process of forgery by tracing, which
can be detected under magnification by minute changes in direction of
the 'controlled' movement, as opposed to the more rapid, 'ballistic'
movements of normal writing. In speech 'the large breathing movement
of the entire phrase is a slow, "controlled" movement during which the
rapid pulses of the syllables occur, like ripples on a wave'.

In a ballistic movement, to quote Stetson at length,

the entire movement consists of a single pulse. It is impossible to change the
movement during its course. The member is indeed thrown from one limit
to the other like a projectile, as the name implies. A study of the action of the
muscles in such ballistic movements shows that the movement is started by
a sudden contraction of the positive muscle-group which immediately relaxes.
During at least half of the course of the movement neither of the antagonistic

---

[1] Defined (3) as 'due to an abdominal pulse which integrates a single stressed syllable
or a few syllables grouped about a single stressed syllable'.
[2] Cf. also Lehiste 1970, 8.

muscle-groups is contracted, so that the moving member flies free. At the end of its course the movement is usually arrested by the contraction of the negative muscle-group. The movement is a movement by momentum.

Thus for Stetson (33):

The syllable is constituted by a ballistic movement of the intercostal muscles. Its delimitation is not due to a 'point of minimal sonority' but to the conditions which define a movement as one movement. *In the individuality of the syllable the sound is secondary; syllables are possible without sound. Speech is rather a set of movements made audible than a set of sounds produced by movements* (my italics).

However, as Stetson elsewhere emphasizes (1945, 90), the consonant and vowel sounds are 'not mere beads strung on a string'. The syllabic pulse generally has the effect of setting the vocal cords in vibration, and the vowel may then be viewed as an essential accompanying articulation[1] which modulates the resulting glottal tone; the consonants, on the other hand, are auxiliary and non-essential movements, which however, when they occur, may have a function in the syllabic process. The ballistic movement of the chest pulse is described as beginning with a 'release' and ending with an 'arrest'; both release and arrest may be effected by the intercostal muscles alone, as in a syllable consisting of a single vowel (type V); but the release may be assisted by a simultaneous consonant stroke (type CV), and the arrest may be effected by a consonant stroke alone (type VC), which blocks or restricts the egress of air from the lungs; in a syllable of type CVC both consonantal functions are operative (Stetson, 7, 50).

The advantages of this theory over the 'sonority' or 'aperture' theories of the syllable have been well stated by Stetson himself (171 ff.). But we may note in particular that it does not rely upon identification and classification of the constituent oral articulations – it is in a sense 'generative' rather than 'taxonomic' (cf. Stetson, 6);[2] and as current

---

[1] Essential since the air must pass through the buccal cavity, with some consequent filtering of the signal, the precise nature of which will vary with tongue and lip positions: cf. Joos 1948, 49 ff.

[2] But, as observed by Brown (1972, 40; cf. 1970, 5), 'the concept of the syllable has not yet been introduced into the theory of generative phonology in a way which exploits its potential for accounting for the phonetic distribution of underlying elements': cf. Harms 1968, 116 ff; Bell 1970b, 74, 82 n.7; Sampson 1970, 602. In a tagmemic study by Gudschinsky & Popovich, however (1970), 'The syllable is then used as the matrix for the distribution of the phonemes and as a conditioning environment for some of the variants'; cf. also Harrell 1962.

models of grammar treat syntax rather than morphology as central, Stetson's theory gives the syllable primacy over the consonants and vowels, which are defined by their function in relation to the ballistic movement of the chest pulse. The division between syllables is the division between chest pulses, and the allocation of consonants to one syllable or another is determined by their releasing or arresting functions. A sequence of consonants may operate in an arresting + releasing function; but they may also operate together as a complex arrest or release (cf. Stetson, 83 ff.). There is then no theoretical problem in a syllable of the type [steps], where [st] and [ps] are respectively complex releases and arrests, as against in e.g. *piston* or *popsy*, where the same sequences are divided between syllables. The 'problems' of cases like κτεί(νω) reside only in the fact that certain types of sequence are more amenable to complex function on account of their relative articulations (including their 'aperture'), and so tend to occur in such functions more commonly than other sequences.[1] For example, a syllable such as Eng. *ply* [plai] or *try* [trai] is 'normal', in de Saussure's terms, only in so far as 'the liquid (*l*, *r*) is so open a conformation that it permits the pulse of the syllable movement to begin' (Stetson, 84);[2] in an English syllable like *spy* [spai] 'the fricative occurs during the preparation of the beat stroke' (of the primary oral articulation [p]). Languages vary greatly in this respect;[3] unlike Greeks, for example, many English speakers, for whom the type *spy* is 'normal', find difficulty in cases like *psi*, where 'the accessory sound occurs during the back stroke'. On the other hand, for many languages, or periods of languages, the *spy* type is anomalous, and the syllabic structure is modified accordingly: thus classical Latin *sc(h)ola*, *spiritum* are later found in the forms *iscola*, *espiritum*, with a prothetic vowel to which the first consonant can be attached (whence, in western Romance languages, e.g. Sp. *escuela*, *espíritu*, Fr. *école*, *esprit*); and a word like Eng. *school*, when borrowed into modern Indian languages, takes on such forms as *iskūl* (with prothesis) or *sikūl* (with the sequence broken by an 'anaptyctic' vowel): cf. Sharma 1971, 64 ff.

Similar considerations apply to the type κτεί(νω), Russ. *tkat'*, where

---

[1] For some statistics on plosive + liquid see Bell 1971, 47.

[2] In a more recent visual-acoustic study it has been shown experimentally (Truby 1964, 104) that in a word like Eng. *play* there is 'physiological pre-positioning of the tongue to the lateral resonance articulation *before* the lips burst open for the audible phase of the initial plosive...the tongue assumes its most extreme lateral articulatory position some 50 msec (on the average) before *any* sound is heard'.

[3] Cf. Zirin 1970, 22 f.

'the beat strokes occur so close together that they fuse with each other in arresting or releasing the syllable movement'. Syllables such as Efik *mkpa* 'death' or Zande *mgba(ku)* 'adze' are even further removed from English speech-habits, yet are extremely common in a number of African languages.[1] The rules governing initial consonant sequences may be quite complex; in Georgian (Vogt 1958, 29 ff.) a plosive may be followed by a plosive articulated further back in the mouth only if it has the same glottal characteristics (voiced, aspirated, or glottalized); but heterogeneous sequences may occur if the relative places of articulation are reversed, as e.g. in *t'bilisi* 'Tiflis' (voiceless aspirated followed by voiced plosive with progressive articulatory order). By Stetson's theory the 'problems' of such cases are reduced to practical matters of articulatory adjustment in particular languages,[2] and are of no general theoretical significance to the definition or delimitation of the syllable.

It does not necessarily follow that marginal elements of the syllable will always be exactly coterminous with the beginning or end of a chest pulse, and this may be a particularly common source of disagreement on syllabic boundaries, particularly on the part of the hearer. The complexities of coordination between oral and thoracic movements is such that a clear delimitation at the level of 'competence' may be more or less blurred in performance, and one might more cautiously speak of the relative 'adherence' of marginal to nuclear elements.[3] But provided that this reservation is borne in mind, there should be no danger in continuing to use the traditional terminology of 'division', 'boundary', etc.

The advantages of Stetson's theory for our own purposes will soon become apparent, and further details will be discussed at the appropriate points. It has already been found of value by a number of writers, including de Groot (1932, esp. 98), Pike (see below), Jakobson & Halle (1968, 423), and by Zirin (1970, 17) in a specifically 'prosodic' connexion. But it has not been without its critics, who have particular misgivings about Stetson's physiological experimentation, much of which had been carried out in the 1920s and left a good deal to be desired in the light of modern techniques: thus especially Ladefoged 1958; 1967; Lieberman 1967, 26, 191 ff. Even such criticism, however, is tempered by a recognition of the significance of Stetson's work (e.g. Ladefoged 1958, 3); another critic, Fry (1964, 217), acknowledges that 'the essence

---

[1] Cf. Westermann & Ward 1949, 66 f. For further examples see Bell 1970b, 33 ff.
[2] Cf. Huffman 1972.
[3] See especially Bell 1970b, 49 ff.

of rhythm and syllabification in speech is in fact movement', and that the results of later work 'do suggest that Stetson was at least looking in the right place for evidence of syllabic action, that is in the movement of the speech muscles'. Fry's principal criticism is that 'the muscles used in speech are so numerous, the interaction of the various systems so complex that we should hardly expect to find syllabification controlled by a single muscle or even by the respiratory muscles alone'.[1] Pike, in an earlier work (1943, 53 f.), makes a number of detailed criticisms of Stetson's theory, but does not find it generally incompatible with his own ideas, and defines the syllable (116) as 'a single movement of the lung initiator, which includes but one crest of speed . . . Physiologically, syllables may also be called chest pulses'; and more recently (1967, 365 ff. nn.) Pike has come out in positive defence of Stetson against some of Ladefoged's criticisms, and with some reservations adopts his theory for his 'etic' (vs 'emic') purposes.

At the very least, in Ladefoged's terms (1958, 2 f.), 'the major part of Stetson's work should be considered as a theory attempting to explain how the respiratory muscles are involved in speech, rather than an account of the observed action of these muscles': cf. Twaddell 1953, 451 ff. and Laziczius' recognition (1961/1966, 224) that 'in more recent phonetic literature there is no other work as instructive in this respect as Stetson's'. For our purposes, provided that the model has the necessary descriptive adequacy, we need not insist on more than its theoretical validity;[2] and in fact the model will be found to have great explanatory power. We shall continue to refer to such concepts as 'chest pulses' etc., but with the caveat that the physiological definition of these terms need not be exactly what their literal sense implies.[3]

---

[1] This particular criticism is supported by the fact that apparently 'quite normal syllabification patterns occur in the speech of some patients with essentially complete paralysis of the respiratory musculature who use an iron lung for respiration' (Lehiste 1970, 109).

[2] Cf. Fromkin 1968, 51: 'the purpose...of any such model is to explain the phenomena, and it is justified in so far as it does make events understandable'.

[3] Cf. A 1969, 195.

4   Length and quantity

Certain primary prosodic features may now be considered in the light of a motor theory of the syllabic process – length, quantity, and (in a separate chapter) stress.

Vowel length

Very many languages, including Latin, Greek, and Sanskrit, make a significant distinction between categories of 'long' and 'short' vowels, as *mālus* vs *mălus*, λήγω vs λέγω, Skt *pŭrāṇas* 'ancient' vs *pūrāṇas* 'filling'. It has sometimes been assumed that, as the terminology suggests, the distinction is simply one of temporal duration. But phonetic studies of spoken languages in which this distinction is made show that, whilst 'long' vowels do tend to be of longer duration than 'short', and normally are so in comparable environments, the actual durations fluctuate to a considerable degree, and it is doubtful whether the hearer could always use them as *sole* criteria for judging the category to which a particular vowel sound belongs.[1] Moreover the relationship of the *perceptual* dimension of 'length' to objective duration seems not to be a simple one, and is not yet fully understood.[2]

QUALITATIVE FACTORS

Differences of 'length' are often linked with differences of *quality*.[3] In Latin, for example, *ĭ ŭ ĕ ŏ* had more open articulations than *ī ū ē ō* respectively;[4] in Attic Greek ε probably had a quality midway between that of η [εε] and ει [ee];[5] in Sanskrit short *ă* is regularly stated by the

---

[1] Environmentally determined fluctuation is liable to be particularly marked (e.g. before voiced vs voiceless consonants: cf. Chen 1970), though, as an allophonic feature, it is of less importance than free fluctuation (cf. Nooteboom 1971, 284 f.). Kerek (1968, 40) cites Fónagy for the observation that in Hungarian 'the objectively measured duration of short stressed vowels often equals the duration of unstressed long vowels'. Cf. Trubetzkoy 1935/1968, 38; Fischer-Jørgensen 1941, 175.

[2] Fry 1968, 386.

[3] Cf. Lehiste 1970, 30 ff.   [4] A 1965, 47 ff.

[5] A 1968a, 84 ff.

ancient phoneticians to have a close ('*saṃvṛta*') articulation as compared with the more open ('*vivṛta*') long *ā*,[1] and a qualitative distinction of this type is preserved in the modern Indo-Aryan languages. Indeed it may sometimes be difficult or even impossible to say that a particular vowel is the long correlate of a particular short vowel, and vice versa (cf. A 1959, 245 ff.). In English the distinctions of vowel length are particularly clearly associated with qualitative differences; and many modern writers take the view, as Kurath (1964, 18), that 'length is not a distinctive feature in the vowel system of MnE'.[2] That such qualitative differences have a long history in English is suggested by the divergence that has occurred between originally correlative pairs of short and long vowels, amplified by the operation upon the long vowels of the 'Great Vowel Shift' which characterized the development from Middle to Modern English; thus, for example, [æ] in *man* vs [eɪ] in *mane*, [e] in *men* vs [ii] in *mean*, [ɪ] in *bit* vs [aɪ] in *bite*. The original relationship is in many cases still indicated by the historical orthography, and is still functional in grammatical processes (e.g. *profane/profanity, obscene/obscenity, divine/divinity*),[3] and these two factors account for the native intuition which regards the diphthong [aɪ] of *bite*, for example, as an instance of 'long *i*'.

Such differences of quality between long and short vowels are generally attributed to a 'tense' as opposed to 'lax' articulation respectively, the latter being characterized by an attenuation of various processes in the vocal tract;[4] thus, as Trnka says of English (1966, 21), 'In order to feel a vowel as a long one, we must hear it pronounced tensely, the length alone being insufficient to produce this effect'. Tenseness tends generally to be associated with durational length, but exceptions are found. In Modern Icelandic both tense and lax vowels[5] (the former including diphthongs) occur in both long and short varieties; in stressed syllables, the short duration is normal when followed by more than one consonant, the long duration otherwise. For example, the lax vowel of *vita* 'to know' and the tense vowel of *víta* 'to blame' are both of relatively long duration; whereas the lax vowel of *kaldur* 'cold' and the tense

---

[1] A 1953, 57 f.
[2] Cf. e.g. Gimson 1970, 94 ff.
[3] Cf. Chomsky & Halle 1968, 50.
[4] See especially Jakobson & Halle 1964. For a critical survey of the concept of tenseness see Lebrun 1970.
[5] In Icelandic 'broad' and 'narrow' (earlier 'heavy' and 'light'). The tense vowels derive from Old Icelandic long vowels and diphthongs, and the lax vowels from short. Even when derived from simple long vowels, tense vowels are (with the exception noted below) in varying degrees diphthongal: cf. Haugen 1958, 66 ff.

vowel of *kálfur* 'calf' are both of relatively short duration.[1] In such cases a classification by some such criterion as tenseness, to the exclusion of length, is clearly indicated.

TIME RATIOS

Some traditional statements about length go so far as to describe the long vowels as having twice the duration of the short. In some languages the average values may happen to approximate to this ratio;[2] but the fluctuation is so great that it could hardly form the basis of any phonological equation; and the traditional statements are in fact based on a confusion of criteria (and in some cases probably of length and quantity). As will be seen at a later stage, a sequence of two short vowels (or two 'light' syllables) may, in certain languages and under certain conditions, carry the same accentual patterns as a single long vowel (or a 'heavy' syllable); historically also two short vowels in hiatus may contract into a single long vowel. Such synchronic or diachronic equivalences may provide a basis of alternation in certain types of metre (see pp. 255 ff.). But they do not in any way imply a *durational* ratio of 2:1 for long vowels (or 'heavy' syllables) to short vowels (or 'light' syllables).

The tradition of this proportional relationship of vowel durations seems to begin with the Greek musical writers (e.g. Aristides Quintilianus, *De Mus.*, 32, 41 f. W-I), for whom short vowels have the value of one time unit (χρόνος πρῶτος) and long vowels two. But musical conventions are one thing and normal speech (as opposed to singing) another – 'It is plain that the equivalence of a musical crotchet to two quavers . . . is something not to be found in the actual sounds of speech' (Beare 1957, 38). A similar doctrine is found in the Old Indian phonetic treatises,[3] where a short vowel is described as having the value of one *mātrā* ('measure') and a long vowel the value of two. Whatever may be the utility of the *mātrā* device for phonological purposes, to transfer it to the field of phonetic duration can only lead to confusion; and in some of the later treatises attempts are even made to allocate absolute as dis-

---

[1] Cf. Einarsson 1945, 4 ff. There is, however, a tendency for some tense vowels, when short, to drop their diphthongal element; and conversely for lax vowels, when long, to develop a diphthongization (of 'rising' type): cf. Einarsson 1945, 11; Steblin-Kamenskij 1960, 42 ff. In other words, diphthongization tends in general to be associated with length rather than with tenseness *per se*, though 'falling' diphthongs are associated only with tenseness.

[2] Lehiste 1970, 33 f.   [3] A 1953, 83 ff.

tinct from relative values; 1 *mātrā* is said, for example, to be equivalent in length to the call of the blue jay, and 2 *mātrās* to that of the crow – rather as if one were to define vowel length in terms of centiseconds. But in the earlier and better Indian treatises no such absolute definitions are attempted.

In the classical languages, including Sanskrit, diphthongs are for the most part phonologically and metrically equivalent to long vowels; so that whatever is said about the latter may generally also be taken to apply to the former.

NON-TEMPORAL APPROACHES

There have been various attempts to define the length distinction in non-durational terms.[1] One such theory posits a difference in the type of progression from the vowel to the following syllabic margin (e.g. in terms of 'weak' vs 'strong' cut-off, or 'loose' vs 'firm' or 'close' transition), the contrast being 'between a syllabic which is allowed to run its full course and one whose duration is cut short by the commencement of the succeeding consonant' (Trubetzkoy 1935/1968, 37).[2] Fischer-Jørgensen (1941, 180) criticizes this theory on the grounds that the alleged phonetic distinctions are so fine that the phoneticians themselves cannot agree on what they hear, or even whether they hear anything, and that instrumental aids have produced no evidence of such features. To the present writer it seems, however, that this theory, in its general principles, comes closer than any other to one which we shall later adopt (pp. 62 ff.) as providing the most effective explanatory model of vowel length; some of its shortcomings are discussed on p. 197 n. 2.

Consonant length

Length distinctions are also operative in consonants, having semantic function in many languages, including Latin and Greek (e.g. *agger* vs *ager*; ὅρρος vs ὅρος). In some languages 'geminate' consonants have a distribution similar to that of single consonants; they may, for instance, occur initially and finally as well as medially: some examples from the N.E. Caucasus are Lakk *ččan* 'foot' vs *čan* 'little'; Avar *icc* 'spring' vs *ic* 'moth'; Tabassaran *qqör* 'hare' vs *qör* 'crow', *jiff* 'copper' vs *jif*

---

[1] For a summary see Fischer-Jørgensen 1941.
[2] Cf. Jespersen 1913, 202 f; Jakobson 1937a/1962, 257; Lepscky 1962, 236 ff; Trnka 1966, 22.

'snow' (Trubetzkoy 1931); examples from Berber may be found in Mitchell 1957, 193 ff. In such cases they may be more appropriately described in terms of tense vs lax articulation[1] – rather as in the case of the Icelandic vowels described above; as Mitchell comments (1957, 197), 'What may be called relative phonetic length may often be included among the exponents of gemination', but 'It is impossible to reverse the procedure and consider phonetic length as the criterion for the category'.[2] However, in the languages of immediate concern to us 'geminates' occur only medially,[3] where for all descriptive prosodic purposes they are entirely comparable with other sequences of two consonants (e.g. as regards the accent placement of *medŭlla*, which is the same as that of *uenŭsta*, as against *mĕrŭla*). They may therefore be treated simply as cases of CC,[4] and require no special consideration. Historically it may be noted that they commonly replace an original sequence of dissimilar consonants, as in Latin *sella* < **sed-lā*, Greek τέτταρες, τέσσερες < **kʷetw~* (cf. Skt *catvāras*), Pkt *kaṭṭaï* < Skt *kartati*.

Syllabic quantity

Before attempting a motor interpretation of the length distinction in vowels, we may give some preliminary consideration to the question of *quantity*. But first it may be noted that the qualitative tense vs lax distinction in English also correlates with a distributional difference which it shares, for instance, with German and Dutch. This can be seen most clearly in the case of monosyllabic full words, where lax (short) vowels never occur in final position, being always followed by at least one consonant; whereas tense vowels (long vowels and diphthongs) may occur finally as well as before consonants.[5] Thus, with lax vowels: *bid, bed, bad, pot, put*, etc; but with tense vowels: *pea, do, far, law, fur, pay, pie, toy, low, cow*, etc., as well as *peat* etc.[6] For this reason Kurath refers to the lax English vowels as 'checked' and the tense as 'free'.

[1] Trubetzkoy 1926, 23 f.
[2] Cf. also Mitchell 1960, 375 n.2 on Arabic final geminates as being not necessarily longer but having greater tension and firmer contact.
[3] Latin *hŏcc* is confined to the position before initial vowel (A 1965, 75 f.); and Greek initial ρρ etc. is confined to the position after final vowels (A 1968a, 42 and p. 219).
[4] Cf. Trubetzkoy 1931, 9 f.
[5] Kurath 1964, 17; Trnka 1966, 22.
[6] Cf. Gimson 1970, 90 f. Note also the tendency, in animal imitations, to add a consonantal closure to forms not having a long (tense) vowel, as e.g. *wuff, yap* (beside *moo* etc.): cf. Hála 1961, 111.

$\breve{V}C = \bar{V}$ (vs $\breve{V}$)

From these limited data the picture emerges of some kind of equivalence between sequences of the types $\breve{V}C$ and $\bar{V}$ (the latter indicating both tense (long) vowels and diphthongs); and a similar equivalence underlies a number of phonological characteristics of English. For example, the stress placements in the words *dialéctal, duodénal, suicídal* vs *diágonal, litúrgical, conjéctural* indicate that, beginning with the penultimate vowel, a sequence [ekt] is equivalent to a sequence [iin] or [aɪd], but that a sequence [ən] or [ɪk] or [ʊr] is *not* equivalent to these – in other words, that a sequence $\breve{V}CC$ is equivalent to $\bar{V}C$, but $\breve{V}C$ is not. By Chomsky & Halle (1968, 29) sequences of the types $\breve{V}CC$ and $\bar{V}C$ are classified as 'strong clusters' and those of the type $\breve{V}C$ as 'weak clusters'.

The tense/lax distinction cannot in itself explain the equivalence of sequences of the types $\bar{V}C$ and $\breve{V}CC$; and Chomsky & Halle's conflation of them as 'strong clusters' simply on grounds of their phonological behaviour provides no explanation of *why* they are equivalent.

Certain parallels between English and Latin in these matters will doubtless have been noticed. In Latin, in monosyllabic full words, long vowels and diphthongs may occur in final position, as *dā, quī, quae*, etc., but short vowels only when followed by at least one consonant, as *dăt, quĭd, ĕst*, etc. A striking example is provided by the names of the letters of the alphabet; the names of the 'continuant' consonants, in which (from Varro onwards) the vowel precedes, have a short vowel (*ĕf, ĕl, ĕn, ĕs*, etc.), whereas the names of the plosives, in which the vowel follows, have a long vowel (*bē, cē, dē*, etc.); similarly, in the names of the vowels the long vowel is used as generic.[1] In Latin generally, as in English, there is an equivalence of the medial sequences $\bar{V}C$ and $\breve{V}CC$ as against $\breve{V}C$. This may be seen, firstly, in the accentual placement – which is on a penultimate syllable containing the vowel of a sequence $\bar{V}C$ (e.g. *refécit*) or $\breve{V}CC$ (e.g. *reféctus*), but on the antepenultimate where the penultimate contains the vowel of a sequence $\breve{V}C$ (e.g. *réfĭcit*); and secondly, in the metrical values, since both *refēcit* and *refĕctus* may, for example, end a hexameter, whereas *refĭcit* may not.

Historically, all three types of sequence are differently reflected in the Latin developments of medial vowels as regards the occurrence or degree of 'weakening' (i.e. closure). $\bar{V}C$ shows no weakening (e.g. *refēcit, relātus* remain unchanged from their prehistoric forms); $\breve{V}CC$

---

[1] There is clear evidence from occurrences in verse (e.g. Lucilius, Terentianus Maurus): Strzelecki 1948, 9; Kuryłowicz 1958, 381.

shows partial weakening (as far as the mid degree, ĕ: e.g. *refăctus* →
refĕctus; *retĕntus* remains unchanged); V̄C shows full weakening (to the
close degree, ĭ: e.g. *refăcit* → *refĭcit*, *retĕneo* → *retĭneo*): see further
pp. 133 f. But descriptively there are no prosodic grounds for distinguishing V̆CC from V̄C.

Similar equivalences may be established for Greek. Here too V̄C and
V̆CC are metrically equipollent, as against V̆C. The equivalence is also
reflected, for example, in the formation of the comparative and super-
lative of adjectives: both ὠμός (stem V̄C) and λεπτός (stem V̆CC) retain
the short thematic vowel ο (ὠμότερος, λεπτότερος), whereas σοφός
(stem V̆C) lengthens the thematic vowel to ω (σοφώτερος), evidently in
some form of rhythmic compensation.[1]

A parallel situation existed in Sanskrit, as is known from the statements of native treatises; it is also attested by metrical equivalences and
contrasts, and by the placement of the dynamic accent which superseded
the earlier (free) melodic accent. The effects of such accentuation are
seen in developments in the Indo-Aryan languages: e.g. (with dynamic
accents marked) *kámalam* 'lotus' → Hindi *kámal*; *aráṇyam* 'desert' →
Pkt *aráṇṇa-* → Gujarati *rān*; *páñcamaka-* 'fifth' → Guj. *pãcmɔ*;
vyākhyánam 'explanation' → Pkt *vakkhána-* → Hi. *bakhán*. Developments in the Iranian languages point to a similar situation there also.[2]
We have already seen that English has basically comparable accentual
characteristics to those of Latin; and in fact they are not confined to the
Indo-European field. In Arabic, for example, accentuation is based on
equivalences and contrasts between different types of sequence in a
manner closely similar to that of Latin (and even more so to that of
Indo-Aryan: see pp. 156 ff.); in Semitic languages in general, as Mitchell
notes (1957, 191), 'It is often convenient . . . to recognize the quantitative
equipollence of syllables whose structure differs according to whether
elements of length are referred to consonant or vowel'.

Also significant is the very common historical process whereby the
reduction of a consonant sequence to a single consonant tends to result
in lengthening of a preceding short vowel by 'compensation', i.e.
V̆CC → V̄C. In Latin, for example, **īsdem* → *īdem*, acc. pl. **-ŏns* →
-ōs. In Greek **ἐσμι* (cf. Skt *asmi*) → Doric ἠμι, Attic εἰμι; acc. pl. τονς
(as in Argive) → Doric τως, Attic τους, Lesbian τοις (with diphthongization). From Indo-Aryan examples have already been seen in Pkt

---

[1] Cf. Galton 1962, 281 f; A 1962, 50; 1967a, 147 n.1; Zirin 1970, 68 n.10.
[2] Meillet 1900; Kuryłowicz 1958, 369 ff.

kaṭṭaï → Hindi *kāṭe* and Pkt *araṇṇa-* → Guj. *rān*.[1] From a comparative point of view the same alternation may be seen, for example, in Doric σελᾱνᾱ = Lesbian σελάννᾱ (< *σελᾱσνᾱ). The descriptive complementarity of the two types of sequence has also been noted in Icelandic (p. 47; for Scandinavian in general cf. Lehiste 1970, 42, 49).

The equivalence of the medial $\bar{V}C$ and $\breve{V}CC$ sequences in the classical languages has long been recognized. It may in fact be rather more broadly stated than we have done so far. $\bar{V}C$ may be restated as $\bar{V}C_0$, where C_0 = any number of consonants, including zero (e.g. Latin *diĕi, relā́tus, redā́ctus, redĕmptus*); and $\breve{V}CC$ as $\breve{V}C_2$, where C_2 = at least 2 consonants (e.g. *refĕctus, excĕrpsit, contĕmptrix*); $\breve{V}C$ may also be restated as $\breve{V}C_{01}$, where C_{01} = not more than 1 consonant (e.g. *médĭus, mínĭmus*). It is the equivalence, metrical and phonological, of $\bar{V}C_0$ and $\breve{V}C_2$, in joint opposition to $\breve{V}C_{01}$, that has given rise to the concept of *quantity*, as distinct from vowel length. Like length, this also is a binary feature, with a 'superior' grade represented by $\bar{V}C_0$ and $\breve{V}C_2$, and an 'inferior' grade represented by $\breve{V}C_{01}$.

HEAVY ('LONG') VS LIGHT ('SHORT')

It will be convenient first to consider the Indian doctrines on this matter. The two grades are referred to as 'heavy' (*guru*) and 'light' (*laghu*); a typical statement[2] categorizes as heavy a long vowel, or any vowel together with a following consonant-group (*saṃyogas*), and as light a short vowel not followed by a consonant-group. It will be noted that Sanskrit here makes a clear terminological distinction between the degrees of quantity and those of vowel length, which, as in the western tradition, are termed 'long' (*dīrgha*) and 'short' (*hrasva*). Some confusion does, however, occur, and the terms 'heavy' and 'light' tend to be applied to the vowels of the relevant sequences as well as to the sequences as a whole.[3]

The Greek grammarians use the one pair of terms (μακρός, βραχύς) to refer both to vowel length and to quantity. But the two concepts are, initially at least, clearly distinguished. Moreover, unlike the Indians, they explicitly state the degrees of quantity as characterizing *syllables*. Thus in Dionysius Thrax (17 U)[4] a 'long' syllable is one which contains a long vowel or a diphthong or which contains a short vowel fol-

---

[1] Cf. also Turner 1970; Sharma 1971, 102 ff.
[2] *Taittirīya-Prātiśākhya* xxii. 14 f.
[3] A 1953, 85 ff.
[4] Cf. Zirin, 43 f.

lowed by two consonants; and a 'short' syllable is one which contains a short vowel not followed by two consonants. The ambiguous terminology, however, inevitably leads later writers into confusion. In the first instance, a 'long' syllable containing a long vowel (or diphthong) was felt to be somehow more 'naturally' long than one containing a short vowel; and this conception was expressed in terms of the philosophical opposition of φύσει 'by nature' vs θέσει 'by convention' respectively (e.g. Dionysius Thrax 17 U).[1] θέσις, however, can also mean 'position', and could so be understood as referring to the position of the short vowel before two (or more) consonants in the 'long' sequence $\breve{V}C_2$. This interpretation is reflected in the Latin translation of θέσει by *positu* or *positione* (vs *natura*), whence also our own terminology of 'by position' (vs 'by nature'). Combined with the ambiguous terminology of quantity and length,[2] this led eventually to the idea that, instead of *syllables being 'long'* 'by position', the *vowels* of such syllables *were lengthened* 'by position' – which, of course, they were not: in a word like λεκτός the ε remains short as it does in λέγω; it is the syllable containing the ε which is 'long'. The misunderstanding is already evident in Quintilian,[3] and becomes common in the Middle Ages;[4] it continues through the Renaissance, recurs most surprisingly in de Saussure (1916/1960, 60), and is still unfortunately encountered in some modern handbooks.

The Greek and Latin statements on quantity do not in general make any reference to the *structure* of the syllables concerned, although, as we have seen, they did discuss the question of syllabification. There are, however, rare exceptions. Dionysius Thrax, in the above-mentioned treatment of quantity, describes one of the circumstances in which a syllable may be 'long by position' as 'when it ends in a single consonant and is followed by a syllable which begins with a consonant, as e.g. ἔρ.γον'.[5] The same approach is also found in Hephaestion (*Ench.*, 1 ff. C), exemplified by ἄλ.λος. But both Dionysius' and Hephaestion's statements reveal the difficulties caused by an inadequate theory of syllabification. For whereas Greek doctrine correctly prescribes the divisions ἔρ.γον and ἄλ.λος, words such as Ἕκτωρ, ἔξω are divided Ἕ.κτωρ, ἔ.ξω (on the basis of the initial occurrence of the sequences

---

[1] Cf. Zirin, 68 ff.
[2] In addition to the use of the term 'length' to refer to quantity, 'quantity' is nowadays sometimes used in the sense of vowel length.
[3] Zirin, 51 f.   [4] Hiersche 1957.
[5] Fränkel 1960, 148 f; Zirin, 44.

κτ, ξ); and so a syllabificatory treatment of 'positional' quantity must add the rule (as in both Dionysius and Hephaestion) that a syllable is 'long' if the next syllable begins with two consonants. The orthographic, non-phonetic basis of their doctrine of syllabification is also revealed by the necessity for a further rule that in e.g. ἅλς ἐπάγη, with word division after the two consonants, a syllable is 'long' if it ends in two consonants.

PRE-PAUSAL $\breve{V}C$

It is more surprising that the Indians do not attempt a syllabificatory analysis of quantity, since their rules for syllable division have a sounder basis. One point which they mention, however, deserves notice, since it will be of relevance later. If, as the Indian doctrine would permit, one were to adopt the view that a syllable is light if it ends in a short vowel, but is otherwise heavy (i.e. if it ends in a long vowel or a consonant), then we should expect the final syllable of a word ending in $\breve{V}C$ to be light if followed by a word with initial vowel (since, by the syllabificatory doctrine, the consonant will belong with the following vowel), and heavy if followed by a word with initial consonant (since the first of two consonants is said to go with the preceding vowel); and this is in fact the case. But we should also expect that such a syllable would be classifiable as heavy *before pause*,[1] e.g. at the end of a sentence, since there is no following vowel to which the consonant could be attached.[2] The Indian treatises are in general rather equivocal on this subject, but the *Taittirīya-Prātiśākhya* (xxii.14) does quite clearly include such syllables amongst the 'heavy'. In the ancient western writers there is no specific mention of the matter. Dionysius of Halicarnassus (*De Comp.*, 75 ff. UR) in four cases implies that final ∼ $\breve{V}$n

---

[1] In philological works one commonly encounters the term '*in pausa*' for this location. This has no authority in Latin grammar (where not even the term *pausa* is found), and is in any case inappropriate: one might expect, say, *ante* (or *ad*) *pausam*, or *in fine* (as Quintilian, ix.4.93). The term '*in pausa*' seems to derive from Max Müller, who, in his translation of the *Ṛk-Prātiśākhya* in 1856 (394, cxix), used 'in der Pause' as a rendering of the Sanskrit '*avasāne*'; the Latin form '*in pausa*' appears in his *Sanskrit Grammar for Beginners* (1866), from which it passed into other grammars. The Sanskrit word is indeed the locative of *avasānam* 'pause'; but the locative is here used with its conventional technical value (in the abbreviated grammatical style) in the sense of 'before' (just as, for example, the ablative is used with the meaning 'after'). No such convention prevails in the case of the Latin 'locative' expression *in*+Abl., and Bopp (in his *Grammatica critica linguae Sanscritae* of 1832) regularly uses the more appropriate '*ante pausam*'. For further details cf. A 1962, 99 f.

[2] Cf. Kent 1948; Fränkel 1960, 148 f; Irigoin 1967, 72 n.8; Zirin, 57 f.

(e.g. in πᾶσιν) may be 'long'; but on the other hand Hephaestion (*Ench.*, 14 C) implies that the final syllable of ὕπνος is 'short'. Metrical evidence is here not easy to invoke, since the verse line tends to be treated phonologically like a sentence, so that internal sentence (and clause) endings are generally not so treated;[1] and the verse end is commonly 'indifferent' for rhythmic purposes (see pp. 296 ff.); but there does seem to be some evidence for the 'long' value of pre-pausal ~V̆C in both Latin and Greek. This will be more conveniently discussed in the context of a detailed study of the individual languages (pp. 130 f; 204 ff.).

TIME RATIOS

The most traditional approach to the question of quantity, more particularly to the equivalence of syllables 'long' by 'nature' and by 'position', as opposed to 'short' syllables, is in terms of duration – as in the case of vowels. But this leads to immediate difficulties. For, as Dionysius of Halicarnassus observes (*De Comp.*, 57 f. UR), the first syllables of ὁδός, Ῥόδος, τρόπος, and στρόφος are all 'short' for metrical purposes, and σπλήν and ἤ are both 'long', although 'some are longer than long and some are shorter than short'. Dionysius does not elaborate on the matter; but in Aristides Quintilianus (41 f. W-I) we find an attempt to justify syllabic quantity in terms of the lengths of the sounds involved. A short vowel, as we have already seen, was given the value of 1 'time unit', and a long vowel the value of 2; but in addition a consonant is said to have the value of $\frac{1}{2}$ unit.[2] The question of the two types of long syllable can then be stated in the terms: $\bar{V} = 2$; $\breve{V}CC = 1 + \frac{1}{2} + \frac{1}{2} = 2$; $\therefore \breve{V}CC = \bar{V}$. But this is a specious solution; for it simply ignores the fact that by this doctrine there would be a whole range of values, from e.g. ὁ = 1 to σπλήν = $\frac{1}{2} + \frac{1}{2} + \frac{1}{2} + 2 + \frac{1}{2} = 4$; and there would be no reason for drawing a distinction between 'short' and 'long' at any particular point on the scale: indeed the 'short' sequence of, say, στρόφος (CCCV̆C = 3) would be a whole unit longer than the 'long' ἤ ($\bar{V} = 2$) or ἐξ ($\breve{V}CC = 2$).[3]

The situation is to some extent clarified by later writers. Choeroboscus, in his commentary to Hephaestion's *Enchiridion* (180 C), explains that the 'rhythmicians' (who were concerned primarily with the

---

[1] Cf. *Hermann 1923, 94; Fraenkel 1928, 344 f; Safarewicz 1936, 96; Kuryłowicz 1966; and pp. 113 ff.

[2] A doctrine also found in the Indian treatises: A 1953, 84.

[3] Cf. A 1968a, 99 f; Zirin 47.

musical implications) are using the term χρόνος πρῶτος in a quite
different sense from the 'metricians and grammarians'.[1] For the former,
he says, each sound has its durational value, and so the syllables may
have a variety of lengths; whereas the latter treat any 'long' syllable
as having 2 units, and any 'short' as having 1; that is, they transfer
the concept of this relationship from vowel length to syllable quantity.
But still this does nothing to explain *why* syllables so apparently
different in terms of C/V structure should be equivalent. An attempted
explanation by Longinus (Prolegomena to Hephaestion, *Ench.*, 87 C)
says that the metricians are basing themselves, not on any actual
measurements of length, but rather upon *function* (δύναμις) – by
which he presumably means their metrical distribution. But this is
really a circular explanation, since we still have to explain why different
syllable types should have the same metrical functions. In a similar
discussion by Marius Victorinus (vi, 39 f. K: Zirin, 52), Longinus'
distinction between duration and function is paralleled by a distinction
between '*spatium*' and '*ratio*', but the phonetic explanation of the
latter is hardly enlightening: 'ut dicimus omnes Germanos longos
esse, quamuis non sint omnes eiusdem staturae: sic dicimus etiam
has syllabas in genere esse non in spatio longarum seu breuium
syllabarum'.

A similar transfer of concept from vowel length to syllable quantity
was also made by the Indian metricians; but the commentaries come no
nearer to explaining the reason for the metrical equivalence of types of
syllable which, by their own rules, are different in duration. As stated
by one of these, the *Vṛttamuktāvalitarala* ('Pearl-necklace of Metre')
(Varma 1929, 89), it is simply so 'by tradition'.

A further difficulty for the durational theory of quantity is presented
by certain types of consonant sequence, particularly plosive + liquid
(and, e.g. in Greek, plosive + nasal), which in certain languages and
dialects fail to 'make position'; that is to say, a sequence V̆PL (where
P and L = plosive and liquid respectively) may produce a 'short' and
not a 'long' syllable, as is shown by metre and, for example, by accent
placement in Latin (*tónĭtrus* being accented like *mónĭtus* and unlike
honĕstus). In English, Chomsky & Halle (1968, 82 f., 241) have to
recognize that, for the purpose of rules relating to placement of stress
and to tenseness vs laxness of vowels, their category of 'weak cluster'
must be extended to include the sequence V̆Cr in some cases; thus, for

---

[1] Cf. also Goodell 1901, 6 f.

example, *cérebral* [∼ɪbr∼] like *pérsonal* [∼ən∼], with antepenulti-mate stress, unlike *paréntal* (∼ent∼] with penultimate; or *putrefy* like *purify*, with long (tense) vowel in the first syllable, as against *justify* with short (lax) vowel. A further English parallel is provided by the process of 'glottal reinforcement',[1] primarily of plosive consonants, which is a common feature of some types of English speech. A con-sonant is not normally reinforced if followed by a vowel, but it is if followed by another consonant (or, incidentally, by pause: cf. p. 55). An exception to this rule occurs, however, with the sequence plosive + liquid (also + semivowel); in such cases the plosive is reinforced *only* if the preceding vowel is stressed, as e.g. in *pétrol* [∼ ʔtr∼] or *cýclist* [∼ ʔkl∼], or if a grammatical boundary intervenes between the plosive and liquid, as e.g. in *uproot* [∼ ʔpr∼] or *at least* [∼ ʔtl∼], but *not* in forms like *acróss* [∼kr∼] or *replý*ᵢ [∼pl∼] (by contrast with *succéss* [∼ ʔks∼]).

The equivalence of V̆PL to V̆C can hardly be due to any *inherent* durational feature of L, since the reversed sequence LP regularly does 'make position' in Latin and Greek:[2] note also the stress placement in English *immórtal*. Moreover, by a durational theory certain variations due to grammatical boundaries would be quite anomalous. Thus, for example, in early Latin verse, where intramorphic PL regularly do *not* 'make position', they regularly do so when a word or morph boundary falls between them, as e.g. in *ab-ripi, ab lenone* (cf. pp. 20, 140); similarly in Aristophanes, contrary to the usual 'Attic shortening' κλ κμ etc. 'make position' in forms of the type ἐκ-λιπών, ἐκ μάχης; and in Homer, where such sequences normally *do* 'make position', they rarely do so in the 'weak' half of a foot if they are preceded by a word boundary (cf. pp. 210 ff., 217 ff.). Thus a grammatical boundary *before* such sequences would appear to shorten them, but *between* such sequences to lengthen them. It is not denied that this may be the case; but the durational theory provides no explanation of why it should apply only to these sequences. One is again reminded of the parallel in English glottal reinforcement, which occurs, for example, with the [k] of *fork left* but not with that of *four clefts* (Higginbottom 1964, 137).

The durational approach to quantity has been revived in various guises in recent times (e.g. Verrier in 1914, Sturtevant in 1922, Schmitt

---

[1] Higginbottom 1964.
[2] Cf. Zirin, 56.

in 1934).[1] The approach may be typified by Verrier's idea that, in addition to the syllable proper, there is a 'quantitative syllable' measured from the beginning of one vowel to the beginning of the next; so that, as Zirin illustrates it, the first line of the Aeneid would be divided into 'quantitative syllables' as follows:

arm.av.ir.umqu.ec.an.ōtr.oi.aequ.īpr.īm.us.ab.ōr.īs.

But the anomalies to which this approach must lead have already been demonstrated; and for an explanation of the treatment of the PL sequences Sturtevant (1922, 47) has to fall back on the 'laws of versification', which 'establish certain relative time values for Greek and Latin sounds and groups of sounds' – an explanation that is no better than the 'tradition' of the Indian treatise. It is therefore difficult to see how it can be maintained, as by Dale (1964, 20 n.9), that 'What the Greek *ear* actually measured, of course, was not "the syllable", as we in our print-and-paper-limited fashion take it, but. . .the time taken to move from the beginning of one vowel-sound to the beginning of the next'. Just who 'we' are who conceive of the syllable in terms of 'print and paper' (where it is not normally indicated) is obscure; and the positive part of the statement is unsupported by any argument more convincing than 'of course'.

A criterion of quantity has been proposed by Jakobson which does indeed base itself on the structure of syllables, and also on the concept of the vocalic 'mora' (corresponding to the Indian *mātrā* and the Greek χρόνος πρῶτος): 'In metrical patterns like Ancient Greek and Arabic, which equalize length "by position" with length "by nature", the minimal syllables consisting of a consonantal phoneme and one mora vowel are opposed to syllables with a surplus (a second mora or a closing consonant) as simpler and less prominent syllables, opposed to those that are more complex and prominent' (1960, 360). This approach also, however, leaves unexplained why even a single consonantal 'surplus' following the vowel should create 'length' of syllables just as an additional vowel mora, whereas any amount of consonantal 'surplus' preceding the vowel (as in στρό.φος) should be irrelevant; moreover the invoking of 'prominence' involves circularity, since it is just this which

---

[1] For references and further discussion see Zirin, 61. Taranovski (1963, 198 f.) draws attention to the chaos created in Slavic metrics by a durational theory, the so-called 'musical bar theory', originating in the ideas of Westphal and developed especially by S. S. Šervinskij.

we are trying to explain; and the factor of 'complexity' seems altogether too wide and vague a criterion.

Then there is the theory of Marouzeau (based on an idea by Juret), which similarly operated with syllabic structure (1954; 1955: discussed in detail by Zirin, 61 ff.). A sequence V̆CCV̆, for example, would be divided as V̆C.CV̆; but in accounting for the 'length' of the first syllable V̆C Marouzeau does not make the duration of the syllable itself the relevant factor, since he finds instrumental measurements to invalidate this criterion. He suggests instead that the closing and holding stage of the first consonant, added to the closure and hold of the second, creates a 'suspension', the total duration of which is allocated by the hearer to the first syllable, whereas only the opening of the second consonant is allocated to the second syllable. Consequently the syllable V̆C will be interpreted as 'long', but CV̆ as 'short', even though this may not accord with actual duration. This is an ingenious device; but apart from any other weakness of the theory (cf. Zirin, 62 ff.), it relies too heavily on psychological factors of perception, which cannot as yet be measured, and so simply shifts the problem instead of solving it. As it stands it is vulnerable to the jibe directed at some earlier durational approaches by Thomson (1923, 424): 'How could an interval for dinner between two speeches make the first one long?'

It remains to note the equivalence of 1 'long' to 2 'short' syllables, which, according to Longinus and Choeroboscus in the commentaries already referred to, is assumed by the metricians (and grammarians) as against the rhythmicians, for whom there are no such exclusively binary ratios. Its possible bases will be discussed more fully at a later stage (pp. 255 ff.); but one important point may here be made. There are two quite distinct types of metrical equivalence; one (sometimes termed 'contraction') in which the 'long' is an optional replacement of a basic 2 'short' (as e.g. in the dactylic hexameter); and the other (usually termed 'resolution') in which the 2 'short' are an optional replacement of a basic 'long' (as e.g. in the Greek iambic trimeter or Latin senarius). Moreover, contraction is not in general subject to limitation by the incidence of word boundaries, whereas resolution is subject to more or less stringent regulation on this account; and contraction is a characteristic of the 'weak' part of the foot, whereas resolution is primarily a characteristic of the 'strong' part. Meillet, however, confuses the issue by speaking of both types of equivalence as 'resolution', and suggesting that true resolution (as e.g. in iambics) is simply a 'necessary licence' extended from the contraction found in hexameters (1923, 43 f.). Equally mistaken is Meillet's citation of these equivalences as evidence for the purely durational nature of quantity in verse, since it is immediately weakened by his own recognition that the 'strong' position is less clearly marked by two 'short' syllables than by one 'long'. The necessity of separating the two types of equivalence is also emphasized by Safarewicz (1936, 73 ff.); Kuryłowicz (1948/1960, 207); Dale (1958, 102); Parker (1968, 268).

In Old Indian the metrical equivalence of 1 heavy to 2 light syllables is of a rather different type from either of the western forms. It is not found in Vedic, and is relatively uncommon in classical Sanskrit, the predominant metres being of a syllabic type ('*akṣaracchandas*'), in which the quantities are more or less strictly regulated. In the classical language, however, metres do occur of the '*mātrāchandas*' type, in which the number of syllables is varied by basing the verse on the number of quantitative *mātrās* (heavy = 2, light = 1). But it is hardly possible in these metres to say that either the 1 heavy or the 2 light is the basic element; for in some there is no recognized foot structure; and in the Āryā, for example (which is recognized as a '*gaṇacchandas*', 'foot verse'), some of the 4-*mātrā* feet may have all the possible alternative forms, viz. $\Sigma\Sigma\Sigma\Sigma$, $\Sigma\Sigma$, $\Sigma\Sigma\Sigma$, $\Sigma\Sigma\Sigma$, and $\Sigma\Sigma\Sigma$.[1]

From this point onwards, to avoid possible confusion between vowel length and syllable quantity in theoretical discussion, we shall adopt the Indian terminology of *heavy* and *light* to refer to syllables,[2] as against *long* and *short* to refer to vowels,[3] even in languages other than Sanskrit. For purposes of symbolization, the traditional superscript longum and breve ($\bar{V}$, $\breve{V}$) will be used to indicate vowel length,[4] but a subscript longum and inverted breve to indicate syllable quantity (Σ, Σ), though for convenience these will be placed only below the vowel

---

[1] Keith 1928, 418.

[2] As A 1953, 85; 1964, 4 f; Nagy 1970, 3 n.3; *Newman 1972, 3 and n.2. The terms 'strong' and 'weak' are used by Miyaoka (1971, 220) for exactly comparable quantitative distinctions in Eskimo. In modern metrics 'heavy' and 'light' are sometimes also used of stressed vs unstressed syllables as the basis of accentual poetry: e.g. Stankiewicz 1960, 78; Lotz 1960, 140.

[3] Housman, for instance, who was well aware of the distinction between vowel length and syllable quantity, nevertheless tends to confuse the issue for the reader (as 1928) by writing *nullā spes*, etc.

[4] Except in phonetic and phonemic transcriptions, where geminated symbols are used.

of the syllable when this is indicated.[1] Thus, if we were to follow the suggestions of p. 55, a syllable type symbolized as CV̆C would be a *heavy syllable* containing a *short vowel*; and Latin *rĕcĕntēs* would exemplify all three possible combinations of length and quantity.

A motor approach

In turning to motor theory for a possible explanation of the problems of length and quantity, we may note that even Meillet, embarrassed by the implications of the durational theory which underlies his arguments, was led to redefine it (1923, 9) in terms of a syllable being 'long' or 'short' according to whether the speaker *felt* it as long or short, the distinction being not so much a matter of external physical measurement as of an internal process which is somehow also communicated to the hearer. As it stands, this is more of a subterfuge than a theory, with no indication of how this 'feeling' of syllabic type could be objectively described; but at least it located the most promising area of investigation.

VOWEL LENGTH IN MOTOR TERMS

It will be remembered that by Stetson's theory the syllabic pulse may be arrested by the chest muscles or by an oral (consonantal) articulatory stroke; so that syllables of the types $\sim$V and $\sim$VC might both be said to be arrested, one thoracically and the other orally.

In sequences of the type $\sim$VCCV$\sim$ the first C is commonly found to arrest the first syllable and the second C to release the second syllable. But if both consonants are of identical articulation, i.e. geminate as e.g. [pp], then at higher rates of utterance the 'crowding' of articulations causes the arresting consonant to drop; the arresting movement is overtaken by the following release (Stetson 1951, 67 ff.). The dominant rôle of release over arrest may also be seen from the fact that if sequences of the type $\sim$*eat, eat, eat*$\sim$, or $\sim$*at, at, at*$\sim$, are speeded up, the arresting consonant tends to shift to the releasing function, giving $\sim$*tea tea tea*$\sim$, $\sim$*ta ta ta*$\sim$ etc. (Stetson, 40 f.). When 'singling' or 'shifting' of this kind takes place, it may happen that the syllable becomes chest-arrested (here symbolized $^+$), i.e. $\sim$VC.CV$\sim$ or $\sim$VC.V$\sim$ $\rightarrow$ $\sim$V$^+$.CV$\sim$. Stetson assumes that this must always happen; but at this point we introduce an amending hypothesis which

[1] As A 1966a, 111 n.2.

will be relevant in a number of connexions – namely that in such cases the arrest of the syllable may effectively vanish, and that consequently we may have sequences of the type $\sim V^o.CV\sim$ (where ^{o} indicates absence of thoracic arrest). In a ballistic simile we might compare this to the case where A throws a ball, and B, instead of catching it (and then throwing it to C), knocks it on to C without arresting its flight.

We may now relate this hypothesis to a further circumstance, noted by Stetson and others, in connexion with the contrast of short and long vowels. Stetson (43) observes that the quality of a short vowel cannot be prolonged,[1] and that it consequently depends upon rapidity of articulation. He further notes (67) that with increasing rate vowel quality tends to change, since 'less and less time is given in which to approximate the specific shape of the vocal canal', and comments particularly on the tendency of English to reduce to the 'neutral' vowel [ə].[2] Such an 'incompleteness' of articulation has been commonly observed as a characteristic of short, lax vowels as compared with their long, tense counterparts. Thus for Jakobson & Halle (1964, 100) the lax articulation involves 'a smaller deformation of the vocal tract from its neutral, central position', whereas the tense vowels (like tense consonants) not only 'show primarily a longer time interval spent in a position away from neutral' but also 'display a greater deformation of the vocal tract';[3] from the acoustic standpoint also (Jakobson, Fant & Halle 1952, 36 f.) not only do 'the tense vowels have a longer duration than the corresponding lax' but also 'In a tense vowel the sum of the deviation of its formants from the neutral position is greater than that of the corresponding lax vowel'.

Thus rate of articulation may be seen as linked with differences of vowel quality, and specifically with such differences as characterize tense vs lax vowels.[4] But if one accepts the basic tenet of Stetson and others that the syllable is the prime motor unit of speech, it seems reasonable to look for the factor governing such rate[5] in the syllabic process rather than in a vague 'accelerator' control; and the hypothesis is here proposed that, where a distinction is made between long, tense

[1] Cf. Trubetzkoy 1938, 158 f; Fischer-Jørgensen 1941, 177.
[2] Cf. also Lehiste 1970, 140.
[3] Cf A 1959, 241.
[4] Excluding cases such as modern Icelandic (see p. 47), where the tense/lax distinction is quite independent of duration.
[5] In a linguistically distinctive function, i.e. as opposed to the *overall* rate of utterance, which is another, 'paralinguistic' matter.

vowels and short, lax vowels, the difference is one of the presence vs absence of thoracic arrest. Stetson himself virtually implies this in the case of the distinction between syllables of types $\sim\bar{V}C$ and $\sim\breve{V}C$: thus (104; cf. also 42), 'When the syllable is arrested primarily by the consonant, the vowel is said to be lax. But if the syllable is arrested in part by the chest muscles, the vowel is counted "tense"'; and this latter equation, $V^+ =$ tense $(\bar{V})$, will of course also apply to syllables of type $\sim\bar{V}$, where Stetson's general theory postulates an entirely thoracic arrest. The amendment of Stetson's theory introduced above makes it possible to extend the former equation, $V^o =$ lax $(\breve{V})$, to syllables of the type $\sim\breve{V}$ as well as $\sim\breve{V}C$. In other words, the relatively slow articulation associated with the long, tense vowels may be seen as a consequence of thoracic arrest, and the relatively fast articulation associated with the short, lax vowels as a consequence either of oral arrest or of 'overtaking' by the release of the next syllable (the 'knocking-on' effect).[1] Physiologically this seems a reasonable hypothesis in view of the larger and less mobile musculature involved in the thoracic arrest, which requires a prolongation of the vowel whilst it is reaching its maximum contraction. Duration thus becomes simply an incidental feature of vowel 'length', which is primarily determined by the syllabic process.

SYLLABIC QUANTITY IN MOTOR TERMS

If this is accepted, then in languages which distinguish $\breve{V}$ from $\bar{V}$ the difference will be, in motor terms, a distinction of V^o from V^+. In which case syllables ending in $\breve{V}$ (V^o) will be opposed, *qua* unarrested (orally or thoracically), both to syllables ending in $\bar{V}$ (V^+) and to syllables ending in $\breve{V}C$ (V^oC), which are arrested (thoracically and orally respectively). And if we adopt the basic traditional rule of syllabic division in the classical languages, that of two successive consonants the first generally belongs to the preceding syllable, but that a single intervocalic consonant belongs to the following syllable, it will follow that in these languages *heavy syllables are arrested syllables and light syllables are unarrested syllables*. We are thereby enabled to explain 'why there are precisely two syllable types in Latin verse' (Zirin, 64); and we need no longer concede (as Zirin) that 'from a purely phonetic point of view

---

[1] The occurrence of pre-pausal $\breve{V}$, implying V^o independently of these conditions, may be seen as a special characteristic of this position, with relaxation ('vanish') of the syllabic pulse rather than arrest.

this number is arbitrary', nor necessarily that 'more is involved than phonetics'.

Kuryłowicz (1948/1960, 219) rightly comments that the vowel length of, say, Latin $\bar{e}$ is only a special case of the 'long' syllable, one which is 'non-entravée', i.e. in our terms not orally arrested; we need not, however, agree with Kuryłowicz that it is only through the intermediary of $\bar{e}$, and its quantitative equivalence to e.g. $\breve{e}t$, that the latter is opposed as a 'long' syllable to $\breve{e}$ as a 'short'; for us both $\bar{V}$ and $\bar{V}C$ are equally and intrinsically heavy, *qua* arrested, and it is the syllabic arresting factor which explains their quantitative equivalence.[1] Nor is it necessary (as Zirin, 72 ff.) to assume an analysis of long vowels as $\breve{V}C$; such an analysis is possible for closing (falling) diphthongs (see below) and perhaps also for close vowels (i.e. [ii], [uu] = /ij/, /uw/), but it becomes phonetically implausible in the case of open vowels.[2]

Summary of motor definitions

It may be useful at this point to summarize our proposals regarding motor definitions of length and quantity:

Long vowels ($\bar{V}$) are vowels of syllables which are thoracically arrested ($\sim V^+$); they tend to be of tense quality.

Short vowels ($\breve{V}$) are vowels of syllables which are not thoracically arrested, viz. which are orally arrested ($\sim V^oC$) or whose arrest is overtaken by the release of the next syllable ($\sim V^o$); they tend to be of lax quality.[3]

Heavy syllables (Σ) are syllables which are arrested, either thoracically ($\sim V^+$) or orally ($\sim V^oC$).

Light syllables ($\underset{\sim}{\Sigma}$) are syllables which are unarrested ($\sim V^o$).

Some consequences are that short vowels can occur in either light or heavy syllables ($\sim V^o$ or $\sim V^oC$), long vowels only in heavy syllables ($\sim V^+$); and that heavy syllables can contain either long or short vowels ($\sim V^+$ or $\sim V^oC$), light syllables only short vowels ($\sim V^o$).

[1] It is however true that the concept of quantity only arises for languages with distinctions of vowel length (cf. *Newman 1972, 4, 26); for otherwise there would simply be an opposition of 'open' vs 'closed' syllables.

[2] Cognate considerations lead e.g. Trager & Bloch (1941: cf. Bloch & Trager 1942, 50 f.) to treat both diphthongs and long vowels in English as sequences of $\breve{V}$ followed by /j/, /w/, or /h/ (e.g. [aa] = /ah/) on the grounds that (234) 'the six short-vowel phonemes occur with a strong stress only in checked syllables, whereas the long vowels and diphthongs occur also in free syllables'.

[3] The different alternative mechanisms associated with shortness of vowels could potentially involve durational and qualitative differences; such may well underlie the differences in the development of medial short vowels in Latin in heavy (arrested) and light (unarrested) syllables: see pp. 51 f., 133 f.

With certain types of articulation there could possibly be some fluctuation as between thoracic and oral arrest. A typical case would be that of closing diphthongs, e.g. [ai], [au], in which the second element is, on the one hand, sufficiently open ('vocoidal') to permit of entirely thoracic arrest, but also sufficiently close ('contoidal') to permit of oral arrest; then the difference between a pronunciation of e.g. Latin *maior* (inscr. MAIIOR) as [maj.jor] or [mai.jor] would simply depend on the type of syllabic arrest,[1] i.e. as V^oC or V^+. Alternatively in such cases one could envisage a simultaneous oral and thoracic arresting action.

Hypercharacterization

There is also the possibility of 'double arrest', i.e. both thoracic and oral in sequence ($\sim V^+C$). But there is a tendency in some languages to eliminate at least certain of these, as being 'redundant' from the point of view of the ballistic movement. Such syllables are 'hypercharacterized' and, as Kuryłowicz comments (1948/1960, 220), the consonantal closure adds nothing to the quantity. A Latin example is seen in such developments as *caussa*, *cāssus* (Cicero, Vergil) to later *causa*, *cāsus*, involving a reduction of the type $\sim V^+C . CV \sim$ $\rightarrow$ $\sim V^+ . CV \sim$,[2] with dropping of the oral arrest. In Greek, on the other hand (by 'Osthoff's Law'), there is a development of e.g. *γνωντες* to *γνόντες*, involving a reduction of the type $\sim V^+C . CV \sim$ $\rightarrow$ $\sim V^oC . CV \sim$, with dropping of the thoracic arrest.[3] The descriptive effects of such reductions may be seen in the 'laxing rule' of English (Chomsky & Halle 1968, 171 f., 241), whereby 'vowels are nontense in position before certain consonant clusters': thus e.g. *descrĭption* (vs *describe*), *wĭsdom* (vs *wise*), *convĕntion* (vs *convene*), *lŏst* (vs *lose*). In terms of the motor theory of the syllable, the tendency to reduce hypercharacterized syllable endings may be seen as an avoidance of 'controlled' as against 'ballistic' movements (see p. 41). In a syllable $\sim V^+C$ the arrest of the ballistic movement tends to be completed (thoracically) before the final C, and the syllable has to be continued by a controlled action: 'In such cases the consonant occurs with the latter part of the syllable movement but is not an integral part of it. Such consonants are often

[1] Cf. A 1965, 39 n.1.
[2] Cf. A 1965, 36.
[3] See further Lejeune 1955, 188 f. and p. 222. For similar reductions in Hausa by 'syllable-overload rules' cf. Klingenheben 1928, 282 ff; *Newman 1972, 16 and n.13; and for Arabic Fleisch 1950, 248 ff.

noticeable in singing where the prolongation of the vowel leaves the consonant dangling' (Stetson, 58 f.).[1]

Particularly uncommon is the case where a vocoidal articulation is prolonged beyond the extent required for thoracic arrest; hence the reduction in Greek of the 'long diphthongs', both prehistorically (by Osthoff's Law) and historically, as e.g. *Ζηυς → Ζεύς, κλήις → κλείς; similarly Old Indian $\bar{a}i$, $\bar{a}u$ → ai, au (A 1953, 62 ff; 1962, 31 ff.).

Pre-pausal V̆C again

We may now return to the question of the sequence V°C in the position before pause. On the face of it we should expect it to form an orally arrested syllable (cf. p. 55); but another possibility may also be considered. The consonantal stricture must of course sooner or later be released; but such release may be delayed or otherwise effected in a manner dissociated from the syllabic movement of the utterance;[2] in which case the consonant has effectively only an arresting function, and the syllable in question is arrested. But the release of the stricture may be integrated with a continuation of syllabic movement, forming the release of a new syllabic pulse, which is linguistically uncharacterized (but may produce a non-significant whispered or murmured vocalic sound, as often e.g. in Fr. *petite, malade*, etc.).[3] In this circumstance it is conceivable that the final consonant would lose its arresting function, and so leave the preceding syllable unarrested. Something like this may perhaps occur in languages which distinguish between single and double final consonants,[4] as e.g. in Icelandic *man* 'maid' vs *mann* 'man' (acc.), where the absence of consonantal arrest in the first word is further suggested by the fact that the vowel is lengthened (cf. p. 47). By the Indian phoneticians, on the other hand, the unreleased nature of Sanskrit consonants both before another consonant and before pause is specifically noted under the term '*abhinidhāna*';[5] and the plosives in particular are described as 'arrested' (*āsthāpita*)

---

[1] In Latin *cāssus → cāsus* etc. the dropping of the consonant would eliminate a situation termed 'unusual' by Stetson (8), where 'a vocal movement of the controlled type begins...in the utterance of a fricative and is finally merged into a ballistic pulse'.

[2] Cf. Heffner 1950, 172 f.

[3] Cf. Sharma 1971, 68: 'In Panjabi its plosion is clearly heard, though the following vocalic exponent is quite indeterminate, not sufficient to form a new syllable; it may be called an incipient syllable' (cf. 139 f.).

[4] Other than the lax/tense distinction mentioned on p. 50.

[5] A 1953, 71 f; 1962, 97 f.

and as 'obscure, weakened, deprived of breath and voice'. It is significant that in pre-pausal position the distinctions of voice and aspiration are neutralized; and the 'weakness' is further indicated by the fact that subsequently all such consonants are lost (e.g. Skt *vidyut* 'lightning' → Pkt *vijju*). This is evidently a matter which must be investigated individually for each language (see pp. 130f., 204 ff.).

Syllabification again

Stetson's theory does not in itself provide criteria, given a particular sequence of vowels and consonants, for predicting where the arrest and release points will come, since the whole basis of the motor principle is that the sounds make the syllabic movement audible but do not determine it. Each language has its own rules in this matter,[1] but certain general underlying principles can be traced. The classical languages show considerable agreement with one another, and the basic traditional rules seem on the whole to be justified in the light of such generalizations. Firstly, there is a tendency for syllables to have a consonantal release assisting the chest pulse, and consequently for a single intervocalic consonant to release the following syllable rather than arrest the preceding one;[2] one may note, for instance, the tendency in English to maintain and extend the 'linking *r*' where a following word begins with a vowel – e.g. *four days* = [fɔɔ deiz] but *four hours* = [fɔɔrauəz], thence 'intrusively' in e.g. *saw(r)ours* = [sɔɔ(r)auəz]; alternatively a glottal stop may be inserted to provide the consonantal release, as [sɔɔʔauəz]. In French there is the well-known phenomenon of 'liaison' (*vingt ans* = [vɛ̃tɑ̃], etc.), which tends to be extended in colloquial speech. Semivowel 'glides' are also common in many languages to avoid what would otherwise be a 'hiatus'; in Hindi, for example, a consonant-ending verb-stem such as *bhāg-* 'flee' has a preterite *bhāgā* and a subjunctive *bhāge*; but a vowel-ending stem such

---

[1] Cf. Zirin, 66; and for contrast of Hindi and Panjabi, Sharma 1971, 137.

[2] Cf. Zirin, 63. For Pulgram (1970, 47 ff., 66 ff., 75) this is just one aspect of principles of 'maximal open syllabicity' and 'minimal coda and maximal onset'. Note also the typological generalization of Jakobson (1958/1962, 526) that 'There are languages lacking syllables with initial vowels and/or syllables with final consonants, but there are no languages devoid of syllables with initial consonants or of syllables with final vowels' (similarly Jakobson & Halle 1956, 37; cf. Bell 1970b, 178; 1971, 44, 90, 101). Against *Sommer's rejection of this universal (1970) see Darden 1971; cf. also Dixon 1970. The primacy of the CV type is also argued by Bondarko (1969) on the grounds that it is 'the minimal unit for optimal realization of distinctive features'; and by MacNeilage & DeClerk (1969, 1233) on grounds of motor control.

as *khā-* 'eat' inserts a *y* in the preterite *khāyā* and (optionally) a *v* [ʋ] in the subjunctive *khāve*.[1] 'Hiatus' may thus be seen as involving absence of a consonantal reinforcement of the syllabic release, and the various devices mentioned above as functioning to supply such reinforcement.[2] The same underlying tendency will account for the last of a sequence of consonants functioning as the releasing consonant of the following syllable. The most basic patterns of syllable division are thus ~ V . CV ~ and ~ VC . CV ~ .

Complex elements

Secondly, there is a tendency for some sequences of consonants to form complex releasing or arresting combinations more readily than others, for reasons connected with their individual articulations. The ballistic stroke of the syllable is assisted by a single releasing consonant in so far as the latter creates a sudden transition from stricture to aperture of the vocal tract, viz. from C to V,[3] involving a build-up of the air pressure resulting from the chest pulse followed by a more or less rapid release, which serves to accelerate the stroke by a kind of 'choke' effect. But such transition is also possible, and therefore allows and assists the syllabic pulse to develop, if the syllable begins with two consonants of which the second is of markedly greater aperture than the first, as in the case of plosive + liquid referred to on pp. 43, 57;[4] for the liquids 'combine closure and aperture, either intermittently or by barring the median way and opening a lateral by-pass' (Jakobson, Fant & Halle 1952, 20). Nasals also, although they involve, like plosives, a complete occlusion of the oral passage, nevertheless by lowering the velum allow the passage of air through the nose. From the acoustic standpoint, 'The oscillograms of nasals and of sounds like L and R exhibit many

[1] Cf. A 1962, 61.
[2] Cf. the proposals referred to on p. 32 for considering all syllables as commencing with a consonant, including zero. For further examples see Hála 1961, 104 ff; the common tendency for hiatus to contract in the absence of intervocalic 'glides' etc. is also seen by Hála as a manifestation of the same principle; cf. Bell 1971, 96 f., who however notes that loss of intervocalic consonants often leads to hiatus: but such loss is probably to be attributed to oral articulatory processes not directly linked with syllabic function.
[3] Cf. Twaddell's reference (1953, 423) to the 'rapid crescendo' characteristic of post-pause (as opposed to pre-pause) allophones; also Pulgram 1970, 81.
[4] The idea of relative aperture in this connexion is already foreshadowed by Aristides Quintilianus (43 W-I), who states that, the first member being 'of thicker sound' (παχυφωνότερος), the second as being 'thinner' (λεπτότερος) is 'elided and suppressed' (ἐκθλίβεταί τε καὶ πιέзεται).

traits similar to those of vowels' (Tarnóczy 1948, 71). And semivowels, whose articulation is basically the same as that of close vowels, are clearly also of a relatively open conformation compared with, say, a plosive or fricative consonant.

Such functioning of these types of sound is characteristic of many languages. Latin, Greek, and English have already been mentioned in this connexion, and further attention will be paid to the classical languages (pp. 137 ff., 210 ff.). A particularly interesting parallel is provided by Icelandic, where, as already described, stressed vowels are relatively long if followed by a single consonant, and relatively short if followed by more than one consonant. We could now interpret this in the sense that a single intervocalic consonant releases the following syllable, and that the preceding vowel is consequently lengthened as a result of thoracic arrest: i.e. the pattern is $\sim V^{\circ}C.CV\sim$ or $\sim V^{+}.CV\sim$. But in addition vowels are lengthened before consonant sequences of the type voiceless obstruent $+ r$ or semivowel: e.g. in the initial (stressed) syllables of *titra* 'to shiver', *vökva* 'to water', *Esja* (name of mountain).[1] In other words, such sequences are syllabically equivalent to single releasing consonants. Similar considerations apply, though with a different chronology, to *l* and *n*. Former geminate voiceless plosives have been simplified in modern Icelandic, and the loss of the arresting consonant has been compensated for by so-called 'pre-aspiration' (i.e. a *voiceless* lengthening of the preceding vowel): thus e.g. *brattur* 'steep', formerly [brat.tʏr] → mod. [brah.tʏr] = [braḁ.tʏr]; and the same phenomenon is found in the case of the sequences voiceless plosive $+l$ or *n*, e.g. *epli* 'apple' = [ɛhplɪ], *vitni* 'witness' = [vɪhtnɪ].[2] The shortness of the voiced element of the vowel indicates that the earlier syllabification was [ɛp.lɪ] etc.,[3] and the subsequent need for compensation by pre-aspiration reflects a shift in the syllabification to [ɛh.plɪ], i.e. with the consonant sequence forming a complex release for the following syllable.[4]

---

[1] Einarsson 1945, 4 f; Haugen 1958, 82 f. (Icelandic *v*, though not strictly speaking a semivowel, is weakly articulated).

[2] Cf. Einarsson 1945, 16 ff.

[3] Whereas in the case of sequences with *r* or semivowel the vowel length and absence of pre-aspiration indicate that the syllabification was already [tɪɪ.tra] etc. before the period when pre-aspiration was operative. In e.g. *brattra* (gen. pl. of *brattur*) pre-aspiration does occur, because the development will have been from [brat.tra] (with short vowel before consonantal arrest) to [brah.tra] (by simplification of geminate and compensation).

[4] For other doctrines of syllabification in Icelandic cf. Haugen 1958, 84 f.

In Swedish, Sigurd (1955) has studied the degree of 'vowel-adherence' of the various consonants; for example, *l* is of higher rank than *k*, since syllables may begin with *kl*(V) and end with (V)*lk*, but not vice versa; and a distributional analysis establishes precisely the liquids, nasals, and semivowels as standing highest in rank. In fact the reverse order of consonants tends to form complex arrests from that which tends to form complex releases;[1] for a relatively open consonantal articulation may only partially arrest the syllabic movement, and so permit a following consonant of greater stricture to complete the arrest (and not constitute a 'controlled' appendage: see p. 66).

Thus de Saussure's concept of 'aperture' (see p. 39) is indeed relevant to the syllable[2] – but it is only an ancillary factor to the chest pulse, and does not in itself create or define the syllable.

An intervocalic consonant sequence of, say, the type PL does not, however, necessarily function as a releasing combination; a syllabification $\sim$VP.LV$\sim$ is equally as possible as $\sim$V.PLV$\sim$ since P can perfectly well arrest and L release a syllable; and languages vary one from another, and from period to period, in the functioning of such sequences (as has just been seen in Icelandic and will later be shown for the classical languages). Moreover, since either alternative is phonetically possible, it is not surprising that, even within a given language and period, there may be variation between one and the other treatment in congruence with grammatical function; specifically, a morph boundary may impose a syllabic boundary, so that a morph-initial PL may be required to release a syllable, whilst the same sequence divided between morphs may be required to arrest one syllable and release the next. If such a sequence is preceded by a short vowel, the syllable to which that vowel belongs will consequently be light ($\sim$V^o.CCV$\sim$) or heavy ($\sim$V^{o}C.CV$\sim$) respectively, as already seen on p. 58.

A sequence such as LP may, of course, similarly either function in combination to arrest a preceding syllable, or to arrest a preceding and release a following syllable (i.e. $\sim$VLP.V$\sim$ or $\sim$VL.PV$\sim$). But since the preceding syllable will then be arrested (and so heavy) in either case, such differences of function are less relevant prosodically than in the case of the order PL (see however p. 68).

[1] Cf. the tendency in Panjabi for $C^x{}_\partial C^yV\sim$ $\rightarrow$ $C^xC^yV\sim$ and for $\sim VC^y{}_\partial C^x\rightarrow$ $\sim VC^yC^x$ where C^y is of greater aperture than C^x (Sharma 1971, 58 ff., 82).
[2] Cf. Bell 1970b, 23: 'The sublaryngeal speech mechanism and the grouping af articulatory gestures are probably both involved.'

If quantity is defined in terms of syllabic arrest vs non-arrest, then releasing consonants are clearly irrelevant to the definition. Moreover, if (as the chest-pulse theory assumes) every syllable has a thoracic release, the function of a syllable-initial consonant is in support of and simultaneous with that release ('the consonant movement fuses with the syllable movement': Stetson, 57 f.) – unlike the indcpcndently arresting rôle of a syllable-final consonant; the releasing consonant thus adds nothing to the basic syllabic structure, whereas the arresting consonant does. From the durational standpoint, in fact, according to Stetson (46), 'The releasing consonant never adds to the length of the syllable and it actually accelerates the syllable movement'.

The more specialized applications of this theory of the syllable to phenomena presented by the classical languages will be mentioned in their appropriate places. But it is hoped that enough has already been said to show that the syllable, at least as defined in terms of motor phonetics, can hardly be dismissed as a mere 'print-and-paper' construction (cf. p. 59). Rather does it provide, at the very minimum, a basis for the explanation of a number of otherwise disparate phenomena; and as thus defined it tends to support the conclusions towards which, by other routes, a number of experimental phoneticians have recently been led; for example, Lisker, Cooper & Liberman 1962, 98: 'Usually, the encoding of motor commands into shapes and movements of the tract is a complex transformation, one that could not be computed, even in principle, without taking account of interactions over stretches of the order of syllabic length'; Fry 1964, 219: 'There is a certain amount of circumstantial evidence which points to the likelihood that the syllable acts as the unit of motor control'; Fromkin 1966, 196: 'One possible conclusion is that the minimal linguistic unit corresponding to the motor commands which produce speech is larger than the phoneme, perhaps more of the order of the syllable' (similarly Lenneberg 1967, 109, 115); Boomer & Laver 1968, 9: (a study of slips of the tongue) 'suggests that syllable structure and rhythm are also more than just linguistic constructs and can be plausibly considered to be central aspects of the neural control programme in speech'; MacNeilage & DeClerk 1969, 1217: 'The results suggested that syllabic factors are influential in the "premotor" command structure of speech.' Similar observations are found in Fromkin 1968 (63), where it is also suggested (57) that, whereas the phoneme may be the minimal unit in the 'competence mode', the syllable is the minimal unit of 'performance'; and in this connexion Lehiste (1970, 155) further comments that 'A competence model can be a static model; a performance model must be a dynamic model'. Such a 'generative' rôle of the syllable also underlies the statement by Abercrombie (1964a, 6) that 'The rhythm is already *in* the air-stream, in fact, before the actual vowels and consonants which make up words are superimposed on it'.

Finally it should be noted that the theory of the syllable does not in itself account for the equivalences in certain metrics of one heavy to two light syllables. The origins of these will be sought elsewhere (see pp. 255 ff.); but in one type of such equivalence a motor theory of the syllable will be found to supply an essential underlying factor (see pp. 169 ff., 197 ff., 318 ff.).

5   *Stress*

We may now consider certain modulations applicable to the syllabic pulses or to the process of their audible emission.[1] We shall, for the purpose of the languages concerned, examine only the most common of these modulations, which are also in a sense the most basic, since probably no language fails to exhibit them (although their functions may vary from language to language) and they utilize mechanisms which are in any case inherently involved in speech. Adopting the terminology of radio telephony, we may call these 'amplitude modulation' and 'frequency modulation'. We shall first consider the former type, since it is more closely related to the motor processes which we have just discussed.[2]

Amplitude modulation is manifested in language by what is most commonly termed 'stress'. It has, however, been widely observed[3] that what is interpreted by the speaker or hearer as stress has no simple correlation with amplitude as acoustically registered or loudness as auditorily perceived: Trager's statement (1941, 133) that 'Stress intensity is manifested as relative loudness' is a considerable oversimplification. Most commonly it is associated with other factors, notably duration and pitch; and in some cases these criteria may prove to be more potent cues to stress from the listener's point of view than simple increases of loudness; amongst other things the 'inherent amplitude' of particular sounds is liable to affect the loudness patterns, and in order to interpret these in terms of stress the hearer would have to apply appropriate 'corrections'.[4] The complexity of the possible

---

[1] Cf. Stetson 1951, 36 f.
[2] For a discussion of the wide range of possible modifying features see Crystal 1969, 126 ff. Some of these, though treated by Crystal (in the context of English) as 'paralinguistic', may function linguistically in various languages – e.g. 'creak', 'breathy voice' (cf. Abercrombie 1967, 101).
[3] Cf. Crystal 1969, 113 ff; Lehiste 1970, 106 ff.
[4] Lehiste 1970, 118 f. Peterson & McKinney (1961, 81) note that in utterances of equal quality but falling pitch, peaks of power occur where harmonic frequencies pass through formant centre frequencies – i.e. quality (especially of vowels) may help to determine power output.

cues involved has been commented upon by many observers: e.g. Gimson 1956; Fry 1958; Soderberg 1959, 114; Vanvik 1961; *Cook 1961, 63; Wang 1962; Lehiste 1970, 125 ff. In this respect it has a parallel in the 'accent' of music as described by Cooper & Meyer (1960, 7): 'a product of a number of variables whose interaction is not precisely known'; the purposes of the present study, however, will not permit us simply to set the matter on one side as 'a basic axiomatic concept which is understandable as an experience but undefined in terms of causes'.

The plurality of cues has often led to the view that what is termed 'stress' is not even basically a matter of amplitude at all; and alternative definitions have been given, most commonly in terms of pitch; thus, for example, Bolinger 1958a, 149: 'The primary cue of what is usually termed STRESS in the utterance is pitch prominence.'[1] Most supporters of this view do, however, recognize that it is not simply a matter of *high* pitch, but rather of a *change* of pitch;[2] nor need the change necessarily be *upward*;[3] and Jongen (1969, 322) notes a case in Flemish where the syllable interpreted as stressed is the one which *precedes* the rise of pitch.[4] Žirmunskij (1966, 90), having commented that 'the syllable which is dynamically stronger is usually melodically higher', goes on to add the cautious parenthesis '(or lower, in certain languages)'.[5] And already in an admirable note to a famous paper of 1875 (= Lehmann 1967, 161 f.) Verner demonstrated from Swedish examples the possibility of a strong stress on a low pitch followed by weak stress on a high pitch.[6]

Variation in the stress/pitch relationship may result in wrong judgements of accent placement in foreign languages;[7] in Hindi, for example, stress is most commonly associated with a downward step of pitch; in a sentence such as *vah jā rahā hai* 'he is going' the stress and associated low pitch occur on the syllable *jā*, and the highest pitch on the weak syllable *hā*;[8] but the English speaker tends to hear the latter as the most prominent, and in speaking Hindi tends to stress it more strongly than the *jā*.

---

[1] Cf. Wang 1967, 93 n.2 (citing J. D. McCawley); Faure 1970, 49 f., 82 ff.
[2] Cf. Gimson 1956, 147.   [3] Bolinger 1958a, 149; 1958b, 175.
[4] Cf. also, for Polish, Jassem 1959, 263.
[5] Cf. Chatman 1965, 50.
[6] Cf. (on Schwabian) Schmitt 1953, 18; (on Slovene) Halle 1971, 15; and in general Kalinka 1935, 325, 349; Nooteboom 1971, 285 f. (with further refs.).
[7] Cf. Fónagy 1958, 54 f.   [8] Firth 1950, xxxvi.

The variability of the potential cues to stress afforded by pitch should itself indicate the necessity for not confusing the two phenomena.[1] In this connexion a suggestive distinction is made by Schmitt (1953, 17), who characterizes pitch as an acoustic effect, but stress as a motor activity.[2] The acoustic and auditory effects of this activity include wave-amplitude and loudness; but, as Schmitt recognizes, the correlation is not always direct and, as we have seen, may include other features. In a strong denial of the primacy of pitch in the definition of stress (whatever its potency as a cue), Stetson (95) makes the point that in music 'It is possible to make abrupt pitch changes within a musical figure without changing the stress pattern'; but that in speech it is not surprising if stress should involve changes in pitch simply as incidentals, for 'the heavy stroke of the accent involves the chest pressure and is apt to change the pitch because the laryngeal musculature is often affected by tensions in the other musculatures of speech'.[3]

An attempt to find a more positive and less variable acoustic correlate of stress has been made by Lehto (1969, following Sovijärvi 1958), the relevant criterion being not the overall maximum of intensity but an increase during the 'beat phase' ('Stossphase') of the syllable; but Lehto recognizes that as a starting point for such studies 'the only possible criterion for what can be called stressed' is 'the opinions of native listeners'.

Fónagy (1958) concludes that stress is not definable in acoustic terms, and that the listener simply uses the various cues as a basis for judging the degree of force employed by the speaker; in this connexion we may recall the distinction made above by Schmitt, and assume as a working hypothesis that, whereas in the case of pitch the relationship between audition and interpretation, however complex, is relatively direct, stress is primarily interpreted in indirect, 'kinaesthetic' terms, i.e. in terms of the movements the hearer himself would make in order to produce the perceived effect.[4] Much of the confusion regarding the nature of stress probably arises from the fact that it is used to denote

[1] Cf. Jones 1962, 256 §912 and note.
[2] Cf. Faure 1970, 57.
[3] For more specific observations see Lehiste 1970, 82, 125, 144.
[4] Cf. Abercrombie 1964a, 7; Lieberman 1968, 162. Some writers, however, would extend such a motor theory of perception to speech more generally, including intonation: cf. especially Stevens 1968; Liberman, Cooper, Studdert-Kennedy, Harris & Shankweiler 1968; Lieberman, Sawashima, Harris & Gay 1970, with refs; in which case one might describe the difference between stress and pitch interpretation in terms of 'more or less' (of the motor component) rather than 'either/or'.

'both an aspect of the articulatory or motor side of speech and also a feature of the sounds perceived by the hearer' (Fry 1958, 126; cf. *Cook 1961, 42 ff.); as sound received 'it denotes a complex of perceptual dimensions', but (129) 'particularly in the case of a listener receiving his native language, it is probable that the listener's kinaesthetic memories play some part in his reception of speech. If this is so, it is likely that the contribution will be particularly strong in the case of stress judgments since rhythm of all kinds has a powerful motor component.'[1] The situation is thus similar to that described for another phonetic feature by Fischer-Jørgensen (1967, 138 f.): 'None of these cues is necessary, and none is sufficient alone. We are thus faced with a situation where a large number of instable acoustic cues correspond to a single physiological difference and to one functional feature.'

Following the trend of the statements cited above, it is here proposed to assume for stress a motor definition, based on criteria of production rather than acoustic or auditory effect. In fact such an approach is by no means new; the remarks of Lloyd (1906) already pointed in this direction and deserve to be recalled: (85) 'The idea of stress is never, in the main, acoustic, but muscular'; (93) 'While loudness is a part of the apprehension of a sound through the sensory nerves of the hearer, stress is a part of the apprehension of it by the motor nerves of the speaker'; (94) 'It may be doubted in fact whether that rudimentary consciousness of stress, which is instinctively common to all learners and teachers of language, is not just as accurate, for this purpose, as any external mechanical record which has yet been contrived ... no account of language is complete, which does not connect completely the motor consciousness of the speaker with the sensory consciousness of the hearer'. The 'muscular' aspect of stress has been given particular priority by Vanvik (1961), who includes as a criterion (and even (30) the 'ultimate criterion') the potentiality of concomitant isolated and/or large gesture.[2] Strong stress, as already noted by Jones (1962, 245 §909 and note), 'is usually accompanied by a gesture with the hand or head or other part of the body'; Jones has also drawn attention to the fact that such stress need have no direct acoustic effect[3] – 'A strong stress may even occur on a silence, e.g. on the stop of a voiceless plosive', and the example is cited from English of one type of pronunciation of '*Thank you*', viz. ['ḳkju], where a 'syllabic k without plosion is stressed

---

[1] Cf. also Classe 1939, 12 ff; Rigault 1962.
[2] Cf. also Robinson 1971, 41.   [3] Cf. Jones 1954, 2 n.1.

although it has no sound; the stress is generally shown by a gesture';
pitch characteristics of the following syllable may here also play a
part. Overt gesture is a feature primarily of emphatic stress; but whether
or not gesture is present, it might be said that, by its power to require
a kinaesthetic interpretation, stress is particularly apt to evoke in the
hearer an identification with the speaker, and so is naturally fitted to
perform the function of emphasis.

We have now to consider, however, in more detailed terms, the
possible mechanisms by which stress is produced. After discussing the
difficulties of defining stress in acoustic or auditory terms, owing to
the influence of the superimposed segmental sounds, Wang (1962, 72)
concludes that 'the complexities of these results ... will provide a
suitable motivation for looking for stress determinants elsewhere,
e.g. in the subglottal activities'. We can perhaps be rather more specific.
It is generally agreed that the unit with which stress is most closely
associated is the *syllable*; it might seem reasonable, therefore, to seek
its definition in the same area of motor activity as we have already
assumed for the syllable, namely in the action of the chest muscles.
However, the chest pulse in itself cannot define stress, since syllables
show different degrees of stress, and only a relatively few of them have
strong stress. The stress process must therefore be seen as a *reinforcement* in some way of the syllabic chest-pulse.[1] But it is probably not
yet possible to specify with certainty the nature of this reinforcement:
'Some of the difficulties are that output records are hard to interpret
and that the insertion of needle electrodes produces an awkward amount
of discomfort to the subject' (Wang 1962, 73). The most usual assumption is that the stress reinforcement is effected by the abdominal
muscles;[2] for Stetson (3) the abdominal pulses generate 'feet', which
consist of 'a single stressed syllable, or a few syllables grouped about a
single stressed syllable'. Doubts about the function of these muscles
have, however, been expressed by Lebrun (1966b; c), and the matter
can hardly be considered as settled. We shall therefore refer to the
stress mechanism in non-committal terms simply as a 'stress pulse'.

A stressed syllable can then be defined as a chest pulse reinforced
by a stress pulse (which perhaps constitutes the culmination of an
'abdominal pulse'). We may then go on to consider certain possible
consequences of this coordination of pulses.

[1] Cf. Stetson, 95 f; Fónagy 1958; Ladefoged 1967, 46.
[2] E.g. Stetson, *passim*; Pike 1957.

In Stetson's terms (67) 'Stress affects the factors of the syllable on which it falls; all the auxiliary movements tend to increase in amplitude'. If we consider the releasing elements of the syllable, these effects are readily observed in English, where, for example, voiceless plosives releasing a stressed syllable are more strongly articulated, with an increase in aspiration; and where the release of such a syllable is not supported by a phonemic consonant, the tendency, under emphatic stress, is to provide such support by means of glottal plosion.[1] The vocalic nucleus of the stressed syllable normally receives greater expiratory force, and tends to 'increased articulatory precision' (Fant 1957, 47). The point of maximum intensity varies from language to language,[2] but most common (and normal, for example, in English) is the diminuendo type, where the peak is reached relatively early in the syllable.[3]

It appears that the arrest of the stress pulse is at least assisted by the arrest mechanism of the syllable itself; hence, if the stress is to characterize a single syllable, the syllable will tend to be arrested. The consequences of this interaction are widely attested. Vanvik (1961, 40) observes that 'Physiologically there seems to be a need for what R. H. Stetson called an arresting consonant after short vowels occurring in stressed syllables'; Trubetzkoy (1935/1968, 37) notes that in some Germanic languages (including English)[4] open, stressed final syllables are always 'long'; for Fant (1957, 43) 'The tendency towards lengthening is the most obvious feature observed as a physical correlate to stress'.[5] Stetson himself (103 ff.)[6] has a number of relevant comments: in a stressed syllable 'the preceding consonant is drawn in to assist in the preparation of the heavy stroke, and if the vowel is "short", the following consonant is drawn in to assist in the arrest of the heavy stroke'; 'the heavy stroke runs into the releasing consonant stroke of the next syllable and so converts it into a double consonant. Since the syllable movement is arrested by this obstacle,...increase of stress will not greatly lengthen the vowel'; but 'If the syllable involved has a "long" vowel (i.e. a vowel that can be prolonged), the increased force of the

[1] More particularly in initial position. Medially one may observe a glottal or pharyngal constriction.
[2] Pike 1957; Jones 1950, 134, 149 ff.
[3] Jones 1950, 150; Kurath 1964, 151.
[4] Cf. Kurath 1964, 41; Trnka 1966, 22.
[5] Cf. Fry 1958, 135; Lehiste 1970, 36 ff.
[6] Cf. 1945, 57.

stress shows in the increased length of the chest pulse, and the vowel is somewhat longer'.

Historically these principles may be seen at work in the common tendency for stressed syllables to preserve or develop an arrest, either by consonant-doubling (giving an oral arrest) or by vowel-lengthening or diphthongization (associated with a thoracic arrest). Thus, against the general Romance tendency to simplify geminate consonants, Italian *vacca* (with geminate preserved), *femmina* (with geminate developed), and syntactically e.g. *la Città(d)del Vaticano.*[1] The thoracic alternative, which is the more common, may be seen, for example, in the pronunciation of late Latin /dębérę/ (< cl. *débére*) as [deˈβee.rɛ], with lengthening of the vowel in the stressed second syllable as opposed to the unstressed first, and subsequent diphthongization attested by Fr. *devoir*; whereas in e.g. /méttęrę/ (< cl. *míttere*), with geminate consonant and so oral arrest [ˈmet.tɛ.rɛ], there is no such lengthening or diphthongization, and the result in French is *mettre* [mɛtʀ]. Similar stress lengthening is seen in English, where e.g. O.E. *nǎcod* → Mid.E. *nāked* (mod. [ˈneikɪd]), and it is a characteristic feature of many modern languages, e.g. Italian, Russian, Greek.

In some languages the choice between thoracic and oral arrest of a stressed syllable may vary from dialect to dialect (cf. p. 52); cases are commonly cited from Norwegian, where in the west the former is general, but in Oslo and the east the latter (cf. Nynorsk *koma* [∼ ɔɔm ∼] vs Bokmål *komme* [∼ ɔmm ∼]).[2]

Vowel or consonant lengthening due to stress is to be clearly distinguished from inherent length where this is in significant opposition to shortness; as Weinrich points out (1958, 182), in classical Latin *tēla* [ˈtee.la] the vowel length is phonologically relevant, whereas in late Latin /téla/ [ˈtee.la] (→ Fr. *toile*) the length is only phonetic,[3] as it is in the three modern languages referred to above.

It is, however, possible to have a more 'staccato' mode of utterance, in which the stress is arrested without involving syllabic arrest, and so involves a less appreciable increase in duration. Spanish seems to

---

[1] Such 'syntactic doubling' also occurs after unstressed conjunctions and proclitics, e.g. *a casa* = /akkása/: cf. Hall 1964, 553; but in the case of disyllables, since it is confined to end-stressed words, stress must be an operative factor. Note also that doubling occurs before plosive+liquid (e.g. *va(p)presto*).

[2] Sommerfelt 1933, 324; Broch 1935, 111; Martinet 1955, 141 f; Popperwell 1963, 115.

[3] Cf. Ebeling 1968.

present a case of this type, where (unlike in Italian, for example)[1] vowels ending stressed syllables, though generally longer than those of preaccentual syllables, tend if anything to be slightly shorter than vowels ending unstressed final syllables; thus for *paso* Tomás (1963, 199 ff.) gives vowel durations of 10.8:10.8 cs., and for *peseta* 6.5:10:11.7 cs., and comments that the duration of the stressed vowels is similar to that of short vowels in e.g. German.[2]

Phonetic lengthening of vowels under stress must inevitably tend to neutralize a phonological opposition between short and long vowels of similar quality,[3] where duration is one of the identificatory criteria; such neutralization will be the more complete if, as we have suggested, thoracic arrest is a characteristic both of phonological long vowels and of vowels lengthened under stress; and the confusion of the two categories will be complete in cases where the lengthening of a vowel results in a change of quality to one identical with that of a corresponding phonological long vowel[4] associated with tense articulation. Gemination of consonants in the same circumstances must have the effect of neutralizing the opposition between long (geminate) and short (single) consonants.

It has in fact been considered exceptional for languages to have phonologically significant, independent distinctions both of length and of stress;[5] and it has been noted by Juilland (1948, lv) that in late Latin it was precisely the loss of length distinctions that created the independence of the stress accent;[6] conversely in late Greek, when the independent melodic accent changed to stress, it was accompanied by a loss of length distinctions (A 1968a, 88 f.). Where cases of coexistence are found, Trubetzkoy suggests (1935/1968, 37) that they are subject to a limitation whereby the distinction between short and long vowels is found only before consonants, the contrast there being one of transition, as described on p. 49. English is cited as an example of this limitation, where, as already noted, final stressed short vowels do not occur, nor generally do medial stressed short vowels in hiatus, i.e. followed by

[1] Cf. Hall 1971.
[2] Cf. also Dalbor 1969, 244 f.
[3] Cf. Spence 1965.
[4] Cf. the results of contraction ($\breve{V} + \breve{V} \rightarrow \bar{V}$) or compensatory lengthening ($\breve{V}C \rightarrow \bar{V}$) in Latin, Greek, and Sanskrit (A 1959, 244 f; 1962, 30).
[5] Jakobson 1926/1962, 624; 1931/1962, 135 f; 1937a/1962, 258; Trubetzkoy 1938, 160; Krámský 1966; Jakobson & Halle 1968, 425.
[6] The principle is earlier recognized by Vendryes (1902, 63), who further notes that the same basic idea underlies the arguments of Dietrich (1852).

another vowel.[1] An alternative attempt to save the rule has been made by treating English vowels as having distinctions of tenseness and not of length: thus Jakobson 1931/1962, 135 n.66. Another explanation which might be adduced is that to a large extent English stress is non-phonemic, being predictable by a combination of phonological and grammatical rules (cf. p. 17; e.g. Chomsky & Halle 1968; Halle & Keyser 1971). More relevant, however, may be the fact that stress in modern English can operate in a manner which does not require a significant lengthening of a short vowel (for further discussion see pp. 194 ff.).

[1] An exception is provided by one pronunciation of words like *ruin, fluid, suet,* which however have monosyllabic (diphthongal) variants, or disyllabic with long vowel in the first syllable (cf. Jones 1962, 234 § 869). In any case there is no *distinction* between long and short vowels in this position.

6   *Pitch*

In considering frequency modulation we encounter fewer problems of production theory. Such modulation is effected primarily by variation in the rates of vibration of the vocal cords, giving rise to variation in the fundamental frequency of the transmitted sound. But what is relevant to speech is not so much this acoustically measured frequency as the correlated sensations of 'pitch' as perceived by the hearer; and these are affected by other factors in addition to frequency.[1] 'The perceptual correlates have proved to be of great complexity' (Jensen 1961, 41) and have been found to include, for instance, loudness, duration, and vowel quality.[2] 'Experimental phonetics cannot be used to demonstrate what is and what is not perceived by the ear' (Jensen 1958, 189), and systematic descriptions of pitch phenomena generally have a perceptual rather than an acoustic or physiological basis; they are 'descriptions of idealized patterns distilled out of speech events rather than, say, what can be measured directly from narrow band spectrograms' (Wang 1967, 96). But since the native listener himself intuitively performs such 'idealizations', there is no inappropriateness in this method. Moreover, unlike in the case of stress, there is no immediately compelling reason to assume an indirect, motor interpretation of the perceived sound, even though the cues involved may be just as complex. In short, it might be stated as a working (if perhaps oversimplified)[3] hypothesis that the criteria of stress are to be sought primarily in the speaker, but those of pitch primarily in the listener; and it is probably by means of auditory rather than kinaesthetic feedback that the speaker achieves the desired pitch effects; the greater difficulties of the deaf with intonation than with stress may be symptomatic of this difference.[4]

Another contrast between stress and pitch may be noted. Stress, as we have seen, operates on the syllable as a whole, including its consonants, and arresting consonants play a particular rôle in the process. Thus in Latin, for example, a word of the type *re.fĕc.tus* is

---

[1] Cf. Crystal 1969, 108 ff.   [2] Cf. also Lehiste 1970, 62 ff.
[3] See p. 76 n. 4.   [4] Cf. Stetson 1951, 95.

stressed in the same way as *re.fé.cit*, the sequence [ek] being for purposes of stress equipollent to the long vowel [ee]. Pitch, however, can operate only on such elements as are capable of carrying fundamental pitch differences, i.e. in the production of which the vocal cords are in vibration – which means primarily the vowels: 'Fundamental frequency tends to medium value during articulation of consonants, the marked rises and falls being made during vowel articulations' (Fry 1968, 389). The observation of this fact has a long history, at least in India; in his commentary on the phonetic treatise of the ṚgVeda, Uvaṭa notes that 'The relation of quality–qualified exists between pitches and vowels, not however between (pitches and) consonants' (Cardona 1968, 456).[1] Voiced sounds other than vowels (more particularly if they are of relatively open articulation, as liquids and nasals: cf. pp. 43, 69) are also capable of participating in pitch variation;[2] Pike (1948, 7) notes that 'a (pitch) glide may end on a voiced consonant in the same syllable', a point already made by the Indian treatise *Vaidikābharaṇa* (A 1953, 83).[3] What, however, is clearly out of the question is that pitch should operate on a voiceless consonant, as e.g. [k].[4] Thus in Greek a word like ἕκτος [hék. ~] can *not* carry the same pitch pattern as e.g. οἶκος [ói. ~] (see further p. 153);| and so the relationship of these forms is, from a modulatory point of view, utterly different from that of *refectus* and *refécit* in Latin.[5]

In their linguistic functioning, pitch phenomena are relative and not absolute; they are liable to wide variation depending upon the other pitches in their environment. In languages where words are said to have significant pitch patterns, a given pattern may vary from context to context, 'and if we require a single lexical entry we shall be faced with the problem of selection' (Sharp 1954, 168) – in fact, as Sharp most strikingly demonstrates, the significantly different patterns are manifested not so much in the individual words themselves as in the different 'contonations' of the sentence frameworks in which they are embedded.

The functions for which pitch phenomena are employed vary from language to language; they may, in so-called 'tonal' languages, have lexically distinctive function, utilizing differences of level and/or contour (cf. p. 92 and Wang 1967); they may perform the 'culmina-

---

[1] Similarly *Paribhāṣenduśekhara* 79 f.
[2] Cf. Wang 1967, 95.
[3] On variation between languages in the extent to which non-vocalic elements may carry pitch features cf. Lehiste 1970, 84.
[4] Cf. Borgstrøm 1938, 261.   [5] Cf. Zirin 1970, 75, 79.

tive' function of word accentuation; and they may characterize the 'intonation' of longer stretches of speech, notably the sentence, which commonly interacts with the pitch patterns of words in the two other functions: cf. Jensen 1961, 32.

In the present study we shall be primarily concerned with the accentual functions of pitch. For our knowledge of these phenomena in a 'dead' language we are of course dependent on graphic indications and/or the recorded statements of native writers. In both cases all but the most obvious features of contextual variation are likely to have been 'normalized', and we are thus presented with what may be phonetically a greatly oversimplified picture. Such problems as arise are consequently for the most part concerned with the interpretation of the evidence, and with the adequacy of alternative modes of description, rather than with any complexity of the phonetic phenomena themselves.

7 Accent

The Latin *accentus* (see p. 3) is based on the Greek προσῳδία, which in its earlier linguistic use had referred to the melodic (pitch) characteristics of words; but as applied to Latin it in fact designated dynamic (stress) characteristics (see pp. 151 ff.); and in current sub-technical usage 'accent' is often employed almost as a synonym of stress – especially in relation to emphasis. It is also commonly used in a non-technical sense to refer to a particular (more often dialectal or 'foreign') mode of pronunciation. And, like the Greek προσῳδία, it is frequently extended to designate the accent *marks*, even when these have nothing to do with pitch or stress (as e.g. in French).

In technical linguistic usage the term 'accent' has a clearly defined basic meaning, on which there is little disagreement; but misconceptions are occasionally encountered in regard to its more specific functions. The most general property of accent in this technical sense is its *culminative* function; it is a phonetic 'peak' or 'climax' occurring typically in every word – though in some languages it may characterize the individual morphemes of compound words,[1] and conversely it may be subordinated to phrase or sentence patterns. In English, for example, words such as *downstairs, home-made, fourteen* are accented, in isolation, on both syllables;[2] but in e.g. *fourteen shillings* the accent is on the first syllable, and in *just fourteen* on the second (Jones 1962, 253 f. §§ 931 ff.). Primarily, however, the accent is a feature of the word, in that it tends to occur once and once only in what are grammatically and semantically identifiable as words; so widespread is this circumstance that accentuation may be employed as a phonological criterion for the status of 'word' where grammatical criteria are ambivalent. We have encountered a class of forms which, by at least some grammatical criteria, might be classed as words, but which from the phonological point of view, including accentuation, cohere more or less closely

---

[1] Cf. Martinet 1954, 14.
[2] Double accentuation is also found in English in a few non-compound words, particularly proper names, e.g. *Berlin, Chinese, sardine* (Jones 1962, 252 f. §§929 ff.).

with a word preceding or following; such forms have sometimes been terms 'clitics' ('enclitic' and 'proclitic' respectively: see pp. 23 ff.).

In this culminative function the purpose of the accent has sometimes been seen as 'concentration of attention', tending to compensate for the fact that 'attention is discontinuous and intermittent' (Bolton 1894, 155);[1] in these terms it may be said to have the effect of grouping together, with itself as the focus of attention, a sequence of syllables having a single semantic function – in other words, to 'individualize' the semantic units (thus e.g. de Groot 1931, 126; Martinet, 14 f; Trost 1964, 127).

But other functions of accent are also frequently noted.[2] If in a given language the accent normally occurs at a particular point in the word (e.g. initial as in Czech or Icelandic or Hungarian; final as in Armenian; penultimate as in Polish), it is to this extent *demarcative*. In the cases mentioned, the occurrence of the accent generally indicates that a word commences or ends with the syllable in question, or ends with the next syllable. In Latin, although there are regular rules for accent location, the situation is rather more complex, and the accent is only partially demarcative (even if one only considers words of more than two syllables); the occurrence of accentuation on a light syllable indicates that a word ends with the next syllable but one (e.g. *fácilis*); accentuation on a heavy syllable indicates that a word ends with the next syllable if that syllable also is heavy (e.g. *compóno*), but if it is light, a word may end either with that syllable or with the one following (e.g. *compóne, compónere*); and the occurrence of disyllables and monosyllables in fact makes the demarcative function even less effective.[3] 'Some languages lay great stress on the strict delimitation and separation of words and morphemes, while others do not regard these things as being so very important' (Trubetzkoy 1935/1968, 46); and in general the demarcative function of the accent does not seem to rank very highly.

The demarcative function is in any case only possible when the location of the accent is fixed by regular rule. If, on the other hand, the accent is 'free', in the sense that its position is not phonologically predictable, another function is rendered possible, the so-called *distinctive* function. In Spanish, for example, it is capable of distin-

[1] Cf. Hendrickson 1899, 201.
[2] Cf. Trubetzkoy 1935/1968, 34; Jakobson 1937/1962, 254 ff; Martinet, 19 ff.
[3] Cf. also Pulgram 1970, 31 f. and n.13.

guishing the meanings of *término* 'end' (noun), *termino* /∼í∼/ 'I end', and *terminó* 'he ended'; in Russian between *pláču* 'I weep' and *plaču* 'I pay'; in English between *ímport* (noun) and *impórt* (verb); in classical Greek between ὄρος 'mountain' and ὀρός 'whey';[1] in modern Greek between πίνω /píno/ 'I drink' and πεινῶ /pinó/ 'I'm hungry' or γέρος 'old man' and γερός 'healthy'. In many cases such freedom is, however, subject to some limitations: in Greek, for example, the accent is limited to the last three syllables of the word.

But the importance of the distinctive function of the accent tends to be exaggerated. As Martinet suggests (13 f.), one can hardly consider it as a primary function when one has to conduct an extensive search to come up with at the most a few dozen pairs of words distinguished exclusively by their accent – most of which in any case could generally not occur in comparable contexts. And Martinet goes on to note that, historically speaking, one cannot establish semantic needs as underlying the development of 'free' accentuation. It may come about quite fortuitously; in late Latin, for example, it resulted from the loss of length distinctions in vowels, so that patterns of the type ΣΣ̣Σ and ΣΣ̱Σ[2] (e.g. *réfĭcit*, *refēcit*), where the different accentual positions are determined by differences of length/quantity, develop to Σ́ΣΣ and ΣΣ́Σ (/réfeket/, /reféket/), where the different accentuations are environmentally unconditioned, i.e. free.[3] It might be argued that the accentual distinctions thus established are in some way a compensation for the lost length distinctions, but their effectiveness is minimal compared with the latter; the most one can say is that, freedom of accent having been established, it *may* fulfil a distinctive function.

But even when they so function, the status of accentual features is quite different from that of the segmental distinctive features which characterize the phonemic vowel and consonant units. In a pair of words such as Eng. *god* and *cod* the initial consonants are distinguished by the presence or absence of the feature of voicing – which, however, is also relevant to consonants elsewhere in the word, e.g. the final consonants of *led*, *let*; the feature may occur more than once, e.g. in *god*, or not at all, as in *cot*; whereas in e.g. *ímport* vs *impórt* the accentual feature must occur once and once only. As Garde neatly expresses it

---

[1] Cf. p. 3 n.2; for further examples see Lupaş 1967, 17 f.
[2] Σ̣, Σ̱ = syllable containing short, long vowel.
[3] *Phonetically* the accented vowels were of longer duration, but this is an allophonic *consequence* of the accentual stress and not an independent, phonological feature (see p. 80).

(1968, 8), in the case of a distinctive feature we must know, for each relevant segment, whether it is there or not ('s'il est là ou s'il n'y est pas'), but for an accentual feature whether it is there or elsewhere ('s'il est là ou s'il est ailleurs'). In Martinet's terms (16) the accent is not 'oppositive' but 'contrastive'. Its value does not derive from the paradigm, i.e. the system of oppositions operative at a given point in the chain (e.g. voiced vs voiceless as in the initials of *god* vs *cod*; nasal vs oral as in the initials of *mad* vs *bad*), but from the syntagm, i.e. by contrast with the rest of the chain (e.g. the accented ~ *mú* ~ in *remunerative*, by contrast with the unaccented portions *re* ~ *nerative*). In other words, in *mad* vs *bad* nasality is opposed to orality (non-nasality) in the initial position; but in *ímport* vs *impórt* the accent on the initial syllable of the former word is not opposed to its absence in the latter; opposition would occur only if *ímport* were distinguished from an accentless word *import*, which it is not.

The point has also been made in recent years that in languages with 'free' accent the location of the accent is largely determined by the grammatical (morphological) structure of the word (cf. p. 17 and Kiparsky 1967a; Garde, 108 ff; Worth 1968; Nicholson 1970), so that the primary difference between 'free' and 'fixed' accentuation is that the former can, in certain cases, help to indicate the morphological structure. In Greek, for example, final accentuation characterizes the participle of the strong aorist (e.g. λιπών, as against indic. ἔλιπον or pres. part. λείπων), and the genitive and dative of certain 3rd-declension nouns (e.g. ποδός, ποδί, as against acc. πόδα); retraction of accent characterizes the vocative of certain nouns, e.g. ἄδελφε beside ἀδελφός; penultimate accentuation characterizes the perf. part. passive, e.g. λελυμένος. In Italian (Garde, 124 ff.), although the accent is 'free', there is a general rule that, given a class of 'accentable' morphemes, the later predominate accentually over the earlier in the word, giving, for example, *opera* (antepenult.), *operoso* (penult.), *operosità* (final). Reference has already been made to the claim of Chomsky & Halle that, given the grammatical structure of a word (including its trans-formational derivation), the 'free' accent of English is also in principle predictable. However, although the morphemes in such cases may have 'accentual properties' (Garde, 110 ff.), as e.g. Gk perf. part. passive -μέν-, the *accent* remains a prerogative of the *word* in which it occurs.

It should be noted (as by Martinet, 14) that the well-known occurrence of 'secondary accents' in many languages does not affect the general principle that each accentual unit (normally the word) has one and only one accent. Such secondary 'accents' are no more than automatic phonetic features whose form and place of occurrence are determined by reference to the 'main' accent; in Hungarian, for example, where the main accent is regularly on the first syllable of the word, a 'secondary accent' tends to fall on alternate following syllables – thus in a 5-syllable word such as *boldogtalanság*[1] 'misery' main stress falls on the initial and secondary stresses on the antepenultimate and final.[2] In English the principle is represented by what Chomsky & Halle (1968, 78 f.)[3] term the 'Alternating Stress Rule', as e.g. in *baritone* ['bærɪˌtoun], organize ['ɔɔgəˌnaiz]. In Hindi, words with final accentuation have secondary accents, under certain conditions, on the next syllable but one preceding, as e.g. *pareśān* 'distressed' [ˌpəree'ʃaan] (Mehrotra 1965, 103). In classical Greek a special case is seen in the subsidiary accentuation of enclitic combinations such as ἄνθρωπός τις. The probability of such phenomena in Latin will be discussed later (pp. 188 ff; cf. A 1969, 200 ff.).

By Garde (53 ff.) these features are simply termed 'echoes' of the true accent, and are rightly distinguished from secondary accents of the type seen in e.g. German *Bürgermeister* ['b~ˌm~], *Spielzeug* ['ʃ~ˌts~], which are grammatically and not phonologically determined. Nor does the term 'secondary' *necessarily* imply that such 'echoes' are phonetically weaker (cf. p. 293 and A 1966a, 123); its more important implication is that they are predictable from and determined by the main accent. To take a more exotic example, in the (Uto-Aztecan) Tübatulabal language of California (Voegelin 1935, 75), 'Alternation of stress in general is oriented from the main stress, which is not acoustically more prominent than other stressed vowels, but merely serves as a convenient point of departure in describing the rhythmical pattern'; thus in the word ['ïmbïŋ'wiba'ʔat] (translated as 'he is wanting to roll string on his thigh') the main stress falls on the final syllable, and the 'secondary' stresses (though phonetically just as prominent) are determined by regular rules with reference to this point.[4]

---

[1] The acute accent sign in Hungarian indicates vowel length, not accentuation.
[2] Sauvageot 1951, 25 f.   [3] Cf. Halle & Keyser 1971, 26 ff.
[4] In cases where a 'secondary' stress accent is also less strong than the main accent, it might be less liable to have the syllabic consequences discussed on pp. 80 ff; note, however, the development seen in e.g. Latin *peregrinus* → It. *pellegrino*, *academia* → *accademia*, with doubling of consonant after presumed secondary stress.

Thus far we have been discussing accent without attempting to specify the range of its possible phonetic realizations. The negative principle is stated by Garde (52) that the accent must *not* utilize a feature which is also distinctive in the language; and conversely (51) that it would be burdensome to add to the language a supplementary feature solely for contrastive, culminative purposes; so that (Pulgram 1969, 37) 'In general, accent is produced by an increment or enhancement of a phonic quality already inherent in the phone'. And the features that turn out to be so utilized are, not surprisingly, the two 'modulations', of frequency and amplitude, discussed above – the two 'prosodic' features par excellence; as Martinet comments (16), the accent impinges upon the hearer's attention because it is effected by phonetic features which are 'assez peu délicats'.

We have already noted the tendency for the cues to stress to include variations of pitch (as well as of duration); but, as has been insisted, this does not justify an assumption that the two types of accent are really one and the same; and the different natures of the processes involved are reflected in different types of rule regarding the placement of accent (cf. pp. 83 f., 153). We shall, therefore, not accept what Thomson (1923, 57 f.) criticized as a 'general-hash theory' of accent, in which pitch, stress, and duration are inextricably intermeshed; and it is difficult to interpret in a meaningful way the statement by Kabell (1960, 14), regarding the rival descriptions of the Latin accent as comprising stress or pitch, that the truth probably lies somewhere between the two views.[1]

It was mentioned that the accent, as such, is contrastive and not oppositive. It can, however, happen that the feature utilized for accentual purposes may permit of variation and so create oppositions within the accented syllables. Most commonly this is the case with pitch. In Greek, for example, in forms such as φῶς 'light' vs φώς 'man', or οἶκοι 'houses' vs οἴκοι 'at home', there is an opposition between two pitch patterns in the accented syllables, viz. falling (indicated by the circumflex) vs rising (indicated by the acute). Much rarer are such oppositions in connexion with a stress accent; but they are attested in Danish and in Latvian by 'uninterrupted' vs 'interrupted' expiration, the latter being effected by glottal constriction (Danish '*stød*').[2]

In a number of languages the features which in other languages are

[1] Cf. also Galton 1962, 291 ff.
[2] Trubetzkoy 1935/1968, 33 f., 40; 1939/1969, 175; Martinet, 19.

utilized for accentual purposes may be used for oppositional, distinctive purposes in any syllable of the word, and are then of course not available for accentual function. Again this is primarily the case with pitch. In such contexts the different levels or movements of pitch are commonly known as 'tones', and the languages so utilizing them as 'tone languages';[1] such languages are widely attested, for example, in S.E. Asia, Western and Southern Africa, and North America.[2] Utilization of stress features in this function is extremely rare, but is reported by Pike & Kindberg (1956) for the Peruvian language Campa.[3]

There are thus, following Martinet (22), three types of language in regard to the utilization of frequency modulation:

1. Tone but no accent.
2. Accent but no tone.
3. Accent and tone (in the accented syllable).

In the third category, however, it is often possible to eliminate the tonal opposition – which marginally breaches the universal stated by Garde (52) – by means of a different analysis of the phenomena. If the opposition is between two different pitch contours, the element which carries the opposition (normally a vowel or diphthong) may sometimes be analysable as comprising two *morae*; in a case such as Gk φῶς vs φώς, for example, the ω would be thus analysed: in ῶ, with falling pitch, the accent (identified as *high* pitch) would be said to occur on the first mora, but in ώ, with rising pitch, on the second mora. There would then be no *opposition* of pitch patterns, and so no 'tone', but rather a difference in the *location* of the pitch accent.[4] It has some-times been suggested that languages naturally divide from this point of view into 'syllable languages' and 'mora languages' – but this has rightly been denied by Martinet (51), who points out that the concept of the mora (unlike that of vowel or syllable) does not correspond to a phonetic reality, but is a purely analytical device; there are languages in which the use of the mora facilitates a clear description of the phono-logy, and others in which it does not – but that is all. A similar view is taken by Garde, with special reference to grammatical criteria (143 ff.); the difference between βᾶς and βῆς, for example, is grammatically parallel to that between λιπών and λίπῃς, viz. as participle vs subjunc-tive (cf. p. 19); there is, therefore, good reason for considering the

---

[1] Cf. Woo 1969, 2 ff.   [2] Pike 1948, *passim.*
[3] Cf. Garde, 40 f.
[4] Cf. Cook 1972, 31. For a comparable analysis of tone in Crow cf. Hamp 1958, 321 f.

accentual difference in the former pair as a difference of location just as it clearly is in the latter pair. And in fact there is a wide range of accentual phenomena in Greek which are far more economically describable in terms of the mora than of the syllable (or syllabic nucleus) as a whole.[1]

With regard to stress accentuation, we have noted a reference to the 'increased articulatory precision' by which it is accompanied; and a related phenomenon is commented on by Jakobson (1937/1962, 259), namely the occurrence of richer vowel systems in the accented syllable.[2] In a study of Hindi accentuation, Kuryłowicz (1968b) has suggested that the accent may in some languages be redundant, in as much as it is no more than a corollary of the phonemic structure, which itself creates a 'rhythmic centre' by virtue of one syllable differing from all others in respect of the system of oppositions operative within it. There may also, according to Kuryłowicz, be *negative* 'rhythmic centres' (in the sense of having minimal systems of oppositions); and if such a negative centre is constituted by the final syllable, the pre-final portion of the word then becomes a positive centre by contrast. This situation is held to account for the location of the Indo-Aryan stress accent, and Latin is also cited as a parallel. At least in the case of Latin, however, it seems doubtful whether such phonemic distributional criteria can account for accent location; for in fact the system of vowel oppositions in final syllables is richer than in medial syllables, and richest of all in initial syllables. Jakobson (1937a/1962, 259) does indeed recognize that in Latin (and e.g. most Turkic languages) one may have 'bi-culminative' forms, with positive 'rhythmic centres' in Kuryło-wicz's sense in the initial and the accented syllables – but even this may misrepresent the true situation. For in Latin the effect of the prehistoric initial stress accent was drastically to reduce the oppositions of short vowels and diphthongs in medial syllables (virtually to nil in the case of light syllables), whereas the grammatically functional final syllables were less subject to such reduction.[3] As a result of the later shift in accentual location, the classical Latin accent, governed by the 'penultimate rule' (see pp. 155 ff.), came to fall on the phonemically *least* rich, medial syllables of the word. It does not, therefore, seem justifiable to assume any general correlation of accentual with phonemic

[1] Cf. also pp. 236 ff. and Jakobson 1937a/1962, 262 ff; Kuryłowicz 1958, 106 ff; A 1966b, 12 f; 1968a, 111 ff; Bell 1970b, 66 ff.
[2] Cf. also Lehiste 1970, 140 ff.
[3] Cf. pp. 51 f., 133; Vendryes 1902, 299 f; Enríquez 1968.

systems. More cautious is the observation by Garde (51) that, whereas phonemic features (e.g. vowel qualities) may, by neutralization in unaccented syllables, constitute negative correlates of accentuation, only prosodic features may positively characterize the accent. But even such negative correlations may, as the case of Latin demonstrates, be completely upset by historical processes of accent shifting determined by quite other and often obscure factors. Whether phonemic distinctions are or are not neutralized *may* indeed be determined by accentuation (as the *prehistoric* Latin developments or the distribution of the 'neutral' vowel in English clearly show), but the reverse is extremely dubious.

The accentual and differential functions of the two modulations do not exhaust their employment in language. For instance, in a language with stress accent words may also have an independent pitch pattern, as in certain Mongol dialects according to Polivanov (1936, 80). Conversely, in a language with pitch accent or tonal distinctions words may also have an independent stress pattern: thus in Bantu (Schmitt 1953, 21; Doke 1954, 43 f; Bell 1970b, 64);[1] in Taos, of New Mexico (Trager 1941, 143); in Amuzgo, Chinantec, and Zapotec, of Mexico (Pickett 1951; Robbins 1961; Merrifield 1963; Bauernschmidt 1965); in Gurung, of Nepal (Pike 1970, 157); and in Mandarin Chinese (Woo 1969, 14 ff.). More recent studies, in fact, tend to neutralize, by answering it, the rhetorical question posed by Nietzsche (Halporn 1967, 240): 'But where is there a language which could keep an *intensio vocis* apart from the accent, a rise in tone from a marked emphasis?'

Particularly common, however, are the cases where, regardless of whether the language has a pitch or a stress accent, or whether or not it has tonal distinctions, longer stretches of utterance (notably the sentence) have characteristic pitch patterns of their own – generally referred to as 'intonations'.[2] In some languages the intonational pitch contour may vary functionally, as e.g. in English, where a falling terminal pattern is characteristic of statements and 'wh-' questions, and a rising pattern of 'yes-or-no' questions. In some languages the contour may always take the same general direction (though with possible functional variations in range or details of form); thus, for example, with rising pattern Norwegian (Popperwell 1963, 177 f.), and with falling pattern Abaza (A 1956, 131 ff.). Similarly sentences may tend

---

[1] Cf., on Bambara (of W. Africa), Woo 1969, 34 ff.
[2] See especially Lehiste 1970, 95 ff.

to particular types of stress patterning, which may influence that of the constituent words (cf. p. 86). Conversely, the details of the sentence patterns of pitch and/or stress are liable to determination by the patterns of the individual words; in English, for example, in the normal pattern of a declarative sentence, 'The stressed syllables form a descending sequence of notes, the first being on a rather high level pitch and the last having a falling intonation' (Jones 1962, 282 §1022).

In addition, stress, often combined with pitch features, may be utilized for emphatic contrast of particular words in a sentence (for English cf. Jones 1962, 298 ff. §§1049 ff.); and combinations of pitch, stress, duration, and a variety of qualitative features may be employed to give emphasis for intensity and for the expression of attitudinal implications (cf. Jones 1962, 309 ff. §§1060 ff; Lehiste 1970, 151; and especially Crystal 1969, *passim*).

In this study we shall be concerned mainly with the prosodic characteristics of individual words, but it will be necessary from time to time to take account of variations determined by the prosodic sentence patterns in which they are embedded.

8 Rhythm

The wide variety of meanings of the word 'rhythm' has already been mentioned (p. xii); and de Groot (1968, 541) has commented that it 'is frequently used for any kind of repetition or periodicity in the physical world, also for any kind of correspondence in aesthetic experience, and, generally, for practically anything connected with experience as long as it is not clearly defined'. In a general sense the word has often been used for other than audible phenomena; in defining the Greek ῥυθμός, for example, Aristides Quintilianus (31 W-I) refers to visible manifestations (e.g. dancing), audible (e.g. music), and tangible (e.g. the arterial pulse).[1]

In its earliest uses, as Benveniste (1951) has argued, the term ῥυθμός means little more than 'form', being commonly equated with σχῆμα, though with a characteristic specialization of use. For whereas σχῆμα generally denotes a fixed, unchanging form, ῥυθμός tends to be found in contexts referring to the pattern assumed at a given moment by a mobile, changing medium. But in Plato the term undergoes an important development of meaning; it is used to designate the form of the movement itself, and in particular a regular ordering of such form – as, for example, in dancing – comparable with harmony as the ordered combination of musical sounds (thus e.g. *Phil.* 17D; *Symp.* 187B; *Laws* ii 665A); it is a κινήσεως τάξις, 'an ordering of movement', which is closely associated with the idea of measurement (μέτρον)[2] and of number (ἀριθμός: cf. Castillo 1968, 287)[3] – whence also the Latin use of *numerus* as the equivalent of ῥυθμός.[4]

In definitions of the modern term 'rhythm', both generally and in its specific reference to language, the motor factor has been repeatedly

---

[1] Galen also cites Herophilus for a comparison of the diastole (vs systole) of the pulse with the 'arsis' (vs 'thesis') of music (see p. 100) as being that element of perceived movement which strikes the appropriate sense (ix, 464 Kühn).

[2] Cf. also Aristotle, *Prob.* 882b: πᾶς ῥυθμὸς ὡρισμένη μετρεῖται κινήσει.

[3] E.g. Plato, *Phil.* 17D; also Aristotle, *Rhet.* 1408b: ὁ δὲ τοῦ σχήματος τῆς λέξεως ἀριθμὸς ῥυθμός ἐστιν.

[4] For further accounts cf. Schroeder 1918; Sturtevant 1923; Waltz 1948.

emphasized: e.g. Goodell 1901, 91 f; de Groot 1930, 227; and more recently Fry 1958, 129; 1964, 217; Abercrombie 1964a, 7 ('All rhythm, it seems likely, is ultimately rhythm of bodily movement'). But patterned movement in many non-linguistic contexts is associated with more or less strict temporal regularity – e.g. in the rhythms of inanimate and animate nature, in human physiological rhythms such as those of the pulse, respiration, or walking, and in the arts of music and dance. As a result the term rhythm comes to be applied to the pattern of intervals between movements, or between their beginnings or peaks, or to the pattern of durations of movements, rather than to the qualitative pattern of the movements themselves; and through the intermediary of song this quantitative conception of rhythm is often transferred from the context of music to that of the linguistic art of poetry, and thence to language itself, until finally duration has sometimes been conceived as the primary parameter of rhythmic definition. Thus for Quintilian (ix.4.46) 'numeri (= ῥυθμοί) spatio temporum constant' and are specifically differentiated from metre, which depends in addition on 'ordo' – 'ideoque alterum esse quantitatis uidetur, alterum qualitatis'; for unlike metre, according to Quintilian (ix.4.48), rhythm does not even distinguish between dactyl and anapaest, 'tempus enim solum metitur, ut a sublatione ad positionem[1] idem spatii sit'.

In recent years there has been increasing criticism of the inadequacies of a temporal definition of rhythm in language and poetry, as of syllabic quantity and vowel length (see pp. 46 ff., 56 ff.); thus, for example, de Groot (1968, 542 ff.): 'By a certain school "rhythm" is defined as isochrony of successive intervals[2]... it does not apply to any type of verse in any language that we have knowledge of'; and Crystal (1969, 29): 'It is now clear that the temporal thesis is untenable... There were no objective measurements put forward in support of the temporal theory when it was propounded, and when these did come to be made, it was readily demonstrable that great variations in terms of temporal length existed...'; similarly Chatman 1965, 42 f., and already Hendrickson 1899, 209 n.2: 'Without the moulding power of rhythmic movement a purely quantitative rhythm cannot be sustained in language.'

It is notable that even some of those who set out with the assumption of a temporal basis of rhythm tend to find that its inadequacies require

---

[1] These terms translate the Greek ἄρσις and θέσις respectively.
[2] For such views in regard to English cf. Faure 1970, 70 ff.

the introduction of some other factor. In antiquity, Aristides Quintilianus (31 W-I) defines rhythm as a 'structure of time units combined according to a certain arrangement' (σύστημα ἐκ χρόνων κατά τινα τάξιν συγκειμένων); but he goes on to recognize that the similarity of musical sounds in themselves makes the texture of the music 'expressionless' (ἀνέμφατος) and causes the attention to wander; and that there must therefore in addition be certain 'incidents' (πάθη) which make apparent the 'δύναμις' of the composition and 'stimulate the attention in an ordered manner' (τεταγμένως κινοῦντα τὴν διάνοιαν). In modern times similarly Ezra Pound (1951, 198 f.), having defined poetic rhythm as 'a form cut into time, as a design is determined space', went on to recognize that syllables have not only differing durations but also different 'weights', and that these factors together constitute 'the medium wherewith the poet cuts his design'. In his study of the origins of Greek metres Meillet assumed 'un rythme fondé uniquement sur la succession de syllabes longues et brèves' (1923, 11), but was forced to acknowledge (26) that 'la langue opère, non avec des durées objectives, mais avec le sentiment qu'ont les sujets parlants d'une opposition entre syllabes brèves et syllabes longues' (cf. p. 62) – and even this fails to explain how, for instance, a spondee can have rhythm, since only 'short' syllables are (23) 'capables de fournir des temps faibles nets'. Dale also, whilst adopting a militantly durative-quantitative attitude to Greek verse rhythm (e.g. 1968, 4 f.), is forced to admit that one of the 'longs' in the spondee 'must have been distinguishable from the neighbouring longs, or the clarity of the rhythm would suffer' (1964, 16); she recognizes also (1958, 102) that dactyls and anapaests appearing as variants of iambic feet must be distinguished from those appearing as variants of trochaic feet, since their confusion would 'obscure their total difference in essence and in rhythmical effect'.[1] But for such problems Dale proposes the hardly adequate solution of undefined 'special time values' (1964, 16); and West (1970) even suggests that in order to understand Greek metre we need to distinguish *seven* different syllabic quantities. It is true that 'some phonetic features may be binary, others ternary, etc.', and that 'some (say Stress) may require as many as five or six phonetic values'

---

[1] Cf. also Hendrickson 1899, 208 f. (citing Latin grammarians); Sturtevant 1923, 327; Irigoin 1959, 70; Pohlsander 1964, 161. In Thomson's terms (1926, 3, 5 n.), 'it is not accurate to say once a quantity is to be always a quantity...If – ∪ ∪ means neither ᷄∪∪, nor – ᷄∪, nor – ∪᷄, it means nothing at all to be heard in speech; and – ᷄∪ is certainly *not* a dactyl'. See further pp. 328 f.

(Postal 1968, 59 n.6); but as Postal points out (60 f.) in a criticism and development of principles first proposed by Jakobson, it is likely that a systematic phonological representation involves only binary values;[1] and in fact it is hoped that in subsequent pages many of the problems raised by West will find their solution in the recognition of a number of binary contrasts rather than a single multi-valued scale. Amongst classical scholars who have explicitly recognized the inadequacies of a temporal doctrine of verse rhythm may be mentioned Hermann (1818, 5 f.), Wilamowitz (1924, ii, 270), and Fraenkel (1928, 6 ff.); in Hermann's words, 'caussa absoluta in numeris vi quadam exprimenda contineatur necesse est, quae seriem aliquam temporum incipiat'.

The recognition of non-temporal factors as essential to the creation of rhythm does not in itself preclude a belief in isochrony; it may, for example, be held that rhythm is created by the recurrence of such factors at regular intervals in time (thus e.g. Abercrombie 1964a, 5 ff; 1964b, 216 ff.), though some of the criticisms cited above refer to this modified temporalism as well as to purely durational theories of rhythm based on the length of the recurring elements themselves. Even a motor theory of length and quantity could be reconciled with such a belief; but it is hoped that in fact the explanations to be offered for the various problems treated will make temporal considerations redundant.

For the rhythmic 'incidents' it would be natural to look to the basic prosodic features of stress and pitch which perform the accentual functions of culmination and 'grouping in attention'. As between the two there is general agreement in casting stress for this rôle; thus, for example, Classe 1939, 12; Stetson 1945, 71; Abercrombie 1964a, 6; Fry 1968, 368; Crystal 1969, 29; Robinson 1971, 38; and already Hermann 1818, 6, with special reference to the rhythm of classical verse ('Id autem, quo exprimitur ea vis, non potest non in fortiore notatione alicuius unius temporis positum esse: idque *ictum* vocamus'). Some writers have explicitly denied the relevance of pitch to rhythmic patterning: thus Meillet 1900, 271; Thomson 1923, 26; Stetson 1945, 71; and to the argument (put forward, for example, by Goodell 1901, 158; Kabell 1960, 2, 212) that in certain types of music, notably the pipe-organ, stress (if one excludes mechanical swell effects) is

[1] Cf. the point made by Halliday (1963, 9 n.1) in regard to stress, that, if asked, a speaker may say that he can distinguish 'what are being *called* four degrees of stress, but would analyse them as something else; but the question is so framed as to preclude this answer'.

impossible[1] and yet rhythm is perceived, Thomson replies that by one means or another the *perception* of stress is in fact induced in the hearer; but even in such cases, as Stetson observes (1951, 95), musical accentuation is not achieved by *melodic* manipulation.

Implicitly or explicitly underlying this identification of stress as the basis of rhythm is the conception of rhythm as movement, and of stress, in the production of audible linguistic phenomena, as the motor activity par excellence;[2] in Žirmunskij's view (1966, 89) 'the perception of rhythm is more closely connected with motor impressions (although received through the medium of speech) than with purely acoustical sensations'; and it has been suggested (pp. 76, 83) that a distinction between kinaesthetic and direct auditory perception may characterize the basic difference between stress and pitch modulation. Already Aristides, in the passage referred to on p. 98, cites as the relevant 'incidents' of rhythm the contrasting features of 'loudness' (ψόφος) and 'quietness' (ἠρεμία); as commonly in ancient musical and metrical discussion, the audible factors are associated with accompanying visible movements of hand or foot, viz. raising (ἄρσις) and lowering (θέσις). By transference these words are frequently also applied to the musical or metrical phenomena themselves; and in modern times attempts have been made to see in the terms certain motor implications (specifically of stress) for the linguistic performance of Greek and Latin verse. But discussion on this basis has not surprisingly been inconclusive, especially as the applications of these terms to particular musical or metrical elements underwent mutual reversal in the course of antiquity and the resulting confusion of meanings still prevails.[3] The matter will be argued on quite other grounds in subsequent discussions.

Stress has also been identified, at least by some scholars, as the rhythmic basis of other 'quantitative' verse forms. For classical Arabic there is much dispute; but on grounds, inter alia, of the number of 'neutral' syllables permitted, Weil concludes (1960, 675 f.) that 'quantity alone cannot have been decisive for rhythm. Therefore, with it we have – not only in a regulating but in shaping capacity – stress'. And for Hungarian it is recognized even by such a 'quantitative' interpreter as Horváth (Kerek 1968, 46) that, when spondees occur in

[1] Cf. also Roussel 1954, 30.   [2] Cf. Fry 1958, 129.
[3] Cf. Hendrickson 1899, 206 ff; Beare 1957, 58 ff; A 1966a, 117; and particularly Dale 1968, 210 ff.

iambic verse, it is 'only the successive occurrences of stress that make one sense the iambic rhythm'.

However, whilst one may admit the dominant rôle of stress in the creation of audible patterns, it would be confusing to appropriate to this (or any other) factor so widely and variously used a title as 'rhythm'. The question 'What is Rhythm?' is only too liable to turn into a dispute about the use of a word; it is not a question which, for our purposes, we need to answer; it has performed its service as a cover-term suggestive of the general area of investigation, and in the detailed discussions of particular features which follow it seems safer to eschew the term altogether and to refer simply to 'pattern', determined as necessary by such specifications as 'dynamic', 'melodic', 'quantitative', etc.

The simplest form of audible sequence is that of undifferentiated pulsation, as e.g. of a metronome,[1] where there is a mere alternation of + and −, of the presence and absence of the signal;[2] but since such alternation is in any case essential to the existence of the sequence (as opposed to a continuum), it can hardly be termed a pattern unless varied by some other formative factor.[3] In language similarly, the simplest sequence would consist of the mere succession of syllables, involving a chain of chest pulses or, in other words, an alternation of nuclear elements (primarily vowels) with marginal (releasing and arresting) elements.[4] But again the patterning of such a sequence requires a formative factor, which may be provided, for example, by grammatical boundaries, by pauses, or by the incidence of stress. A more complex form of patterning based on the syllable might utilize the potentiality of different types of syllable and syllabic component – e.g. tense vs lax nuclei, or heavy vs light syllables (in motor terms, arrested vs unarrested). Combinations of formative factors are also conceivable – e.g. of pitch with type of syllabic nucleus,[5] or of stress with type of syllable. An audible patterning based on variations in

---

[1] Cf. Sachs 1953, 16.

[2] Cf. Cicero, *De orat.* iii.186: 'distinctio et aequalium aut saepe uariorum interuallorum percussio numerum conficit; quem in cadentibus guttis, quod interuallis distinguuntur, notare possumus'.

[3] We here exclude from consideration the imposition of pattern by the *hearer* upon an otherwise amorphous sequence; this is a well-known perceptual phenomenon, and by psychologists it is the subjective activity that is commonly taken as the defining feature of 'rhythm' even though it may have objective stimuli.

[4] Cf. Park 1968, 108.

[5] Cf. Jakobson 1960, 360 f.

duration is utilized by the Morse Code; but, as already indicated, there seems to be no firm evidence for such a patterning as a functional feature of natural languages.

Finally, the terms 'rhythm' and 'pattern' need not necessarily be confined to *regular* manifestations of the relevant factors – though at least an underlying regularity is presumably characteristic of their artistic manipulation; the point is already recognized by Aristoxenus, who reserves the title ῥυθμός for *eu*rhythmic pattern, but acknowledges that the substrate material, the ῥυθμιζόμενον, is susceptible of shaping in all kinds of ways (*El. Rhyth.* ii.8 = ii, 78 f. W).[1] In a language such as modern Greek, for example (with 'free' stress accent), the stress patterning of normal speech is essentially 'irregular' in the sense that the number of syllables between the stresses is highly variable. But in any verse form which utilizes stress as its patterning factor ('accentual' verse) its incidence must have a basis of regularity, for example by tending to occur on alternate syllables, or so many times in the line, or according to some other system of regulation; as Eliot commented in a critique of 'vers libre' (1917, 519), 'freedom is only truly freedom when it appears against the background of an artificial limitation'. This question of regulation vs irregularity will again arise in the context of the next chapter.

[1] Cf. Westphal 1883, 12.

9 Metre

It is not here intended to provide a full survey of so wide and controversial a subject, but rather to give a minimal background of general theory to which the characteristics of the particular languages may later be referred. As already stated (pp. 12 ff.), metrical phenomena cannot be ignored, since, especially in the case of 'dead' languages, the relationship between poetry and ordinary language may provide clues to the prosodic patterning of the latter; and in any case verse form is a form of the language, albeit specialized in function, and entitled to some consideration as such. However, details, as opposed to general principles, of particular verse forms, even in the languages under special scrutiny, will be investigated only when they are relevant to the language itself. We shall, moreover, be concerned principally with 'spoken' verse, as opposed to lyric, since in the latter (at least in Greek) linguistic considerations are liable to be subordinated to musical; as Cicero observed (*Or.* 183), 'a modis quibusdam cantu remoto soluta esse uideatur oratio maximeque id in optimo quoque eorum poetarum qui λυρικοὶ a Graecis nominantur, quos cum cantu spoliaueris, nuda paene remanet oratio'.

Stylization

Whilst poetic language may be considered in general as a stylization of ordinary language, there is general agreement that verse involves more specifically a stylization of prosodic patterns. It is sometimes suggested that the only features admissible for such stylization are such as are semantically relevant in the language; this appears to be the implication of Jakobson 1933, 135 and of Stankiewicz 1960, 78 (cf. p. 12). This view, however, is expressly refuted by de Groot (1968, 537) and in general by Chatman (1965, 30: 'any attempt at a theory of metre is obliged to consider all features of the language which might have metrical relevance'). Much indeed depends on the definition of 'relevance'; and semantic relevance does not in fact seem to be a necessary criterion for the features utilizable in metre.

'Stylization' implies the artificial regulation of features which occur in less regular patterns in ordinary language; but such regularity in itself could result in a monotony destructive of art.[1] As a corollary, Halle & Keyser (1966, 190; 1971, 165 ff.) object, for example, to the traditional 'iambic foot' theory of the English 'iambic pentameter', since it establishes a mere doggerel as the norm and implies that certain 'lines which abound in the writings of the best poets are metrically deviant'.[2] And in fact it is a characteristic of the major verse forms to incorporate a measure of controlled diversity: 'It is this contrast between fixity and flux, this unperceived evasion of monotony, which is the very life of verse' (Eliot 1917, 518). Such a result may be achieved in a variety of ways; but before discussing these it will be useful to make certain basic distinctions of levels to which we may subsequently refer.

Poetic levels

First, there is what we may call the *form* of the verse, which defines it in the most general sense, e.g. as 'sonnet', 'Sapphic', 'elegiac couplet', etc. It is simply a label which, in Hollander's words (1959, 294), 'serves to set up a literary context around an utterance, directing the reader to give it a certain kind of attention'.

From the form of the verse in this general sense we may distinguish the more specific *structure* of the individual instance, whether of a particular poem within a genre, or of a line within a poem.[3] Such a structure represents the particular choice of the alternatives offered within the general form.

Both form and structure are entirely abstract, and may be said to constitute the domain of METRE. In this respect they are to be distinguished from the *composition*, which is the implementation of the structure in terms of its linguistic realization.[4] Such a distinction corresponds to Jakobson's 'verse design' vs 'verse instance' (1960, 364), or Halle's 'meter' vs 'mapping' or 'actualization' (1970, 64).[5] More generally it might be said that it is at the level of composition that verse becomes poetry, or that artistry is superimposed on artifice.

---

[1] Cf. Leech 1969, 122.
[2] Cf. Park 1968, 108 ff; Halle 1970, 70 ff; Robinson 1971, 31 f., 52 ff.
[3] Cf. Žirmunskij 1966, 86 f.   [4] Cf. Halle & Keyser, xvi, 140.
[5] For a particularly interesting illustration of the value of this distinction (in Finnish) see Kiparsky 1968.

Finally, and importantly, the composition has to be distinguished from the *performance*, by a particular person, and even on a particular occasion. The separation of these two levels has been insisted upon by numerous writers. Jakobson (loc. cit.) distinguishes the 'verse instance' from the 'delivery instance'; for Chatman (1960, 150) it is a question of the 'poem' vs the 'interpretation'; for Stankiewicz (74 f.) of 'type' vs 'token'; in de Groot's words (1968, 548), 'The reciting of a poem is an individual momentary act of Realization'; and for Halle & Keyser (1971, 171 f.) 'The correspondence rules are not instructions for poetry recitations. They are, rather, abstract principles of verse construction whose effect on the sound of the recited verse is indirect.'[1]

The potential variety of performance in general is noted by other writers, e.g. Leech 1969, 122; and it is today commonly agreed that performance by the *author* is not necessarily definitive; Stankiewicz (75), in criticizing the views of Sievers on the status of the 'Autorenleser', argues that 'The shortcoming of this approach lies in the identification of the poem, which constitutes a replicable, invariant structure, with its acoustic implementation in the concrete performance';[2] and in the sleeve-note to his recording of *Four Quartets*[3] Eliot himself writes, 'A recording of a poem read by its author is no more definitive an "interpretation" than a recording of a symphony conducted by the composer'.

The point has also been made that composition and performance belong to two quite different fields of study, the first to versification and the second to declamation: thus Porter 1951, 21 f; Stankiewicz, 75.

For a classical exemplification of the four-fold distinction of levels we may take, as *form*, the iambic trimeter of Greek tragic dialogue; as one of its *structures*, the variant with heavy first 'anceps' ($\Sigma\Sigma\Sigma\Sigma\|$ $\Sigma\Sigma\Sigma\Sigma\|\Sigma\Sigma\Sigma\Sigma$); as *composition*, line 279 of Euripides' *Orestes* (ἐκ κυμάτων γὰρ αὖθις αὖ γαλήν' ὁρῶ); and as *performance*, the rendering of it by Hegelochus on an occasion made notorious by Aristophanes (*Ran.* 303 f.).

---

[1] See further Hrushovski 1960, 178 f; Taranovski 1963, 198 f; Wellek & Warren 1966, 142 ff; Beaver 1968, 319.
[2] Cf. Chatman 1960, 165 f.
[3] H.M.V. CLP 1115.

Rules and variations

It has been mentioned that diversification of poetic pattern may come about in various ways. Firstly, the form itself may permit, as a normal feature of its constitution, a more or less wide range of alternative structures in particular poems or lines; though if the form is to have any meaning, there must always be some general principle of arrangement underlying the variety of structures – for example, in the Greek or Latin dactylic hexameter, the occurrence of six feet, of a heavy first element in each foot, and of a 2-mora second element (Σ or $\Sigma\Sigma$)[1] except in the final foot, and of at least one of a system of caesurae.

There may also be limitations on the number of certain variants occurring in the line, e.g. generally no more than one 'resolution' per line in iambics before Euripides' later plays.[2] And it is commonly found that the end of the line is more restricted in permissible variants than the rest; even in the relatively variable Vedic verse it is noted that 'in all metres the rhythm of the latter part of the verse is much more rigidly defined than that of the earlier part' (Arnold 1905, 9);[3] and in classical Arabic verse the variants at the end of the half and full line 'have to appear regularly, always in the same form' (Weil 1960, 669). In the Finnish *Kalevala* the strictness with which the principal rule of metrical/accentual agreement applies 'increases from zero to 100 percent as we progress from the first foot to the fourth' (final): Kiparsky 1968, 138; similarly on Russian verse Bailey 1968, 17 (cf. the Latin situation discussed on p. 154). Of many Greek examples one may mention the anapaestic systems of tragedy, where spondaic variants are generally common, but where the last full foot of the final line is almost invariably a pure anapaest.[4] In a broader context, there may also be tendencies to regularization in the closing lines of poems – in English, for example, 'a reestablishment of the norm, the most probable and therefore the most stable arrangement of stresses' (Smith 1968, 160). Conversely the beginning of the line is commonly the most tolerant of 'licence'.[5] In the English iambic pentameter the 'reversal' of stresses in the first foot is so common as to qualify, even by tradi-

---

[1] The common metrical use of the term 'mora' in respect of *syllables* must be distinguished from that of its phonological use as applied to *vowels*.
[2] Zieliński 1925, 142; Descroix 1931, 110, 128.
[3] Cf. Kuryłowicz 1970, 426 f; Nagy 1970b, 14.
[4] For Latin cf. Wilkinson 1940, 31, 41 ff; 1963, 121.
[5] Cf. Fraenkel 1928, 269 n.

tional metrics, as a consecrated variant of the form, but is generally excluded from the second and fifth feet.[1]

Another type of diversification results from choices exercised at the level of composition, which superimposes linguistic pattern on the abstract metrical structure. In accepting that verse form and structure have their origins in the language, it is of course implied that certain general characteristics of the language are already taken account of at these levels: 'notatio naturae et animadversio peperit artem' (Cicero, *Or.* 183: cf. Wilkinson 1963, 95); and to quote Stankiewicz (74), 'Poetic works, unlike sculptures and paintings, are not tangible, concrete things. They depend on their implementation, on reading or oral delivery.' For example, such structural features of verse as 'quantity' or 'stress' are meaningful only in terms of their linguistic realization; and the concept of the 'line' itself implies (in traditional verse forms) that this will normally be delimited by some grammatical boundary. But clearly a great deal of the linguistic implementation is not so taken into account, and provides the possibility of variation at the level of composition rather than structure. Variation is of course immediately and inevitably provided by the fact that each line has a different lexical, grammatical, and phonological constituency or texture. Such variety, however, is a simple consequence of the fact that the material of verse is language and not some less infinitely variable medium; in itself, therefore, it is of no artistic consequence. Certain of these features may nevertheless be deliberately manipulated for expressive purposes and thereby create special types of variety within the framework of the structure; examples would be the use of assonance or alliteration, or of different placings of clause and sentence boundaries (with the phonological implication of different intonational and/or stress patterns).

But at this point we encounter a certain indeterminacy in the distinction between structure and composition. What in one language may be matters of composition may in another be matters of structure. In modern English poetry, for example, alliteration is a case of the former type, available to the poet for his own individual purposes, whereas in Old English and some other forms of Old Germanic verse it had the status of an obligatory structural feature;[2] and whilst in English verse

[1] Cf. Jespersen 1900/1933, 250 ff; Shewring 1933, 49; Wimsatt & Beardsley 1959, 598; Gross 1964, 31. For a new interpretation see Halle & Keyser, 174 f; cf. also Beaver 1971.
[2] Cf. Lehmann 1956, 3 ff., 23 ff., 72 f; Halle & Keyser, 147 ff.

stress is a basic element of structure, it would be theoretically possible for a verse form which based itself on some other feature, such as syllabic type, or pitch, to vary the stress pattern of the line at the level of composition. In quantitative verse, the types of syllables are specified in the structure, whereas in purely syllabic verse the types of syllable are indifferent and it is only their number that is structurally relevant; variation of syllabic type may then be employed for stylistic purposes in composition.[1] Similarly one verse form may leave the poet free to vary the distributions of internal grammatical boundaries, whereas another may specify (positively) that such boundaries normally fall at particular places in the line ('caesurae' or 'diaereses'), and/or (negatively) that they should *not* occur at certain points ('bridges' or 'zeugmata');[2] 'Porson's Law' is a famous example of the latter type of requirement (see p. 304).

When one speaks of structural requirements or norms, it is not necessarily implied that all or any of these are codified and stated in metrical treatises or traditional teaching; metrical 'rules' are in the first instance descriptive, being abstracted from the compositional practice of poets, and only subsequently may they take the form of positive or negative prescriptions.

The allocation of features as between structure and composition must, as we have seen, be determined separately for each language; and it must be recognized that, as with alliteration, the status of a given feature may vary from period to period within the same language. But, given that a feature is relevant at the level of structure, the question remains whether the feature need be fully determinate at this level. If, for example, in accentual English verse it emerges that the pattern of the iambic pentameter does not normally include a 'trochaic' second foot, or in the quantitative Greek epic hexameter that a word with spondaic ending may not terminate at the end of the fifth foot, and if in fact we encounter an exception to the 'rule' in a poet recognized as such, should we amend our account of the 'permitted' structures accordingly, or should we say that this is an occasional or individual idiosyncrasy of composition, and strictly speaking 'unmetrical' or 'deviant'? It would probably be generally agreed that the level of structure should concern itself with all such variants as admit of a significant degree of generalization, but not with rare variations, especially if there are obvious non-structural causes for their occurrence.

[1] Park 1968, 109.   [2] Maas 1966, 33.

On this basis we would, for example, within the framework of traditional English metrics, consider as occasional deviations in composition the inversion of the second foot in English iambics, occurring only 34 times in Shakespeare as against over 3,000 examples of the inverted first foot; and one would consequently exclude such inversion from the alternatives statable at the level of structure. Similarly and even more obviously with the Greek example, which occurs only once (if at all) in the whole Homeric corpus (see p. 286). Such deviations can sometimes be attributed to particular circumstances, including the desire for special effects or the need to incorporate recalcitrant linguistic material (especially proper names, which cannot be replaced by metrically more amenable synonyms). As an English example of the former, Keyser (1969, 390 f.) suggests that there is a 'metrical pun' in Keats' 'How many bards gild the lapses of time', where 'the poet is purposely moving outside of the meter in order to caricature metrically the sense of the line' (Halle & Keyser, 171);[1] for the latter one may instance the anaclasis (inversion) of the first foot in Aeschylus, *Sept.* 488, 547, to accommodate the names Ἱππομέδοντος and Παρθενοπαῖος ($\Sigma\Sigma|\Sigma\Sigma\|\Sigma$).

Another type of 'deviation' concerns not so much the statistical or typological insignificance of the cases as the fact that the variants involved are peculiar to or particularly frequent in an individual author. One may in such a case either recognize a special 'idiolectal' form or structure of verse, or treat it as a compositional deviation. In some cases, however, such deviations may foreshadow a later more general acceptance of the innovation, and will then become normal structural variants.

One common type of innovation consists in the regularization of what had hitherto been nothing more than tendencies of composition, until they become norms of structure;[2] such, for example, is the case with 'Naeke's Law' in Callimachus, which virtually normalizes the Homeric tendency to avoid spondaic word-ending at the fourth-foot diaeresis (see p. 286); or with the Horatian treatment of the Sapphic, which normalized the heavy fourth syllable and the caesura after the fifth – an innovation which ultimately proved to have unforeseen consequences for the form as a whole (see pp. 347 ff.).

Lastly, there is variation at the level of performance, which is so obvious as hardly to need comment.[3] But at this level we move out of

[1] For Greek see p. 311.   [2] Cf. Stankiewicz, 80.
[3] See e.g. Chatman 1960, 150.

the realm of versification; 'the subjective interpretation of a poem cannot be taken as a measure of its objective properties' (Stankiewicz, 74).

TENSION

In the context of poetic variation one often encounters reference to a factor called 'tension'. The term is, however, used in various ways, referring to different levels or relationships between levels. One common use concerns the relationship between the various structures permitted within a form. Generally speaking, it is assumed that there will be an 'optimal' or 'ideal' structure which sets up 'a pulsation of expectation' (Barkas 1934, 9); and when some other structural alternative is selected, there is said to be a 'tension' between the 'invariant' and the variant, between the ideal and the actual.[1] The concept of the ideal structure may be based on the statistical frequency of a particular type of line; or on a learnt, traditional knowledge of the ideal.[2] But neither of these conditions is essential; the ideal line may occur in composition only rarely – or conceivably not at all; it may simply be intuited as that structure which comprises the most regular recurrence of the structural elements, as e.g. the 'iambic' line consisting entirely of iambi. In using such terms as 'optimal' or 'ideal' one does not necessarily express any value judgement regarding their desirability; the ideal line may even be thoroughly undesirable (cf. p. 104 and Park 1968, 108 ff; Robinson 1971, 55).

If, however, the tension becomes too ubiquitous, the underlying 'invariant' becomes obscured, and 'the variations cease to be variations, in the absence of a scheme' (Stutterheim 1961, 232).[3] One particular limitation on the occurrence of tension has already been noted, namely the tendency to harmonize the ideal and the actual at the end of the line. This may be seen from one point of view as an aspect of 'climax' (cf. pp. 117 ff.), and from another as providing a regular pattern of demarcative signals for a division of the poem into lines.[4]

A similar type of tension would also apply to cases of 'deviation', where there is conflict between the compositional deviant and the ideal or some other variant at the level of structure.

[1] Cf. Thompson 1961, 170; Wilkinson 1963, 95.
[2] Cf. Epstein & Hawkes 1959, 56; Hrushovski 1960, 178 f.
[3] Cf. Halle & Keyser, 143: 'Lines in which all and only the most complex correspondence rules are utilized...would exceed the threshold of the reader's ability to perceive the pattern.'
[4] Park 1968, 113.

Poetic tension is sometimes described in quasi-musical terms as a kind of 'counterpoint' or 'syncopation'.[1] Regarding the latter, Wilson (1929, 65)[2] observes that 'to give a syncopated effect the melody must have some accompanying sound emphasizing the rhythm it contradicts', whereas (67) 'poetry, being a "one-part" music, cannot be syncopated; it has nothing to mark the beat'. In its more limited sense, 'syncopation' is perhaps an inappropriate metaphor in connexion with poetry, since the tension is not between two simultaneous patterns *in praesentia*, but rather between one pattern *in praesentia* and the other *in absentia* – between the actual and the ideal, or between the deviant and the norm. Even in music, however, the term may in fact be used with an extended sense which makes it appropriate to poetry: 'the feeling of regularity may be established by the succession of a number of normal measures, with the result that the listener's mind continues the regular throb or grouping and feels the disturbance of the new throb or grouping superposed on this, as it were' (Scholes 1970, 1002).

Rather different are the implications of the 'counterpoint' image, which introduces a possible source of 'tension' which we have not so far considered; for counterpoint does not imply a conflict between identical features, as of the musical accents in syncopation, but rather the artistic combination of different melodic patterns. As applied to verse, one could envisage a form of which the pattern is determined by some particular prosodic feature x, such that there is another feature y whose distribution in the language is partially coincident with that of x. In such a situation one could speak of tension between x and y where the two factors failed to coincide in composition, and of 'concord' or 'harmony' where they coincided and so reinforced the metrical pattern; and such a 'counterpoint' between the patterns of the two features could arguably be manipulated by the poet for artistic ends. Schmitt (1953, 37) uses the term with reference to ancient quantitative verse; and Eliot (1942, 12) suggests that 'to the cultivated audience of the age of Virgil, part of the pleasure in the poetry arose from the presence in it of two metrical schemes in a kind of counterpoint'. In Latin the two features in question are syllabic arrest (heavy quantity) and accentuation; the linguistic incidence of the latter is connected with that of the former, but in such a way that there is only partial coincidence between them; and what Eliot has particularly in mind is

[1] Cf. Fowler 1966; Malof 1970, 17, 132 f.
[2] Cf. Beare 1957, 24.

the Latin hexameter – a matter which will be discussed more fully later (pp. 335 ff.).

We have not discussed the performance level in regard to tension; and Jakobson (1960, 366) emphasizes that tension exists 'independently of its different implementations by various actors and readers'. But the reader has in some way to deal with the elements which give rise to the tension. He may, for example, when faced with variation from the ideal, or with deviation, either read the composition as he would in normal speech (a 'prose' reading as it is sometimes called) or regularize it in the direction of the norm (a 'metrical' reading), or he may in some way compromise between the two extremes: 'The adjustment of these two things to one another in any particular line can never be final; each reader must deal with this tension as best he can, in his own voice' (Thompson 1961, 170).[1]

In the case of 'counterpoint', tension does not *necessarily* involve conflict, since the relevant features involved are different from one another and so may be capable of coexistence; a 'prose' reading, therefore, could also be a 'metrical' reading, and vice versa. But one can envisage a type of metrical reading in which the feature y is made to coincide with x (or with certain patterned occurrences of x) and is otherwise suppressed; for example, accentual peaks, instead of occurring at their normal positions in words, might be made to recur at regular intervals determined by the metrical structure. Such a 'scanning' mode of performance would perhaps be encouraged by a situation in which, for example, coincidence naturally occurred (i.e. even in a 'prose' reading) over part of the line, and/or in which y was kinaesthetically a more powerful shaper of rhythm than the feature x on which the metrical structure was based. The situation is not, as we shall see (pp. 337 ff.), entirely hypothetical.

But it must again be emphasized that the poetic tension (and its obverse of concord or harmony) resides in the various levels of the *poem*, and their interrelationships, regardless of the particular performance; there is thus an element of unconscious wisdom in the words of the professor parodied in Anatole France's *Jocaste*:[2] 'Remarquez, Messieurs, l'harmonie des vers de Sophocle. Nous ne savons pas comment on les prononçait, nous les prononçons tout de travers; mais quelle harmonie!'

---

[1] Cf. Leech 1969, 122.
[2] Cited by Norberg (1965, 496).

Line and colon; caesura and enjambment

The beginning of this chapter referred to the linguistic foundations of verse in general; and we now continue with an examination of possible more specific relationships between the units of verse and language structure. The major verse unit relevant to such a consideration is the 'line' (also sometimes called 'verse'). Of the Homeric hexameter line Kirk (1962, 60; cf. 1966, 106) notes that it 'tends to be more or less self-contained in meaning; its ending usually coincides with a major or minor pause, the end of a sentence or clause or at least the point at which a predicate is divided from its subject'; of the earliest Latin verse, with special reference to the Saturnian, Leo (ap. Prescott 1907) observes that 'verse and sentence are identical', and that even in 'Kunstpoesie' (with special reference to Plautus) 'words in the sentence intimately connected in thought were not separated by the verse unless the separation was justified by special considerations'; and even where identity is not complete, the line is commonly seen as an 'ideal' or 'metrically normalized' sentence.[1] In Vedic verse similar considerations apply to the '*pāda*'[2] which exhibits various characteristics of the linguistic clause or sentence. For example, the finite verb is accented in the Old Indian language if it begins a sentence, but not generally otherwise – except if it begins a *pāda*; vocatives likewise are accented (on their initial syllable) only at the beginning of a sentence *or* of a *pāda*.[3] Kuryłowicz (1966; 1970) also contrasts the cohesion *within* the line, effected by extending the 'internal' junctural features of compounds to the 'external' juncture of words, with the lack of such cohesion *between* lines (e.g. hiatus and general absence of 'synaphea').[4] Conversely Brożek (1949, 118 f.) has shown that in Greek tragedy (but not comedy) hiatus is markedly avoided in cases of enjambment, i.e. where successive lines are grammatically cohesive and so preclude the potentiality of pause between them. The unity of the line is also stressed by Fraenkel (1928, 344 f.), with special reference to the artificiality of elision and 'iambic shortening' across changes of speaker.[5] There are in fact striking parallels between the metrical line and the linguistic sentence:

[1] Cf. Drexler 1967, 20.
[2] = constituent line of stanza; the word means 'foot', but in the sense of 'quarter' (figuratively from the quadruped), since the principal Vedic stanzas have four lines. On the western metrical 'foot' see p. 122.
[3] Cf. Kuryłowicz 1948/1960, 207 n.13.
[4] Cf. Schein 1967, 9.   [5] Cf. pp. 149, 180, 227 and Safarewicz 1936, 96.

the very recognition of 'enjambment' as a matter worthy of comment presupposes that it contrasts with the norm; and in Greek tragedy, for example, its occurrence has been seen as generally having a deliberate poetic motivation (thus Brożek 1949, 102 ff.).[1]

If the line is ideally the metrical equivalent of the sentence, it is tempting to look for metrical parallels to lower-level units of grammatical structure, for example the clause or phrase. One would not expect the evidence for such parallels to be as clear as in the case of the line, since the grammatical units in question do not have the clear-cut status of the sentence as an independent utterance (with the phonetic implication of potential extended pause at its end). In many verse forms, however, there are more or less clear tendencies for the line to divide into two or more *cola*, the divisions between which are generally termed *caesurae* (τομαί) or, where they coincide with the end of a foot, *diaereses*.[2] The terminology has, of course, been derived from the descriptions of classical verse, and in what follows we shall have such forms mainly in mind.

The divisions between cola are basically grammatical boundaries at the level of clause or phrase, and tend to occur at more or less strictly regulated points in the line; but by no means all lines show caesurae in this sense (though some writers would restrict the term to such cases: e.g. Shipley 1938, 151 ff.). As Drexler points out (1967, 20 ff.), there may be considerable variation in the grammatical type and strength of caesurae, e.g. as between clause and phrase; and from the caesura between, say, a noun and a predicative adjective, representing the grammatical boundary between subject and predicate, one may come to admit as acceptable a caesura between a noun and an attributive adjective, i.e. between two grammatical constituents at a lower level; and it is not a long step from this 'licence' to the admission of mere word boundaries as meeting the requirement of caesura. There are indeed even cases where the boundaries between 'clitics' (or 'appositives' more generally) and a full word may be admitted in this function,[3] e.g. Sophocles, *El.* 921 (see p. 26). In general, however, such extreme extensions are avoided,[4] and the colon remains 'normatively and essentially a unit of meaning' (Porter 1951, 22).

[1] On enjambment in Homer see especially Kirk 1966, 105 ff.
[2] Sometimes specialized in the sense of a division of the line into two equal halves (cf. Drexler 1967, 22).
[3] On the status of γάρ in this respect cf. p. 26; and on monosyllables in general O'Neill 1939, 265 f.   [4] Cf. Koster 1953, 17 f., 57; Maas 1966, 86.

Even though not all lines show coincidence of cola with major grammatical units, nevertheless the most frequent divisions between words tend to occur at points where higher grammatical boundaries are also commonest. In Homer, for example, there is a word-end in the third foot in nearly 99% of cases (100% in Callimachus), and this is precisely the position in which higher grammatical boundaries occur more frequently than elsewhere within the line.[1] For Vergil, Shipley (1938, 151 ff.) sees evidence for the semantic rather than purely metrical basis of the cola in the uncompleted lines, of which only 1 out of 58 is not complete in sense; and similarly for Ausonius' *Cento Nuptialis*, where the grammatical unity of the first section is also regularly complete.

The colon as such (or its delimiting caesurae) is a metrical feature, based on grammar,[2] and manifested in composition; and the point has often been made that any question of its *phonetic* implications is the concern of performance.[3] Chatman, however (1960, 165 f.), reserves the term 'caesura' (as also 'enjambment') for a feature of performance only,[4] so that 'it might be more proper to speak of a line as "suggesting" or "signaling" caesura and enjambment than "having" it'. Sturtevant, on the other hand (1924a), starting from the premiss that every feature of metre must have phonetic implications for performance, states that no such phonetic correlates are in fact perceptible, and consequently that the caesura is a 'philological ghost'. Though Sturtevant's premiss is doubtful, the question of phonetic implication does deserve some consideration.

Those who assume some performance correlate of the metrical caesura are generally careful to state that they do not necessarily mean 'pause' (thus Chatman, loc. cit; Fränkel 1960, 149 ff.); and other writers seek to show that pause *cannot* be implied. For if it were, the syllable preceding the caesura should be subject to the same principles as apply at the end of the line; there would then, as Bolling says (1913, 160), 'be no reason for objecting to the metre of a line such as *Πάτροκ-λον κλαίωμεν.: τὸ γὰρ γέρας ἐστὶ θανόντων*', since the syllable ~μεν would be subject to the 'indifference' of quantity which applies at the end of the line (see pp. 296 ff.); whereas, in fact, closer junctural features

---

[1] De Saussure 1899; Porter 1951, 22 f; Fränkel 1960, 127 f.
[2] Cf. Denniston 1936; Drexler 1967, 20.
[3] E.g. de Groot 1935, 118.
[4] For Chatman caesura = 'the occurrence of terminal junctures *intra*linearly' and enjambment = 'the absence of *inter*linear terminal junctures'.

are implied at grammatical boundaries in the line than would occur in normal speech (an instance of the 'cohesion' of the line referred to above); and in avoiding such lines 'the poet has subjected himself to limitations stricter than those demanded by the nature of the sounds'.[1] The same point is made by Meillet (1923, 10); Drexler (1967, 20) speaks of 'synaphea of cola'; and Fränkel (1960, 149) points out that in Homer even at syntactical breaks one finds, for example, light quantity with final long vowels and diphthongs before an initial vowel ($\sim \bar{\breve{Y}} + V \sim$; cf. p. 224) and heavy quantity with final short vowels before an initial consonant sequence ($\sim \breve{Y} + CC \sim$) – just as in the case of closely connected words; and similarly with elision.

In Pulgram's terminology (cf. 1970, 31, 86) one might say that the line is treated as a single 'cursus' instead of a sequence of separate cursus such as the same utterance would involve in normal speech. A particularly interesting illustration of this principle has been noted by Soubiran (1966b)[2] in connexion with the 'bucolic diaeresis' (at the end of dactylic IV) in both Greek and Latin hexameters. When this coincides with a major grammatical boundary ('punctuation'), Soubiran shows that, both in Homer and in Vergil, for example, there is a clear preference for word junctions of the type $\sim \breve{V}C + V \sim$ as opposed to $\sim \breve{V} + CV \sim$. This could be explained in terms of an avoidance at this point of the potentiality of pause implied by the grammatical structure; for in order to ensure the light quantity of the word-final syllable preceding the diaeresis in the former type of junction it will be necessary to envisage a close juncture, and so no pause, between the final consonant and the initial vowel of the following word.[3] Moreover, although

---

[1] But, if the accentual tradition is correct, the accent (as a feature irrelevant to the verse structure) *does* follow normal rules: e.g. *Il.* i 237 φύλλά τε καὶ φλοιόν· νῦν αὖτέ μιν υἷες 'Αχαιῶν, where the pre-caesural syllable is heavy by synaphea, but its accent follows the pre-pausal rule (acute, not grave).

[2] Cf. also Hellegouarc'h 1969.

[3] Soubiran has also found a similar though less clearly defined principle of cohesion to apply before spondaic V where the line ends with a quadrisyllabic word in Greek and in Vergil and later Latin poets, presumably due to 'sa masse et son rythme indécis' (of the last word) and to the fact that otherwise 'ce mot long et lourd risque d'être senti comme une sorte de corps étranger' (1969a, 329). Cohesion is also observed by Soubiran in terms of the rule (1969b, 147) 'Si une proposition s'achève avec les pieds II ou III de l'hexamètre latin, elle doit être reliée à la suivante par une élision ou une liaison de type cv'.

In Latin from Vergil onwards there is also a strong tendency (particularly marked in Lucan) for the word preceding the bucolic diaeresis to be a pyrrhic (ΣΣ) rather than a dactyl or a longer word with dactylic ending; this might perhaps be understood in the sense that it serves further to weaken any impression of a 'dying fall'

a spondaic IV with diaeresis is not avoided in Latin (cf. p. 336), there is a strong preference for a dactyl before 'punctuation' (Soubiran 1966b, 23); it may here be significant that a heavy final syllable before the diaeresis would be heavy regardless of whether it ended in $\bar{V}$, $\bar{V}C$, $\bar{V}CC$, or $\breve{V}C(+CV\sim)$, and so would provide no requirement of close juncture with the following word. Whatever may be the precise reasons underlying these tendencies, they surely reflect the artificial cohesion of the line, with the result, as Soubiran sees it (1966b, 48), that there is an antagonism between metre and syntax.

But this relates to a particular position in the line, and other writers have seen evidence for a vestige of phonetic implication, and more specificially pause, in at any rate certain caesurae. Kent, for example, (1948) discusses the 54 cases in Vergil where $\sim\breve{V}C$ before initial vowel counts as metrically heavy (e.g. *Aen.* ii 563 *et direpta domŭs et parui casus Iuli*), and concludes that this is due to a pause, so that the consonant arrests the preceding syllable, thereby rendering it heavy (see pp. 55 f., 67 f.), instead of releasing the following syllable and so leaving the preceding syllable light – 'the poet holds the consonant with the word which it ends' (307).[1] Such cases, as Kent shows, tend to come at syntactical caesurae or before conjunctions, and in this respect follow the same pattern of distribution as hiatus (as opposed to the usual elision), e.g. *Aen.* i 16 *posthabita coluisse Samo: hic illius arma*. With regard to hiatus in the Iliad a similar point is made by Mette (1956), who argues that 'hiatus gives the chief proof of the objective reality of the ancient τομαί'.[2] This view might also be supported by the contrast, noted for the Homeric narrative hexameter by Drewitt (1908), between the commonness at main hemimeral (mid-foot) caesurae of 'overlong' syllables (see p. 66) and the rarity of what he calls 'dovetailed length', i.e. where a word ending in a short vowel depends for heavy quantity on the presence of a consonant sequence at the beginning of the next word $(\sim\breve{V}+CC\sim)$; for (102) 'it is uncomfortable to rest on an open short vowel'.

For classical verse it is also possible to state some general principles regarding the *location* of the caesurae, and so the relative lengths of the

---

at this point by precluding an accentual reinforcement of the IV pattern as $\acute{\Sigma}\Sigma\Sigma$; in *Aen.* vi 432, for example, the accentual pattern is $\sim$*úrnam móuet, ille siléntum*, with IV $\sim$*nam móue*$\sim$ as against the less preferred $\sim$*árgui(t. Heu*$\sim$) of *Aen.* iv 13.

[1] Cf. Zirin 1970, 57.
[2] Cf. Dale 1957, 33.

cola, in the case of the main spoken metres (iambic trimeter and dactylic hexameter):

(i) A division of the line into equal lengths is avoided.
(ii) When the line consists of two cola, the second tends to be longer than the first.
(iii) When the line consists of three cola, the second tends to be longer than the first, and the third longer than the second.[1]

The avoidance referred to in (i) is generally seen as reflecting a desire not to create the premature appearance of cadential (line-end) patterns.[2] This principle, however, is also applicable to other than bisections; thus, in Greek hexameters, 'Hermann's Bridge' (or the 'law of the fourth trochee'), whereby a word boundary is avoided at IVb_1, may be seen as precluding an anticipation of the final foot (envisaged as a 'catalectic' $\Sigma\Sigma$).[3]

With regard to (ii), this results in a preference for the 'penthemimeral' caesura (i.e. at IIIa, with a dominant variant at $IIIb_1$ in the hexameter), giving a proportion $2\frac{1}{2}:3\frac{1}{2}$ feet for the line,[4] as e.g. *Il.* i 88 οὔ τις ἐμεῦ ζῶντος: καὶ ἐπὶ χθονὶ δερκομένοιο. In Greek tragedy the penthemimeral caesura, involving, in Descroix's terms (1931, 256), 'la répartition idéale des syllabes 5+7',[5] accounts for 4/5 of all cases; in Aeschylus' *Supplices*, for example, there are 346 cases as against 86 for the hephthemimeral (at IVa),[6] which latter Descroix (267) sees as constituting a mere 'coefficient de variété', designed to break the monotony of a single type.[7] Similar considerations apply to the hexameter. The preponderance of caesurae in III in Homer has

---

[1] On the question of four-cola lines see Kirk 1966, 73 ff.
[2] Cf. p. 116 n.3 and Park 1968, 114.
[3] Cf. p. 303 and A 1966a, 129 n.1.
[4] If one counts the final foot of the hexameter as a full foot; otherwise $2\frac{1}{2}:3\frac{1}{4}$. For the $IIIb_1$ variant the figures are $2\frac{3}{4}:3\frac{1}{4}$ or 3.
[5] Cf. Schein 1967, 23.
[6] The proportion of penthemimeral caesurae in each play of Aeschylus varies from 76–85% and in Sophocles from 74–83% (Schein 1967, 34, 63, and Tables X–XI).
[7] The penthemimeral caesura of the iambic trimeter may be seen as corresponding to the central diaeresis of the trochaic tetrameter (cf. p. 314); if it were the case that the iambic line was derived from the trochaic (by dropping the initial cretic), then there would of course be no synchronic significance in the position of the favoured caesura, since it would simply represent a historical survival; on this, however, see Descroix 1931, 303 f.

Descroix also argues (160 f.) that the number of syllables, and not only the metrical feet and their subdivisions, was relevant; since, if the number of syllables in the first half of the line is extended by 'resolution', the hephthemimeral caesura is avoided.

already been mentioned, and indeed seems already to have been observed by Varro (O'Neill 1942, 160). Fränkel (1960, 105) adds the further point that strong grammatical breaks are twice as common in the first half of the line as in the second. In Vedic also, whilst there is no requirement of a caesura in the shorter lines (of 5 or 8 syllables), there is a caesura after the 4th or 5th syllable in lines of 11 and 12 syllables.

With regard to (iii), the tendency is towards a proportion $1\frac{1}{2}:2:2\frac{1}{2}$ feet, e.g. Eur. *Hipp.*, 621 ἢ χρυσὸν: ἢ σίδηρον: ἢ χαλκοῦ βάρος; Ennius, *Ann.* (?) *Marsa manus,: Peligna cohors,: Vestina uirum uis*. In Homer, Porter (1951, 45) finds that 84% of such tripartite lines divide into cola of 6:8:10 morae respectively, i.e. in the same proportions as the feet of the trimeter. It is generally agreed that these tendencies have an aesthetic purpose of 'climax';[1] related to this (and often supporting it) is the tendency observed by Hirt (1927, 126) for an adjective to go with the last of a list of nouns (especially proper names); e.g. *Il.* iv 52 Ἄργός τε Σπάρτη τε καὶ εὐρυάγυια Μυκήνη. Similarly in Sanskrit, e.g. (in the Nala episode of the Mahābhārata) *Damayantīṃ Damaṃ Dāntaṃ Damanañ-ca suvarcasam*, 'D., D., D., and the splendid D.'

The phenomenon of climax is not however confined to verse, and has been seen as just one manifestation of a general stylistic tendency of the Indo-European sentence, often known as the 'law of increasing members' ('Das Gesetz der wachsenden Glieder') after the title given to it by Behaghel (1909, 139).[2] The tendency had indeed already been noted in antiquity;[3] thus Demetrius (*De Eloc.* i.18) says that 'in compound sentences the final colon should be the longer', and Cicero (*De Orat.* iii.186) 'aut paria esse debent posteriora superioribus, extrema primis, aut, quod etiam melius et iucundius, longiora'. Behaghel suggests that this principle is only one of refined speech, since there is less evidence of it in Plautus than, say, Vergil. For more recent times Wilkinson (1963, 176) cites 'Friends, Romans, countrymen'; but in a more prosaic context one may note 'Ladies and gentlemen' (as against 'men and women'), and Wilkinson's French example of 'Dubo... Dubon...Dubonnet'.

A parallel is also to be found in the rule of Sanskrit grammar given by Pāṇini (II.ii.34) that in copulative ('*dvandva*') compounds the

[1] De Groot 1935, 106; Porter 1951, 45; Fränkel 1960, 106; Wilkinson 1963, 97.
[2] Cf. Lindholm 1931, 25; Wilkinson 1963, 97, 175 ff. It is, however, not only Indo-European: on the Finnish *Kalevala* cf. Sadeniemi 1951, 27 ff; Kiparsky 1968, 138.
[3] Cf. Hofmann–Szantyr 1965, 722 f.

element with the fewer syllables comes first, as e.g. *plakṣa-nyagrodhau* 'ficus infectoria and ficus indica'. The commentary goes on to mention that when the number of syllables is equal, their quantity determines the order: thus e.g. *kuśa-kāśam* 'poa cynosuroides and saccharum spontaneum'. These rules may, however, be overridden by semantic considerations, as that 'the more honourable' comes first in e.g. *mātā-pitar(au)* 'mother and father', or the names of elder and younger brother (e.g. *Yudhiṣṭhirārjunau* 'Yudhishthira and Arjuna'), or the names of castes, which 'are placed according to their priority', as *brāhmaṇa-kṣatriya-viṭ-śūdrāḥ*, without regard to length. There are, of course, parallels to such exceptions in other languages, and Wilkinson (1963, 177) notes that in Latin 'more important things and persons come first', as e.g. *Aeneas Anchisiades et fidus Achates* (*Aen.* viii 521). Finally, a division of the line into equal cola may typify a particular genre of verse; Jakobson, for example (1952, 56 f.), states that in the 'recitative forms of Common Slavic versification...the symmetrical measures were used for laments, the asymmetrical for epics'; and Nagy (1970b, 33) sees this as an explanation of the central diaeresis of the elegiac pentameter.

We have discussed the strong tendency for the line to end with a grammatical boundary of some kind, generally a strong boundary such as that of the sentence; and Porter (1951, 22 f.) tentatively refers to this as a special kind of caesura. In Greek hexameter verse, for example, as Maas (1966, 87) comments, 'there is a tendency to avoid postpositives at the end of the line, possibly because they are rare at the end of a sentence'. As in the case of intralinear caesurae, 'enjambment' (i.e. more or less close grammatical connexion between the final word and the first of the next line) does, however, sometimes occur, e.g. Soph., *O.C.* 498 f. ~μίαν‖‖ ψυχὴν~, or *Ant.* 524 f. ~φιλεῖ‖‖ κείνους~; rarer are cases involving proclitic or 'prepositive'+full word, as *Ant.* 27 f. ~τὸ μὴ‖‖ τάφῳ καλύψαι~ (even *Ant.* 409 f. ~τὸν‖‖ νέκυν~), which in drama, as observed by the ancients, are relatively common only in Sophocles.[1] Even less common are postpositives at the beginning of a line;[2] exceptionally rare also, of course, are cases of the type Horace, *Serm.* i.ix 51 f. ~*est locus uni-*‖‖*cuique suus*~; and particularly of the type cited by Hephaestion (Π. ἀποθέσεως μέτρων, 15 C), e.g. Simonides ~ἡνίκ' 'Αριστο-‖‖γείτων "Ιππαρχον κτεῖνε~

---

[1] Cf. Maas 1966, 85; Schein 1967, 75.
[2] Descroix 1931, 286 ff; Maas 1966, 86; Schein 1967, 6.

or Nicomachus ~ Ἀπολλό-|||δωρος~ (cf. Choeroboscus, 144 C). For, as Hephaestion observes, 'every line (normally) finishes with a complete word, so that such cases are reprehensible' and can only be justified by the fact that otherwise the names will not fit the metre; only for comic effect is this practice extended, as e.g. Eupolis ~ οὐ γὰρ ἀλλὰ προ-||| βούλευμα βαστάζουσι~.

A particular form of enjambment involving elision, as e.g. Soph., *O.T.* 332 f. ~τί ταῦτ'|||| ἄλλως ἐλέγχεις; ~,[1] was specially noted by the ancients under the title of εἶδος Σοφόκλειον (e.g. Choeroboscus, 144 C). It is otherwise rare in Greek,[2] as also in Latin, where it is mainly employed by Vergil, e.g. *Aen.* vi 602 f. ~ *cadentique|||| imminet* ~.[3] But elision seems, in Greek verse, to play a special rôle in relation to the caesurae generally; it has, for example, been suggested that 'bisected trimeters' were more acceptable if an elision occurred at the diaeresis, as e.g. Aesch., *Sept.* 252 οὐκ ἐς φθόρον σιγῶσ' ἀνασχήσῃ τάδε;: it is in fact termed by Porson (1802, Praef. xxv) a 'quasi-caesura' (cf. p. 311). The significance of elision here has been doubted by Goodell (1906, 161); but it has been noted by O'Neill (1939, 278) that 'quondam penults made final because of elision do not acquire the metrical significance of true finals'; he finds elision rare at the penthemimeral caesura in iambics (as also Descroix 1931, 266 ff.), thus supporting Hermann's principle 'elisio non officit caesurae',[4] whereas it occurs in over half the cases of central diaeresis; similar statistics apply to Homer, elision being very rare at the favoured caesurae in III. From a negative standpoint these facts could be explained by assuming that, in normal speech, elision was primarily a feature of closely connected words (cf. the ms practice referred to in n. 1 below), so that it would be inappropriate where there is the potentiality of pause in performance (as at a caesura), and conversely would tend to mitigate an undesirable break by precluding the possibility of pause (as at a central diaeresis). More positively it might perhaps be argued that, whether or not actually realized in performance (cf. Rossi 1968), the non-elided form is at least psychologically present and so tends to give the impression of a word boundary one syllable further on, so that an elision at the central diaeresis would suggest a hephthemimeral caesura (e.g. in the

---

[1] In the Laurentianus the consonant preceding the elision is in all cases placed at the beginning of the following verse: cf. Körte 1912.
[2] Maas 1966, 87.
[3] Cf. Raven 1965, 27, 93.
[4] Rossi 1968, 233.

above example III σιγῶσ' suggests III–IVa σιγῶσα);[1] and conversely elision at a caesura would suggest the word boundary elsewhere and so weaken the caesura. These, however, must remain matters of speculation; the phonetic implications of elision will be taken up in more detail in connexion with the particular languages.

The foot

Finally we have to consider the unit termed a 'foot' in the tradition of western metre. It seems that the term is taken from the 'movements of the human foot in its simplest form of progress' (Dale 1968, 211), i.e. its progressive raising and lowering (cf. Aristotle, *Prob.* v 885b πᾶσα πορεία ἐξ ἄρσεως καὶ θέσεως συντελεῖται); it could then be applied to a minimal binary cycle of contrast in the sphere of language or music; and in fact the two phases of the metrical (or musical) 'foot' do receive in antiquity the names of ἄρσις and θέσις, a terminology which would also be appropriate in connexion with the practice of 'beating time'; in the words of Marius Victorinus (vi, 43 K), 'pes est certus modus syllabarum, quo cognoscimus totius metri speciem, compositus ex sublatione et positione'.[2] This principle of 'alternation' is crucial to the manifestation of prosodic pattern, since without it there is only formless succession;[3] in modern times, Chatman (1960, 160 n.9) defines the function of the foot as being 'to explain the sequential norm and variations of points and zeroes'.[4] It follows, therefore, that a foot in this sense cannot consist of a single element – a point already made by Aristoxenus, who observes that a single mora involves no separation (διαίρεσις) into parts, and that without such separation (i.e. into ἄρσις and θέσις) there can be no foot[5] (*El. Rhyth.*, 81 W);[6] and in applying the principle to Greek music Aristoxenus goes on to say (84 W)[7] that in 'continuous rhythm', i.e. in which a particular

---

[1] For a 'quasi-penthemimeral' cf. Soph., *Aj.* 969 τί δῆτα τοῦδ' ἐπεγγελῷεν ἄν κάτα; (Rossi 1968, 233), where IIb τοῦδ' suggests IIb–IIIa τοῦδε.

[2] Cf. Diomedes, i, 474 K.

[3] Cf. pp. 101 f; Maas 1966, 32. This point seems not to be appreciated by *Burger (1957, 15 f.), who denies the existence of any contrast between 'temps forts' and 'temps faibles'.

[4] Cf. also de Groot 1930, 227.

[5] Aristoxenus in fact uses πούς in a wider sense, viz. as a 'measure' rather than a foot in the metrical sense; the latter corresponds to Aristoxenus' πούς ἀσύνθετος (cf. Westphal 1883, 20, 28; Dale 1968, 212).

[6] Cf. 75 W and *Williams 1911, 36.
  Cf. Westphal 1883, 35 f.

pattern is repeated, not even a 2-mora sequence can qualify as a measure, since the beats would come too close together (τὸ γὰρ δίσημον μέγεθος παντελῶς ἂν ἔχοι πυκνὴν τὴν ποδικὴν σημασίαν). As examples of permissible measures are given the 3-mora iambus (ratio 1:2) and the 4-mora dactyl (ratio 2:2). Westphal (1883, 37) points out that in modern music also there are scarcely any examples of a duple measure in which neither beat may be divided, as e.g. in $\frac{2}{8}$ time with no semiquavers. So far as poetry is concerned, there are probably reasons other than mere temporal 'crowding' for the non-occurrence of the pyrrhic foot as an element of repetitive or 'periodic' metre – reasons related to the impossibility (in Latin and Greek) of implementing the requirement of alternation within such a foot: indeed even the dactyl is admissible not on the basis of its greater length but because one of the 2-mora elements is differently constituted from the other. These points will be considered in more detail at a later stage; but we may here remark, as suggested on p. 98, that the spondee, viewed as a purely quantitative pattern, can hardly be termed a 'foot' in its own right, since there is no contrast between the two heavy syllables as such, and so no alternation; as Pohlsander says (1964, 161), 'the spondee has no real existence of its own (i.e. there is no spondaic metron), but must always be considered the contracted form of some other metrical unit'. In this connexion also we may note the definition of verse by G. M. Hopkins as 'Speech wholly or partially repeating the same figure of sound'; in citing this, Jakobson (1960, 358 f.) goes on to state that 'Such a figure always utilizes at least one (or more than one) binary contrast of a relatively high and relatively low prominence effected by the different features of the phonemic sequence'. Jakobson's view is fully in accordance with the principle we have already enunciated, but Hopkins' own 'sprung rhythm' is scarcely an exemplification of it; for, as Hopkins explains it, a sprung-rhythm foot 'has only one stress, which falls on the only syllable, if there is only one, or, if there are more...on the first'. The result of this admission of one-syllable feet is, in Whitehall's terms,[1] 'the free occurrence of juxtaposed stresses without intermediate unstressed syllables' (i.e. with no alternation in terms of the patterning feature of English verse); as interpreted by Fussell, 'the poet working in sprung rhythm is composing almost as if the spondee were a base rather than a substitute foot';[2] and Fussell's tentative

---

[1] Fussell 1965, 71.
[2] Cf. also Gross 1964, 28.

assessment of Hopkins' innovation is that it 'belongs less, perhaps, to the history of English versification than to the history of British personal eccentricity'.[1]

The foot has a very different status from the other units of metrical structure with which we have been concerned, the line and the colon. These latter, as we have seen, have more or less close grammatical correlates in the language itself, and their boundaries tend to coincide with linguistic boundaries at the compositional level. With the foot it is quite otherwise; it is a unit of structure[2] rather than of composition or performance, or of appreciation – as was well observed by Cicero (*Or.* 173), 'nec uero multitudo pedes nouit nec ullos numeros tenet', and by Quintilian (ix.4.114), 'neque uero tam sunt intuendi pedes quam uniuersa comprensio...ante enim carmen ortum est quam obseruatio carminis'. We have spoken of the foot in the context of metrical form and structure, and there seems no inherent objection to this; it was already recognized from an early date, e.g. by Plato and by Aristophanes (as also was the 'metron');[3] but one should perhaps at this point enter the caveat that the poet's analytical awareness of the abstract metrical pattern of his poetry is a widely variable factor, and this is likely to be particularly true of those metrical units which are not also units of composition.

There can, however, be some less direct correlations between the foot and linguistic units. If, for example, the same phonetic feature is utilized as the exponent of word accent in the language and as the positive element of metrical alternation, then the foot will correspond to the word in the sense that both are units comprising one 'accented' element and one or more unaccented: the foot will in fact be a kind of 'metrical word',[4] but their boundaries need not coincide. If the relation-

---

[1] However, the charge of eccentricity should perhaps be limited to the context of *modern* English versification (as opposed, say, to Anglo-Saxon); and it would be possible to claim a patterned basis for such verse if one accepted a temporal theory of the foot, as e.g. Abercrombie (cf. p. 99), for whom 'As in Latin verse, all the feet within a piece of English verse are of equal length or quantity' (1964a, 10); but we have already sided with the critics of 'temporalism' in considering it not to be adequately substantiated, and in looking to other factors as criteria for pattern.

[2] Cf. Chatman 1960, 160 n.9.

[3] Already attested by Herodotus (cf. Schein 1967, 15). The term is generally applied to a higher unit of alternation than the foot, involving more than one positive term (cf. Maas 1966, 38 f.); most familiar is the metron of the iambic 'trimeter' ($\|\underset{\smile}{\Sigma}\Sigma|$ $\Sigma\Sigma\|$), which incorporates the alternation between variable odd feet (i.e. with 'anceps' $\underset{\smile}{\Sigma}$) and invariably iambic even feet.

[4] Cf. Kuryłowicz 1966.

ship is more indirect, e.g. if the metrical and linguistic 'accents' are simply both determined by the same factors, their positions need not coincide. The structure of the metre will then not be apparent from the linguistic accents themselves, and for oral analytical purposes, as in teaching, the quasi-word status of the foot in such cases may be implemented in performance – i.e. each foot may be pronounced as a 'word', with its positive element phonetically 'accented', regardless of the positions of the word accents, producing a 'metrical' reading of the type theoretically envisaged on p. 112. This will be discussed more fully in connexion with the Latin hexameter (pp. 340 ff.).

Part II

THE PROSODIES OF LATIN

IO   *Syllable structure: Quantity and Length*

Both arrested and unarrested syllables occur, the former with either thoracic or oral arrest: e.g. *dō* (CV⁺), *dăt* (CVᵒC), *-nĕ* (CVᵒ).

~VCV~ and ~V̆CCV~ (general)

As regards the arresting or releasing function of consonants in other than pre- or post-pausal position, the traditional basic rules of syllabification[1] would imply that a single consonant between vowels releases the following syllable, and that of two consonants between vowels the first arrests the preceding syllable and the second releases the following syllable.[2] Thus the syllabic pattern of e.g. *făcĭlĕ* will be CVᵒ.CVᵒ.CVᵒ, of *dēpōnō* CV⁺.CV⁺.CV⁺, and of *cŏntĭngĭt* CVᵒC.CVᵒC.CVᵒC. If arrested syllables are identified with 'heavy quantity' and unarrested syllables with 'light quantity', the traditional syllabifications are supported by metrical and accentual evidence, as well as by the traditional rules of quantity. Thus, for example, *cŏrpŏră* (CVᵒC.CVᵒ.CVᵒ) indicates by its antepenultimate accent that the second syllable is light, and by its beginning a hexameter that the first syllable is heavy, as also follows from the traditional rule of quantity that a short vowel followed by two or more consonants creates a heavy syllable, but otherwise a light syllable. The rules of syllabification may also apply across word boundaries;[3] so that in (hexameter ending) ~*scīrĕt dără iŭssŭs* (*h*)*ăbēnās* the syllabic pattern is CCV⁺.CVᵒC.CVᵒ.CVᵒ.CVᵒC.CVᵒ. CVᵒ.CV⁺.CV⁺C, equating with a quantitative pattern ΣΣΣΣΣΣΣΣΣ.

The allocation of a single intervocalic consonant to the following syllable is in agreement with the general tendency towards oral rein-

---

[1] Excluding the cases discussed on p. 29. See also pp. 137 ff. on certain consonant sequences.

[2] Note that intervocalic *z* normally stands for double [zz], and so involves arrest + release (A 1965, 46).

[3] This is general where VCV sequences are involved; on other sequences cf. pp. 139 ff.

forcement of release; and we may assume that, just as the syllabic pattern of e.g. *bŏna* was demonstrably (by metrical evidence) *bŏ.na*, so that of *fāma* was *fā.ma*.

Quantity of pre-pausal ~ V̆C

As regards pre-pausal ~ V°C, we have seen that in Sanskrit its value as an arrested syllable seems well established; and Gauthiot (1913, ch. v) sees this as a general Indo-European characteristic. In Latin the unreleased nature of the final consonant is suggested by the loss of final *s* and *t* in various dialects and at various periods; but our interest in this matter centres on its consequence for syllabic quantity, since, if prepausal ~ V°C is arrested, we shall expect such syllables to count as heavy.

Metrically the final syllable of a line is generally 'indifferent' as to quantity, and so provides no indication; and within the line syntactical boundaries tend to be obscured phonologically by the artificial 'cohesion' already discussed. There are, however, a few phenomena which indicate that in Latin pre-pausal ~ V̆C (~ V°C) was in fact equated with heavy quantity. If, as Kent suggests, the heavy quantity at caesurae in lines such as *Aen.* ii 563 (see p. 117) or *Ecl.* x 69 (*omnia uincit amŏr; et nos cedamus amori*) is due to pause, then this is an indication of the heaviness, and so arrested nature, of pre-pausal ~ V°C. There is also suggestive evidence from the elegiac pentameter, where quantity at the end of the line does not seem to be altogether 'indifferent'. It has often been pointed out that the final syllable seldom ends in a short vowel without a following consonant (e.g. Raven 1965, 108; Drexler 1967, 109). In Tibullus and Propertius such syllables occur in this position only in around 4% of lines; and in Ovid, if one excludes the words *ego, mihi, tibi, sibi* (where the final vowel of the datives may be long), the figure reduces to a mere 1% (Platnauer 1951, 64); in the *Fasti*, for example, there are 23 cases in nearly 2,500 lines (Martin 1953, 141). On the other hand syllables of the type ~ V°C (e.g. *erĭt*) are equally acceptable with those of type ~ V⁺(C) (e.g. *meō, deōs*) and so may be presumed equally heavy.

There is also accentual evidence. We have seen (p. 51) that in Latin (as in English) there are no monosyllabic full words ending in a short vowel. Since in enclitics such finals do occur (*-quĕ, -uĕ, -nĕ*), this peculiarity is presumably due to the fact that full words in isolation require an accent, and in monosyllables this must inevitably fall on a final syllable. From this it seems to follow that an isolated monosyllable ending in V⁰ cannot carry the accent (see further p. 178); but on the other hand monosyllabic full words ending in V⁰C freely occur (e.g. *dăt*, *quĭd*), just as those ending in V⁺(C) (e.g. *dā*, *quōs*), and are presumably accentable. And since accent in Latin is determined by quantity, ∼ V⁰C must (unlike ∼ V⁰) be comparable with ∼ V⁺(C), and so equatable with heavy quantity.

Quintilian (ix.4.107) cites as an example of cretic quantitative pattern (ΣΣΣ) the final word of '*Quis non turpe dīcĕrĕt?*', but considers the final syllable as a case of 'breuis pro longa', i.e. as qualifying for heavy quantity only by the principle of indifference, thereby implying that it is inherently light. But Quintilian's views on such matters would inevitably be governed by traditional doctrine regarding syllables 'long by position', which took no account of syllabification, and, guided by the more obvious evidence of non-final syllables, stated it as a general rule that a short vowel must be followed by two or more consonants if the syllable were to count as heavy.[1] Quintilian's statement, therefore, can hardly be cited as evidence against the heavy quantity of pre-pausal ∼ V⁰C. Dale (1964, 20 n.9) also sees evidence for the equivalence of pre-pausal ∼ V⁰C to ∼ V⁰ in Seneca, *Oed.* 449–65, where a sequence of acatalectic dactyls all end either in V⁰ or V⁰C, and none in V⁺(C);[2] but here again it is quite possible that we have an artificial regulation based on the traditional rules.

Vowel length

Thoracic arrest, as already suggested in general terms, is in Latin associated with tenseness and relative length of the nucleus, i.e. with what are traditionally termed the 'long' vowels, and is invariably equated with heavy quantity in all positions (on the evidence of accent, metre, and traditional statements of quantity). The vowels of such syllables contrast with those of other types, whether arrested or unarrested; for in syllables ending with V⁰C (orally arrested) or V⁰ (unarrested) the absence of thoracic arrest is associated with laxness and relative shortness of nucleus, i.e. with the traditional category of

---

[1] It is presumably for this reason that doubt is never expressed about the quantity of pre-pausal syllables ending in V⁰CC, as e.g. in *prodĕst*, *delĕnt*, *indĕx*.

[2] *leo* at 457 presumably = *lĕŏ*.

'short' vowels. The tenseness is in turn responsible for the long vowels occupying a larger, more 'centrifugal' perimeter of articulations (cf. p. 63; A 1959, 241 ff; 1965, 47 ff.). The relationship between the short and long vowel systems may be represented schematically as follows:[1]

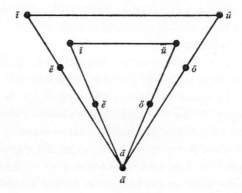

It will be seen that the diagram places short *ĭ* and long *ē* closer to one another than to long *ī* and short *ĕ* respectively; and similarly with the *o* and *u* vowels. The similarity of *ĭ* and *ē* is shown by the occurrence, even in republican inscriptions, of E for short *ĭ* and I for long *ē* (e.g. TREBIBOS, MENUS, MINSIS for *trĭbibus, mĭnus, mēnsis*). The relatively open articulation of short *ĭ* is also shown by its frequent rendering in Greek as ε (e.g. Λεπεδος, κομετιον, Δομετιος, Τεβεριος = *Lepĭdus, comĭtium, Domĭtius, Tĭberius*), and conversely by the rendering of Greek ε by Latin I (e.g. PHILUMINA = Φιλουμένη). The similarity of short *ŭ* and long *ō* is likewise illustrated by COLOMNAS, SOB, OCTUBRIS, PUNERE for *colŭmnas, sŭb, octōbris, pōnere*; and the relatively open articulation of *ŭ* is shown by the use of *u* to render Greek o (e.g. *purpura, gummi* = πορφύρα, κόμμι).

An audible difference between the qualities of long and short *i* is clearly observed by Velius Longus in the 2 c. A.D. (vii, 49 K); and in the same century the specific similarity between short *ĭ* and long *ē* is noted in a statement attributed to Terentianus Maurus (Pompeius, v, 102 K): 'Quotienscumque *e* longum uolumus proferri, uicina sit ad *i* litteram.' The relatively open articulation of short *ĕ* is also indicated (in the 4–5 c.) by a statement of Servius (iv, 421 K) that its quality was similar to that of *ae*, which had developed to a monophthongal

---

[1] Cf. the acoustic diagram given for Czech by Lehiste (1970, 31).

[εε], midway between *ē* [ee] and *ā*. The greater tenseness of long back vowels is commonly also associated with a greater degree of lip-rounding, and this is specifically referred to by Terentianus (vi, 329 K) in comparing the long with the short *o*.

In late Latin vowel length/tenseness eventually ceased to function as a distinctive phonological feature (see p. 80), and it is significant that the former long *ē* and *ō* then merged with the former short *ĭ* and *ŭ* to give generally in Romance /ẹ/ and /ọ/ respectively, distinct from Romance /i/ and /u/ (derived from former long *ī* and *ū*) and from Romance /ę/ and /ǫ/ (derived from former short *ĕ* and *ŏ*).[1]

When phonetic differences are as great as those between, say, Latin short and long *i*, one might perhaps question the validity of treating them as in any way the 'same' vowel. The reasons for doing so are often complex (A 1959, 243, 245 ff.), and vary from language to language. In the case of classical Latin, however, it could be said that long *ī* is the most close and front vowel in the long system, and short *ĭ* is the most close and front in the short system; and similarly with the other pairs.[2] Grammatical alternation may also be relevant, as, for example, in establishing the relationship of the *ĕ* in *lĕgo* with the *ē* in *lēgi*. Historical factors may further encourage identification; for example, the fact that the contraction of *ĕ+ĕ* results in *ē* (as *nĕ+hĕmo → nēmo*); or that compensatory lengthening of *ĭ* results in *ī* (as **ĭs-dem → īdem*). For the native speaker's intuition of such relationships, and for the establishment of orthographic norms, a combination of phonological and grammatical considerations is likely to have been decisive.

So far as the short (lax) vowels are concerned, there is no descriptive reason for distinguishing the qualities of those in unarrested syllables (~ Vᵒ) and in arrested syllables (~ VᵒC), as e.g. the *ĭ* vowels of *re.tĭ.ne.o* and *re.sĭs.to*. But historically the development in the two cases was different (cf. pp. 51 f.). In unarrested medial syllables the short vowels underwent drastic changes under the influence of the prehistoric strong initial stress. Basically all were reduced to a single grade of aperture – close,[3] within which the qualitative differences of backness or frontness were determined by their environment. In certain labial

---

[1] This situation probably already prevailed in the colloquial at the time of Servius' statement cited above.

[2] Cf. A 1962, 30.

[3] Cf. the development in northern dialects of Modern Greek, where unstressed /e/, /o/ → /i/, /u/, and original /i/, /u/ are lost entirely: Thumb 1912, 8 f; Newton 1972, 182 ff.

environments the result was a back rounded quality [ʊ], as e.g. in *occŭpo* < * ∼ *căp* ∼ ; in others a more centralized and/or unrounded quality resulted, which was at first identified with *ŭ* but later with *ĭ*, as e.g. in *aucupium*, later *aucipium* (the so-called 'intermediate vowel': A 1965, 56 ff.). But in most environments the result was a front quality [ɪ], regardless of its origin: thus e.g. in *abĭgo* < * ∼ *ăg* ∼ , *collĭgo* < * ∼ *lĕg* ∼ , *capĭtis* < *capŭt* ∼ , *nouĭtas* < *nouŏ* ∼ , as well as original *ĭ* maintained in e.g. *pestĭlens*. Other environmental effects are seen in e.g. *pepĕri* < *păr* ∼ , where the *r* is responsible for more open articulation: and in *filiŏlus*, where the *ŏ* is due to the combined influences of preceding *i* and following 'dark' *l* [ł] (A 1965, 33 f.). In some words the vowel is lost altogether ('syncope'), as in *dexter* (beside δεξῐτερός), *pergo* < * ∼ *rĕg* ∼ ; in others the quality seems to be determined by the initial syllable ('vowel harmony'), as in *alăcer*, *celĕber*; and very often grammatical analogy has restored or preserved the original form, as in *impătiens* (after *pătiens*): but note normal phonetic development in *insĭpiens* < * ∼ *săp* ∼ .

Such developments indicate a particularly weak or relaxed articulation of the vowels in question; the weakening was, however, less marked if the syllable was arrested by a consonantal articulation. For example, original *ă* closed only to *ĕ* and original *ĕ* was preserved, as in *perfĕctus* < * ∼ *făc* ∼ , *attĕntus* < * ∼ *tĕn* ∼ , beside *perfĭcio* and *attĭneo*; and back vowels remained back, as in Old Latin *eŏntis* (cf. ἰόντος), which later → *eŭntis*. This suggests that in unstressed positions the short vowel in an arrested syllable was articulated with greater precision than in an unarrested syllable. Long vowels, i.e. with thoracic arrest, were not subject to change of any kind; thus *relātus* retains its *ā*. The first elements of diphthongs, however, followed the same pattern of development as short vowels in arrested syllables; thus **inclaudo* → **incloudo* → *inclūdo*; **incaido* → *inceido* (*SC de Bacch.*) → *incīdo*.[1]

---

[1] This seems incidentally to suggest that, at the period of weakening, the second elements of diphthongs had a consonantal function, i.e. formed an oral arrest rather than accompanied a thoracic arrest. Where the digraph *ae* is followed by a vowel, as in *Gnaeus*, the second element represents either a vocalic followed by a semivocalic articulation [∼ai.ju∼] or a double semivowel [∼aj.ju∼], as in the case of words like *maior* (see p. 66). The same applies to Greek words in Latin containing *u*-diphthongs, as e.g. *Agaue* = [a.gau.wee] or [a.gaw.wee] (cf. p. 207 and Hoenigswald 1949b; A 1965, 42).

Complex pausal releases and arrests

The oral (consonantal) releases and arrests of Latin syllables may be either simple or complex. In an isolated word such as *dăt*, both release and arrest are simple, and in *stănt* both are complex. In native Latin words there occur after pause complex releases of the types *s*+plosive or /w/ (e.g. *sto, spes, suadeo*), plosive or *f*+liquid (e.g. *tremo, fremo, plus, fluo, breuis, glisco*), and triconsonantal complexes of the type *s*+plosive+liquid (e.g. *stringo, splendens*). Complex arrests before pause, as one might expect, tend to show a reverse order of elements (see p. 71); thus, for example, liquid (or nasal)+plosive or *s* as in *fert, uult, pars, tunc, dant*; plosive+*s*, as in *caelebs, nox*; and liquid+plosive +*s*, as in *falx, stirps*; but the order *s*+plosive is also found, as in *post*.

~ V̆CC(C)V ~ (non-pausal sequences)

When intervocalic consonant sequences are found such as occur neither initially nor finally at pause, one may assume (again in accordance with traditional rules) that they constituted arrest+release; so that *factus, amnis*, for example, would be analysable as *făc.tus, ăm.nis*. An analysis *făct.us* etc. is less probable in any case, since it would create a complex arrest (and of a type not found in Latin final syllables) at the expense of oral reinforcement of release; and *fă.ctus* is ruled out both on grounds of the non-occurrence of initial *ct* and, more conclusively, by the heavy quantity attested for the first syllable. With such sequences may also be included all double consonants; thus e.g. *mĭtto = mĭt.to*, with consequent heavy quantity of the first syllable.

Where sequences of three consonants are involved, the central one is usually of lesser aperture than one or both of the flanking consonants: e.g. *sculptus, spectrum, antrum, fulcrum*. The difference in aperture between the first and second consonant (C^1C^2) also is generally greater or smaller than that between the second and third (C^2C^3). If it is greater, one might suppose that there would then be a greater tendency for the sequence C^1C^2 to form a complex arrest than for the sequence C^2C^3 to form a complex release; and vice versa. One might therefore expect syllabic patterns of the types *sculp.tus, spec.trum, an.trum*. This agrees with the typology of word-initial sequences in Latin, and is in accordance with the traditional doctrine and inscriptional practice (Kent 1932, 63 and 64 n.6). It also agrees well with the observation that, in the only circumstance where it can be proved (viz. after short vowel), the sequence plosive + liquid, and only this sequence, functions internally as a complex release (see below). For this last reason one would also presumably syllabify *sartrix* (where the C^1C^2 and C^2C^3 aperture differences are equal) as *sar.trix* rather than *sart.rix*; and conversely a form such as *sextus* or *extra* would be syllabified as *sex.tus*, *ex.tra*, rather than *sec.stus*, *ec.stra*, because the sequence *st(r)* does *not* function internally as a complex release in the only circumstance where it can be tested (see below).

Where sequences unattested initially or finally at pause are divided by a grammatical boundary, the syllabification will, a fortiori, be of the type *ăb-duco*, *nĕc. tibi*, involving heavy quantity for the preceding syllable.

~ V̆CC(C)V ~ (pre-pausal sequences)

We have then to consider the syllabic functioning between vowels of consonant sequences which *are* also found initially or finally at pause. The latter case presents no special problems, since, for example, a word of the type *mŭltus* scarcely admits of a syllabification other than *mŭl.tus* or *mŭlt.us*, either of which involves heavy quantity for the first syllable; and of these *mŭl.tus* is the more probable as providing an oral release for the second syllable; a syllabification *mŭ.ltus*, giving light first syllable, would be anomalous in terms of initial groups, and in fact in such words the first syllable is always heavy. The same arguments will apply to a word such as *nexus*, indicating a syllabification *nĕc.sus*; and in the case of a three-consonant sequence, as in *cărpsit*, there is the additional criterion of relative apertures discussed above, so that all indications are in favour of a syllabification *carp.sit*.

~ V̆CC(C)V ~ (post-pausal sequences)

When we turn to sequences which are also found initially, it is necessary to distinguish between

(a) their 'non-junctural' occurrence, i.e. where the sequence of consonants together with the preceding vowel contains no grammatical boundary; and

(b) their 'junctural' occurrence, i.e. where a grammatical boundary does so occur:

(a) NON-JUNCTURAL

These can be tested for syllabic function where the preceding vowel is short, by the criterion of quantity (as indicated by metre or by accent placement).

1. *s+plosive*. In the case of this sequence quantity is regularly heavy, so that a word such as *pĕstis* is to be syllabified as *pĕs.tis*, with the consonant sequence constituting arrest+release,[1] which agrees with inscriptional practice though conflicting with ancient doctrine (see p. 29). In the case of a three-consonant sequence as in *ăstra*, heavy quantity could indicate either *ăs.tra* or *ăst.ra*; but the principle of relative apertures would indicate the former (see also below).

2. *Plosive (and f)+liquid*. A special case is presented by the sequence plosive+liquid. For the evidence of early Latin verse and of accent placement is quite clear that a syllable containing a short vowel followed by such a sequence was regularly *light* in quantity. These sequences must therefore have functioned as complex releases of the following syllable: thus *tenĕ.brae*, *pă.tris*, *pŏ.plus*; and further support is given to the above syllabification of *ăstra* as *ăs.tra*. It is not, however, true that this function also applies to the group *f+liquid* (e.g. in *uăfri*, *cinĭflones*), as suggested by Postgate (1923, 7) and Raven (1965, 25).[2] This false doctrine goes back to the Latin grammarians (A 1965, 90 n.), who equated the Latin *f* with the Greek φ, which in classical Greek was a plosive [ph] and not, as later, a fricative. The non-junctural sequence *f+liquid* functions only as arrest+release, giving invariably heavy preceding syllable; the difference in function between this sequence and plosive+liquid may be related to the fact that the difference in aperture between *f* and a liquid is less than that between a plosive and a liquid, and so the former sequence is less capable of providing the sudden transition from stricture to aperture which characterizes oral reinforcement of the ballistic release of the following syllable. On de Saussure's scale, for instance (1916/1960, 44 ff.), the

---

[1] The possibility of *pĕst.is* is discounted as involving a second syllable without oral reinforcement of release (see above).

[2] Cf. also Hoenigswald 1949a, 274.

sequence plosive + liquid would represent an increase in aperture from zero to 3, but fricative + liquid only from 1 to 3. The sequence plosive + nasal forms a complex release only in Greek words, in imitation of Greek practice (see pp. 210 ff.): thus *cy̆.cnus* giving light quantity at Horace, *Carm.* iv. iii 20 (on de Saussure's scale such a sequence would represent an increase in aperture from zero to 2).

The attested early Latin treatment of the sequences plosive + liquid is evidently an innovation, replacing a yet earlier, prehistoric treatment in which such sequences functioned like others as arrest + release, and not as a complex release. The vowel of the middle syllable of *intĕgra*, for example, shows that the syllable must have been arrested at the time of vowel weakening, i.e. *intĕg.ra*, since it has the same quality as in e.g. *infĕc.ta* and not as in *infĭ.cit*. At Plautus, *Rud.* 1208 there occurs the phrase *porci săcres*, in which the metre demands that the first syllable of *săcres* be heavy, i.e. *săc.res*; and it has been suggested by Timpanaro (1965, 1084 ff.) that this may be a survival, in an 'espressione sacrale e arcaica', of the prehistoric syllabic patterning of such sequences.

At a later period, and under the influence of Greek practice, it became permissible to adopt for metrical purposes the alternative of treating syllables containing a short vowel followed by plosive + liquid as being of heavy quantity, i.e. as implying a function of arrest + release for such sequences. Thus at Vergil, *Aen.* ii 663 one finds *pă̄tris* and *pă̄trem* following one another in the same verse, as if implying *pă.tris*, *pă̄t.rem* respectively. It has been suggested that originally this practice applied only to Greek words and otherwise metrically intractable Latin words (Skutsch 1964, 91 ff.); but already in Ennius one finds, for instance, *nĭ̄grum* with heavy first syllable.[1] It need not be supposed that such a treatment for purposes of verse composition would necessarily be reflected in performance; but one point of interest here arises. In words such as *uolŭcres*, *perăgro*, *latĕbras*, *manĭplis* the position of the accent depends on the treatment of the plosive + liquid sequence, which will normally have been *uó.lŭ.cres*, etc., with light penultimate syllable requiring accent on the antepenultimate. But the treatment *uo.lŭc.res*, with heavy penultimate, is admitted in verse even at the end of a hexameter line, where agreement is usually sought between the linguistic accent and the metrical strong position; so that in such cases the poet appears to envisage a performance of this type,

[1] Cf. Timpanaro 1965, 1075 ff.

giving accentuation on the penultimate, i.e. *uo.lŭc.res*. This seems in fact to be accepted by Quintilian (i.5.28): 'euenit ut metri quoque condicio mutet accentum: *pecudes pictaeque uolucres*;[1] nam *uolucres* media acuta legam'; but the more general view of the grammarians is that this is a compositional licence not reflected in performance; thus e.g. Servius (on *Aen.* i 384 ' ~ Libyae deserta *peragro*'): '*per* habet accentum...; muta enim et liquida quotiens ponuntur, metrum iuuant, non accentum'.[2]

In this connexion finally may be mentioned the combination *qu*, which normally does not permit a preceding syllable with short vowel to be treated as heavy, and probably stands for a single, labio-velar consonant [kʷ] (A 1965, 16 ff.). Occasional exceptions do, however, occur, as e.g. *lĭquidus* with heavy first syllable at Lucretius, i 349, perhaps indicating a pronunciation [lik.wi ~].

(b) JUNCTURAL

1. *s + plosive (and /w/)*. Where a morph boundary falls between the two consonants, as in *dis-tineo*, the syllabic boundary also falls here, i.e. *dĭs.tineo*, with consequently invariably heavy quantity for the preceding syllable. The same syllabification applies (at least after a short vowel) where a morph boundary falls before the consonant sequence, as in *re-spiro = rĕs.piro*, provided that it is not also a word boundary. In this latter case the syllabic boundary in early Latin seems to have coincided with the word boundary, giving a light preceding syllable if the vowel were short.

Later poets, however, are faced with a dilemma (Hoenigswald 1949a). For in their Greek models the sequence *s + plosive* normally functions as arrest + release, so ensuring heavy quantity for the preceding syllable even after a word boundary. Exceptions are nearly all due to the exigencies of otherwise metrically intractable words, as, in hexameters, Σκάμανδρος, σκέπαρνον. This conflict between Greek and Latin junctural habits led classical Latin poets to avoid altogether the sequence of a word-final short vowel and a word-initial *s + plosive*,[3]

---

[1] Vergil, *Geo.* iii 243.

[2] Schoell 1876, 113 ff; A 1965, 90. In late Latin, as the evidence of Romance developments shows, there was a shift of accent from e.g. *ténebrae* to *tenébrae*. But this can hardly mean that the syllabification was then *te.neb.rae*, since the Romance evidence also indicates an *open* syllable, i.e. without oral arrest. For discussion and bibliography see Leumann 1928, 182; Timpanaro 1965, 1088 ff.

[3] Even in Greek the conflict between phonetic and word boundaries in these cases seems to have led to some restriction on their occurrence in verse: cf. p. 216.

except in the case of intractable words (as in the Greek models): thus e.g. Catullus, lxiv 357 (hexameter ending) *undă Scamandri*.[1] Sometimes the normal Greek practice is imitated, as in Catullus, lxiv 186 *nullă spes*, implying a syllabification ~ *ăs.p* ~ ;[2] and sometimes the native Latin treatment is maintained, as in Vergil, *Aen.* xi 309 ~ *ponitĕ. spes* ~ (where, however, the syllabification ~ *ĕ.sp.* ~ is aided by the major grammatical boundary).[3] A striking feature of the situation is that no poet freely permits himself *both* the Greek *and* the Latin treatments.[4]

It is significant that such sequences are not avoided in the 'anceps' (position admitting *either* Σ̲ *or* Σ̲) of metres in which this applies, as in the iambic trimeters of Phaedrus and Seneca; for here either syllabic treatment is equally acceptable from a metrical point of view. Nor is any problem presented by the word-initial group *su* /sw/, since this does not occur in Greek and so provides no contrary model to the normal Latin treatment, which regularly makes this a complex syllabic release, leaving unarrested the preceding final syllable of a word ending in a short vowel, which is consequently light: thus e.g. Ovid, *Met.* ix 692 *silentiă suadet.*

2. *Plosive + liquid.* The syllabification of this sequence is strongly influenced by grammatical boundaries, and generally speaking does not distinguish between word boundaries and morph boundaries within the word. If the grammatical boundary falls between the two consonants, the sequence regularly functions as arrest + release, even in early Latin verse, resulting in invariably heavy quantity for the preceding syllable: thus e.g. *ăb-ripi* = *ăb.ripi*, *ăb lenone* = *ăb.lenone*. But if the grammatical boundary falls before the consonant sequence, the sequence functions as a complex release, leaving a preceding short vowel un-arrested. Even in classical Latin verse a syllabic division of the sequence in such cases (as e.g. *rĕ-trahit* = *rĕt.rahit*) is comparatively rare

---

[1] There is a similar avoidance of word-initial *z* after final short vowel, presumably because in the Greek models *z*, as = [zd] (A 1968a, 53 ff.), was normally treated as arrest + release; in Latin initial *z* = simple [z] (A 1965, 45 f.), but the pattern of the model is followed, and in Vergil the avoidance is breached only by the intractable (*nemorosă*) *Zacynthus* (*Aen.* iii 270) as in Homer, *Od.* i 246 ὑλήεντι Ζακύνθῳ. A case such as Juvenal, v 45 *ponerĕ zelotypo* presumably reflects the actual Latin pronunciation with simple [z].

[2] This is most common in 'studied imitation of Greek lines' (Raven 1965, 24).

[3] A number of cases are noted by Housman (1928) for Horace: e.g. *Serm.* I. ii 30 *in fornicĕ stantem*, and even (I. v 35) *praemiă scribae.*

[4] For further discussion of this see Collinge 1970, 197 ff.

(Hoenigswald 1949a, 273 n.15)[1]; it is especially rare if a word boundary is involved, as Catullus, xxix 4 *ultimā Britannia*, and as Raven observes (1965, 25) 'may usually be seen as a conscious "Grecism"'.[2] A parallel to such differences has already been cited from English (pp. 20 f.).

3. *f + liquid*. Although there is no reason to think that in non-junctural contexts this sequence was ever treated as other than arrest + release, its behaviour at morph-boundaries is similar to that of plosive + liquid;[3] the only cases occurring involve such a boundary before the sequence. Within a word, as e.g. in *rĕ-freno, rĕ-fluit*, the sequence is more often treated as a complex release, leaving a preceding syllable with a short vowel unarrested and so of light quantity;[4] and at word boundaries this treatment is general: rare exceptions are Ennius, *Ann.* 577 *populeā fruns*,[5] Catullus, iv 18 *impotentiā freta*, implying ~ *ăf.r* ~.

When Latin grammarians state that light quantity may occur before the sequence *f* + liquid, they in fact invariably cite cases where a word boundary precedes the sequence (for references see A 1965, 90 n.); and Bede, though he gives the rule (vii, 230 K), acknowledges the invalidity of such examples in establishing a general principle.

Hypercharacterization

This phenomenon (described on p. 66) is not uncommon in Latin, though we have seen that there is some tendency to reduce its incidence. The number of cases is, as also in Greek, increased by vowel contraction, as e.g. in *cōn.tio, nūn.tius*[6] < **couentio, *nouentios*; but reduction by vowel shortening is common in late Latin (see A 1965, 75 n.2); a prehistoric tendency to reduction is also seen in the development of e.g. **amāntem, *uidēndos → amăntem, uidĕndus*.

What is sometimes mistermed 'hidden quantity' in fact refers to vowel length in hypercharacterized syllables, as e.g. in *nōs.co, scrīp.si, āc.tus, mīl.le*, where quantity would be heavy regardless of vowel length and so does not in itself afford evidence of the length of the vowel, which is known from other evidence (A 1965, 65 ff.).

[1] It appears to be more common where the liquid is *l*; in Vergil, for example, 3 cases vs none with *r*; in Lucretius 8 cases vs 2 with *r*.

[2] Cf. Collinge 1970, 200.   [3] Cf. Collinge 1970, 193 n.2.

[4] Invariably so in Vergil; but in Lucretius heavy quantity is rather more common than light (8 cases vs 5).

[5] Cf. Skutsch 1964, 93; Timpanaro 1965, 1080.

[6] Syllabification of consonant sequences is assumed to be the same as after short vowels.

11   *Word juncture* $(\sim V + V \sim)$

The above discussions of syllable structure have included reference to the prosodic implications of certain types of juncture involving consonants and consonant sequences. Another type of word juncture, which is particularly relevant to syllabic and quantitative patterning, is that in which a word having a final vowel or diphthong in its basic, pre-pausal form[1] is collocated with a following word having an initial vowel or diphthong.

Since word-final *m* in most cases probably represents a nasalization of the preceding vowel (A 1965, 30 f; Soubiran 1966, 47 ff.), the combination vowel + *m* at word end is also for this purpose to be classified as a vowel.[2]

We have already noted the tendency for the release of the chest pulse to be assisted by an oral articulation, and have seen some of the devices utilized to achieve this end and so to avoid junctural 'hiatus'. In some languages there is a particular tendency to avoid the sequence of a *long* vowel and another vowel, or in other words a thoracic arrest followed by a thoracic release without oral reinforcement; and in such cases the first vowel may be shortened ('vocalis ante vocalem corripitur'). This is a characteristic feature of Sanskrit vowel sandhi; for example, the process whereby *rājā + iva → rājeva* requires an intervening rule whereby final *ā* before initial vowel → *ă*, since otherwise the result would be **rājaiva* (A 1962, 37). This descriptive rule presumably reflects a historical development, and in fact in the case of final close vowels this situation is still largely preserved in Vedic, where *patnī + acchā → patnĭ acchā* (A 1962, 35 f.).[3] The remaining hiatus in

---

[1] In fact of the diphthongs only ~*ae* is involved, and in hexameters most commonly as a nom. pl. ending, the dat./gen. si. being relatively rare in such junctures. Wyatt (1966, 669) suggests that this reflects the situation in Greek as regards 'epic correption' of nom. pl. ~αι vs dat. si. ~ᾳ/η (cf. p. 224 and A 1968a, 91, 94).

[2] The original consonantal value appears to be preserved in e.g. Ennius, *Ann.* 243 *dum quidem unus homo*; Horace, *Serm.* I. ii 28 *cocto num adest* (A 1965, 81 n.3).

This was already well observed in antiquity; thus Śākalya ap. Pāṇini, vi.1.127 'iko 'savarṇe hrasvaśca', i.e. 'close vowels followed by a dissimilar vowel (remain) and a short vowel (is substituted for a long)'.

this case is particularly tolerable in so far as a close vowel [i] or [u] provides the articulatory posture for a semivocalic, oral reinforcement of the release of the next syllable – thus e.g. *patnĭyacchā* (or, in other terms, generates a semivocalic glide, which effectively eliminates the hiatus). Alternatively the process may be seen as a transfer of the second mora of the close long vowel (which in other environments accompanies the thoracic arrest) to an oral releasing function in the next syllable; this would then be parallel to the process seen in the so-called 'shortening' of diphthongs before vowels, whereby $/\sim ai + V\sim/ \rightarrow /\sim a.jV\sim/$, etc., as commonly in Homer (e.g. καὶ ἀναίτιον, with light first syllable). For further discussion of Greek see p. 224; and on Sanskrit A 1962, 37 ff.

In classical Latin verse hiatus is primarily a characteristic of Greek imitation (cf. Raven 1965, 28). But in early Latin verse it is common at caesurae and diaereses, i.e. where there is often the potentiality of pause: cf. p. 117 and Drexler 1967, 18, 48 f; shortening of long vowels may be seen in monosyllables in certain environments (the so-called 'prosodic hiatus'), as e.g. in Plautus, *Merc.* 744 *nam quī amat quod amat sĭ habet id habet pro cibo*; instances of this type are also occasionally found in classical Latin, as e.g. *Aen.* vi 507 *tĕ, amice, nequiui.*[1]

The devices so far mentioned for modifying the hiatus have all preserved the number of syllables in the individual underlying forms. But far more common in Latin verse is the implied elimination of hiatus by reduction of the two syllables in juncture to one, generally known by the title of 'elision', though mostly referred to by the grammarians as '*synalife*' (συναλοιφή). The grammarians seem to speak in terms of simple elimination of the final vowel or diphthong of the first word (Sturtevant & Kent 1915, 141 ff.). When the vowel is short, such a process would find a parallel in Greek (see pp. 226 f.), and one may compare the treatment of the definite article in French or Italian. It is, moreover, supported by metrical considerations in Latin itself. For in a corpus of some 53,000 hexameter lines (Ennius to Ovid) collated by Siedow (1911)[2] elision of final short vowels is found before light initial syllables (which the metre also requires to be light) in 3,797 cases out of a total of 9,871 elisions of short vowels. This would be

---

[1] It has, however, also been argued (Soubiran, 373 ff.) that in all these cases it is rather a matter of contraction of the two vowels into some kind of long element, giving rise to one heavy instead of two light syllables, and so no hiatus.

[2] Cf. Brunner 1956; A 1965, 79 ff.

unthinkable if such elided vowels were in speech not normally eliminated but contracted in some way with the following initial; for such
contraction would be expected to result in a *heavy* syllable (in *Aen.*
ix 580 *spiramenta animae*, for example, the required quantitative
pattern is produced only on the basis of an implication $\sim t$' *ănĭmae*,
not $\sim ta\_animae = \sim tānĭmae$).

Soubiran, nevertheless (151 ff.), would restrict the process of elimination to final *ĕ*, and primarily to the enclitics (*-que*, *-ne*, *-ue*), which are
more frequently elided than any other category, and which incidentally
have doublets without final vowel (cf. *ac, nec*; *tanton*; *neu*); Soubiran
also accepts extension of the process to certain other 'grammatical
words' which in early Latin verse have forms without final vowel
(e.g. *nemp(e), und(e), ill(e), ist(e)*; also *proin(de), dein(de)*: cf. Drexler
1967, 58 ff.). In all other cases (as also in the case of other than short
final vowels) Soubiran argues for a 'partial pronunciation' of the final
vowel (55 ff., 648), such that it 'counted metrically as zero, but continued to be heard, the two vowels in contact being pronounced with a
single impulse'. We must, of course, be careful to distinguish between
composition and performance; and it is not inconceivable that, in a
sequence of two vowels in juncture, the first might be treated as eliminated even though in performance both vowels would be fully pronounced.
We have, however, also to remember the principle that metrical features
are based on features of ordinary language; and metrical elimination by
elision could hardly be so well established if it did not reflect some
linguistic reality. It could just possibly be argued that it is simply an
extension by compositional licence of the cases admitted by Soubiran;
but the extension is remarkably wide. What does seem most improbable,
in the case of a final short vowel followed by an initial short vowel *in a
light syllable*, is Soubiran's compromise referred to above; for if the
pronunciation of both vowels 'with a single impulse' means anything,
it means some kind of diphthong – and a diphthong (or a long vowel)
involves heavy quantity. Soubiran's view, which goes back more than a
century, to Ahrens and Hermann,[1] is in fact not very different from that
of Bridges in regard to English verse, namely that the elided vowels are
'heard in the glide, though prosodically asyllabic'.[2] We shall see that
such an interpretation could well apply to certain types of juncture in
Latin, but hardly to those cases where light quantity is required. It
will therefore be assumed that elision in the sequence $\breve{V}_x + \breve{V}_y$ implies

---

[1] Rossi 1968, 233.   [2] Chatman 1960, 163.

→ $\breve{V}_y$; in which case it is likely that more generally $\breve{V}_x + V_y \rightarrow V_y$ (i.e. even in those cases where the second syllable is thoracically or orally arrested, and so heavy).

Elisions of long and nasalized vowels and of diphthongs in verse are not much less common than those of short vowels (6,800 cases as against 9,871 in the corpus), but the positions of occurrence are more restricted. They occur before a light syllable in only 905 cases, of which only 84 before position b_2 of a dactyl, as against 1,455 cases of short vowel elisions at this point.[1] Of those which occur before position b_1 about half involve conjunctions or common adverbs of spondaic form (notably *ergo, quare, quando, certe, longe, immo, porro, contra*); the next largest category at this position is that of words ending in *ī*. Only a small proportion involve inflexional endings other than *ī* or *ū* (a number of them in any case being in closely knit or idiomatic combinations such as *aequō animo*, where the inflexional ending of the first word is of little significance).

From this the most probable conclusion seems to be that simple elimination of final long (and nasalized) vowels and diphthongs in juncture was *not* normal in speech, and was generally found only where they carried no considerable semantic load. In which case it is likely that such junctions normally resulted in some kind of long vowel or diphthong, which would invariably involve heavy quantity (regardless of the original quantity of the word-initial syllable) and so would be excluded from the metrical positions in which light quantity was demanded. The junctural process here will then have been one of contraction, though one can only surmise what the qualities of the resultant juncture may have been in each case. Some clues may be afforded by the results of contraction in internal junctures, as e.g. *dē-ăgo* → *dēgo*, *co(m)-ăgo* → *cōgo*, *prō-ĕmo* → *prōmo*, *mā(u)ŏlo* → *mālo*, *co(m)-ĭtus* → *coetus*, *prae-ĭtor* → *praetor*.[2] The exceptions, where metre implies elimination of a final long or nasalized vowel,[3] are supported

---

[1] Before heavy syllables, elision of long vowels etc. is no less common before short vowels than before long vowels – indeed it is (contrary to the teaching of some textbooks) considerably more common (in Vergil by a factor of about 3:1): cf. Sturtevant & Kent 1915, 153 f.

[2] At *word*-junctions, however, there is no evidence in verse for implications of the type $V + \breve{V} \sim \rightarrow \breve{V} \sim$ (which would alter the basic quantitative pattern of the second word in respect of other than a final syllable): cf. p. 146 n.1.

[3] The greater frequency of such cases after a heavy syllable (i.e. before position b_1 as against b_2) may be related to the greater frequency of spondaic common adverbs etc. as against iambic; and perhaps more generally to a reluctance to reduce $\Sigma\Sigma$ to Σ.

by the evidence of 'fossilized' combinations such as *animaduerto* <
animum + *aduerto*,   *magnŏpere* < *magnō* + *opere*,   *cauaedium* < *cauum* +
aedium (Varro, *L.L.* v.161), CVRAGO < *curam* + *ago* (cf. Sturtevant &
Kent 1915, 129 ff., 141).

The fact that final long *close* vowels were more readily elidable than
others before metrical positions requiring light quantity seems to
indicate that they did *not* normally contract with the following initial
vowel; and the most likely conclusion is that they were reduced to
semivowels [j], [w] ('synizesis') and so did not affect the quantity of
the following syllable; thus e.g. Catullus, lxxxv 1 *odī* + *ĕt* (*amo*) →
[oodje ∼]; Lucilius, 1095 *ritū* + *ŏculisque* → [riitwo ∼]. Such a process,
however, by conversion of the vowel to consonantal function, might
be expected to affect the quantity of a preceding light syllable by
shifting the consonant preceding the original vowel from releasing
into arresting function, i.e. ∼ V⁰.CV + V ∼ → ∼ V⁰C.CV ∼. This
effect is seen in the internal synizesis of Vergil, *Aen.* v 432; xii 905
gĕnua = [genwa], or ii 16 *ǎbiete* = [abje ∼], with heavy first syllables.[1]
And in fact junctures of this type following a light syllable (as e.g.
Horace, *Serm.* 1. i 59 *tantŭlī* + *ĕget*) are exceptionally rare; in the Aeneid,
for example, a final *ī* is elided before b₁ (where it follows a heavy
element) in 25 cases (compared with 4 for final *ā* and 5 for final *ō*),
but before b₂ (where it follows a light syllable, viz. b₁) not at all:
cf. Soubiran, 311. This tends to support the supposition of synizesis,
which of course would not affect the quantity of a preceding *heavy*
syllable – the context in which elision of a long close vowel most
commonly occurs.

The conclusion from verse practice (at least in hexameters) therefore
seems to be that the general treatment of vowel juncture in Latin was as
follows:

(i) final short vowels: *loss* ('apocope').
(ii) final long vowels other than *ī*, *ū* (including diphthongs): *contraction* (but
in certain grammatically/semantically determined cases: *loss*).
(iii) final *ī*, *ū*: '*synizesis*'.

---

[1] There do not, however, appear to be cases of metrically required heavy quantity
being created in a penultimate syllable by synizesis at external (word) junctions
(cf. p. 145 n.2). *Short ĭ* had a more open articulation than the corresponding long
vowel, and in the only cases where it occurs finally may have been particularly
open (cf. Kent 1932, 103); it occurs in elision after light syllables (e.g. *ubi* + V ∼)
and so suggests loss rather than synizesis.

The special treatment of *ī, ū* has a parallel in Sanskrit; for open final vowels contraction is here normal (there is no apocope), but for close final vowels followed by a dissimilar vowel the result is synizesis, as e.g. *mṛdu+asti → mṛdvasti* (A 1962, 35).

A further breakdown of the statistics cited above gives an indication of the general comparability of nasalized vowels with non-nasal long vowels and diphthongs.[1] For whereas elisions of short vowels before light syllables total 3,797, elisions of nasalized vowels in these positions total only 498, which is comparable with the figure for long vowels and diphthongs (407). However, occurrences of final *m* in general (considering all contexts) are much less frequent than those of final non-nasal long vowels or diphthongs; and in spite of this, elision of final nasalized vowels before the position b_2 of a dactyl is about three times as frequent as that of non-nasal long vowels and diphthongs (64 as against 20). The final nasalized vowels thus appear, from this point of view, to occupy an intermediate position between short and long.

The figures from Siedow on which the above conclusions have been based are restated below in tabular form:

	$\Sigma'\Sigma$	$\Sigma'\underset{\smile}{\Sigma}$	$\Sigma'\underline{\Sigma}$	Totals
~V̆	2,342	1,455	6,074	9,871
~V̄	387	20	2,574	2,981
~Vm	434	64	3,321	3,819

Soubiran has pointed out, moreover (244 f.), that in Vergil the nasalized vowels are elided about twice as frequently, in proportion to their overall occurrence, as are other long vowels *or short vowels* (excluding enclitics); and also that they tend to occur with a higher than average frequency at the ends of lines (i.e. in the quantitatively 'indifferent' position, and where there is no 'synaphea'). Thus, whilst they are certainly not classifiable as short vowels, there seems to have been a tendency to place them more frequently than at random in positions where their length was indeterminate; for further discussion cf. Soubiran, 207 ff.[2]

---

[1] Cf. the Indian classification (e.g. by the *Taittirīya-Prātiśākhya*: A 1953, 42) of syllables containing nasalized vowels as metrically equivalent to those containing long vowels.

[2] It has been suggested by Fink (1969, 450 f.) that final *m* was reduced to some kind of (? nasalized) labial fricative, of which the stricture tended to be relaxed; the hypothesis is unsupported, but is reminiscent of the developments of Sanskrit *m*

The aspirate *h* at the beginning of a word does not normally prevent elision, perhaps on account of its being treated not as a consonant but as a breathy modification of the following vowel (cf. A 1965, 43; and on Greek p. 229). However, both in early and in classical Latin verse it has been observed that hiatus is rather more common before *h*~ than before unaspirated vowels; and that in classical verse forms of the deictic *hic* (pronominal and adverbial) tend otherwise not to be placed after a final long (or nasalized) vowel or diphthong – i.e. in contexts where one might normally postulate contraction. From this it could be argued, as by Soubiran (97 ff.), that initial *h* in careful, cultivated speech tended to be preserved as a consonant, and was articulated particularly clearly in a deictic form, whereas it tended to be effaced in colloquial speech. Elision before *h*~ might then imply the phonetic absence of the aspirate rather than simply a non-consonantal ('prosodic') function (cf. p. 11). Where such elision occurs in verse, it could reflect colloquial tendencies, and/or a compositional extension from cases where the two words were closely connected and where consequently the *h* tended to be effaced in the same way as between vowels within words (A 1965, 43 f; cf. 1968a, 52 f.).

If *h* were to function as a consonant, it would be expected to create heavy quantity when it follows ~$\breve{V}$C; and in fact at caesurae the treatment of ~$\breve{V}$C as heavy is more common before *h*~ (in proportion to its overall occurrence) than before initial vowels; in Vergil, for example, 14 cases of the type *terga fatigamŭs hasta* (*Aen.* ix 610) beside 40 of the type *et direpta domŭs et*~, whereas initial *h* in Latin as a whole is about 10 times less frequent than initial unaspirated vowels. But in a large majority of cases *h*~ does not, of course, 'make position' in this way; the explanation of this presumably lies in the same factors as account for elision before *h*~ in classical Latin verse; additionally it could be that in any case *h* would tend to form a complex release with the preceding consonant (rather as the sequence plosive + liquid), resulting in a simple aspirated consonant.[1]

A special case is presented by 'prodelision' or 'aphaeresis', which occurs when a final vowel is followed by the copula *est* (or *es*). The evidence of the grammarians, inscriptions, and manuscript tradition indicates that in such cases it was the initial *ĕ* that was eliminated in the

in some dialects: see A 1953, 40 ff; 1962, 81 f; cf. also Apabhraṃśa *kaʋala* < *kamala*, etc. (Hemacandra, iv 397): modern Hāṛautī has [kəw̃əl].

[1] In all cases there is an intervening grammatical boundary, but the very open articulation of the *h* might cause this to be overridden.

juncture;[1] thus e.g. *Aen.* xi 23 *sub imost* (cod. Mediceus); C.I.L. XII, 882 *Raptusque a fatis conditus hoc tumulost,* where ~ *que* + *a,* involving normal elision, is written in full, but *tumulo* + *est* is written in the prodelided form. The same applies to the nasalized vowels: e.g. Lucretius, ii 94 *probatumst*; sometimes written without ~ *m,* e.g. Vergil, *Geo.* iii 148 *Romanust* (Fulvianus; ~ *umst* Romanus); C.I.L. X, 5371 *molestust.*[2] The same phenomenon is also found in early Latin verse and in inscriptions at the junction of final *s* with *est,* as e.g. Plautus, *Merc.* 833 *Interemptust, interfectust, alienatust. occidi*; C.I.L. I, 199, 17 *uocitatust* (166 B.C.). This is no doubt to be connected with the 'weakness' of final *s* in early Latin, for which there is other evidence (A 1965, 36; Drexler 1967, 61 f.), though perhaps also motivated by the proximity of the two sibilants, i.e. ~ *us* + *est* → ~ *us* + *st* → ~ *ust* (cf. Soubiran 163 n.2 and refs.).

We have seen that exceptions to elision are found at caesurae and diaereses (as also, of course, at the ends of lines), where the potentiality of pause avoids the hiatus situation. Conversely, the occurrence of elision in verse at major grammatical boundaries, and especially at change of speaker, must be an artificiality[3] – one of several such which tend to the internal cohesion of the line: e.g. Terence, *And.* 298 PAM. *Accepi: acceptam seruabo.* MYS. *Ita spero quidem* (Soubiran, 478); similarly elision of interjections (as *hem*: Rossi 1968, 237).

That in normal speech there were in fact special processes of juncture, involving the reduction of two syllables to one when forms with final and initial vowels occurred in sequence, is well attested by statements in Cicero and Quintilian amongst others.[4] From Quintilian's statement (ix.4.33 ff.) it appears that in literary prose such junctures were less regularly applied than in verse, even within phrases ('nonnumquam hiulca etiam decent faciuntque ampliora quaedam, ut "pulchra oratione acta"'); but where they did occur, it seems likely, on the evidence of tendencies in verse, that they followed the general principles suggested above; in which case exceptions to these principles in verse, as e.g. complete elimination of final long vowels in other than the categories

---

[1] Soubiran, 162 ff.

[2] Soubiran (149) also suggests the possibility of this treatment extending to other 'grammatical' words (e.g. prepositions, conjunctions) – which would solve the problem of such junctions as in *Aen.* i 90 *Intonuere pŏlī et crebris* ~ , where synizesis of the ~ *ī* would result in an unmetrical heavy preceding syllable (see above); cf. also Soubiran 521, 527 f; Shipley 1924, 145 ff.

[3] Cf. Sturtevant & Kent 1915, 132.

[4] A 1965, 78; Soubiran, 68 ff; Drexler 1967, 15 ff.

and contexts referred to, may be considered as simple compositional licences.

The treatment of elision in the *performance* of verse inevitably depends on the mode of performance adopted (see pp. 340 ff.). If a 'prose' reading is employed, strict metrical pattern, especially in hexameters, will be disrupted in any case, and the occasional absence of juncture corresponding to the metrically required elision will only slightly affect the degree of such disruption. If, on the other hand, a 'scanning' reading is adopted, clearly the elisions must be realized in all cases, including the elimination of final long vowels when essential to the metre; this point is expressly made by the grammarian Sacerdos (vi, 448 K): 'inter syncopen ergo et synalifam hoc est, quod syncope ab ipsis ponitur poetis, nantes pro natantes; synalifa autem a nobis uel pronuntiantibus uel pedes scandentibus fit, cum a poeta plenum uerbum ponatur. "*mene incepto*" nos scandimus "*menincepto*"; "*monstrhor*" nos percutimus, cum poeta posuerit "*monstrum horrendum*"'. What, however, can hardly be supported, in the absence of any demonstration of its phonetic feasibility, is the idea of a 'compromise' rendering of elision in which both the presence and the absence of the elided vowel are somehow combined in an articulation which is at once audible and at the same time free of any prosodic consequences in the phonological sense.

12   *Accent*

(a) TYPOLOGY

There is little disagreement that the prehistoric accent of Latin was a stress accent, which fell on the initial syllable of the word. Its effects have already been seen in the loss or 'weakening' of vowels in pre-historically unaccented syllables, a process which is a typical conse-quence of strong stress in some other languages (e.g. English). There is, however, some controversy regarding the nature of the classical Latin accent which replaced it – namely, whether it was manifested by stress or by pitch, by 'amplitude' or 'frequency' modulation. The latter assumption, which has been made mainly by French scholars, appears on the face of it to be supported by statements in many of the ancient sources, as e.g. Varro (cited by Sergius, iv, 525 ff. K): 'Ab altitudine discernit accentus, cum pars uerbi aut in graue deprimitur aut sublimatur in acutum.' But it is quite clear that the Latin ter-minology is simply translated from the Greek (*accentus* = προσῳδία, *acutum* = ὀξύ, *graue* = βαρύ); and more than this, in the grammarians' accounts generally the whole detailed system of Greek accentuation is taken over and applied to Latin. Except by Cicero (Schoell 1876, 33 f.), the Greek περισπώμενον is regularly adopted as (*circum*)*flexum* (Schoell, 79 ff.); and Varro (iv, 528 ff. K) even includes the problematic 'middle' accent (μέση, *media*: cf. p. 253). The Greek rules for the selection of acute vs circumflex are also applied to Latin; thus Pompeius (v, 126 K) distinguishes *árma* vs *Músa*, as e.g. ἄρμα vs Μοῦσα, and Priscian (ii, 7 K) distinguishes *hámīs* vs *hâmus* as e.g. κώμοις vs κῶμος. It is incon-ceivable that Latin should have developed a system of melodic accentua-tion that agreed in such minor detail with Greek, and we can only assume that the grammarians have slavishly misapplied the Greek system to the description of Latin.[1] The very similarity of the Latin statements to those which apply in Greek is therefore an embarrass-ment rather than a support to the idea of a melodic accent for Latin.

In fact not all the grammarians follow the Greek model. In Servius

---

[1] Cf. Lepscky 1962, 204.

(iv, 426 K) we find the clear statement, 'Accentus in ea syllaba est *quae plus sonat*', which is amplified by reference to a 'nisum uocis' (cf. also Pompeius, v, 127 K). Such descriptions are admittedly late (from *c.* 400 A.D.), but no later than some of those prescribing a melodic accent, and may well go back to an earlier source (Sommer 1914, 27).

Developments in the Romance languages, with their losses of unaccented vowels (e.g. *ciuitátem* → It. *città*), suggest stress as the accentual feature of late Latin; in Probus (4 c. A.D.) one finds, for example, such directions as '*oculus,* non *oclus*' (cf. It. *occhio*); significant also is the use of the term *accentus* by Sidonius (5 c. A.D.), *Ep.* VII. xii 3: 'cum plausuum maximo accentu', which must surely imply amplitude. It seems unlikely that the prehistoric dynamic (stress) accent would have been replaced by a melodic accent and then quite soon again replaced by a dynamic accent (Pulgram 1954, 225; Drexler 1967, 14). The absence of vowel loss under the influence of the classical Latin accent is sometimes cited as an argument against stress at this period; but (i) a dynamic accent does not necessarily and always have this result, (ii) such effects may depend on the strength of the stress,[1] and (iii) they take time to operate (in Germanic, for example, it has been estimated that the rate of loss in final syllables is only about one mora per half-millennium). In any case some such effects are in fact to be observed even in connexion with the classical accent, as e.g. in *disciplína* (beside *discípulus*); moreover, the conservatism of normative spelling may well conceal instances of syncope or lead us to ascribe them to a later period; there were probably many 'popular' forms of the type *caldus* (< *calidus*), like English [pliis] for *police*, which have simply gone unrecorded (Pulgram 1954, 223).

Another aspect of 'weakening' in historical times that is suggestive of a dynamic rather than a melodic accent is the process of so-called 'iambic shortening', which is discussed in detail below (pp. 179 ff.); cf. Pulgram 1954, 221.

There is also a strong internal reason, already noted in a general context, for believing the Latin accent to have been different in type from that of ancient Greek, which is almost universally agreed to have been a melodic accent. For in Greek the location and variety of accent depend only upon those elements of the syllable which can carry

---

[1] Kerek (1968, 123 nn.14, 15) observes that, whereas stress conditions in Hungarian appear to have been unchanged over centuries, there has been a singular lack of reduction, and suggests as a 'plausible explanation' the weakness of the stress as compared with English or German.

variations of pitch, i.e. primarily upon the vowels and diphthongs. Thus e.g. αὖλαξ is accented properispomenon like τοῦτο, and not paroxytone like αὕτη in spite of the fact that the final syllable of the first word is heavy; all that is relevant is that the vowel of its final syllable (α) is short;[1] similarly δίσκος is paroxytone like ξίφος, and not properispomenon like ῥῖγος or οἶκος, in spite of its first syllable being heavy, because the accented vowel (ι) is short and the σ cannot carry variations of pitch. In Latin, on the other hand, it is syllabic quantity alone that is relevant; it makes no difference whether the heaviness of the syllable results from a long vowel or diphthong, i.e. thoracic arrest, or from consonantal (oral) arrest; the fact that in e.g. *re.féc.tus* the *c* [k], unlike the continuation of the long *ē* in *re.fḗ.cit*, cannot carry variation of pitch is irrelevant. The contrast with the Greek system could hardly be greater, and speaks strongly in favour of stress (which characterizes the whole syllable) rather than pitch (which characterizes only certain elements of it).

It has further been claimed (Trubetzkoy 1939/1969, 182) as a general typological rule, based on the observation of a large number of living languages, that the distinction between melodic and dynamic accentuation correlates with the distinction between languages whose prosodic phonology is based on the mora and languages in which it is based on the syllable; with the reservations made by Martinet (see p. 92), Greek falls into the former category, whereas, as will be argued, Latin does not. At least in terms of analytical typology, therefore, Latin is to be classed with languages which, in general, have dynamic rather than melodic accentuation.

Finally there is the evidence of verse composition. In early Latin (scenic) verse, even on a cautious interpretation, 'A regard for accent ...seems to be established' (Harsh 1949, 108). More specifically, 'the early dramatists try hardest to avoid clashes of ictus and accent, Plautus above all' (Pulgram 1954, 233); it is of course impossible for the poet always to achieve coincidence of accented syllables with a particular element of the foot, and Pulgram (233 n.3) cites Ritschl for the observation that such coincidence occurred only 'quoad eius fieri posset'.[2] If one considers each word as an isolate, then there are certainly wide divergences, even in early Latin verse, between metrical

---

[1] Cf. Tronskij 1962, 48 (already observed by Choeroboscus, *Schol. in Theod.*, i, 384 f. H).
[2] Cf. also Bentley's 'quoad licuit' (p. 342).

and accentual patterns. But the coincidence is likely to have been greater if one were to take into account the shifts of accent which probably occurred in particular syntactical groupings, as well as secondary accentuations; for example, a word group such as *ad scribendum adpulit* (Terence, *And.* 1) might well have been treated like a single word for purposes of both primary and secondary accentuation – i.e. *ad scríbend(um) ádpulit*, as e.g. *indíligéntia*; and the syntactical accentuation of prepositional phrases has already been discussed (p. 25). There is little direct evidence on these matters;[1] but detailed hypotheses have been put forward by Fraenkel (1928) and Drexler (1933) which would result in a close coincidence of patterns. Many of these proposals have indeed been disputed (see e.g. Kalinka 1935, 347 ff; Vandvik 1937; Lepscky 1962, 211 f; Soubiran 1971); certainly their case is overstated, and Fraenkel later recanted much of what he had written on the subject;[2] but it remains likely that the general principle is valid.

In classical Latin verse, based more closely on Greek models, the situation is different. In the hexameter non-coincidence is more common than coincidence in the first part of the line. This may be seen as a deliberate artistic effect or, as by Fraenkel (1928, 331), a simple neglect of the matter, resulting partly from a divorce of poetic from normal language. But what is undeniable is the tendency for coincidence to occur (and to be sought with increasing success) in the latter part of the line, as a manifestation of 'the ubiquitous desire that the basis of a verse should emerge clearly at the end' (Wilkinson 1963, 121). No such coincidences are found in classical Greek verse, where the melodic accent is generally agreed to be irrelevant to the metrical patterns (see p. 261). The Latin accent must therefore be different in type. And specifically it is much more probable that the amplitude modulation of stress, which, like the metrical patterns, is related to syllabic quantity, would be relevant to such patterns than would be the frequency modulation of pitch, which is not so related.[3] One is disposed, therefore, to agree with Enk (1953, 94) that 'a regard for coincidence of ictus and accent can only be understood if the accent had an element of stress'.

[1] Cf. Sturtevant 1923, 55.
[2] Cf. **Williams 1970, 427.
[3] Cf. *Skutsch 1913, 188; Fraenkel 1928, 350; Harsh 1949, 108.

(b) INCIDENCE

The classical Latin accent was a fixed accent, its position within the word being determined by regular phonological rules to which grammatical structure was rarely relevant. The rules for its location were explicitly stated by Latin writers, though they tended to be unnecessarily complicated by the attempt to incorporate distinctions which were relevant to their Greek models but not to Latin. Thus e.g. Quintilian, i.5.30:

In every word the acute is confined within a range of three syllables, whether they be the last or the only ones in the word, and specifically to the penultimate or antepenultimate of these. Moreover, the middle one of the three, if long, may be either acute or circumflex; but a short in the same position will have grave tone, and so will place the acute on the syllable preceding it, i.e. the antepenultimate.

In more modern terms the rule may be stated as (Kent 1932, 66): 'A long penult was accented, as in *pepércī, inimícus*; but if the penult was short, the antepenult received the accent, as in *exístimō, cōnfíciunt, ténebrae*', with the addition that 'Disyllables were necessarily accented on the penult, as in *tégō, tóga*'.

The position of the accent in words of 2+ syllables is thus governed by syllabic quantity (of the penultimate); and very similar rules may be found in some other dynamically accented languages. Some partial parallels have already been noted in English (p. 51),[1] though here grammatical considerations are more directly relevant. For *verbs* in English Chomsky & Halle (70) set up a basic, approximate rule (no. 19) as follows:

Assign main stress to
(i) the penultimate vowel if the last vowel in the string under consideration is non-tense and is followed by no more than a single consonant;
(ii) the last vowel in the string under consideration if this vowel is tense or if it is followed by more than one consonant

– or in the formulaic notation of Rule 20:

$$V \rightarrow [\text{1 stress}] \Big/ \left\{ \begin{array}{l} \underline{} C_0 \begin{bmatrix} -\text{tense} \\ V \end{bmatrix} C_0^1 \\ \left\{ \begin{bmatrix} \underline{} \\ +\text{tense} \end{bmatrix} \right\} C_0 \\ \underline{} C_2 \end{array} \right\}$$

[1] For the recognition of such parallels by writers from the 17 c. onwards see Chomsky & Halle 1968, 59 n.3.

and they observe (n.15) 'the essential identity of (19) and the rule governing stress distribution in Latin'. The verbal accent rule thus stated places the accent on final or penultimate syllables (as e.g. in *astónish, detérmine*; *maintaín, decíde*; *collápse, convínce*); but the authors note that the same basic rule applies to *nouns*, with the difference that a final syllable containing a non-tcnse (lax) vowel is ignored for the purposes of accent location (37 n.26, 44 ff., 72):[1] thus e.g. *cínema, aspáragus, ásterisk*; *aróma, horízon*; *veránda, appéndix*.[2] The basic nominal rule of English thus comes particularly close to the general Latin rule,[3] but with the exception that, if the final syllable contains a tense vowel (or diphthong) followed by a consonant, the stress falls on the final syllable, as e.g. in *machíne, domaín, brocáde, cheroót* (Chomsky & Halle, 45, 77 f.).[4]

A rather less complex parallel is provided by Arabic. If one considers this language as having heavy and light syllables defined in the same way as for Latin, i.e. as being respectively arrested (thoracically or orally) and unarrested, then for 'classical' Arabic,[5] as for Latin, the accent generally falls on the penultimate syllable if heavy and on the antepenultimate if the penultimate is light. But in words of 3 + syllables, if both the penultimate and antepentultimate are light, the

---

[1] Halle & Keyser, however, (1971, 76 ff.) attempt to bring verbs (and adjectives) under the same rule as nouns.

[2] On e.g. *eclípse* cf. Chomsky & Halle, 45 f; Halle & Keyser 1971, 81. Other exceptions are variously explained by Chomsky & Halle; for example, in *módesty* the final *y* is treated as a glide and not a vowel (39 ff; cf. Halle & Keyser, 32 ff., 40 and n.).

[3] One must, however, beware of oversimplifying the English rules; Wilkinson, for example, in noting the parallel with Latin (1963, 90 f.), comments that 'Récondite is...surely a solecism, perhaps induced by "reckon"'; but, as Chomsky & Halle show (153 ff.), this is only one of a number of such cases, including e.g. *éxorcize, mérchandise, fráternize, ággrandize, íllustrate, Býzantine*, for which various explanations have been proposed. In some such cases forms may vary as between speakers or dialects (cf. the variants *recóndite, aggrándize, Byzántine*) or periods (e.g. *illústrate* up to the 19 c: Halle & Keyser 1971, 132 f.). The desire for too direct a correlation between Latin and English in this respect caused English metrical theorists in the 16 and 17 c. to be much perturbed by the fact that words such as *carpenter, Trumpington* were not accented on their penultimate (cf. Park 1968, 85; Attridge 1972, 145 ff; and p. 273); Chomsky & Halle (85 f.) treat *cárpenter* as ending in its underlying representation *-entr* (cf. the related *carpentry*).

[4] On e.g. *Néptune* cf. Chomsky & Halle, 45 f. Where no consonant follows, as e.g. in *window, ménu*, the final syllable tends to be ignored for purposes of the rule; as Chomsky & Halle point out (39, 45), the tense vowel in such cases is not in opposition to a corresponding lax vowel.

[5] Or, since there is doubt about the stress of classical Arabic, it might be preferable to speak of the 'koine' (cf. Ferguson 1956, 386), or the 'historic stage common to the dialects' or 'predialectal stage' (Birkeland 1954, 9).

accent probably regressed beyond the antepenultimate to fall on a heavy syllable (or, failing that, on the initial syllable regardless of its quantity). These rules have undergone modification in modern colloquials, but remain determined by distinctions of quantity.[1] The accent now generally falls on the penultimate, whether heavy or light: thus cl. $\Sigma\acute{\Sigma}\Sigma$ → mod. $\Sigma\acute{\Sigma}\Sigma$ (and cl. $\Sigma\acute{\Sigma}\Sigma$ remains); but the accent falls on the antepenultimate if both it and the penultimate are light (thus $\acute{\Sigma}\Sigma\Sigma$), unless the preantepenultimate is also light, in which case the accent falls on the penultimate: thus $\Sigma\acute{\Sigma}\Sigma\Sigma$ but $\Sigma\Sigma\acute{\Sigma}\Sigma$.[2] There is one feature in which Arabic, both ancient and modern, is markedly different from Latin, and recalls a characteristic of English referred to above. If the final syllable is 'overweight', as having thoracic + oral arrest ($\sim V^+C = \sim \bar{V}C$)[3] or double oral arrest ($\sim V^oCC = \sim \breve{V}CC$), the accent falls on the *final*. Discussions of Arabic phonology in fact tend to use the terms 'short', 'medium', and 'long' corresponding to our 'light', 'heavy', and 'overweight'.[4]

In Old Indian, the accent was originally a free melodic accent, having the same Indo-European inheritance as the classical Greek accent. But this accent was subsequently lost, and developments in Middle and Modern Indian indicate that it was replaced by a quite distinct fixed dynamic accent. That this existed already in Sanskrit is suggested by certain accentuations prescribed in the *Phiṭsūtra* of Śāntanava, which are at variance with the Vedic, and by such a rule as that (ii.19) 'a heavy syllable of a polysyllabic word (is accented) when followed by one or two light syllables'.[5] The rules for the new accent are in general similar to those of Latin; the accent falls on the penultimate if heavy, and on the antepenultimate if the penultimate is light. But, as in classical Arabic, in words of 3 + syllables, if both penultimate and antepenultimate are light, the accent recedes as far as the preantepenultimate ($\acute{\Sigma}\Sigma\Sigma\Sigma$). The same pattern is largely applicable to the

---

[1] Following statements regarding the colloquial refer more specifically to the Cairo variety: cf. also Lecerf 1969, 170 ff.

[2] Cf. Gairdner 1925, 71 ff; Firth 1948, 138 f; Birkeland 1954, 9; Ferguson 1956, 386; Mitchell 1956, 110 f; 1960, 370 ff; Harrell 1961, 15; Abdo 1969, 82. But, as Mitchell points out (1960, 376), the purely quantitative phonological rules are subject to modification by qualitative factors (e.g. vowel qualities) and by grammatical considerations.

[3] Cf. our 'hypercharacterized' syllables.

[4] Alternatively Mitchell (1960, 372) speaks of non-final syllables in terms of 'short' and 'not-short', and final syllables in terms of 'long' and 'not-long'.

[5] Cf. Jakobi 1899, 567 f.

modern languages. In Hindi, for example, *tarāvaṭ, nirañjan* are stressed on the penultimate (ΣΣ́Σ), but *sumati* on the antepenultimate (Σ́ΣΣ); and the stress recedes to the preantepenultimate in *kámalinī*. There is, however, also a similarity to the Arabic situation in that, as generally stated, a final heavy syllable derived from an Old Indian penultimate heavy syllable bears the stress: thus e.g. Hindi *camā́r* < Skt *carmakā́ras*. This might be seen as a simple historical survival, and descriptively unproductive (just as Latin *illíc* < *illíce*: cf. A 1965, 87); but if the syllable in question is not 'overweight', the stress recedes: thus e.g. Skt *vilámbas* → Hindi *bílam*. This principle also results in the final stress being maintained in recent loans from Persian having similar syllabic patterns: thus e.g. *dīvā́n, pasánd,* and may even lead to transfer of stress, as in *agást* = Eng. *Aúgust*[1] (in English nouns, as we have seen, the final stress rule only applies to ~ V̄C).

Thus, even if the modern Indian rule has historical origins, it has developed into a fully productive synchronic principle. Rather similar considerations may in fact also apply to Arabic. By Abdo (1969, 70 ff.) pre-pausal forms like *kitā́b* 'book' are treated as derived (descriptively) from the context form *kitā́bun* (to which the normal penultimate rule applies), and the deletion of the ending leaves the position of the accent unchanged. But words which in cl. Arabic end in ~ V̂ʔ (long vowel + glottal stop) in pre-pausal position lose the stop in modern dialects; the vowel is then shortened, and the accent recedes to the penultimate (Birkeland 1954, 10 f; Abdo 1969, 76); thus e.g. *ṣaḥrā́ʔ* 'desert' → *ṣáḥra*. The continued final accentuation of forms such as *kitā́b* in modern dialects is therefore not simply a historical relic, but has a descriptive (synchronic) phonological basis related to the current structure of the final syllable.

Apart from the general parallelism of the English, Arabic and Indian systems to that of Latin, their special feature of final accentuation may be suggestive with regard to certain Latin phenomena yet to be discussed.

The Latin accentual rules as stated above apply to 'full' words, as opposed to proclitics or enclitics, which, as already mentioned, form an accentual unity with the full word to which they adhere (e.g. *Caesár-ne* as *lantérna, ád forum* as *árborem*); in other words, the latter normally involve 'syntactical' accentuation. A few uncertainties remain, however, in the case of enclitics (most commonly *-que*). According to the gram-

---

[1] On these developments cf. Jakobi 1913, 220; Turner 1921, 343 f; Master 1925, 83 f; Jaina 1926, 319 ff; Mehrotra 1965, 101 ff; Sharma 1971, 146 f.

marians (A 1965, 87 f.) the accent in such cases always shifts to the last syllable of the full word; thus e.g. Varro (cited by Martianus Capella, iii 272): '...particulas coniunctas, quarum hoc proprium est acuere partes extremas uocum quibus adiunguntur'. This rule implies, for example, *Mūsắque, līmĭnắque*, where the position of the accent in the combination is different from what it would be in a single word of the same syllabic pattern (as e.g. *mŭnĕra, dīmĭdĭus*). But generally the examples which the grammarians actually cite are of the type *uirúmque*, where the accent is the same as for a single word of this pattern (e.g. *relínquo*). It has been suggested (and this seems highly probable) that the extension of the rule to the earlier cases is simply another example of the grammarians' copying of Greek models, since in Greek one has e.g. Μοῦσά τε, χρήματά τε (Tucker 1965, 461; Liénard 1969, 556); and the evidence of verse is strongly against such a general rule. For in the cadence of the hexameter line, where agreement between metrical and accentual patterns is the norm, one commonly finds such cases as *suspéctaque dóna* (just as e.g. *notíssima fáma*).[1] In the case of the type *līminaque* it has been plausibly suggested that the accent remained in the same position as in the isolated full word, i.e. *lĭminaque*; to this Wagener (1904) has added the further hypothesis of a secondary accent on the enclitic (*lĭminaquĕ*), in order to explain such versifications as *liminaque laurusque dei∼*.[2] This primary accentuation is also suggested by such cadence patterns as ∼ *Satúrniaqu(e) árua* (Williams 1950; Soubiran 1966a, 464 ff.).

However, in this last type of combination the enclitic is elided; and it has often been suggested that elision in general could have the effect of causing a regression of accent in cases where the word (or word + enclitic), deprived of its final vowel, would otherwise be anomalously accented. Thus in Plautus, *As.* 394 *ad tonsor(em) ire dixit* an accentuation *tonsór* would be anomalous, and so it is suggested that the accent regresses to the preceding syllable. This suggestion, first explicitly put forward by Hermann (but also perhaps implied by Bentley, who at Terence, *And.* 1 marks *ad scríbendum áppulít*),[3] was accepted by a majority of nineteenth- and twentieth-century scholars (including Fraenkel, e.g. 1928, 14, 268 f.), but does not on the whole seem well founded, as Soubiran in particular has demonstrated (459 ff.).

---

[1] Cf. Kent 1932, 68; Liénard 1969, 554.
[2] Greek influence is, however, here also involved: cf. Collinge 1970, 200, and pp. 219 ff.
[3] 1726, ii; cf. Soubiran, 457 f.

For example, the apocope of final *ĕ* in *illĭc(e)* does *not* lead to an accentuation *illĭc*;[1] elision in many cases probably does *not* imply loss of final vowel but rather coalescence with the following initial (see pp. 145 ff.); and the general rules governing 'resolution' in early Latin verse require that in a line such as Plautus, *As.* 76 *et id ego percŭpĭ(o) obsequi gnato meo* the disyllabic sequence *cŭpĭ* should not be final in the word (by the 'law of the split anapaest': see pp. 167 f.)[2] – so that *percupi(o)* is *not* metrically comparable with e.g. *percupit*.

The arguments in favour of accentual regression are based on the assumption of close agreement in early Latin (scenic) verse between accentual and metrical patterns, which in itself is at least probable; but, unfortunately for the doctrine of regression, if *all* relevant cases of elision are considered, and not selectively cited, such regression is *un*favourable to agreement twice as often as it is favourable (Soubiran, 475). In fact many of the cases in which elision seems to be responsible for a shift of accent may really be cases of *syntactical* accentuation (as *ad scríbend(um) ádpulit*: cf. p. 154), which may have been extended for metrical purposes to less closely connected groups of words (cf. Fraenkel 1928, 352). As Drexler points out (1967, 17 n.17), Plautus, *Stich.* 143 suggests an accentuation *cónsili(a) éloquar*, but *As.* 115 *consíli(a) exórdiar*.

Returning to the hexameter, and the cadence type *Saturniaqu(e) arua*, it is significant that, where no enclitic is involved, as e.g. *Aen.* iii 581 *intremer(e) omnem*, such patterns are extremely rare in more cultivated poetry (this is the only example in Vergil, there is one in Statius, and there are none in e.g. Ovid, Tibullus, Propertius, Lucan).[3] It therefore seems that an accentuation *Satúrniaqu(e)*, *líminaqu(e)* was normal, or at least permissible, for enclitic combinations; and, since it appears *not* to have been acceptable in the type *intremer(e)*, that this accentuation was *not* due to the effect of elision; for if it were, it should equally result in *íntremer(e)*, which there would consequently be no reason for avoiding in the hexameter cadence; the fact that such forms are there avoided indicates that their normal accentuation was *intrémer(e)*.

Soubiran also suggests (466 f.) that a comparable enclitic accentuation may have been permissible in the type *totasque*, viz. as *tótasque* (beside the more normal *totásque*); the evidence for this is seen in such

[1] Cf. Schoell 1876, 60, 140 ff.   [2] Cf. Lindsay 1922, 92, 94; Rossi 1968, 238.
[3] Soubiran 1959; 1966a, 460 f.

'hypermetric' lines as *Geo.* iii 377 ~ *totasqu(e)|||| aduoluere* ~, which are well attested in Vergil (21 cases); for examples *not* involving an enclitic are much rarer (*umor(em)*, *Latinor(um)*, *horrid(a)*, *sulpur(a)*), of which the last two are in any case irrelevant to the question).

The conclusion seems to be, therefore, that full word + enclitic was generally accented as a single word; but that alternative pronunciations were at least conceivable and metrically acceptable, in which the enclitic was treated as more or less separable and so as not affecting the isolate accentuation of the full word.[1]

Reformulation of rules

The traditional formulation of the rule for the location of the Latin accent implies an apparently anomalous situation in so far as an *antepenultimate* light syllable is accentable under the same conditions as a heavy, viz. if followed by a light syllable ($\Sigma\acute{\Sigma}\Sigma$ as $\acute{\Sigma}\Sigma\Sigma$), whereas a *penultimate* light syllable, unlike a heavy, may not be accented, except in disyllabic words ($\Sigma\acute{\Sigma}\Sigma$ but not $\Sigma\acute{\Sigma}\Sigma$). It might be argued that any anomaly in the situation resides in the mere fact of accentuation of a light syllable (cf. A 1965, 86), since, as we have seen (pp. 79 ff.), the general tendency is for stressed syllables to be arrested; and that such accentuation is simply a *pis aller* in the absence of any heavy syllable in the accentable part of the word, and so stands outside the basic system. But a pattern of accentuation so viable in terms of its frequency of occurrence can hardly be considered as in any way 'exceptional', and demands a description and explanation in its own right.[2]

A well-known attempt to simplify and rationalize the positional rule is that of Jakobson (1937a/1962, 259; 1937b/1962, 270; cf. Trubetzkoy 1939/1969, 174; Bell 1970b, 68), which utilizes the concept of the mora, applied not with reference to vowel length (see p. 92) but to syllabic quantity, a light syllable being counted as 1 mora and a heavy syllable as 2. Jakobson's formulation of the rule is that (in words of 2 + syllables)

---

[1] Cf. pp. 25 f., 114, and Soubiran's citation (466 n.1) of the abbreviation *S.P.Q.R.* It has in fact been argued by Tucker (1965) that the 'normal' accentuation was a relatively late development, and that the 'isolate' accentuation was general in Plautus and Terence, citing as evidence the 'iambic shortening' of *égŏn(e) patri*, *ită(e)st*, *uidĕ(s)n(e)*.

[2] A preliminary study from which the following discussion is developed was presented in A 1969.

the accent falls on the syllable which contains the second mora from the end of the word excluding the final syllable; in Trubetzkoy's terms, the accent falls *on* this mora. If we mark each mora by °, these formulations will account for the accentuation of all the relevant patterns, i.e. (a) ΣΣ̈Σ, (b) Σ̈̈Σ̣̈Σ, (c) Σ̣̈Σ̣́Σ. This certainly provides a neat form of statement; but may there not perhaps be in it more of symbolic sleight-of-hand than of phonological validity? The sole justification for setting up the *syllabic* mora in Latin[1] is to explain the location of the accent; yet heavy syllables of which the relevant mora is the *first* element (in (a)) are phonologically identical with heavy syllables of which the relevant mora is the *second* element (in (b)):[2] there are no grounds for distinguishing the *lā* of *lătius* from that of *relātus*, both simply being stressed. If we aim to make phonological statements which are at least capable of reflecting the intuitive processes of the native speaker, it seems hardly probable that a concept which implies different analyses of identical syllables could form the basis of the accentual rules when it is irrelevant elsewhere in the phonology. As has been pointed out by Chomsky & Halle (1965, 122), implicit in Jakobson's more recent phonological theory (concerned with 'distinctive features') is the assumption of a certain 'naturalness', in the sense that 'the rules will apply to classes of segments which can, in general, be easily and simply specified in terms of feature composition'. But from this point of view also the mora-based analysis of Latin accentuation is hardly satisfactory. In an analysis of long *vowels* as comprising 2 morae (as e.g. in Greek), the morae correspond to phonetically homogeneous elements; and the same applies to diphthongs in so far as both elements are vocoidal; but the criterion of homogeneity cannot apply to VC sequences of the type occurring, for instance, in the second syllable of *re.fĕc.tus* or the first syllable of *pŏs.ci.mus*, since the first mora would consist in each case of a vowel but the second of an obstruent.

Having set up the concept of the syllabic mora for the analysis of the Latin accent, Jakobson goes on to identify this as a basis within Latin itself for the metrical equivalence of 1 heavy to 2 light syllables, without recourse to the hypothesis of Greek influence (see pp. 255 ff.). But, apart from the inherent dubiousness of the concept, it does not in any case adequately account for Latin metrical peculiarities in this respect;

---

[1] We are, of course, referring to the language itself, without at this stage considering metrical matters.
[2] Cf. Zirin 1970, 77.

and it is hoped that an alternative analysis of the accentual phenomena will prove also to have greater explanatory power with regard to metrical matters.

Accentual matrices

We may, in the first instance, envisage an accentual 'matrix' consisting of either 1 heavy syllable or 2 light syllables, in which phonetically the stress is of the (in fact most common) 'diminuendo' type (see p. 79), i.e. rising to its peak near the beginning of the matrix. In the case of a heavy syllable this will imply, for example, *relātus* = [re.ˈlā͞a.tus], the arrest of the stress pulse being coordinated with the thoracic arrest of the syllable during the latter part of the vowel; or *refĕctus* = [re.ˈfĕk.tus], where the arrest of the stress is coordinated with the oral arrest of the syllable by the consonant [k]. From the standpoint of 'naturalness', the analysis in terms of morae would be incompatible with such a phonetic assumption, in so far as the dominant mora would sometimes coincide with the minimal point of intensity, e.g. *sáecŭla* = [ˈsā͞i.ku.la] but in mora terms /sā̊i.kŭ.la/.[1] It may be noted that Voegelin, who employs the mora in his description of Tübatulabal stress (1935, 75 f.), with the rule that 'counting backward from the main stress, every second mora is stressed where possible', has to recognize that 'This is not always possible because stress falls on the beginning of the accented vowel, so that an alternate stress will fall on the third mora when the series long vowel (2 morae) – short vowel (1 mora) is followed by a stressed vowel'.

The proposed equivalence for accentual purposes of 1 heavy and 2 light syllables is liable to be seen (mistakenly, as it is hoped to show) as simply another instance of a phenomenon familiar to students of Greek and Latin poetry (in which connexion the term 'mora' is also commonly used) – so familiar that it is sometimes taken for granted as almost a universal truth; as Quintilian says (ix.4.47), 'una enim syllaba ⟨longa⟩ par est ⟨duabus⟩ breuibus...longam esse duorum temporum, breuem unius, etiam pueri sciunt';[2] and more recently Sonnenschein

[1] Zirin (1970) adopts an approach that has much in common with the above (treating ΣΣ or Σ̱ as the 'accentual group', defined as 'the accented syllable and any syllable which falls between it and the final syllable'); but he nevertheless retains the mora concept for the pattern Σ̱ΣΣ, where (78) 'in order to keep the rule simple the antepenult must be considered to consist of ◡◡, e.g. *quaátenus*'.

[2] Cf. Drexler 1967, 12 n.

(1925, 119), 'The substitution of two short syllables for one long is rooted in the rhythmic sense of man'.

Poetry apart, it has been observed that there is 'a tendency in Latin toward a binary rhythm in which short syllables tend to occur in pairs' (Zirin 1970, 77; and cf. especially Safarewicz 1936, 73 ff.). A notable case is provided by the dichotomy of 4th-conjugation verbs into those which have a stem ending in short *ĭ* (which → *ĕ* before *r*) and those which have long *ī*; thus on the one hand e.g. *căpĕre, făcĕre*, and on the other e.g. *audīre, dormīre, ăpĕrīre, sĕpĕlīre*. There is clearly a relationship between the length of the stem vowel and the quantitative pattern of the root; in most cases the stem vowel is short when the root has a single light syllable, but long if the root has a heavy syllable or two light syllables.[1] As an explanation of such a *linguistic* distinction between the types *căpĕ(re)* ($\Sigma\Sigma$) and *ăpĕrī(re)* ($\Sigma\Sigma\Sigma$), one obviously cannot accept the suggestion made by Kent (1946, 99) that the long vowel was necessary to the latter, but not the former, 'to avoid a succession of three short syllables, which made metrical difficulties'. A more convincing explanation is that *ăpĕ(rīre)* ($\Sigma\Sigma$) is equivalent to *au(dīre)* (Σ) and non-equivalent to *că(pere)* (Σ), and that a light syllable as in *căpere* tends to occur in combination with a following light syllable, thereby requiring a short stem-vowel. A similar situation has also been seen in the distribution of the 2nd-conjugation perfect ending in -*ŭi*, which is almost invariable where the root then has a single light syllable (as e.g. *mŏnŭi, dĕcŭit*), but is not normal in other cases, which mostly have perfects in -*si* (as e.g. *auxi, mulsi*).[2]

It may, however, be noted that e.g. *impĕdīre, fulgŭrīre* also have long stem-vowels, in spite of the fact that the syllable of the root preceding the stem vowel is light (as in *căpĕre*) and is not preceded by another light syllable (as in *ăpĕrīre*). The possibility therefore arises that the pattern of *căpĕre* etc. is due not simply to the fact that the radical syllable immediately preceding the stem vowel is light, but rather to the fact that it is in some common forms light *and accented*,[3] e.g. *căpis, căpit, căpio* – which is not the case with any of the other classes of verb (e.g. *audis, ăpĕris, impĕdis*).[4] In which event, it is not so

---

[1] Cf. Niedermann 1908; for exceptions see Graur 1939.

[2] Cf. Burger 1928, 22 ff; Safarewicz 1936, 76.

[3] Viz. in disyllabic forms and in trisyllabic forms whose second vowel is in hiatus and so short regardless of its original length.

[4] It has been argued that in some cases of the type *căpĕre* the short stem-vowel is inherited from Indo-European (cf. Buck 1948, 272); but the matter is much disputed,

much a case of the binary 'cohesiveness' of ΣΣ, but rather of Σ́Σ; that is, it has an accentual and not simply a quantitative basis.[1]

A comparable cohesiveness of an accented light syllable with a following light syllable may be seen in the shift of accent from classical to colloquial Arabic. For whereas Σ́ΣΣ → ΣΣ́Σ, Σ́ΣΣ remains unchanged; and whereas Σ́ΣΣΣ → ΣΣ́ΣΣ, Σ́ΣΣΣ → ΣΣ́ΣΣ.[2] If one treats other than an 'overweight' final syllable as light (cf. p. 157 and n.4), this may be interpreted as indicating that, unlike Σ́Σ, the sequence Σ́Σ is a unit which, like Σ̆ (phonetically [Σ̄̆]), must either as such retain the accent or lose it: the peak of stress cannot be shifted from one element of the unit to the other, i.e. from [Σ́Σ] to [ΣΣ́], any more than it could be changed from [Σ̄̆] to [Σ̆̄].[3]

It is in fact doubtful whether one can establish in Latin a simple binariness of ΣΣ, or an equivalence of ΣΣ to Σ, without an accentual basis. One's tendency to believe in such a simple binariness no doubt arises from the so familiar *metrical* equivalence of ΣΣ to Σ; this is a feature more particularly of dactylic verse, where dactyls and spondees are for the most part freely interchangeable, and has no positive relationship with accent. In *árma uirúmque cánō*, for example, the two ΣΣ sequences comprise (i) a post-accentual + a pre-accentual syllable, and (ii) a post-accentual + an accented syllable. Moreover, as is well known, there is an increasing tendency in the development of the Latin hexa-

and it seems in any case that the type has been extended in Latin in accordance with purely Latin phonological characteristics (note occasional survivals, as Lucr., i 71 *cupīret*, where the analogy of *cŭpĭs* etc. has not been extended).

[1] The equivalence of *ăpĕ(rīs)* to *áu(dīs)* etc. in certain respects, though undeniable, is in fact irrelevant to this particular problem; for, as we have seen, the long stem-vowel also occurs in the type *impĕ(dīs)*, where no such equivalence is involved.

[2] Thus in Mitchell's formulation (1960, 374) preceding word-boundary has the same function descriptively as preceding heavy syllable.

[3] The principle applies also to words in which the old accent was yet further regressive; thus (based on Mitchell's examples (1960) of the Egyptian pronunciation of classical forms):

Σ́ΣΣΣΣ → ΣΣΣ́ΣΣ, but Σ́ΣΣΣΣ → ΣΣ́ΣΣΣ;

Σ́ΣΣΣΣΣ → ΣΣΣΣ́ΣΣ, but Σ́ΣΣΣΣΣ → ΣΣ́ΣΣΣΣ.

These apparently contradictory shift-rules can be easily accounted for by treating Σ̆ and Σ́Σ as accentual units, and stating that the stress progresses *in steps of a unit* as far as it can, thus:

Σ́ΣΣΣΣ → ΣΣ́ΣΣΣ → ΣΣΣ́ΣΣ;

Σ́ΣΣΣΣ → ΣΣΣ́ΣΣ (and can shift no further);

Σ́ΣΣΣΣΣ → ΣΣΣ́ΣΣΣ → ΣΣΣΣΣ́Σ;

Σ́ΣΣΣΣΣ → ΣΣΣ́ΣΣΣ → ΣΣΣΣΣ́Σ (and can shift no further).

meter to achieve agreement between metrical and accentual patterns in the cadence of the line, as e.g. in *prīmụs ạb ọ̄rīs*. As such agreement suggests, the metrical pattern is a 'falling' pattern, in the sense that the 'strong' part of the foot (which in the cadence is reinforced by the linguistic accent) is the initial portion; and this is invariably a heavy syllable; so that the equivalence of $\Sigma\Sigma$ to Σ is a characteristic only of the 'weak' part of the foot. In fact the cadence type *Geo.* iii 84 $\sim et$ *tremịt ạrtus*, where the sequence $\Sigma\Sigma$ is represented by an accentual unit (*trémị(t)*), becomes progressively avoided in cultivated verse, and has been seen by Soubiran (1959, 45 ff.) as generally serving special expressive purposes, notably an 'effet de mouvement subit et brusque', as also in the case of the similarly accented (elided) $\sim intrémer(e)$ *ómnem* (cf. p. 160). It is important to remember also that in the hexameter the basic form of the foot is $\Sigma\Sigma\Sigma$ (as generally required in V) and *not* $\Sigma\Sigma$ (which in itself forms no pattern: cf. p. 98); Σ is therefore a substitute for $\Sigma\Sigma$ and not vice versa; in other words, it is a case of contraction and not resolution.

But we have been dealing with classical patterns based closely on Greek models. In the earlier hexameters of Ennius one does find a very few cases in which (in I) $\Sigma\Sigma$ is substituted for Σ in the strong position (e.g. *Ann.* 490 *capitibu(s) nutantis* $\sim$);[1] here we do have resolution (of a heavy syllable into 2 light), and in the iambic and trochaic metres of scenic verse, as in Greek, such resolution is common.

The conditions of resolution are much more strictly governed than those of contraction, both in Greek (see pp. 316 ff.) and in Latin. In Plautus and Terence resolution may be applied both to the strong and to the weak part of any foot except the last. Unlike in hexameters, there is a tendency (though its precise extent is arguable) for accentual patterns to coincide with metrical patterns throughout the line,[2] i.e. for accent to coincide with the 'strong' part of the foot.[3] It is probably this factor which accounts for the extended tolerance of spondaic feet in Latin iambic and trochaic metres, these being admitted even in the second feet of iambic metra (and the first of trochaic), where they are not permitted in Greek; for 'it is *highly* significant that a spondee in this position *rarely* involves word-accent on the originally short element' (i.e. the weak position: Raven 1965, 37).

[1] Also perhaps in *Ciris* 434 *coralio fragili et lạcrịmoso electro* (Maas 1957).
[2] Excluding the first foot (cf. Drexler 1965).
[3] Here definable as that part of the foot which may not consist of a single light syllable, i.e. initial in trochees, final in iambics.

Thus the pattern $\Sigma\acute{\Sigma}$ is here normal in iambics, but not $\acute{\Sigma}\Sigma$; in other words, the patternless quantitative succession of heavy syllables in the metre is given form by accentual placement in composition. This tendency to accentual/metrical coincidence displays a particularly significant facet in relation to resolution. For in the strong position, when $\Sigma\Sigma$ is substituted for Σ, 'there is a strong tendency for word-accent to coincide with the first syllable...and *not* to fall on the syllable immediately preceding or following this point – i.e. $\times\overset{\frown}{\smile}$ is regular, $\overset{\prime}{\times}\overset{\frown}{\smile}$ and $\times\overset{\frown}{\smile}\acute{}$ are avoided' (Raven 1965, 45).[1] It seems certain that this peculiarity also must have a linguistic rather than a purely metrical basis, since it relates not to the quantitative metrical pattern of the line but rather to the prosodic pattern of the composition (see especially Drexler 1965, 21; 1967, 45). In other words, since the unresolved strong position tends to coincide with accent, $\acute{\Sigma}$ (phonetically [$\overset{\prime}{\Sigma}$]) is normally substituted by $\acute{\Sigma}\Sigma$, a formulation which further underlines the accentual nature of the equivalence.[2]

Substitution of $\Sigma\Sigma$ for the *weak* position is not a characteristic of Greek tragic verse; but in Greek comedy anapaests may substitute for any but the final foot in iambics (cf. pp. 330 ff.); and in early Latin scenic verse such substitution may occur even in combination with a resolved strong position, producing a proceleusmatic foot ($\Sigma\Sigma\Sigma\Sigma$). Such extension might be viewed as in some sense a 'licence', but restrictions on the conditions of its occurrence could in part at least reflect even here some features of an accentual basis. In Plautus and Terence the 'rule' has been observed (going back to Hermann, Ritschl, and Lachmann) that a resolved weak position in iambic and trochaic metres should not consist, in part or whole, of the end of a longer word; thus a resolved iambic foot is not normally composed as follows: $\sim\Sigma|\Sigma\Sigma,\Sigma|\sim$ or $\sim\Sigma|\Sigma,\Sigma\Sigma|\sim$; the rule is commonly referred to as the 'Law of the split anapaest' (though it also applies to the proceleusmatic sequence, with resolved second element as well). Exceptions do indeed occur, but they are relatively infrequent, and most common in the beginning of the line.[3] Since no such avoidance is found in the anapaests

---

[1] The admission of senarius endings of the type $\sim$*dicere uolui femur* need not conflict with this rule; $\sim$*re uo*$\sim$ need not here constitute a resolved strong position; $\sim$*re*, in spite of its light quantity, may alone fill the position, as appears to be permitted at this point in the line (cf. e.g. $\sim$*fingere fallaciam*): Exon 1906, 34; Fraenkel 1928, 262 ff; Drexler 1965, 58 ff; 1967, 37.

[2] Cf. Cole 1969, 22 ff. on the Saturnian.

[3] Cf. Maurenbrecher 1899, 25 ff; Drexler 1965; 1967, 41 f.

of anapaestic metres (where the $\Sigma\Sigma$ is basic in the weak position), there is clearly some operative factor other than purely quantitative metrical structure; and an accentual factor may possibly be relevant (cf. Exon 1906, 31). For the effect of the rule is to exclude resolution where the first syllable of the $\Sigma\Sigma$ sequence would be post-accentual, since the word-ending would be accented $\sim\Sigma\Sigma\Sigma$ or $\sim\Sigma\Sigma$; we have already seen (p. 160) that this rule does not apply where the word ends in two light syllables *plus an elision*, for the accent in such cases will fall on the first of the two remaining light syllables, as e.g. $\sim per$-*cúpi̯(o) obsequi* $\sim$. Some of the more common exceptions, e.g. of the type $\sim$ *inter e̯os* $\sim$, may be only apparent, and explainable by syntactical accentuation (*intér eos*).[1] In fact in a large number of cases the resolution $\Sigma\Sigma$ of weak position is, like that of strong position, accented $\Sigma\Sigma$; this is the case if the resolution consists of a pyrrhic word, or part of an anapaestic(-ending) word (or syntactical group); and in some other cases, where the $\Sigma\Sigma$ is pre-accentual, as e.g. in *regiǫ́nibus*, it is possible that the first syllable bore a *secondary* stress (see pp. 188 ff.).

Since a weak position filled by a single heavy syllable shows no tendency to be accented (indeed rather the reverse, since such a tendency would work against the clear preference for coincidence of accent and strong position), the accentual peculiarities of the resolved weak position can hardly be due to any deliberate attempt to procure coincidence of accent with this part of the foot. It could rather be the case that only by virtue of their accentual unity are the two light syllables felt appropriately to substitute for a heavy; and that when such substitution is extended from the strong position (where the unresolved heavy also tends to be accented), there remains nevertheless a feeling for the accentual basis of their coherence, which precludes such substitution where it could not possibly form an accentual unit, viz. in post-accentual position. In many cases a requirement of accentual unity in the weak position must conflict with the tendency to accentual/metrical coincidence in the strong position; for example, a metrical pattern $\Sigma\Sigma\Sigma$ manifested in iambics by $\sim |fa̯ci̯at|$ (*bene*) (Plautus, *As.* 945), whilst satisfying the 'split anapaest' rule, apparently thereby fails to achieve accentual/metrical coincidence, since the normal accentuation is *fáciat*. But here, as perhaps in many such cases, the syntactical accent of the word group is likely to have been *faciát bene*,[2] i.e. the same pattern

---

[1] For other exceptions see Drexler 1967, 41.
[2] Cf. Fraenkel 1928, 48.

as in *Poen.* 1216 ~ *bęnę fęceris.* In which case (leaving aside the possibility of secondary stress) one might conclude that the requirement of cohesion between the two light syllables in weak position could be satisfied by their *potential* accentual unity (i.e. in other syntactical environments).

Whilst the above provides a possible explanation of the 'split anapaest' rule in Latin terms, it should at the same time be remembered that a similar rule also applied to the Greek comic iambic trimeter. The Greek metre, like Latin, admits anapaests to the even as well as the odd feet, but, unlike Latin, does not admit spondees to the even feet. In the weak position of the even feet, therefore, the two light syllables in Greek can hardly be substitutes for a heavy – so that the rule may have a quite different basis from that suggested above for Latin; and its strict observance in the Greek models, especially Menander (see Lindsay 1922, 88; Maas 1966, 69), might help to explain the rarity of exceptions in Latin, as also some of the cases where an accentual explanation is dubious. But the equivalent resolution in trochaics (dactyl for trochee or spondee) is almost unknown in Greek (p. 330), and so can hardly account for the Latin rule in its application to this metre.

In general it seems clear that in early Latin scenic verse, as in the language itself, the equivalence is not just $\Sigma\Sigma = \Sigma$, but basically $\acute{\Sigma}\Sigma = \acute{\Sigma}$; it is an accentual phenomenon, and not simply a quantitative matter as in the Greek hexameter or its derivative Latin form.

When this equivalence is interpreted in phonetic terms, it raises an important point of general principle. For the arrest of a stress pulse tends to be coordinated with the arrest of a syllabic pulse. In the case of an accented monosyllabic matrix $\acute{\Sigma}$ ($= [\grave{\acute{\Sigma}}]$) this presents no problem; but it is otherwise in the case of the disyllabic matrix $\acute{\Sigma}\Sigma$. For if the stress were arrested in the first syllable, it would most typically be associated with an arrest of that syllable; but an oral arrest in the case of a word such as *ágere* would result in ['ag.ge.re], and thereby neutralize a distinction between short and long consonants which was phonologically relevant in Latin (cf. *ággere*); similarly a thoracic arrest, with lengthening of the vowel, would result in a neutralization of the distinction between e.g. *uéneris* and *uēneris*. And the evidence of verse shows that no such lengthenings took place. There remains the possibility of ' staccato' stress (pp. 80 f.), with a rapid and independent arrest involving no significant vowel-lengthening; but if this were normally the case in

Latin, it is not clear why Σ̌ should not behave accentually just as Σ, e.g. why a penultimate light syllable should not be accented, or why light monosyllables should not occur. One is led, therefore, to examine the hypothesis that Σ̌ was indeed unarrested, and so conforms to our general dichotomy of heavy vs light syllables on the basis of the presence or absence of arrest; in which case, if we exclude the 'staccato' mode, we have to envisage the possibility of an arrest of stress *after* the accented light syllable: and since (in words of 2+ syllables) Σ̌ occurs only in the environment Σ̌Σ, and not Σ̌Σ,[1] more particularly in combination with a following *light* syllable.

Disyllabic stress

On the phonetic level, then, we have to consider the idea of a *disyllabic stress pulse* operating on the disyllabic accentual matrix; symbolically, if we were to mark the arrest of stress by a grave accent, the mono-syllabic matrix would then imply [Σ̀] and the disyllabic matrix [Σ́Σ̀]. This rather unconventional suggestion calls for more extended discussion.[2]

The idea that a stressed light syllable is in some way 'incomplete' is already found in Sonnenschein's explanation of forms like *cáue* filling a resolved strong position in early Latin verse (1911, 10): 'When the speaker or reader...is confronted with the short syllable *ca-*, he cannot stop there but is compelled by the demands of his ear (which expects a long syllable) to take in the next syllable as part of the rise.' More recently and objectively Kuryłowicz (1948/1960, 206 f; 1949/1960, 294 ff; 1958, 328 f.) has referred to the unaccentability of a single light syllable in Latin, correlated with the absence of light monosyllabic words, and has proposed this as an explanation of the substitutability of Σ̌Σ for Σ̌ in early Latin verse. Kuryłowicz also draws attention to a similar phenomenon in some types of old Germanic verse, associated with similar linguistic conditions, and suggests (1948/1960, 207) that this indissoluble unity of an 'ictus'-bearing light syllable with the following syllable is a characteristic transferred from

---

[1] On disyllabic words see pp. 185 f.

[2] Cf. Fraenkel's hint (1928, 269 n.4), not further pursued, of the phonetic inadequacy of a marking of the type Σ́Σ. The closest approximation to this idea, under the well-chosen title 'pyrrhic accent', is found in FitzHugh 1923, amid a welter of otherwise nonsensical matter (cf. Kalinka 1935, 312 for recognition that 'the occasional fertile seed may have strayed among the wildly luxuriant weeds' of this author's works).

the accentuation of the spoken language; he further emphasizes, as we have done, that the metrical equivalence $\dot{\Sigma}\Sigma = \dot{\Sigma}$ based on this is something quite different from the equivalence $\Sigma\Sigma = \Sigma$ in classical Latin verse, which is taken over from Greek and is applicable only in the weak position. Kuryłowicz therefore considers words of the type *páter* as 'syllabic compounds', structurally intermediate between monosyllables and disyllabic words with heavy first syllable.

The phonetic (as opposed to phonological) literature on stress is less extensive than one could wish. But there are at least some indications from living languages that the model of a disyllabic stress pulse for Latin is not phonetically unrealistic. One may begin with Sievers (1901, 209), who claimed to have observed, for both German and English, that disyllabic words with short vowel in the first syllable followed by a single consonant (e.g. *fasse*, *hammer*) are 'expiratorily monosyllabic' but contain two 'sonorant' syllables, i.e. that they constitute (225) 'sonorant syllable groups with percursive expiration' ('Schallsilbengruppen mit durchlaufender Exspiration'); and that the syllabic boundary in such cases falls within the intervocalic consonant, which thus belongs to both syllables.[1] Sievers also mentions that speakers of some other languages (e.g. Italian, Russian, Greek) have difficulty in reproducing this mode of utterance, and tend, in accordance with their native speech-habits, to place the syllabic boundary before the intervocalic consonant; whereas such a division in English and German mostly occurs only when a 'weak' syllable is followed by a 'strong', or vice versa (e.g. *appeár*, *befínden*; *seáling*, *Seéle*). It will be noted that the non-Germanic languages referred to do not have significant distinctions of vowel length, and are thus free to lengthen the vowel of the stressed syllable in order to provide a thoracic arrest (cf. pp. 79 f.).

More recently Newman (1946, 183 f.) has contrasted words of the types *veto(ed)* vs *echo(ed)* ([vii ~] vs [e ~]) in terms of a distinction 'full middle stress' vs 'sonorous weak stress' in the second syllable, and has observed an accompanying distinction of aspirated vs unaspirated in the intervocalic consonant.[2] Durand (1955, 233) has noted that in a word such as *Bobby* there is a rise of abdominal pressure on the initial [b] which then falls over the whole of the rest of the word, and concludes that one could consider the word as composed of a single syllable, even though this would be contrary to generally received

[1] Cf. also Eliason 1942, 146.
[2] For tenseness distinctions in other types of consonant cf. Hoard 1971.

opinion. And in experiments on air flow during speech, with English-speaking subjects, Draper, Ladefoged & Whitteridge (1960, 1842) have observed persistence of activity after the stressed syllable, which has the effect of 'checking the expulsion of air by the elastic recoil of the thorax'.

In Czech, it was noted by Broch (1911, 295 ff.) that the 'stress-wave' tends to extend into the following syllable (or part of it) in the case of words beginning $(C)\breve{V}CV \sim$, i.e. with light first syllable; this contrasts with the types $(C)\breve{V}CV \sim$ and $(C)\breve{V}CCV \sim$, i.e. with heavy first syllable, where the stress is completed within that syllable. On this situation Broch commented (297) that it is evidently difficult for the stress to be limited to a light first syllable. Czech is also referred to by Chlumský (1935, 99) as exemplifying a distinction between syllables and 'rhythmic, respiratory groups', for which Brücke (1871) is credited with the first observation. And Vendryes concludes from a study of the Germanic and Czech phenomena that 'the place of intensity is the long syllable; length attracts intensity and intensity creates length; when, as a result of special conditions, intensity is attracted to a short syllable without being able to lengthen it, it seeks to resume its rights by annexing to itself the whole or part of the following syllable' (1902, 132).

In Finnish, Sovijärvi (1958, 364) notes that when the first (stressed) syllable is 'short', a weaker 'beat phase' (see p. 76) also occurs in the second syllable, whereas this does not generally happen if the first syllable is 'long'. With this one may compare the analysis of Dutch speech-rhythm by Boer (1918), who states that, whereas a 'long' stressed syllable may be followed by another stressed syllable, this cannot occur in the case of a 'short' stressed syllable; so that, whereas a sequence $\underset{\sim}{\Sigma}\Sigma$ may constitute two 'speech measures' $(\acute{\Sigma}\acute{\Sigma})$, a sequence $\underset{\sim}{\Sigma}\Sigma$ may only constitute one $(\acute{\underset{\sim}{\Sigma}}\Sigma)$.

The examples cited in the various languages to illustrate such extensions of the stress process into the syllable following a stressed light syllable tend predominantly to have following syllables which are in some sense 'weak'; and for Czech Chlumský notes that in disyllables of the type *nevím*[1] 'I don't know', where the second syllable in the literary language has a long vowel, the colloquial tends to shorten it (1928, xi of résumé). This pattern of co-occurrence, with stressed light syllable followed by 'weak' syllable, is also seen in certain aspects of the

---

[1] The acute in Czech orthography indicates length, not stress (which is on the initial syllable).

descriptive phonology of English. There is, for example, the 'laxing' rule as stated by Chomsky & Halle (50 ff: rule 79): V → [–tense] /—CV̆CV (cf. also 180: rule 19b), i.e. the stressed vowel becomes lax if followed by an unstressed (and also lax) vowel in the next syllable – but not otherwise: thus e.g. *profånĭty, serĕnĭty, derĭvătive* (beside *profane, serene, derive*). Chomsky & Halle also refer to the alternative (American) pronunciations of the first two syllables of *presentation* (cf. p. 18 n.), with (a) lax stressed vowel /e/ + reduced vowel /ə/, and (b) tense stressed vowel /ii/ + unreduced vowel /e/; and they consider the failure of the laxing rule to operate in (b) as part of 'a rule of great generality' (161 n.123). They further note the laxing seen in the first syllables of disyllabic words with final close vowels, as *mĕnu, vălue, tĭssue, nĕphew* (195), as well as *pĭty, cĭty* (245 n.6); laxing is not 'normal' in disyllables, and Chomsky & Halle propose to deal with such cases by treating the finals as /ue/, /eɛ/ (with subsequent 'e-elision'), thereby converting the words into trisyllables, where the laxing rule will apply.[1] From the phonetic standpoint, however, it may be worth noting that (in my own pronunciation, at least) the final vowel in such cases is normally lax (i.e. [ˈmenju] etc: also [kənˈtinju]), and that in the one exception noted by Chomsky & Halle, *Hebrew*,[2] where the first vowel is tense, the second vowel in my pronunciation is also tense, i.e. [ˈhiibruu].[3] In words like *ávenue, révenue, résidue*, where the final vowel is not preceded by a stressed V̆C, my pronunciation (supported by Jones 1967) is generally with tense [uu].[4]

Another cognate matter is incidentally referred to by Chomsky & Halle in connexion with the non-reduction (e.g. to /ə/) of the final vowel of a word like *climax*, 'because of the tense vowel in the preceding syllable' (146 n.100); they point out the existence (in American English) of variants such as /ǽrəb/ vs /éiræb/ for *Arab*, i.e. lax + reduced vs tense + full vowel,[5] and cite J. L. Fidelholtz as having pointed out 'this minor regularity'.[6] Fidelholtz has enlarged on this point in correspondence, and has stated as a broad general rule that in disyllabic

---

[1] Cf. also Halle & Keyser, 79 f.   [2] See also p. 195 n. (on *guru*).

[3] Jones (1967, s.vv.) indicates some of the examples with final [u(:)], i.e. optional length, but Hebrew only with [u:].

[4] Note also noun *áttribute* with ~[u:t] beside verb *attribute* with (optional) ~[ut].

[5] Cf. Kenyon & Knott 1944, s.v.

[6] Cf. Halle & Keyser, 71 f; also paper announced by Fidelholtz for LSA Annual Meeting 1970 under the title 'Why *Arab* may rhyme with *scarab* and *Ahab*, but not *dare grab* or *may rub*'; and his 'English vowel reduction', unpublished paper MIT 1967, cited by Halle & Keyser, 184.

words lax vowel in the second syllable does not reduce if the first syllable is (in Chomsky & Halle's terms: see p. 51) a 'strong cluster' – in our terminology, 'heavy': thus e.g. *matrix, syntax, wombat, incest*; but that it does reduce if the first syllable is a 'weak cluster', i.e. light: thus e.g. *cherub, method, nomad* (/nɔ́məd/; compare also the alternative /nóʊmæd/ without reduction).[1] He notes also that in words with tense vowel[2] in the final syllable stress shifts to the first syllable if it is heavy (thus e.g. *céntaur, túrmoil, réptile*), but if not, not (thus e.g. *divíne, maríne, cigár*: contrast (American) variant /síigaar/).

Examples such as those cited above are relatable to the intuitions described by Abercrombie (1964b, 218 f.): 'There is felt to be something anomalous in a syllable which is stressed and yet short, followed by an unstressed one which is long...My impression is that nowadays there are some types of English where Type A (sc. the 'foot' ♩ ♪) is not found.' We shall return to this tendency in English subsequently.

The descriptive phonology of English thus points to a special connexion between stressed light syllables and weak vowels in following syllables, whereas no such special connexion applies where the stressed syllable is heavy. The descriptive rules are, as commonly, paralleled by historical rules of sound change, which naturally have been discussed by linguists of earlier date, both for English and German (though we shall concentrate on the former). In connexion with Modern English loans from French, Sweet, for instance, discusses the tendency to shorten long vowels (or keep stressed short vowels from being lengthened) when followed by a single consonant and a weak vowel (1891, 297): e.g. *method, cavern* (beside *cave*), *pleasure* (beside *please*); and he observes more generally (299) that 'the combination short strong (i.e. stressed) vowel + short consonant occurs in English only before a weak vowel': thus in e.g. *filling, lesser, many, cupboard*, and, with 'syllabic consonant' in the second syllable, *cattle, written, trouble*. In Late Middle English (Sweet 1891, 257) short vowels before a single consonant followed by another vowel were normally lengthened, as e.g. in *nāme, mēte* (< Early Mid.E. *ă, ĕ*), but are often preserved in

---

[1] Exceptions involve e.g. words ending in a single non-obstruent consonant, where reduction is general (*nasal, urban, nectar*, etc.); similarly mostly with *u* = [ə] in final syllable (e.g. *Venus, eunuch, bismuth*).

For *nomad* Jones 1967 (ed. Gimson) surprisingly gives ['nəuməd] and ['nɔmæd], where earlier editions (as 9th, 1948) give the (in my observation) more normal alternatives noted above.

[2] +C (see p. 156).

Late as well as Early Mid.E. before a single consonant followed by *i*
or by *e* + liquid/nasal, as e.g. in *măni, pĕni, bŏdi; cŏper, sădel, sĕven*.
This 'back-shortening', as he calls it, Sweet attributes to the length
being shifted to the final vowel or syllabic consonant; this dubious
explanation he attempts to support by the observation that in a 'drawled'
pronunciation of words like *pity* (cf. Sweet 1891, 300; Luick 1897,
440; Sonnenschein 1925, 136 n.) the lengthening is thrown on to the
final (Sweet ·*pitii*). Such a phenomenon, however, could be equally well
explained by treating the 'drawl' as an extension of the accentual
matrix, which in the case of a heavy, monosyllabic matrix would be
applied to the end of that syllable (e.g. in a word like *party* → ['paaa.ti]),
but in the case of a disyllabic matrix to the end of its terminal syllable.
A reminiscence of Sweet's hypothesis is found in the explanation
proposed by Eliason 1939 and Eliason & Davis 1939 to explain the
failure of the first vowel to lengthen in e.g. *body, heaven, dinner,
baron*, and the actual shortening in e.g. *sorry, devil, linen, other*. This
situation is attributed to a secondary stress on the final syllable; but
there is no clear evidence for this, and indeed, where more than minimal
stress does occur on the final syllable, as in e.g. *climax, peacock*, the
first vowel is *not* shortened, and it has to be admitted (Eliason, 79)
that 'the historical evidence seems to be somewhat at variance with the
experimental data for the failure of vowel lengthening in type $\overset{\prime}{\times} \overset{\smile}{\times}$'.[1]

It has also been suggested that the failure of the lengthening rule in
these cases is ultimately due to inflexional paradigms in which trisyllabic forms (with regular short vowel) would alternate with disyllabic
forms, i.e. **bāron:bărones* → *băron:bărones*; cf. Eliason & Davis
1939, 51 ff; Chomsky & Halle, 253). One need not deny the support
of such analogical models, but it does not seem that they are a necessary
condition for the phenomena in question. It is true that the non-
lengthening is not regular (e.g. *bācon* beside *mŭtton*), and that the
conditions of variation are not clearly established, but it does seem to
reflect a tendency that recurs, in both native and borrowed forms, at all
periods of the English language. Already in Anglo-Saxon the neuter
plural ending ~*u*, which is dropped after a heavy syllable (e.g. *hūs*
'houses', *folc* 'nations'), remains if the preceding syllable is light
(e.g. *scĭpu* 'ships'); similarly in masc. sing. *sŭnu* 'son', fem. sing.
căru 'care' (beside *hand*, etc.); and ~*u* < ~*w* survives in e.g. *sĭnu*
'sinew' but is lost in *mǣd* 'meadow' (cf. pl. *mǣdwa*): Sweet 1891,

[1] Cf. also Bliss 1953, 36 ff.

302 ff; Abercrombie 1964b, 218 f. This indicates that the final short vowel survives by virtue of a close accentual unity with a preceding light syllable, which does not apply where the preceding syllable is heavy.[1] There is admittedly nothing anomalous about a form like *bācon*; but in the light of the characteristics we have noted, the long vowel is not essential to the manifestation of accent when followed by a weak final syllable.

In dealing with similar phenomena Luick (1898, 350) speaks of words like *body* as having short stressed vowel with 'percursive' expiration (cf. p. 171), as against the monosyllabically stressed first syllable of *greedy* (Luick 1897, 440 distinguishes such cases as having 'acute' vs 'circumflex' accentuation respectively). He also treats similarly the shortening seen in e.g. *crĭminal, sĕverity* (vs *crime, severe*) – 'although they are perceived acoustically as two syllables, they form expiratorily only one'. Luick (1898, 352) follows Sievers (cf. 1901, 225) in suggesting that in such cases we have 'stark geschnittene Akzent', i.e. in which the consonant articulation intervenes while the vowel is still at the syllabic peak; and he further notes the subsequent tendency in trisyllabic words towards syncope of the second short vowel, as e.g. *butler, bodkin* < Mid.E. *boteler, bodekin*, which, by closing the syllable, produces a heavy first syllable with monosyllabic stress.

There are thus clear indications – phonetic and phonological, descriptive and historical – that the idea of a disyllabic stress matrix is not an unnatural one; that in such cases the first syllable is light (unarrested); and that there is a preference for the second syllable to be in some sense 'weak'. The hypothesis of two light syllables as the alternative stress matrix in Latin is thus also in accordance with tendencies found elsewhere. A possible phonetic motivation for the preference regarding the second syllable may be seen in the tendency (already assumed for single heavy syllables) to avoid 'hypercharacterization'. In the disyllabic matrix the peak of stress falls on the short (lax) vowel of its first syllable, which is the nucleus of the matrix; the vowel of the second syllable then functions as an accompaniment of (thoracic) arrest. If this vowel is short, the combination of the short in the first syllable and the short in the second is equivalent to a long vowel in the monosyllabic matrix (of which the latter part accompanies the

---

[1] This is part of a more general tendency of West Germanic to syncope of short close vowels after heavy stressed syllables: cf. further Boer 1918; Kuryłowicz 1949/1960, 296.

thoracic arrest). A long vowel (or diphthong) in the second syllable would therefore produce the equivalent of an 'overlong' vowel or diphthong – which is anomalous, involving a prolongation of the vowel beyond the extent required for thoracic arrest.[1] The closure of the second syllable by one or more consonants would also have a 'hypercharacterizing' effect (cf. pp. 66, 141); one need not, however, anticipate that the tendencies against such an effect (involving a consonant after the thoracic arrest) would be as strong as against the prolongation of a vowel beyond the arrest. In fact the historical reductions seen in single hypercharacterized syllables of the type $\sim V^+C$ are far from universal, and tend more particularly to apply to cases where the consonant is of 'sonant' type (liquid or nasal), as e.g. in Greek *γνων.τες → γνόν.τες*, Latin **amān.tem → amăn.tem*. For purposes of classical Latin accentuation both thoracically and orally arrested syllables ($\sim V^+$ and $\sim V^oC = \sim \bar{V}$ and $\sim \breve{V}C$) are indeed equally excluded as second elements of the disyllabic matrix; but we shall also encounter evidence in certain types of Latin for a difference in treatment between the two categories (pp. 182 ff.).

If the hypothesis proposed for Latin is adopted, i.e. if the accentual matrix is either monosyllabic [$\overset{\circ}{\Sigma}$] or disyllabic [$\overset{\circ}{\Sigma}\overset{\circ}{\Sigma}$], one may consider a reformulation of the rule for the location of the classical Latin accent. For words of 2+ syllables it may now be stated as a simple rule of progression: THE ACCENT OCCUPIES THE LAST MATRIX IN THE WORD, EXCLUSIVE OF THE FINAL SYLLABLE.

This rule will generate word-final sequences possessing the following patterns of relationship between stress and quantity (and only these):

(a) $\Sigma\overset{\circ}{\Sigma}\Sigma$
(b) $\overset{\circ}{\Sigma}\Sigma\Sigma$
(c) $\overset{\prime}{\Sigma}\overset{\circ}{\Sigma}\Sigma$

A pattern of the type $\Sigma\overset{\circ}{\Sigma}\overset{\prime}{\Sigma}$, for example, is precluded by that part of the rule which excludes the final syllable from the matrix. The generated patterns are in full accordance with the data, as also are the exclusions.

For monosyllabic words the rule could be made to apply by adding to the second clause the proviso: IN WORDS OF MORE THAN MATRIX

---

[1] Note that the 'contraction' of two vowels in juncture (e.g. in Sanskrit: A 1962, 30) never results in more than a 2-mora vowel, even though the uncontracted forms total 3 or 4 moras (e.g. *rājā + āsīt → rājāsīt*): cf. (on Luganda) *Tucker 1962, 150.

LENGTH. It will then generate the pattern $\hat{\Sigma}$, since a monosyllable cannot be of more than matrix length. But no accentuation is generated for Σ, since the matrix would be incomplete; and this also, as we have seen (pp. 51, 131), is in accordance with the data, since no such independent monosyllables occur in Latin. Beside Greek οὖ, πρό, for example, Latin has *tū*, *prō*.[1] Enclitics consisting of a light syllable are of course admissible, since they are by definition unaccented,[2] forming the final syllable of a longer accentable complex, as e.g. *uirum-que* = [wi.rúŋ. kʷe]. Also perhaps of significance here is the vowel-shortening seen in the first element of 'fossilized' enclitic combinations such as *quŏque*, *sĭquidem*; this could be interpreted as an indication of the (descriptive) semantic indivisibility of such forms, as against *quō-que*, *sī quidem*; the shortening, in other words, would ensure that the first element could not be accented by itself, and so could not constitute an independent meaningful form.[3]

If we apply the rule to disyllables, it will generate [$\hat{\Sigma}\Sigma$] and, by virtue of the proviso, [$\hat{\Sigma}\hat{\Sigma}$] (since $\hat{\Sigma}\hat{\Sigma}$ is not of more than matrix length). But it fails to generate an accentual pattern for $\Sigma\Sigma$, since it is of more than matrix length and the final syllable is therefore excluded. This would preclude an accentuation [$\Sigma\hat{\Sigma}$]; and an accentuation [$\hat{\Sigma}\hat{\Sigma}$] or [$\hat{\Sigma}\hat{\Sigma}$] would conflict with the definition of permitted matrices. It will immediately be evident that this failure runs counter to the data, since forms such as *ămŏ*, *sĕnĕx* commonly occur;[4] and the traditional rule is that all disyllabic words are accented on the initial syllable: thus e.g. Quintilian i.5.31: 'Est autem in omni uoce utique acuta, sed numquam plus una nec umquam ultima, ideoque in disyllabis prior.' This tradition is supported by classical verse practice in so far as in the cadence of the hexameter an ending of the type ∼ *ĕō magis acrem* (Lucr., i 69) is as rare as e.g. ∼ *speciēs ratioque* (Lucr., ii 61; vi 41) or ∼ *sōlī mihi Pallas* (Vergil, *Aen.* x 442) – which suggests at least that the final syllable of an iambic word was not accented in such contexts.[5]

A special case has therefore to be made for disyllables of this type. But before considering further the classical situation regarding such

---

[1] Kuryłowicz 1948/1960, 206; 1949/1960, 296. Cf. the observation that in 'non-tonal' dialects of Danish apocope of disyllables results in a 'dynamic circumflex' – but only if the word contains a 'long sonorous sound' (Ringgaard 1963).

[2] For a close parallel in Maori cf. Holmer 1966, 164 f.

[3] For further discussion cf. Sommer 1913, 129; Vollmer 1917b; Drexler 1967, 55 ff.

[4] Forms of the type *ămăt* might also be cited here, though they would conform to the rule when followed by an initial vowel, since the second syllable will then be light.

[5] See, however, pp. 186 ff.

words, it will be instructive to examine the treatment of them in early Latin, which will suggest that the proposed rule tended in fact to operate in these also.

Iambic shortening

Latin inherited a number of disyllabic forms with the pattern $\Sigma\Sigma$. But there are indications that they were in some way anomalous in terms of the accentual system as it developed in historical times. The evidence for this lies in the diachronic process known as 'iambic shortening', and the cognate phenomenon of 'brevis brevians' in verse composition. The effect is to weaken the second syllable and so, in terms of our tentative rule, to create a normal disyllabic matrix. Thus earlier *ĕgō, cĭtō, mŏdō* were reduced to *ĕgŏ, cĭtŏ, mŏdŏ*, and **bĕnē, mălē, dŭō* were reduced to *bĕnĕ, mălĕ, dŭŏ*[1] – whereas, for example, *ambō, longē* (with heavy first syllable) remained unaffected, since the accentual pattern [$\hat{\Sigma}\Sigma$] was in no way anomalous. In Plautus and Terence there is evidence for a much wider extension of this process than appears from classical Latin verse; for words like *ămā, pŭtā* (to cite their classical forms) are found occupying the same resolved positions in the foot as are words of structure $\Sigma\Sigma$, i.e. as if *ămă, pŭtă* – whereas, for example, *laudā, mandā* (with heavy first syllable) do not permit the final vowel to count as short; nor indeed do words like *sĭmŭlā, ăbĕrō* (with *two* light preceding syllables), which would be accented [$\hat{\Sigma}\Sigma\Sigma$].

These more extended manifestations of the process were at one time assumed to be a purely metrical phenomenon, and this view is still occasionally encountered (thus Beare 1957, 163 ff., esp. 167). But it has now for some time been generally recognized that the process, like other metrical conventions, must have some basis in the language; thus, for example, explicitly Jachmann 1916, 63; Sturtevant 1919, 237; Lindsay 1922, 49 ff; Skutsch 1934, 92 f; Safarewicz 1936, 91; Drexler 1967, 49 f; 1969a, 35; Soubiran 1971, 409 f; and the assumption is implicit in the discussions by most other writers. Beare criticizes the view expressed by Laidlaw (1938, 16) that 'in everyday speech the Romans found difficulty in giving full value to a long (unaccented) syllable succeeding a short (accented) syllable in the same word',

---

[1] The short $\sim ă$ of fem. sing. and neut. pl. (*magna*, etc.), as against e.g. Vedic $\sim ā$, is also generally held to be due to such a shortening, beginning in iambic words (**bŏnā → bŏnă*, etc.) and then extending to other types.

on the grounds that (1957, 163 n.1) 'It is probably true that *we* find it hard to pronounce *mălē*.[1] Laidlaw, Lindsay and many other British scholars seem to think that Latin was pronounced like English.' But we have seen that the process in question, though it is indeed characteristic of English, is in fact of much wider application, and can be given a plausible phonetic explanation; already in 1913 Sommer (128) cites Thurneysen for an explanation of the Latin phenomenon in terms of the 'expiratory syllable'.

This, however, does not exclude the possibility that, like certain other features (e.g. elision), the scope of the process was to some degree extended in verse beyond its linguistic justification. This must, for example, have been the case if a change of speaker intervened between the two syllables;[2] for it would imply that the stress pulse initiated by one speaker was arrested by the other! The occurrence in verse of forms involving 'brevis brevians' in resolved *weak* positions might also be seen as an extension beyond normal linguistic practice; but it is no more so than that of the ordinary pyrrhic patterns to which they are equivalent.

It was suggested by Jachmann (1916, 63 ff.) that the shortening process was a characteristic primarily of colloquial speech, and that this would explain why Ennius, like later hexameter writers, excluded it from his poetry, as 'a vulgarism inappropriate to his elevated style'.[3] Vollmer (1917a, 136) lays emphasis on the syntactic operation of the process, and sees its disappearance in later poetry as one aspect of the general divorce of poetry from normal speech, with quantity being determined within the word-isolate rather than the word group.[4] This syntactical effect is most commonly seen in cases where a monosyllable ending in $\breve{V}C$ stands before an initial vowel;[5] Drexler (1969a, 28, 36; 1969b, 356)[6] also sees syntax as significant in so far as an iambic word is generally 'shortened' only if it is closely related to what follows. The further point is made by Mańczak (1968) that the words most

---

[1] Fehling (1967, 180) comments on the difficulty of German speakers in pronouncing Latin words such as *pălūs* with correct vowel length in the second syllable, because 'German has no simple "iambic" words with initial accentuation'.

[2] The occurrence of such cases is disputed: cf. Lindsay 1922, 57 ff; Fraenkel 1928, 345; Safarewicz 1936, 96.

[3] For rare exceptions cf. Vollmer 1917a; Lindsay 1922, 42; Drexler 1967, 50.

[4] Cf. Fraenkel 1928, 331, 346 f.

[5] Also an elided disyllable, as e.g. *tĭb(i) ĕueniat*. Cf. Sommer 1913, 128; Safarewicz 1936, 83.

[6] Cf. Soubiran 1971, 409.

commonly affected are those with the highest frequency of occurrence; of 3,578 cases in Plautus 88% (3,138) are provided by only 24 different words; and only 32% of words which, on grounds of their syllabic structure, might be subject to the process are in fact affected (167 out of 524); amongst other cases, one may note that shortening of the locative *domi* is frequent as compared with other iambic forms of *domus* (cf. Drexler 1969a, 73 ff.). Thus, as Mańczak observes, the shortening is not to be compared with the type of 'sound-law' which operates with absolute regularity; and he points out the occurrence of similarly 'irregular' reductions in words of high frequency in the development of Romance.[1] One may therefore consider the process of 'iambic shortening' as a tendency rather than a rule.[2]

As generally stated for early Latin verse, the shortening process applies not only where the *preceding* light syllable bears the accent, but also where the *following* syllable is accented – as e.g. *ămĭcítiam, uĕrĕ-bămini* (where original long vowel is indicated for the second syllable by *ămĭcus, uĕrĕbar*, etc.). It is difficult to envisage a single phonetic basis which would explain both categories of shortening – Drexler's statement (1969b, 347) that the accent 'stretches its shadow' as far as the third syllable preceding or following it hardly constitutes a phonetic explanation; and it must be admitted that many problems remain unresolved. But as in the case of original pyrrhic patterns (e.g. in *rĕgĭŏnibus*: cf. p. 168), the linguistic unity of the two syllables in many of the pre-accentual cases is possibly accounted for by the presence of a secondary stress-peak on the first of them (thus [ámìkítìà], [wérèbâa-minii]). In some such cases the shortened vowel has become general in the language, as e.g. in *pătĕfácio, călĕfácio*[3] (for original *ē* cf. Plautus, *Ps.* 21 *contābēfacit*);[4] but in the majority of cases the long vowel has been restored (or preserved) in classical Latin by analogy with related forms with different accentuation (*ămīcítia* by analogy with *ămĭcus*, etc.).

The process of 'iambic shortening' was not a characteristic of the prehistoric period with initial stress, since forms like *ămīcus, ăuārus* preserve the long vowel in the second syllable; and the operation of the

---

[1] Cf. also for other languages A 1958, 127 f. n.70 and refs.
[2] Cf. Soubiran 1971, 409; 'chez Plaute, les lois strictes existent moins que des tendances'.
[3] With further reduction by syncope in e.g. *calfacio, olfacio*, producing a heavy syllable in place of the two light.
[4] See also Lindsay 1922, 39, 47.

process in forms like *bene, modo* can hardly have been much earlier than 200 B.C; for these derive from **dŭĕnēd, mŏdōd*, etc. – but final ~ *d* is retained after a short vowel (*illŭd*, etc.), and its loss after a long vowel does not occur until around this date (cf. Old Latin *rectēd, marīd, sententiād*, etc.); if the process of shortening were earlier, we should therefore expect **bĕnĭd, mŏdŭd*, etc.[1] Kalinka (1935, 390) suggests that the process in general operated for not much more than a century, from mid-3 c. to mid-2 c. B.C.

Even during the period of its operation the shortening process, as already suggested, seems not to have applied to all strata of society; nor does it seem anywhere to have been a regular rule, except in certain categories of very common words. In many cases grammatical analogies are likely to have inhibited its operation (giving, say, *ămā* after *laudā, bŏnō* after *magnō*), as generally in classical Latin.[2] And syntactical accentuation is likely to have precluded its operation as often as it induced it (*ín fŏrō*, for example, would preclude shortening to *fŏrŏ*). Tempo, as dictated by metre or situation, seems also to have been a determining factor, the shortening being characteristic of more rapid enunciation (Soubiran 1971, 409, 411).

There remains an important feature of the process of which we have not so far taken account. The equivalence in early Latin verse of nor-mally iambic to pyrrhic ($\Sigma\Sigma$) forms is not confined to forms ending in a vowel (as e.g. *ămā*), where the original quantity of the second syllable is due to thoracic arrest. It is also common where the second syllable is heavy by virtue of *oral* arrest, as in e.g. *ădĕst, sĕnĕx*. And in longer words, where the pyrrhic equivalence applies before the main stress (where secondary stress may have been operative), it is in fact much more common with second syllables of this type, as e.g. in *uŏlŭptátes*,[3] *iŭuĕntúte, gŭbĕrnábunt*;[4] such second syllables also predominate in cases where the light first syllable is constituted by a monosyllabic word, as e.g. in *sĕd ŭxŏrem, ŭt ŏccĕpi*. The equivalence is also frequent

---

[1] Kent 1932, 107 n.5; Kuryłowicz 1958, 383 f.

[2] The later 'end-shortening' seen in e.g. *dīxĕrŏ, findŏ, nēmŏ* is quite a different matter (even if it has spread from originally iambic words like *uŏlo*); beginning in Augustan times, it is by the 4 c. A.D. prescribed by Charisius (i, 16 K) and Marius Victorinus (vi, 28 K) as regular for verbs other than monosyllables.

[3] Syntactic accent will of course account for the equivalence in e.g. *uŏlŭptás mea* (as against *mea uŏlŭptas*: cf. Beare 1957, 162 f.). A few cases, as *Phĭlĭppi, fĕnĕstrae, săgĭtta*, have been held to indicate a survival of the prehistoric initial accent (cf. Drexler 1969a, 214 ff., 240).

[4] Cf. Drexler 1969a, 214.

in cases where the final syllable of a disyllabic word is orally arrested by virtue of the next word beginning with a consonant, as e.g. in (strong position) *ŭtĕr uostrŏrum*, (weak position) *dĕdĭt dŏnō*.[1]

There seems, however, to have been a tendency for the equivalence not to operate where the second syllable was 'hypercharacterized'. Thus it is rare in the case of words ending in ~ *ns* or ~ *x*, as e.g. *ămāns*, *fĕrōx* (Drexler 1969a, 115 ff; Soubiran 1971, 410), i.e. where there is both a consonant sequence and a long vowel; similarly *fŏrās*, *fŏrīs*, *fŏrēs* show the pyrrhic equivalence more often before initial vowel than before initial consonant (Drexler 1969a, 79, 150). Cases such as Terence's *ex Graecis* BONIS *Latinas fecit non bonas* (*Eun.* pr. 8) are thus somewhat exceptional.[2]

The equivalence is rather more common in cases where the two vowels are in hiatus, or separated only by the semivowel /w/ (as e.g. *nouo*), which might indicate that it was particularly appropriate where the interruption was minimal (cf. on Greek pp. 323 f.); but the possibility of synizesis or contraction in many such cases, giving in effect a heavy monosyllable, makes the interpretation uncertain (Drexler 1969a, 106, 172 ff., 240 ff.).

Skutsch (1934, 92 f.) observes that, if the light second syllable resulting from iambic shortening is no different from an original light syllable, then the quantitative basis of the verse is not thereby infringed: i.e. a shortened *ămā* really is a pyrrhic *ămă*. This certainly will apply to cases where vowel shortening is involved; but the situation is surely different when the second syllable is heavy 'by position', i.e. by virtue of oral arrest. In some cases the quantitative verse-pattern might conceivably be preserved by a shift in the syllabic boundary, as, say, *ĕgĕ.stātis* or *uŏlŭ.ptātes*: but this could hardly apply to cases such as *gŭbĕrnābunt* or *ădĕst* (*benignitas*).[3] The operation of the poetic 'brevis brevians' in fact extends beyond the range of linguistic 'iambic shortening'; but the preponderance of cases involving orally arrested syllables makes it unlikely that they are merely a licence extended from cases with thoracic arrest (long vowels). On the other hand such syllables can hardly become light except by losing their oral arrest, i.e. their closing consonant(s) – which manifestly does not happen;[4] there is, for example, no reduction of the consonant sequence ~ *rn* ~ in *guberna-*

---

[1] For full lists and references see Brenot 1923.
[2] Cf. Lindsay 1922, 48 f.
[3] Cf. Lindsay 1922, 45; Pighi 1950; Drexler 1967, 51 n.53.
[4] Cf. Kuryłowicz 1949/1960, 295.

bunt. The disyllabic accentuation, therefore, in so far as it is reflected by early Latin verse practice, seems not necessarily to require that the second syllable be light, but only that it must contain a short (lax) vowel, whether originally or by 'iambic shortening'.

It might be argued that, this being so, one should expect the normal accentuation of words like *uŏlŭptas* to be *uŏlŭptas* and not *uŏlúptas*, since [wólùp] could then constitute an accentual matrix. But this does not follow. The possibility of even an orally arrested syllable (where no vowel-shortening is required) acting as the second element of a disyllabic matrix may well not have arisen until after the fixation of the historical accent: and even if an accentuation *uŏlŭptas*, with disyllabic matrix, had existed (after the period of regularly initial stress), it could well have been shifted quite early to *uŏlŭptas*, with monosyllabic matrix [lŭp], after the pattern of all other types of word with heavy penultimate syllable (as e.g. *ăuắrus, dēlĕctat*).

To the extent that orally arrested syllables remained arrested even when forming the second element of a disyllabic stress matrix, the purely quantitative basis of early Latin verse must in fact have been infringed. But since, as will later be argued (pp. 339 ff.), such a basis of classical Latin verse is an artificial product, and not derived from native phonological characteristics, it is not surprising if early scenic verse, with its closer adherence to colloquial speech, should be more tolerant of accentual patterns sometimes taking precedence over quantitative. In a senarius such as (Plautus, *Men.* 16)

$$tant(um)\ ad|\ narran|d(um)\ argū|ment(um)\ adest|\ benig|nitas$$

the accentual unity of the word *ádĕst* [ΣΣ] renders it acceptable to fill a resolved element in spite of the fact that the quantitative pattern of IV is then a cretic (ΣΣΣ).

If, as metrical evidence suggests, orally arrested syllables functioned more readily than thoracically arrested syllables as second elements of a disyllabic stress matrix (presumably because the latter require an additional process of vowel-shortening, i.e. loss of arrest), one has to accept an accentual distinction between the two types of heavy syllable in this context. This, however, does not weaken previous arguments regarding their equipollence as *mono*syllabic matrices; and a similar type of distinction has already been noted for English, where there is evidence for a difference between syllables containing weak vowels (regardless of following consonants) and syllables containing strong vowels, as regards their capacity for forming the second element of an accentual matrix. One may also recall, within Latin itself, the different 'strengths' of the two types of heavy syllable as indicated by the different prehistorical developments of their vocalic nuclei (p. 134).[1]

It may be concluded, therefore, that for a certain period and in certain forms of speech a disyllabic accentual matrix could be constituted in Latin not simply by two light syllables, but also by a light syllable followed by an orally arrested syllable; even for such forms of speech, however, a light syllable followed by a thoracically arrested syllable could not form a matrix; and in order to conform to a tendency in favour of such matrices, at least in common words, it was necessary for the second syllable to lose its arrest. Only in this latter case, in fact, is it strictly correct to speak of iambic *shortening*.[2]

Staccato stress

The point has already been made that in other forms of Latin speech there is no evidence for any generalized operation of the shortening process; which must almost certainly mean that words of the type *ămā*, where the second syllable was thoracically arrested, did not have disyllabic accentuation. How then were they accented? The logical conclusion would seem to be that the first syllable, though light (un-arrested), nevertheless carried a monosyllabic stress, which would thus be of the 'staccato' type referred to earlier (pp. 80 f.). This means in effect that in some forms of Latin this staccato type of accentuation was common in iambic words, but in other forms of the language tended to be avoided: one is reminded of Abercrombie's observation about English (p. 174), to which we shall return yet again later. Thus some speakers would have pronounced [ámà] and others (perhaps of higher social level) [âmaa]. In the case of orally arrested second syllables, as e.g. in *sĕnĕx*, it remains an open question whether the latter class of speakers would have pronounced them as [sêneks] etc. or, like the former class, as [sénèks]. The general basis of the accentual system,

---

[1] Diphthongs seem to have functioned as $\check{V}C$ (cf. p. 134 n.), and are also subject to 'brevis brevians', e.g. in *nŏuae*, and pre-accentually in *Clŭtaeméstra* (Liv. Andr.).

[2] Such shortening does, of course, involve a loss of length distinctions; and it has been suggested that a language in which length is significant would not normally neutralize such distinctions in the interests of stress. But the cases here involved apply only to a limited category of word-patterns; internally (e.g. *ămīcitia*) the pheno-menon is relatively uncommon, and in final position will rarely have been semantically significant (cf. A 1960; 1962, 17 ff.).

however, as we have now formulated it, suggests that all speakers will have pronounced invariably pyrrhic words, e.g. *ăgĕ*, as [ágè] etc.

Eventually, with the loss of distinctive vowel-length in Vulgar Latin, thoracic arrest, with concomitant extension of vowel duration, became available as an exponent of accentual stress, and all disyllabic matrices were consequently contracted to monosyllabic: thus e.g. cl. *ăgĕ* [ágè] → *áge* [a͡age].

End-stress

A further possibility has also to be considered for classical Latin. It has been observed (Drexler 1967, 93 ff.) that at caesurae of the dactylic hexameter iambic words in particular tend to be followed by a syntactic boundary, as e.g. *cănō* in *arma uirumque cano, Troiae qui primus ab oris*, whereas other types of word are commonly in more or less close connexion with what follows, as e.g. *fātō* in *Italiam fato profugus*, or *nĭtĭdō* in *sub nitido mirata die*. As regards the penthemimeral caesura, Perret (1966, 121) has noted that, whereas Homer places 13% of his iambic words at this point, and Callimachus only 4%, Vergil places no less than 42% here. Drexler finds similar tendencies applicable at the central caesura of the pentameter. From this the conclusion might be drawn that the difference of treatment reflects a difference of syntactic accentuation – i.e. that iambic words tended to have final accentuation before a pause.[1]

In the interior of the Latin hexameter or pentameter this might not appear a justifiable conclusion, since concord between accent and strong position is far from general in the earlier part of the line. But there are also factors involving the *end* of the pentameter which, in such a position, could well be significant. It is well known that in the Latin elegiac pentameter there was an increasing tendency to have a final disyllabic word, reaching a figure of practically 100% in Ovid;[2] and it has been generally recognized that this must have some special purpose – most probably the achievement of concord between metrical

---

[1] Drexler is, however, careful to point out (1967, 114) that this *is* only a tendency, and not a rule. The fact that there is no such indication for the cadence of the hexameter (see p. 178) could be accounted for by the fact that the requirement for a syntactical break at this point would rarely arise; in general, a caesura at Va restricts the possibilities of accentual/metrical agreement in the subsequent portion of the line.

[2] Propertius shows an increase from 63.2% in Book i to 98.3% in Book iv (Sturtevant 1924b; cf. also Veremans 1969, 761 ff.).

and accentual patterns;[1] it can hardly be dismissed, as by Axelson (1958, 135), as the mere 'technical over-uniformity of a hyper-elegant virtuoso'. It also seems highly improbable that, as suggested by G. A. Wilkinson (1948, 74 f.), this practice was intended to *avoid* agreement at the end. It will have had the effect, certainly, of ensuring that in the rest of the coda there would be agreement between accent and strong position – thus e.g. *cármine| dóctus a|met* as against (with trisyllabic ending) *ómne gé|nus pere|at*. But there still remains the problem of the final disyllable itself, which seems no more amenable to agreement than any other type of word, leading Sedgwick, for example (1924, 336) to state that 'of all Latin metres the pentameter most flagrantly violated spoken accent at the critical point'.[2] This difficulty may have been slightly reduced by the increasing tendency to use unemphatic 'sentence enclitics' and pronouns in this position (e.g. *erat*, *tibi*), the proportions of which increase from 2.5% in Tibullus to 25% in Ovid (Wilkinson 1940, 39); for, if these were unaccented, they would at least not produce a *counter*-metrical effect. But perhaps more significant is the fact that the final syllable is normally heavy (see p. 130), i.e. the word is a true iambic and not a pyrrhic, and the quantity in this position is not therefore 'indifferent'. The end of the pentameter is, of course, the end of the couplet, and so normally followed by a strong syntactical break. This may be seen, as Drexler (1967, 110 ff.) specifically suggests, as connected with the internal tendencies already mentioned; and it raises in a more significant way (since accentual agreement in the coda is a widespread phenomenon) the possibility that disyllables of the pattern $\Sigma\Sigma$ tended in such an environment to be end-stressed, i.e. [$\Sigma\acute{\Sigma}$]; in which case they would clearly be preferable at this position in the verse to the type $\Sigma\Sigma$, which, if accented at all, could be so only counter-metrically, i.e. as [$\acute{\Sigma}\Sigma$].[3]

If this explanation is correct, it provides a parallel in Latin iambic

---

[1] E.g. Sturtevant 1924b; Wilkinson 1963, 123 ff; Drexler 1967, 108 ff.

[2] Also Beare 1957, 174, 192.

[3] The case of the pentameter suggests consideration of iambic line-ends in iambic and (catalectic) trochaic verse. In the case of longer words there will be no accent in the last two syllables, and so at least no conflict; and in very many cases iambic (or pyrrhic) words here are closely connected with what precedes and so are liable to lose their stress by syntactic accentuation (e.g. *in foro*, *animúm meum*, *quantúm potest*). Fraenkel, however (1928, 21 f.) takes it as 'self-evident' that one will not look for agreement at this point.

The relevance, if any, of the 'Bentley-Luchs law' (cf. Drexler 1967, 36) to this question is not evident.

words before pause to the final accentuation already noted for words
ending in 'overweight' syllables in English, Arabic and modern
Indian.

It is also a notable tendency of the Ovidian pentameter to end the
two sections with a rhyming epithet and noun, e.g. *flammaque in arguto
saepe reperta foro*. Such repetition of an inflexion, in closely connected
words in hyperbaton, in itself tends to endow it with a certain prominence.[1] Moreover, rhyme is a typical feature of accentual verse, as
e.g. in Germanic;[2] and in Sedgwick's words (1924, 335) 'It is recurrence
of stress, not of verse ictus, which causes rhyme'. At the very least,
as Lanz says (1931, 235), 'although they may not actually be stressed, –
yet the musical pleasure derived from the riming vowels is sufficient
to attract our attention, and thereby to produce the impression that
they are stressed'. This feature, then, may be a further indication of an
increasingly felt need to ensure prominence of the final syllable of the
pentameter, for which the selection of pure iambic words was one
important device.

Secondary stress

The absence of 'iambic shortening' in prehistoric Latin is shown by
the persistence of long vowel in e.g. *ăuārus*, in spite of the prehistorically
stressed initial light syllable; such a word must therefore have had
monosyllabic, 'staccato' stress, i.e. [âwaa~] (cf. Kuryłowicz 1968c,
193). But there is no reason to assume that disyllabic accentuation may
not have applied in words with pyrrhic beginning, as e.g. *făcĭlis*
[fákì~]. This consideration may help to explain a well-known peculiarity of accentuation suggested by early Latin verse. For here words of
the type *făcĭlĭus* are most commonly found with their first two syllables
filling a resolved strong position – which suggests an accentuation
făcĭlĭus [fákì~] (as against later, classical *făcĭlĭus* [~kílì~]).[3]

It is commonly held that the historical accent originated in a secondary rôle (e.g. Kent 1932, 66), the secondary stress having had the
function of limiting the extent of unaccented portions of the word.

---

[1] On the possible origins in epic formulae of the word-ordering involved see Conrad
1965.
[2] Note the specialization of meaning in English *rhyme/rime* < O.Fr. *rime* < *rhythmus*
(cf. Park 1968, 6 f; Attridge 1972, 88 ff.).
[3] Cf. A 1969, 200 ff. On exceptions in early Latin, and later developments, cf. Thierfelder 1928.

For example, one might have had prehistoric accentual patterns of the types *détĕrios* [déetérìos], *rélātos* [rêlâatos], *dēdicātio* [déedikâatioo], *régiṓnes* [régìôônees], with initial main stress, and secondary stress in the position of the historical accent. In disyllables, and in trisyllables with light penultimate, the historical accent agrees with the prehistoric: e.g. *fḗci*, *fḗcerat*, *fácio*; and one may assume that in such cases the relevant post-accentual portion of the word was of insufficient mass to require any secondary stress.

But in that case the same principle might be expected to apply to a tetrasyllable with tribrach beginning such as *făcĭlĭos* [fákìlios], which from this point of view is comparable with *fécĕrat* [féekerat], since the post-accentual portion is of identical structure ($\sim \Sigma\Sigma$). And incidentally, if one were to impose a secondary stress in the position of the classical accent, i.e. [fakílìos], its peak would clash with the cadence of the main prehistoric stress. We should therefore expect there to be no secondary prehistoric stress, and the historical accentuation to be [fákìlius], which is in fact implied by early Latin verse.

This explanation could also apply to another peculiarity of such verse; for pentasyllabic words of pattern $\Sigma\Sigma\Sigma\Sigma\Sigma$ there is a strong tendency for the verse to imply an accentuation $\Sigma\Sigma\Sigma\Sigma\Sigma$, e.g. *adsímĭlĭter* [atsímìliter], but for words of pattern $\Sigma\Sigma\Sigma\Sigma\Sigma$ regularly an accentuation $\Sigma\Sigma\Sigma\Sigma\Sigma$, e.g. *mălĕfĭcĭum* [malefíkìũ] as in classical Latin. For the prehistoric accentuation of the former would have been [âtsímìliter] (which, with weakening of the prehistoric accent, → [atsímìliter]); but the imposition of a prehistoric secondary stress in the same position in the latter type (with disyllabic main accent [málèfikiõ]) would lead to clash with the main stress. Such a word is comparable with a tetrasyllable such as *dētĕrĭus*, prehistorically [déetérìos], and consequently will be expected to be stressed prehistorically as [málèfíkìõ] (→ hist. [malefíkìũ]). Sturtevant (1919, 243) points out that many words of this latter type are compounds with a trisyllabic second element, which might therefore be independently accented; but this hypothesis is unnecessary and unsupported: if it were valid, one would also expect early Latin verse to indicate an accentuation such as *ĭnṓpĭa*, which it does not (even though its compound status is emphasized by the analogical retention of the unweakened *ŏ* from *ŏpes*); in any case by no means all such words are compounds with transparent second elements (e.g. *dŏmĭcĭlĭum*; cf. Ahlberg 1900, i, 27 ff.).

The classical shift of accent in the types *facilius*, *adsimiliter* might perhaps be seen as eliminating the anomaly that such forms alone had a stress peak on the fourth syllable from the end.[1]

The evidence of early Latin verse also, as we have seen, suggests the possibility that there was a pattern of secondary stress as well as the main accent in longer Latin words in the historical period.[2] The general principle of such stressing seems to be that the portion of a word preceding the main accent was treated as a word for purposes of secondary stress[3] (unless it consisted of a single syllable);[4] thus e.g. *rĕgĭŏnĭbus* [rḛgìŏonibus], *sŭspĭcābar* [sûspikaabar], *mĭsĕrĭcórdĭa* [mḭsèri-kórdia], *uĭnōsíssĭma* [wînoosíssima], *mălĕfĭcĭum* [mãlèfíkium] (and, with classical accent, *ădsĭmílĭter* [ãtsimíliter]). Such secondary stressing will also have been effective in the classical hexameter in providing accentual/metrical agreement in the coda when (exceptionally) this contains a polysyllabic word such as *Lāŏdămīa* [lãàodamîia] or *abscondantur* [ãpskondântur].[5] With very few exceptions (e.g. words of the

---

[1] The formulation of the rule on p. 177 then becomes possible. However, one could now introduce an amendment which makes the rule more general in application. It has been suggested that a disyllabic matrix may have been constituted not only by $\underset{\smile}{\Sigma}\underset{\smile}{\Sigma}$ but also by $\underset{\smile}{\Sigma}\breve{\Sigma}$, i.e. light syllable + heavy syllable with short vowel (= oral arrest): *sĕnĕx* may have been pronounced as [séneks], and e.g. *uoluptátes* may have had a secondary stress of the type [wŏlùp ∼]; and support is lent to this possibility by certain parallels in English (see pp. 173 ff., 191 ff.). In this connexion we have already suggested (p. 184) historical explanations of the fact that a word like *uoluptas* is nevertheless stressed on the penultimate. By means of a redefinition the descriptive rule can be made to take account of pronunciations of the type [$\underset{\smile}{\overset{\prime}{\Sigma}}\breve{\Sigma}$] without having to define the disyllabic matrix differently for the main stress of longer words (viz. as $\underset{\smile}{\Sigma}\underset{\smile}{\Sigma}$) and for disyllabic words and secondary stress (which would additionally require $\underset{\smile}{\Sigma}\breve{\Sigma}$): *the matrix can be invariably stated as $\underset{\smile}{\Sigma}\breve{\Sigma}$*. For in e.g. *uoluptas*, where the potential matrices are disyllabic [wolup ∼] and monosyllabic [∼ lup ∼], the progressive formulation of the rule correctly ensures that the accent will fall on the latter and not the former.

[2] Cf. Fraenkel 1928, 352; Tucker 1965, 454.

[3] Cf. the closely similar rule given for secondary (and tertiary) stresses in Arabic by Abdo (1969, 73 ff.).

[4] It may incidentally be doubted whether, in prehistoric Latin, both main and secondary stresses would survive when their peaks fell on immediately successive syllables, as e.g. in *relātos* [rêlãàtos], *dēlectat* [dêelèktat], *dēterios* [dêetérìos]; and such forms could possibly have set the pattern for the more general demise of the initial stress as the main accent.

[5] Cf. Liénard 1969, 559. It has, however, been suggested by Exon (1906, 32; 1907) that inflected forms such as *consuluisti* took a secondary stress on the same syllable as the main accent in shorter forms of the word, i.e. *consŭlúisti* after *consúluit*; in support of this grammatical influence he cites the fact that such forms are as much avoided by Vergil in the coda as are sequences of the type *spē uŏlŭērunt* (where the stressing would presumably be *uŏluérunt*).

pattern ΣΣ̈ΣΣ̣Σ) such a secondary stressing will fall on the beginning of the word, i.e. the position of the prehistoric accent, and so would generally support the principle enunciated by Lindsay (1894, 409) that 'The change from the old accentuation to the new would be, in reality, nothing but a usurpation by the secondary accent of the prominence of the main accent'. One difference would be that, at least in the language represented by early Latin verse, the presumed prehistoric 'staccato' stress would be changed to disyllabic stress (e.g. *uoluptates* [wôluptâatees] → [wőlùptâatees]), leading occasionally to actual 'iambic shortening' as in e.g. *amicitia* [âmiikítìa] → [ắmìkítìa].[1]

EXCURSUS A

Iambic shortening and staccato stress in English

The preceding chapter has proposed for Latin a disyllabic stress-matrix [Σ̂Σ̣] (or [Σ̂Σ̣])[2] as well as a monosyllabic [Σ̂]; but it has at the same time been recognized that, at least for some speakers, the 'staccato' pattern [Σ̂(Σ)] may also occur, and this possibility has also been presumed for the initial stress of prehistoric Latin. Numerous attested parallels have been cited for the disyllabic pattern. But it remains to seek the support of a living parallel for the coexistence with this (and with the non-staccato monosyllabic [Σ̂]) of such a staccato pattern. The search for a parallel has led to a phonetic re-examination of certain features of English, which do seem to attest such a possibility.

In the perception of syllabic structure and of stress in general, we have already noted the rôle of kinaesthetic memory; and in dealing with the fine distinctions of motor activity involved in this particular problem, no instrumental techniques appear to exist at present such as might provide more objective results than kinaesthetic impression. For Broch, dealing with similar phenomena in 1911 (299), the most valid

[1] In classical Latin, however, one could envisage the possibility of a staccato secondary stress, i.e. [âmiikítìa] (as for the main accent of e.g. *ămā* [âmaa]), since there is no shortening of the second vowel.

[2] See p. 190 n.

observations were those of 'a scientifically trained native', and the same opinion has been expressed more recently by Lehto (1969, 14). In what follows, therefore, the phonetic observations are based primarily on kinaesthetic examination of my own speech habits; and it must be left to readers to examine their own behaviour in these matters and to decide whether what is here stated applies also to their own speech. Some preliminary testing on a variety of audiences suggests that it may.

We have observed for English the tendency to alternation between the monosyllabic stress-pattern (as in *profane*, which we may now symbolize as [~fêin]) and the disyllabic (as in *profanity* [~fǽnì~]). In the latter the first syllable of the matrix is a light (unarrested) syllable and the second a syllable containing a 'weak' vowel; 'weak' vowels may now be more specifically identified with Arnold's 'lenis' (as opposed to 'fortis') vowels, defined as those which are 'normally rhythmically weak', and comprising primarily /i/ and /ə/ (Arnold 1957, 235).[1] Syllables containing fortis vowels we may hereafter, where necessary, symbolize as Σ, and those containing lenis vowels as $\underset{\circ}{\Sigma}$. It has also been observed that in nouns like *relaxation*, where the second syllable retains a full (fortis) vowel owing to derivation from an under-lying form *reláx*, the first syllable, which has secondary stress, has a long (tense) vowel: thus [ˌriilækˈseiʃən]; similarly *detestation* [ˌdiites-ˈteiʃən], *emendation*, *authenticity* (cf. *authéntic*). Whereas, if the vowel in the second syllable is a lenis vowel, owing to its not being derived from an underlying form in which it is stressed,[2] the first syllable has a short, lax vowel, as e.g. in *devastation* [ˌdevəsˈteiʃən], *demonstration*. These two types of pattern we may now interpret as (a) [dîitestêiʃən] etc., with monosyllabic secondary stress where the second syllable has a fortis vowel, and (b) [děvəstêiʃən] etc., with disyllabic secondary stress where the second syllable has a lenis vowel: i.e. (a) = [$\hat{\Sigma}\underset{\circ}{\Sigma}$~], (b) = [$\overset{\prime\prime}{\Sigma}\underset{\circ}{\Sigma}$~].[3]

To the examples of primary stress already cited from Fidleholtz (p. 174) one may add the alternative pronunciations of *negro* as /niigrou/ and (southern U.S.A.) /nigrə/ (→ *nigger*): cf. Kenyon & Knott 1953,

---

[1] Syllabic [ɾ], [ḷ], [ṇ], [ṃ] may be treated for this purpose as /ər/ etc: cf. Gimson 1970, 53.

[2] Or not being orally arrested (e.g. *defamation*, *preparation*, with weakening in spite of *defáme*, etc.).

[3] Of course only monosyllabic stress is possible if the first syllable has oral arrest, and so cannot be light, even if the second syllable has a lenis vowel, as e.g. in *compensa-tion* [kɔ̂mpənsêiʃən] = [$\hat{\Sigma}\underset{\circ}{\Sigma}$~].

s.v; or of *provost* as (civil and academic) /prɔ́vəst/ and (military colloquial) /proúvou/ (cf. /prəvoú-maaʃəl/). These we may now interpret
as e.g. [nîigrou] vs [nígrə̀] etc., and the earlier examples as [êiræb] vs
[ǽrəb], [noûmæd] vs [nɔ́məd], [wɔ̂mbæt] vs [tʃérəb], etc: the contrast
in all cases is between [Σ̲Σ̲] and [Σ̲́Σ̣̲̀].

In addition to /i/ and /ə/, which are by far the most common of the
lenis vowels, /u/ and /o/ are also found in this function (as reduced
forms of the fortis /uu/ and /ou/): cf. Arnold 1957, 235. The difference
recognized by Newman (see p. 171) and Chomsky & Halle (1968,
190 f.) in the stress levels of the second syllables of words like *veto*
on the one hand, and *echo* or *motto* on the other, may then be interpreted in terms of monosyllabic vs disyllabic stress, as [vîitou] vs
[ékò], [mɔ́tò]; one need not, as Chomsky & Halle, assume different
underlying representations '/vētɔ/' vs '/mɔto/', since the differences
of stress level and vowel quality in the final syllable will be an automatic
concomitant of the different stress patterns associated with heavy vs
light initial syllable, i.e. [Σ̲Σ̲] vs [Σ̲́Σ̣̲̀].[1] Similar considerations apply
to cases such as *Hebrew* vs *menu* (see p. 173), which we may now
interpret as [hîibruu] ([Σ̲Σ̲]) vs [ménjù] ([Σ̲́Σ̣̲̀]); and again the special
derivations proposed by Chomsky & Halle are rendered unnecessary.[2]

---

[1] Cf. also Hoard 1971.

[2] A stress pattern of the type [ménjù] assumes that the first syllable is light and so
unarrested, i.e. that the syllabic division is *not* [menₐju] (similarly in the case of
[nígrə̀]). In other words, the sequence Cj (like plosive + r) is here behaving in the
same way as a single C. But in longer forms, where the syllable after the stress
peak is not final, as in *speculate, emulate, tabulate, regulate, insinuate, copulate,
accurate,* my own pronunciation tends to an arrested syllable, with consequent
monosyllabic stress, i.e. [spek̂.juleit] etc; in *communal,* for example, my pattern is
[kɔ̂m.junəl] contrasting with that of *common(er)* [kɔ́mən(ə)]. Exceptions are provided
by e.g. *visual, educate,* where for me a pattern [vîẑ.juəl], [éd̂.jukeit] occurs only in
very careful speech; the disyllabic pattern, however, is related to a tendency to
assimilate the consonants, as [víʒùəl], [éd̂ʒùkeit]; and this in turn raises the question
of the status of the affricates /dʒ/ and /tʃ/ as single consonants (see e.g. Trnka 1966,
6 f; St. Clair 1972), which does in fact seem to be supported by the stress patterning.
    Thus, for example, *badger, lodger, midget, prejudice, tragedy, hatchet, pitcher,
satchel* have disyllabic stress and do *not* divide as [bæd.ʒə], [hæt.ʃit] etc. – thereby
contrasting with the compounds *hat-shop, cat-show,* etc., and with other combinations
of plosive + /ʃ/, as e.g. *caption* [kæ̂p.ʃən], *action* [æ̂k.ʃən]. /ts/, /dz/, on the other
hand, function as two consonants; *Betsy, Patsy, Stetson* pattern as [bet.si] etc.,
in contrast with *Betty* [bétì], *Bessy, patchy* [pǽtʃì], etc., and do *not* contrast with the
compounds *wet-suit, hot-seat,* or with other combinations of plosive + /s/, as e.g.
popsy [pɔ̂p.si], *flaccid* [flæ̂k.sid]. One may also contrast the prosodic patterning of
ketchup [kétʃəp] with that of the alternative *catsup* [kæt.sʌp] (note also the alterna-

We may now return to the point made by Abercrombie (p. 174) that there appear to be some types of English in which a pattern comparable with our $\Sigma\underline{\Sigma}$ does not occur with initial stress. Some of the examples considered above indicate a tendency to weaken the vowel of the second syllable in such cases, thereby permitting disyllabic stress, as e.g. /~ou/ → /~o/ in *motto* [mɔ́tò]. Examples of weak /o/ internally are seen in *calomel, allocate*, giving patterns of the type [kǽlòmel] which are entirely comparable with e.g. *caramel* [kǽrəmel]. In these internal positions alternative pronunciations with /ə/ are admissible even in RP (cf. Jones 1967, s.vv.); and such an alternative occurs in final position in the colloquial use of the word *fellow* (= 'chap'). In non-RP (e.g. Cockney) such final reductions are common, as in *arrow, barrow, follow, hollow, marrow, motto, piano, shadow, swallow, tomorrow, widow, yellow*, pronounced as [bǽrə] etc. In referring to this, Sivertsen (1960, 93) comments that the *un*reduced vowels occur mainly in 'less homely words', instancing *photo, radio, Soho*; but these latter, unlike the former, have heavy first syllables, and one could add e.g. *banjo, bingo, cargo, polo, solo* (not all in fact 'unhomely'). This is not to say that final weakening may not also take place for reasons other than the tendency to disyllabic stress: it is found, for example, in *window, potato, tomato*; Fidelholtz suggests that in certain other exceptional cases frequency of use is a factor tending to induce reduction, and it may be so here.

Other vowels than /ou/ may have reduced variants in current English; in RP, for example, [prɔ́dəkt] is common for *product*, with /ə/ replaced the fortis /ʌ/; in non-RP, *placard, blackguard, record* (noun) are commonly heard as [plǽkəd] etc., with /ə/ replacing the fortis /aa/, /ɔɔ/ of RP;[1] and for *nephew*, which in RP commonly reduces to [névjù], Gimson (1970, 147) cites the further reduced non-RP /nevi/,[2] i.e. /~juu/ → /~ju/ → /~i/.

What seems to emerge from these facts is a tendency in English to reduce the occurrences of the initially stressed sequence $\underline{\Sigma}\underline{\Sigma}$. In the case of Latin, where the comparable sequence $\underline{\Sigma}\bar{\Sigma}$ (i.e. with second syllable containing long vowel) does occur, we have suggested that it

tion here of light syllable + lenis vowel with heavy syllable + fortis vowel). Similarly *sudsy* patterns as [sʌd.zi] in contrast with *muddy, fuzzy, pudgy* [pʌdʒì], etc., and in the same way as *fubsy* [fʌb.zi], *exit* (in the pronunciation [ég̑.zit]).

[1] Cf. also the general American pronunciation of *clapboard* as [ˈklæbə⁽ʳ⁾d] (Kenyon & Knott 1953, s.v.).

[2] Similarly in non-RP /edikeit/.

was implemented with a 'staccato' stress, i.e. [$\hat{\underline{\Sigma}}\bar{\Sigma}$], which is completed within the bounds of the light syllable, as compared with the 'legato' stress of monosyllabic [$\hat{\Sigma}$] or disyllabic [$\hat{\Sigma}\check{\Sigma}$]. The relatively exceptional nature of such patterns might be compared with that of the 'Scotch snap' in music, in which the accented notes are shortened and the unaccented lengthened, as opposed to the more normal 'metric alteration' whereby the accented notes are made 'not only a little stronger but also a little longer' (cf. Sachs 1953, 296 ff.).

If such initially stressed sequences of type $\underline{\Sigma}\underline{\Sigma}$ as do occur in English are implemented with a special 'staccato' mode of stressing, as suggested for the parallel situation in Latin, then we should expect to be able to detect some phonetic difference between the mutually comparable first portions of such pairs of words as the following:

	$\underline{\Sigma}\underline{\Sigma}$	vs		$\underline{\Sigma}\check{\underline{\Sigma}}$
record	[rêkɔɔd]		*reckon*	[rékən]
comment	[kɔ̂ment]		*common*	[kɔ́mən]
asset	[æ̂set]		*acid*	[ǽsìd]
suburb	[sʌ̂bəəb]		*cupboard*	[kʌ́bə̀d]
sapphire	[sæ̂faiə]		*Sapphic*	[sǽfìk]
Leppard	[lêpaad]		*leopard*	[lépə̀d]
Hatchard	[hæ̂tʃaad]		*hatchet*	[hǽtʃìt]
product(a)	[prɔ̂dʌkt]		*product*(b)	[prɔ́də̀kt];[1]

and perhaps similarly, though less clearly, between the secondarily stressed elements of

$$
\left.\begin{array}{ll}
\textit{annexation}(\text{a}) & [\text{æ̂ne}\sim] \\
\textit{annotation}(\text{a}) & [\text{æ̂nou}\sim]
\end{array}\right\} \quad \text{vs} \quad
\left\{\begin{array}{ll}
\textit{annexation}(\text{b}) & [\text{æ̀nì}\sim] \\
\textit{animation} & [\text{æ̀nì}\sim] \\
\textit{annotation}(\text{b}) & [\text{æ̀nò}\sim]
\end{array}\right.
$$

My own impression, after a good deal of kinaesthetic introspection and auditory monitoring, is that there are clear articulatory and audible differences involved, though their precise specification is less certain. In the first place, the articulation of the first syllable in the type $\underline{\Sigma}\underline{\Sigma}$ is more tense and energetic than in the type $\underline{\Sigma}\check{\underline{\Sigma}}$; and if one articulates a word such as *reckon* with the first syllable as in *record*, the result sounds and feels quite unnatural. Moreover, if one takes a word of type $\underline{\Sigma}\check{\underline{\Sigma}}$ such as *suffix* /sʌfiks/ and pronounces it in a 'contrastive' manner (i.e. to distinguish it from *prefix*, *affix*, etc: cf. Sharp, 1960, 134), the result is to render the first syllable similar to that of a $\underline{\Sigma}\underline{\Sigma}$ word

---

[1] Sanskritists might compare their pronunciation of the loan-word *guru* in English (/gúruu/ = $\underline{\Sigma}\underline{\Sigma}$) with that of the Sanskrit neuter adjective *guru* (= Gk βαρύ), where the final vowel must be short, i.e. $\underline{\Sigma}\check{\underline{\Sigma}}$.

such as *sapphire* or *suburb* as normally pronounced; and since contrast involves emphasis of the syllable in question, this tends to support the impression that there is greater intensity in the first syllables of $\Sigma\underline{\underline{\Sigma}}$ words than of $\underline{\underline{\Sigma}}\Sigma$ words. It is also my impression that in the $\Sigma\underline{\underline{\Sigma}}$ forms the first syllable tends not to be orally arrested, i.e. really is 'light', or in other words that the syllabic division tends to come between the vowel and the following consonant (cf. Sharp's syllabification of the 'contrastive' pronunciation of *suffix* as [ˈsʌ.fiks]).[1]

We have seen that /i/ is classifiable as a lenis vowel, as e.g. in *rabbit*; but it can, unlike /ə/, also occur in fortis positions, e.g. as in *bitter*. Chomsky & Halle (1968, 36) draw attention to the fact that in a word such as the noun *progress*, with an underlying verb form *progréss*, the vowel in the second syllable is not weakened to /i/ as in e.g. *tigress* /táigris/, where there is no such underlying form.[2] In nouns such as *permit*, *convict* the underlying verbal forms *permít*, *convíct* themselves have /i/ in the second syllable; but in these cases, as expressed by Chomsky & Halle (1968, 96), the nouns have second syllables with 'tertiary' and not 'zero' stress levels (cf. Halle & Keyser 1971, 39f.); whereas 'zero' stress is found in words like *hermit*, *verdict*, which have no underlying forms with stressed second syllable. The observation that there is a difference of intensity between the second syllables of the nouns *permit*, *convict* and of *hermit*, *verdict* seems to be justified;[3] and this provides us with the possibility of yet other contrasts between the articulations of word-types $\Sigma\underline{\underline{\Sigma}}$ and $\underline{\underline{\Sigma}}\Sigma$, in which the vowels of the second syllables as well as the first are comparable in quality. A word such as *panic* /pǽnik/, for example, having no underlying form with final stress, has the lenis value for the vowel of the second syllable; but in the noun *addict* /ǽdikt/ a derivation from the verbal form *addíct* gives the possibility of a pronunciation with fortis /i/ in the second syllable, i.e. having an intensity comparable with that of a fortis vowel such as the /e/ in *annex* /ǽneks/. Such a fortis /i/ (occurring in other than main or secondarily stressed position) we may mark as /i̠/. If we then take a sentence such as *The addict panicked* /ði ǽdi̠kt pǽnikt/,

[1] This conclusion tends to support Sharp in his criticism of the traditional rejection of a syllabification of *bedroom* as [ˈbe.druum] (see p. 32).

[2] Cf. (noun) *insert* /ínsəət/, with /əə/ maintained from verb *insért*, but *concert* /kɔ́nsəət/ only in the sense of 'union', i.e. when descriptively derivable from verb *concért* – otherwise, in the sense of 'musical entertainment', /kɔ́nsət/, with weakening to /ə/ (cf. Jones 1967, s.v.).

[3] Though I judge that 'zero' may also be possible for *permit*, *convict* (but not 'tertiary' for *hermit*, *verdict*).

it is found (at least in my own speech) that the prosodic pattern of /ǽdi̯kt/, as regards *both* its syllables *and* the transition between them, cannot be applied to /pǽnikt/ without the latter sounding and feeling unnatural. In other words, the pattern of /ǽdi̯kt/ is [Σ̂Σ̱], and that of /pǽnikt/ is [Σ́Σ̱].

Let us now consider the syllabification of the disyllabic, 'legato' form [Σ́Σ̱]. A number of phoneticians in the past have distinguished between two types of transition from vowel to following consonant, or 'syllabic cut-off' as Trubetzkoy termed it (see p. 49). In the 'close' transition it is stated, for example, that the consonant forms an integral part of the VC sequence, whereas in the 'loose' transition it is 'dispensable' (and so belongs syllabically with the next vowel: cf. Fliflet 1963, 191).[1] The use of this distinction as a criterion for vowel length has already been referred to as of dubious value (see also n. 2 below), but it does appear to correspond to the differences of syllabification associated with 'staccato' stress ([Σ̂Σ̱]) vs disyllabic 'legato' stress ([Σ́Σ̱]), the former being characterized by a 'looser' transition from V to C than the latter. The corollary of this (i.e. 'closer' transition in the case of disyllabic stress) has in fact already been stated specifically in connexion with 'percursive expiration' (Sievers 1901, 225; cf. pp. 39, 171, 176); in such cases it is also stated, for example, that the inter-vocalic consonant comes at the syllabic peak (Sievers, loc. cit.), or is 'ambisyllabic' (Eliason 1942, 146), or is 'felt as constituting in itself the syllable boundary...or...as containing the syllable boundary' (Fliflet 1963, 191). There is no question of the first syllable being identifiable with an orally arrested syllable (even though 'close' VC transition is presumably involved there also);[2] the first syllable of e.g. *hammer* [hǽmə̀] is quite distinct from that of *hamper* [hǽmpə]; it is rather that the consonant [m] in [hǽmə̀] simply *interrupts* the peak–arrest sequence

[1] Similarly Malmberg (1955) suggests, on the basis of auditory–acoustic evidence, that the appreciation by the hearer of whether a vowel belongs to a following or preceding consonant depends on which end of the vowel formant pattern is 'inflected' by the consonant.

[2] In a thoracically arrested syllable 'loose' transition is involved, since the ballistic movement is completed before the consonantal articulation. But the value of this as a criterion of vowel length is neutralized for English stressed syllables by the existence of the staccato forms referred to: certainly there are transitional differences as between e.g. *packer* [pǽkə̀] and *Parker* [páàkə], but I do not find any such clear differences as between the latter and the staccato *Packard* [pǽkaad]; and in unstressed position, there is presumably 'loose' transition from the short vowel of a light, unarrested syllable to the following consonant (cf. p. 171). For possible teneseness distinctions in the consonant see Hoard 1971.

[ǽ–ə], without arresting the first syllable and so also arresting the stress pulse at this point.

In a language with 'free' stress accent, as English, it seems to be normal for the disyllabic stress to be associated with an intervocalic consonant (cf. p. 81); although cases such as [rúìn] do occur (cf. Sharp 1960, 134), they are only alternatives to other pronunciations, and never contrast with the pattern more normal in English, in which hiatus is preceded by a long (stressed) vowel, as [rú̯ùin]. It does not, however, seem that such an oral articulation is universally necessary to the disyllabic stress (cf. Hála 1961, 118);[1] in Latin, a language with 'fixed' accent, there seems no reason to assume such a necessity, since there is evidently no objection in early Latin verse to the 'iambic shortening' of words such as ĕō, scĭō. The consonant requirement of English may therefore be due only to the typological characteristic whereby in other than preconsonantal position the distinction between short and long vowels is neutralized, with the long vowel being normal under stress.

The possibility remains, however, that an intervocalic consonant facilitates the disyllabic stress by providing an automatic interruption of the vowel sequence, which, particularly under the unifying effect of the stress pulse, might otherwise tend to coalesce (cf. colloquial Latin *ain* for *ais-ne*, and *reice* at Vergil, *Ecl.* iii 96). The whole hypothesis of disyllabic stress in fact implies a second 'syllable' which is not definable within the general terms of the motor theory, since it consists only of an arresting function. Its distinction from the preceding syllabic peak must presumably depend on its having an independent peak of 'sonority'; in which case there must be some intervening marginal feature to separate them. Such a feature would of course be provided by a consonant; in some other cases, as when the second vowel is more open than the first, the margin might be provided by an automatic glide (thus perhaps Latin *scĭăt* = [skíʲàt]); but in other cases, as e.g. *ăĭt* [áìt], the necessary interruption would have to be provided by other (? subglottal) means.

Indeed, *it may be that from a motor point of view we should consider a 'disyllabic' stress-matrix not as comprising two syllables, but rather as a unitary, 'interrupted' heavy syllable.*[2] Since the special conditions attaching to the second 'syllable' apply only where stress is involved

[1] To avoid possible confusion, note that Hála seems to use the term 'staccato' to refer to this type of stress, rather than in the sense here adopted.

[2] Cf. Pickett 1951, 61 on 'phonetic' vs 'phonemic' syllables in Zapotec, which shows several similarities to the Latin stress system.

(otherwise, for example, $\underset{\smile}{\Sigma}\bar{\Sigma}$ in Latin or $\underset{\smile}{\Sigma}\underset{=}{\Sigma}$ in English may freely occur), it is evident that the unity is dependent on stress; and it is therefore not surprising that in early Latin verse the 'resolution' $\underset{\smile}{\Sigma}\breve{\Sigma}$ should be substitutable for $\bar{\Sigma}$, since both are, in a motor sense, monosyllabic. The substitution in classical Latin verse of the 'contraction' $\bar{\Sigma}$ for $\underset{\smile}{\Sigma}\underset{\smile}{\Sigma}$, uncorrelated with stress, is, as we have repeatedly emphasized, not a native feature but derived from Greek (see pp. 255 ff.); we shall see, however, that *resolution* in Greek also has a basis similar to that of Latin (pp. 318 ff.).

The foregoing examination of the English phenomena leads one to believe that the hypothesis for Latin of a 'staccato' form of stress in the first syllables of 'unshortened' iambic forms is phonetically not unrealistic. The English examples form, moreover, as in Latin, a relatively exceptional class as compared with the cases where stress is associated with a matrix longer than a light syllable, i.e. 'legato' [$\acute{\bar{\Sigma}}$] or [$\acute{\Sigma}\Sigma$]; and, again as in Latin, the 'staccato' [$\hat{\acute{\Sigma}}\underset{=}{\Sigma}$] sequences tend, particularly in colloquial speech, to be eliminated in favour of the pattern [$\acute{\Sigma}\underset{\circ}{\underset{=}{\Sigma}}$], thereby providing a close parallel to the phenomenon of 'iambic shortening'.

Part III

THE PROSODIES OF GREEK

13 Syllable structure; Quantity and Length

Greek in general shows similar patterns to those of Latin, and our account will follow as far as possible the same order of treatment. Both arrested and unarrested syllables occur, the former with either thoracic or oral arrest; thus, for example, in monosyllabic words, ποῦ (CV⁺), τίς (CVᵒC), οὔ (CVᵒ). Monosyllables of the last (unarrested) type occur freely in Greek, unlike in Latin (where they are found only as enclitics).

~ VCV ~ and ~ V̆CCV ~ (general)

According to the traditional rules, a single consonant between vowels releases the following syllable, as in Latin, and of two consonants between vowels the first arrests the preceding syllable and the second releases the following syllable. Thus the syllabic structure of e.g. πᾰτέρᾰ will be CVᵒ.CVᵒ.CVᵒ, of δηλώσει CV⁺.CV⁺.CV⁺, and of σύνδεσμος CVᵒC.CVᵒC.CVᵒC. If arrested syllables are equated with 'heavy quantity' and unarrested syllables with 'light quantity', the traditional syllabifications are generally supported[1] by metrical evidence, as well as by the traditional rules of quantity. Thus, for example, χερσί (CVᵒC.CVᵒ) indicates by its beginning a hexameter that the first syllable is heavy, and χεροῖν (CVᵒ.CV⁺C) by its ending an iambic line that the first syllable is light, as also follows from the traditional rule of quantity that a syllable containing a short vowel followed by two or more consonants is heavy, but otherwise light. The rules of syllabification may also apply across word boundaries: so that in e.g. (hexameter ending) ~τοῖσιν μὲν ἐνὶ φρεσὶν ἄλλα μεμήλει the syllabic structure is CV⁺.CVᵒC.CVᵒ.CVᵒ.CVᵒC.CVᵒ.CVᵒ.CVᵒC. CVᵒ.CVᵒ.CV⁺.CV⁺, equating with a quantitative pattern Σ̱Σ̱Σ̱Σ̱Σ̱Σ̱Σ̱-

---

[1] Excluding those discussed on p. 29. See also pp. 210 ff. on certain consonant sequences.

ΣΣΣΣΣ, just as if the word boundaries were not present. This matter, however, is discussed in more detail below.

The allocation of a single intervocalic consonant to the following syllable is in agreement with the general tendency towards oral reinforcement of release; and we may assume that, just as the syllabic pattern of e.g. φόνος was demonstrably (by metrical evidence) φό.νος, so that of φωνή was φω.νή.

The bases of the metrical equivalence of two light to one heavy syllable are discussed on pp. 255 ff. and 319 f.

Unlike in Latin, accentuation cannot generally be used in Greek as a criterion of quantity, since the position of the Greek accent is limited by vowel length and not by syllabic quantity.[1]

We have already noted (p. 52) that in the formation of comparatives, for example, Greek shows internal evidence for a prosodic equivalence of syllables ending in V^oC to those ending in V^+, in joint contrast with syllables ending in V^o.

Quantity of pre-pausal ~ V̆C

As in Latin, the general expectation is that pre-pausal ~ V^oC would involve syllabic arrest and so heavy quantity. The unreleased character of Greek final consonants is particularly suggested by the fact that only three, all continuants, survive in absolute final position (ν, ρ, ς): cf. ἔφερε beside Skt *abharat*, etc; pre-pausal (as pre-consonantal) οὔ (or οὐχί) beside pre-vocalic οὐκ; μέλι, παῖ, γάλα beside μέλιτος, παιδός, γάλακτος.[2] In the letter-names ἄλφα, βῆτα, etc. the final consonant of the Semitic *aleph*, *bēt*, etc. is preserved only by the addition of a 'protective' α-vowel, which sets the consonant in a releasing instead of an arresting function. Similarly, interjections requiring an occlusive arrest, corresponding to our '*st!*', '*pst!*', could not be integrated into the Greek

---

[1] Indirect evidence is occasionally offered, under the conditions of Wheeler's and Vendryes' Laws (cf. A 1967a, 50 ff.). For example (by Vendryes' Law) the difference of accentuation in Attic between ἕτοιμος and ἀρχαῖος is related to different quantities of the first syllable, as also (by Wheeler's Law) is the accentual difference between τειχίον and λίθιον. But exceptions (more particularly to Wheeler's Law) weaken these correlations (e.g. πεδίον).

[2] See further Ward 1946 (in modern Greek only ς is really viable in pre-pausal position). For the syllabic function of final consonants in Greek it may perhaps also be significant that in Mycenaean spelling the surviving final consonants are omitted just as are continuants at the end of a syllable within the word (e.g. *te-o* = θεός, θεόν as *pa-ka-na* = φάσγανα, *a-pi* = ἀμφί): cf. also Householder 1964; Beekes 1971.

language with a final consonant; instead a vowel was added; and in this case the consonant was doubled in order that the first syllable should contain the required arrest: thus σίττα, ψύττα, where the final ~τα is simply a means of securing the syllables σίτ, ψύτ.[1] In other words, these syllables were equated with the arrested syllables of σίτ.τα, ψύτ.τα, but the unreleased plosives (τ) were not viable in Greek before pause.

The correlation with heavy quantity is not easily demonstrable, since for metrical purposes the quantity of syllables at the end of a line is generally 'indifferent'; and within the line syntactical boundaries tend to be obscured phonologically by artificial 'cohesion'. There are, however, some indications that in Greek pre-pausal ~V̆C (~V°C) was in fact equated with heavy quantity (in addition to the implication by Dionysius of Halicarnassus referred to on pp. 55 f.). Firstly, there is a tendency in the Greek pentameter ending (though not so strongly developed as in Latin: see p. 130) to avoid final syllables ending in a short vowel, i.e. unarrested syllables; it is noted by Martin (1953, 141) that out of 1,512 pentameters in Bergk's *Anthologia Lyrica* only 98 end in this manner; and on the other hand no distinction is made between syllables with thoracic arrest (i.e. long vowel) and with oral arrest (i.e. short vowel + consonant). Another indication may perhaps be seen in the patterns of 'resolution' as occasionally admitted in foot V of tragic iambics. This most often involves the line ending with a quadrisyllabic word or complex: e.g. Aeschylus, *Pers.* 448 ~ φιλόχορος, 501 ~ διὰ πόρον; *Eum.* 40 ~ θεομυσῆ, 780 ~ βαρύκοτος; Sophocles, *Phil.* 1302 ~ πολέμιον, 1327 ~ ἀκαλυφῆ; Euripides, *Hel.* 511 ~ βασιλέᾱ, 991 ~ τρεπόμενος.[2] Such resolutions are relatively common in the later plays of Euripides (cf. Zieliński 1925, 174, 191); but out of around 30 cases occurring *none* have final syllables ending in ~V̆, whereas orally arrested syllables are as admissible as thoracically arrested.[3]

---

[1] Cf. Schwyzer 1931; Wyatt 1970, 52. The vowels are simply linguistic representations of the syllabicity (nuclear function) of [s]. ὤόπ, φλαττόθρατ are examples of unintegrated onomatopoeia (Ward 1946, 103).

[2] Cf. Seidler 1812, 380 ff; Descroix 1931, 163.

[3] The same applies to the few examples in the other tragic authors. The possibility cannot be excluded that the non-occurrence of ~V̆ is due to chance; but if certain general conclusions about Greek prosodic patterns are correct (see pp. 320 f.), the absence of proceleusmatic (ΣΣΣΣ) words in this position would be explainable. A trimeter cited by Aristotle, *Phys.* 194a does end with ἐγένετο, but this is generally assumed to be from comedy (cf. e.g. Aristophanes, *Pax* 674 ~ πολεμικά; Menander, *Dysc.* 108 ~ ἀνόσιε). If this is in fact a tragic rule, it is unobserved by Porson in his criticism of Hermann (Watson 1861, 261): 'As Mr. Herman has not given any

Another type of metre in which the principle of 'indifference' is not fully operative is the choliambic (see pp. 299 ff.). In the work of Herodas, for example, final syllables ending in a short vowel are relatively uncommon (72 out of 598 according to Werner 1892, 26; cf. also 14 f.), and Werner concludes, 'Herodam ut ceteros Graecorum choliambographos in ultima versuum sede raro sibi concessisse syllabas exeuntes in brevem vocalem'. Syllables of the type $\sim \breve{V}C$ are comparatively more frequent (around 160),[1] and so, if these figures are significant, are rather more readily classifiable with the remaining syllables (of type $\sim \bar{V}(C)$), which would imply that they were heavy rather than light. But the differences in this case are perhaps not great enough to exclude mere statistical probability as a factor in the occurrence of the various types.[2] In Babrius, accentual peculiarities (see p. 267) normally result in the final syllable having a long vowel. There are, however, a few cases of final $\sim \breve{V}C$ (as well as $\sim \alpha \iota$, $\sim o\iota$), as e.g. πίστιν; whereas the rare examples of final $\sim \breve{V}$ are all in poems which on other evidence are manifestly corrupt (e.g. cxvi: cf. Rutherford's comment, and page xc of his Introduction).

There may also be some evidence from lyric, if it is admitted that there are cases where the metre requires a heavy syllable, without 'indifference', at period-end. Within periods there is synaphea (metrical continuity) between lines, and no 'indifference', so that the requirement of a final heavy syllable can be met by a syllable of type $\sim \breve{V}C$ only if the next line begins with a consonant; thus e.g. in Aristophanes, *Nub.* 564, χορόν has final heavy syllable on account of πρῶτα beginning the next line. But at period-end, σέβουσῖν (600, responding with 567 μοχλευτήν) is permitted to stand in spite of the next line beginning with ἤ. If, as Irigoin (1967) assumes, the metre (choriambic) requires a heavy syllable here, it would support the view that a final syllable of type $\sim \breve{V}C$ before pause 'is and remains closed' and so heavy; and Irigoin goes on to comment that 'metricians regrettably tend to consider a final closed syllable with short vowel as short; phonetically, before pause, a closed syllable can only be long'. Such an interpretation of

striking instances of this resolution in his incomparable treatise, I shall try to supply the defect:

Ὁ μετρικὸς, ὁ σοφὸς, ἄτοπα γέγραφε περὶ μέτρων.
Ὁ μετρικὸς ἄμετρος, ὁ σοφὸς ἄσοφος ἔγενετο.'

[1] Werner's figure of 199 includes the 'short diphthongs' αι and οι, for which, however, the analysis $\breve{V}C$ is uncertain.
[2] Cf. Cunningham 1971, 219 f.

pre-pausal ∼V̆C is strongly opposed by Dale (1964, 20 n.9), who castigates it as mere 'fashionable doctrine' and 'modern theory', and espouses as self-evidently right a concept of quantity which there has already been occasion to criticize (pp. 58 f.). Dale would presumably have considered the position in question as 'indifferent', and so potentially light (cf. Dale 1968, 26); but it would then be necessary to show that a syllable of type ∼V̆ could also occur there. It seems preferable to investigate the situation for each language in the light of the evidence rather than to rely on general preconceptions; and for Greek at any rate Irigoin's views seem to be rather better supported than Dale's.

Vowel length

Thoracic arrest is associated with long vowels, as in Latin, and is invariably equated with heavy quantity in all positions, as shown by metre and by traditional statements. The vowels of such syllables contrast with those of other types, whether arrested or unarrested; for in syllables ending with V°C (orally arrested) or V° (unarrested) the absence of thoracic arrest is associated with short vowels. However, unlike in Latin, there is no clear evidence that the short vowels occupied a smaller, less 'centrifugal' perimeter of articulation (cf. A 1968a, 59). For example, the Latin short *ĭ* vowel is commonly transcribed by the Greek ε instead of ι (e.g. κομετιον = *comitium*), which suggests that Greek ῐ was of a closer quality than *Latin ĭ*, and so not markedly different from that of the corresponding long vowel. However, whilst in the short-vowel system back and front axes never accommodated more than three grades of aperture, in the long-vowel system of classical Attic the front axis (and at an earlier period the back) accommodated four (A 1959, 244 ff.).

In the case of diphthongs, since the second element is closer than the first, it could theoretically form an oral arrest; but it is at the same time of sufficiently open aperture to accompany a thoracic arrest: both would of course result in heavy quantity.[1]

---

[1] In the case of αυ and ευ it is evident that latterly the second element had a consonantal function, since its aperture was eventually reduced to that of a fricative (thus in Modern Greek e.g. αὐτός, γεῦμα = [aftos], [ˈjevma]). Final digraphs before an initial vowel probably do not represent a diphthong at all, since the second element functioned as a consonantal (semivocalic) release for the following syllable, thereby avoiding hiatus and involving light quantity: thus e.g. μοι ἔννεπε = [mo.jen∼];

Complex pausal releases and arrests

The oral (consonantal) releases and arrests of Greek syllables may be either simple or complex. In an isolated word such as τίς both release and arrest are simple, and in θρίξ both are complex. The following complexes are found after pause: σ + plosive (e.g. στενός, σφαγή, σβέννυμι, ζυγόν);[1] σ + nasal (e.g. σμίνθος); plosive + σ (e.g. ξένος, ψόφος); plosive + liquid or nasal (e.g. κράτος, βλέπω, κνέφας, τμῆσις, δμώς); plosive + plosive (e.g. κτῆμα, πτῶσις, βδόλος, χθών, φθόνος); nasal + nasal (e.g. μνήμη); and triconsonantal complexes of the type σ + plosive + liquid or nasal (e.g. στρέφω, σφραγίς, σπλάγχνα, σκνίψ).[2] The inventory of complex post-pausal releases is considerably larger than in Latin, but complex pre-pausal arrests are notably restricted, viz. to sequences of which ς is the final member, namely ξ, ψ, λς (ἅλς);[3] and triconsonantal μψ (χρέμψ), γξ (σφίγξ), ρξ (σάρξ).[4]

~ V̆CC(C)V ~ (non-pausal sequences)

When consonant sequences are found intervocalically, such as occur neither initially nor finally at pause, one may assume (again in accordance with traditional doctrine) that they constituted arrest + release. ἄρτος, for example, would be analysable as ἄρ.τος; a syllabification ἄρτ.ος is improbable, because a complex arrest would thereby take precedence over oral reinforcement of release; and ἄ.ρτος is ruled out both on grounds of the non-occurrence of initial ρτ ~ and by the heavy quantity attested for the first syllable. Here also are to be included all double consonants, as e.g. πέττω = πετ.τω.

> medially, the second element of the digraph represents either a *double* semivowel (i.e. αἰδοῖος = [ai.doj.jos]; ἀγαυός = [a.gaw.wos]) or a vowel followed by a semi-vocalic 'glide' (i.e. [~oi.jo~], [~au.wo~], etc.): cf. Arg. αθαναιαι, Cor. ευϝαρχοσ (A 1968a, 77 ff.). Heavy quantity results in either case, though simplification of the geminate may occur, leading to loss of the arresting element and so to light quantity (as e.g. commonly in the second syllable of δείλαιος or the first of τοιοῦτος).
>
> That prevocalic ει has a different value from preconsonantal ει is shown by the fact that the two subsequently develop quite differently (for details see A 1968a, 69, 79).

[1] ζ = [zd]: cf. A 1968a, 54 ff; Nagy 1970, 126 f.

[2] There also survive dialectally the sequences δϝ ~ (Cor. δϝενια = Δεινίου) and ϝρ ~ (e.g. Arc. ϝρησισ = ῥῆσις). There are numerous gaps in the actual occurrences of each category: there are, for example, no cases of σγ ~, σν ~, τκ ~, δλ ~, σπν ~.

[3] Dialectally also ~ρς (Cret. μαιτυρσ; Alcman μάκαρς); ~νς (e.g. Cret. acc. pl. ελευθε-ρονς): the correct Attic form of ἕλμινς is ἕλμις.
ὦλξ is only a grammarians' construct, based on acc. ὦλκα(ς).

Where sequences of three consonants occur, the decision may be taken on the basis of their relative apertures (see p. 135); thus, for example, ἐχ.θρός, ὄμ.βρος, ἄρκ.τος, πλαγκ.τός. Where the articulations flanking the central consonant are of equal aperture, as e.g. in σπλάγχνα, ἄρθρα, practice may have varied from dialect to dialect, since we know that, where this can be tested (i.e. after short vowel: see pp. 210 ff.), the sequence plosive + liquid or nasal functioned in some dialects as a complex release, in others as arrest + release; and in dialects of the former type this factor could even have involved a syllabification πέρ.κνός, in spite of the fact that ρ evidently had a greater aperture than ν.

Where sequences unattested in initial or final position at pause are divided by a grammatical boundary, the syllabic division must a fortiori have been of the type ἐν.τείνω, ἐκ.κινῶ. This environment also provides examples of types of sequence (mostly containing σ) which are not otherwise found; thus e.g. ἔκ-στασις, ἐν-σείω, ἐν-σπείρω, προσ-ψαύω, ἐκ-πτύω, where the syllabic division presumably coincided with the grammatical.[1]

~ V̆CC(C)V ~ (pre-pausal sequences)

We may now deal with the syllabification between vowels of consonant sequences which *do* also occur either initially or finally at pause. Those which can occur *only* finally are very few, viz. λς, μψ, γξ, ρξ, and present no special problems. For words such as ἄλσος, κομψός can only admit of analyses ἄλσ.ος or ἄλ.σος, κομψ.ός or κομ.ψός or κομπ.σός. ἄ.λσος and κο.μψός are excluded by considerations of quantity and the occurrences of initial sequences. The criterion of oral reinforcement of release tends to exclude ἄλσ.ος and κομψ.ός;[2] and the decision as between κομπ.σός and κομ.ψός may be taken on grounds of the relative apertures of the flanking consonants, which would be in favour of the former.[3]

---

[1] In cases of weaker disjuncture (cf. A 1962, 19 n.) such sequences were simplified in various ways; thus perf. pass. inf. *πεπλεκσθαι → πεπλέχθαι; aor. *enskʷete → ἔσπετε (cf. pres. *ensekʷe → ἔννεπε); fut. *διδασκσω → διδάξω.

[2] The same may be assumed to apply to the sequence ρσ, which, though not occurring finally in Attic, is of the same general type as λσ (i.e. liquid + σ): therefore e.g. θάρ.σος.

[3] Similarly e.g. ἕλκ.σις (ἕλξις).

~ V̆CC(C)V ~ (post-pausal sequences)

In considering sequences which can occur initially, it is necessary to distinguish between

(a) their 'non-junctural' occurrence, i.e. where the sequence of consonants together with the preceding vowel contains no grammatical boundary; and

(b) their 'junctural' occurrence, i.e. where a grammatical boundary does so occur:

(a) NON-JUNCTURAL

1. *General.* In the case of 2-consonant sequences, the quantity of the preceding syllable is heavy even if the vowel is short; e.g. in ἄστυ, ὄζος, κόσμος, λέξις, πεπτός, τέμνω; we may therefore assume either ἄσ.τυ or ἄστ.υ, etc., of which the former analysis is favoured by considerations of oral release of the following syllable. The consequent syllabifications ἄσ.τυ, λέκ.σις, πεπ.τός, etc. are contrary to ancient doctrine (ἄ.στυ etc.), which, however, must be considered as phonetically inapplicable (pp. 29 f.). For 3-consonant sequences the criterion of relative apertures could again be applied; thus, for example, ἄσ.τρον, ἰσ.χνός.

2. *Plosive + liquid or nasal.* In Greek, unlike Latin, nasals in general behave in much the same way as liquids in the post-plosive environment. In prehistoric Greek it is evident that (as in prehistoric Latin) the sequences in question were divided as arrest + release, giving a heavy preceding syllable in all cases; for adjectives such as πυκνός, μακρός form their comparatives as πυκνότερος, μακρότερος, with *short* 'linking' vowel o, just as e.g. in λεπτότερος, ὠμότερος, and unlike in σοφώτερος (with long linking ω).[1] In Homer also this is the usual treatment; a syllable containing a short vowel followed by plosive + liquid or nasal has light quantity most commonly *metri gratia*, where a word could not otherwise be accommodated in the metre (e.g. ἀφροδίτη)[2] – and even then only where the sequence involved is plosive + ρ or voiceless plosive + λ. For Homer, therefore, we may assume normal syllabifications of the type πατ.ρός, τέκ.νον.

---

[1] Cases such as ἐρυθρώτερος, ἐμμετρώτερος, εὐτεκνώτατος are later formations (see below on Attic).

[2] For other cases, some of which may be of more recent origin, cf. Wathelet 1966. The isolated case φαρέτρης (normally φαρέτρη) at *Il.* viii 323 may be explained as a means of avoiding spondaic-ending words at end of foot (see pp. 286 ff.).

But in classical Attic a different treatment seems to have prevailed. For in both tragedy and comedy light quantity is found freely occurring in such environments, implying a syllabification πα.τρός, τέ.κνον, etc., with the sequence acting as a complex release. This treatment is traditionally known, therefore, as 'Attic shortening' (*correptio Attica*). It is particularly characteristic of comedy, and may be presumed to reflect the spoken colloquial of the time; the alternative treatment might be seen as due to the influence of epic tradition, which would appropriately be stronger in tragedy.[1] An incidental reflex of the Attic treatment, apart from metre, is seen in the Attic accentuation of ἄγροικος, which is like that of ἕτοιμος and unlike ἀρχαῖος; for the Attic shift, by 'Vendryes' Law', from properispomenon to proparoxytone is characteristic only of words having a *light* antepenultimate syllable.

In consequence of their involvement as second members of a complex releasing sequence, the liquids and nasals were recognized by the Greeks themselves as a special category of consonants, to which they gave the name ὑγρός (e.g. Dionysius Thrax, *Ars Gramm.*, 14 U; Hephaestion, *Ench.*, 5 C). Scholiasts' explanations of the word are various, but the most general opinion seems to be that it means 'fluid' in the sense of 'unstable', with reference to their values for quantitative metrical purposes. In Latin this term was translated by *liquidus*, but since in Latin it did not apply to the nasals, the word came to refer, as in current phonetic terminology, only to the 'liquids' *r* and *l*; in this sense it remains a useful term, since a class-definition of these consonants in articulatory terms is a somewhat complex matter.

From the statistics given by Schade (1908) one may derive the following overall figures[2] for the occurrence of *correptio Attica*, i.e. of light quantity where a short vowel is followed by one of the sequences plosive + liquid or nasal. In the trimeters and tetrameters of Aristophanes, *correptio* occurs in 1,262 cases as against 196 cases of heavy quantity (= a ratio of 6.4/1). In the trimeters of Aeschylus, Sophocles, and Euripides the figures are respectively 214/66 (= 3.25/1), 438/189 (= 2.3/1), 1,118/493 (= 2.25/1).[3] The tendency to *correptio* is thus

---

[1] The epic practice is also normal in the early iambographers.

[2] Schade, however, does not distinguish between junctural and non-junctural occurrences.

[3] For *correptio* Schade's figures refer only to 'weak' position in the foot, i.e. they exclude the rare cases of light syllables in 'resolution'; and for heavy quantity they refer only to 'strong' position, since the weak position is either light or 'anceps' and so cannot determine heavy quantity.

more than twice as strong in comedy as in tragedy; but even in the latter it is much more common than heavy quantity. The ratios show a surprising disparity between Aeschylus and Sophocles in this respect; but the area of disagreement is reduced if it is noted that, excluding the so-called 'heavy groups' (see below), the two noun-stems πατρ- and τεκν- account for over half of the examples of heavy quantity in Sophocles; apart from these, therefore, Aeschylus and Sophocles show similar ratios.[1]

However, not all sequences of plosive + liquid or nasal were equally prone to treatment as complex releases (involving light quantity for a preceding syllable with short vowel). The Homeric exceptions to heavy quantity, as already noted, did not extend to groups involving nasals, and included the lateral λ only where it was preceded by a *voiceless* plosive. And even in Attic *correptio* does not normally occur in cases of voiced plosive + λ or nasal (i.e. βλ, γλ, γν, γμ, δν, δμ).[2] For this reason such groups were termed by Schade (1908) 'coniunctiones graves' – a felicitous term in the light of our current use of 'heavy', since they almost invariably[3] involve heavy quantity. If one excludes such groups, a short vowel preceding plosive + liquid or nasal in Attic comedy is seldom associated with heavy quantity; and Maas (1966, 76) suggests that, where exceptions occur, 'we can conclude that the tragic manner is being parodied'.[4]

The difference in treatment between voiced and voiceless plosives may possibly be related to the greater tension and 'plosivity' of the latter. The difference between the nasals and liquids may be related to the fact that, whereas in the liquids there is incomplete or discontinuous oral closure, in the nasals oral closure is complete and continuous and only the nasal passage is open. Of the two liquids, ρ involves an intermittent, alternating closure and aperture (trill), whilst λ involves a partial closure (with lateral aperture). The various treatments suggest that for purposes of complex release function the relevant Greek consonants may be set on a scale of stricture (or tension)/aperture as follows:[5]

---

[1] Descroix 1931, 17; Page 1951, 42 f.

[2] δλ, βν, βμ do not occur, having become by assimilation λλ, μν, μμ (cf. Lac. ἐλλά beside ἕδρα; σεμνός beside σέβομαι; τέτριμμαι beside τρίβω).

[3] An isolated exception is βὔβλου at Aesch., *Supp.* 761.

[4] Figures excluding the 'heavy groups' are given for a selection of tragic works by Descroix (1931, 15), and show a considerable increase in the proportions of light quantity over the figures given by Schade.

[5] Cf. also de Saussure 1916/1960, 71 ff; Descroix 1931, 17 f; Delattre 1944; Grammont 1946, 99; Bell 1970b, 142.

$$
\text{(1st members)}
\begin{cases}
\text{Voiceless plosives (π τ κ φ θ χ)} \\
\\
\text{Voiced plosives (β δ γ)}
\end{cases}
$$

$$
\text{(2nd members)}
\begin{cases}
\text{Nasals (ν μ)} \\
\\
\text{Liquids}
\begin{cases}
λ \\
ρ^{1}
\end{cases}
\end{cases}
$$

3. *Other special sequences.* The above scale omits one remaining consonant, the fricative σ, which on the basis of its degree of stricture
would naturally be placed between the plosives and the nasals. It does
not generally figure in discussions of the present type since it was
insufficiently different in stricture/aperture from the plosives to function as second member of a medial complex release. As first member,
however, a rare exception is found in Pindar's treatment of the first
syllable of ἐσλός (< ἐσθλός) as light, implying a syllabification ἐ. σλός
(thus at *Pyth.* iii 66; *Nem.* iv 95; but heavy at *Pyth.* viii 73). Original
medial sequences of σ + liquid or nasal are not attested, having all been
assimilated prehistorically (except at juncture, e.g. δύσ-λυτος, δύσ-νοος);
but the fact that the resulting forms regularly have heavy preceding
syllable (either by vowel or consonant lengthening) indicates that such
sequences functioned prehistorically as arrest + release and not as
complex release: thus e.g. *asme (cf. Skt *asmān*) → Lesb. ἄμμε, Dor.
ἄμε, Att. ἡμᾶς; *χεσλιοι (cf. Skt *sa-hasram*) → Lesb. χέλλιοι, Ion.
χείλιοι, Att. χίλιοι.

There are also rare cases of light quantity before μν, as (?) at Aesch.,
Ag. 991 ὑμνῳδεῖ (lyr.). μν, unlike νμ, can form an initial sequence;
and the special treatment may be connected with the greater mobility
of the tongue-tip than the lips, a factor which could incidentally also
account for the initial occurrence of πτ and κτ (lesser mobility of back
of tongue for κ), and the non-occurrence of τπ ~ , τκ ~ .[2]

There are parallels in other languages to the divisions and order of
the scale suggested by the Greek phenomena. In English, if one
considers the converse complex *arrests*, it is found that words occur(red)
with final *rn, rm, ln, lm* (e.g. *burn, harm, kiln, helm*), but not with final
nr, mr, nl, ml – which is congruent with a greater aperture for the
liquids than for the nasals; and words are found with final *rl* (e.g. *curl*),

[1] For the relative aperture of ρ note also its occurrence in 'resolution' (pp. 317,
323, 326, 331).
[2] Cf. Sievers 1901, 205 f.

but not with final *lr*[1] – which reflects the relative placing of the two liquids. In Latin (cf. p. 141 n.) heavy quantity in the type *rĕpletur*, though rare, is more common than in the type *rĕtrahit*. In Icelandic, vowel lengthening takes place before voiceless plosive + *r*, but pre-aspiration before voiceless plosive + *l* or *n*; and this has been interpreted (p. 70 n.) as indicating that the former group functioned as a complex release at an earlier period than the latter.

Also omitted from the scale of stricture/aperture is the semivowel ϝ [w] ('digamma'), which survived historically in some Greek dialects, and was still relevant to quantity in some forms of verse, including Homer (for details see A 1968a, 45 ff.). As a semivowel, its articulation would be similar to that of a close vowel, and we might expect to place it on the scale after the liquid ρ.[2] In many dialects sequences having ϝ as second member were assimilated and simplified; if, before this process, the sequence formed a complex release, we should not expect the simplification to have any effect on the length of a preceding vowel. But if the sequence had functioned as arrest + release, the preceding syllable would have been invariably heavy; and if it contained a short vowel, the quantity could be preserved after simplification only by compensatory lengthening of the vowel, i.e. by substituting a thoracic for an oral arrest. We find that the results vary from dialect to dialect and period to period. For example, the sequences ν, λ, ρ + ϝ result in compensatory lengthening in Ionic but not in Attic: thus beside Corc. ~ ξενϝοσ we have Ion. ξεῖνος but Attic ξένος;[3] beside Boe. καλϝοσ, Ion. κᾱλός but Att. κᾰλός; beside Arc. κορϝα, Ion. κούρη but Att. κόρη. This indicates that in Attic, unlike Ionic, such sequences had before simplification been treated in the same way as plosive + liquid or nasal, i.e. as complex releases.[4] A similar situation is indicated for δϝ if Att. ὀδός: Hom. οὐδός are from *ὀδϝος;[5] also for σϝ in Att. ἴσος, Ion. ἶσος beside Cret. etc. ϝισϝοσ (where the σ is 'secondary',

---

[1] Cf. Sievers 1901, 204 f; Greenberg 1965, 17, 22, 29.

[2] Cf. Sommer 1909, 173. Note, however, that the initial sequence ϝρ occurred in Greek, as also originally in English (e.g. *wrought*). The reverse initial sequence is seen in e.g. Fr. *roi* [rwa]. Sievers (1901, 204) assumes that in the case of [wr ~] the [w] must have a particularly strictural articulation; but alternatively the [w] may represent simply a labial rounding simultaneous with the liquid (cf. the articulation of modern English initial (*w*)*r*-).

[3] An Attic comparative such as κενότερος to κενός (Ion. κεινός) would have been inherited with short linking vowel o (and not ω) from Common Greek κεν.ϝο ~, and this would have been maintained even after the Attic syllabificatory change to κε.νϝο ~.

[4] Cf. Lejeune 1955, 263.   [5] Cf. Wyatt 1969, 226 ff.

i.e. from original **ts*).¹ The Attic treatment of plosive (and σ)+semi-vowel also finds a parallel in Icelandic, where (p. 70) vowel lengthening occurs in e.g. *vökva, Esja*, thereby implying a complex function for the sequences in question.

However, other combinations of consonant+ϝ had undergone prehistoric assimilations, and reflect syllabification as arrest+release in all cases, generally by consonant doubling: thus **kw* → [kkʷ] (→ ππ), as in ἵππος (cf. Myc. *i-qo*) beside Skt *aśvas*; **tw* → [ttʲ] (→ ττ, σσ), as in Att. τέτταρες, Ion. τέσσερες (cf. Ephesus τεΤαραϙοντα: A 1958, 115; 1968a, 57 f.) beside Skt *catvāras*; (original) **sw* → [ww], as in Aeol. ναῦος (cf. p. 207 n.) beside ἔνασ-σα.² Similar considerations apply to prehistoric groups involving the semivowel [j], as e.g. **t(h)j* in Lesb. μέσσος, Boe. μεττοσ (cf. Skt *madhyas*), which is the same development as for **ts*;³ **sj* in τοῖο (=[tojjo])⁴ beside Skt *tasya*; **-lj* in ἄλλος, beside Lat. *alius*.

Finally, the form ἀνδροτῆτα, occurring in Homer where a light first syllable is metrically required, is not of course a case of the sequence νδρ functioning as a complex release. The form is metrically anomalous, and the embarrassment has been relieved by the substitution of ἀδροτῆτα in many mss.⁵ There are possible solutions from linguistic prehistory; the form is presumably related to ἀνήρ and so derives from **n̥ro* ~ or **n̥r̥* ~ (cf. Hoenigswald 1968). The former should give ἀρο~, which is metrically correct, but would be isolated and so subject to analogical substitution by ἀνδρ~, as in ἀνδρός, ἀνδρεία, etc.⁶ The latter could at an early stage have given ἀν̥r̥ ~, with still syllabic r̥⁷ (cf. Skt *nr̥ṣu* = ἀνδράσι, etc.), which thus would also permit the preceding syllable to remain light; and the development of r̥ → ρο, and of the glide-consonant δ, would be subsequent to the fixation of the formulae in which the word occurs. As Hoenigswald suggests, the underlying form is no doubt archaic and so may represent a 'precious relic'. The latter solution appears to imply a stage of linguistic development even earlier than that of Mycenaean (cf. Ruijgh 1970, 312); but, as Wathelet points

---

¹ See however Wyatt 1969, 192.
² Also with vowel lengthening in Dor. ϝᾶϝος (Ion. νηός, and with 'quantitative metathesis' Att. νεώς).
³ Att.-Ion. μέσος is due to a later simplification of σσ.
⁴ Thence [tojo] → [to.o] → Att. τοῦ; but cf. also Kiparsky 1967c, 629 ff.
⁵ For acceptance of this reading, however, see Beekes 1971, 353 ff.
⁶ Cf. Szemerényi 1964, 109: 'We may infer an original alternation **H₂ner/*H₂n̥r-* (resulting in Gk. ἀνερ-/*ἀρ-, levelled to ἀνερ-/ἀνρ-).'
⁷ Wathelet 1966, 170 f.

out, the Mycenaean writing system would in any case be ill-suited to represent syllabic liquids; and on the basis of variations in Mycenaean spelling Heubeck (1972) suggests that these in fact were still unchanged in Mycenaean. The same considerations could apply to some other cases in which Homer treats, exceptionally, a syllable containing a short vowel followed by plosive + liquid as light, as in ἀβρότη (metrical 'amendment' for ἀμβρότη) < *ἀμῠτη; similarly ἀβροτάξομεν (cf. Wathelet 1966, 160 ff.).

(b) JUNCTURAL

1. *General.* When a morph boundary falls between two members of a consonant sequence, the syllabic boundary also falls here, with consequently heavy quantity for the preceding syllable even though its vowel is short: thus, for example, in προσ-τάσσω, ἐκ-σῴζω, ἐκ τούτου (and, a fortiori, when a morph boundary falls *after* the sequence, as in ἔξ-εστι[1]).[2]

When a morph boundary within a word falls *before* the sequence, the syllabic boundary nevertheless falls between the consonants, with resultant invariably heavy quantity, as e.g., with preposition προ-, προ-σ.τάτης, πρό-κ.σενος (πρόξενος), πρό-π.τωσις. However, where a word boundary is involved, there is some variation. Normally, as in the case of intra-word boundaries, the consonant sequence functions as arrest + release; but occasionally, and generally only *metri gratia*, a preceding word-final syllable ending in a short vowel is treated as light: e.g. Hom. ἔπειτα σκέπαρνον,[3] implying a treatment of σκ as complex release.

In certain metrical positions there is an evident antipathy to the procurement of heavy quantity by a word-final short vowel followed by an initial consonant sequence. In Homer this applies with particular rigour to the end of foot IV,[4] and generally of II, in both cases where

---

[1] The syllabic division here is presumably ἐκ.σεστι, in accordance with the general tendency to oral reinforcement of release.

[2] But in VCV sequences morph boundaries do not normally affect syllabic division; note however, e.g. Cret. συννεῖ (3 sing. subj. of σύνειμι), with gemination of ν to procure a syllabic division συν.~ and thereby preserve the phonological integrity of the morpheme συν (Lejeune 1955, 300); for literary examples cf. Maas, 79.

[3] For other examples see Maas, 78. At *Od.* vii 89 ἀργύρεοι δὲ σταθμοί is, as Maas observes, 'suspect, because θμ also is surprising' (Bentley proposed ἀργύρεοι σταθμοὶ δ'). On the case of initial ζ = [zd] see p. 140 n. At Theoc., xxix 20 ἅς κε ζόης, with ζ apparently in its later value of [z], the line is almost certainly corrupt (Hermann proposed κεν ἔης).

[4] According to Maas (77) it never occurs here; but Drewitt (1908, 104) finds two cases – both involving monosyllables and in the same construction: *Il.* xxiv 557 ἐπεί με πρῶτον and *Od.* xvii 573 ἐπεί σε πρῶθ' (cf. Stifler 1924, 340 f.).

the final syllable would be in 'weak' position. In non-lyric iambics and trochaics the antipathy is general,[1] and is especially rigorous in the case of disyllabic words with heavy first syllables; thus a line beginning ἀνδρὶ στρατηγῷ (Aesch., *Ag.* 1627) or ending κοινᾷ χθονός (Eur., *Phoen.* 692) is exceptional (Maas, 77). The reason for these avoidances may possibly lie in the relationship between the stress patterns of normal speech and metrical patterns, which will later be discussed in some detail. At this point it may just be noted that in Homer spondaic word-endings at IV are in any case relatively rare; the most common cases of their occurrence involve words or phrases of the type Ἀχαιοῖς, ἐφ' ἵππων, περὶ πάντων, i.e. constituting or ending with a pattern ΣΣΣ in which moreover the final syllable is hypercharacterized, i.e. contains a long vowel or diphthong followed by a consonant,[2] whose end *must* consequently coincide with the end of a foot; their favourite position is at line-end, where the quantity of the final syllable is 'indifferent' (cf. Stifler 1924, 366). This does not apply to cases where the word ends in V̆C,[3] which admit of an alternative pattern ΣΣΣ (and so a different place in the line) if the next word begins with a vowel, as e.g. ἄριστον (by contrast with Ἀχαιῶν) in *Il.* i 244 χωόμενος ὅ τ' ἄριστον Ἀχαιῶν οὐδὲν ἔτεισας; and where the word ends in V̆, even more possibilities are open, viz. before an initial consonant or a vowel in hiatus (as *Il.* i 565 ἀλλ' ἀκέουσα κάθησο, ἐμῷ δ' ἐπιπείθεο μύθῳ), or before a vowel with elision (as *Il.* i 583 ἔπειθ' ἵλαος). With regard to the restriction in iambics and trochaics, it could be said that there are more opportunities for words of the pattern ΣΣ̆ (as ἀνδρί) to function metrically as ΣΣ than for words of the pattern ΣΣ̆ (as χερί) to function as ΣΣ.[4]

2. *Plosive + liquid or nasal.* As in Latin, the syllabification of this sequence is strongly influenced by grammatical boundaries. If such a boundary falls between the two consonants, the sequence regularly functions as arrest + release, resulting in heavy quantity of a preceding syllable even if the vowel is short. This is already recognized by ancient

---

[1] Weak position provides no evidence, on account of 'anceps'.
[2] Cf. Drewitt 1908, 103 ('Overlength in the diaeresis is surprisingly common'). From the references given by Stifler for *Il.* i–vi, around ⅔ of the cases are of this type (over 90 out of *c.* 150 exx. of the pattern ΣΣΣ).
[3] At the foot IV diaeresis, if one excludes monosyllables, Stifler's references provide only 14 exx. for the whole of Homer (7 of these in name formulae). On this, and also on words ending with vowel or diphthong, see further pp. 287 ff.
[4] Cf. Newton 1969, 370.

writers, as Hephaestion (*Ench.*, 6 C): 'If, however, the "mute" is final in the first syllable, and the liquid is initial in the second, the syllable is no longer "common" but outright long.' Thus in e.g. ἐκ μάχης or ἐκ-λιπών the first syllable can only be ἐκ. ∼, and therefore arrested and heavy, even in Attic.

If the grammatical boundary falls before the sequence, in Homer it may very occasionally function as a complex release, giving light preceding syllable if its vowel is short: e.g. in πρωτό-πλοον, πρ̥-τρα-πέσθαι, ἐ-κλίθη, κε̥-κρυμμένα. In some such cases, e.g. προτραπέσθαι, the word involved would otherwise be intractable in a hexameter, and this consideration generally applies in the quite common cases where a word boundary is involved (as before words with iambic beginning, e.g. προσηύδα, θρόνους, which can only occur in hexameters if a light syllable precedes). Some such cases may possibly reflect an original 'syllabic' liquid: e.g. in *Il.* iii 422 ἐπὶ (ϝ)ἔργα̥ τράποντο, where ρα is derivable from *r̥ (cf. Wathelet 1966, 160 ff.). On the other hand, however, in the weak position of the foot, *heavy* quantity seldom depends on a following initial sequence of plosive+liquid or nasal, although it frequently does in strong position (as e.g. *Od.* i 107 πεσσοῖσι̥ προπάροιθε). The general principles involved here are presumably the same as in the case of other types of sequence discussed above.

In Attic, word-final short vowels regularly involve a light syllable, even in tragic dialogue, before an initial 'light group'; and the same applies with few exceptions to intra-word morph junctions;[1] which indicates that in such cases the sequence normally formed a complex release. Before initial 'heavy groups', on the other hand, light final syllables are rare; and especially so at intra-word junctions (Descroix 1931, 20 f.).

The degrees of incidence of 'correptio Attica' may be generally summarized by the diagram opposite (A 1968a, 105), which takes comedy as its central axis, and displays along different dimensions the rôles of the various factors – dialect/genre, voice (of plosives), stricture/aperture (of liquids and nasals) – on which the incidence depends.

3. *Other sequences with liquid or nasal.* There are rare cases in which the sequence μν is permitted to function as a complex release (cf. p. 213) where a grammatical boundary precedes: e.g. Eur., *I.A.* 68

---

[1] Cf. Descroix 1931, 18; Page 1951, 24 and n.25.

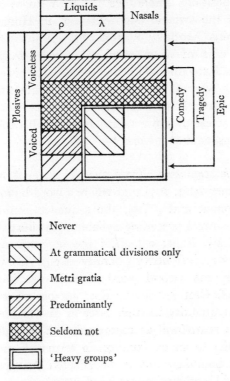

	Never
	At grammatical divisions only
	Metri gratia
	Predominantly
	Seldom not
	'Heavy groups'

Incidence of 'correptio Attica'.

θυγατρὶ μνηστήρων; they are particularly rare at intra-word junctions, as μξ-μνῆσθαι at Aesch., *Pers.* 287 (lyr.).

The sequence *s + liquid or nasal was assimilated at a prehistoric date, and after pause or consonant was simplified to a single consonant. But its original intervocalic function as arrest + release, even when preceded by a grammatical boundary, is still reflected in the fact that a heavy syllable may be formed with a preceding word-final short vowel, as e.g. *Il.* xii 159 βέλεᾰ ῥέον (cf. Skt *srav-*, Eng. *stream*), *Il.* xiii 754 ὄρεῖ νιφόεντι (cf. Eng. *snow*). For ρ this treatment is also general in dialogue of Attic tragedy and comedy, and spellings with ρρ are occasionally found in inscriptions.[1] At intra-word junctions this treatment was evidently regular, and resulted in double consonant, as e.g. Hom. ἔ-ρρεε, ἔ-ννεον (cf. Skt *snā-*), Att. ἔ-ρρευσε. However, the analogy

---

[1] As in some mss of Homer where a preposition is involved (and so a close connexion between the words): e.g. καταρρόον for κατὰ ῥόον.

of word-initial positions sometimes led to a single consonant being introduced after the syllabic augment: e.g. in Homer ἔλαβε beside ἔλλαβε (cf. Aegina λhαβον= λαβών< *sl~); in Attic this became general in the case of λ or nasal – thus only ἔλαβε, ἔνειφε, etc. – though it remained exceptional in the case of ρ. In this connexion it may be relevant that whereas there are stems originating from simple initial *l or nasal (e.g. λείπω, νέομαι: cf. Skt ric-, nas-), which therefore involve no arrest of a preceding syllable, all cases of ῥ~ derive from original consonant sequences.[1]

4. *Sequences with semivowel.* From the evidence of Homer it might appear (cf. Sommer 1909, 177) that where a word boundary intervened between a consonant and ϝ [w], the sequence could function as a complex release, since a preceding syllable with short vowel sometimes counts as metrically light: e.g. *Il.* i 106 κρήγυ**ο**ν εἶπας, *Il.* vi 151 ἄνδρε**ς** ἴσασιν (as against heavy quantity in e.g. *Il.* i 108 εἶπα**ς** ἔπος), where historically the second word in each case is known to have begun with ϝ (cf. Cret. ϝειπόντι, Boe. ϝίστορ, El. ϝεπος). Sommer explains the light quantity in such cases as due to the relatively high 'sonority' of the semivowel as compared with that of the preceding consonant (parallel to an explanation in terms of aperture). But for the grammatical boundary not to be effective in separating the two consonants would be otherwise unprecedented in Greek, and Sommer's explanation is in fact as unnecessary as it is mistaken. There are clear indications (cf. Chantraine 1958, 120 ff; Shipp 1972, 44 f.) that initial ϝ was in the process of disappearance during the epic period (inscriptions indicate that it was a less viable feature of Ionic than of Aeolic). There are, for example, frequent cases of elision before words having etymological initial ϝ, as e.g. *Il.* i 19 εὖ δ᾽ οἰκάδ᾽ ἱκέσθαι (cf. Arc. ϝοικοσ); few of these can be easily emended away, and many of them clearly involve adaptations, in an age when initial ϝ was no longer a feature of living speech, of formulae originating at a time when it was (e.g. fem. φωνήσασ᾽ ἔπεα after masc. φωνήσας (ϝ)έπεα). In fact a majority of the cases where, in weak position, heavy quantity is achieved at a word boundary of the type ~V̆C w~ involve either formulae or following enclitics (which form a phonological unity with the preceding

---

[1] *sr* or *wr*. For the latter cf. τᾆ ῥήματα (Aristophanes, *Ran.* 1059); *Od.* xxii 46 ὅσᾶ ῥέзεσκον – but also ἔ-ρεзε (*Il.* ii 400), on which Choeroboscus comments (*Schol. in Theod.*, ii, 44 H) that it is διὰ τὸ μέτρον.

word). The most likely explanation, therefore, of the fact that an apparent sequence ～V̆C w～ does *not* always result in heavy quantity is simply that the second word did not, at the time of composition, have an initial ϝ; it began with a vowel, and the preceding final consonant therefore acted as a simple syllabic release.

The situation is different where intra-word morph boundaries are involved. Here a morph beginning with ϝ would, by its bound nature, be invariably in contact with the final consonant of the preceding morph with which it was grammatically connected; the disappearance of the ϝ might therefore be expected to have prosodic consequences which would not generally apply to free forms (words). However, the situation does not in fact arise. It could be expected in the case of perfect participles in -ώς, where the presence of an original ϝ is indicated by e.g. Goth. *-wōþs*, Skt *-vān* (and by the υ of the fem. -υῖα).[1] An original *γεγον-ϝως might then be expected to give, at least in Ionic, *γεγουνως (with compensatory vowel-lengthening); and *λελυκ-ϝως to give, even in Attic, *λελυππως (with double consonant: cf. ἵππος). In fact no such compensatory heavy quantity is found. That this is not due to the group Cw acting as a complex release (in any case improbable in the junctural context) is shown by the fact that κϝ does not here develop to π.[2] The reason must therefore be that the pattern of the forms without original ϝ, which constitute the rest of the perfect paradigm (e.g. γέγονα, λέλυκα), has ousted the expected developments by analogical pressure.

Intra-word junctures of the type ～V̆C-j～ regularly involved heavy quantity, as would be expected from their non-junctural developments; e.g. *t-j* in Att. μέλιττα, Aeol., Ion. μέλισσα, beside μέλιτ-ος;[3] *k-j* in φυλάττω, φυλάσσω beside φύλακ-ος.

When Cw occurs as a word-initial sequence, it may in Homer, like plosive + liquid or nasal, have quantitative effects on a preceding word ending in a short vowel, as e.g. *Od.* i 203 οὔ τοι ἔτῑ δ(ϝ)ηρόν, *Od.* ix 236 ἡμεῖς δὲ̱ δ(ϝ)είσαντες, and even *Il.* iii 172 φίλε̱ ἑκυρέ, where ἑ̱～ = ϝϝἑ～ < *swe～, with double consonant preserved, though

---

[1] Also Myc. *te-tu-ko-wo-a* = *tetukhwoa* (cf. τετευχότα).

[2] Or Myc. *q*.

[3] The geminates in Attic and Ionic (as compared with μέσος: p. 215 n. 3) are attributable to the grammatical boundary delaying the phonetic development, so that by the time the geminate stage had been reached (a) Attic had converged with Boeotian in the relevant reflexes, and (b) the simplification rule σσ → σ had ceased to operate in Ionic. Cf. p. 21 and A 1958, 119 n.31.

initial, in a fossilized expression (A 1968a, 46 f.). The indication is that the sequence functioned as arrest + release in early Greek even when preceded by a grammatical boundary. But in weak positions in verse similar restrictions applied to those which have been mentioned for other sequences.

At intra-word junctions, a morph-initial Cw behaves as expected in cases where it can be tested. In Homer, the sequence δϝ requires heavy quantity of a preceding syllable – achieved in the texts either by vowel-lengthening or by consonant-doubling: e.g. δείδιμεν for δέ-δϝιμεν, ἔδδεισα for ἔ-δϝεισα; it follows, therefore, that the sequence functioned as arrest + release. But in Attic there is no such lengthening, hence δέδια, ἔδεισα, implying complex release (also apparently for this sequence even in Ionic: cf. Lejeune 1955, 71).

The double consonants at both intra-word and proclitic junctions in Boe. θιοππαστοσ, τα ππαματα may be due to an original initial sequence *kw, indicating a functioning of this sequence as arrest + release; and the same would apply to the prehistoric sequence *k in Hom. ὅτε̤ (σ)σεύαιτο and ἐπισσεύεσθαι (cf. Skt cyav-).

Hypercharacterization

Syllables in which thoracic arrest is followed, within the syllable, by one or more consonantal articulations, are well attested in Greek: e.g. πλῆτ.τω, θώρᾱξ; and their number is increased if words of the type πρωκτός are syllabified as πρωκ.τός (as after a short vowel) rather than πρω.κτός.

At a prehistoric period, however, there are indications that such syllables were felt to be anomalous in cases where the consonant was a 'sonant' (liquid, nasal, or semivowel), and the vowel was accordingly shortened ('Osthoff's Law'): cf. p. 66. The reason for this particular change presumably lies in the relatively large aperture of the 'sonants', which permitted them to behave syllabically in the same manner as vowels, e.g. by accompanying a thoracic arrest of the syllable.[1] In which case either the syllabic peak would continue for the whole duration of the vowel, and would so be anomalously long; or, if the latter part of the vowel functioned normally as a 'coda', i.e. accompanied the thoracic arrest and so concluded the ballistic movement, the 'sonant' would

---

[1] Note also that in early Greek even the liquids and nasals were capable, as syllable-finals, of carrying variations of pitch (pp. 242 f.).

then tend to form an extra peak of sonority.[1] By shortening the vowel, a normal peak would be obtained and the 'sonant' would function as the arresting element.

When the same sequences of long vowel + sonant occurred before a vowel, no such anomalies arose, since the sonant would then function as an oral reinforcement of the release of the next syllable, and the first syllable would end normally with a long vowel, i.e. thoracic arrest: e.g. γνῶ.ναι, πατρῶ.jος (πατρῶιος). The vowel was not shortened before word-final sonants in any environment (thus regularly ἔγνων, dat. sing. ∼ωι etc.), perhaps by generalization from environments in which the sonant was followed by a vocalic word-initial to which it was attached (τῶ jανδρί = τῶι ἀνδρί, etc.).[2]

At a later stage, further sequences of the types eliminated by Osthoff's Law came into being, e.g. by contraction, as ἔ-ελθον → ἦλθον, τιμά-οντες → τιμῶντες, ἀοιδή → ὠιδή, προ-αυδᾶν → πρωὐδᾶν, or by analogy, as subj. φέρωνται after φερώμεθα, φέρησθε (Lejeune 1955, 189).[3] In this case the sequences involving liquids and nasals survived, but the semivowels continued to be an embarrassment, being the most vocoidal of the sonants (cf. p. 67) – hence the name 'long diphthongs' for the sequences ωι, ωυ, etc. By the early 4 c. B.C. preconsonantal ηι had merged with ει: thus e.g. κλείς for Old Attic κλήις. Soon afterwards the same development appears in inflexional endings (e.g. dat. sing. βουλει, 3 sing. subj. ειπει), but is reversed from *c.* 200 B.C. by an analogical restoration of the long vowel from other cases and persons/ numbers in which it was not followed by ι (e.g. βουλῆς, εἴπητε). But the 'long diphthongs' were evidently no longer viable, and about the same time a new development supervenes whereby they lose their semivowel element: thus ᾱι, ᾱυ, ηι, ωι → ᾱ, η, ω.[4] The preservation of the semivowel in texts was then purely orthographic, and its lack of phonetic value is reflected in the Byzantine practice of writing the ι subscript (ᾳ, ῃ, ῳ) instead of adscript.

So at this later period the anomaly of the sequence was eliminated by reducing it to a single long vowel, functioning normally as syllabic peak + coda.

---

[1] Cf. p. 177.
[2] Cf. the treatment of final αι and οι as = 1 mora for accentual purposes (p. 238 n.).
[3] Alternatively the analogy may have prevented the operation of Osthoff's Law.
[4] For evidence see A 1968a, 82.

14 Word juncture ($\sim V + V \sim$)

The maintenance of hiatus, without any change in the basic forms, is well attested in Homer (even when one discounts cases where the next word in fact began with ϝ). In the case of final long vowels or of diphthongs this is most common in the strong position of the foot, and more particularly at a caesura; in foot III around 700 cases are attested.[1] In the case of a final 'long diphthong', as e.g. *Il.* xvi 734 σκαιῇ ἔγχος, one might rather consider it as a sequence of long vowel + semivowel, i.e. [$\sim$εεje$\sim$] etc; and in the case of other diphthongs as either short vowel + double semivowel, e.g. *Il.* iii 40 ἔμεναι ἄγαμος = [$\sim$ajja$\sim$], or as diphthong + semivocalic glide, i.e. [$\sim$aija$\sim$]. In the case of vowels of close or mid aperture (short or long) it is also possible that an automatic transitional glide intervened, as e.g. *Il.* xvii 196 παιδὶ(*j*)ὄπασσε, *Il.* vi 388 ἐπειγομένη(*j*)ἀφικάνει, *Il.* i 333 ὁ(*w*)ἔγνω – as commonly happens in sequences of this type.

Apart from certain forms which normally occur with hiatus (see below), short vowels in hiatus are most commonly found at the IIIb$_1$ ('trochaic') caesura, at Ib$_2$ (especially if followed by pause: e.g. *Il.* ix 247 ἀλλ' ἄνα, εἰ μέμονάς γε), and at IVb$_2$ ('bucolic diaeresis').[2]

In weak position it is normal in Homer for final vowels and diphthongs to be 'shortened' in hiatus (hence the term '*correptio epica*' for this phenomenon, sometimes also called 'weak hiatus'). By far the most common cases involve the diphthongs $\sim$αι and $\sim$οι, of which around 6,500 examples are thus attested. Since, however, diphthongs do not have 'short' counterparts, it is here rather a case of the second element shifting into a consonantal releasing function for the next syllable, leaving the first element (a short vowel) as syllable-final; thus e.g. ἄνδρα μοι ἔννεπε = [$\sim$o.je$\sim$], κλῦθί μευ ἀργυρότοξ' = [$\sim$e.wa$\sim$]; and the cases of actual shortening of long vowels in such a context (e.g. πλάγχθη ἐπεί) have often been seen as an analogical extension from the diphthongal cases.[3] However (see p. 142) the

[1] Chantraine 1958, 89.   [2] Chantraine 1958, 90.
[3] For discussion and references see Rossi 1968, 234.

phenomenon of 'vocalis ante vocalem corripitur' is also a possible phonetic process in its own right.

The 'shortening' of a 'long diphthong' is more surprising, since the second element might be expected to act as a consonant in releasing function and so leave the vowel long, as in strong position: for both treatments cf. *Il.* i 30 ἡμετέρῳ ἐνὶ οἴκῳ ἐν Ἄργεϊ; such 'shortening' is less common than that of other diphthongs or even of long vowels, and might be seen either as an analogical extension or as involving loss of the second element with consequent shortening of the vowel.

Shortening is not indicated in literary texts, but occasional examples are found in inscriptions: e.g. Cret. με (= μὴ) ενδικον, Meg. επειδε ικεσιοσ (Lejeune 1955, 292).

In Attic verse hiatus is practically confined to interjections, interjectional vocatives (as παῖ), interrogative τί, and (in comedy) περὶ and ὅτι and in the phrases εὖ οἶδα/ἴσθι, μηδὲ/οὐδὲ εἶς/ἕν.[1]

The general avoidance of hiatus is not confined to verse; Maas observes that it applies also to the prose of e.g. Isocrates, 'and dominates great parts of it almost without a break until the late Byzantine period'; Plato shows a progressive tendency to restrict hiatus to 'prepositive' words (Maas, 84), and this is a general rule in Demosthenes; it applies also to some of the works of Aristotle.

Another means of preserving the number of syllables in the basic forms, but without hiatus, is the insertion of a glide consonant (other than the automatic semivocalic glides referred to above). This is confined to particular categories of words, mainly in which alternants with and without a final consonant were inherited. The most common such case is the 'ν ἐφελκυστικόν' or 'paragogic *n*', as e.g. in dat. plur. πᾶσι(ν), 3 sing. ἔδοξε(ν), which seems to be primarily of Ionic origin (but not used by Herodotus). It is incidentally also sometimes used before an initial consonant to secure a heavy syllable (as e.g. ἔδδεισεν δέ, ἔστιν θάλασσα), and in fact it is found in inscriptions (contrary to Byzantine teaching) almost as often before consonants as before vowels. ς is also occasionally found in a 'hiatus-bridging' function: e.g. οὕτω(ς) and Hom. πολλάκι(ς), ἀμφί(ς). Another isolated example is the κ of the prevocalic variant οὐκ, which had been lost in other environments (cf. p. 204); Arcadian εικ (beside preconsonantal ει) may represent an extension of this (Lejeune 1955, 286);[2] one could

---

[1] Descroix 1931, 26 ff; Maas, 90.
[2] The κ may, however, be a relic of the particle κε.

compare the case in English, where final *r* has been generally lost, but preserved before initial vowel (as in *more and more* [mɔɔr ən mɔɔ]), and by some speakers is extended to other words ending in similar vowels (as e.g. *law and order* [lɔɔr ən ɔɔdə]).

Other treatments of the juncture of final and initial vowels involve the reduction of the two syllables to one. The most common cases of this type are generally referred to as 'elision'. Unlike in Latin, there seems little reason to doubt that what was involved was complete loss of the final vowel of the first word. It is practically restricted to short vowels, and of these ʊ is never elided, whilst elision of ι is primarily a feature of verbal endings. In literary texts the loss is indicated, apart from its omission in writing, by the use of the apostrophe sign; in inscriptions, however, the vowel is frequently written even where metre shows that it must have been elided (e.g. πατρισδεστιεφεσοσ = πατρὶς δ᾿ ἐστ᾿ Ἔφεσος); in general, the more 'official' the text, the more does it tend to give the full spelling. That complete loss is involved in elision is further indicated by the result in the internal juncture of compounds (ἐπάγω etc. < ἐπ(ι)-ἄγω), and also by the fact that the following syllable, if originally light, remains so after elision (whereas, if a combination of vowels were involved, the result should be a long vowel or a diphthong, giving heavy quantity: see below). Apparent elision of a diphthong is seen in e.g. βούλομ᾿ ἐγώ (*Il.* i 117: primarily in verbal endings of epic, lyric, and comedy); but this may represent a loss of the second (semivocalic) element and consequent elision of the final short vowel remaining.[1] A parallel to this may be seen in Old Indian (where coalescence rather than elision is the general rule); for example, a sequence such as *vāi asāu* implies a juncture form *vāyasāu*, from which the *y* (which we know from the ancient authorities to have been weakly pronounced – '*laghuprayatnatara*') is then dropped, giving in classical Sanskrit a hiatus form *vā asau*; but in the Vedic hymns the words occasionally go on to coalesce, giving a junctural form *vāsāu* (A 1962, 38 f.).

Although there seems to be little doubt about the loss of the 'elided' vowel, there are indications that a juncture of the type $\sim \text{VC}(\breve{\text{V}}) + \text{V} \sim$ (with elided $\breve{\text{V}}$) was felt to have different implications from the type $\sim \text{VC} + \text{V} \sim$ (with final C and so no elision). For example, in tragic trimeters a breach of 'Porson's Law' (see p. 311) is occasionally admitted

---

[1] Sommerstein (1971, 214 n.154) produces good arguments for considering that such elision was not a normal characteristic of careful Attic speech.

if an elision is involved;[1] and other peculiarities of elision have been discussed in connexion with caesurae (pp. 121 f.). It is clear from metrical evidence that when a vowel was elided the preceding consonant performed a normal releasing function in respect of the following syllable, since the preceding syllable in a sequence of the type $\sim VC(\breve{V})$ $+V\sim$ remained light; and it would be reasonable to assume that elision was normally a feature of continuous utterance, in which there was no pause between the words involved. This may account for part at least of the objection felt to the notorious mispronunciation of γαληνʼ ὁρῶ[2] as γαλῆν ὁρῶ (see p. 105). According to the scholia this resulted from a shortness of breath on the part of the actor, and so may indicate that he paused after the ν, thereby precluding its releasing function for the following syllable and so the possibility of interpreting the sequence as resulting from elision. At an intended pause, elision must of course have been an artificiality of composition – particularly when it occurred at change of speaker, as e.g. Soph., *El.* 1502 OP. ἀλλʼ ἔρφʼ. ΑΙ. ὑφηγοῦ (with, in addition, transfer of aspiration from the second speaker to the first!).

Much less common than elision is the process of 'prodelision', in which it is the short initial vowel of the following word that is deleted after a final long vowel or diphthong, as e.g. in ἦ ʼμός. It applies mainly to initial ε of tragedy and comedy.[3]

The remaining types of juncture involve the coalescence of final and initial into a long vowel or diphthong; they mostly, though not exclusively, involve words in close grammatical connexion with one another (notably where the first is a 'prepositive'). Various more or less artificial subcategorizations of such coalescence are recognized by the grammarians; most general is a distinction according to whether or not the coalescence is indicated in writing. This distinction in turn may rest on the consideration that in the negative case the resulting sound was one that did not occur in other than junctural contexts – e.g. perhaps a 'rising diphthong' [ea] in Ar., *Thesm.* 476 μὴ ἄλλην. The term usually adopted for this kind of coalescence is συνίζησις;

---

[1] Cf. Sobolevskij 1964, 50.

[2] Accentuation of the elided γαλην(ά) is uncertain. Tradition has it that the accent is 'thrown back' on to the preceding syllable: but see Laum 1928, 420 ff. Tronskij (1962, 81) suggests that in such cases, assuming a gradual rise of pitch towards the accented syllable, the penultimate syllable did in fact have a higher pitch than the one preceding it.

[3] For details and interesting restrictions see Platnauer 1960.

but the process does not correspond to that generally described nowadays as 'synizesis', which is the reduction of the first vowel of a sequence to a semivowel. This is clear from the fact that the first syllable of e.g. ἐπεί in ἐπεὶ οὐ (*Od.* iv 352) remains light, whereas a juncture of the type ἐπjοὐ might be expected to give a heavy first syllable; and conversely the syllable resulting from συνίζησις is heavy even if the initial syllable of the second word is basically light – as in εἰ μὴ ὁ κελεύσας (Eur., *Or.* 599), which cannot therefore stand for [∽ mjo ∽]. As regards the actual phonetic values of these coalescences, however, we can for the most part only guess at them in the light of general phonetic probabilities.

The other cases (which are marked in writing) are further subdivided by the grammarians according to whether (a) a process of vowel-contraction is involved, as e.g. μὴ οὖν → μῶν, τὰ ὅπλα → θὦπλα, μοι ἐστι → μοῦστι; or (b), more rarely, the second vowel is ι or υ, and simply combines with the preceding vowel to form a diphthong (as τὸ ἱμάτιον → θοἰμάτιον). Type (a) is generally referred to as κρᾶσις and (b) as συναίρεσις. In either case such coalescences are generally marked in the current (originally Alexandrian) system by the 'κορωνίς', which is identical in form with the 'ἀπόστροφος'.[1]

The ancient terminology is, however, often inconsistent and confusing.[2] Nor is it always possible to determine whether a juncture involves coalescence or prodelision; for example, mss vary between μη 'ς and the 'crasis' form μῆς – where the point is merely graphic, since the pronunciation will be the same in either case; some phonetic difference is involved, however, as between χρῆσθαι 'τέρῳ and χρῆσθ-ἀτέρῳ (Ar., *Pax* 253: Brunck and Bekker respectively), as also between μὴ 'δικεῖν and the 'συνίζησις' form μὴ ἀδικεῖν (Eur., *Hec.* 1249; Aesch., *Eum.* 85). In a case such as λέγω· 'πὶ τοῦτον (Soph., *Phil.* 591: cf. Lejeune 1955, 291) prodelision is supported by the fact that the juncture occurs at a major grammatical break, where elision is found but coalescence does not otherwise occur in Greek verse. One can perhaps see the reason for this. If such a break implies (as in normal speech) a pause in performance, then both elision and prodelision are indeed, as noted above, artificial to the extent that their phonetic motivation depends upon continuity of utterance; but *coalescence* at pause is *impossible*. In the composition of Latin verse

---

[1] It has also come to be identical in shape with the 'smooth breathing'.
[2] Descroix 1931, 29 f; A 1968a, 92 f.

this consideration was evidently no deterrent (see pp. 145, 149 f.), which suggests a lesser regard than in Greek for congruence of composition and performance.

In all types of juncture the initial aspirate ('rough breathing') is prosodically irrelevant. It does not, for example, hinder elision or coalescence, and in sequences of the type $\sim VC + hV \sim$ it does not create heavy quantity for the preceding syllable.[1] When preceded by a voiceless plosive consonant (i.e. οὐκ or by elision e.g. ἐπ', κατ'), the aspiration is transferred to the consonant, resulting in an aspirated plosive; thus e.g., internally, in καθημέριος; at word-junctions spellings of the type καθ' ἡμέραν, with the aspiration also marked on the vowel, are redundant and are due to a Byzantine 'normalization' (they are not general in those inscriptions which otherwise indicate the aspiration of vowels). Where the preceding consonant is of a type that has no aspirated counterpart, the practice in compounds suggests that the aspiration was there generally lost (only occasionally παρ*h*εδροι, προσ*h*εκετο = προσηκέτω, etc.);[2] and this may sometimes also have been the case at word-junctions, more particularly if the words were in close grammatical connexion; a suggestion of this may be seen in the statement attributed to Herodian (ii, 48 L) that the word φίλιππος was, as an adjective (where the two elements are semantically separable), pronounced with aspiration of the second member, but not as a proper name.

Finally, considerations both of juncture and of quantity rule out the assumption sometimes made that the 'smooth breathing' indicates something more than mere absence of aspiration – more specifically a glottal stop. For such an occlusive articulation would inevitably preclude elision or coalescence, and if preceded by a final consonant would make the preceding syllable heavy in all cases – which manifestly does not occur. The 'smooth' sign was originally introduced by the Alexandrian grammarians simply to direct attention to the correct reading in forms like ὅρος (as against ὄρος), and had no positive phonetic implications (A 1968a, 50 ff.).

---

[1] Hiatus is surprising in the Homeric formula πότνια "Ηρη at end of verse. It has been suggested (cf. Chantraine 1958, 92) that this might reflect a prehistoric form in which the original initial consonant (? *s or *j) still survived and had not yet changed to *h*.

[2] Note however, in both inscriptions and literary texts from the 4 c. to 1 c. B.C., the form οὐθείς (and μηθείς) beside fem. οὐδεμία and earlier οὐδείς, which suggests a devoicing and aspiration of the δ → θ (Lejeune 1955, 290).

15 *Accent*

(a) TYPOLOGY

Certain differences between the accentual rules of Latin and Greek (see p. 153) point to a difference in type of modulation, and more specifically to a modulation of frequency rather than amplitude in Greek. Other indications tend to the same conclusion. From the time of Plato (e.g. *Crat.* 399A) a binary accentual opposition is recognized to which are generally applied the terms ὀξύς (→ *acutus*) and βαρύς (→ *grauis*). Of the two terms it is the former which is applied to the positive, culminative feature, occurring on one and only one syllable in each full word, and so being sometimes referred to as the κύριος τόνος, i.e. the 'accent proper'. If ὀξύς were here interpreted as referring to amplitude, and so in auditory terms as 'loud', the opposed βαρύς should mean 'quiet' – which it does not; indeed, as Sturtevant points out (1940, 94), it tends to mean the reverse, being applied to sounds which are both low and loud, as e.g. βαρυβρεμέτης 'loud-thundering' as an epithet of Zeus; and a passage in the *Phaedrus* (268D), referring to music, indicates that Plato understood the terms as applying to features of pitch. Similarly from a passage in the *Rhetoric* (1403b) it is clear that Aristotle considered accentuation as a type of ἁρμονία, whereas loudness is referred to as μέγεθος (with μέγας and μικρός as its two poles). The actual words used to denote accentuation in Greek are themselves suggestive of its nature; of these τάσις or τόνος (lit. 'stretching') may be taken to derive their meaning from the string tension whereby the pitch of a musical instrument is varied, the 'sharp' accent being commonly associated with ἐπίτασις 'tightening', and the 'heavy' with ἄνεσις 'slackening' – terms which are also applied to stringed instruments (e.g. Plato, *Rep.* 349E); and the common term προσῳδία, of which the Latin *accentus* is a literal translation, has a clear reference to the melodic nature of the Greek accent (see p. 3).

These indications are further supported by the close parallelism of the Greek accent to that of Vedic, which was unmistakably described by the ancient Indian phoneticians in terms of 'high' and 'low' pitch,[1] and of 'tense' and 'lax' vocal cords (cf. A 1953, 87 ff.). In spite of numerous divergences, the Greek and Vedic accentual systems must be derived from a common Indo-European origin – as seen, for example, in their close agreement in the nominal paradigm:

Nom. sing.	πατήρ	*pitá*
Voc. sing.	πάτερ	*pítar*
Acc. sing.	πατέρα	*pitáram*
Dat. sing.	πατρί	*pitré*
Dat. plur.	πατράσι	*pitŕ̥ṣu* (loc.).

To the ὀξύς of Greek corresponds the Indian *udātta* ('raised') pitch, and to the βαρύς the *anudātta* ('unraised'). Remnants of this original system are still found in some modern Baltic and Slavonic languages (notably Lithuanian and Serbo-Croat);[2] but it is Vedic that has preserved it most faithfully, to the extent that, in Kuryłowicz's words, 'Pour comprendre l'accent grec il suffit de partir d'un état à peu près védique' (1958, 7).

Musical evidence

There seems to be supporting evidence also from some surviving fragments of musical settings of Greek texts. Aristoxenus observes that there is a natural melody of speech based on the word accents (*Harm.*, 17 W); but in singing, according to Dionysius of Halicarnassus, this melody is subordinate to the requirements of the music. Dionysius mentions the choral lyrics of Euripides as displaying this most clearly, and cites an example from the *Orestes* (140–2: *De Comp.* xi, 41 f. UR). It so happens that another choral fragment of this play (338–44), with a musical setting that may be the original, has been preserved on a papyrus; it is badly mutilated, but it tends to support Dionysius in so far as there is little correlation between the linguistic accents and the music. On this Mountford (1929, 165) has commented that the absence of correlation is not surprising, since 'if the same melody were sung to the strophe and antistrophe of a choral ode, it would frequently happen that the rise and fall of the melody would be contrary to that of the

---

[1] For a discussion of the metaphorical use of the terms 'high' and 'low' in relation to pitch in western antiquity cf. Jan 1895, 58 f., 143 ff.

[2] The melodic accents of certain modern Scandinavian and Indo-Aryan languages (Swedish, Norwegian; Panjabi, Lahnda) are of secondary and independent origin.

pitch accents of the words; for strophic correspondence did not extend as far as identity of accentuation'.[1]

Though the facts seem clear enough, this rationalization of them has not found favour with all scholars. Winnington-Ingram (1958, 42) has pointed out that it is not certain that the same melody was repeated in strophe and antistrophe. In a recent study Wahlström (1970, 8) suggests that it is 'dangerous to generalize from the compositional practice of a notoriously avant-garde composer like Euripides'; and from an accentual analysis of passages from the lyric poets he seeks to show that there is a tendency to accentual responsion between stanzas, which is particularly marked towards the ends of lines and so suggests that the poet was taking the musical setting into account. The agreement between stanzas is not complete, but Wahlström comments (22) that 'it would have been an inhumanly difficult task to compose large-scale poetry which responded perfectly both accentually and metrically and which in addition was good literature'.

Whatever may be the truth regarding the musical settings of strophic poetry, the situation seems quite clear in the case of the musical inscriptions from Delphi (probably late 2 c. B.C.), in which there is a marked tendency to agreement between the music and what we deduce to have been the melodic patterns of speech.[2] The same applies to the epitaph of Sicilus, found at Aidin, near Tralles in Asia Minor, in 1883. This inscription (not earlier than 2 c. B.C., and probably 1 c. A.D.) was in better condition than any other ancient musical fragment, and the notation survived intact; the stone was brought to Smyrna, but disappeared in 1923, having been photographed in the preceding year (cf. *BCH* 48 (1924), 507; there was a report of its reappearance in 1957). A modern transcription (after Crusius 1894a) appears opposite.[3]

So far as the high pitch is concerned, a syllable which would bear the acute accent is generally marked in the musical inscriptions to be sung on a higher note than any other syllable in the word (note the treatment of e.g. ὅλως, ὀλίγον, χρόνος in the Aidin inscription). Regarding the range of variation between low and high pitches in speech, there is a well-known statement by Dionysius of Halicarnassus (*De Comp.* xi, 40 f. UR) to the effect that 'the melody of speech is measured by a

[1] Cf. Borthwick 1962, 160; Pöhlmann 1966, 212; Dale 1968, 204 ff.
[2] Cf. Winnington-Ingram 1955, 57 ff; 1958, 41 ff; Pöhlmann 1960, 26; Pearl & Winnington-Ingram 1965, 187.
[3] The song has been recorded in H.M.V. *The History of Music in Sound*, Vol. 1.2 (HLP 2).

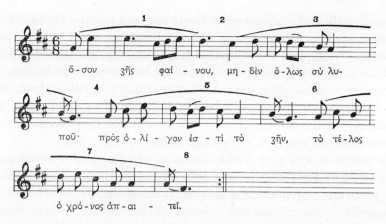

ὅ - σον   ζῆς   φαί - νου,   μη - δὲν ὅ - λως   σὺ λυ-

ποῦ·   πρὸς ὀ - λί - γον ἐσ - τὶ τὸ   ζῆν,   τὸ τέ - λος

ὁ χρό - νος ἀπ - αι - τεῖ.

single interval, approximately that termed a "fifth", and does not rise
to the high pitch by more than three tones and a semitone, nor fall to
the low by more than this amount'. Descriptions of the melodic range
of Norwegian, a language with a comparable accentual system, average
around a sixth;[1] and modern recitations of the R̥gVeda show a range
of a fifth, which is 'not much different from that used in emphatic
speech' (Gray 1959, 87).

Although there was evidently a similarity between music and the
accentual patterns of Greek, it is also certain that the changes of pitch
in speech were more gradual than in singing; one would expect this
from experience of modern languages having a melodic accent, and it is
expressly stated by Aristoxenus (*Harm.*, 10 f. W), who distinguishes
between continuous change (συνεχής) and change by intervals (δια-
στηματική), and notes that a speaker who employs the latter type of
pattern is said to be singing rather than speaking (an intermediate
style is recognized for the reading of poetry by Aristides Quintilianus,
5 f. W-I). The graduality of melodic change in one context at least is
confirmed by the evidence of Vedic; for we know from the ancient
phoneticians that the syllable immediately following a high pitch
(*udātta*) did not bear a level low pitch but a falling glide, starting at a
high pitch and finishing low, to which they gave the name *svarita*
'intoned' (described by some authorities as a '*pravaṇa*', lit. 'downhill
slope': cf. A 1953, 88). Since such a glide was automatic in this context,
it is to be considered structurally (as it was by the Indians) simply as a
variant of the low pitch (*anudātta*); the fact, therefore, that it is not

[1] See e.g. Haugen & Joos 1952, 41 ff; Popperwell 1963, 151 f.

specially indicated or discussed in Greek does not rule out the likelihood of its existence in this language also; and support for it is to be seen in certain tendencies of the musical fragments, e.g. the second syllable of ὅλως in the Aidin inscription, where the long vowel is to be sung on two notes in descending order.[1] There is some musical evidence also for a tendency to rising pitch in the syllable preceding a high; but 'the tendency to fall from the accented syllable is distinctly stronger...than the tendency to rise to it' (Winnington-Ingram 1955, 66).

In Greek as well as in Vedic, however, when a syllable contained a long vowel or diphthong it could carry a falling melodic pattern without any preceding high pitch, in which case it was marked in Greek with the 'circumflex' (περισπώμενος)[2] instead of the 'acute' accent mark. Phonetically this independent falling glide was probably identical with the dependent glide following a high pitch, and the Indian writers use the same term *svarita* for both. The Greek musical inscriptions tend to treat both in the same way: note, for example, the setting of λυποῦ, ζῆν, ἀπαιτεῖ in the Aidin inscription, where the long accented vowel is in each case marked to be sung on two notes in descending order; the first of the two notes in such cases is generally the highest in the word.[3]

The 'contonation'

If one considers the falling glide as a feature of the phonetic realization of the accent, the combination of high pitch + fall can be envisaged as a single unit, which one may term a 'contonation' (A 1966, 10; cf. Kiparsky 1967, 75 f.). It then follows that Greek had both a disyllabic type of contonation (as in e.g. ὅλως, βαίνω, μόνον, ἄνθρωπος, ἄνεμος) in which the high pitch is in one syllable and the glide in the next, and a monosyllabic type (as in e.g. λυποῦ, δῶρον) in which the peak and glide are in the same syllable, the peak forming the starting point of the glide. These two types of melodic 'contonation' are reminiscent of the two basic ('legato') types of dynamic accent in Latin (pp. 163 ff.).

---

[1] Cf. Turner 1915, 196.

[2] Lit. 'bent round'. The term could be interpreted in a phonetic or a graphic sense. There is a dubious Byzantine tradition that it originally referred to the shape of the mark, having been substituted for the name ὀξύβαρυς ('acute–grave') by Aristophanes of Byzantium upon changing the shape from ᴧ (a combination of the two components) to ⌒ in order to avoid confusion with the consonant Λ.

[3] Cf. Winnington-Ingram 1955, 57.

The mora

In the case of long vowels or diphthongs in final syllables, there could be a phonological opposition (before pause or enclitic: see below) between the monosyllabic contonation and a high pitch without falling glide – as e.g. between gen. sing. λυπηρᾶς and acc. plur. λυπηράς, εἷς 'one' and εἰς (aor. part. of ἵημι).[1] As an alternative to recognizing two different types of melodic movement on such vowels, it would be possible to analyse them in the ͵manner described on pp. 92 ff., i.e. as comprising two 'morae', on either of which the high pitch may be located. In the case of the vowels marked 'circumflex', the morae are accented high + low, the low having automatically its falling variant; in support of this analysis one may note the use by Greek writers of such terms as δίτονος, ὀξύβαρυς, or σύμπλεκτος for this accentuation; and also that Aristotle does not mention the circumflex at all, presumably because it is simply a combination of the two basic types high and low (*Poet.* 1456b; cf. *Rhet.* 1403b), as is specifically stated at some length by Choeroboscus.[2] In the case of the long vowels marked 'acute', the morae are accented low + high (whatever may have been the precise phonetic variant of the 'low' in this environment, e.g. ? rising). Historical support for these analyses may be seen in the fact that, for example, an original πάϊς contracts to give παῖς (with circumflex) whereas δαΐς contracts to give δᾴς (with acute).[3] We have already seen that an analysis in terms of morae also simplifies the descriptive statement of certain other phenomena in Greek (pp. 19, 92); as a further example, the accentual relationship of vocative Ζεῦ to nom. Ζεύς can be said to be the same as that of πάτερ to πατήρ, in spite of the difference of marked accent on Ζεῦ and πάτερ: in both cases the high pitch simply shifts in the vocative to the first mora that can carry it. Moreover, as will be seen, it vastly simplifies the statement of limitation on the 'recession' of the accent.

In recent years this analysis of the Greek accent has been utilized in the explanation of one of the greatest problems of Greek metrics – the origin of the equivalence in dactylic hexameters of a single heavy syllable to two light. Since, however, other and non-accentual

---

[1] Cf. Lupaş 1967, 15.

[2] Cf. Vendryes 1929, 45 f. Choeroboscus incidentally also recognizes the accentual equivalence of the circumflex to the high + low on successive syllables.

[3] For further discussions of analysis by morae cf. Jakobson 1931/1962, 120 f; Trubetzkoy 1935/1968, 33 f; Halle 1971.

solutions are possible, this matter will be discussed separately (see Excursus B).

(b) INCIDENCE

Unlike the Latin accent, the Greek was 'free' in the sense that its position was not phonologically predictable – though various grammatical rules apply to particular categories of words.[1] But, unlike in Old Indian, phonological constraints operated to limit the range of positions in which the accent could occur, most notably a rule of 'recession', limiting the distance from the end of the word. In Old Indian it was possible to have an initial accent even on words such as *ábubodhiṣāmahi* 'we wanted to learn' (1 plur. mid. impf. desid. of *budh-*), or *úddālakapuṣpabhañjikā* 'breaking of the *uddālaka* flower' (name of a game: cf. Pāṇini, vi.2.74); but Greek has, for example, ἀνεπίθετος, φερόμενος corresponding to Old Indian *ánapahitas*, *bháramāṇas*.[2]

Limiting rules

Statements of the Greek rule in traditional terms tend to be rather involved; for example (from a typical school grammar),[3] 'The acute may stand on any of the last three syllables, the circumflex only on the last or last but one. But the acute cannot stand on the last but two, nor the circumflex on the last but one, unless the vowel of the last is short.' Thus accentuations of the types ἄνθρωπος, ἀνθρώπων, καλός, δῶρον, καλῶν, are admissible, but not *ἄνθρωπων or *δῶρων. By contrast with Old Indian, Aristophanes creates a word of 78 syllables (*Eccl.* 1168–75 λεπαδο...πτερύγων), which is nevertheless accented only on the penultimate.

By introducing the concept of the mora, Jakobson was able very considerably to simplify the rule, with a formulation: 'The span between the accented and the final mora cannot exceed one syllable' (1937b/1962, 263).[4] In terms of the description we have given of the Greek accent as a 'contonation' which includes the falling glide, and as

---

[1] Cf. Kiparsky 1967a; Warburton 1970a, 108.
[2] Vendryes, 54.
[3] Cf. A 1966b, 12.
[4] For discussion and a suggested improvement in terms of 'moric vowels' see Mouraviev 1972; the proposed rules, however, are of great complexity.

having either a monosyllabic or a disyllabic form, the rule can be yet
further simplified to the statement that '*Not more than one mora may
follow the contonation*' (A 1966b, 13). In δῶρον, for example, the
contonation occupies the first syllable, and in ἄνθρωπος the first two
(since the glide continues to the end of the second syllable), leaving
only one mora (the short vowel o) at the end of the word in each case;
in ἀνθρώπων or δώρων, the contonation occupies the last two syllables,
and so nothing follows; in the inadmissible *ἄνθρωπων or *δῶρων *two*
morae (the long vowel ω) would follow and thereby break the rule.[1]

A remarkable anticipation of this mode of formulation deserves to be
mentioned. The following statement is found in C. Lancelot's *Nouvelle
Méthode pour apprendre facilement la langue grecque* (1st edn, Paris,
1655; citation from the 9th edn, 1696, 549): 'la dernière syllabe qui
suit le Circonflexe, ne peut estre longue par nature: parce que cette
dernière syllabe ayant déjà esté précédée d'un rabaissement, qui est
dans le Circonflexe mesme, elle ne peut avoir deux mesures'.

It is clear that a simple rule restricting the accent to the last three
syllables is inadequate; before Jakobson had formulated his rule,
however, there had been a proposal to state the limitation in terms of
the last three morae.[2] On the face of it this involves too great a restriction, since it would seem to imply that forms of the type ἄνθρωπος
are inadmissible (the high pitch standing on the *fourth* mora from the
end (1 + 2 + 1)). But the formulation is defended on the following
grounds. There is a rule of Attic (usually termed, though inappropri-
ately, the 'final trochee' rule)[3] whereby, if the high pitch occurs on a
penultimate syllable containing a long vowel or a diphthong, it must
occur on the first mora (i.e. the accent must be circumflex and not

[1] Apart from the case of words ending in ‿αι and ‿οι (see below), exceptions arise
as a result of Attic-Ionic 'quantitative metathesis' after the date of fixation of the
accent; thus (i) in genitives in ‿εω of 1st decl. masc. nouns, e.g. Ἀτρείδεω < ‿ηο <
‿αο; (ii) in words of the 'Attic' declension, e.g. ἵλεως < ‿ηος < ‿αος (whence by
analogy also oblique cases, as Μενέλεῳ); (iii) in genitives in ‿εως of 3rd decl.
nouns with ι and υ stems, e.g. πόλεως, πήχεως < πόληος etc. (whence by analogy also
gen. plur. πόλεων etc.). Accentuation of this type is further extended, by analogy
with the Attic declension, to compounds such as δύσερως, εὔκερως, φιλόγελως,
ἔκπλεως. Though in some cases the anomaly is removed by 'synizesis' (πόλεως etc.),
metrical treatment shows that this is not always the case, even where the word would
permit it. See further Vendryes, 202, 264; Lupaş 1967, 16.
[2] Vendryes, 53 ff; cf. Garde 1968, 145.
[3] It refers to vowel lengths and not syllable quantities, and so can apply to what is in
fact a spondee, as e.g. λαῖλαψ (cf. Bally 1945, 22 f.).

acute) if the final vowel is short;[1] if the final vowel is long, then by the general limiting rule the high pitch must occur on the second mora (i.e. acute accent). Thus e.g. δῶρον vs δώρων (cf. παῖδες beside Doric παῖδες, Attic contraction ἑστῶτες beside Homeric ἑσταότες). Consequently the occurrence of circumflex or acute on penultimate long vowels or diphthongs is automatically determined by the length of the final vowel. Rare exceptions, as οἶκοι (nom. plur.) vs οἴκοι (loc. sing.), λῦσαι (infin.) vs λύσαι (optat.) are best dealt with by grammatical rules which allot different mora values to the final diphthongs.[2] This being so, it is argued, there is no phonological opposition of acute and circumflex on penultimate syllables, and so there are no grounds for treating their vowels as comprising two morae.

It seems likely that the limitation of recession is based on phonetic considerations, in terms of the extent of low-pitched utterance that is permitted to follow the contonation;[3] and it is surely unrealistic to imply that a penultimate long vowel would not be counted as long in words like ἄνθρωπος simply because accentual variation (in *other* types of word) is automatically determined in this position.[4] A preferable formulation seems to be that of Jakobson; and the contonational account is perhaps even more satisfactory: for the equipollence of long and short penultimate vowels (as regards limitation of recession), as e.g. in κακόγλωσσος and κακόβιος, is then due simply to the phonetic condition that a glide does not end in the middle of a vowel, and so ends in each case at the same distance from the end of the word.

In Aeolic the variation between acute and circumflex is automatic in *all* cases, since in full words the accent invariably recedes to its full limit; thus e.g. θῦμος, θύμου (beside Attic θυμός, θυμοῦ), but also in

---

[1] The rule is also sometimes applied by grammarians and mss to the results of crasis, although the general rule here is that the second word retains its accent unchanged. Thus one finds both τἆλλα and τἄλλα, χοἶδε and χοῖδε, etc. (Vendryes, 250).

[2] Cf. Kuryłowicz 1958, 112, 130, 154; Kiparsky 1967b, 124 f. In general ∼οι and ∼αι are to be considered for accentual purposes (like ∼ον, ∼ος, etc.) as = ∼V̆C, i.e. as = 1 mora. Contrary cases could be considered as involving morphological divisions, e.g. locative ∼ο-ι (similarly optative: cf. λύσαιμεν beside ἐλύσαμεν, etc.): see also Bally 1945, 20, 33 f. In support of this note the accentuation of loc. ᾿Ισθμοῖ (which must imply 2 morae in the final syllable) as against nom. plur. ἰσθμοί (which need not, since the acute can occur on a 1-mora vowel). For a contrary view see Sommerstein 1971, 165 n.96.

[3] One would of course reject, with Vendryes (54 f.), the explanation of the scholia on Dionysius Thrax (39 H) that one's *breath* could not possibly suffice for further regression of accent (cf. also Cicero, *Or.* xviii.58).

[4] Cf. Galton 1962, 283; Mouraviev 1972, 114.

monosyllables, so that there can be no opposition of the type φῶς vs φώς – only φῶς is possible. It may be said that in Aeolic the mora is therefore irrelevant, and that only *syllables* are necessary to accentual description (thus Garde 1968, 148); but the fact remains that the law of *limitation* is even here most simply stated in terms of the mora.

Whilst the regulation of accentual placement in Greek is statable primarily in terms of vowel elements, two rules, of unexplained causation, require reference to quantity. One of these, 'Wheeler's Law' (Wheeler 1885, 60 ff.), states that words which were originally accented on their final mora ('oxytones') show regression to the penultimate syllable if the word has a dactylic ending: thus e.g. ποικίλος, ἀγκύλος beside Old Indian *peśalás*, *aṅkurás* (cf. Greek καθαρός, παχυλός, ἁμαρτωλός, etc.). Analogy has reduced the effect of this law in some directions, but extended it in others.[1] The other rule, 'Vendryes' Law' (Vendryes, 263), applies primarily to Attic, and states that a word with properispomenon accent, as e.g. ἑτοῖμος, retracts the accent to the preceding syllable if this is light: thus Attic ἕτοιμος, as against e.g. ἀρχαῖος, where the first syllable is heavy.[2] There is a near parallel to the 'law' in some Old Indian texts. The contraction of e.g. *evá +* *etád* normally gives *evaìtád* (where ` indicates the 'independent' *svarita* accent, parallel to the Greek circumflex); but in the Śatapatha-Brāhmaṇa the accent recedes to the preceding syllable, thus *évaitád*, with acute (*udātta*) on the first syllable. The effect is that the *svarita* on the penultimate, originally independent, now becomes dependent. But, unlike in Attic, the ŚB shows no restriction to cases where the preceding syllable is light. A point of interest is that the *udātta* thus arising does not count as such to the extent of neutralizing a preceding *udātta* (as normally in this text: see below): thus e.g. *agním évābhīk-ṣamāṇaḥ*, where *évā~* < *evà~* < *evá + a~*.

---

[1] Cf. Vendryes, 148 f; A 1967a, 50 f.

[2] To judge from grammarians' references to an Old Attic τροπαῖον, the law would seem to be relatively recent; in which case it would presumably be later than the Attic vowel-contractions. Yet it does not apply to forms like φιλοῦμεν, ἐμοῦγε where the circumflex arises from contraction. From a purely descriptive point of view this would present no difficulty, since one could simply apply the retraction rule before the contraction rule (cf. Sommerstein 1971, 166, 204); but, given the historical premiss, this would imply that, even after the contractions, speakers still analysed φιλοῦμεν, ἐμοῦγε as φιλέομεν, ἐμέογε (and so did not apply the retraction rule) – which seems a dubious explanation: cf. in general p. 18 and in particular p. 258.

The law seems to have applied even outside Attic, and so to be of some antiquity, in the case of adjectives in ~αιος, ~ειος, ~οιος (e.g. βρότειος beside ἀνδρεῖος).

Enclitics

Certain additional rules are required for the combination of full words
with enclitics, where the latter form a more or less complete phonological unity with the former. In a sequence such as ἀγαθός ἐστιν,
πατήρ σου, λέγω τι, φιλῶ σε, the accent of the full word serves as the
accent of the combination without breach of the general rule. Where,
however, the accent of the full word, if applied to the combination as a
whole, would breach the rule of recession, a secondary accent was
added to the full word in order, so far as possible, to bring the post-
accentual sequence within the limitations of the rule: thus ἄνθρωπός τις,
ἄνθρωποί τινες, οἶκός τις, οἶκοί τινες, etc.

There were, however, limits to the extent to which this could operate.
In cases like καλῶς πως, καλοῦ τινος, καλῶν τινων, for example, the
rule is breached but it is impossible to add a secondary accent to the
main word. In e.g. οὕτω πως a secondary accent on the second syllable
is impossible, since this syllable carries the glide element of the main
accent; to this principle the Śatapatha-Brāhmaṇa provides a parallel
in so far as a high pitch followed in juncture by another high pitch is
reduced to a low – i.e. successive high pitches are inadmissible. In
e.g. οἶκοί τινων the secondary accent still leaves the rule breached on
account of the long vowel in the final syllable of the. enclitic; in this
case it is usual to say that the length of the final vowel in enclitics is
irrelevant; but it may simply be a case of an accentual *pis aller*, just as
the absence of secondary accentuation in καλῶς πως, οὕτω πως, etc.

In combinations of full word and enclitic the full word invariably
retains its main accent unaltered. Thus in e.g. φώς τις the combination
does not follow the rule of the 'final trochee' and change to φῶς τις
as e.g. *ἑστώτες → ἑστῶτες. Only when the two elements become
effectively a single word does the final-trochee rule apply (by a process
termed by the grammarians ἐπέκτασις); thus, according to Herodian,
the combination τούς + enclitic δε, when fused to form the demon-
strative pronoun, results in an accentuation τούσδε;[1] similarly the
combination ἐγώ + γε, when fused into a single pronominal word,
follows the final-trochee rule to give *ἐγῶγε, which subsequently
changes (by Vendryes' Law) to ἔγωγε. A well-known example which
illustrates this principle is the name Οὖτις (acc. Οὖτιν) adopted by
Odysseus to deceive the Cyclops; as a proper name, and so a unitary

[1] Vendryes, 92.

word, it undergoes 'epectasis' and so follows the final-trochee rule, thereby contrasting with the pronoun οὖτις consisting of negative+ enclitic. Thus at *Od.* ix 408 Polyphemus says Οὖτίς με κτείνει, but his fellow Cyclopes, overlooking the epectasis, reply (410) εἰ μὲν δὴ μῆτις (or ? μή τίς) σε βιάζεται... [1]

An exception to the general rule that enclitics are unaccented is seen in the grammatical tradition regarding paroxytone full words followed by disyllabic enclitics. In such cases a secondary acute on the final syllable of the main word is, as we have seen for οὖτω‿πως, impossible.[2] But the tradition states that a secondary accent was placed on the final syllable of the enclitic – thus e.g. μεγάλοι‿τινές, παίδοιν‿τινοῖν (the alternation of acute on short vowels vs circumflex on long being probably by analogy with e.g. ποδός vs ποδῶν).[3]

This accent is surprising, especially as it does not apply to the exactly parallel case with monosyllabic main accent, as e.g. καλοῦ‿τινος, καλῶν‿τινων (though Hermann here proposed to accent the final of the enclitic by analogy with the cases of disyllabic main accent). Vendryes (83) attempts to remove the difficulty of καλοῦ‿τινος etc. by arguing that in the combination the final syllable of the full word is not a true final, and therefore (cf. pp. 237 f.) was not subject to accentual oppositions; so that the circumflex here is not a 'real' circumflex; ἀληθῶς‿ποτε, for example, is really equivalent to ἐδηλώσατε. This, however, seems hardly a convincing way of obviating the difficulty.[4]

There remains a possible explanation based on numbers of syllables, assuming a rule that not more than two unaccented syllables may follow the syllable containing the high pitch (which would then exempt καλοῦ‿τινος etc.). In most cases involving more than two syllables the situation would be met by secondary accentuation on the full word, as ἄνθρωπός‿τις, οἶκοί‿τινες, etc; but since in the case of μεγάλοι‿τινές etc. this is impossible, and since to accent the first syllable of the enclitic would make it identical with a full word (as e.g. interrogative τίνες, or 'existential' ἔστι), the only solution, it might be argued, was to accent the final. The admission of purely syllabic criteria into an otherwise mora-based accentual system seems a high price to pay for an explanation; however, it may be that reasoning of this kind underlies

---

[1] Postgate 1924, 28; Lupaş 1967, 17. Similarly Euripides, *Cycl.* 672 ff: ΚΥ. Οὖτίς μ' ἀπώλεσ'. ΧΟ. οὐκ ἄρ' οὐδείς ἠδίκει, etc; cf. Aristophanes, *Vesp.* 184 ff.

[2] Cf. Tronskij 1962, 67.

[3] Vendryes, 82.

[4] Cf. Sommerstein 1971, 208 ff.

the doctrine of the grammarians regarding the accentuation μεγάλοι τινές etc; and it may also have been reinforced by a further consideration which will be discussed (p. 249).[1]

There is one case in which the rule prohibiting acute accent on successive syllables of the full word seems to be broken. According to the grammarians φύλλα τε, Λάμπε τε in Homer are to be accented φύλλά τε, Λάμπέ τε – to which Herodian adds such examples as ἄλλός τις, ἔνθά ποτε, τυφθέντά τε. In the *Venetus* of the Iliad one finds πύργός τε (xxii 462); and at least some grammarians prescribed ἄνδρά μοι at the beginning of the Odyssey. Such secondary accentuation would be normal if the main accent were a circumflex and not, as here, acute. But in Proto-Indo-European morphology sequences of the type V̆ + liquid or nasal were treated in the same way as diphthongs (analysable as V̆ + semivowel); they had, for instance, weak unaccented alternants in which the vowel was dropped and the liquid or nasal itself became a syllabic nucleus – e.g. indic. *bhéreti* 'he bears' (Skt *bhárati*): past partic. *bhr̥tós* (with r̥ preserved in Skt *bhr̥tás*); indic. *gʷhénti* 'he strikes' (Skt *hánti*): past partic. *gʷhn̥tós* (Skt *hatás*), just as e.g. *gᶻʷhéjeti* 'he destroys' (Skt *kṣáyati*): past partic. *gᶻʷhitós* (Skt *kṣitás*, Gk φθιτός), where the vowel *i* is the syllabic form of the semivowel *j*. This syllabic functioning of the liquids and nasals, completely parallel to that of the (semi)vowels, indicates their sonorant nature in Proto-Indo-European,[2] and so their potentiality for carrying variations of pitch to the same extent as the second member of a diphthong; and in modern Lithuanian, which distinguishes falling from rising accents, one still has e.g. *vilkas, mir̃ti, kum̃pas, kañdis*, with high pitch on the liquid or nasal, just as on the second element of a diphthong in e.g. *eĩti, braũkti* (and as opposed to fall of pitch in *tìltas, pìnti*, etc.).[3] In Norwegian similarly, the liquids and nasals following a vowel are described as 'prolonging the vowel glide' (Popperwell 1963, 169). To the extent that this potentiality was preserved in Homeric Greek, the first syllable of a word such as πυργος or ἐνθα was capable of having either a rising or a falling pitch-pattern (acute or circumflex), and by the final-trochee rule the falling pattern is required – so that an accentuation πύργος, ἔνθα really stands for πῦργος, ἔνθα, or in parallel

---

[1] For the accentuation of an enclitic (though in a syllable-based system) one may compare modern Greek, where e.g. φέρε τονε = /fére tóne/ (but here with accent on the penultimate): Warburton 1970a, 113.

[2] Cf. in general p. 69, and Trubetzkoy 1939/1969, 170 f; Stetson 1951, 36 f.

[3] On Serbo-Croat also cf. Halle 1971, 9.

with the marking of εἶτα, for example, πύργος, ἔνθα. The contonation was thus monosyllabic, and complete on the first syllable; so that a secondary accent was required before an enclitic, and could be accommodated on the final of the main word: thus ἔνθά τε as εἶτά τε etc. Such an interpretation is also supported by the Delphic hymns, where syllables of this type behave in the same way as diphthongs in so far as they may be sung to two notes (e.g. Δεελφίσιιν, ἀαμβρόταν).[1]

This accentuation, however, became extended analogically by the grammarians, who were unaware of its phonetic basis and so applied it to other cases of 'trochaic' ending: hence e.g. ὄφρά τοι, ὅσσά τε (also occasionally in mss), whereas consonants such as φ or σ are incapable of carrying melodic variation. This extended treatment is also found applied in the mss of some later authors, as e.g. in the *Laurentianus* of Sophocles.[2]

From the enclitic accentuations so far considered one should probably distinguish the unemphatic forms of the plural pronouns ἡμεῖς and ὑμεῖς, which are generally full words. The unemphatic forms (occurring in acc., gen., and dat.) are accented as ἥμας, ἥμων, ἥμιν, etc.[3] These are usually considered as enclitic, but with special rules on account of the long vowel in the first syllable. Such an explanation is unsatisfactory, since elsewhere in Greek the length of vowel in the penultimate is irrelevant to the limitation of recession;[4] it seems preferable simply to see this as a regression of accent in unemphatic (but not accentually enclitic) forms. They may originally have been true enclitics, as was the finite verb (thus in Vedic, except at the beginning of a line or sentence: e.g. *agním īḷe* 'I praise Agni'). Of the verbs in Greek only certain forms of εἶναι and φάναι preserve their enclitic status, the rest having become full words with recessive accent.[5] If the same is true of the plural unemphatic pronouns in Greek, there is (from the accentual point of view) no more cause to consider them as enclitics than there is so to consider a verb such as ἦσαν or ἔφη.

---

[1] Vendryes, 50; cf. Galton 1962, 288. [2] Vendryes, 85 f.
[3] Vendryes, 96; cf. Barrett 1964, 425.
[4] Nor does this accentuation apply to the phonologically comparable enclitics εἰμι, εἰσι, φημι, φησι, φᾶσι.
[5] Cf. Postgate 1924, 30 f. In modern Cypriot the verb is enclitic after the negative and adverbs: e.g. /ém barpati/ 'he doesn't go', /epsés irtamen/ 'we came yesterday' (Thumb 1912, 29).

Synenclisis

Where more than one enclitic occur in succession ('synenclisis'), there is disagreement about the accentual treatment. The grammatical tradition says that all are accented except the last: thus e.g. *Il.* v 812 ἤ νύ σέ που δέος ἴσχει, and Herodian constructs a sequence of six – εἴ πέρ τίς σέ μοί φησί ποτε. He does, however, comment (i, 563 L) that such extended synenclisis is rare, because one needs a pause in the continuity of 'breath'. The rule is considered suspect by Vendryes (88 f.),[1] who points out that the *Venetus B* of the Iliad accents only alternate enclitics, as ἤ νυ σέ που, etc. – a practice approved by Hermann and Göttling; more recently Barrett, in his edition of the *Hippolytus* (1964, 426 f.), finds the grammatical tradition 'wholly improbable' and proposes to treat such sequences as if they constituted a single full word, with secondary accents where necessary, e.g. ἤγγειλέ γε μοί ποτε[2] – which produces effectively the same result as alternation, and which he finds to be in general agreement with the medieval mss of the play. There remains, however, much uncertainty in this matter.[3] Where two enclitics were in close grammatical or semantic connexion, it is possible that they may have been felt to form an accentable unit (cf. p. 250), and so actually were accented in speech; in which case an accentuation such as πώποτε (whether written as one word or two) is probably correct: cf. modern Greek τίποτε 'something, nothing'.

The grave accent-mark

At this point it is necessary to return to the question of accent *marking* in Greek. The tradition of such marking seems to have started in Alexandria around 200 B.C., and at first, to judge from papyri, it was used sporadically and mostly to resolve ambiguities. The high pitch on a short vowel was rendered by the acute sign, as in e.g. λέξαι; the same sign was also used when the high pitch occurred on the second mora of a long vowel or diphthong, as in e.g. (optat.) λήξαι; but when the high pitch occurred on the first mora of a long vowel or diphthong, thereby inducing the 'compound' accent (monosyllabic contonation), this was marked with the circumflex sign, as in e.g. (infin.) λῆξαι.

[1] Cf. Tronskij 1962, 72 f.
[2] For modern Greek cf. Warburton 1970b, 38 ff. (e.g. /ðiórθosé mu to/, /ðóse mú to/).
[3] Cf. Warburton 1970a, 118 ff. For acceptance of the tradition cf. Chandler 1881, 280 ff; Sommerstein 1971, 21 ff.

In one early system of marking, every low pitch was indicated by the grave sign, e.g. Θεόδωρὸς; but such a practice was clearly uneconomical and inelegant,[1] and was later replaced by the current (Byzantine) system whereby only the high (or rising) and compound pitches are indicated (by the acute and circumflex signs respectively). An intermediate development is seen in some papyri which write the grave signs only where they precede an acute (e.g. φιλὴσὶστέφανον), and in some cases omit the final acute sign (e.g. πὰγκρὰτης). This last practice is reminiscent of the marking system of the ṚgVeda, which marks the *anudātta* preceding an *udātta*, and the dependent *svarita* following, but not the *udātta* itself: thus e.g. *agnínā* appears as *a̱gninā̀* (and at the beginning of a half-line all *anudāttas* preceding the first *udātta* are marked, as e.g. *va̱i̱śvā̱na̱ram = vaiśvānarám*).

In the Byzantine system, however, the otherwise disused grave sign was substituted for an acute where this occurred on the final mora of a word ('oxytone'), except in the case of interrogatives (as τίς) or when followed by an enclitic or pause: thus e.g. ἀγαθός ἐστιν, ἔστιν ἀγαθός·, but ἀγαθὸς ταμίας. There has been much discussion as to what this substitution implies from a phonetic point of view[2] – e.g. whether it implies a full or partial lowering of the pitch,[3] or is merely a graphic peculiarity.[4] Debrunner (1930, 54) suggests as one possibility a loss of pitch characteristics but retention of whatever intensity the acute may have had;[5] one might also envisage the possibility of a falling pitch-pattern on such syllables, but distinct from that of the circumflex or post-acute.[6] Complete neutralization is rejected by Lupaş (1967, 14) on the grounds of its improbability in such a line as Soph., *O.T.* 130 ἡ ποικιλῳδὸς Σφὶγξ τὰ πρὸς ποσὶ σκοπεῖν; but this is not necessarily a conclusive argument.[7]

We have argued that in other than oxytone words a high pitch was followed by a falling glide to complete the contonation. In Vedic, when

[1] Cf. Herodian, i, 10 L; *Schol. in Dion. Thr.*, 153, 294 H.
[2] See e.g. Tronskij 1962, 75; A 1966b, 11 f; Wahlström 1970, 6.
[3] The grammarians use the expression κοιμίζεται, or τρέπουσα εἰς βαρεῖαν (cf. Herodian, i, 10, 551 L; Apollonius Dyscolus, 36 S).
[4] Thus e.g. Laum 1928; for criticism see Schmiel 1968, 66 f.
[5] Cf. also Galton 1962, 286 ff.
[6] Cf. Trubetzkoy's note (1935/1968, 38 n.1) on Ganda (E. Africa), where 'the "low" tone is always realized by means of a steeply-falling intonation which differs from the actual phonological "falling tone", first, as regards the "depth" of the final part and, second, in the fact that it can affect not only long but also short (monomoric) syllables'.
[7] Cf. Sommerstein 1971, 207 n.149.

the high pitch occurred at the end of a word, the glide was carried by the initial syllable of the next word; thus in a sequence such as *RV* x 14, 12 *urūṇasā́v asutŕ̥pā* the glides are placed as shown by the R̥gVedic marking: *u̯rū́ṇasāv àsu̯tr̥pà̍*, with the initial syllable of the second word carrying the glide from the final high pitch of the first word. But in Greek the word developed a more autonomous phonological status than in Vedic.[1] One aspect of this is the tendency to generalize a single variant of each word, as seen, for example, in the loss of final plosives (p. 204) in all environments, which probably originated in pre-pausal position; against the invariable τό of Greek, Old Indian shows such multiple variants as *tad, taj, tat, tac, tan, tal*, determined by the initial of the following word. There was also a clearer demarcation in Greek between 'close' and 'open' juncture, in the sense of characterizing transitions respectively within and across word boundaries; for example, the implications of consonant sequences for quantity show marked differences in the two cases; and there was no need in Greek, as there was in Vedic, for a special '*pada*' (word-isolate) tradition to ensure correct word-division in the transmission of oral texts.[2]

An exception to the general practice regarding the grave accent-mark is found in the case of following enclitics, since these formed a more or less close phonological unity with the preceding full word; so that in a sequence ἀγαθός ἐστιν the first syllable of the enclitic ἐστιν could in fact carry the falling glide (in the terminology of the grammarians, the enclitic 'awakens' (ἐγείρει) the acute accent which is elsewhere 'put to rest' (κοιμίϑεται) as a grave). But an accentuation *ἀγαθός βασιλεύς would involve the glide being carried by the initial syllable of the following (full) word, i.e. the extension of the terminal portion of the contonation across a word boundary. This would have been contrary to general Greek junctural tendencies, being character-istic of close and not open juncture; and it is here that the original contonational system, as preserved in Vedic, would have broken down in Greek. On the assumption that a high pitch could not be followed by a low without a transitional glide, the situation could be resolved only by a lowering of the final pitch to a level where it was no higher than the

---

[1] Galton 1962, 280 f; A 1966b, 11.

[2] Cf. *Atharva-Prātiśākhya* iv.107: 'The study of the word-isolates is designed to teach the beginnings and ends of words, and their correct form, accent, and meaning.' For instance, where the '*saṃhitā*' (continuous) text, with its morphological variants and cross-junctural accentuation, reads *mahā́mā̐dityonamàsopasadyò* (*RV* iii 59, 5), the '*pada*' has *mahā́n ā́dityaḥ namàsā upa-sadyàḥ*.

initial of the following word; and this is presumably the essence of the phenomenon indicated by the grave sign.

If the following word begins with a high pitch (e.g. ἀγαθὸς ἄνθρωπος, καλὸν δῶρον), it is not immediately clear why a high final pitch should be lowered, since no fall would be involved in any case. It may, however, have been a general requirement (except after pause) that the high pitch should contrast with a preceding low; and this would not be possible for an initial high if the voice were still at a high pitch carried over from the preceding word. We have seen that in the Śatapatha-Brāhmaṇa this is precisely the context in which a final *udātta* was reduced to *anudātta*; and it was Meillet's opinion (1905, 245 ff.) that the lowering of final acutes in Greek in fact originated in this particular environment.

The general practice of the musical fragments is that a syllable which would be marked grave is set not lower than other syllables in the same word; but the intervals are small, 'and it is more characteristic for the syllables of a grave-accented word to be set to the same note' (Winnington-Ingram 1955, 66); the grave syllable is also normally not set higher than the initial of the following word, whether accented or unaccented.

Once again the above approach to the problem finds an early anticipation in the work of Lancelot (see p. 237), who explains (op. cit., 22):

après avoir ielevé la voix sur une syllabe, il faut nécessairement qu'elle se rabaisse sur les suivantes;...on ne le figure jamais que dans le discours, sur les mots aigus...qui dans la suite changent leur aigu en grave,...pour montrer qu'il ne faut pas relever la dernière, laquelle autrement porteroit jusques sur le mot suivant, & feroit le mesme effet qu'aux Enclitiques, qui est de les unir avec le mot précédent.[1]

A parallel to the Greek situation in this respect is provided by Serbo-Croat, where, according to Trubetzkoy (1939/1969, 193 f.), the accent has a rising pitch-pattern and the following syllable is held at the same level as the end of the accented syllable; moreover, 'This involvement of the following syllable is absolutely essential for the phonetic realization of free accent in Serbo-Croatian. Freedom of accent is therefore limited by the fact that it cannot occur on a word-final syllable.'[2]

One may also compare Borgström's statement on Norwegian (1938,

---

[1] Cf. op cit., 547: '...ils ne l'élèvent pas tout à fait, parce que cet élèvement paroistroit tellement au respect du mot suivant, qu'il sembleroit l'unir à soy, ce qui ne se peut faire qu'aux Enclitiques'.

[2] Cf. also Halle 1971, 6.

261), that 'a high peak can only occur if one or more unaccented syllables follow the accented syllable; in accented final syllables there takes place only a more or less incomplete tonal movement, which is most similar to the low peak. If, for example, a monosyllabic word, e.g. *jā*, is spoken with a high peak in hesitating, conditional assent, it is apprehended as disyllabic: *jā`a'*; this is further supported by Broch's observation (1935, 83) that 'the compound intonation is never heard in a genuinely monosyllabic word…If I pronounce it with the beginning of the compound intonation, it sounds impossible as a complete word to a Norwegian ear; the ear instinctively expects a continuation of some kind or other.'

Intonation; Enclitics (and proclitics) again

The retention of the acute before pause is not explainable simply in terms of word accent, since the contonation is inevitably incomplete in this environment. It is most probable, therefore, that this should be interpreted, in part at least, as a feature of sentence prosody rather than of accent alone.[1]

One could possibly just assume that the general requirement that an accentual peak be followed by a fall was in some way neutralized by a pause (e.g. that here there would be some kind of 'silent fall'). A more positive and realistic hypothesis might be that the sentence intonation required a rise in pitch to occur on the last syllable before pause unless it conflicted with the word-accentual characteristics of that syllable. It would thus not be possible in the case of a perispomenon, as καλῶς, or a paroxytone, as φέρω, in both of which the final syllable carries an accentual falling pitch. In a case such as καλός or καλήν the intonational rise would agree with the accentual rise and would support its occurrence without a following fall. One would presumably, on this reckoning, have to assume also an intonational rise on the final syllables of e.g. δῶρον or ἄνθρωπος. Such an implication would not necessarily be contradicted by the fact that we do not find pre-pausal accent-markings δῶρόν, ἄνθρωπός, etc; for the final rise would here be intonational and not accentual, and might only be indicated where it is also accentual, as in καλός etc.[2] But on the other hand Trubetzkoy may be right in assuming that the intonational rise only occurred if the word contained no other (accentual) high pitch; in other terms, the intonation pattern

[1] Cf. Trubetzkoy 1939/1969, 238.   [2] Cf. Sommerstein 1971, 206 f.

would simply require that a high pitch occur at some point in the final word.

Cases of the type καλός could in turn possibly account for traditional accent-markings of the type μεγάλοι τινές, which in other than pre-pausal environments appear as μεγάλοι τινὲς etc. A pre-pausal enclitic τινες, even though *unaccented*, would be pronounced with an intonational rise on the final syllable, i.e. *phonetically* as τινές, the same as an *accented*, full word such as καλός. In other environments the latter appears as καλὸς; and if the grave sign in fact implies complete neutralization of accent, i.e. low pitch, καλὸς would have the same pattern phonetically as (enclitic) τινες. As a result, the grave sign might come to be applied, mistakenly, to give τινὲς in those cases where the post-accentual elements of the combination full word + enclitic exceeded the normal number of syllables. Following on from this, the enclitic might be assumed to have an acute accent (and not simply rising intonation) before pause – thus μεγάλοι τινές.[1]

Similar considerations might have applied to the rare cases where an indefinite which is normally enclitic comes to stand initially in a phrase, and so seems to require an accent, which would however have to be distinct from that of the interrogative: thus ποτὲ μὲν...ποτὲ δὲ.[2] It may be that other speakers, and not only grammarians, would intuitively have interpreted the situation in this way: note modern Greek ποτέ 'ever, never', stressed on the final syllable as well as in the enclitic combination ποτέ μου 'never in my life',

An explanation of this type may also apply to 'proclitics', i.e. words (mostly of high frequency of occurrence) which cohere closely with the following full word and so tend to form an accentual unity with it. Such a category was not recognized by the ancients, and the ms traditions regarding them may well be mechanical and arbitrary:[3] for example, unaccented ὁ, ἡ beside accented τό; εἰς, ἐκ beside πρός, ἐπὶ, etc; οὐ beside μὴ (it may be noted that all the unaccented forms are monosyllables beginning with a vowel).[4] Herodian mentions that there is no difference in accentuation between ἐπιμείλια and ἐπι μείλια (δώσω) – i.e. the ἐπι is unaccented in either case. As prefixes they certainly

---

[1] The proposals in this paragraph arise out of suggestions made in personal communication by Dr Alan Sommerstein.

[2] Cf. Vendryes, 105.　　　　　　　　[3] Vendryes, 66 f.

[4] Postgate 1924, 62; on οὐ, however, see p. 253. For the identification of the article as a proclitic see especially the excellent argument of Sommerstein 1971, 178 ff. (against Vendryes, 76).

have no accent of their own: thus e.g. ὑποδμώς, καταγράφω; when a prefix apparently carries an accent, it is only by virtue of the word with its prefix functioning as a single unit: thus e.g. ὑπόνομος, κατάγραφε; and by 'epectasis' the same may apply to cases where a proclitic preposition is fused with the following word: thus πρόπαλαι, διάπεντε, with regression of accent, as opposed to e.g. παραχρῆμα, παραπολύ, with the full word retaining its accent.[1] It is also to be noted that in Aeolic, where the accent is normally recessive (θῦμος, πόταμος, σόφος, etc.), this does not apply to prepositions and certain conjunctions, which, according to the grammarians, there 'retain the acute accent'.[2]

An explanation of these apparent contradictions between the traditional marking (which tends to accent the proclitics) and other evidence (which suggests that they were unaccented) might be as follows. By the grammarians the phenomena of *en*clitic accentuation were seen in terms of the enclitic 'leaning' on the preceding full word (ἐγκλίνειν) and transferring to the last syllable of the latter the burden of its accent (ἀναβιβάζειν: cf. Vendryes, 76); when this was not possible, as e.g. in λέγω τι, the transfer was said to take place only 'in the mind' (Herodian, i, 564 L: νῷ μόνῳ νοεῖται τὰ τῆς ἐγκλίσεως). On the basis of such an interpretation a *pro*clitic, when followed by an *en*clitic, would tend to be given an 'enclitic' accent on its final syllable: thus e.g. περί μου, πρός τε ἀλλήλους. This accent might then in turn be misinterpreted as equivalent to the main accent in e.g. καλά τε, and consequently converted to a grave before a full word, as in περὶ πάντων etc. It is, however, again quite conceivable that the reasoning attributed to the grammarians might also have applied intuitively to other speakers and so have been reflected in at least some actual pronunciations, to the extent of giving a high pitch on the final of the proclitic in περί μου etc. Such a treatment would be the more likely in cases such as this, where the combination of a preposition and a governed enclitic might be felt grammatically to qualify as an accentable unit. Note also in late Greek the compound adverb περίπου, the accentuation of which is supported by modern Greek; in the case of prepositions before full words, however, the accent mark, which tends to persist in the orthography, is not generally reflected in actual speech.

In such cases of enclitic accents on proclitics the accent is always oxytone, even when the general rules of recession would permit a perispomenon. This peculiarity may arise from the fact that in the case

---

[1] Vendryes, 68, 93.　　　　　　　[2] Vendryes, 69.

of full words the only condition under which a single accent indicative of enclisis can occur is when the full word is oxytone, as e.g. ἀγαθός τις, λιπών τε (in e.g. καλῶς τε or μεγάλη τις there is no indication of enclisis).[1] The oxytone would thus come to be envisaged as the 'enclitic accent'; and if our analysis of the phonetic nature of the accent is correct, such an accent would have particular 'linking' properties, in so far as it requires the falling part of the contonation to extend over the first syllable of the enclitic. By analogy (perhaps in speech as well as in grammatical doctrine) a combination of the type οὐ τις would then be accented as οὔ τις,[2] just as φῶς τις, and not (except by epectasis) as οὖ τις; similarly ὥς περ, ὥς τε, etc. Perhaps symptomatic of this interpretation of the enclitic accent is the occasional tendency in some mss, noted by Postgate (1924, 70), to replace a final circumflex by an acute before enclitic: e.g. ὧν τε for ὧν τε.

In general it may be said that, whereas both proclitics and enclitics are in principle unaccented, the former are without accentual influence on the main word whereas the latter may require the main word to carry a secondary accent, or may protect its accent against neutralization. This difference in effect is a simple consequence of the fact that Greek accentual rules operate from the ends of words and not from their beginnings. The general distinction may also be illustrated from modern Greek, where certain forms, e.g. μας, can operate both as enclitics (possessive pronoun) and as proclitics (direct or indirect object), with different accentual consequences; thus (Warburton 1970a, 112):

(i) ὁ γείτονάς μας το πούλησε 'our neighbour sold it';
(ii) ὁ γείτονας μας το πούλησε 'the neighbour sold it to us'.[3]

Interrogatives

In considering terminal intonation (before pause), it has been implied that in certain circumstances this had a rising pattern in Greek, regardless of the meaning of the sentence. In English such an intonation is primarily a characteristic of yes/no questions; but in Norwegian, for

---

[1] The same also applies to secondary accents; for, as a result of the limiting rules of recession, these can only occur if the vowel of the final syllable of the main word is short (as ἄνθρωπός τις, δῶρόν τι), and so can only be acute. On ∼αι, ∼οι see p. 238.

[2] But see also p. 253.

[3] Additionally, as Warburton notes, there may be assimilation of the final consonant of a full word to a following enclitic, and of a proclitic to a following full word: thus e.g. μας μίλησε 'he spoke to us' = /maz mílise/, ὁ φίλος μας μίλησε 'our friend spoke' = /o fíloz mas mílise/.

example, even 'sentences which contain ordinary, definite, decided statements end on a rising melody...There is, consequently, a pronounced rise in pitch within the last word of the sentence. Should the sentence end in a Tone Group, the rise in pitch can be even greater'; so that 'Norwegian often strikes foreigners as an unending series of question-marks' (Popperwell 1963, 177 f.). This leads us to consider the case of the oxytone interrogatives τίς and τί, which do not reduce their accent to grave within the sentence. As stated by Apollonius Dyscolus (*Pron.*, 28 S), the accent here may be considered as having not a distinctive but an interrogatory function – or in other words to be not an accentual but an intonational feature. One may compare the case reported for Ganda by Trubetzkoy (1935/1968, 38 n.1), where the rising tone occurs 'only in interrogative verb-forms and this has nothing to do with word phonology, but rather belongs in the field of sentence phonology'. It is also noted by Ultan (1969, 54), in the course of a study of interrogative systems in some 79 languages, that 'Although data on QW (question-word)-accent are scarce, 20 languages have fortis stress or sentence stress, high pitch, rising contour, or a combination of stress and high pitch on the QW. These languages are evenly distributed.'

One could therefore view the acute accentuation of τίς, τί simply as an example of this general tendency: the same could apply (at least in emphatic contexts) to the negative οὔ (see below). The only problem is that longer interrogative words show no special peculiarity of accentuation (e.g. τίνα, πότε, πῶς, ποῖος, πότερον), unless perhaps, as suggested by Postgate (1924, 10), these words carried a specially high melodic peak. Though this is not mentioned by ancient authorities, it is by no means impossible.

One other, though more complicated, explanation might be considered. Two respects in which all the interrogative words, including τίς and τί, could be said to fall into the same accentual category are (i) they are all maximally recessive, and (ii) they are all accented as in the pre-pausal position; in addition (iii) they all tend, as in many languages (cf. Ultan 1969, 48, 55), to gravitate to the beginning of the sentence. Now conditions (i) and (iii) are also characteristic of certain common vocatives, as ἄδελφε, πόνηρε, γύναι, Ζεῦ beside nom. ἀδελφός πονηρός, γυνή, Ζεύς (cf. also in Vedic e.g. *RV* i 1, 9 *ágne, sūpáyanó bhava* beside nom. *agníḥ*). Condition (ii) presumably also applies to vocatives, even when the influence of the nom. accent maintains oxytone accentuation, as e.g. ὦ 'γαθέ. In addition, vocatives tend to stand outside the sentence proper:[1] note e.g. the place of δὲ in Eur., *Or.* 622 Μενέλαε, σοὶ δὲ τάδε λέγω; in Vedic too a verb following an initial vocative is treated as beginning a sentence, and is so accented: e.g. *RV* iii 28, 1 *ágne, juṣásva no havíḥ*. The recessive accentuation is also characteristic of the ironic question ἄληθες; and the exclamation χάριεν[2] – which are clearly independent utterances.

These peculiarities and parallelisms could lead to a hypothesis that the interrogative words of Greek, though overtly not independent of the sentence, might be considered so at some deeper level of structure,[3] and for this reason have the phonological characteristics of finality as well as initiality.[4]

According to Herodian (i, 504 L) the negative οὐ also had an acute accent in all positions (i.e. was not in fact a proclitic); and this view gains some support from Aristotle, who (*Soph. El.* 166b; cf. *Poet.* 1461a) appears to distinguish the negative from the enclitic pronoun οὐ ('of it')[5] by the accent, and specifically in terms of higher pitch (λέγοντες ὀξύτερον).[6]

The 'middle' accent

Finally, in a number of the ancient discussions of the Greek accent, beginning with Aristotle, we find references to a 'middle' accent (μέσος). This has been variously identified as (a) the glide forming the second half of the circumflex (Grammont 1948, 388); (b) the glide on the syllable following the high pitch (Blass 1890, 133); (c) the circum-

---

[1] Cf. Postgate 1924, 31. [2] Cf. Postgate 1924, 92.
[3] Cf. on πότερον Kretschmer 1938, 38.
[4] The overt, surface-structure situation in a little-known language is of some interest in this connexion. In Abaza (N.W. Caucasus) 'substantive' interrogative sentences are unusual in having their interrogative words at the end; but these words are independent to the extent that they constitute main clauses, linked to a relative clause constituting the rest of the sentence. Thus e.g. 'Who will go?' = *y-ca-wš dəzda*, lit. '*rel.*-go-*fut.* who (is it)?'; 'What did you give her?' = *y-lə-w-t-z zaɡ°'əya*, lit. '*rel.*-her-you-give-*aor.* what (is it)?': cf. also Fr. *qu'est-ce que...?* ('adverbial' interrogation is incorporated in the verb: e.g. *w-anbá-ca-wš* 'when will you go'?, lit. 'you-when-go-*fut.*?'). In all Abaza interrogatory (and exclamatory) sentences there is a rising–falling terminal intonation, as against simple fall in affirmative sentences (A 1956, 133).
[5] Or possibly the relative οὔ.
[6] Cf. Postgate 1924, 63.

flex as a whole (Hoenigswald 1954, 209 ff; cf. Vendryes, 44);[1] (d) the accent marked grave, replacing the final acute within the sentence (cf. Sturtevant 1940, 100); and (e) any level of pitch intermediate between the highest and lowest (cf. A 1968a, 112 f.). But since the ancient writers themselves probably use the term in different senses, it is unprofitable to speculate further on its meaning. In any case it certainly does not signify any structurally relevant melodic features over and above those which have already been discussed.[2]

[1] The same identification is made by some Byzantine grammarians.
[2] Cf. Tronskij 1962, 44.

EXCURSUS B

The equivalence of one heavy to two light syllables in Greek hexameters

An outstanding problem of Greek metrics concerns the origin of the equation $\Sigma = \Sigma\Sigma$ in dactylic hexameters. It is, as has been argued (pp. 48 ff., 60 f.), unrealistic to base this on purely temporal considerations; and, if such were its basis, it is difficult to see why it should apply only in weak and not in strong position. In this connexion one can hardly avoid reference to the notorious passage in Dionysius of Halicarnassus (*De Comp.* xvii, 71 UR), where he reports the view of the 'rhythmicians' that the heavy ('long') syllable of strong position in dactyls is in some degree shorter than the sum of two 'shorts', being termed on this account ἄλογος 'irrational' as opposed to τέλειος 'complete'. Dionysius also mentions a type of anapaest (termed κυκλικός) differing from the normal, which is a mirror-image of the dactyl with its 'irrational long'. Amongst discussions relevant to this matter may be mentioned Goodell 1901, 168 ff; White 1912, 5 f; Pipping 1937; Koster 1953, 82 ff; Rossi 1963a; Parker 1965; Irigoin 1965; Maas 1966, 37; Dale 1968, 6 f. Dionysius' statement has sometimes been used to explain the negative side of the problem, i.e. the metrical *non*-equivalence of $\Sigma\Sigma$ to Σ in strong position in hexameters. But, firstly, the basic pattern of the hexameter is dactylic, not spondaic (as indicated, inter alia, by the preponderance of dactyls in the cadentially important foot V); so that, as cannot be too often emphasized, it is not a matter of 1 heavy being 'resolved' into 2 light, but of 2 light being 'contracted' into 1 heavy. And secondly, it may be that Dionysius is not here making a general metrical statement, but rather a stylistic observation applying to a particular type of line such as that which he cites (the entirely dactylic *Od.* ix 39 Ἰλιόθεν με φέρων ἄνεμος Κικόνεσσι πέλασσεν) – a type of line which he elsewhere (xx, 92 UR) describes as being particularly rapid, 'so that some of the feet do not differ much from trochees', in this case citing the famous *Od.* xi 598 αὖτις ἔπειτα πέδονδε κυλίνδετο λᾶας ἀναιδής. As Rossi points out (1963a, 44), in ch. xvii Dionysius is writing of metrical matters, but after citing his anapaestic example (κέχυται πόλις ὑψίπυλος κατὰ γᾶν) he says: περὶ ὧν ἂν ἕτερος εἴη λόγος: 'Where', asks Rossi, 'will the discussion be resumed? Precisely in ch. xx', where Dionysius treats of stylistics (τὸ πρέπον).

A 'shortening' of the heavy syllable beginning a dactyl is certainly a possibility, more especially if it were associated with stress (see pp. 286 ff.). One is reminded of the English 'laxing rule' seen, for example, in the accented syllables of words of Romance origin such as *críminal*, *sevérity* beside *crime, severe* (see p. 176); for native words one may note Old English *ǣrende* → Mid.E. *ěrende* (errand), *hǎligdæg* → *hǒliday* (beside *hōly*); the tendency persists in Modern English, where (Gimson 1970, 262) 'Vowels...in accented syllables which form the hub of a rhythmic group are shortened according to the number of unaccented syllables (especially following) in the group. Thus, the /aɪ/ of /taɪd/ (*tide*) shows progressive shortening in such rhythmic groups as *tidy*, *tidily*...'[1] But whatever may be the true implications of Dionysius' words, it is perhaps safest simply to recognize, as Parker (1965, 319), 'the impotence of modern scholarship in the face of ancient muddle', and 'the unsuitability of Dionysius' statement as a basis for theorizing'. One can hardly use it (as e.g. Maas 1966, 37; West 1970, 186) in support of an in any case unrealistic temporal explanation for the equivalence of Σ and ΣΣ in weak position and non-equivalence in strong position.

One proposal for a non-temporal explanation bases itself on accentual factors. For accentual purposes, as we have seen, there are grounds for analysing the Greek long vowels and diphthongs into two morae, as against one mora for the short vowels. And it has been suggested by Jakobson (1937b/1962, 269) and subsequently by Ruipérez (1955, 79 ff.) that it is this proportional relationship which underlies the metrical equivalence. It is generally held to be a Greek innovation, and more specifically Ionic.[2] It is a striking fact that it is not a feature of Aeolic verse;[3] and in Aeolic (see p. 238) different rules of accentuation applied, such that acute and circumflex were never in opposition to one another, but simply automatic alternants. The variation in Aeolic between θῦμος and θύμου is automatically determined by the length of the vowel in the final syllable; it is not phonological but only phonetic, and might be argued not to justify an analysis into morae. This contrasting accentual situation in Aeolic, where the metrical equivalence is also

---

[1] Cf. Jones 1962, 237 §886.
[2] Meillet 1923, 43.
[3] Cf. Martin 1953, 95; Cole 1969, 60 and n.84.

lacking, has been held to support the idea of an accentual basis for the metrical equivalence in non-Aeolic verse.[1]

It must, however, be recognized that this theory will only account directly for a *vocalic* equivalence of $\breve{V}$ and $\breve{V}\breve{V}$ and not for a *quantitative* equivalence of Σ and $\Sigma\Sigma$. It will account for the latter only in so far as 'naturally' heavy syllables are concerned, i.e. those containing a long vowel or diphthong, but not in the case of 'positionally' heavy syllables, i.e. those containing a short vowel. One would therefore have to assume an extension of the equivalence principle in the latter case.[2]

It may be doubted whether oppositions of melodic accent could form a basis for quantitative metrical principles: cf. the comment of Meillet (1900, 271), 'Le ton ne peut servir de base au rythme que quand il s'est transformé en accent d'intensité.' In which case another and simpler basis for the equivalence might be considered more probable – namely, the process of vowel contraction, whereby e.g. ἐφίλεε → ἐφίλει, τιμάετε → τιμᾶτε, δηλοόμεθα → δηλούμεθα;[3] it may be noted incidentally that such contraction is a prime source of the circumflex (monosyllabic) accentuation, and has been cited as historical support for the mora analysis, since $\breve{V}\acute{\breve{V}}$ contracts to $\acute{V}$ and $\breve{V}\breve{V}$ to $\hat{V}$.[4] This in itself would hardly account for the metrical equivalence, since speakers would not be aware of the historical facts, and in any case it does not only apply to sequences of short vowels: e.g. φιλέουσα → φιλοῦσα, ȝήετε → ȝῆτε, ȝήωμεν → ȝῶμεν (so that one could not even assume a descriptive rule $\breve{V}\breve{V} \to \bar{V}$ rather than simply $VV \to \bar{V}$). The process of contraction was carried further in Attic than in other dialects;[5] but in the text of Homer some contractions must go back to an early period, since the metre precludes their expansion even in some formulaic contexts.[6] A textual form such as τάρβει, for example, can be restored to τάρβεε when the relevant syllable occurs in weak position (e.g. *Il.* iv 388; *Od.* vii 51); but this does not apply to, say, φιλεῖ in *Il.* ii 197 ~φιλεῖ δέ ἑ μητίετα Ζεύς (strong position) or to τάρβει in *Il.* xxi 288 ~μήτε τι τάρβει (end of line and so $\Sigma\Sigma\Sigma$ is impossible). The textual ἀγρίου. πρόσθεν δὲ~ (*Il.* xxii 313) demands ἀγρίο̲ο̲, and in weak position generally ~oo *can* be restored for genitive

---

[1] E.g. Jakobson 1937b/1962, 269. The argument is misunderstood by Dale (1957, 21).
[2] Zirin 1970, 68 ff.
[3] Cf. Nagy 1970b, 13, 154.
[4] Kuryłowicz 1958, 107; Zirin 1970, 66.
[5] Lejeune 1955, 235.
[6] Chantraine 1958, 27 ff.

AAR

∼ου;[1] but there are 575 cases where ∼ου occurs in strong position and so *cannot* be expanded. The conclusion seems to be that in the course of epic development contracted (monosyllabic) elements were substituted for uncontracted (disyllabic), but that the influence of the earlier formulae remained strong. That at a later date the true nature of the uncontracted forms was no longer recognized is seen from the phenomenon of 'diectasis';[2] ὁράω, for example, contracted to ὁρῶ, αἰτιάεσθαι to αἰτιᾶσθαι; but the metre demanded two syllables, and to meet this need the vowel was simply repeated to give the textual but non-historic ὁροῶ, αἰτιάασθαι, etc.; similarly φάος → φῶς, whence by diectasis φόως (in cases where the second is heavy by reason of a following consonantal initial).

In the final form of the Homeric text, therefore, contracted and uncontracted forms exist alongside; but this in itself would not account for metrical equivalences of spondee to dactyl which were already established in the earlier formulae. Any explanation along these lines must assume that some predecessor of the Homeric hexameter was based on purely dactylic patterns (except at line-end); that then, in certain words of the poems, vowel-contraction produced spondaic sequences; and that thence the substitution 'extended beyond the original etymological confines of the formulas which generated it, so that new formulas with spondee instead of dactyl became admitted' – a case of the metre 'assuming dynamics of its own and becoming regulator of any incoming non-traditional phraseology' (Nagy 1970b, 154 f., 96: cf. p. 14). At an earlier stage the language must have tended more to dactylic patterns than later, after contractions had taken place; it would, for example, have been easier to compose purely dactylic verses in Mycenaean Greek than in, say, later Ionic or Attic.[3]

Of the explanations so far offered for the metrical equivalence this seems the most plausible; and if correct, the metrical term 'contraction' is a felicitous one. It should, however, be remembered (cf. p. 61) that it is not entirely true to say that the equivalence of Σ and ΣΣ is a monopoly of Greek (and thence Latin), and does not occur in Old

---

[1] Kiparsky (1967c, 632) makes the novel suggestion that the pre-contractual form of the genitive was ∼ŏŏ rather than ∼ŏŏ (by quantitative metathesis from ∼ōŏ) and points to the rarity of cases where ∼οǫ (filling weak position) rather than ∼ου is metrically indicated (only *Od.* xiv 239 ∼δήμου φῆμις: cf. p. 286); he also notes *Il.* ii 731 ∼Ἀσκληπιοῦ δύο παῖδε, where metre requires that ∼ου = ΣΣ, and the curious ὅου at *Il.* ii 325, *Od.* i 70.

[2] Chantraine 1958, 75 ff.   [3] Cf. Maguinness 1963, 209 f; 1971, 162.

Indian (as e.g. Meillet 1923, 43; Kuryłowicz 1968c, 192); the principle is stated with notable conciseness by the Indian metrician Piṅgala (*Chandaḥ-sūtra* i. 14) in the rule *'glau'* (where *g* = *guru* 'heavy', *l* = *laghu* 'light', and ∼ *au* is the dual inflexion). The origins of the Indian equivalence are unknown, but it is clear from the statements of native observers (cf. p. 57) that it was not based on duration.[1]

[1] In musically accompanied poetry or song such equivalences may of course be regularized in duration; thus in Luganda the equivalences are fitted to the regular musical pattern of drum-beats, 'short' syllables being accompanied by one beat, and 'long' syllables by two (*Tucker 1962, 163 ff; cf., on Kimasaaba songs, Brown 1972, 41).

16   *Stress*

(a) ACCENTUALLY RELATED STRESS

(1) Classical correlations

As a result of the fact that variation of pitch is commonly one of the cues to stress, it has sometimes been assumed that conversely the melodic accent of classical Greek must have contained an element of stress: thus, for example, Schmitt (1924, 208 f; 1953, 23 ff.), who assumes for Greek a weak dynamic accent with pitch as only a concomitant feature – even though he elsewhere recognizes (1953, 18 ff.) that pitch is determinable primarily by acoustic criteria but stress by motor activity, and that consequently there need be no universal correlation between them. Support for the idea of an element of stress in the ancient Greek accent is sometimes sought in Latin words borrowed from Greek (e.g. Sturtevant 1940, 103), which are accented on the same syllable as in Greek even though this may be contrary to Latin rules. But in fact most of the alleged examples are of late origin,[1] from a period when the Greek accent itself had indeed changed to a dynamic accent, with consequent neutralization of vowel length; thus in Prudentius (4–5 c. A.D.) metrical requirements indicate *ĭdŏlum*, *ĕrĕmus*, *pŏĕsis* < εἴδωλον, ἔρημος, ποίησις, and the shortness of the medial vowels suggests initial accentuation. But the shortness of these vowels is simply due to the fact that in late Greek, where vowel length was governed by stress, they were unstressed; and, given the quantitative pattern ΣΣ̆Σ, it was inevitable even by Latin rules that such words should be initially accented; it is not the case that Latin took them over at an early period with a pattern Σ̄Σ̄Σ and in consequence of its own stress accent reduced them to Σ́Σ̆Σ (even though in late Latin unaccented vowels were indeed short). Similar considerations apply to Vulgar Latin forms of Greek loanwords as reconstructed on the evidence of the Romance languages.[2]

The only clear example from classical Latin times is *áncŏra* < ἄγκυρα; but here one cannot exclude the possibility of an intermediary in the

---

[1] Vendryes 1902, 159 f; André 1958, 157 f.
[2] For examples see Pulgram 1965.

borrowing (?Etruscan), or the analogy of some other word or words: André (1958, 152) suggests, as another term with a nautical meaning, *ámphŏra*. The example is in any case countered by *crĕpĭda* < κρηπῖδα, and *trŭtĭna* < τρυτάνη, where, as André remarks, 'l'accent grec n'est pour rien'. Evidence is also sometimes cited from the Plautine metrical treatment of *Philippus* (as the name of a coin < Φίλιππος) as if accented *Phílipus*;[1] but whatever may be the explanation of this treatment, it need not have anything to do with the Greek accent, since the same treatment is found for e.g. *Achilles* < 'Αχιλλεύς and even for some non-Greek words, as e.g. *sagitta*.[2] One may therefore accept the statement of Quintilian (i.5.2) that in his youth even the most learned people pronounced a Greek name such as *Atreus* ('Ατρεύς) with the Latin accent on the first and not the second syllable, and his implication that any attention to the position of the Greek accent was a recent pedantry. Elsewhere (i.5.62) he points out that, in spite of the Greek "Ολυμπος, τύραννος, Latin accents these words as *Olýmpus*, *tyránnus*, 'quia duabus longis sequentibus breuem acui noster sermo non patitur'.

The strongest argument against any significant element of stress as a correlate of high pitch in Greek is provided by the fact that in Greek classical verse there appears to be no attempt to achieve agreement between accent and metre in any part of the line in any spoken form. The situation may be exemplified by *Il.* i 84 τὸν δ' ἀπαμειβόμενος προσέφη πόδας ὠκὺς 'Αχιλλεύς.[3] In a recent study Schmiel (1968) has attempted to apply to Homer the same type of analysis as was applied to Vergil by Jackson Knight (cf. p. 338). Employing Knight's terms of 'homodyne' for agreement between accent and strong position, and 'heterodyne' for disagreement, Schmiel suggests that there is more homodyne composition in speeches than in narrative, and that 'vivid' lines are mostly homodyne whereas 'calm' lines are usually heterodyne; these same 'textural' tendencies he finds to be even more pronounced in Sophocles. These are matters on which it is difficult to be objective (it may be noted that for Knight homodyne was associated with 'smoothness' and heterodyne with 'ruggedness'). But even if such correlations of texture and mood could be more objectively established, they would not necessarily imply an element of stress in the accent; since they would not be associated with the metre in general, but only with

---

[1] Lindsay 1922, 40, 77.
[2] Cf. p. 182; also Quintilian i.5.22 f. on *Camillus*.
[3] Cf. Kabell 1960, 3.

particular forms of expressiveness, they need be nothing more than purely melodic ornaments without any dynamic implications.

In connexion with the study of possible correlations between Greek accent and metre, Jakobson has commented (1937b/1962, 270), 'Hitherto, the attempts to clear up the role of the accent in Greek verse suffered from a false assumption that the accent, if it participates in the verse structure, must gravitate toward the downbeat, and also from a too summary, overly simplified treatment of the accent itself'. And if one considers other elements of the accent than the high pitch, certain general tendencies do in fact appear, which are quite different from what has generally been anticipated.[1]

From a sampling of the intersections of accent and metre in classical Attic verse (iambics), the statistical trend is for the acute to occur in *weak* position, whereas the strong position tends to coincide with the circumflex or the syllable *following* an acute (which may be termed the 'postacute') – i.e. with a falling melodic pattern in either case (the *svarita* of the Indians: see p. 234). By way of illustration we may cite the opening lines of Sophocles' *Antigone*, underlining (the vowels in) the strong position of each foot:

Ὦ κοινὸν αὐτάδελφον Ἰσμήνης κάρα,
ἆρ' οἶσθ' ὅ τι Ζεὺς τῶν ἀπ' Οἰδίπου κακῶν
ὁποῖον οὐχὶ νῷν ἔτι ζώσαιν τελεῖ;

The matter has not, however, been pursued to any great lengths, since it appears, as we shall see, to be an automatic consequence of certain other factors and not to arise out of any deliberate choice by the poets.

For falling pitch to be associated with stress would not in itself be surprising; in English intonation, for example, the primary sentence-stress in statements is normally associated with a falling 'nucleus';[2] and in Serbo-Croat, according to Trubetzkoy (1939/1969, 191), 'In contrast with the "rising" accent, which is characterized almost entirely by its musical quality, and which...is not associated with any significant expiratory increment, the "falling" accent is primarily expiratory' (cf. also 226 n.262).

For Greek, it was pointed out by Schmidt a century ago (1872, 204) that the circumflex is naturally distinguished from the acute in so far as it is necessarily associated with heavy quantity, and so, he

---

[1] Cf. A 1967a.
[2] E.g. Gimson 1970, 268 ff.

concluded, corresponds more closely than the other Greek accents to the dynamic accent of German. But in addition, paroxytone words tend to have a long vowel (or diphthong) in the following, final syllable, since it is this condition which precludes proparoxytone or properispomenon accentuation; thus, schematically, $[\sim \acute{\Sigma}\grave{\Sigma}]$ occurs, but not $[\sim \acute{\Sigma}\Sigma\Sigma]$ nor $[\sim \hat{\Sigma}\Sigma]$. By the 'final-trochee rule' (p. 237), if the penultimate vowel is long and accented, and the vowel of the final syllable is short, the accent must be circumflex, i.e. $[\sim \hat{\Sigma}\Sigma]$, which precludes an accentuation $[\sim \acute{\Sigma}\grave{\Sigma}]$ in which there would be a correlation between high pitch and long vowel; this situation is not affected by 'Vendryes' Law' (p. 239), whereby $[\underline{\Sigma}\hat{\Sigma}\Sigma] \rightarrow [\acute{\Sigma}\grave{\Sigma}\Sigma]$, since a falling pitch still occurs on the long vowel, and the acute does not. The situation is neutral in the case of proparoxytone accentuation, since the accented syllable and the following syllable may have either short or long vowels; the accented vowels of oxytone words may also be long or short, but in fact (see pp. 244 ff.) there is generally neutralization of the accent in this case.

If, therefore, any general statistical tendency is to be expected from the Greek accentual rules, it would be for a falling pitch (circumflex or post-acute) to occur on long vowels or diphthongs – and more particularly on the last long vowel in the word – but for a high pitch not to; specifically, the rules favour patterns $[\sim \hat{\Sigma}]$, $[\sim \hat{\Sigma}\Sigma]$, $[\sim \acute{\Sigma}\grave{\Sigma}]$, $[\sim \acute{\Sigma}\grave{\Sigma}\Sigma]$ but disfavour $[\sim \acute{\Sigma}\grave{\Sigma}]$, $[\sim \acute{\Sigma}]$.[1] Long vowels imply heavy quantity, and light quantity implies short vowel; any tendencies to length/accent correlation might therefore be expected to have at least some degree of reflexion in quantity/accent tendencies.[2] This expectation was tested for prose over a number of passages of continuous speech in Plato's *Republic*, and the results (which exclude the 'grave' accent and some other doubtful cases) are summarized in the tables overpage, showing (a) correlations of pitch with the last heavy syllable in the word, and (b) correlations of the last heavy syllable with pitch, expressed as percentages of the total 'population at risk'.[3]

Whilst the tendencies thus revealed are rather striking, they are

[1] 'Wheeler's Law' (see p. 239) also tends to disfavour $[\acute{\Sigma}\grave{\Sigma}\Sigma]$.

[2] Cf. also Kuryłowicz 1970, 429 n. Relevant exceptions to any such parallelism between length and quantity are provided principally by the accentual treatment of words ending in αι, οι (see p. 238) and by words ending in $\breve{V}C$ whose final syllable is heavy before a word beginning with a consonant.

[3] A 1967a, 53.

(a)	on last heavy syll.	elsewhere
% of (i) high pitch (acute)	22	78
(ii) falling pitch (post-acute)	67	33
(iii) falling pitch (circumflex)	77	23
Total (ii)+(iii)	70	30

(b)	under (i) acute	under (ii) post-acute	(under iii) circumflex	(ii)+(iii)
% of last heavy syll.	19	58	23	81
other syllables	66	27	7	34

probably only an incidental effect of the accentual rules, which in themselves are probably not based on any predilections regarding the
incidence of falling pitch (but rather on limitations in terms of morae).
However, they could account for the tendency in verse for falling
pitch to correlate with strong position – automatically in cases where
the weak position was filled by a light syllable or syllables (since light
syllables in any part of the word tend not to carry falling pitch); but
also elsewhere (i.e. in spondaic feet, as e.g. ζώσαιν in *Antigone* 3) *if*,
let us suppose, words were normally stressed on their last heavy syllable
and if verse composition deliberately sought agreement between stress
and strong position. The question of stress in classical Greek will later
be discussed in some detail; but it must be emphasized that any tendency
to correlation between metre and *accent* would then be simply an
incidental consequence of (a) correlation between metre and stress,
(b) correlation between stress and quantity, (c) correlation between
quantity and vowel length, and (d) the also incidental correlation
between accent and quantity.

One can hardly speculate on the extent, if any, to which Greeks were
subconsciously aware of any statistical correlation between stress
(assuming its existence) and melodic patterns. Certainly there seems to
be no evidence for this in classical verse. For a later period, however,
there may be some indications which point to such an awareness.

(2) Post-classical correlations

Firstly, there is the case of Latin words borrowed or represented in
literary Greek, notably by Plutarch, where there is some prima facie
evidence that the Latin accent was taken into account.[1] The clearest

[1] A 1967a, 54 f.

case involves the representation of the Latin penultimate stress by Greek properispomenon, i.e. by a falling pitch on the same syllable: thus e.g. γουττᾶτος, Τουρκουᾶτος, λιγᾶρε, κηλᾶρε, Κυρῖνος = *guttātus*, *Torquātus, ligāre, cēlāre, Quirīnus*. The use of the circumflex here (as against the acute), though not contrary to the tendencies mentioned, is hardly citable as evidence; for, by the 'final-trochee rule', if the Latin accent is to be equated with *any* Greek accent on the penultimate syllable, it must in these words be a circumflex, since the vowel is long. But there are other cases where, if the accentual tradition is correct, the Latin penultimate stress is represented by a Greek *proparoxytone* – e.g. μάκελλον, Μάρκελλος, λούκουντλος, Σέκουνδος, ἔδικτα = *macéllum, Marcéllus, lucúnc(u)lus, Secúndus, ēdícta*. These examples involve a heavy penultimate syllable, which however contains a short vowel and so cannot carry the circumflex in Greek; a possible interpretation of this accentuation would then be that Greek speakers equated the Latin stress with their falling pitch, and achieved this by placing a high pitch, itself involving no stress, on the *preceding* syllable.

It is characteristic of some forms of later verse to develop into more or less regular rules what were in their earlier models only statistical trends; for example, in discussing the localization of quantitative word-types in the Greek hexameter, O'Neill (1942, 121) refers to 'the Callimachean actualization of the potentialities of the *Iliad*'s inner metric' (for details see pp. 286 ff.). Tendencies of a similar type seem to have operated in regard to certain metrical/accentual correlations. If one considers the *Antigone*, 53% of words occurring at the end of iambic trimeters are paroxytone, 17% oxytone, 17% perispomenon, and 13% proparoxytone; which means that the final syllable had a falling accentual pitch in 70% of cases (paroxytone + perispomenon). This situation had already been noted by Hanssen (1883, 235), who commented that 'the rising rhythm at the end of the iambic trimeter must have been connected with the transition from high to low tone'. More particularly he had noted that accentuation of the final syllable of the line was relatively infrequent, giving figures of 29%, 32%, 30%, and 27% for Aeschylus, Sophocles, Euripides, and Aristophanes respectively. Hanssen had not, however, appreciated the significant difference of melodic pattern symbolized by the acute and circumflex accents, and so had classed these together; the frequency of the final *acute* accent alone would of course be markedly lower even than this (cf. our figure of 17% for the *Antigone*). Hanssen then goes on to observe that in late trimeters, of the Roman and Byzantine periods, the tendency to avoid accentuation of the final syllable gradually becomes an almost unexceptional rule: for Gregory Nazianzen (4 c. A.D.), Paulus Silentiarius (6 c. A.D.) and Georgius Pisides (7 c. A.D.) the figures reduce to respectively 19%, 11%, and 1.1%; and in even later writers to 0.1%. Such a rule must of course at these late dates have been entirely artificial, since by the 4 c. A.D. the change from a melodic to a dynamic accent was almost certainly established (Gregory himself also composed hymns in metres which have regard to such an accent), and so the regulation of the accent must have been counter-metrical in effect.

Similar normative tendencies are to be observed in elegiac pentameters. Hanssen notes that the avoidance of final accentuation is more marked at the end of the pentameter line than at the end of its first colon – thus in the early elegy an average of 18% as against 34%, which he interprets as deliberate: 'at the end of the pentameter, in order to characterize the rising rhythm, conflict was sought between the grammatical accent and the verse-ictus'. Whether deliberate or not, the tendency is later developed into a rule, so that in Alexandrian works the final accentuation reduces to an average of 12%, in the Roman period to an average of 6%, and in Byzantine times to less than 1.5%. Even at an earlier period, when the melodic accent was certainly still in existence, some individual writers had already established the avoidance as a rule – thus in Antipater of Sidon (late 2 c. B.C.) the figure is little more than 1.5% (as against 36% at the end of the first colon); similarly Antipater and Philip of Thessalonika (1 c. A.D.); which led Wackernagel to comment (1925, 50): 'This cannot of course be fortuitous;...but must depend on the fact that at the end of the elegiac couplet a fall of pitch was preferred, and poets of particularly acute hearing made out of this a law for themselves.'

The same applies to other late and less familiar metres having an iambic ending,[1] where a specifically paroxytone accentuation is the main characteristic. The non-fortuitous nature of the correlation has here been noted, for example, by Maas (1922, 582 n.); and it could well be interpreted as showing a preference for a falling pitch on the final syllable. Of certain such lines[2] Dihle (1954, 185) has suggested that the penultimate (light) syllable bore the 'ictus', i.e. constituted

---

[1] Cf. A 1967a, 57 f.
[2] 'Teliambics' (alias 'miuric' (dock-tailed) or 'myuric' (mouse-tailed)), consisting of dactylic/spondaic hexameters with iambic final foot (cf. *Il.* xii 208 ~αἰόλον ὄφιν).

the strong position; this, however, seems improbable, and it is perhaps significant that the only exceptions to the paroxytone accentuation in the cases he is considering involve perispomena – which, by our interpretation, would also involve falling pitch on the final syllable.

Finally, similar correlations are well known as a characteristic of the fables of Babrius, written in the 'scazon' or 'choliambic' ('limping iambic') metre, in which a spondee is substituted for the final iambus. In nearly all cases there is an accent on the penultimate syllable; and this has sometimes been interpreted as evidence for the change from a melodic to a dynamic accent – which is accordingly dated to the time of Babrius (uncertain, but probably around 2 c. A.D.). Other evidence does not rule out the possibility that, in some areas at least, the change may have started about this period; but it is only justifiable to draw such a conclusion from the evidence of Babrius if it is established that the final foot of the Greek scazon has a reversed pattern of strong/weak positions, so that the accented syllable would correlate with the strong position. But this assumption has been rejected by a number of writers for quite other and well-founded reasons.[1] What in any case tends to be overlooked is the fact that the penultimate accent in Babrius is nearly always an acute: a circumflex is there avoided just as is an acute on the antepenultimate – an avoidance which, by the 'final-trochee' rule, results in the final syllable rarely being other than 'naturally' heavy, i.e. containing a long vowel or diphthong. In terms of a melodic accent this would represent a near-absolute rule that the final syllable (i.e. strong position) should correlate with falling pitch, and that the penultimate syllable (i.e. weak position) should correlate with a high and *not* a falling pitch – as in the case of the other metres already mentioned, and as is fully recognized by Hanssen (1883, 241). It is again noticeable that of the exceptions to the rule a number involve perispomenon accentuation, i.e. a circumflex on the final syllable.[2]

In earlier scazons, as in the *Mimes* of Herodas (3 c. B.C.), no such regulation of accent is traceable; nevertheless, paroxytone accentuation at line-end is 2 to 3 times as frequent as any other type. In Herodas there seems no doubt that this is fortuitous – resulting only from the statistical correlations of accent and quantity – but it could have provided the basis for a later generalization.[3]

[1] See A 1967a, 58, and pp. 299 ff.   [2] For details cf. A 1967a, 59.

[3] Cf. Werner 1892, 26; Witkowski 1893, 2 f. Martin (1953, 184 f.) suggests that there is already regularization in Herodas, based on tendencies in Hipponax; but see now Cunningham 1971, 219 f.

In all the cases cited above the accentual peculiarities could in fact be explained as a mechanical regularization of originally fortuitous tendencies. But the possibility remains that at certain of the periods with which we have been concerned, towards the end of the era of melodic accentuation, an actual phonetic prominence had come to be associated with the falling melodic pattern – and that it was this prominence which poets sought to enlist in support of the terminal pattern of their verses.

(3) The dynamic accent

We have mentioned evidence from the work of Gregory Nazianzen that by the 4 c. A.D. the phonetic typology of the Greek accent had undergone a change from melodic to dynamic; for in some of his hymns the tendency is to simple correspondence between accentual peak and strong position. There are similar indications of the transition to a dynamic accent in interior elements of an anonymous early 4 c. Christian hymn (*Pap. Amherst*, ed. Grenfell & Hunt, I.ii); and earlier, in the late 2 c.– early 3 c. A.D., in the hymns of Clement of Alexandria. But there is no convincing evidence before this date.

Rather later metrical evidence is provided by the epic hexameters of Nonnus (*c.* 5 c.), which, like Babrius' scazons, show a preference for final syllables containing a long vowel or diphthong, together with paroxytone accentuation. For these reasons the names of Nonnus and Babrius are sometimes linked in this context; but in Nonnus properispomenon accentuation is also admitted, and what is clearly avoided is a proparoxytone or oxytone. In view of the fact that the hexameter has a *falling* terminal pattern, whereas the scazon probably does *not* (see pp. 299 ff.), the accentual phenomena in the two authors are unlikely to be connected. Moreover, the rules of Nonnus can hardly represent a regularization of earlier statistical tendencies, since in Homer the paroxytone accentuation accounts for little more than one third of lineends and is not much more frequent than proparoxytone. The accentuation in Nonnus, therefore, like that of the 2–4 c. writers mentioned above, is most readily explained in terms of a change from pitch to stress as the modulating feature.

As modern Greek shows, this change was accompanied by a loss of the contrast between monosyllabic (circumflex) and disyllabic (acute) accentuation. The stress is completed within the bounds of the accented syllable, and its arrest is facilitated by a lengthening of the vowel in other than final open syllables; a corollary of this is the loss of phonological distinctions of vowel length (preceded also by a monophthongization of diphthongs);[1] the transition from the one type of accentuation to the other is not unlike that which took place in late Latin, in spite of the fact that there the earlier system also was dynamic (see p. 186). The modern Greek stress accent occurs on the same syllable as bore either the circumflex or the acute: thus γυναῖκα → mod. /jinéka/, ἕτοιμος → mod. /étimos/; in the latter case the development might possibly be seen as involving a contraction of the two elements of the disyllabic contonation into the first of the two syllables: thus (melodic) $[\acute{\Sigma}\grave{\Sigma}]$ → (dynamic) $[\hat{\Sigma}(\Sigma)]$ (and of course in the former case $[\hat{\Sigma}]$ → $[\hat{\Sigma}]$). If such a contraction took place before the ultimate loss of the melodic basis of the accent, i.e. as an elimination of the disyllabic contonation, this might be seen as a preliminary adjustment associated with the change to a dynamic basis. And if in the late melodic-accent period the falling pitch had some degree of stress as a concomitant feature, one could then envisage a coherent sequence of events in the transition from melodic to dynamic accentuation; thus, indicating a combination of pitch and stress by double accent-marks on the cadence:

$$(\text{melodic}) \begin{cases} [\hat{\acute{\Sigma}}] \to [\hat{\grave{\Sigma}}] \\ [\acute{\Sigma}\grave{\Sigma}] \to [\acute{\Sigma}\grave{\grave{\Sigma}}] \to [\hat{\grave{\Sigma}}(\Sigma)] \end{cases} \to (\text{dynamic})[\grave{\Sigma}].$$

One problem would, however, then remain. As may be seen from modern Greek, a dynamic accent replaced both acute *and 'grave'* accents at the end of a word, as e.g. in καλὸς μαθητής = /kalóz maθitís/. One could envisage a change of (melodic) pre-pausal $[\acute{\Sigma}]$ to $[\hat{\Sigma}]$ as part of the general neutralization of accentual differences;[2] and no problem arises if the development from pitch to stress was *not* in fact as outlined above, but if stress simply replaced the melodic accentual *peak* (whether in a monosyllabic or disyllabic contonation), so that melodic $[\acute{\Sigma}]$ and $[\hat{\Sigma}]$ would both directly develop to dynamic $[\grave{\Sigma}]$. But for the 'grave', if it indicated complete loss of melodic accent, the development is less easily understood. It might perhaps arise from a generalization of the pre-pausal (and/or pre-enclitic) form; and it is no doubt true that in ordinary speech pre-pausal forms were far more

---

[1] Cf. A 1967a, 61; 1968a, ch.2 and 88 f.

[2] As suggested on p. 248, the rise in pitch in such cases is probably to be attributed to intonation rather than accent; but where this was the only melodic variation in the word, it would come to be interpreted as an accentual feature.

frequent than would appear from the continuity of literary sentences.[1]
No problem would arise in connexion with the 'grave' if it indicated a
falling melodic pattern (cf. p. 245). But it must be admitted that there
are no particularly compelling reasons for preferring one hypothesis to
another as regards the precise manner of transition from the melodic
to the dynamic accentual system.

The general principle of enclitic accentuation survived the change of
accentual type; for example, in modern Greek μίλησέ μου 'speak to
me'.[2] But just as ancient Greek did not permit high pitches to occur
in immediate succession within a word, so in modern Greek stresses
may not; consequently, whereas in ancient Greek secondary enclitic
accentuation was applicable in e.g. τὴν γυναῖκά μου (since the circumflex implies a fall of pitch within the syllable), no such accent is possible
in the corresponding modern Greek /ti jinéka mu/. It is true that in
this particular case secondary accentuation is in any case unnecessary,
since the effect of neutralizing distinctions of accent and of vowel
length was to convert the original rule of limitation to a simple 3-syllable
rule. But where a secondary accent *is* required, it can no more follow
the main accent in e.g. εἶδα τονε than it can in φέρε τονε – for the use
of the circumflex sign here is purely historical and the accentuation
is /ἴδα tóne/, just as /fére tóne/.[3]

The development of the Greek accentual system is in marked contrast
with that of Indo-Aryan, where the melodic accent vanished without
trace and was replaced by a dynamic accent the location of which was
quite unconnected with that of the former: e.g. Skt *áraṇyam* → Gujarati *rān*, *rājaputráḥ* → Guj. *rāut*, the original melodically accented
syllable having in both cases completely disappeared.

In discussing the typology of the classical Greek accent, evidence was
adduced for its melodic nature from the tendency in some musical
settings for the melody to reflect the accentual patterning of words.
The validity of conclusions drawn from this evidence was strengthened
by the fact that the music in such cases reflects not simply the location
of the accentual peak, but also the different types of contonation. How-

[1] Cf. Vendryes, 41; see also p. 246. On the generalization of pre-pausal forms in
   Indo-Iranian cf. A 1962, 27, 101 ff.
[2] Cf. Warburton 1970a, 112 ff; 1970b, 37 ff.
[3] Cf. Thumb 1912, 28 f.

ever, musical composition *may* also take account of the dynamic
accentuation of words, with melodic features related to the incidence of
word stress. This is a feature of Byzantine music, long after the change
of the Greek accent from a melodic to a dynamic type. The higher
points of the musical melodic curves tend to coincide with word
accents, or the accented syllable may be sung on two notes in a rising
pattern;[1] but no distinction is, of course, made between different types
of accent – acute, circumflex, or grave – since these distinctions no
longer existed in speech. At the end of a musical phrase the accent is
not reflected in this way;[2] but even here it is noticeable that the accented
syllable is often sung on two descending notes, so that it is still marked
by a melodic movement. Coincidence of melody with dynamic word-
accent is also a feature of Gregorian chant, and here too the tendency
is for the accented syllable to be sung on a higher pitch than the following (and often than the preceding) syllable.[3]

EXCURSUS C

The Anglo-Dutch tradition

When in the 14 and 15 c. ancient Greek began to be studied in western
Europe, the teachers were at first primarily Greeks, who naturally
enough used and taught the pronunciation current in their mother
tongue, i.e. virtually that of modern Greek. Reforms in the direction
of a reconstructed classical pronunciation were introduced by Erasmus
and others in the course of the 16 c;[4] but these reforms left the accent
untouched; for even if the reformers had been capable of distinguishing
in theory between dynamic and melodic accentuation, it would have
been quite impracticable for them (as for modern reformers)[5] to
introduce in practice the unfamiliar melodic type of ancient Greek.
Ancient Greek continued, therefore, to be pronounced with a dynamic

---

[1] Wellesz 1961, 349.   [2] Cf. Kabell 1960, 31.
[3] Cf. Reese 1940, 166 f; Park 1968, 12.
[4] A 1968a, 125 ff.   [5] Cf. A 1967b, 98; 1968b, 152 ff.

accent on the marked syllable, and has so continued in most countries up to the present day.[1] The exceptions are Great Britain and the Netherlands (also the Commonwealth and South Africa).

These exceptions have their origin in the doctrines of two Dutch writers in the 17 c. The first of these, Isaac Vossius, was formerly tutor in Greek to Queen Christina of Sweden, and subsequently came to England, receiving an honorary degree at Oxford in 1670. In 1673 he published anonymously at Oxford a treatise *De poematum cantu et viribus rhythmi* in which he stated that the accent marks of Greek had nothing to do with pronunciation (in spite of the evidence of the modern language) and so could be ignored. And eleven years later, in a well-named *Dissertatio Paradoxa,* Vossius' negative ideas on Greek accents were developed into a positive new doctrine by one H. C. Henning (self-Latinized as 'Henninius'), a doctor of medicine from Utrecht. Henning had been impressed by the general similarity of the accentual systems of Latin and of Arabic, particularly as regards their following of the 'penultimate rule'; he was also struck by the similarity of metrical structures in Latin and Greek. He concluded that the 'penultimate rule' was the mark of a 'rational' accentual system, and proceeded to add Greek to Latin and Arabic as allegedly having followed this rule; all modern European languages were, by contrast, classified as 'conventional' in their accentuation, though Spanish and Italian were singled out as being more 'rational' than others, and English as being particularly 'irrational'. Greek, then, according to Henning, was to be pronounced as regards accentuation just as if it were Latin.

This completely unsupported doctrine surprisingly found acceptance both in the Netherlands and in England, where it seems to have been well established by the early 18 c. (though the older system survived in some quarters until about the middle of the century; and 'metamórphosis' is still to be heard). Elsewhere Henning's ideas, after some initial success, were sooner or later rejected as resting upon false arguments, and the 'Modern Greek' system now prevails (with varying degrees of attention and success as regards distinctions of vowel length). The Henninian system was carried from England to America, where it prevailed until the early 19 c. This system was evidently still

---

[1] In Norway this had a strange result. For in Norwegian stress is associated with *low* pitch, so that in the Norwegian pronunciation of Greek the original melodic patterns tend to be reversed (communication from Professor Hans Vogt).

being taught when Longfellow was at school (grad. 1825); for in the poem *Blind Bartimeus* the lines in Greek require stressing according to Latin and not Greek accentuation: thus in the last verse:

Recall those mighty Voices Three,
'Ιησοῦ, ἐλέησόν με!
Θάρσει, ἔγειραι, ὕπαγε!
'Η πίστις σου σέσωκέ σε!

But by the latter half of the century it had succumbed to the German influence in American classical studies. Further support for the change was no doubt provided by the publication of E. A. Sophocles' *History of the Greek Alphabet and Pronunciation* (Cambridge, Mass. 1854), which was, naturally, anti-Henninian in tone.[1]

It appears that some English scholars long before the time of Henning had independently adopted the practice which he advocated. In a letter to Spenser in 1580, Gabriel Harvey[2] expresses his objection to the changing of accents in English words in order to accord with Latin rules (cf. p. 156 n.3): 'In good sooth, and by the faith I beare to the Muses, you shal neuer haue my subscription or consent...to make your *Carpēnter*, our *Carpĕnter*, an inche longer or bigger than God and his Englishe people haue made him'; and he concludes as follows: 'And thus farre of your *Carpēnter* and his fellowes, wherein we are to be moderated and ouerruled by the vsuall and common receiued sounde, and not to deuise any counterfaite fantasticall Accent of oure owne, as manye, otherwise not vnlearned, haue corruptely and ridiculouslye done in the Greeke.'

One result of accepting the views of Vossius and Henning was that the original accents came to be omitted from a number of Greek texts printed in England in the 18 c. – 'as if a gale from the Netherlands had stripped the letters of a superfluous foliage' (Errandonea 1945, 90). Support was lent to this practice by the attack on Greek accents in Richard Dawes' *Miscellanea Critica*, first published in 1745; and in 1759 it was adopted as the official policy of the Oxford University Press. The practice was, however, deplored by many scholars, including John Foster, fellow of King's College, Cambridge, whose admirable essay *On the different nature of Accent and Quantity* was first published in 1762. Later, in his edition of the *Medea* (1801), Richard Porson also

---

[1] Cf. Drerup 1930–1932, 610 ff., 766 ff.
[2] In *Smith 1904, i, 117–19.

insisted on the importance of accentuation, and urged the reader to persist in its study 'scurrarum dicacitate et stultorum irrisione immotus'; the influence of so great a scholar was probably decisive in ensuring that the Greek accents were thereafter respected in English printed texts.[1]

(b) NON-ACCENTUAL STRESS

The argument of section (a) has indicated that in classical Greek there is no evidence of any *inherent* association of stress with pitch. Yet the general probability remains that Greek was like other known languages in having a dynamic patterning of some kind. There are no a priori reasons why such a patterning should not occur independently of the melodic accent, for which parallels have already been cited (p. 94). Even in a language with a dynamic accent there may be other 'linguistically non-functional low-degree stresses' (Kerek 1968, 37 on Hungarian) whose incidence is determined by other criteria than those of accentual stress.

The fact that the Greeks themselves do not mention stress in addition to pitch is not, of course, any disproof of its existence. It would not have been the functional, accentual feature, and so could well not have interested them at a conscious, analytical level. They recognize, for example, a distinction between voiced and voiceless plosives (β δ γ vs π τ κ), since the opposition is semantically functional; but, unlike the ancient Indians,[2] their phonetic acumen was not such as to perceive the *nature* of the voicing process[3] (indeed, not until the latter part of the nineteenth century was this generally recognized in Europe, under the influence of Indian doctrine); and in the case of the nasals and liquids, where voicing was automatic and so non-functional, they make no reference whatever to its presence. A parallel is perhaps provided by classical Arabic; the modern dialects have dynamic accentual systems, yet the early grammarians give no hint of any dynamic patterning.[4] This is generally interpreted as indicating that the classical language lacked any such characteristic; but it may rather be that, as suggested by Mitchell (1960, 369), the grammarians simply 'lacked the interest to devise techniques and categories of the kind necessary for

---

[1] For further discussion cf. A 1967b; 1968a, 134 ff.
[2] A 1953, 33 ff.   [3] A 1968a, 27 f.
[4] Cf. Lecerf 1969, 170.

rigorous observation and analysis'. Stress, after all, still remains one of the more difficult areas of phonetic description; and not until well into the eighteenth century was even the rôle of stress in English verse widely recognized, although 'poets had been writing and readers responding with unerring ears for centuries' (Attridge 1972, 45).[1] Moreover, as a non-accentual feature, it is likely that any such stress in Greek would have been weaker than in a dynamically accented language like Latin; and Latin speakers might well not have recognized it as stress – just as English speakers have difficulty in recognizing the dynamic patterns of Indian languages, which are relatively weak and accompanied by unfamiliar cues in terms of pitch (see p. 75).

The problem is then, *if* any such dynamic patterning existed in classical Greek, how can we know anything about it? It is pointless to make arbitrary pronouncements unsupported by any objective evidence, as was done by Henning (p. 272), who imposed on Greek a pattern of stress derived directly from Latin.[2] Hanssen (1882) concluded that the final syllables of Greek words were stressed if heavy, but that otherwise the penultimate was stressed, regardless of its quantity; this conclusion, however, rests on dubious arguments derived from the melodic accentuation and, as will become apparent, conflicts in part with other evidence.

Evidence: (1) Metre (a priori)

We should be well on the way to discovering the dynamic patterning of Greek if it were established that Greek spoken metres had a dynamic basis or at least tended to dynamic reinforcement. For then, more particularly at the ends of lines, we might expect there to be concord between metrical and speech patterns, so that the former could give a clue to the latter. It is, however, impossible to establish this premiss in advance, however strongly one may feel that it is in accordance with general probability. Ancient discussions are of little help; for (p. 100) the terms ἄρσις and θέσις as applied to the elements of the (metrical) foot do not in themselves necessarily imply a dynamic opposition; they apply primarily to bodily gestures – the rise and fall of the feet in dance, of the hand in 'beating time' – and it would be hazardous to

---

[1] Cf. Fussell 1954, 153 ff.
[2] As more recently Hilberg (1879: see p. 282); Lieger (1926, 9, cited by Kalinka 1935, 331); cf. also Murray 1927, 84.

argue from this to speech dynamics and to say that an audible 'ictus' fell on the strong position – particularly hazardous in view of the tendency for the signification of the two terms to be reversed without notice. Passionate views have been held on either side of the 'ictus' issue, but have generally had little objective basis. Of those who deny the existence of such an 'ictus' in classical verse one may mention Meillet (1923, 10 f.); Schmitt (1953, 30 f.); Lepscky (1962, 209); Dale (1968, 4 f; 1969a, 250). On the other side stand, for example, Hendrickson (1899); Thomson (1923, e.g. 425, 520; 1926, 5 n.); Roussel (1954, 25 ff.); Setti (1963); and other scholars referred to earlier in general discussion (p. 99).[1] It may here be noted that Bentley, famed for his opposition to the idea of an ictus in the Latin hexameter, appears to have held quite the contrary view on iambics and trochaics, Greek as well as Latin (see pp. 343 f.).[2]

Similar divergence of views is found regarding classical Arabic poetry. By many this is considered to be purely quantitative; but from the mode of presentation by Al-Khalīl, the founder of Arabic metrics, and from the number of neutral syllables permitted, Weil concludes (1960, 675 f.) that 'quantity alone cannot have been decisive for the rhythm. Therefore, with it we have – not only in a regulating but a shaping capacity – stress'; and that 'In most lines the ictus and the word-accent will coincide in the same "long"'.

The assumption of an ictus-less and so purely quantitative verse is sometimes bound up with the conception of a decline from ancient to modern times; it is evident in Maas' discussion of the subject (1966, 3 f.), and even more so in Murray (1927, 83): '...in Latin and Greek pronunciation, quantity was the chief variable; while modern uninflected languages have fallen back more and more on the easy careless method of stress'. The strongest expression of this view is that of Nietzsche, who contrasted the ancient with the 'barbarian' rhythms of Germanic: 'Rhythm in the ancient sense is Moral and Aesthetic, the bridle which is put on passion; in short, our type of rhythm belongs to Pathology, the ancient to Ethics': 1912, 336 f. (written 1884).[3] Even when such value judgements are not expressed, it tends to be suggested that our modern 'ears' are in some way less subtle than those of the Greeks; thus Dale (1968, 4 f.) refers to the 'difficulty of training our ear to appreciate, or even to hear, a purely quantitative rhythm'.

---

[1] For a discussion of recent views see also Parker 1970, 60 ff.
[2] Cf. Kapp 1941, 190 f.   [3] Cf. Middleton 1967, 65.

By Stetson (1945, 71) such attitudes have been criticized as invoking an unprovable concept of 'the delicate ear of the ancients'.[1] But so far no very strong disproof of their premisses has been forthcoming. Apart from general arguments (cf. pp. 97 ff.) perhaps the most suggestive indications of some factor additional to quantity as the basis of pattern in Greek verse are:

(i) The fact that the difference between the invariable ('strong') part of the foot and the variable ('weak') part, in all metres where the distinction applies, involves basically a *heavy* syllable as the invariant (contrasting with the weak Σ ('biceps')[2] of dactylics[3] or the Σ ('anceps') of iambics/trochaics); we do not find $\Sigma\Sigma$ or Σ as invariants. In other words, we find spoken metres having basic foot-patterns such as $\Sigma\Sigma$ or $\Sigma\Sigma$, but *not* e.g. $\Sigma\Sigma$ or $\Sigma\Sigma\Sigma$. One could conceive of, say, a 'pure' iambic line which did not permit spondaic feet, i.e. in which the basic pattern would be $\Sigma\Sigma$, with an invariable Σ; but here there would be no contrast of invariable vs variable element (even if the heavy syllable were 'resolvable' into two light, resolution is a strictly regulated device (see pp. 316 ff.) – so that the second element could not be stated as a free variable Σ like that of the dactylic hexameter). This circumstance at least raises the possibility for Greek of the state of affairs described by Kerek (1968, 23) for Hungarian:

That syllable length is readily available...to serve as the quantitative metric principle should not obscure the significant fact that it has another, system-regulated function, namely, that it is a conditioning factor in low-level stress placement; thus there is a good case for assuming that if a native audience not only accepts as 'natural' but possibly expects long syllables as metrical rhythm peaks, it is on account of the *stress* assigned to them due to their length, rather than because of their values as time units;

in other words there is the possibility, as Kerek (38) expresses it, of 'confusion of the metric formula and rhythmic potentials of the linguistic sequences that fill it'.

---

[1] For the terminology cf. p. 306; and earlier e.g. W. Melmoth, *The Letters of Sir Thomas Fitzosborne*, 9th edn (London, 1784; 1st edn Dublin, 1748), xiv, 63 f: 'the delicacy of Tully's ear'; xxxvii, 171: 'Most certain it is that the delicacy of the antients with respect to numbers, was far superior to any thing that modern taste can pretend to; and that they discovered differences, which are to us absolutely imperceptible.' These expressions perhaps derive ultimately from the (hardly complimentary) 'aures delicatas' of Quintilian, iii.1.3.

[2] $= \Sigma$ or $\Sigma\Sigma$.

[3] On anapaestics see pp. 332 f.

(ii) the fact that a spondee may function both in a 'rising' and in a 'falling' verse pattern (as iambic or anapaestic vs trochaic or dactylic). As Snell (1962, 22 n.3) remarks of a line such as Ζεῦ πάντων ἀρχά, πάντων ἀγήτωρ (attrib. Terpander), the succession of equal lengths precludes any recognition of rhythm. It may be true, as Meillet suggests (1923, 26), that in, say, the iambic trimeter, the pattern of a spondaic foot would be marked in some sense by 'la dépression que forme la brève fixe et constante de l'autre pied du mètre'; but others have not seen this as an adequate explanation of the viability of the spondee; and stress on one or other of the heavy syllables has been seen as a more probable solution (cf. pp. 98 f.). Setti (1963, 181 f.) adopts an attitude similar to that of Meillet, in so far as he recognizes as essential to the pattern as a whole the requirement of a pure iambus for one of the feet in each metron (iambic ‖∑̰∑|∑∑‖, trochaic ‖∑∑|∑̰∑‖). But he goes on to ask *how* this renders the pattern perceptible in the ambiguous feet, and concludes that it must be by some means other than mere quantity – though connected with it – and specifically with the expected recurrence of an 'ictus' at one point rather than another.

Similar questions arise with the tribrach, which may represent the 'resolution' of a foot in either a falling (trochaic) pattern or a rising (iambic) pattern. There is also the fact that a dactyl may occur both in a falling (dactylic hexameter) pattern and in a rising (iambic), although a trochee may not so occur.

Evidence: (2) Music

Before attempting to find a more positive indication of the factors which account for these situations in Greek, one further possibility suggests itself, which, one might have hoped, would provide a clue to the presence or absence of 'ictus' in Greek verse. Amongst the surviving fragments of musical settings of Greek texts there are a few instances in which certain notes are marked by a point (στιγμή). As an instruction additional to that of the melodic pattern, it would be reasonable to suppose that such marks indicated musical accentuation, which might then be presumed to coincide with the linguistic stressing of the text. In the anonymous fragment *De Musica* (Bellermann 1840, 21) it is stated: ἡ μὲν οὖν θέσις σημαίνεται, ὅταν ἁπλῶς τὸ σημεῖον ἄστικτον ᾖ...ἡ δ' ἄρσις ὅταν ἐστιγμένον. But as Bellermann comments: 'quaeritur, quid hoc loco sit ἄρσις, quid θέσις, quoniam magna apud veteres est confusio in usu harum vocum...Praeterea confusio ista eo augetur, quod grammaticorum nonnulli uniuscuiusque pedis priorem partem arsim, posteriorem thesim vocant, ictus ratione omnino neglecta.'[1] Bellermann nevertheless concludes that 'magis consentaneum videtur esse, tempus accentu praeditum, quam destitutum notari, perinde ac longiores syllabae notantur, breves notis destitutae sunt'.[2] These conclusions, however, are not accepted by all scholars; and the opposite interpretation is made by Winnington-Ingram (1955, 77 ff; 1958, 8), namely that the function of the στιγμή is 'to mark the ἄρσις of the foot in the ancient acceptation of the term', i.e. the *weak* position.[3] In view of these uncertainties, it is clearly not justifiable to claim the musical markings as evidence for an 'ictus' in the strong positions of verse.[4]

Evidence: (3) Metre (a posteriori)

However, there still remains a possible line of approach to the solution of dynamic patterns in classical Greek, which, whilst relying on metrical evidence, need not assume a priori the existence of a metrical ictus – though its conclusions may render this probable.

If there were regular patterns of stress in Greek words, it is possible that some account would be taken of these in the composition of Greek spoken verse – and, on general grounds, any such regard for linguistic/ metrical congruence might be expected more particularly in the coda of the line. If evidence were forthcoming of selective placement in the line of words of particular quantitative patterns, i.e. in one position rather than in another, quantitatively equivalent position, it would be reasonable to conclude that the composition was having regard not simply to quantity but also to some other factor – and on general phonetic grounds the most likely candidate for identification as this factor would be stress. If this were so, it is most likely that the positive dynamic feature would tend to coincide with the focal 'strong' position of the foot; and a study of the patterns of placement should then enable one to establish a hypothesis about the location of stress in each quantitative pattern-type of word, which might perhaps lead to the formulation of some general rule or rules.

[1] Cf. Rheinach 1894, 367.
[2] Cf. also, on the Sicilus epitaph, *Williams 1911, 33.
[3] Cf. also Kalinka 1935, 295 f.   [4] But see also p. 294.

Previous approaches to the problem

That such a study could lead to results has already been occasionally recognized. In 1885 Goodell (83), in a discussion of English verse, remarked on the question of stress and the Greek accent: 'It is also certain, that, if present at all, this increase of stress accompanying the pitch-accent was in the rhythmical structure of both prose and poetry wholly disregarded in favor of a stronger word-ictus, which latter was made as essential an element of poetic rhythm as the stress-accent of English is in our poetic rhythm.' Goodell did not pursue the matter further, but some specific attempts to locate the linguistic 'ictus' will be mentioned below. From what one knows of stress placement in other languages, it is likely (and assumed by all investigators of the present problem) that it would be governed with some reference to the beginnings and/or the ends of words – more probably the latter; it is therefore encouraging to find even Dale lending some general support to such an enterprise, in so far as (1957, 43) '...finding reasons for observed facts about word-end in Greek metres...will always provide a challenge which we cannot avoid taking up'.

It may be stated at the outset that such a study cannot be expected to lead to a hypothesis that the dynamic patterning of words in Greek was the same as in Latin. For in fact the extent of agreement between strong position and the alleged word-stress would then be little greater than that between strong position and the melodic accentual peak – which we have seen to be non-significant from a compositional point of view in classical Greek. This may be easily tested. In a hundred lines of Greek iambics, taken at random, the marked accent coincided with strong position in the following percentages of cases for each foot:

41   50   55   36   31   31   (Total 244/600)

For the same 100 lines there was coincidence of strong position with the syllable which would be accented by *Latin* rules as follows:

35   72   84   37   31   2   (Total 261/600)

There are some notable differences in the distribution of the percentages between these two sets of figures – but the overall difference is slight and non-significant. Certainly the agreement in the latter case is much less than in, say, the Plautine senarius,[1] where there seems

---

[1] Cf. Langen 1888, 403, 406.

(though to a disputed extent) to be deliberate matching of accent with verse-pattern (pp. 153 f.). The low percentage for foot VI is of course due to the inevitable word-end at end of line, so that only a monosyllable could possibly produce a stress in the final strong position.[1] The high percentages for feet II and III are due to the occurrences of caesurae in III and IV, which involve word-end one syllable after the strong position; agreement in III is augmented because, even when there is no caesura in IV, the regularly light weak position of IV ensures that a trisyllabic word following the caesura in III will be accented by Latin rules on its first syllable; for example, in *Ant.* 14

μιᾷ θανόντοιν ἡμέρᾳ διπλῇ χερί,

giving a Latin accentual pattern

Σ́Σ,|Σ́Σ́|Σ:Σ́|ΣΣ,|Σ́Σ,|Σ́Σ

The epic hexameter is slightly more favourable to agreement with Latin accentual rules: but even so such agreement averages only around 60%. Here there tends to be the highest measure of agreement in the last two feet, as a simple consequence of the fact that, by mere statistical probability, the last word is often of two or three syllables; thus e.g. ~ νόστιμον ἦμαρ (Σ́ΣΣ,|Σ́Σ) or ~ γλαυκῶπις Ἀθήνη (Σ|Σ́Σ,Σ|Σ́Σ). Soubiran (1959, 49 n.33) notes that in *Il.* xxiii 73.5% of lines end in such a manner, so that a majority of agreement is inevitable.

These facts incidentally quite undermine the allegedly practical arguments of some supporters of the Henninian pronunciation of Greek (p. 272), who defend it against its rival on the grounds that, if one adopts the stressed rendering of the *Greek* accents in reading Greek prose, it is necessary to change to a different system, based on quantity, in reading Greek verse if any rhythmical effect is to be produced; whereas the *Latin* accentuation of Greek, being already, as they say, 'according to quantity', is immediately suited to this purpose. It is true that the Latin accent is based, like the verse-patterns, on quantity; but the particular rules for its location produce no significant agreement between it and the occurrence of strong position in verse. A word like, say, θυγάτηρ, if stressed on its second syllable, would

---

[1] The proportion here would be considerably increased if one were to extend to Greek the special syntactical end-stress of iambic words before pause which may have been a feature of Latin (see pp. 186 ff.).

admittedly conflict with the verse-pattern of a hexameter beginning
Ἄτλαντος θυγάτηρ~ (Σ̆Σ̆|Σ,Σ̆Σ̆|Σ:); but a Latin accentuation does no
better (ΣΣ́|Σ,Σ̆Σ́|Σ:).

The hypothesis put forward by Hanssen (1882: see p. 275) could
lead to a greater measure of agreement – but its potential for this
purpose is diminished by the fact that the quantity of final syllables is
assessed on the basis of the pre-pausal form (treating ~V̆C as light)
and disregards contextual variation; and that, if the final syllable is
not heavy (by his reckoning), the stress falls on the penultimate even if
light. It will produce much greater agreement than the Latin formula
in a line such as *Ant.* 18

ἤδη καλῶς καί σ᾽ ἐκτὸς αὐλείων πυλῶν

(Σ̆Σ́,|Σ̆Σ́,|Σ,Σ́|Σ:Σ|Σ̆Σ̆,|Σ̆Σ́),

but demonstrates its limitations in e.g. *Od.* i 39

μήτ᾽ αὐτὸν κτείνειν μήτε μνάασθαι ἄκοιτιν

(Σ́,Σ́|Σ,Σ|Σ́:Σ́|Σ,Σ|Σ̆Σ́,Σ|Σ́Σ),

where it improves on the Latin accentuation in the case of κτείνειν,
but is no better in αὐτόν, and worse in μνάασθαι; or in *Ant.* 169

παῖδας μένοντας ἐμπέδοις φρονήμασιν

(Σ́Σ,|Σ̆Σ́|Σ:Σ|Σ̆Σ́,|Σ̆Σ|Σ́Σ),

where Hanssen's stresses in the first two words are as for Latin, in
ἐμπέδοις different but of the same degree of metrical concord, and
in the final word less conducive to agreement.

Previous attempts to found a hypothesis of linguistic stress on metrical
evidence have been made, at a wide interval, by Hilberg (1879) and
Miller (1922). The former scholar gathered together a valuable selection
of relevant material over the period from Homer to Tzetzes, paying
special attention to the poetry of Nonnus. From a study of this material
Hilberg drew the conclusion that final syllables of Greek words were
phonetically weak, and from there went on to claim (265 ff.), as Henning
had done earlier, that Greek originally had a system of stress completely
identical with that of Latin.[1] But these conclusions involve some strange
interpretations of the data, which have been criticized by other scholars
(cf. Hanssen 1882, 259 f; Ehrlich 1912, 155 ff; Miller 1922, 169 ff;
*Hermann 1923, 107 f.). And we have seen that such a hypothesis does

---

[1] 275: 'Das ursprüngliche Betonungssystem der griechischen Sprache ist somit dem
der lateinischen Sprache vollständig gleich.'

not support the idea of an agreement between linguistic stress and verse-pattern. Miller's study, like that of Hanssen, led to an acknowledgement of the possibility of stress on final heavy syllables, but was marred by the improbable assumption of dynamic word-patterns such as $(\Sigma)\acute{\Sigma}\acute{\Sigma}(\Sigma)$, with stresses on immediately successive syllables.

Apart from these studies there is the work of Zander (1910, especially 439 ff. '*de ictu*'), which, however, was based primarily on the more ambiguous evidence of rhythmical prose. Zander also admits stressing of heavy final syllables in certain cases, but assumes that spondaic endings before pause were always stressed on the penultimate.[1] He supports this claim on the metrical side by reference to the scazon (469 n.), about which, however, we shall have more to say later. A particular weakness of Zander's study from our present point of view is that it is more concerned with the dynamics of word-sequences as a whole than with the dynamic patterns of individual words.

A new approach

It therefore seems worth making a further attempt to see whether there is any clear pattern of selection in the placement of words in the lines of spoken verse, such as would suggest a preference for particular syllables of words to coincide with the strong positions of feet. Universal trends would lead one to pay particular attention to the endings of lines; but to begin with it would be advisable to leave out of consideration words containing the final syllable of the line, in view of problems connected with the principle of 'indifference', to which we shall return later. Monosyllables also may be omitted from the study (except in so far as they form part of enclitic or proclitic combinations), since they involve no *contrast* of stress within their own structure.

One could begin by studying an extended corpus of verse, and marking the strong position in each case (by a grave sign);[2] thus, for example, in one of the iambic trimeter lines of such a corpus:

(ω) κοὶνον αὐταδὲλφον ἰσμηνὴς (καρα);

or in a hexameter line:

ἀνδρα μοι ἐννεπε μοὺσα πολὺτροπον (ος) μαλα (πολλα).

---

[1] 468: 'Ad pausam ita descendit spondaicae vocis exitus, ut ictus sit paenultimae.'

[2] *Greek accents (and breathings) are omitted in subsequent discussion in order to avoid confusion and an excess of diacritics.*

If one were to consider only these two lines, there would be 2 examples of the word-pattern $\bar{\Sigma}\underline{\Sigma}$ (κοῖνον, μοῦσα), 2 of $\bar{\Sigma}\underline{\Sigma}\bar{\Sigma}$ (ἄνδρα μοι, ἔννεπε), and 1 each of $\underline{\Sigma}\underline{\Sigma}$ (μαλα), $\underline{\Sigma}\underline{\Sigma}\bar{\Sigma}$ (ἰσμηνής), $\underline{\Sigma}\underline{\Sigma}\underline{\Sigma}\underline{\Sigma}$ (πολύτροπον), $\underline{\Sigma}\underline{\Sigma}\underline{\Sigma}\bar{\Sigma}$ (αὐταδέλφον); and a similar classification and count of patterns could then be extended to a corpus of any length.[1]

However, much of the resulting statistics would be irrelevant for our purpose. For many word-types, simply by reason of their quantitative structure, can only occur in particular places relatively to the strong and weak positions of feet; if they are to be used at all, they *must* be placed there.[2] For example, a trochaic word $\bar{\Sigma}\underline{\Sigma}$, whether in the rising, iambic verse-pattern or in the falling hexameter, *can* only be placed in such a way that its heavy syllable will coincide with strong position and its light syllable with weak position – in iambics $\underline{\Sigma}|\bar{\Sigma}$ or in hexameters $|\bar{\Sigma}\underline{\Sigma}$. This applies to all words where a single heavy syllable is flanked (on either or both sides) by 1 or 2 light syllables; thus in fact in all but two of the cases in the two lines cited ($\bar{\Sigma}\underline{\Sigma}$, $\bar{\Sigma}\underline{\Sigma}\bar{\Sigma}$, $\underline{\Sigma}\underline{\Sigma}\underline{\Sigma}\underline{\Sigma}$, $\underline{\Sigma}\underline{\Sigma}\underline{\Sigma}\bar{\Sigma}$); and of the remainder the word-type $\underline{\Sigma}\underline{\Sigma}$ in the hexameter is restricted to weak position, leaving only the pattern $\bar{\Sigma}\bar{\Sigma}\bar{\Sigma}$ (molossus) whose placing is not uniquely determined by purely quantitative considerations.

Our main attention, therefore, must be concentrated on words comprising a succession of heavy syllables, or of more than two light syllables. The much greater frequency of the former in verse makes it appropriate to consider them first.

(i) HEAVY SYLLABLES

If we consider the portion of a hexameter following the IIIa (penthemimeral) caesura, a spondaic word could potentially occur, from a purely quantitative standpoint, in any of the bracketed placings:

$$\sim\,\vdots\,\underline{\Sigma}\mid\bar{\Sigma}\ \ \underline{\Sigma}\mid\bar{\Sigma}\ \ \underline{\Sigma}\mid\bar{\Sigma}\ \ \Sigma$$

A molossus could occur as follows:

$$\sim\,\vdots\,\underline{\Sigma}\mid\bar{\Sigma}\ \ \underline{\Sigma}\mid\bar{\Sigma}\ \ \underline{\Sigma}\mid\bar{\Sigma}\ \ \Sigma$$

---

[1] There is of course the possibility that stress systems in different dialects (as epic and Attic) might differ in certain respects. But unless the search for a common system proves abortive, we need not assume such differences a priori.

[2] Cf. Newton 1969, 361.

In an iambic trimeter the following alternative placements are potentially admissible for a spondaic word:

$$\sim: \underset{\smile}{\Sigma} \mid \underset{\smile}{\Sigma} \quad \overline{\Sigma \parallel \underset{\wedge}{\Sigma}} \quad \Sigma \mid \underset{\smile}{\Sigma} \quad \Sigma$$

In iambics the molossus can only occur in such a position that the pattern is $\underset{\smile}{\Sigma}\underset{\smile}{\Sigma}\Sigma$.[1] But in hexameters, where either $\underset{\smile}{\Sigma}\Sigma\Sigma$ or $\Sigma\underset{\smile}{\Sigma}\Sigma$ is possible, the latter is rare, even though such words could very readily follow the IIIa caesura, and though words of this pattern are quite common: Ludwich (1885, 224 ff.) finds in 2,407 lines of Homer only 3 examples of the pattern $\Sigma\underset{\smile}{\Sigma}\Sigma$ as against 392 of $\underset{\smile}{\Sigma}\Sigma\underset{\smile}{\Sigma}$; from Stifler's references (1924, 332 ff.) for diaeresis at spondaic IV in the first six books of the Iliad, there appear only 6 instances of a molossus; and O'Neill's figures for 2,000 lines of Homer provide only 1 instance (1942, 144). In the whole of Homer Ludwich notes some 48 cases of $\Sigma\underset{\smile}{\Sigma}\Sigma$ (248 ff.); but of these half are proper names (e.g. 6 instances of Θηβαίου, 8 of Πατρόκλεις), 4 involve the phrase Λυκίης ευρείης, and a number should probably be 'decontracted' (e.g. Πατρόκλεες). In any case the situation clearly supports Ludwich's wider conclusion (254) that 'in all hexameter poets of the best period the general "accentuation" of the molossus is that which places the verse-ictus on the initial and final syllables; bringing the middle syllable of the molossus into the arsis is so far as possible avoided by all' (cf. also 243 f.).

The dispondaic word-form ($\Sigma\Sigma\Sigma\Sigma$), is also of interest. From its commonness at the ends of lines,[2] Ludwich had evidently concluded that its normal 'accentuation' was $\underset{\smile}{\Sigma}\Sigma\underset{\smile}{\Sigma}\Sigma$; he was therefore surprised to find some 75 cases indicating $\underset{\smile}{\Sigma}\underset{\smile}{\Sigma}\Sigma\Sigma$ (250 ff.), and concluded (252) that 'a correct judgement of these cases is impossible so long as the "accentual" rules in Homer are not thoroughly investigated for all word-classes, with special reference to *final* syllables', going on to express the hope that such a study would not be long delayed. If, however, we ignore the cases at absolute line-end, what is significant is that in the whole of Homer only 2 examples occur of the pattern $\underset{\smile}{\Sigma}\underset{\smile}{\Sigma}\Sigma\underset{\smile}{\Sigma}$.[3]

For spondaic words in both hexameters and iambics, however, where either $\underset{\smile}{\Sigma}\Sigma$ or $\Sigma\underset{\smile}{\Sigma}$ could occur, both placements are in fact found, with the former outnumbering the latter over the lines as a whole, but

---

[1] Cf. Newton 1969, 363.   [2] Cf. Erhlich, 173; O'Neill, 177.
[3] O'Neill, 177.

only by about 2:1. These results for the spondee might lead one to decide that the whole enterprise is likely to be inconclusive; but first one should consider in more detail the circumstances of occurrence of the less favoured placing, i.e. $\bar{\Sigma}\bar{\Sigma}$. An important point overlooked by Newton (1969, in a critique of A 1966a) is the necessity to consider not merely general numerical factors but also distributional factors (relating to position in the line) and qualitative factors (relating to the actual types of words involved).

The hexameter

We may begin with the hexameter, and start from the coda – or rather, since we are for the present excluding the absolute final position, from V. A spondaic word ending at this point would involve a pattern $\bar{\Sigma}\bar{\Sigma}$. But according to Stifler (325), if one excludes cases of 'decontraction' into a dactyl (see pp. 257 f.),[1] this occurs only once (if at all) in the whole of Homer,[2] viz. at *Il.* x 299 ~ ειᾱσ᾽ Εκτωρ, – which, however, (a) involves an elision and (b) appears in only one ms ('P²¹ teste Ludw' O.C.T; others have ειᾱσεν). Nor are there at this point any spondee-*ending* words, i.e. of pattern $\Sigma|\bar{\Sigma}\bar{\Sigma}|$ or $(\Sigma)\Sigma|\bar{\Sigma}\bar{\Sigma}|$. It is true that spondaic V is much less common than dactylic – about one in 18 lines (cf. Maas, 59); but over the whole of Homer this is equivalent to a total of nearly three books; and word-end at V is not otherwise uncommon. So the rarity of spondee-ending words at this point can hardly be fortuitous.

From V we proceed to IV. Word-end here is quite common; but it has long been noted that in Greek hexameters such word-end is much more common if the foot is a dactyl than if it is a spondee. The situation may be described in various ways. It is true that spondaic IV is less common than dactylic; but even so spondaic word-endings here are much less frequent than might be expected. Where there is a word-end at this point, dactyls outnumber spondees in Homer in the approximate ratio 8:1, whereas when there is no word-end the ratio is only about 3:1. According to O'Neill's figures, only about 4.5% of spondaic or spondee-ending words end at this point,[3] as against over 50% of words with dactylic ending. The preference for a dactylic IV with word-

---

[1] Cf. Ehrlich, 160; Shipp 1972, 206 f.

[2] Cf. also O'Neill 1939, 276; 1942, 170 f.

[3] O'Neill treats all final syllables of the verse as heavy; if words with light final syllable are excluded from the figures for end of line, the percentage will of course be slightly larger, but not to such an extent as to invalidate the general principle.

end was a particular characteristic of bucolic verse, whence the term 'bucolic diaeresis';[1] in Theocritus' Idylls, for example, dactylic feet with word-end outnumber spondees by a ratio around twice that of Homer, and occur in about 75% of lines.

There remain arithmetically a fair number of spondaic word-endings at IV in Homer, in fact of the order of 1,000; but a more detailed study of these is suggestive. The general rarity of molossi with pattern ΣΣ̱Σ (most of which are accounted for by this position) has already been noted. A fairly complete study of the situation can be made with the help of Ehrlich, 160 ff. and Stifler. Ehrlich details all cases in Homer of spondaic words with 'naturally' heavy final syllables filling IV; as will be seen later, it is these 'naturally' heavy finals which account for the vast majority of cases, and these total 445 for spondaic words. References for all types of spondaic and spondee-ending words which end at IV are given by Stifler for *Il.* i–vi, with outline statistics for the rest of Homer, including citations where the final is heavy 'by position'.

We may first consider the case of spondaic words filling IV. A notable feature here is that a large number of such words are pronouns, such as αυτους, ημεις, and other words which in many languages have pronominal affinities, as e.g. παντων, αλλοις (cf. the semi-pronominal declension of Latin *totus*, *alius*, or Sanskrit *sarva-*, *anya-*). This fact could possibly be relevant in so far as such words tend to be of relatively high frequency of occurrence, and as a corollary are in some languages subject to special modes of utterance, which may be historically reflected in 'weakening';[2] in the Odyssey some cases are also accounted for by the copula, as e.g. φιλος ειη,[3] to which similar considerations may apply. But in any case the requirements of the caesura mean that a spondaic word filling IV is preceded by a word of structure Σ̱ or ΣΣ̱ or Σ̲; and the majority of these types of word are proclitics or other forms closely connected with what follows (e.g. conjunctions), in the approximate proportion 8:1:[4] thus e.g. επ' ωμων,

---

[1] Cf. O'Neill, 166 ff.

[2] Cf. A 1958, 127 f., n.70 and refs. In connexion with these and the 'appositives' discussed below, note that the class of 'free' words recognized by Hilberg (1879, 2) as permitting exceptional metrical treatment comprises proper names, pronouns, numerals, pronominal adverbs, conjunctions, prepositions, and interjections, with the observation that 'All metrical laws which apply to "free" words apply also to "non-free" – but not vice-versa'. Note also that Greek grammarians list the anaphoric pronoun αυτον as an enclitic (cf. Vendryes, 95 f.).

[3] Cf. Ehrlich, 167.

[4] Cf. Ehrlich, 166.

και αλλους, περι παντων, αμα λαω, εξ ιππων, η κυκνων; other cases involve such categories as anaphoric and relative pronouns, numerals, and common adverbs, which, like the more generally recognized 'proclitics', tend to be subordinated phonetically to the full word which follows;[1] Dottin (1901), for example, points out that such categories are closely parallel to those which cause initial mutation in Celtic.[2]

If one considers such forms as constituting a single phonological unit with the following word, one is dealing with structures of the types $\Sigma\Sigma\Sigma$, $\Sigma\Sigma\Sigma\Sigma$, and $\Sigma\Sigma\Sigma$ respectively rather than with simple spondees. Of the remaining cases some involve close grammatical connexions, as noun + adjectival or genitival attribute, e.g. στιχας ανδρων, πολιν ακρην; and Ehrlich notes (160 f.) that, where looser connexions are involved, the spondee is often followed by a strong syntactic break, which, he suggests, facilitates its treatment as at line-end: e.g. *Il.* xviii 406

η νυν ημετερον δομον ικει · τω με μαλα χρεω

Conversely[3] the spondaic word may be in close connexion with what follows, as e.g. αλλων μυθον, and so might be considered to form a combination which would be treated as a single word and thus effectively would not involve word-end at IV.

After excluding the cases mentioned above, the number of relatively independent spondaic words filling IV is remarkably small – from Ehrlich's lists about 15–20 with 'naturally' heavy finals, depending on one's interpretation: e.g. σχεθον ιππους, φιλον ελθειν, ζευξ' ιππους, σακος οισω, τλη μιμνειν; and of these some could be considered as forming complex units, e.g. phrases such as κακα πασχειν. One may therefore accept Ehrlich's conclusion (167) that 'in principle the poet avoids spondaic words in the 4th foot' – in other words, that the pattern $\Sigma\Sigma$ is abnormal. More positively, the pattern $\Sigma\bar{\Sigma}$ in Homer occurs freely and without restriction.

It has, however, to be admitted that the recognition as unitary combinations of appositive (or other closely connected form) + spondaic

---

[1] Cf. Sobolevskij 1956; 1964, 51 f; and the class of 'Appositiva' set up by Fränkel 1960, 142 ff. (supported by Bulloch 1970, 260).

[2] Cf. also the classes of words which do not generally alliterate in Old English verse as do stressed 'full words' (Halle & Keyser 1971, 155 n.7).

[3] Cf. Stifler's 'Type 3' (332 f.).

word creates further examples of the molossus, which (p. 285) is rare in the case of single words ending at IV. From Ehrlich's lists there appear around 50 examples of such combinations; but it may be significant that with rare exceptions (as the formula βουν ηνῖν at *Il.* x 292; *Od.* iii 382) the monosyllable is in fact an obviously 'weak' prepositive form, as in e.g. εξ ιππων. The effect of locating the combination in this way is to set the prepositive in weak position; and it could be that the resulting 'abnormal' molossic pattern (Σ)ΣΣ was for this reason more readily accepted in such cases. The same consideration would apply to the less common case of postpositives, as e.g. βουλης εξ, which, if taken as combinations, result in a pattern ΣΣ(Σ); here also the appositive occupies weak position, and in addition the main word has its 'normal' pattern.

The total number of molossic words and combinations ending at IV is around 100. Since there are few examples of independent spondaic words here, this means that most of the rest of the *c.* 1,000 cases of spondee-ending words or combinations must be of the pattern ΣΣΣ or ΣΣΣΣ. And here a point of great significance arises, to which some reference has already been made (p. 217). In only 14 cases does the word or combination end in a syllable of type ~V̆C. Of these 7 involve proper names or name-formulae: Βατιειαν, Πυλαιος (τ' οζος Αρηος),[1] βοωπις (ποτνια Ηρη) (× 2), περιφρον (Πηνελοπεια) (× 3); 2 involve pronominals (ποτι δ' αυτον, αμα δ' αλλον); the remaining examples are εᾱνον (× 2), μελαιναν, αεθλον, επεεσσιν. To these might perhaps be added 18 examples of combinations with postpositions, as μαχης εκ, δομοις εν (of which 13 involve εκ) or with enclitic (κοτυλην τις) – where, however, the special considerations might apply which have already been mentioned in the case of molossi.

The evident avoidance of the case in question is an aspect of the law named after F. Wernicke, who, in his edition of Tryphiodorus in 1819 (173) stated that if foot IV is a spondee and is followed by word-division, the final syllable must be heavy 'by nature' and not 'by position'. In fact, as we have seen in the case of spondaic and molossic words or combinations, word-end at IV tends to be avoided even if it is heavy 'by nature'; 'Wernicke's Law', therefore, can hardly be due to any peculiarity of 'positional' quantity in itself.[2] In a majority of cases where the pattern (Σ)ΣΣΣ ends at IV, we have noted (p. 217)

---

[1] Where in any case the enclitic effectively creates a word-end ~V̆CC.
[2] Cf. Ehrlich, 175; Stifler, 335 ff; O'Neill, 168 ff.

that the final syllable is not only 'heavy by nature' but also 'hyper-characterized', i.e. contains a long vowel or diphthong followed by a consonant. Such words can otherwise only be placed at the end of the line; and Stifler has argued (336) that this is the normal place for forms of pattern $(\underline{\Sigma})\underline{\Sigma}\underline{\Sigma}\underline{\Sigma}$ with final $\sim \bar{V}(C)$, and that they tend to be placed in the 'avoided' IV position only if the end position is occupied by another such form (as in $\sim$ ανησει θυμος αγηνωρ) or if the last two feet are occupied by a formula or expression characteristic of this position (as in $\sim$ ελασση μωνυχας ιππους).

The forms with 'naturally' heavy (and especially hypercharacterized) final syllables therefore contrast with those having 'positionally' heavy finals in so far as the latter, by being placed before an initial vowel, are converted to forms with *light* final syllable and so can occur in other positions in the line, where the pattern will then be $(\underline{\Sigma})\underline{\Sigma}\underline{\Sigma}\Sigma$; here they occur with complete freedom, in the same way as any other trochaic or trochee-ending forms.

Forms ending in a long vowel or a diphthong could also potentially be placed elsewhere, before an initial vowel, which would have the effect of permitting 'epic shortening' (p. 224). The finals which most generally display this treatment are the diphthongs αι and οι; the cases of their failure so to shorten in weak position are described by Chantraine (1958, 89) as 'infime', by contrast with the long vowels η and ω which remain long in weak position in around 5% of cases, and the 'long diphthongs' ῃ and ῳ, which remain long in some 20% of cases. In the whole of Homer the cases of 'shortening' of final αι and οι number around 6,500. It is therefore surely significant that of the occurrences of the forms $(\underline{\Sigma})\underline{\Sigma}\underline{\Sigma}\underline{\Sigma}$ ending at IV those with final syllable ending in αι or οι are particularly few. From Stifler's references for *Il.* i–vi there appear 15 examples – but of these no less than 12 are accounted for by the same formula μελαιναι (νηες) in the catalogue of ships in Book ii (one is reminded of the English compound accentuation of the Norse '*lóng-ships*'), leaving only Αχαιοι (× 2) and νεοσσοι. This figure contrasts with the *c*. 90 examples with hypercharacterized final syllable,[1] and compares well with the figure for final $\sim \breve{V}C$. It is thus clear that forms of the pattern $(\underline{\Sigma})\underline{\Sigma}\underline{\Sigma}\underline{\Sigma}$ are employed in the 'avoided' IV position only *in indirect proportion to their potentialities*

---

[1] For this purpose one may add in such cases as πολυαιξ (with final $\sim \breve{V}CC$), and also note that the postposition εκ (as in μαχης εκ) would, before a vowel, require the form εξ and so not admit the treatment $\underline{\Sigma}\underline{\Sigma}\underline{\Sigma}$ before vocalic initial (nor would the prepositional εκ μαχης be possible in a hexameter).

of occurrence elsewhere.[1] In other words, the pattern (Σ̱)Σ̱Σ̱Σ̱ is *in principle* as unacceptable to end at IV as is the simple spondaic Σ̱Σ̱.

In the foregoing discussions word-ends ⁓ει and ⁓ου have all been treated as monosyllabic; but in an undeterminable number of cases (see pp. 257, 286) these will, at the time of composition, have represented disyllabic Σ̱Σ̱; and this would yet further reduce the number of exceptions to the avoidance.

The nature of the exceptions examined has tended to support yet more strongly the often noted facts about the 'bucolic diaeresis'; and in later hexameters these relatively few exceptions are further reduced in number – especially in Callimachus and Nonnus. Thus, for example, according to O'Neill's figures (142, Table 10) words of pattern Σ̱Σ̱Σ̱ in Homer end at IV in around 7% of their occurrences, but in Callimachus this reduces to a mere 0.2%. The avoidance is sometimes referred to as 'Naeke's Law', after this scholar's observation of it for Callimachus in 1835 (*RhM* 3, 516 f.).

It is sometimes stated that there is a more general avoidance in hexameters of spondaic foot followed by diaeresis (e.g. Chantraine 1958, 153). We have already seen that spondaic word-endings at V are practically non-existent (which incidentally weakens Soubiran's suggestion (1966b, 29) that the avoidance at IV is due to a dislike for dividing the line into a tetrapody + dipody).[2] At III such endings are virtually precluded by the requirements of the caesura. But as we proceed towards the beginning of the line, we may, on general grounds, expect any regulation to be less rigorous. At II spondaic endings are also rare, and the apparent avoidance here is sometimes termed 'Hilberg's Law' after his observation that in Alexandrian and later poetry spondaic word-ends in this position are almost entirely confined to particular word-classes (1879, 129, 263); but it had already been pointed out by B. Gisecke in 1864 (*Homerische Forschungen*, 128 ff.) that, in the case of words beginning before foot II, dactylic endings are also rare here. O'Neill's figures show that, in Homer, of spondee-ending words only around 1.6% end at this point[3] as against about 4.5% at IV;

---

[1] In Nonnus and to some extent in Callimachus, however, 'epic shortening' is restricted – in Nonnus being permitted only in the first foot, so that words such as ἅμαξαι are inadmissible (Maas, 80: cf. p. 268). The reasons for this restriction, which has no precedent in Homer, are not clear.

[2] Cf., however, Parker 1966, 20.

[3] They are more frequent, however, in the Odyssey than in the Iliad: cf. O'Neill, 172; Ehrlich, 172 (spondaic words filling II in 1.84% of lines in the Odyssey as against 1.05% in the Iliad).

but of words with dactylic ending also only some 5% end here as against over 50% at IV; so that the scarcity of spondee-ending words here is probably not in itself significant.[1]

In foot I, of course, the forms in question cannot be longer than spondaic; such cases in fact occur about once in every 10 lines; from O'Neill's figures, about 20% of the occurrences of such forms are placed here.

It thus emerges that spondaic words are located metrically as $\bar{\Sigma}\bar{\Sigma}$ almost only (a) at the beginnings of lines, where we should not in any case look for very regular coincidence between speech and metrical patterns, and (b) at the extreme ends of lines, where a special factor has yet to be considered. Elsewhere the location $\bar{\Sigma}\Sigma$ is normal, with a clear avoidance of $\Sigma\bar{\Sigma}$. Since there is a similar avoidance in principle of $(\Sigma)\Sigma\bar{\Sigma}\Sigma$ and $\Sigma\Sigma\bar{\Sigma}$, it is evident that there is some characteristic of final Σ which makes it unsuited to weak position in the foot. The question remains, how to interpret this.

For Porter (1951, 20) 'The easiest assumption is that long final syllables are somehow more effectively long than other long syllables' (similarly West 1970, 186). But the general implausibility of purely temporal contrasts has already been emphasized – and particularly improbable is such a contrast *within* the category of heavy syllables. O'Neill's interpretation is no more acceptable; he recognizes (1939, 265) that such syllables 'must have possessed phonetic properties and metrical values that the initial and medial syllables of longer words did not have'; but he concludes that the phonetic property in question was *pitch*. This, however, is clearly untenable; since classical Greek poetry took no account of the melodic *accent* for metrical purposes, it seems highly improbable that it would take any account of *non*-accentual pitch. Moreover the accentual and presumed non-accentual pitch-patterns would inevitably have been in complex interference with one another.[2]

A tentative conclusion

We are left, therefore, with *stress* as the most probable phonetic characteristic of final heavy syllables.[3] Word-endings $\bar{\Sigma}\Sigma$ and $\Sigma\Sigma\bar{\Sigma}$ regularly

[1] Cf. also Maas, 61.
[2] Cf. Todd 1942, 31 ff.
[3] Newton (1969, 361) concedes, perhaps too readily, to the hypothesis of such stress that it would not 'in any sense be refuted by the observation that in words of the form ∪ − − ictus coincides with the first long'; the more detailed analysis above

show the metrical placement patterns $\underline{\Sigma}\underline{\Sigma}$ and $\underline{\Sigma}\underline{\Sigma}\underline{\Sigma}$ (as they must if they are to be admitted to the hexameter line at all); and if we accept that this reflects their normal stressing, we may state a more general rule that *the last heavy syllable in the word was stressed* (i.e. not only where such syllable is the final syllable of the word). In addition we find words with the patterns $(\underline{\Sigma})\underline{\Sigma}\underline{\Sigma}\dot{\underline{\Sigma}}(\underline{\Sigma})$ and $(\underline{\Sigma})\underline{\Sigma}\underline{\Sigma}\underline{\Sigma}\dot{\underline{\Sigma}}(\underline{\Sigma})$; if such patterns imply stressability of certain heavy syllables in addition to the last, it could be covered by a rule of secondary or alternating stress,[1] i.e. that stress also fell on the next preceding heavy syllable separated from the last by an interval, the intervals in the material so far studied being $\underline{\Sigma}\underline{\Sigma}$ and $\underline{\Sigma}$, to which a study of iambics/trochaics will add $\underline{\Sigma}$. Since the presumed Greek stress was not a culminative, accentual feature, there would be no reason to suppose that the 'secondary' stress was necessarily less strong than the 'main' stress; so that the latter might only qualify as 'main' in so far as it forms the pivot for locational statements.

Words ending in $\underline{\Sigma}(C)\breve{V}$ will of course generally have a trochaic ending $\underline{\Sigma}\underline{\Sigma}$ and so, in terms of our hypothesis, would generally be stressed as $\sim\dot{\underline{\Sigma}}\underline{\Sigma}$. As noted on p. 217, the occurrence of such words with the final syllable made heavy in weak position (by reason of a following word with initial consonant sequence, i.e. in the pattern $\sim\underline{\Sigma}(C)\breve{V},C.CV\sim$) is particularly avoided, being mainly confined to foot I; and this may be seen as due to the fact that such words are, above all others, capable of occurring in the form $\sim\underline{\Sigma}\underline{\Sigma}$ and so avoiding the undesirable pattern $\sim\dot{\underline{\Sigma}}\underline{\Sigma}$. In addition, however, their use in this context would not simply involve a lack of concord between strong position and a presumed linguistic stress ($\sim\underline{\Sigma}\dot{\underline{\Sigma}}$), but the conflict would be occasioned by an in any case infrequent stressing of the words in question (which would generally be $\sim\dot{\underline{\Sigma}}\underline{\Sigma}$): e.g. *Od.* xiv 385 πόλλᾰ̆ (χρήματ᾽ ἀγόντα~). Where such words ended at a strong position (i.e. in the pattern $\sim\underline{\Sigma}(C)\breve{V},C.CV\sim$), the less common stress-pattern would again be implied, but here at least it would not also be in disagreement with the strong position: e.g. *Od.* ii 102 $\sim$ πολλᾰ̆ (κτεα-τίσσας); and such instances are tolerated rather more often:[2] of words of structure $\underline{\Sigma}(C)\breve{V}$ in Homer 8,827 cases occur in the pattern $\underline{\Sigma}\underline{\Sigma}$ as against 288 in $\underline{\Sigma}\dot{\underline{\Sigma}}$ and 96 in $\dot{\underline{\Sigma}}\underline{\Sigma}$.[3]

presented for occurrences of this type (pp. 289 ff.) tends if anything to give positive support to the hypothesis.

[1] On general parallels in phonological alternation cf. Lightner 1971, 227 and n.3.

[2] They are, however, rare in iambics and trochaics (see p. 217).

[3] Ehrlich, 175 ff.

In some cases the placing of a word-final ∼ V̆ in strong position will of course be inevitable if the word is to be used at all in hexameters, as e.g. *Il.* i 8 ∼ ερῐδῐ̣ (ξυνεῆκε μαχέσθαι).

No account has been taken of monosyllables, since they could contain no internal contrast of stress. Many of them in any case are of categories that probably tended to be unstressed; and O'Neill concludes (1939, 265), on the basis of their distribution in verse, that they 'had less metrical significance than the final syllables of longer words'.

If the stress process in Greek was similar to that of Latin or English (pp. 170 ff.), we might expect that pyrrhic words (ΣΣ) would have much the same characteristics as heavy monosyllables, i.e. at most a disyllabic stress and so no contrast. In fact in hexameters they can only occur in weak position, and are there freely admitted. Sequences of more than two light syllables cannot occur in hexameters, except by occasional metrical licence in the case of words which could not otherwise be used: thus e.g. επιτονος at the beginning of *Od.* xii 423,[1] with the first syllable treated as heavy. This licence is not extended to tribrach words (ΣΣΣ), which by suitable contextualization can occur in the alternative form ΣΣΣ̱ (or ΣΣ'): cf. ερῐδῐ above and e.g. επε᷁ᾱ (πτεροέντα) or επε' (ἀλληλοῖσι).

We have already accepted that the Greeks themselves make no mention of stress. But there is just possibly a hint in Aristotle (*Rhet.* 1409a), where he is discussing two types of paean (Σ̱ΣΣΣ and ΣΣΣΣ̱) and their rhythmical effect. He states that these have opposite values, the first being appropriate at the beginning of a sentence and the latter at the end; and he explains the appropriateness of the latter by saying: 'For a short syllable, being incomplete (ἀτελής), mutilates the cadence (ποιεῖ κολοβόν); the sentence should close on a long syllable and its end should be manifested, not by the scribe or a marginal note, but by the rhythm.' This statement would at least be compatible with a stress-pattern ΣΣΣΣ̱ (and difficult to reconcile with, say, a Latin accentuation ΣΣ̱ΣΣ). Another debatable possibility of ancient support comes from the rhythmical marking of musical texts. We have seen (pp. 278 f.) that there is considerable doubt whether the στιγμή bears any relation to verse-ictus; but in a discussion of the Sicilus epitaph Rheinach (1894, 367 f.) observes that the use of rhythmical signs was indispensable in a text which does not conform to any standard metrical scheme;

---

[1] Cf. Chantraine 1958, 103; Wyatt 1969, 221.

and, referring to the 'bacchiac' (ΣΣΣ̱) sequences in this text (οσον ʒης, συ λυπου, ∼τι το ʒην, απαιτει), he comments that without such indications one could not have guessed that, as the marks suggest (cf. also Crusius' transcription, p. 233), it is not the first of the two heavy syllables in these sequences that is to be 'prolonged', but the *second*; and he further notes that the rhythmical value of the spondaic φαινου (with στιγμή on the second syllable) 'n'est pas moins imprévue'. If our tentative conclusions about stress in Greek are valid, however, these markings are precisely what one might expect in a setting which paid attention to the dynamic as well as the melodic characteristics of the language.[1]

Final ∼ V̆C

Our discussion has implicitly assumed that the dynamic patterns of Greek words, especially those ending in ∼ V̆C, would have varied with their environment, since their final syllables would have alternated between heavy and light according to whether the next word begins with a vowel or a consonant(-sequence): cf. Aristides Quintilianus, 44 W-I. Thus e.g. νηᾰς = ΣΣ in *Il.* ii 493 νηας τε προπασας, but ΣΣ̱ in *Il.* i 306 νηας εϊσας; similar alternations are metrically required in connexion with the 'epic shortening' of final long vowels and diphthongs, which may be presumed to have had a basis in ordinary speech. Such variation in itself provides no argument against the hypothesis. The presumed stress is not an *accentual* feature; and there is no particular difficulty for the hypothesis even in the fact that the stress-pattern of the whole word may depend on the following word (e.g. ανθρωπος = Σ̱Σ̱Σ̱ or ΣΣ̱Σ̱). For the generation of sentences, whether at the grammatical or phonological level, does not take place syllable by syllable, nor even word by word; relatively long stretches of utterance are prepared in advance, and the relationship of the earlier to the later elements in actual phonation is taken account of just as that of the later to the earlier. To take a grammatical example: in Latin the gender concord of an attribute must be determined in advance of the actual

---

[1] It may or may not be fortuitous that the final syllable in all these cases also bears a falling accentual pitch (cf. p. 262). The other examples of the στιγμή in this text involve iambic and (once) tribrach sequences, as ολως, ο χρονος; the heavy syllables are in each case set to two notes, and if one follows Rheinach in restoring two στιγμαί, one is marked over each of the three notes in these cases; it may possibly be (as Spitta, cited by *Williams 1911, 32) that the first note here represents an 'anticipation of an accent', i.e. a syncopation of the rhythm. For further discussion see Martin 1953, 48 ff.

utterance of a postponed noun – e.g. 'et *hic* quidem Romae, tamquam in tanta multitudine, *habitus* animorum fuit'. At the phonological level: in English, the melodic pattern of a word in a sentence depends to a large extent on the structure of the sentence as a whole, including following words; the word 'see', for example, has a quite different pattern in the normal pronunciation of 'I could see something' and in 'I could see éverything', having a falling pitch in the former and a level pitch in the latter. Phonemically, the principle is clearly demonstrated by the phenomenon of 'spoonerism', which presupposes the preparation of the second element of the metathesis before the phonation of the first. Even accentual placement may sometimes vary with context – for example the stress-patterns of 'fundamental' in 'a fúndamental prínciple' and in 'a fundaméntal mistáke' (cf. p. 86). There is therefore nothing unreasonable about assuming for Greek a stress-patterning which, in certain types of word, may show a binary variation dependent on context, such context being limited to the immediately following word. It implies simply that the pattern of chest pulses and arrests is prepared in 'blocks' longer than a single word; and whilst in colloquial speech there would no doubt be changes of mind resulting in prosodic 'errors' just as in grammatical anacolutha, this is hardly relevant to the types of utterance represented in more formal poetry.

EXCURSUS D

The principle of 'indifference'

In considering the hexameter, we have not so far examined the situation with regard to the *final* foot of the line, since here special principles are involved.

According to Aristides Quintilianus (44 W-I) the final syllable of the line in any metre is 'indifferent' (ἀδιάφορος),[1] i.e. may be either heavy or light as the poet wishes.[2] It seems reasonable to assume that this is not a mere poetic invention, but, like other metrical characteristics,

---

[1] Sometimes referred to nowadays as 'final anceps': cf. Rossi 1963b.
[2] Cf. Hephaestion, 14 C; further citations in Rossi 1963b, 61 f.

had some ultimate basis in speech;[1] and since it is the ends of lines that are involved, more specifically in phenomena peculiar to the position before pause, e.g. at ends of sentences (cf. pp. 113 ff., 120 f.). It is perhaps significant that when in iambics there is 'episynaloephe' (elision at end of line: cf. p. 121), and so *no* pause, the final syllable must be heavy (i.e. is *not* indifferent) even without the transferred consonant, as e.g. Soph., *O.T.* 791 f. ～γενος ‖‖ δ' ατλητον～.[2]

Let us now consider the kind of rule for the terminal stressing of Greek that would be required in order to account for the principle of 'indifference' in verse, bearing in mind that it should be applicable to *all* spoken metres. A possible such rule might be as follows:

Pre-pausal ('terminal') words are stressed according to a rule of alternation operating progressively from the main stress of the preceding word, and not in accordance with the general rules for word-stress based on inherent patterns (though the two would often coincide). *The alternation follows the same general principle as that which operates regressively for the secondary stressing of other words* (p. 293). Transposed into dynamic terms, such a rule would be rather like that of the intonational 'nuclear tail' following the 'nuclear syllable' in English, which is described by Crystal (1969, 207 f: cf. also 223) as 'usually continuing the pitch movement unbrokenly until the end of the tone-unit. In such cases, being wholly conditioned by the nuclear tone, the tail has no inherent linguistic contrastivity.'[3]

One additional feature requires to be assumed, namely the possibility, where the rule of alternation would determine it, of stress on a *light* pre-pausal syllable, if preceded by a single light syllable. Such stress would be contrary to the proposed general rules for word-stress in Greek; but it would be dynamically exceptional only to the same extent as is melodically the final high pitch before pause (p. 248) – it would lack the syllabic arrest generally associated with the stress pulse, just as the pre-pausal high pitch lacks the contonational cadence which is elsewhere required.

These hypothetical rules would admit, inter alia, the following possible patterns of stress in relation to terminal quantitative patterns (word-

---

[1] The explanation offered by Aristides (loc. cit.) is clearly inadequate – namely, that where no word follows it is impossible to determine the quantity of a final syllable.

[2] Cf. Brožek 1949, 115 f.

[3] A roughly comparable principle also governs 'secondary lengthening' of word-final open syllables (before enclitic) in Eskimo: Miyaoka 1971, 224 f.

divisions are not indicated, since various such divisions could result in the same stress-patterns; but some particular divisions would preclude the possibility of particular patterns):[1]

(a) ~ Σ́ Σ Σ́Σ̆Σ́   (c) ~ Σ́ Σ Σ́ΣΣ́

(b) ~ Σ Σ́ Σ ΣΣ   (d) ~ Σ Σ́ Σ ΣΣ

We have now to consider the applicability of such a hypothesis to the principle of indifference in verse.

If one assumes coincidence of strong position and linguistic stress in the cadence of the line, pattern (a) would imply that in iambics (or catalectic trochaics) the final disyllable could consist of a pyrrhic (ΣΣ) as well as an iambus (ΣΣ). In fact rules relating to word-division ensure that pattern (a) is virtually always applicable (see pp. 304 ff.); and the principle of indifference here admits just the predicted alternative, as in e.g.[2]

(iambic) Soph., *Ant.*   517   ~ἀλλ᾽ αδέλφος ὤλετὄ
                          52   ~αὐτος αὐτουργῷ χερΐ
                          190   ~τοὺς φιλοὺς ποιούμεθᾰ
(cat. troch.) Eur., *Bach.* 617   ἔλπισῒν δ᾽ εβόσκετὄ.

Pattern (d) would imply that in (acatalectic) trochaics (or catalectic iambics) the final disyllable could consist of a spondee (ΣΣ) as well as a trochee (ΣΣ). These metres are less common, but here again the principle of indifference admits the expected alternative, as in e.g.

(trochaic) Anacreon, fr. 88 Diehl[2] ~κοῦφα τὲ σκιρτῶσα παῖ3εις
(cat. iamb.) Arist., *Ran.* 911 ~καθῖσεν ἔγκαλύψας.

Pattern (b) would imply that in the dactylic (elegiac) 'pentameter' a light final syllable would not be stressed (since it is preceded by more than a single light syllable) and so there would be no coincidence of stress with the strong position of the catalectic (half) final foot (basically Σ̲);[3] there may even be more positive conflict if (see p. 318 and n.) the sequence ΣΣ can form a disyllabic stress-matrix, since pattern (b) would then show a stress-peak on the penultimate syllable. It may therefore be significant that here (cf. p. 205) there is a tendency *not* to apply the principle of indifference, and to prefer a heavy syllable, which

[1] For example, a division ~Σ,ΣΣΣ would preclude (a), and ~ΣΣ,ΣΣ would preclude (d): cf. p. 286 and below.
[2] The marking ˅ indicates coincidence of strong position (`) and of stress (').
[3] On the analysis of the pentameter cf. Goodell 1901, 30 ff.

ensures the unambiguous stress-pattern $\sim\acute{\Sigma}\Sigma\acute{\Sigma}\Sigma$ corresponding to a metrical $\sim\acute{\Sigma}\Sigma\acute{\Sigma}\Sigma$. However, the fact that the pattern $\sim\Sigma\Sigma\acute{\Sigma}\Sigma$ is here admitted at all might possibly reflect an alternative treatment of terminal stresses, connected with the requirement of an exclusively dactylic second colon; for the pattern $\acute{\Sigma}\Sigma\acute{\Sigma}\Sigma\sim$ at the beginning of the colon might be effective in establishing not simply an alternation of stress/non-stress, but specifically a pattern of *disyllabic* unstressed intervals, which could then induce a terminal pattern $\sim\Sigma\Sigma\acute{\Sigma}\Sigma$, over-riding the restriction proposed above.

Pattern (b) could in theory also imply that in anapaestics[1] a light final syllable would involve non-coincidence, for the same reasons as in the dactylic pentameter. In fact between the lines of anapaestic systems (mostly dimeters) there is regularly 'synaphea', so that the indifference principle would not apply in any case. The final ('paroemiac') line, however, is catalectic, retaining only the first syllable (basically Σ) of the final foot, i.e. $\sim |\underset{\smile\smile}{\Sigma\acute{\Sigma}}\|\Sigma\Sigma\acute{\Sigma}|\Sigma$; and in this line pattern (d) would produce a stress on the penultimate syllable regardless of the quantity of the final; so that the latter may be expected to show indifference, i.e. to admit $\underline{\Sigma}$ as well as Σ – and this is in fact the case:

Aesch., *Ag.* 47 ηρᾶν στρατιῶτιν αρῶγᾶν.

The same applies to the anapaestic tetrameter catalectic, e.g.

Arist., *Nub.* 1002 $\sim$ εν γὔμνασιοῖς διατρΐψεις.

Pattern (c) may be relevant to the 'choliambic' or 'scazon', which differs from the normal iambic trimeter in substituting a heavy for a light penultimate syllable, as e.g. Hipponax, 1 Diehl ακουσαθ' Ιππωνα-κτος, ου γαρ αλλ' ηκω. It is sometimes assumed that in the last foot the quantitative pattern is reversed, i.e. that there is an 'Umknickung des Rhythmus' with consequent 'Zusammenstoss der Arsen', so that the basic pattern is $\sim\|\Sigma\acute{\Sigma}\|\acute{\Sigma}\Sigma$.[2] But ancient authorities lend little support to this interpretation;[3] they mostly describe the last foot as a spondee rather than a trochee, and apply the same 'limping' epithet to a spondee substituted for an iambus in other feet, where there is no question of any reversal of pattern;[4] and Hoerschelmann (1894) has drawn attention to a passage in Ovid (*Rem.* 377 f.) which refers to the

[1] Which, however, are for the most part only marginally classifiable as spoken metres (cf. p. 333).

[2] E.g. Christ 1879, 363.

[3] Cf. Beare 1957, 236.

[4] A 1966a, 138 f.

two types of iambic, normal and 'limping', simply as 'fast' and 'dragging the final foot' respectively: 'iambus seu celer extremum seu trahat ille pedem'.[1] This description, as indeed the 'limping' metaphor, seems more suited to a slowing down of the tempo than to a change from rising to falling pattern.[2]

If we assume that the basic metrical pattern is in fact $\sim \|\Sigma\underset{\cdot}{\Sigma}|\Sigma\underset{\cdot}{\Sigma}$, with no reversal of strong and weak positions, there will be coincidence of strong position and stress in the final foot only if the final syllable is heavy, i.e. the principle of indifference should not apply if such coincidence is to be achieved; for the alternation rule does not admit a stressed light syllable preceded by a heavy syllable. It has been seen (pp. 206, 267) that Babrius has a heavy final syllable almost without exception. The requirement in his case could be due primarily to accentual conventions, but it is also at least a preference in earlier writers in this metre, and so tends to indicate that some objection was felt to applying the indifference principle.

In Latin choliambics the situation is admittedly different; for in Latin the accent will in any case have required a penultimate heavy syllable to be stressed, regardless of the quantity of the final[3] – which may therefore be either heavy or light, as e.g. in

miser Catulle, desinas ineptíre,

but for reasons quite other than the indifference applicable to certain Greek metres. Here indeed a reversal of stress-patterns would be inevitable in performance,[4] and it may be suspected that Ovid's description is based more on Greek metrical teaching that on actual observation of the recitation of Latin choliambics. It may be symptomatic that Latin metricians specify an iambic V in choliambics, thereby clarifying the pattern at this point –

'ne deprehensae quattuor simul longae
parum sonoro fine destruant uersum'

---

[1] Cf. Horace on spondees in general (*A.P.* 251 ff.):

> 'syllaba longa breui subiecta uocatur iambus,
>   pes citus...
> tardior ut paulo grauiorque ueniret ad aures
> spondeos stabilis in iura paterna recepit.'

[2] Cf. also Chaignet 1887, 207 f; Crusius 1892; 1894b; Wackernagel 1925, 50 ff.

[3] Cf. Cicero, *Or.* 214 '*persolutas* – dichoreus (= double trochee); nihil enim ad rem extrema illa longa sit an breuis'.

[4] Cf. A 1967a, 58.

(Terentianus Maurus, vi, 397 K; cf. C. Bassus, vi, 257 K). This rule is in fact rigorously followed by Latin poets after Varro. The restriction would be less relevant in Greek if, as has been argued, the penultimate heavy syllable there has the effect only of a retardation and not a reversal of pattern; it is not mentioned by Greek metricians, nor respected by Greek poets (e.g. Theocritus, *Ep.* 19 ο μουσοποιος ενθαδ' Ιππωναξ κειται).

The principle of the Greek choliambic will of course also apply to the 'limping' form of the trochaic tetrameter catalectic (e.g. Hipponax, 70 Diehl αμφιδεξιος γαρ ειμι κουχ αμαρτανω κοπτων).

There remains the question of indifference in the hexameter. By pattern (a) it is implied that a dactylic terminal stressed as $\sim \acute{\Sigma}\Sigma\acute{\Sigma}$ would not occur in speech, since the alternation rule would require stressing of the final syllable regardless of its quantity, i.e. $\sim \acute{\Sigma}\Sigma\acute{\Sigma}$. And, with rare possible exceptions,[1] dactylic endings do not occur in verse,[2] except in the interior of lyric systems, where they are in synaphea and so not to be treated as pre-pausal.[3] The normal ending of a hexameter is in fact $\sim \acute{\Sigma}\tilde{\Sigma}$, with indifference, which would be supported by the stress patterning of type (d). But there are two interpretations of this.

As stated by Hephaestion (20 f. C), the line is catalectic by the omission of the final syllable of the dactyl – i.e. the last foot is basically a trochee, for which a spondee may be substituted by the principle of indifference.[4] Another interpretation, however, is that the final foot is basically a spondee, i.e. a full foot, substituting for a dactyl as in the interior of the line, with the trochee admitted as a substitute for the spondee by the indifference principle.[5] As Rossi observes (1963b, 63 f.), there is no practical point in treating either alternative as basic; but it may nevertheless be of some interest to probe the motivations of the competing interpretations.[6]

[1] Cf. Dale 1964; 1968, 157 f., n; Maas, 29.
[2] If they did, there would be no reason why the final syllable should not be indifferent, thus admitting a cretic $\acute{\Sigma}\Sigma\acute{\Sigma}$, as stated by Hephaestion (20 f., C; cf. Quint., ix.4.104). This is, however, disputed (cf. Dale 1964, 30; 1968, 157 f., on δυσπαιπαλους in Archilochus fr. 116 Diehl³ (Hephaestion, 50 C); also Kalinka 1935, 428).
[3] Cf. Dale 1968, 26, 35 f.   [4] Cf. also Kalinka 1935, 426; Snell 1962, 7 f.
[5] Cf. Maas, 29, 43, 59. Maas is not, however, entirely satisfied with this interpretation, and adds a note (29) 'But it would be better to note it (sc. the final syllable) as a "finale", and to denote it by the symbol $\frown$'; and Dale (1964, 17 f.), whilst rejecting the trochaic interpretation, treats the final simply as 'anceps' ($\times$).
[6] For a parallel controversy in antiquity, but having a rather different basis, see Rossi 1963b, 65 f.

The rejection of the 'trochaic' interpretation rests on the doctrine that (contrary to ancient teaching) the principle of indifference permits '(syllaba) brevis in (elemento) longo',[1] i.e. a light to substitute for a heavy syllable, but never 'longa in brevi.'[2] This doctrine, however, seems to be a mere dogma, without any clear evidence to support it. It is, perhaps, in part inspired by the 'temporal' conception of verse pattern, in terms of which it might be supposed, with highly dubious phonetic reasoning, that 'a short final syllable may have been made prosodically long by the presence of a pause after it' (Maas, 29).[3] It may possibly derive ultimately from Quintilian, ix.4.93 f: 'neque enim ego ignoro, in fine pro longa accipi breuem, quia uidetur aliquid uacantis temporis ex eo, quod insequitur, accedere'; Quintilian, however, goes on to admit that his ears continue to perceive a difference between long and short before pause, and mentions that some have carried the doctrine to its logical (and absurd) conclusion that, if this is so, a final long should also receive the addition of a mora on account of its position ('quo moti quidam longae ultimae tria tempora dederunt, ut illud tempus, quod breuis ex loco accipit, huic quoque accederet'). With regard to this doctrine of 'lengthening by pause' one can hardly do better than quote the words of Lucot (1969, 83): 'Comment un silence pourrait-il conférer une longueur, même illusoire, à une brève dont l'émission est terminée avant qu'il ait commencé?'

In iambics it might be reasonable to say that the heavy final is 'basic' and the light a 'substitute' in so far as a word-final sequence $\sim \underline{\Sigma}\underline{\Sigma}$, unlike $\sim \underline{\Sigma}\underline{\Sigma}$, would stress its final syllable in any case, even without the privilege of pre-pausal location; whereas the pattern $\sim \underline{\Sigma}\acute{\underline{\Sigma}}$ may occur only on account of the terminal alternation rule. But in hexameters the situation is quite different. A word-final spondee would not generally be stressed $\sim \acute{\underline{\Sigma}}\underline{\Sigma}$, but $\sim \underline{\Sigma}\acute{\underline{\Sigma}}$; the pattern $\sim \acute{\underline{\Sigma}}\underline{\Sigma}$ may occur only by virtue of the terminal alternation rule. A trochaic ending, on the other hand, would be stressed $\sim \acute{\underline{\Sigma}}\underline{\Sigma}$ in any case, and so might be considered to have the stronger claim to be considered as the 'basic' form of the final foot.

In general, one cannot but be suspicious of a doctrine which envisages a light as substituting for a heavy syllable regardless of whether it is in strong or weak position.

---

[1] On the terminology see Rossi 1963b, 64.

[2] Cf. Pohlsander 1964, 171; Dale 1964, 17; 1968, 26; Maas, 29.

[3] Cf. Dale 1968, 157 n: 'short + Pause has the effect of a long'.

Moreover, it seems unreasonable to suppose that in a metre which seeks clarity of pattern towards its close (as seen, for example, in the care exercised in the location of word-boundaries, and in the strong preference for a dactylic V) the ambiguous spondee should be chosen as the basic form of its ultimate cadence. The basic, falling pattern of the hexameter is set by its dactyls. We have suggested that a pre-pausal $\sim\underline{\Sigma}\underline{\Sigma}\underline{\Sigma}$ did not occur in speech; but the falling pattern could be clearly preserved by catalexis of the final light syllable, which leaves a trochee as the underlying form of the final foot.[1]

The considerations applicable to the dactylic hexameter will also apply to the ending of catalectic anapaestics (which we have already implicitly interpreted in terms of a basically light final syllable).

In the case of the acatalectic trochaics mentioned under pattern (d), it might be maintained that, as the final foot is the second foot of a metron, it could be considered as basically spondaic just as well as trochaic, since the last syllables of internal metra are 'anceps'; but again it seems perverse, at the end of a line, to choose the ambiguous spondee rather than the unambiguous trochee as basic. And in any case such an interpretation could hardly apply to the iambic tetrameter catalectic, also discussed under (d); for the curtailed final foot is the second of a metron, and in iambic metra it is only the *first* syllables which are 'anceps', so that the second foot must be a pure iambus; and when such a foot is curtailed, the remaining syllable can only be light, except in so far as the indifference principle permits it to be otherwise. This in fact seems to provide the clearest evidence of all for the admissibility of 'longa in brevi'.

The practical outcome of this study of the principle of indifference is as follows. If it has a basis in natural speech, it is possible to frame a quite simple hypothesis for terminal stress-patterning which would account for all the observed operations of the principle. And if this hypothesis is correct, then in all the major spoken metres there will have been close agreement between the metrical patterns of the coda and the dynamic patterns of the composition in normal speech. In the case of the hexameter this would continue the agreement which we have found to be

---

[1] This interpretation incidentally fits in with Snell's interpretation (1962, 8) of Hermann's Law (whereby word-end is avoided at IVb_1) – namely that poets disliked producing the effect of a catalectic dactylic tetrameter followed two feet later by the same cadence at the end of the line.

strongly favoured in foot IV and almost unexceptional in V. If this is accepted, over the hexameter as a whole there would be agreement between verse and speech about 95% of the time,[1] the disagreements being principally confined to I.

Whatever the basis of the principle, however, the fact remains that it represents a neglect in the terminal position of purely quantitative criteria; what our own hypothesis suggests is that the operative criterion was in origin dynamic.

This will be an appropriate point to enter a caveat, the need for which has been well recognized by *Jones (1971, 296). No previous or subsequent statement in this discussion should be taken to imply that Greek verse was basically stressed verse. From a structural standpoint it was quantitative, and certain of its features can only be accounted for in these terms (e.g. the admission of 'anceps' only at one place in the iambic or trochaic metron): but the compositional practice of serious spoken poetry is best explained in terms of a desire to ensure that in performance the quantitative patterning should be reinforced rather than contradicted by the linguistic stress.[2]

The iambic trimeter

Porson's Law. We next examine the situation in other than final feet in the other main spoken metre, the iambic trimeter of tragedy. Beginning, as in the case of the hexameter, with V, we immediately encounter the most famous of all compositional rules – 'Porson's Law', alternatively known as 'Porson's Canon' or the 'Law of the Final Cretic' – of which, nevertheless, it has been commented: 'Yet was no "law" human or divine ever so isolated or unintelligible' (Knox 1932, 36). In fact it is hoped to demonstrate that this 'law' is fully intelligible in terms of the hypothesis of linguistic stress already set up on the basis of hexameter practice, and so to reinforce the observation by Schein (1967, 32) that 'Early Greek spoken verse-forms...have much more in common than is generally realised'.[3]

In a note on line 347 of his edition of Euripides' *Hecuba* in 1797, Richard Porson first refers to the rarity of word-division in the middle of a spondaic V, an observation repeated two years later in a note on line 1464 of the *Phoenissae*. The full statement of the 'law' came in

---

[1] A 1966a, 122.
[2] A stronger statement may, however, be justified in connexion with 'resolution' (see pp. 316 ff.).
[3] Similarly de Groot 1935, 147, with special reference to foot V of hexameters and iambics; cf. Maas, 35.

1802 in a Supplement to the Preface of a second edition of the *Hecuba* (xxx).[1] Here Porson stated it as a general rule of the tragic trimeter that if a 'cretic' word at the end of the line ($\sim,\Sigma\Sigma\Sigma$) were preceded by other than a monosyllable, than V must not be a spondee. That this rule was not known to Porson at an earlier date may be seen from the Greek iambics which he composed for the Craven Scholarship in 1781, which contain two breaches of the rule in successive lines.[2] There is no direct evidence that the rule was known to the Greek metricians, though the apparent respecting of it by Horace and Seneca (see p. 335) may indicate, as Maas suggests (95), that these authors are following such a prescription.

Porson himself was satisfied with simply observing the phenomenon. But Hermann, in his own edition of the *Hecuba* in 1800 (line 341), took Porson to task for not attempting an explanation, and ventured to supply one of his own. At the end of each verse, he suggested, the lungs are almost empty, and so any interruption of the flow of speech is to be avoided; and a word-division following a heavy syllable he supposed to involve an especially long pause, which would be intolerable at this point. In the rather more colourful statement of Elmsley, a supporter of Hermann, reference is made to 'the exhausted lungs of a corpulent performer' (Watson 1861, 172 f.). Such an explanation can hardly be taken seriously; Hermann did, however, go on to consider, with more plausible reasoning, why a monosyllable preceding 'Porson's Pause' was admissible, and in this connexion made the following points of interest;

(i) the monosyllables in question belong syntactically with the following word;

(ii) a monosyllable beginning V ensures a word-division at the end of IV. In this position the inter-word pause assumed by Hermann follows the 'arsis' (strong position) of the foot, which in Hermann's view carried an audible 'ictus' and so would in any case normally be prolonged; whereas the opposite would be the case in the middle of V.[3]

[1] Reproduced in Figure I (p. 308).
[2] See Watson 1861, 33.
[3] 'commode fit, quia haec syllaba, ut arsis, ictu gravatur, ob eamque caussam ita iam per se producitur, ut paussa illa, quae finiendo vocabulo fit, in eumdem locum aptissime incidat. Quod non est in sequente, i.e. prima quinti pedis syllaba, quae ictu destituitur, atque unice continuando numero inservit, omnem non necessariam productionem repudiat.'

The rationalization of Porson's Law in terms of an inter-word interval has again been proposed in recent times by Perret (1960, 590); and both he and Snell (1962, 6) have been led specifically by the conditions of the law to suggest that heavy syllables in Greek were in some way of more marked quantity when final, and so were inappropriate to the weak, 'thesis' position. We have noted an identical suggestion by Porter (see p. 292) in connexion with feet IV and V of hexameters. Bill (1932, 22 ff.)[1] proposes an explanation which is reminiscent of Hermann's in so far as he supposes a break in a spondee to be somehow stronger than in an iambus, but continues by suggesting that such a break would weaken the effect of the obligatory caesura in III or IV. This explanation has been refuted by de Groot (1935, 142 ff.).

The improbability of purely temporal explanations of metrical rules has already been emphasized; and the restrictions observed under Porson's Law can be immediately explained by the hypothesis already framed on the basis of the hexameter. For a word-division in the middle of a spondaic V of the iambic trimeter involves the occurrence of a heavy word-final syllable in the first, 'weak' half of the foot; a final heavy syllable would, it has been assumed, carry stress in speech, and so poets might be expected to avoid placing such a syllable in the weak position if performance of the line were to end with a regular dynamic pattern,[2] i.e. if the strong positions of the verse were to be reinforced by the linguistic stresses. Moreover, in the case of other than monosyllables the effect of the 'prohibited' placing would be to introduce an unstressed syllable into the strong position of IV. One would thus have a cadence pattern of the type

$$\sim |\bar{\Sigma}\bar{\Sigma}\|\acute{\bar{\Sigma}},\acute{\bar{\Sigma}}|\bar{\Sigma}\acute{\bar{\Sigma}}$$

The required agreement is, however, achieved if V is not divided, and/or is iambic: thus e.g.

$$\sim |\bar{\Sigma},\acute{\bar{\Sigma}}\|\bar{\Sigma}\acute{\bar{\Sigma}},|\bar{\Sigma}\acute{\bar{\Sigma}}$$

$$\text{or} \sim |\bar{\Sigma},\acute{\bar{\Sigma}}\|\bar{\Sigma},\acute{\bar{\Sigma}}|\bar{\Sigma}\acute{\bar{\Sigma}}$$

Such an explanation does not depend on an unspecified preference by the 'delicate ear of the ancients' (see p. 277) – invoked in precisely this context by Descroix (1931, 317); and we need not even share Maas' doubts as to whether our modern ears would 'be able to sense that a

---

[1] Cf. also Witte 1914.
[2] Cf. de Groot 1935, 142, 147, 151.

breach of Porson's Law was a mistake' (57). It is not of course suggested that poets consciously followed a formulated rule in this matter, but simply that in composing 'well-formed' verses they avoided combinations and placings of words which would result in the dynamic patterns of the cadence conflicting with the quantitative metrical patterns.

Newton (1969) suggests that, assuming a certain 'strategy' of composition, the placing of words by Sophocles can be accounted for by a 'randomized' routine, requiring no reference to any other factor such as stress – but has to admit that 'with regard to "Porson's Law", its intention, and that of other similar "bridge" rules remain unexplained'. It is precisely such 'bridges' that are most demanding of an explanation; one can hardly dismiss Porson's Law as (Newton, 368) 'an obscure iambographic practice'. Elsewhere (369 f.) Newton observes that Sophocles shows no tendency to avoid words of the pattern ⎺⎺⎺, which, in iambics, must involve conflict of stress and strong position by our general rules; what, however, he fails to point out is that such forms are only placed before the caesura (see p. 313), and *never* (by Porson's Law) in the cadence.

The exceptions to Porson's Law are also of some interest. These mainly involve a class of words which were in fact specifically excluded from the statement of the rule, namely monosyllables in Va. The reason for their acceptability was probably not so much the fact of their being monosyllables as the fact (already recognized by Hermann) that they belonged to a category which formed a close phonological unity with the following word – i.e. 'proclitics' (in an extended sense), the same category as we have seen (p. 287) to be acceptable as exceptions in the hexameter; and it has already been proposed by Sobolevskij (1956; 1964) that a characteristic of such words was their lack of inherent stress (their stressing or otherwise being dependent on the structure of the whole combination).[1] Thus a combination such as Aesch., *Supp.* 949 εξ ομματων or Eur., *Hipp.* 1063 ους ωμοσα, *I.A.* 49 τρεις παρθενοι would be stressed as a single unit, giving a pattern ⎺⎺⎺⎺, which, at the end of an iambic line, does not conflict with the metrical pattern of strong and weak positions. The conjunction γαρ seems also thus to function if it is interposed between connected items, as e.g. Eur., *And.* 230 των κακων γαρ μητερων = ⎺|⎺⎺,‖⎺⎺|⎺⎺ (for 'enclitic' use see below). These same considerations could also apply to words of this

---

[1] On the behaviour of such words in the clausulae of stress-accented Greek prose cf. Skimina 1930, 2 f. and refs.

FIGURE I

Pp. xxx–xxxiii of Porson's *Hecuba*² (1802) with Hermann's annotations (see pp. 305, 310).

xxx SUPPLEMENTUM AD

Καὶ ὡς ἰσθέων γε τὴν τυραννίδα ἐγκωμιάζει. Habuit in animo Troad. 1177. Γέρων τε καὶ τῆς ἰσοθέου τυραννίδος. Notus est Ariphronis Sicyonii Pæan apud Athen. XV. fin. Τᾶς τ' εὐδαίμονος ἀνθρώποις βασιληΐδος ἀρχᾶς. Sic editiones Casauboni, qui tamen ex Epitome legit ἰσοδαίμονος, quod habent etiam Plutarchus de Virt. Mor. p. 450. B. Sextus Empiricus adv. Mathem. XI. 49. In editione Aldina Athenæi est ἰσοδαίμονος, quod Typothetæ videtur erratum, qui ϛ (id est σο) cum ϛ confuderit. Diverso sensu dixit ἰσοδαίμονα Pindarus Nem. IV. 137.

Hactenus hæc. Nunc ad aliud cæsuræ genus accedimus, quam potius *pausam* ideo nominare libet, quoniam versus qui cæsurarum supra memoratarum nullam habeat, necessario minus modulatus est; versus vero qui *pausa* careat, non est continuo immodulatus. De versibus iis loquor, ubi quintus pes in duas voces distribuitur. Tirones vero ea, quæ de hac re dicturus sum, pro supplemento accipient notæ meæ ad Hec. 347. Κρύπτοντα χεῖρα καὶ πρόσωπον ἔμπαλιν. Sic primus recte edidit Kingius pro τούμπαλιν. Nempe hanc regulam plerumque in senariis observabant Tragici, ut, si voce, quæ Creticum pedem efficeret, terminaretur versus, eamque vocem hypermonosyllabon præcederet, quintus pes iambus vel tribrachys esse deberet. Non potuerunt igitur talem versum Tragici scribere, qualis est Κρύπτοντα χεῖρα καὶ πρόσωπον τούμπαλιν, aut Ἄτλας ὁ χαλκέοισι νώτοις οὐρανόν, aut Τὸ μὴ μᾶτευον δ' ἐκ μεταίχμων ἀσφράγιον, certe noluere, si modo vel diversa orthographia vel alia verborum positura vitare possent *In scenam missos cum magno pondere versus*.

xxi PRÆFATIONEM.

Res eadem est, si Creticus in trochæum et syllabam dissolvitur; vel si Cretico in syllabam longam et iambum dissoluto, syllaba longa est aut articulus aut prepositio, aut quævis denique vox, quæ ad sequentia potius quam præcedentia pertineat.

Κῆδός δὲ τοιμῶν καὶ σὸν οἰκέτ' | ἐστὶ | δή.
Χαῖρ'· οὐ γὰρ ἡμῖν ἐστι τοῦτο· | σοί γε | μήν.
Καλῶς μὲν εἶπας, θύγατερ, ἀλλὰ | τῷ καλῷ·
Δεινός χαρακτὴρ κἀπίσημος | ἐν βροτοῖς.

Et sic habe de τίς, πῶς, interrogantibus; ὡς, οὗ, καὶ et similibus, ut partim monui ad Phœniss. 1464.

Verum si secunda quinti pedis pars ejus sit generis, ut precedenti verbo adhæreat, et ambo quasi unam vocem simul efficiant, non jam amplius necesse erit, ut verbum precedens brevi syllaba terminetur. Ac primo pauca citemus exempla, ubi syllaba iambum precedens sit vox enclitica.

Σπεύδομεν, ἐγκονῶμεν· ἤγου μοι | γέρον. Hecub. 511.
Ἔτικτε γάρ μ' ἔτικτεν, ὤμοι μοι | κακκάκων. O.C. d. 976.
Προσέρχεται τόδ' ἐγγύς· οἴμοι μοι | τάλας. Philoct.744 (787 Br.)
Κρίνω σε νικᾷν καὶ παραινέσαί μοι | καλῶς. Œdipt.
Πείθειν ἐπᾴδων· ἰωτῇ ἐφαρμόσει μοι | ὥσπερ. Iph.Ad.nom. (1122.)
Πᾶς φής; τίν' εἶπας μῦθον; αὖθίς μοι | φράσον. Helen.408. (411)
Ἀ δ' εἶδαθ' εἶχον σηφάθ', ἄκουσόν μου | πάτερ. Ion. 632. (545)
Ἔστω φρενῶν λέγουσα πείθω νιν | λόγῳ. Agam.
Τί παισθεύσεις δαφοῦ, ἐξ οὗ συ | γράφεις. Prom.632.
Καὶ μὴν ἐκεῖνος οὐκέτ' ἔσται σοι | βαρύς. Eum.Cl.1119 (1116)
Βίον δ' ἐπαιτῶν εἶρ' ἀγύρτης τις | λάτρις. Rhsf.715. in-eodosfr.
Ἐμάστγον, ὦ γεννάῖ' κάρφω τοι | ὥστε. Philoct.797. (801 Br.)

Eum.Alc. 1490-1491. Heut. 511. 632.

Iph.Bul. 1163. (Jc. do xónon) p. XXXV.

xxii SUPPLEMENTUM AD

Ex hac classe excipienda sunt duo loca.

Cum νω et σφω significent ἡμεῖς δύο et ὑμεῖς δύο, nimis emphatica sunt, quam ut enclitica fiant. Legendum igitur σφῶ νῦν σωτῆρ βλάβης, et ὡς πρὶν σφω πατρί. Melius ἄρα νῦν σωτῆρ βλάβης, ut σωτῆρα κακῶν Med. 361. ἰσάζουσιν θεραπῶν Phoeniss. 609. Idem ὥσπερ Euripidei versus apud Polluc. VII. 178. numeros corrupit. Κοίλοις ἐν ἄντροις ἄλυχρος, ὥσπερ θὴρ μόνος. Recte MS. ὥστε.

Secundo exempla quaedam demus vocum non encliticarum, sed quae sententiam aut versum inchoare nequeunt.

Sed nulla particula saepius, quam ὤ, in ista sede posita reperitur.

Sophocl. Electr. 413. Εἰ μοι λέγοις τὴν ὄψιν, εἴπαιμι ἂν τότε.
Eurip. Phoen. 1635. Ἀλλ᾽ ἔτι νεάζων αὐτός εὑρήσει ἂν βίον;
1642. Ἐγὼ δὲ ναίων σ᾽ οὐκ ἐάσομαι ἂν χθόνα.
Androm. 937. Βλέπουσ᾽ ἂν αὐγάς παρ᾽ ἐκαρπούτ᾽ ἂν λέχη.
1187. Οὗτος γ᾽ ἂν ὅς σε τοιόνδ᾽ ἔτυχεν ἂν γέρον.
Bacch. 1272. Κλύοις ἂν οὖν τι κἀπονοίμαν ἂν σαφῶς.
Heracl. 457. Μάλιστα δ᾽ Εὐρυσθεύς με βούλοιτ᾽ ἂν λαβεῖν.

PRAEFATIONEM. xxiii

Acute igitur et probabiliter in Hippol. 296. γυναῖκες αἵδε συγκαθίσταιτ᾽ ἂν νόσον, (συγκαθίσταιται enim MSS.) conjecerat Musgravius, quamvis postea vulgatum συγκαθίσταιται defenderit. Certa autem Marklandi emendatio Iph. A. 524.

Ὃν μὴ σὺ φράζῃς, πῶς ὑπολάβοιμ᾽ ἂν | λόγον;

In omnibus his exemplis illud observandum est, ἂν semper verbo suo statim subjungi, idque cum elisione. Unde levi mendo laborat versus Erecthei, φρονεῖς γὰρ ἤδη κἀπποτσούσης ἂν πατρός. Quanquam σώζων apud Tragicos aliquando meminisse significat, longe aptior hoc sensu est media forma. Lege igitur, κἀποτούσαι ἂν πατρός. Similis confusio in Med. 734. μεθεῖσαν et μεθεῖ᾽ ἄν. Verum nisi mutatio sit perexigua, haec et similia loca sollicitari nolim. Sane si MS. bonae notae in Aeschyli versu daret παραινέσας καλῶς, aut in Euripidis ἀκούε μου, πάτερ, non illibenter acciperem. Est versus Alcest. 1106. Χρόνος μαλάξει, νῦν δ᾽ ἔθ᾽ ἥξει σου κακόν, qui ex iis, quae modo dixi, non incommode defendi potest. Verum quis reponere dubitabit e Galeno IV. de Dogm. Hippocr. et Plat. T. I. p. 283, 55. ed. Basil. T. V. p. 152. Charter. quem indicavit Valckenarius Diatrib. p. 28. B. C. Χρόνος μαλάξει, νῦν δ᾽ ἔθ᾽ ἠδώκεις, κακόν. Sed talia, ut dixi, ex mera conjectura non tentanda.

Alia sunt, quae huic regulae non vere officiant, tantum ex perversa orthographiae ratione officere videantur. In hanc classem referenda puto exempla, ubi οὐδεὶς inter quartum pedem et quintum dividatur.

category longer than monosyllables, as e.g. Eur., *Phoen.* 747 ουδεν θατε-
ρον = $\acute{\underline{\Sigma}}\|\underline{\Sigma}\acute{\underline{\Sigma}}|\underline{\Sigma}\acute{\underline{\Sigma}}$.[1]

The principle would similarly apply to cases where Vb is occupied
by a monosyllabic word forming a phonological unity with a preceding
full word – or, as defined by Porson (1802, xxxi f.), by a word such as
cannot begin a sentence or verse.[2] Such a class of words we might, with
Sobolevskij, term 'enclitics', though recognizing, as he does, that one is
thereby extending the term beyond its Alexandrian application only
to words in which the (absence of) melodic accent is involved; 'postpositives' might be a less ambiguous term (cf. p. 289). This class would
include, for example, postposed particles and conjunctions (as μεν,
δε, γαρ, δη, ουν, αυ);[3] so that in a line ending θνητοις γαρ γερα
(Aesch., *Prom.* 107) or ημιν αυ χαριν (*Prom.* 821) the word-division
and consequent stress-patterning would be $\acute{\underline{\Sigma}}\|\underline{\Sigma}\acute{\underline{\Sigma}},|\underline{\Sigma}\acute{\underline{\Sigma}}$ and not
$\underline{\Sigma}\|\acute{\underline{\Sigma}},\acute{\underline{\Sigma}},|\underline{\Sigma}\acute{\underline{\Sigma}}$.[4] The principle need not be confined to monosyllables,
but could explain the admission of longer words of similar function,
as e.g. a postposition in ων ουνεκα (Eur., *Ion* 65, where in addition the
relative tends to be proclitic) or negative pronoun in νουν ουδενα
(Soph., *Ant.* 68; cf. proclitic use above), giving a pattern $\|\underline{\Sigma}\acute{\underline{\Sigma}}|\underline{\Sigma}\acute{\underline{\Sigma}}$ and
not $\|\acute{\underline{\Sigma}},\acute{\underline{\Sigma}},|\underline{\Sigma}\acute{\underline{\Sigma}}$.[5]

It is of interest that Hermann, in a ms note in his own copy of Porson's *Hecuba* (1802, xxxii)[6] attempted to turn a number of such cases
to the advantage of his own theory (see p. 305) by pointing out that a
sequence such as θνητοις γαρ γερα is preceded by a punctuation, i.e.
a pause, which would allow one to draw breath before it ('caussa est
in praegressa interpunctione, quae facit, ut sequentia maiore cum
spiritu pronunciari possint').

There are also a few exceptional cases where a breach of Porson's

---

[1] See also (on 'split anapaests') p. 331.
[2] Note Martinet's observation (1952, 216) that Celtic 'lenition' (cf. Dottin, cited
p. 288) is largely a characteristic of words which could not occur at the beginning of
an utterance.
[3] In fact a commentator on Dionysius Thrax (*Schol.*, 466 H) describes μεν, δε, and
γαρ as enclitics; cf. also the accentuations ούκουν, τοίγαρ (Vendryes 1929, 107).
Sobolevskij (1964, 56) also notes the special accentuation with double grave in
some mss of such forms as μὲν, ἐπεὶ, μὴ, etc., which he interprets as an indication of
weak stress.
[4] This prosodic fusion of proclitics and enclitics with main word is, as we have seen
in the case of e.g. Russ. *ú morja*/*u mórja* or Pol. *pisátby*/*pisał-by* (pp. 25 f.), only
one alternative, and the other possibility has been envisaged in hexameters (p. 289).
[5] Cf. p. 332.
[6] Cambridge University Library, *Adv.c.83.32* (reproduced in Figure I).

Law seems to be facilitated by an elision at the word-division: e.g. Soph., *Phil.* 22 ~σημαιν' ειτ' εχει;[1] Eur., *Cycl.* 304 ~εχηρωσ' Ελλαδα. This was already hinted at by Porson (1802, xxxii), who also (xxv) noted the special function of elision in 'bisected trimeters'. It may be that the close phonological connexion between the words, in so far as elision implies absence of pause (cf. pp. 121, 227), caused them to be stressed as a single unit; in which case the heavy syllable rendered final by the elision would not be treated as a word-final, and so (in the cases arising under Porson's Law) would not be stressed; the pattern of e.g. εχηρωσ' Ελλαδα would then be |ΣΣ̱‖ΣΣ̱|ΣΣ̱ and not |ΣΣ̱‖Σ̱,Σ̱|ΣΣ̱, and there would be no conflict between dynamic and metrical patterns.

In the very exceptional case of Eur., *Ion* 1 Ατλας ο χαλκεοισι νωτοις ουρανον various emendations have been proposed; alternatively it has been suggested (Soubiran 1966a, 540 n.1) that the breach of Porson's Law (in our terms the dynamic/metrical conflict) is here deliberate and has the intention of conveying an impression of heaviness: one may recall the lines from Pope's *Essay on Criticism*:

> When Ajax strives some Rock's vast weight to throw
> The Line too labours, and the Words move slow.[2]

Porson's Law is not respected in comedy. Which means, if our hypothesis is correct, that comedy was *either* less averse from the distortion of natural dynamic patterns in performance, *or* was less concerned than more serious genres, as epic and tragedy, that the line (or at least the coda) should have a regular dynamic pattern. On general grounds the former conclusion seems improbable; the characteristic preference for 'correptio Attica' in comedy is one aspect of its prosodic closeness to the language of the people. The latter conclusion, as an a priori probability, was a factor in selecting tragedy rather than comedy as a basis for the testing of our hypothesis; for the dynamic element in Greek would not have been (as in Latin) a basic, accentual feature, necessarily apprehended by even the least sensitive speaker and hearer; to this extent some element of 'delicacy' may perhaps be involved. It was both non-functional and probably weak (as compared with, say, English or even Latin), and so, if taken account of at all in composition, was more likely to be so in more elevated or formal styles. In fact this seems the more probable conclusion; for there are also other require-

---

[1] conj. Porson σημαινειν.   [2] Cf. Freeman 1968, 77.

ments of tragic composition which are not observed by comedy – for example, the not uncommon neglect of the caesura and the frequency of resolved feet (including the admission of anapaests in all but the last, and most significantly of a dactyl in V, with consequent reversal of the rising quantitative pattern even in the cadence of the line). So that, whilst adopting the same general quantitative structure as tragedy, and accepting and extending its licences, comedy shows considerably less regard for its subtler constraints. Passages in comedy which respect such constraints (e.g. *Ran.* 470–8; *Av.* 1706–19)[1] are also tragic in general style; and conversely a number of breaches of Porson's Law by Euripides 'are shown to be comic in style not only by this licence but by the frequent resolution of longa and by changes of speaker inside the line' (Maas, 70). On *Pax* 180 Hardie (1920, 77) observes that Hermes, as befits a god, speaks in tragic style, and, when Trygaeus knocks at the gates of Olympus, begins ποθεν βροτου με προσε-βαλ'~ ; (intending to finish the line with something like εξαιφνης φατις): but, being startled by the appearance of the ἱπποκάνθαρος, exclaims ωναξ Ηρακλεις, with a disregard of Porson's Law typical of comedy.[2] We cannot, therefore, accept the objection by Newton (1969, 368) that 'if spoken Greek was characterized by word stress it seems exceedingly odd that evidence for it should be found in the highly literary productions of Greek tragedy but not in comedy, which one would have expected to reproduce as closely as possible the speech rhythms of the market place'. In comedy the natural dynamic patterns are in no way suppressed or distorted – it is simply that the composition does not display the same care in ensuring that they shall be regular (and indeed to this extent unnatural).

Our hypothesis regarding the stress patterns of Greek words in speech has the effect of revealing Porson's Law as just another aspect of the serious poet's regard for agreement between metrical and dynamic patterning in the cadence of the line, and supports O'Neill's suggestion (1939, 269) that we might 'consider Porson's Canon as having nothing essentially to do with cretic words'. It remains to examine what regard, if any, for such agreement is to be found in earlier portions of the line. In IV and II, the invariably light first element precludes the possibility of stress in weak position (on 'resolved' feet see below). In I certain licences are found, as commonly in this position. There are (mostly

[1] Maas, 69 f.   [2] Cf. Parker 1968, 250.

in proper names) a few cases of first feet consisting of a trochee, as
Aesch., *Cho.* 1049 φαιοχιτωνες ~ ; and substitutions occur here of
types which are abnormal later in the line, e.g. anapaests (elsewhere permitted only to accommodate proper names): see further pp.
330 ff.

The caesura. The only real problem for the hypothesis is presented by
III, when, as frequently, this is spondaic *and* contains a caesura. For the
effect is to place the heavy final syllable of a word in the weak position
of the foot. And heavy final syllables are, it has been assumed, normally
stressed: so that there would here be conflict between metrical and
dynamic patterns[1] comparable with a breach of Porson's Law in V;
and in addition the occurrence of a stressed syllable in IIIa would
involve an unstressed syllable in the strong position of II, thereby
compounding the disagreement.

One possible interpretation would be that in this part of the line
such disagreement simply was not unacceptable. This, however, is
hardly satisfactory; for in IIIb there are strict rules about resolution
(see pp. 316 ff.) which point to a considerable regard for agreement.
Another and preferable interpretation would be in terms of the principle
of 'indifference'.[2] If, as some scholars hold, the caesura had the phonetic
potentiality of pause, it is possible that in iambics, the metre which
Aristotle terms 'the most like ordinary speech' (μάλιστα λεκτικόν),[3]
the stressing of the pre-caesural ΣΣ may have been determined by the
preceding ΣΣ̱Σ of the beginning of the line, i.e. Σ̱Σ, with consequent
agreement of metrical and dynamic pattern. It may or may not be
relevant that Sophocles often uses this position for the repetition of
words, as *O.T.* 216 αιτεις, α δ' αιτεις ~ ; if the second interpretation
is correct, this would imply a difference of stress patterning between
the first and second occurrences of the word, viz. ΣΣ́ vs Σ́Σ: cf. English
'You ásk, but whát you ask ~ ' (with second 'ask' unstressed). It is
pointed out by Platt (1899, 148) that 'The shifting of metrical ictus on
the same word or words...is a favourite ornament in Sophocles', and
in many cases this occurs in positions which imply a contrast of stress
by our general rules, as e.g. *O.T.* 261 κοινών| τε παί‖δων κοί|ν' αν ~ .
For further support for this interpretation see pp. 319 f.

[1] Cf. O'Neill 1939, 258 ff; Newton 1969, 368, 370.
[2] Contrary to the general implications of p. 115.
[3] *Poet.* 1449a; cf. *Rhet.* 1408b; also (including trochaics) Hermogenes, *Rhet. Gr.* vi,
232 Rabe; Meillet 1923, 21.

Where elision occurs in such cases, as e.g. Aesch., *Supp.* 195 ξενους αμειβεσθ', ως ∼, the situation would be anomalous even by the present hypothesis, since elision in normal speech would be a negation of pause, and the principle of indifference should not apply. But it is no more anomalous than the occurrence of the elision itself at an implied pause as here.

The trochaic tetrameter

The general rules relating to word-divisions in the tragic iambic trimeter also have their counterparts in the tragic trochaic tetrameter catalectic, which, as Porson observed, could be considered as an iambic trimeter with a preceding cretic: thus:

Trimeter: Σ Σ|Σ Σ‖Σ Σ|Σ Σ‖Σ Σ|Σ Σ
Tetrameter: ΣΣ|ΣΣ‖Σ Σ|Σ Σ‖Σ Σ|Σ Σ‖Σ Σ|Σ

Porson in fact states that his 'law' applies also to this metre (1802, xliii), an observation in which he had been anticipated by Hermann (1800, 112: 'eadem prorsus ratio est in fine trochaicorum tetrametrorum apud tragicos'). In the tetrameter it involves the general avoidance of word-end at VIb if this foot is a spondee; where there is a word-end at this point, the foot is a trochee in 97% of cases. A similar avoidance is found at IIb, where it is sometimes known as 'Havet's Law' (cf. Maas, 35); Bill (1932 38) terms it a 'Lex Quasi-Porsoniana'; but more recently Torresin (1966) has drawn attention to a posthumously published note of Porson's which establishes it as genuinely Porsonian ('Si prima dipodia tragici tetrametri integris vocibus continetur, secundus pes est trochaeus').

To the IIIa caesura in iambics corresponds a diaeresis at IVb which is regular in trochaics; and here also there is admission of a spondaic foot, with similar implications to those of the trimeter discussed above.

Lyric metres; anapaests

In lyric metres, in view of their association with a musical accompaniment and setting, we should not expect to find the same regard for purely linguistic dynamic patterns, and so the same kind of regulation regarding word-divisions.[1] But even here some traces may be found of the influence of speech-patterns such as we have proposed.

[1] Cf. O'Neill 1939, 280 f.

One may consider the case of dactylo-epitrites, which consist basically of combinations of dactylic hemiepes ($\Sigma\Sigma\Sigma\Sigma\Sigma\Sigma$) and cretic ($\Sigma\Sigma\Sigma$) elements, with 'linking' syllables between them. The link syllable may be either heavy or light; but if it is heavy, it is not normally followed by word-division: for example, one does not generally find the pattern

$$\Sigma\Sigma\Sigma\Sigma\Sigma\Sigma|\Sigma,|\Sigma\Sigma\Sigma$$

$$\text{or}\ \Sigma\Sigma\Sigma|\Sigma,|\Sigma\Sigma\Sigma\Sigma\Sigma\Sigma$$

In a study of these and other similar restrictions in lyric, Parker (1966) sees them as yet another aspect of Porson's Law; she observes that 'word-end after long anceps is subject to some restriction everywhere in serious Greek poetry'; and in an attempt to extend the law to the restrictions on monosyllabic (and so long) 'biceps' (cf. pp. 286 ff.) suggests the possibility that 'the rhythm ... ∪ – – | has a peculiar quality, finality; it is a characteristic clausular rhythm. So ... ∪ – –|– ∪ gives an impression of dislocation, of coming to a halt and starting out again. The law might then be formulated thus: *Whenever a segment of the form* ... ∪ – – – ∪ ... *appears within the verse word end is avoided after the second long:* ... ∪ – ⌢ – ∪ ..., *except at median caesura and diaeresis.*'[1] We agree with Parker in seeing Porson's Law and the other restrictions considered as simply different aspects of one and the same phenomenon,[2] as also with her observation (2) that 'The formulation and the explanation of Porson's Law are inextricably interwoven'. The view of $\Sigma\Sigma\Sigma$ as a clausular rhythm is, however, open to doubt so far as period-end is concerned (cf. pp. 301 ff.); and a simpler and more linguistic explanation of all the phenomena seems to be provided by our hypothesis that heavy final syllables were stressed in speech, whereas both anceps (Σ) and biceps (Σ) are characteristic of *weak* position in verse. To take the case of dactylo-epitrites again: the basic pattern of these lines could be viewed as a varying, but falling pattern catalectic; this pattern would, however, be supported by the speech dynamics only if the link syllable were unstressed, i.e. were *either* light *or* non-final. If, on the other hand, this syllable were heavy and final, and so stressed in speech, it would imply a *rising* dynamic pattern immediately before the word-division, with a reversion to the falling pattern after it. It is this consequence which would be avoided by the restriction in question.

[1] On this exception cf. our discussion of iambics and trochaics.
[2] Cf. also Rupprecht's 'extended Lex Porsoni' (1949, 18): 'If a molossus is followed by one or two short syllables, the second long must not be the final of a plurisyllabic word.'

A similar explanation could be applied to the case of anapaestic systems in tragedy, which occupy a position somewhere between lyric and spoken metres in so far as they are traditionally associated with a marching rhythm (in particular to bring the chorus on and off the stage).[1] In such verses one might expect purely linguistic patterns to be to some extent overridden; but again there are significant restrictions (cf. A 1966a, 136), of which the following is of particular interest. In the full lines of such systems there is normally diaeresis between the metra. The final ('paroemiac') line is catalectic; in this line the rule of diaeresis does not apply; and foot III is almost invariably an anapaest and not a spondee (thus $\underline{\Sigma\Sigma}|\underline{\Sigma\Sigma}\|\underline{\Sigma\Sigma}|\Sigma$). But if foot II is a spondee, a caesura within it is avoided. In terms of our hypothesis, such a caesura would involve a stress in the first, weak part of II (and no stress in the strong position of I), thereby creating a rising dynamic pattern preceding the caesura ($\overset{(\prime)}{\underline{\Sigma\Sigma}}\overset{}{\Sigma}, \sim$) immediately followed by a falling pattern in the rest of the line ($\sim, \underline{\Sigma}\underline{\Sigma}\underline{\Sigma}\underline{\Sigma}$). As Parker also here observes (1958, 84), '−−| suggests to the ear period-end in "rising" movement, and following −∪∪... gives an impression of setting off again in the opposite direction' – which would be a particularly unfortunate effect in the special context of use of the anapaests.

(ii) LIGHT SYLLABLES; RESOLUTION

Thus far we have considered, on the basis of metrical evidence, only the potentialities for stress of *heavy* syllables; and it emerges that one or two light syllables between heavy syllables would *not* be stressed. It need not, however, necessarily be assumed that more extended sequences of short syllables would be devoid of stress contrasts, and it remains to consider whether there exist any rules or strong tendencies for the location of word-boundaries which might give a clue to the possibility of regular patterns of word-stress in such sequences. In spoken metres we can study this possibility only in the 'resolved' feet of iambics or trochaics, where $\Sigma\Sigma$ substitutes for the Σ of strong position; and we shall again concern ourselves primarily with the evidence of tragedy.

In iambics, if we exclude the first foot, there is a very strong tendency for the two light syllables in question to be the first two syllables of a word. In Aeschylus the exceptions number only 12 out of 287 cases, and in Sophocles 22 out of 418;[2] the tendency is also clear in Euripides,

---

[1] Cf. p. 333.   [2] Irigoin 1959, 70 f.

with only 2 exceptions out of 242 in his 'severior' style.[1] What is most rigorously avoided is a word-division between the two syllables (except in so far as proclitics or enclitics are involved). A similar tendency is seen in the trochaic tetrameter – which means that, whereas in iambics the word-division is generally in the middle of the resolved foot ($|\Sigma,\Sigma\Sigma|$), in trochaics it is at the beginning ($\sim,|\Sigma\Sigma\Sigma|$).[2]

A second very strong tendency is for the word to be longer than two syllables. In iambics, in Euripides' 'severior', Zieliński (152) notes 13 exceptions – but all but 3 of these involve proclitics or enclitics (in the broad sense of pp. 287, 307 f.), which, together with the full word, form a longer word-like unit: thus e.g. *Med.* 872 δια| λογων, *Alc.* 802 ο βι|ος, 137 τινα|‿τυχην; cf. Aesch., *Ag.* 600 τον‿ε|μον, Soph., *O.C.* 823 τον‿α|σεβη. Again the same tendency is found in trochaics, as e.g. Eur., *I.A.* 394 ασυνε|τον.[3]

A third notable tendency is for the vowels of the two light syllables not to be separated by more than one consonant – i.e. by a sequence plosive + liquid or nasal (although normal light syllables freely occur before such sequences: see p. 211).[4] Of 4 exceptions in Euripides' 'severior' all involve the sequences *voiceless* plosive + ρ[5] (as e.g. *Hipp.* 1056 ακρι|τον), i.e. the sequences most widely associated with 'correptio Attica' (see p. 219), or in other words the sequences which functioned most like single consonants, as complex releases of syllables. The same applies to all 11 exceptions in Euripides' 'semiseverus'.[6] Similar restrictions appear also to apply to a sequence following the second vowel of a resolved element; of 12 exceptions in the two styles of Euripides referred to only 2 involve plosive + nasal (as *Hcld.* 689 αρι|θμον).

We may thus say that in general two light syllables are admitted in the strong position only on the condition that

(i) they are not separated by a word-boundary, i.e. they 'cohere' within the word;[7]

(ii) they are in contrast with one or more other syllables of the same word;

(iii) there is limited consonantal separation between them (and after them).

[1] Zieliński 1925, 148.
[2] Cf. Irigoin 1959, 72.
[3] Cf. Dale 1958, 103.
[4] Cf. Zieliński, 150 ff.
[5] Described by Zieliński as 'liquidarum liquidissima'.
[6] Zieliński, 160.
[7] Cf. Roussel 1954, 34.

No such requirements as (i) or (ii) apply to the two light syllables of the dactylic hexameter, and Dale is justified in her observation (1958, 102; cf. p. 98) that 'Nor has the "dactyl" or "anapaest" of an iambic trimeter anything to do with the metres properly called by those names'; similarly Parker (1968, 268): 'A "true" long, even if resolved, is still one element, and distinguishable...from the biceps of the dactyl and anapaest, which are genuinely ambiguous.' One must once again firmly reject any identification of the $\Sigma\Sigma$ of *weak* position in dactylic or anapaestic verse with the $\Sigma\Sigma$ of *strong* position in iambics and trochaics. We have already considered the possible bases of the equivalence $\Sigma\Sigma = \Sigma$ in weak position; we have now to consider the basis of the apparently similar but essentially dissimilar equivalence in strong position.

Disyllabic stress

Without further ado it may be said that the conditions of equivalence remind one forcibly of those which apply to the Latin 'disyllabic' accent and its reflexions in early Latin verse, and possibly to English and some other languages (see pp. 165 ff.). Unlike in Latin verse, there is in Greek only an equivalence of $\Sigma\Sigma$ to Σ and never of $\Sigma\Sigma$ to Σ (see pp. 179 ff.); and moreover, as we have seen, the second syllable must be as light as possible (with only limited admissibility of following plosive + liquid sequences). But this could simply reflect the lesser strength of the stress in Greek; and it may be further correlated with the fact that the separation between the two syllables, the 'interruption' of the stress pulse (see p. 198) must be limited (condition (iii) above).

If, on the basis of the evidence from verse, we are to attempt to extend the stress hypothesis in Greek to include the stressing of light syllables, it will clearly be appropriate to consider a succession of two light syllables, as in Latin, as a potential stress 'matrix'; and, again as in Latin, it will be useful to mark the monosyllabic and disyllabic stressed matrices as [$\hat{\Sigma}$] and [$\hat{\Sigma}\hat{\Sigma}$] respectively, to indicate the complex of peak + cadence.[1]

In a tribrach word ($\Sigma\Sigma\Sigma$) the two final syllables do *not* generally substitute for a heavy syllable in strong position. Such a word is not

---

[1] It would then be possible to state the restriction on the hypothesized stressing of pre-pausal light syllables (pp. 296 ff.) in the terms 'unless preceded by a stress matrix'; and to envisage (p. 298) a terminal stress pattern [$\sim\hat{\Sigma}\Sigma\hat{\Sigma}\hat{\Sigma}$] (cf. also pp. 323 f.). It follows that, whenever the restriction is satisfied (i.e. when a stress matrix does *not* precede), a pre-pausal light syllable will be stressed.

equivalent to one of type ΣΣ, since the latter may freely fill an iambic
foot but not (except in I) the former. We cannot therefore propose a
hypothesis that the stressing of tribrach words was [ΣΣ́Σ̀], and so
amend our earlier hypothesis of stress placement simply by changing
'heavy syllable' to 'potential stress matrix'; what the evidence of
verse composition rather suggests is [Σ́Σ̀Σ], since the normal placement
of such words is in iambics ΣΣ|Σ and in trochaics |ΣΣΣ|.

It seems improbable, however, that initiality would have anything
to do with the matter, since in the case of heavy syllables stress is
determined by reference to the *end* of the word. One is led, therefore,
provisionally to restate the hypothesis as follows: *If the final syllable
of a word is heavy, it is stressed; if the final is light, the next preceding
matrix is stressed* (whether monosyllabic or disyllabic). Thus [∼Σ̣́],
[∼Σ̣̀Σ], [∼Σ̣̀ΣΣ], [∼Σ́ΣΣ].

From this it follows that an anapaestic word would be stressed [ΣΣΣ̣́]
(as already assumed), and not [Σ̣́ΣΣ]. Resolutions in iambics are most
common in IIIb;[1] and since IVa is always light, tribrach words are
very common in this position[2] (e.g. in Eur., *Rh.* 444 συ μεν| γαρ
η||δη δεκα|τον αι||χμαзει|ς ετος). IIIa on the other hand may be, and
more often is, heavy; it might therefore be expected that when in such
cases there is a hephthemimeral caesura (at IIIa), IIb would not be
resolved; for it would involve an anapaestic word which, if it were to
produce metrical/dynamic agreement, would have to be stressed
[Σ̣́ΣΣ]. But in fact resolution *does* occur here, as e.g. θυσιαις in Eur.,
I.T. 384 αυτη| δε θυσι||αις η|δεται|| βροτοκ|τονοις. This, however,
raises no new problems, since, as we have seen (p. 313), spondaic
words are also common in this position, appearing to imply either a
stress-pattern [Σ̣́Σ] (perhaps by virtue of the principle of indifference
operating at the caesura) or a dynamic irregularity. The case of the

---

[1] Cf. Ceadel 1941, 73, 85.
[2] Whilst resolution in IV is also quite common, tribrach words are involved remarkably rarely. In Aeschylus and Sophocles (according to Schein's figures) resolutions
in III involving tribrach words total 221, as against 101 for words of type ΣΣΣΣ;
but in IV resolutions number 75 for words of type ΣΣΣΣ as against only 9 for
tribrach words. This may be a reflexion of the 'law of Wilamowitz and Knox' (cf.
Irigoin 1959, 76 ff.), which observes that in the iambographers a verse is not permitted to end with word-divisions located ∼,ΣΣ,ΣΣ or ∼,ΣΣ,ΣΣΣ. The rule is not
respected by the tragedians in the case of unresolved feet, but seems to be applied,
whatever may be the reason (cf. Irigoin, loc. cit.), where resolution is involved – in
effect only in the latter pattern, i.e. avoidance of ∼,ΣΣΣ,ΣΣΣ.

anapaestic words seems in fact to support the former rather than the latter interpretation. For, if the general basis of our hypothesis is correct, ΣΣ̱ may substitute for Σ̱ only by virtue of stressability in speech; there would thus be no justification for using an anapaestic word in resolution if it were stressed (as generally) [Σ́ΣΣ̱], with the ΣΣ̱ element unstressed; the explanation by 'indifference' would imply that in a pre-pausal sequence such as [Σ̀Σ̱,ΣΣΣ̱] the pre-terminal word pattern [Σ̀Σ̱] would, by the proposed alternation rule (p. 297), induce a terminal stressing [Σ́ΣΣ̱].

The same principle will also apply to anapaestic words preceding the central diaeresis (i.e. at IVb) in trochaics, as e.g. πατριδος in Eur., *Phoen.* 607 εξε|λαυνο‖μεσθα| πατριδος.‖ και γα|ρ ηλθε‖ις εξε|λων.[1]

If the formulation of our rules for the stressing of light syllables is correct, there is no reason why it should apply only to an initial di-syllabic matrix; it should, for example, equally well apply to words of the type [Σ́ΣΣΣ̱], with stress placing as shown. Whilst such forms occur much less commonly in verse than do simple tribrachs, they are located in accordance with the presumed stress, i.e. in iambics filling one foot and extending into the next, as |ΣΣΣ|Σ and not as ΣΣ|ΣΣ;[2] thus ετελεσε in Soph., *Tr.* 917 οπως| δ' ετελε‖σε του|τ' επεν‖θορου|σ' ανω; εγενετο in Eur., *Bacch.* 1275 τις ου|ν εν οι‖κοις παι|ς εγενε‖το σῳ| ποσει; Such resolutions are rare in early tragedy;[3] but this may well be related simply to the avoidance of proceleusmatic words; they become very common in the later plays of Euripides.[4] Here also one may include enclitic and proclitic combinations, as e.g. Aesch., *Ag.* 1590 ξενια͜| δε, Soph., *El.* 1361 πατερα͜| γαρ, Eur., *Ion* 931 τινα͜ λο|γον. There is similarly metrical support for a stress-pattern [Σ́ΣΣ̱], as Eur., *I.A.* 846 ψευδομε͜|θα, *Bacch.* 1342 ηθελε͜|τε, *Thes.* fr. 384.2 Nauck εγκεφα͜|λον, though the preference for penthemimeral caesura severely restricts their opportunity of occurrence, since they can occur (excluding I) only by filling III and extending into IV.[5]

By parallelism with the treatment of ΣΣ̱ and ΣΣΣ̱ (see pp. 313, 319) we might also expect to find words of type ΣΣΣΣ̱ preceding the

[1] Cf. Dale 1958, 103; Irigoin 1959, 74.
[2] The latter could normally only occur at end of line: but it does not (see p. 205), perhaps owing to restrictions on the operation of the principle of indifference (see pp. 297, 318) rather than to the present rule.
[3] Descroix, 159.   [4] Zieliński, 178.
[5] See also p. 323.

penthemimeral caesura, implying a (? pre-pausal) stress pattern [Σ̱Σ̱Σ̱Σ̱]; this expectation also is fulfilled, as e.g. γενομενων in Eur., *Tro.* 504 πολλων| γενομε||νων την| ταλαι||ναν ω|φελει.[1] At Eur., *Or.* 294 και νυ|ν ανακα||λυπτ᾽, ω| κασιγ||νητον| καρα the word-type results from elision, and Zieliński (195) comments 'non liquet'. It is, however, exactly parallel to the cases (admittedly anomalous and rather rare) where elision at the caesura is preceded by an unresolved (spondaic) sequence, as αμειβεσθ᾽.

If our hypotheses are correct, we shall expect, further, that the rules of secondary stressing would also apply to disyllabic matrices; specifically, that a preceding matrix will be stressed if separated from the matrix of the main stress. If we first consider only cases where either the main or the secondary stress (but not both) is disyllabic, it would then follow that possible patterns are

$$\text{(a)} \; [\sim \underset{\textstyle\smile}{\Sigma}\underset{\textstyle\smile}{\Sigma}\underset{\textstyle\smile}{\Sigma}\underset{\textstyle\smile}{\Sigma}(\Sigma)(\Sigma)] \qquad \text{(b)} \; [\sim \underset{\textstyle\smile}{\Sigma}\underset{\textstyle\smile}{\Sigma}\underset{\textstyle\smile}{\Sigma}\underset{\textstyle\smile}{\Sigma}\underset{\textstyle\smile}{\Sigma}]$$

We may now investigate whether these predicted patterns are in fact supported by the location of words in verse.

The pattern Σ̱Σ̱Σ̱Σ̱ is in fact extremely common in iambics (cf. p. 319 n.2) and (excluding the pre-caesural occurrences) is regularly located Σ̱Σ̱|Σ̱Σ̱, which would be in agreement with the predicted stress pattern [Σ̱Σ̱Σ̱Σ̱]. Words of this type may begin in III, IV, or (rarely) V.

Zieliński (148), in discussing Euripides' 'severior', states a 'lex de solutione initiali', viz. 'In omnibus pedibus praeter primum syllabae solutae vocabuli initium faciunt', and explains, 'Hoc est: legitimus ictus in vocabulis, qualia sunt θάλαμος, πολέμιος, est *thálamos, pólemios* non *thalámos, polémios*'. This is partly true as far as it goes, but is an oversimplification in terms of our hypothesis; for it applies to e.g. πολεμιος only to the extent that the final syllable is heavy, and so also stressed, the initial stress here being secondary (on the stressing of such a word when the final syllable is light, i.e. Σ̱Σ̱Σ̱, see p. 320).

Words of the more extended form Σ̱Σ̱Σ̱Σ̱Σ̱ are similarly located as Σ̱Σ̱|Σ̱Σ̱|Σ̱, supporting a predicted stress pattern [Σ̱Σ̱Σ̱Σ̱Σ̱], beginning in II or III.

The form Σ̱Σ̱Σ̱Σ̱, though uncommon except in proper names and in later Euripides,[2] does occur, inevitably located Σ̱Σ̱|Σ̱Σ̱, beginning in

---

[1] Zieliński, 178.   [2] Cf. Zieliński, 146, 157 f., 173.

IV, which supports a predicted stress pattern [ΣΣΣΣ̣]: e.g. Soph., *Ant.* 1209 περι‖βαινει| βοης, *Phil.* 932 ικε‖τευω,| τεκνον, *Tr.* 743 αγε‖νητον| ποιειν; Eur., *Alc.* 483 Διο‖μηδους| μετα, *Hcld.* 70 αγο‖ραιου| Διος, *El.* 12 βασι‖λευει| χθονος. The pattern also occurs in trochaics, as e.g. Eur., *Or.* 738 (line end) απεδω‖κεν μο|λων.

The more extended form ΣΣΣΣΣ can and does occur in iambics, beginning in II, as Eur., *I.T.* 314 φιλον| δε θερα‖πειαι|σιν αν‖δρ' ευερ|γετων, supporting a stress pattern [ΣΣ̣ΣΣΣ̣]; here also may occur words of form ΣΣΣΣ followed by a light enclitic, as Eur., *Hec.* 752 Αγαμεμ|νον, ικε‖τευω| σε ~ (also beginning in IV *Hec.* 276 ~ ικε‖τευω| τε σε, with additional enclitic); for trochaics cf. *Or.* 797 ως νι|ν ικετευ‖σω με| σωσαι‖ ~.

It is instructive to compare the location in iambic and trochaic verse of the word-form ΣΣΣ, which can only occur by resolution before caesura or diaeresis (since elsewhere, by our hypothesis, the stress would fall on the final syllable and there can be no secondary stress), with that of the form ΣΣΣΣ (where ΣΣ carries secondary stress, being separated from the stressed final syllable).[1]

Proceeding now to yet rarer word-forms one may cite ΣΣΣΣΣ, as Eur., *I.T.* 1371 ~| ξυναπο‖καμειν| μελη, with its location supporting a predictable stress pattern [ΣΣΣ̣ΣΣ̣]. An example at line-end would be provided, if correct, by Reiske's emendation of Eur., *Bacch.* 1067 ~‖ ελικο|δρομον (for ms ελκει δρομον).

The type ΣΣΣΣΣ may occur at Aesch., *Prom.* 213 ~| υπερε‖χοντας| κρατειν; this was emended by Porson to υπερσχοντας and by Hermann to υπερτερους; but its location ΣΣΣ|ΣΣ would in fact agree with a stress-pattern [ΣΣ̣ΣΣΣ̣] as predicted by our rules. Similar is the combination ~ |υπολα‖βοιμ' αν| (λογον) (LP υπολαβοιμεν) at Eur., *I.A.* 523,[2] which has been emended in various ways to effect a supposed 'rhythmic improvement' (thus Murray, Heimsoeth; cf. Wecklein).

The type ΣΣΣΣΣ is exemplified by Eur., *Hel.* 493 του καλ|λιδονα‖κος ει|σιν~, *Ion* 54 ~χρυ|σοφυλα‖κα του| θεου, located Σ|ΣΣΣ|Σ and thus supporting a predicted stress pattern [ΣΣ̣ΣΣΣ̣]. Before caesura, perhaps by the indifference principle, this pattern may be extended to words of type ΣΣΣΣΣ, as at Eur., *I.T.* 1284 ω να|οφυλα‖κες βω|μιοι‖ τ' επισ|τα̣ται.

---

[1] Cf. Irigoin 1959, 74.
[2] Described by Zieliński (192) as 'admodum memorabilis'.

The type ΣΣΣ̱Σ̱ is exemplified by Eur., *Hel.* 753 τι δη|τα μαν‖τευ-ομε|θα~, *Or.* 444 κυκλῳ| γαρ ει‖λισσομε|θα~, located Σ|ΣΣΣ|Σ̱ and thus supporting a predicted stress-pattern [Σ̱ΣΣ̱Σ̱]. One cannot, therefore, agree with Descroix in seeing these as 'énormités rythmiques' (87) or 'formes vicieuses' (175) or 'd'un galbe audacieux, pour ne pas dire suspect' (184).

If the text is correct at *Bacch.* 278 (ο δ' ηλ|θεν) επι‖ ταντιπα|λον~, the combination would support a predictable stress-pattern [Σ̱ΣΣ̱Σ̱Σ] (Housman επειτ' αντιπαλον), with disyllabic primary and secondary stresses.

We have already seen (p. 320) examples of the word-form ΣΣΣΣ located in such a way as to support the predicted stressing [ΣΣΣ̱Σ]. In most cases, however, a proclitic is also involved (e.g. *I.A.* 846 ου ψευδομεθα), so that they could be included under the type ΣΣΣΣΣ discussed above; and in a number of other cases such words are differently located;[1] thus especially in Aeschylus, e.g. *Eum.* 797 ~ μαρ‖τυρια| παρην, 107 ~ νη|φαλια‖ μειλιγ|ματα, 480 ~ αμ‖φοτερα| μενειν, *Sept.* 1022 ~ τυμ|βοχοα‖ χειρω|ματα, located Σ|ΣΣΣ|, which would seem to imply a stressing [Σ̱ΣΣ̱Σ]. For Sophocles cf. *O.C.* 42 ~ Ευ|μενιδα‖ς ο γ' εν|θαδ' ων (proper name), *Ant.* 418 ~ ου‖ρανιο|ν αχος, *El.* 326 ~ εν‖ταφια| χεροιν. In Euripides it does not occur in the 'severior' style, but is later revived:[2] e.g. *Hec.* 1240 ~ ταλ|λοτρια‖ κρινειν| κακα, *Hel.* 1404 ~ εν|ταφια‖ δουναι| νεκρῳ, *Bacch.* 674 ~ δει|νοτερα‖ βακχων| περι.

The conditions of occurrence in this location are of no small interest. It was observed by Seidler (1812, 385) that in nearly all such cases the two last short vowels are either in hiatus or separated only by ρ (a condition also general even in comedy); the type is in fact well exemplified by the ~ λη|κυθιο‖ν (απω|λεσεν) of *Ran.* 1208 ff. As rare exceptions may be cited Aesch., *Supp.* 388 ~ εγ‖γυτατα| γενους[3] (emended by H. Wolf to αγχιστοι), Eur., *El.* 13 ~ Τυν|δαριδα‖ κορη|ν εχων (cf. *El.* 806), *I.A.* 49 ~ Θεσ|τιαδι‖ τρεις παρ|θενοι (proper names). In Eur., *Phoen.* 79 ~ επ|ταπυλα‖ τειχη| ταδε, *I.A.* 1270 ~ βου|λομενο‖ν ελη|λυθα the separation is by a liquid or nasal.

It thus appears that the condition for a stressing [Σ̱ΣΣ̱Σ] is that the

---

[1] Descroix, 162.   [2] Zieliński, 159 f; but not in V (Descroix, 163).
[3] Note, however, that this form involves the repetition of identical syllables.

separation between the last two short vowels must be minimal (i.e. nil or a consonant of weakest stricture), or, as we might alternatively express it, where we have an 'interrupted' stress-pulse with minimal interruption.[1] Such a 'disyllabic' stress matrix would be particularly similar to a heavy monosyllabic matrix, and this could account for its acceptability in final position, since words of this type would then be closely comparable with those of type [Σ̣Σ̣Σ̣]. Whether the initial heavy syllable is also a condition for this stress-pattern it is not immediately possible to determine, since metrically a word of type Σ̣Σ̣Σ̣Σ̣ cannot in any case be located Σ̣|Σ̣Σ̣Σ̣, but only |Σ̣Σ̣Σ̣|Σ̣ (see, however, p. 326).

In trochaics this treatment of the form Σ̣Σ̣Σ̣Σ̣ occurs at II–III, as Archil., 74.2 ουδε| θαυμα‖σιον~ ; but as other special features also characterize this position (see p. 328), the case is of less consequence.[2] Of greater interest as providing a parallel to iambics would be the trochaic line cited from Hermippus: ες το| Κυλικρα‖νων βα|διζων‖ σπληνο|πεδον α‖φικο|μην. On this Dale (1958, 105) comments: 'Whatever word σπληνόπεδον is corrupted from (σφηνόπεδον is plausibly suggested), the shape appears to break the metron in a form which Hermippus evidently transferred from his comic technique.' Here the intervocalic plosive δ certainly makes one dubious about a stress-pattern [Σ̣Σ̣Σ̣Σ̣] as suggested by its location; but no such objection applies to Aesch., *Pers.* 171 ~‖ γηρα|λεα πισ‖τωμα|τα, which is entirely comparable with e.g. the τυμβοχοα χειρωματα of iambic *Sept.* 1022, and there is no need to assume (as Dale) that 'synizesis' here operates (i.e. that Σ̣Σ̣Σ̣Σ̣ → Σ̣Σ̣Σ̣).

Words long enough to involve tertiary as well as secondary stressing, though not very common, are sufficiently well attested even in tragedy: e.g. Aesch., *Sept.* 19 ~ασ‖πιδη|φορους, agreeing inevitably with a stress-pattern [Σ̣Σ̣Σ̣Σ̣Σ̣];[3] similarly Soph., *El.* 13 ~καξεθρεψαμην, Eur., *Hec.* 882 ~τιμωρησομαι [Σ̣Σ̣Σ̣Σ̣Σ̣]; even quaternary stress is implied by Soph., *El.* 1002 ~εξαπαλλαχθησεται (Σ̣Σ̣Σ̣Σ̣Σ̣Σ̣). Such cases involving disyllabic stress are, however, rare; one may cite Eur., *Hel.* 906 ~αναπληρουμενους for a pattern [Σ̣Σ̣Σ̣Σ̣Σ̣Σ̣]; a pattern

---

[1] For such special conditions governing 'disyllabic' stressing one may compare the situation in Tübatulabal (Voegelin 1935, 76), where 'two short vowels of the same phoneme which are separated by a glottal stop are treated in alternation of stress as a single accentual unit'.

[2] Cf. in I–II Aesch., *Pers.* 720 αμφοτερα~ (Dale 1958, 105).

[3] Whether by general or pre-pausal rules.

[Σ̱Σ̱Σ̱Σ̱Σ̱] is implied in a lyric trimeter by Aesch., *Cho.* 426 επασσυ-
τεροτριβη~. Extended patterns may also be provided as a result of
the combination of proclitic and main word; a particularly interesting
case is Eur., *Cycl.* 681 ~ποτε‖ρας τῆς‖ χερος, where the 'breach'
of Porson's Law can be related to a proclitic value of the interrogative
adjective; so that the whole cadence would be treated as a single
phonological unit, supporting a predictable stress-pattern [Σ̇Σ̱Σ̇Σ̱Σ̱],
just as αναπληρουμενους.

The various restrictions on the occurrence of resolution in tragedy
might be seen as suggesting that disyllabic stress was in general less
clearly defined in contrast with its environment than was the monosyllabic stress of heavy syllables. On this particular matter it is hardly
possible to adduce evidence from hexameters. For a word of the form
ΣΣΣ can there only occur in elision (cf. p. 294), as e.g. επε(α), where it
is effectively a disyllable and so would involve no internal contrast of
stress. Words of form ΣΣΣΣ do occur there, and it has been argued that
their stress-patterning was [Σ̇Σ̱Σ̇Σ̱]; but since (except at line-end by
the principle of indifference) such words in any case involve metrical/
dynamic conflict in hexameters (see pp. 289 ff.), we can draw no conclusions from them about the relative strength of the disyllabic secondary
stress.

It will have been evident, as is well known, that Euripides shows a
progressive increase in the use of resolutions, both as regards number
and type; and it would be easy to see this as simply an increasing
'licence'. The fact remains, however, that if we set up a hypothesis of
stress sufficiently general to explain the locational preferences of
Aeschylus, Sophocles, and Euripides' 'severior', it will also predict
certain patterns which are not actually found there – but which *are*
found in Euripides' 'freer' styles. It may be, therefore, that at least
part of the extension of resolution in these styles is not in fact to be
attributed to increasing 'licence', but rather to an increasing awareness
by Euripides of the less obvious dynamic patterns of Greek speech
and a recognition of their potentialities for verse. It could be, for
example, that to appreciate the prominence of the disyllabic stress in a
pattern [Σ̇Σ̱Σ̱] or [ΣΣ̇Σ̱], where a heavy syllable follows or precedes,
would require a more 'delicate' ear than in the case of a pattern [Σ̇Σ̱Σ]
or [Σ̇Σ̱Σ̱].

LUTHER SEMINARY LIBRARY
2375 COMO AVENUE WEST
ST. PAUL, MINNESOTA 55108

In this connexion we may now also consider the relatively rare cases where a tribrach word is so located (in other than I) as to coincide with an iambic foot, and so, if it were stressed as [$\acute{\Sigma}\acute{\Sigma}\Sigma$] (as previously established), would involve metrical/dynamic conflict. Examples are Aesch., *Pers.* 332 ~και| λιγεα‖ κωκυ|ματα, *Ag.* 1590 αυτου.| ξενια‖ δε~, *Cho.* 1 Ερμη| χθονιε‖~ (but 124 ~Ερ‖μη χθονι|ε~ with 'normal' location $\Sigma\Sigma|\Sigma$); Soph., *Aj.* 459 ~και‖ πεδια| ταδε, *O.T.* 826 ~και| πατερα‖ κατακ|τανειν, 1496 ~τον‖ πατερα| πατηρ, *El.* 1361 ~‖ πατερα| γαρ ει‖σοραν| δοκω; Eur., *Med.* 505 ~ων| πατερα‖ κατεκ|τανον, 375 θησω,| πατερα‖ τε~, *I.T.* 566 ~χαρι|ν αχαρι‖ν απω|λετο, 385 ουκ εσ|θ' οπω‖ς ετεκε|ν αν~, *Or.* 244 ~και| χαριτα‖ς εχων| πατρος, 487 ~μη| προτερο|ν ειναι| θελειν, *I.A.* 1593 ~| ελαφο‖ν ορει|δρομον, *Bacch.* 731 ~ω| δρομαδε‖ς εμαι| κυνες, 18 κειται,| μιγασι‖ν Ελλη|σι~, 662 λευκης| χιονο‖ς ανει|σαν~, and a very few other cases.

These occurrences are, however, mitigated, except in the later plays of Euripides, by two circumstances. First, just as in words of form $\Sigma|\Sigma\Sigma\Sigma$, when located as indicated, there is generally minimal separation between the last two vowels, viz. zero or ρ; at Soph., *O.T.* 719 ~ει‖ς αβατο|ν ορος, where a plosive intervenes, Jebb suggests (though not for this precise reason) that there is a deliberate intention to suggest 'ruggedness'. And secondly, in the large majority of cases there is either a proclitic or an enclitic (in the wide sense of these terms) which effectively creates a word of form $\Sigma|\Sigma\Sigma\Sigma$ or $\Sigma\Sigma\Sigma|\Sigma$ respectively, located as indicated; and since such forms are stressable as [$\Sigma\acute{\Sigma}\Sigma\Sigma$], [$\Sigma\acute{\Sigma}\acute{\Sigma}\Sigma$],[1] there would be agreement of stress with strong position. Moreover, it may not be fortuitous that even in later Euripides, in cases where these circumstances do not apply, the tribrach word ends in a consonant, which means that its light quantity depends on continuity of utterance with the following word (cf. p. 116).

Since [$\acute{\Sigma}\acute{\Sigma}\acute{\Sigma}\Sigma$] seems to have been an admissible alternative to [$\Sigma\acute{\Sigma}\acute{\Sigma}\Sigma$], but [$\Sigma\acute{\Sigma}\acute{\Sigma}$] is relatively rarely implied as an alternative to [$\acute{\Sigma}\acute{\Sigma}\Sigma$]; and since [$\Sigma\acute{\Sigma}\acute{\Sigma}$] is more common when preceded by a proclitic, it may be that in the case of the stressing [$\acute{\Sigma}\acute{\Sigma}\acute{\Sigma}\Sigma$] the first syllable is a relevant factor (cf. p. 324).

[1] At e.g. Soph., *Phil.* 1235 προς θεων| ποτερα‖ δη~, Eur., *Ion* 968 σε και| πατερα‖ σον δ'~ the combined pattern is $\Sigma\Sigma\Sigma|\Sigma$, but since it occurs before the caesura it might be stressable, by the indifference principle, in the same way as $\Sigma\Sigma\Sigma\Sigma$.

LUTHER SEMINARY LIBRARY
2375 COMO AVENUE WEST
ST. PAUL, MINNESOTA 55108

The later 'neglect' by Euripides of the conditions under which tribrach words may occupy a foot may indeed represent a 'licence'; but it could also reflect a development in the language whereby the final disyllabic matrix, at least in continuous utterance, became more generally equivalent to the monosyllabic as regards its capacity for stress, and not simply under the special conditions which had regulated it earlier. In formulaic terms the conditions for optional final stress would then be simplified from $\Sigma\Sigma(C)\breve{V}(\rho)\breve{V}$ to $\Sigma\Sigma\Sigma$, with elimination of the requirements of a preantepenultimate heavy syllable and of minimal intervocalic interruption.

First feet

The situation regarding tribrach words is reversed in the first feet of iambics, even in the earlier poetry. Their 'normal' location here is coincident with the foot, as e.g. πατερα|, ποτερο|ν ~ .[1] Even though a proclitic be involved, the location $\Sigma,\Sigma\Sigma|\Sigma$ ~ (e.g. α δ' ελαβες) is distinctly abnormal except in later Euripides; and the placing of a proceleusmatic as προσεδοσαν $\Sigma\Sigma\Sigma|\Sigma$ (elsewhere normal) is here quite rare. Zieliński's comment (144) is as follows: 'Velut πατέρα vocabulum, cum in ceteris sedibus primâ percussâ pronuntietur (*pátera*), in nostram non venit nisi percussâ secundâ (*patéra*). Non est haec exceptio, sed adversa lex ex ipsius loci natura ducta.' Certainly one can hardly consider this treatment a licence, i.e. as simply admitting occasional metrical/dynamic conflict in the first foot, since it appears as a very definite preference. One could conceivably frame a hypothesis that a stress-pattern [$\Sigma\acute{\Sigma}\acute{\Sigma}$] was encouraged by sentence-initial position, as it was also by a preceding heavy syllable (p. 324), and so would be appropriate at the beginning of the line; one might recall the observation by Mitchell on Arabic (see p. 165 n.) that preceding word-boundary has the same function as preceding heavy syllable – i.e. ποτερον ~ [#$\Sigma\acute{\Sigma}\acute{\Sigma}$] as αμφοτερα [$\acute{\Sigma}\Sigma\acute{\Sigma}\acute{\Sigma}$]. But the avoidance of the pattern [$\Sigma,\Sigma\acute{\Sigma}\acute{\Sigma}$] or [$\Sigma\acute{\Sigma}\acute{\Sigma}\acute{\Sigma}$] is still difficult to understand. Two peculiarities may just be mentioned. The rule of 'minimal separation' again generally applies, as already noted for this position by Müller (cf. Zieliński, 145). The other peculiarity relates to the trochaic tetrameter.

As in iambics the 'normal' location of a tribrach word in other than the first foot is $\Sigma\Sigma|\Sigma$, so in trochaics it is $|\Sigma\Sigma\Sigma|$ (cf. p. 317). But Dale (1958, 104 n.1) observes that there is one (and only one) position where

[1] Zieliński, 144; Descroix, 158.

'resolution ends a word overlapping from a previous metron', viz. between the 1st and 2nd metra, as Eur., *H.F.* 863 οι' ε|γω στα‖δια∼, showing a location Σ‖ΣΣ, with the two final syllables coinciding with strong position. It is of interest, even if its specific relevance is not apparent, to remember that the iambic trimeter is equivalent to a trochaic tetrameter catalectic minus its initial cretic (ΣΣΣ): cf. p. 314. And if the cretic is subtracted from a trochaic beginning such as οι' εγω σταδια∼, the result is an iambic line beginning σταδια∼, which is precisely the preferred type of initial resolution in iambics: and vice versa. It seems possible, therefore, that the iambic and trochaic peculiarities may have the same solution – but what that solution is it would be hazardous to speculate further. The identical nature of the peculiarity in the two cases seems also to suggest that the relationship between the tetrameter and the trimeter may be more than merely analytical.

The case of a dactyl in the first foot of iambics is quite different. For here, especially in earlier tragedy, it is *not* normally formed by a single word coinciding with the foot, as e.g. μητερα. In Aeschylus a dactyl of any form is rare,[1] and continues to be rare in Sophocles, with the exception of the *Philoctetes*, which contains 12; these, however, mostly involve either longer words such as ουδεποτε, ξυλλαβετον, for which a stress-pattern ΣΣΣΣ is probable, or similar proclitic combinations, as ος πατερα, και νεμεσις. Similar considerations apply to the earlier plays of Euripides; there are no first-foot dactyls in the *Medea* or *Heraclidae* and only 1 in the *Alcestis*; in the *Hippolytus* there are 11 – but all of these involve the name Ιππολυτος (cf. Zieliński, 145: 'quo carere tragoedia nostra nullo modo poterat'); and in the 'semi-severus' style dactyls are generally accounted for by proper names, by longer words such as ημετερον, or combinations with a monosyllabic proclitic, as ω θυγατερ (cf. Zieliński, 156 f.); here also one could include such other combinations as πως ο θεος (Eur., *Ion* 365), ουδε παθος (*Or.* 2), ωστε δια τουτον (*Bacch.* 285), και καθ' οδον (*Or.* 550).

It is not the case that a quantitative 'dactyl' necessarily implies a falling dynamic pattern. This has already been suggested for III, where the caesura may result in the preceding heavy word-final syllable being unstressed by the principle of indifference, whilst the initial disyllable of a following word of form ΣΣΣ(Σ) is stressed – thus produc-

---

[1] Descroix, 170.

ing a pattern [$\Sigma\dot{\Sigma}\dot{\Sigma}$] for this foot. And, as we have now seen, the same may apply for different reasons to I. As Descroix observes (175), 'C'est un leurre et une hérésie de parler du mouvement descendant d'un dactyle sans tenir compte des termes qui le composent, de la ou des fins de mots qui l'intéressent'; and what applies to the dactyl in iambics, would apply also to the anapaest in trochaics (cf. the comments of Dale and Parker cited on p. 318).[1] It is not only, as we have seen, word-*divisions* that are relevant to this question (as in III), but also word-*patterns*; so that we should not even agree with Descroix (174 f.) when he comments on Eur., *Andr.* 1157 εξεβαλον εκτος θυοδοκων ανακτορων ($\Sigma\Sigma\Sigma|\Sigma,\Sigma\|\Sigma{:}\Sigma\Sigma|\Sigma\Sigma,\|\Sigma\Sigma|\Sigma\Sigma$) that, whilst the dactyl in III has (as we agree) a rising rhythm, the dactyl in I has a falling rhythm.

Only in cases such as Eur., *Supp.* 93 μητερα has the first foot probably a falling dynamic pattern, which will account for its avoidance in earlier tragedy. The same will apply to such proclitic and enclitic combinations as αυτο‿δε (*I.A.* 1142), ει‿δε‿τι (498), χρη‿δε‿σε (1623), μη‿συ‿γε (*Ion* 1335; *Bacch.* 951). It is even more certain where there is a clear word-division between the two light syllables of the resolution, which could not possibly form a unitary stress-matrix in normal speech;[2] such resolutions are indeed found in comedy, where so many metrical restrictions are relaxed, as e.g. *Ach.* 602 τους‿μεν επι~, *Eq.* 23 αυτο φαθι~, *Eccl.* 795 ταυτα καταθειην~; but even here it is noticeable that in a high proportion of such cases the first word is a pronoun, negative, conjunction, or common adverb – i.e. words of categories which we have earlier seen to be subject to special dispensations – as Descroix comments (188), 'comme si leur qualité leur conférait des droits'.

In view of the relative metrical freedom of comedy we decided not to use it as a basis for establishing hypotheses regarding linguistic stress-patterns. But general tendencies observed in tragedy, though much more frequently departed from, are still clearly detectable. For example, where iambic feet are resolved into tribrachs in Aristophanes, they contain in a slight majority of cases a word-division of the type $|\Sigma,\Sigma\Sigma|(\Sigma)$ as normal in tragedy (1,459 out of 2,654 tribrachs); in 857 cases the tribrach is formed by or comprised within a single word, i.e.

[1] Similarly Irigoin 1959, 70; and cf. p. 98 n.
[2] On 'split resolution' in dramatic lyric see Parker 1968.

(Σ)|ΣΣΣ|(Σ); only 338 are divided as |ΣΣ,Σ| or |Σ,Σ,Σ|, and most of these cases involve close combinations with proclitics or enclitics.[1] Dactylic resolved feet are divided as |Σ,ΣΣ| in 1,004 out of 1,470 cases; in 183 cases the dactyl is formed by or comprised within a single word, i.e. (Σ)|ΣΣΣ|(Σ), but in only 2 of these cases is a word of type ΣΣΣΣ involved, and in 137 the word extends forward beyond the foot. Of 53 examples of the division |ΣΣ,Σ|, 48 are in the first foot.

Anapaestic substitution

We have yet to consider the occurrence of anapaestic feet in the iambic trimeter. In tragedy, Aeschylus all but confines this variant to I, at first predominantly in proper names, but then also in other words, especially in the *Prometheus* (e.g. 89 ποταμων~, 722 κορυφας~, 994 χθονιοις~); in a few cases the word so located could not otherwise be employed (e.g. *Supp.* 713 ικεταδοκου~). In Sophocles the use of anapaests is extended, and, whilst it is still most prevalent in I, it appears also in III and V (though only in proper names) – and, most significantly for our interpretation of the variant, in IV, whilst Euripides further extends it to II: e.g. *Ion* 21 Εριχθονιου~ (cf. 268, 1429), *Hel.* 88 Τελαμων, Σαλαμις δε~, *I.T.* 771 ʒωσ' Ιφιγενεια~; and with other than proper names in the *Cyclops*, e.g. 562 ιδου, καθαρον~, 260 επει κατεληφθη ~.

The anapaest is sometimes considered as an example of resolution (e.g. Maas, 67), i.e. as a substitute for the spondee, with the two light syllables replacing the heavy 'anceps' in the weak position. Such an interpretation would of course be in conflict with our hypothesis that resolution is based on linguistic stress, more specifically on agreement between such stress and *strong* position. However, quite apart from the relative uncommonness of the anapaest in tragedy, as compared with other types of resolved feet, this interpretation is disproved by the fact that the anapaest can occur in the even as well as the odd feet, where a spondee can *not* occur. In other words, the anapaest may be considered an alternative for the iambus, and the ΣΣ not as a 'resolution' of Σ, but as a substitution for Σ (on this see especially Descroix, 194 ff.). In fact, one should perhaps rather envisage the anapaest as a single metrical unit in its substitution for the iambus;[2] it is notable that in trochaics the expected parallel, viz. the dactyl, is excessively rare,

---

[1] Cf. White 1912, 40 f; Maas, 69.
[2] Cf. Descroix, 215.

even in comedy[1] – which suggests that it is not simply a matter of $\Sigma\Sigma$ substituting for Σ, but specifically of $\Sigma\Sigma\Sigma$ substituting for $\Sigma\Sigma$.

In comedy the use of the anapaest is yet further extended, becoming almost as common as tribrachs and dactyls combined, and with the even (II and IV) occurrences only less common than in I[2] – indeed in Aristophanes the anapaest in II is more common than in I; and this in spite of the fact that not even in comedy is a spondee admitted to the even feet.[3] This extension of the anapaest in comedy may perhaps be seen as reflecting a closer approach to the dynamics of natural speech by admitting a greater variety of rising patterns. But in an important respect comedy tends in principle to follow tragedy in its use of the anapaest. There is a general rule that the anapaest may not be 'split' – i.e. that a word-division should not occur after either of the light syllables.[4] This rule might perhaps be interpreted in terms of tempo, as requiring that, in order for an anapaest to be substituted for an iambus, the sequence must be uttered with minimal transitional delay between syllables such as might be occasioned, or suggested, by grammatical boundaries. It is notable that in tragedy, as in the case of resolution, there is also a strong tendency to require that the vowels of the anapaest should not be separated by more than a single consonant; only in Euripides' later plays is the complex plosive + liquid admitted here, and then (except for 2 cases in the *Bacchae*) only the combination voiceless plosive + ρ—a similar restriction to that of resolution, but one which, as Zieliński observes (203), is maintained up to a later period in the case of anapaests. This restriction would fit in well with a desire to ensure the most rapid possible syllabic transitions in the anapaest.[5]

Exceptions to the 'law of the split anapaest' are provided, even in tragedy, by combinations involving proclitics: e.g. Soph., *Phil.* 795 τον ισον~, Eur., *Bacch.* 502 παρ᾽ εμοι~, *Alc.* 375 επι τοισδε~,[6] which in effect constitute a single word. There is a considerable increase

---

[1] Cf. Perusino 1962, 51 ff; Strzelecki 1965, 61 ff.
[2] Cf. Descroix, 201.
[3] For allegedly possible rare exceptions in Menander see Cataudella 1968.
[4] See e.g. Lindsay 1922, 88; Descroix, 210 ff; Maas, 69.
[5] Cf. Descroix, 215. In a study of the choliambics of Herodas, Witkowski (1893, 6) further observes that for anapaests the poet particularly selects words in which one of the transitions consists of zero or the single consonant ρ, 'ut in efferendo anapaestus facile fluat'. But the number of cases there involved is perhaps too low to be statistically significant.
[6] Descroix, 211.

in apparent exceptions in comedy, but here again we encounter much the same categories of words (though of different quantitative patterns) as were cited in connexion with Porson's and Naeke's laws (pp. 307, 287) – including words which, whilst not generally recognized as proclitics, seem to cohere particularly closely with a following word and so to minimize the boundary between them – pronouns, conjunctions (e.g. οτε, αλλα), common adverbs (e.g. παλιν, ταχα, τοτε), 'formal imperatives' (e.g. λαβε, ιθι – especially followed by 'enclitic' δη, νυν), oaths (as e.g. *Plut.* 877 νη τον| Δια τον|| σωτη|ρα∼), numerals (as e.g. *Ach.* 6 τοις πεν|τε ταλαν||τοις∼), and negatives (e.g. ουδεν, μητε): see especially White 1912, 45 f; Descroix, 217 ff; Sobolevskij 1956; 1964. As in the case of Porson's Law, postpositive ('enclitic') function also plays some part, as e.g. *Pax* 203 ∼ τινος ουνεκα, *Lys.* 869 χαριν ου-δεμιαν∼ (for precise iambic parallels see p. 310); and elision is apparently relevant in some cases.[1] In fact the vast majority of 'exceptions' to the law fall into one or other of these categories, and so do not effectively disrupt the rapidity of movement; and after a study of such cases Sobolevskij concludes (1964, 44) that the reason for the 'split anapaest' rule is 'nihil aliud, nisi celeritas anapaesti pronuntiandi, ut inter eius partes nulla mora interponi queat, ne tantula quidem, quanta inter duo vocabula, inter se non cohaerentia, solet esse'.

No such rule, however, applies to the anapaests of anapaestic (as opposed to iambic) verse; for here, as in dactylic verse, the two light syllables of weak position represent neither a resolution nor a substitution – but the basis of the metre; and their contraction into a single heavy syllable is parallel to that of dactylics (see pp. 255 ff.).

Resolution of the strong position in dactylics is extremely rare; it does not appear to follow the rules for resolution in iambics and trochaics, and may be viewed as a simple first-foot licence. Thus perhaps Hesiod, *Op.* 436 δρυος ελυμα∼ (on which, however, see Wilamowitz's note); Homer, *Il.* ix 5, xxiii 195 Βορεης∼/Βορεη∼, on which the scholiast on Hephaestion (323 C) comments: ἔχουσι τοὺς πρώτους πόδας τετραχρόνους ἰσοδυναμοῦντας τῷ δακτύλῳ[2] – but which may have been pronounced as a spondee.[3] For rare cases in lyric dactylics see Dale 1968, 25 n.2.

In anapaestic metres, on the other hand, the substitution of two

---

[1] Cf. Maas, 88.   [2] Cf. Maas 1957.
[3] Cf. Wyatt 1969, 221.

light syllables for the heavy in strong position is more generally admitted, with resulting dactylic feet (and sometimes in lyric proceleusmatic). There appear to be no rules governing word-division in such cases, and probably one should not consider this as on the same footing with the resolutions of iambics or trochaics. The dynamic pattern here in fact may depend not so much on inherent linguistic factors as on a superimposed time and beat. In the case of lyric, music would of course provide these elements; but even in the case of recitative dimeter systems Dale points out (1968, 47 ff.) that they may in origin have been accompanied by a marching rhythm: 'The tramp of soldiers' feet then gives us the normal anapaestic tempo..., i.e. an even stress with no "arsis" and "thesis" of feet... and an exact equivalence of one long or two shorts...The even time-relation of – = ∪∪ would differentiate the rhythm from the dactylic as given by Dionysius' (cf. p. 255). It should, however, be noted that the dactylic substitution in such systems in tragedy is almost entirely confined to the first foot of the metron; the second foot is either an anapaest or a spondee; and since there is normally diaeresis between the metra, each metron will end with a heavy word-final syllable, which, by our hypothesis, will ensure that it ends in a *linguistically* rising dynamic pattern. An apparent regard for such pattern in the final, catalectic line of such systems has already been discussed (p. 316).

SUMMARY OF STRESS RULES

We may conclude by summarizing the main hypothetical stress-rules for classical Greek as suggested by the metrical evidence considered in the foregoing pages:

General

1. A stress-matrix is constituted by (a) one heavy, or (b) two light syllables.[1]
2. Words (or word-like sequences) longer than a matrix have internal contrasts of stress/non-stress.

Primary stress

3. If the final syllable is heavy, it is stressed.
4. If the final syllable is light, the next preceding matrix is stressed; except that in words of form $\Sigma\Sigma\underset{\smile}{\Sigma}\underset{\smile}{\Sigma}$ the final disyllabic matrix may be stressed.[2]

---

[1] In which the nuclei are not normally separated by more than one consonant. For an alternative analysis cf. pp. 198, 327.

[2] If the separation between the nuclei is minimal (generally zero or ρ).

Secondary stress

5. A matrix preceding and separated[1] from the primary stress is stressed.

Terminal stress

6. In terminal (pre-pausal) words, rules 3–5 are neutralized and the following substituted:

  (a) Rule 5 applies progressively from the primary stress of the preceding word;
  (b) Final $\sum_{\sim}$ is stressed by this rule unless preceded by a matrix.[2]

It will have been noted that the location of stress by this hypothesis bears no relation to that of the *modern* Greek stress, which preserves the location of the peak of the ancient *melodic* accent – thus e.g. classical ἕτοιμα, hypothetically stressed [hetôima], modern /étima/; classical βλέπω, hypothetically stressed [blepôo], modern /vlépo/. This is not necessarily an argument against the hypothesis, since the presumed classical stresses are non-accentual and are likely to have been weaker than the accentual stresses of, say, Latin or English or modern Greek. With the advent of stress as an accentual feature, therefore, the 'low-level' stresses could simply have been suppressed. It may, however, be worth recalling that in an earlier discussion (pp. 262 ff.) it was found that falling pitch tended to occur on certain syllables of words, and that these syllables were such as tended to occur in strong positions in verse; so that there could have been some statistical correlation between falling pitch and stress. Moreover, the syllables in question tended to be those for which stress is predicted by the present hypothesis. There is thus the possibility of a statistical, though only indirectly causal, relationship between the hypothetical stress and the classical accent; and in the cases where such a correlation applied, the transition from the classical to the modern accentual system may then have been as outlined on p. 269.

[1] I.e. by $\sum$ (which is not a matrix) or by $\sum_{\sim}$ or $\sum\sum$ (which, though matrices, are not separated from the primary stress and so are not themselves stressable).
[2] For a possible exception to this restriction see p. 299.

Appendix. The Latin hexameter

From the evidence presented in the last chapter it seems probable that the quantitative metrical patterns of formal, spoken Greek verse were if anything supported by the patterns of linguistic stress. In the earlier Latin adoptions of Greek metres various modifications had been introduced to accommodate the accentual and quantitative patternings of the Latin language (see pp. 153 f.); in particular one may note the extension of spondaic feet and of patterns of resolution in iambic and trochaic metres.

At the compositional level, Porson's Law, for example, was irrelevant, since a final syllable of a Latin word, whether light *or* heavy, was normally unstressed and so would not conflict with the requirements of weak position. On the other hand the Latin iambic senarius, which admits spondees (and anapaests) to II and IV, tends to keep them iambic if the end of the foot coincides with word-end. For a spondaic or anapaestic word-ending would involve an accentual stress in the initial (weak) part of the foot, i.e. $\sim|\acute{\Sigma}\Sigma,|$ or $\sim|\acute{\Sigma}\Sigma\Sigma,|$ as against e.g. $\sim\acute{\Sigma}|\Sigma\Sigma,|$.[1] Similarly the trochaic septenarius admits spondees in I, III, and V – but tends to keep them trochaic if there is a word-division inside the following foot; for such a division would involve an accentual stress in the latter part of a spondaic foot, i.e. $|\Sigma\acute{\Sigma}|\Sigma, \sim$ as against $|\acute{\Sigma}\Sigma|\Sigma \sim$. These tendencies Perret (1960) has aptly referred to as 'a Latin equivalent of Porson's Law'.

In later Latin scenic poetry, however, one finds what appears to be a direct imitation of Porson's Law. In the iambic trimeters of Seneca, V is rarely other than a spondee (in which respect the author may be following the prescriptions of metricians on what constitutes a tragic line);[2] and Strzelecki (1938, 16 ff.) has shown that, if there is a word-division inside this foot, the word following the division rarely begins with a consonant unless a monosyllable precedes. On the other hand,

---

[1] Cf. also pp. 186 ff.
[2] E.g. Diomedes, i, 507 K: 'Iambicus tragicus. hic, ut grauior iuxta materiae pondus esset, semper quinto loco spondeum recipit. aliter enim esse non potest tragicus.'

words beginning with a vowel are admitted if the preceding word ends
with a vowel or *m*, in which case there will of course be elision. A similar
tendency has been observed in Horace. These restrictions are quite
irrelevant to Latin, as the republican material shows; and Maas (1966,
95) may be right in concluding that some at least of the Greek metricians
had already observed the conditions of Porson's Law, and that it is their
prescriptions that these later Latin writers are following.

The principle of 'indifference' is in general applicable to Latin
verse. In part it no doubt represents a simple adoption of Greek practice;
but it can hardly have the same linguistic basis as in Greek, whatever
this may have been (cf. pp. 296 ff.). Since final syllables in Latin were
in any case normally unstressed, they would involve no metrical/
dynamic conflict in the hexameter ending regardless of their quantity.
In the pentameter it seems that the principle tended not to operate,
and that composition proceeded on the basis of Latin syntactical stress-
rules (p. 187); in choliambics the principle, which tended not to
operate in Greek, was applicable in Latin (for reasons discussed on
p. 300). In iambics (see 187 n.3) the situation remains doubtful. The
principle does, of course, in any case represent an overriding of purely
quantitative by probably dynamic criteria, and so might have been
particularly attractive to Latin (cf. pp. 339 ff.).

With the adoption of the dactylic hexameter by Ennius and later
poets, Greek metrical models were more closely adhered to than in
early scenic verse. The equivalence of Σ to $\Sigma\Sigma$ in weak position probably had no basis in Latin phonology (see pp. 163 ff., 255 ff.). And
problems arose for composition more particularly from the different
accentual conditions of Latin.

To some extent, even in the hexameter, these differences are simply
reflected in composition. Thus, on the one hand, the tendencies of
'Naeke's Law' (pp. 286 ff.) are ignored in the Latin hexameter. In
Theocritus' Idylls, for example, it has been noted that there is a strong
preference for diaeresis at IV to be preceded by a dactyl rather than a
spondee – a type of line which there occurs in about 75% of cases. In
Vergil, however, even in the Eclogues, spondees are rather more
numerous than dactyls in this context. The contrast between the two
authors was already noted in antiquity by Terentianus Maurus (vi,
389 K): 'plurimus hoc pollet Siculae telluris alumnus...noster rarus
eo pastor Maro', and by Atilius Fortunatianus (vi, 292 K): 'Theocritus hanc metri legem custodiuit, Virgilius contempsit.' The reason

for the compositional difference seems clear; the restriction regarding the 'bucolic diaeresis' is not relevant to Latin, because it makes no difference to the relationship between Latin (accentual) stress and metrical strong position whether a word at this point ends with a dactyl (as e.g. ~ | *dulciạ*| *linquimus arua*) or a spondee (as e.g. ~ *ton*|*dẹnti*| *barba cadebat*) – the accent will in either case fall on IVa (|*dúlcia*|, *ton*|*dénti*|) and so will coincide with the strong position.

In another position, on the other hand, Latin introduces restrictions which were not relevant to Greek. In Homer, as a mere consequence of statistical probability, the final word of the line is commonly of two or three syllables (cf. p. 281) – in slightly less than 75% of cases. In the last two feet of the Latin hexameter, if one excludes monosyllabic and pyrrhic words, such a circumstance would result in agreement between accent and strong position, thus either ~ $\acute{\Sigma}\Sigma,\acute{\Sigma}\Sigma$ or ~ $\acute{\Sigma}\Sigma,\acute{\Sigma}\underline{\Sigma}\Sigma$. And it is therefore highly significant that Latin hexameter writers greatly increase the proportion of cases in which this applies, with progressively greater success. Thus, for example (Sturtevant 1923, 57), in Ennius in 92.8% of cases, Lucilius 95.8%, Lucretius 97.7%, and Vergil 99.8%. By this means agreement between strong position and accent was accordingly achieved with few exceptions in the rhythmically important coda of the line.

Over the rest of the line, however, conflict was far more common than concord (and even increasingly common): thus in Ennius around 41% agreement, Lucilius 43%, Lucretius 38%, Vergil 35%. The contrast between the first and the last part of the line has often been remarked upon; e.g. (apart from such earlier writers as Ritschl and Hermann) Sturtevant 1923; Tamerle 1936 ap. Shipley 1938, 135; Delgado 1963, 161; Herescu 1963, 30; Wilkinson 1963, 120 ff.

Given the accentual conditions of Latin, and the frequency of the masculine caesura, the conflict is well-nigh unavoidable. It has, however, been often stated, and particularly with reference to Vergil, that such contrast between the beginnings and ends of lines became a deliberate device. Sturtevant (1923, 52) suggests that Latin poets 'made a virtue of necessity and actually preferred clash in the earlier part of the verse, in order to give their poetry the air of aloofness from common speech which was traditional in heroic verse'; cf. Wilkinson 1940, 32 (on Ennius); 1963, 121; such an interpretation might find its justification in the principle stated by Descroix (1931, 197) that 'un accord parfait acquiert sa plénitude lorsqu'il succède à une dissonance'.

A particular characteristic of Vergil's development of the hexameter was the increase of discord in IV, and much has been made of his handling of discord and concord in this foot for stylistic, expressive purposes – notably by Jackson Knight (1950): cf. Duckworth 1969, 17 ff., 48 ff. Knight's ideas have been much disputed; and *Greenberg (1967, 13) claims to have shown by a computer analysis that 'Vergil's sequence of homodyned and heterodyned fourth foot in *Aeneid* is not deliberate'. We need not here enter into this controversy: but what does concern us is the mere and undoubted presence of conflict on a large scale. Wilkinson, in emphasizing the desirability of 'tension' in poetry, is careful to say that (1940, 31) 'we must take care not to lose the sound of the underlying metre', and (1963, 93) 'It is only when the opening lines do not make clear what metre is being used, or when the metre gets lost in a continued orgy of exceptions, that the pulse is felt no more and the inward ear gives up': cf. Halle & Keyser 1971, 143 (p. 110 above). But as we have seen, and as emphasized by Kollmann (1968, 299), agreement is the exception rather than the rule – quite exceptional are lines such as *Ecl.* i 70:

Ímpius haéc tam cúlta nouália míles habébit.

It is thus hardly a question, as Wilkinson suggests (1963, 95) of 'the rhythm established by the preceding lines being still felt as an undercurrent'. A particularly striking illustration of the situation is provided if one considers only those cases where there is *contrast* of stress within the foot, i.e. where stress falls on one or other (but not on both) parts of the foot, and notes whether the stress falls on the first (strong) or second (weak) part of the foot. For the first 100 lines of the Aeneid the figures are as follows:

I. 38: 39 II. 4:63 III. 1:57 IV. 29:21 V. 97:2 VI. 99:1

The contrast between II/III and V/VI could hardly be greater, and might be seen to add to the arguments adduced by Maguinness (1963, 209 f; 1971) regarding the unsuitability of the dactylic metre to the Latin language.

However, it can be argued that what we have here is not strictly a conflict, but rather a counterpoint (cf. pp. 111 f.). Whatever the accentual patterns of the words, the quantitative patterning of the metre remains unimpaired, even in the first part of the line; and it is at least a feasible theory that poets might manipulate the contrapuntal possibilities for stylistic purposes. The poet, having learned the rules governing the quantitative structure, would of course be aware of the relationship between that structure and the accentual word-pattern of his composition; and the same would apply to his similarly educated readers or hearers.

But the situation is an artificial one, in which a verse-form developed for one language is applied to another of different phonological type; and it is relevant to ask, even if one cannot answer the question with any certainty, what might have been the reactions of the less sophisticated hearer, who was untaught or half-taught about such matters. Would he have been aware of an underlying quantitative structure which, to say the least, was for the most part not supported by the accentual pattern? It has to be remembered that in ordinary Latin speech, unlike Greek, quantity was closely linked with accent; and it is possible that the untaught speaker would have been aware of quantitative differences only in so far as they were connected with the placement of accent; so that in final syllables, for example, quantity might mean nothing to him. It is by no means self-evident that, as claimed by Frank (1924, 167), 'In Plautus' day every village smith knew his quantity'. *Vowel-length*, of course, with its semantic and grammatical functions, is another matter; and when Cicero (*Or.* 173) says 'omnium longitudinem et breuitatem in sonis sicut acutarum grauiumque uocum iudicium natura in auribus nostris collocauit', there is no reason to see in his words more than a reference to length of vowels. Similarly, Cicero elsewhere (*De Orat.* iii.196) comments on the fact that, although a majority of hearers are untrained in metrical matters, nevertheless, 'si paulum modo offensum est ut aut contractione breuius fieret aut productione longius, theatra tota reclamant'; but this can only refer to vowels and not syllables; for a syllable as such cannot be 'shortened': an orally arrested syllable (as e.g. *pec* in *pectus*) by its very structure can only be heavy; a thoracically arrested syllable, as *nā* in *bonā*, can be reduced to a light, but only by virtue of the shortening of the vowel (*bonă*); and conversely a light syllable can be extended to a heavy – but only by virtue of a lengthening of the vowel (or following consonant). There is nothing to suggest that the untrained Roman ear would have appreciated the *quantitative* (as opposed to phonemic and semantic) differences between, say, *tange* and *tangent*, or the quantitative equivalence of the latter to *tangēs*. The metrical equivalence of light and heavy unaccented syllables under the conditions of 'brevis brevians' (see pp. 179 ff.) may be seen as a further indication of the irrelevance to the speaker and hearer of quantity *per se*, i.e. other than as a concomitant of accent or of significant vowel-length.

Given also the probably greater intensity of stress in Latin, as its accentual feature, it is thus conceivable that the untrained ear would have been more aware of dynamic patterns than of quantitative patterns – perhaps even to the exclusion of the latter. The need felt even by poets for some patterning factor additional to mere quantity is seen in their high regard for the reinforcement of quantity by stress in the last two feet of the line.

It is sometimes pointed out that the clausulae of prose are based on purely quantitative patterns, with no regard for accent (e.g. Beare 1957, 193 ff; Wilkinson 1963, 148 ff., 237 ff; Norberg 1965, 498); but here again we are of course dealing with learned, artistic prose, and also with practices derived from Greek teaching. It would be unwise to attach too much importance to Cicero's statement (*Or.* 168) that it is not only his own ears that delight in rounded periods – 'Quid dico meas? contiones saepe exclamare uidi, cum apte uerba cecidissent'; that not all his hearers were capable of responding to such effects is suggested by the fact that he finds it necessary to pour scorn on those less appreciative of them: 'Quod qui non sentiunt, quas auris habeant aut quid in his hominis simile sit nescio.'

Given, then, the extent of disagreement between accent and strong position in the first part of the Latin hexameter, how could our un-sophisticated hearer be made aware of any pattern in it? One way in which this might be done would be by an artificial mode of performance, in which word-accents were shifted where necessary to coincide with the strong position – in other words by 'scanning', which in the hexameter means treating the foot as a word for accentual purposes (cf. Norberg 1965, 506: 'La phrase *scandere versus* signifie "lire les vers comme en montant une échelle pied à pied"'). That such methods of reading were known in antiquity is shown by the statements of grammarians. Most often cited is that of Sacerdos (vi, 448 K): 'hoc tamen scire debemus, quod uersus percutientes [id est scandentes] interdum accentus alios pronuntiamus, quam per singula uerba ponen-tes. *toro* et *pater*, acutum accentum in *to* ponimus et in *pa*; scandendo uero "inde toro pater Aeneas" in *ro* et in *ter*.[1] haec igitur in metro ideo suam non continent rationem, quia in ipsis nulla intellectus ratio continetur: nam *ropater* nihil significat.' Other relevant statements

---

[1] The idea of a stress on *ter* is of course nonsensical (cf. Beare 1957, 61).

are: Max. Victorinus, vi, 219 K, '"Omnia uincit amor, et nos cedamus amori". scanditur enim sic, *omnia* dactylus, *uincit a* dactylus, *mor et spondeus*'; Priscian, iii, 461 K, 'Scande uersum. *Arma ui rumque ca no Tro iae qui primus ab oris*. Quot caesuras habet? Duas. Quas? Semiquinariam et semiseptenariam...'; 469, 'Scande uersum. *Conticu ere om nes in tentique ora te nebant*. Dic caesuras...' The mode of presentation in Priscian suggests that the 'interdum' of Sacerdos refers to the context of pedagogical practice, though Norberg (1965, 507 f.) suggests that it means simply that the metrical/dynamic conflict affects only some feet of the verse, and that the practice was of wider currency than in the schoolroom.

For a modern instance of the two types of rendering existing side by side one may note Jakobson's account (1952, 24) of the recitation of Serbo-Croat epic in which there is free alternation between the 'prose manner', maintaining the linguistic accents, and 'scansion', following the verse pattern (as well as 'emphatic variations').

Scholars are much divided on the question whether 'scanning', with the placing of a regular, audible 'ictus', was in fact the normal way of speaking Latin verse. In favour of this view may be cited, for example, Hendrickson 1899; Sturtevant 1923, 337 ('Since syllables consist of increments of sound, and since the increments can be added to only by stress, any combining of a syllabic rhythm with a secondary rhythm of feet implies stress'); Fraenkel 1928, 6 f., 331; Pulgram 1954, 232 ('The recurrence of a rhythmic pattern...is the very soul of versification. If a verse has no rhythm, by what criterion may it be called verse?'; '...the ridiculous ictus-less verse...'); Herescu 1960, 27 ('S'il n'y avait pas d'ictus dans la versification, il n'y aurait pas de versification'); 1963, 16 ff; Drexler 1965, 6 f. On the other side may be mentioned, amongst others, *Bennett 1898, e.g. 371; Shipley 1938, 134 ff; Beare 1957, e.g. 237 ('we must abandon our notion of regularly recurring dynamic stresses as the essential feature of verse'); Kabell 1960, 28 f; Lepscky 1962, 214 ('l'ictus vocale non esisteva'); Wilkinson 1963, 94 f; Pighi 1966.

For some writers the problem is mitigated by assuming for Latin a melodic accent (cf. p. 151), which would be more compatible with a non-coincident quantitative pattern (thus Kent 1920; 1922; Moore 1924, 323 ff; Norberg 1965, 505 f; Lucot 1969, 81 ff.); and Kollmann (1968, 301) makes the unlikely suggestion that both dynamic accent and ictus were realized, which would result in many cases in such double-stressed forms as *Tróide, cánó*. Some writers have argued for a stressed ictus on the grounds that in Greek there was nothing to militate against such an ictus, and therefore that Latin would be likely to take over the same rhythm: thus Sturtevant 1923, 337; Allen 1964, 11 – an approach already hinted at by Theodorus Beza (*De Germana pronuntiatione Graecae linguae*, 50 ff.).[1]

But for the most part the argument has hinged either on generalities regarding the need or irrelevance of stress as a marker of metrical pattern, or on the interpretations of statements by ancient rhetoricians and grammarians. Here, however, arguments tend to be obscured by uncertainties regarding the meaning of such key terms as *arsis/thesis*, *ictus, percutio, ferio*, etc., more particularly as to whether they refer to an external 'beating of time' or to a linguistic stress. For bibliography and further discussion see p. 276 and Getty 1963, 120 ff; Beare 1957, 57 ff. (with relevant citations from ancient authors on 63 ff.).

In reading Latin hexameters nowadays the more usual tendency is to realize the word-accents rather than the ictus (though the word-accents may themselves tend to be suppressed in some national pronunciations based on native accentual habits: the French, for example, tend to stress the final syllables of words or word-groups – a point already noted by Erasmus, and Icelanders the initial syllables: cf. Kabell 1960, 43 ff.). In England the accentual reading was reinforced by the support of Bentley (xvii of his 'ΣΧΕΔΙΑΣΜΑ De Metris Terentianis' in *P. Terentii Afri Comoediae*, 1726),[2] whose own approach to the problem, however, contains certain elements of confusion. Bentley observed that the writers of Latin comedy tended to avoid conflict of accent and ictus: 'Jam vero id Latinis Comicis, qui Fabulas suas populo placere cuperent, magnopere cavendum erat; ne contra Linguae genium Ictus seu Accentus in quoque versu syllabas verborum ultimas occuparent'; and he goes on to observe, 'Id in omni metro, quoad licuit, observabatur'. Elsewhere he links the name of Vergil with that of Terence as choosing words and word-orders to obtain 'concinnitas' of strong position and accent; and by way of illustration of the principle he cites, rather surprisingly, the opening lines of the Aeneid, marking the word-accents (*Árma virúmque cáno*, etc.), and states: 'Qui perite & modulate hos versus leget, sic eos, ut hic accentibus notantur, pronuntiabit; non, ut pueri in Scholis, ad singulorum pedum initia...

---

[1] For publication details see p. 345.
[2] See Figure II.

Bentley on Ictus (see p. 342).

XVII

DE METRIS

cum apud Graecos tria loca teneat, apud nos duobus tantum poni potest; aut in penultima ut Praelegístis, aut ea quae a fine est tertia ut Traelegimus. Olympiodorus in Aristotelis Meteora P. 27. Τότε μὲν Γραικοὶ ἐκλήθησαν, τὸ δ᾽ Ἕλληνες. τοῦτο δὲ τὸ θέμα οἱ μὲν θεσσαλοὶ παρώξυνον, Γραικοὶ λέγοντες. ἡ δὲ κοινὴ Διθκόλυς ὀξύνει. Καθόλε δὲ οἱ Ρωμαῖοι παρ᾽ ὅσμα παρώξυνον διὰ τὸν χαρακτῆρα ἰδίαν Τραγεωδίσκους ἐκλήθοι. περὶ τῶ πῶρκια. Hoc est, *Qui olim Graicoi dicti, nunc appellantur Ἕλληνες. Illius autem verbi penultimam Romani acuunt, dicentes Γραικοὶ, sed communis sermo acui ultimam Γραικοὶ. Et universim Romani in quaecumque voce penultimam vel antepenultimam acuunt, propter Fastum & Grandiloquentiam: unde a Poetis dicuntur Τραγεωδίσκοι feroces & superbi.* Ceterum quod hic Fastui tribuit, id dialecto Aeolicae, unde Lingua Latina partem maximam profluxit, rectius imputatur. Aeolenses enim, ut notum est, Βαρύτονα erant; & Θεός, Ἄνηρ pronuntiabant, cum alii Θεός, Ἀνήρ.

JAM vero id Latinis Comicis, qui Fabulas suas populo placere cuperent, magnopere cavendum erat; ne contra Linguae genium Ictus seu Accentus in quoque versu syllabas verborum ultimas occuparent. Id in omni metro, quoad licuit, observabatur; ut in his,

Arma virúmque cáno, Trojáe qui prímus ab óris

Litóras; multúm ille & térris jactátus & álto

Vi súperum, saévae memórem Junónis ob íram.

Qui perite & modulate hos versus leget, sic eos, ut hic accentibus notantur, pronuntiabit; non, ut pueri in Scholiis, ad singulorum pedum initia, *Italám fató profúgus Lavínaque vénit,* sed ad rythmum totius versus. Ubi nulla vox, ut vides, accentum in ultima habet, praeter unicam illam *Virûm:* idque recte ob sequens Encliticon *Que:* quod hic, semel dictum, in Terentio passim fieri animadvertes. Idem efficiunt ME, TE, SE: *Ausculam me, quod verbum audio?* quippe haec Latinis, ut etiam *Rem,* Enclitica sunt, ut Graecis ΜΕ, ΣΕ. Eadem est & Interrogationis vis; sive cum *Ne* Enclitico, sive abjique *Ne.* In hac igitur Enclinicitatis laude palmam omnibus praeripuit Terentius; eanque ut consequi possit, ut & vetitos Ictus effugeret, & vocabula tamen significantiora semper sub Ictu ponerct; non minore studio judicioque verba disposuit, & a prosae orationis ordine decenter invertit, quam mirificus in hac materie artifex ipse Virgilius.

Pri-

TERENTIANIS. XVIII

PRISCIANUS De versibus comicis narrat, *Fuisse quosdam qui obnegarent ulla esse in Terentii Comoediis metra; vel ea, quasi arcana quaedam & ab omnibus doctis semota, sibi solis esse cognita confirmarent.* Ibidem ait, *Omnes quidem Comicos, crebris Synaloephis & Episynaloephis & Collisionibus & Abjectionibus s literae, suisse usu sanctendo versus suos;* TERENTIUM AUTEM PLUS OMNIBUS. Verum profecto hoc est; & causa unica, cur Magistelli isti vel negarent metra esse apud Nostrum, vel ut arcana quaedam venditarent. Quod vero hic queritur & criminatur magnus Grammaticus, non virium est, sed virtus Terentii prima: qui Synaloephas illas data opera confectatus est; quo syllabae ultimae liquescerent coalescerentque cum sequentibus; eoque vetii ac vitiosi in ultimis Ictus artificiose effugerentur. Hac vero Synaloephae, quae tenebras olim Magistris offuderunt, jam in hac Editione, Percussionum intervallis distincta, ne pueris quidem negotium facessent.

Totum autem loc, quod de Ictu in ultimis syllabis cautum fuisse diximus, de secunda tantum Trimetri ἀντιπάλω capiendum; nam in prima & tertia semper licuit; siquidem ista sine venia conclamatum adunque erat de Comoedia Tragoediaque Latina. Cum igitur hunc versum simiciliique apud Nostrum videris,

Malam quod isti à dénique ómnes duini:

cave vitio id poetae verteris; etsi *Malim* illud & *Omnes* si in communi quis sermone sic acuisti, deridiculo fuisset. Nimirum aures vel invitae patienter id ferebant, sine quo ne una quidem in Fabula Scaena poterat edolari. Quin & Graecos ipsos eadem tenuit necessitas, eadem passa est indulgentia. Cum Aristophanes dixit,

Δωλῶ γυναῖκα παρεφρονηκὸς δεσπότα.

Cum Euripides,

Ἥκω νεκρῶν κευθμῶνα καὶ σκότου πύλας,

idem admiserunt in Δωλῶ & Ἥκω, quod Noster in *Malim* & *Omnes:* ipsi enim alibi priorem acuunt, Δωλῶν & Ἥκω.

In secunda igitur Trimetri ἀντιπάλω hoc de quo agimus non licebat. Gellius XVIII, 15. *In Senariis versibus animadverterunt Metrici duos primos pedes, item extremos duos, habere posse singulos integros partes orationis, medios haud unquam posse: sed consulare eos semper ex verbis atque divisis medios haud mixtis atque confusis.* Quotus quisque hoc vel intelligat? nedum ut Senarios per singulos pedes scandendo tempus in hac observatione conterat? At in hac Editione vel aliud agentibus in oculos incurrit; simulque ratio, simulque Metrici isti tacent, plane

d

sed ad rythmum totius versus.' He further deplores the fact that since the Renaissance boys have been forced to learn dactylic verse ('Quo magis est dolendum atque indignandum, jam a literis renatis pueros ingenuos ad Dactylica, quod genus patria lingua non recipit, ediscenda, ferula scuticaque cogi'), whereas the metres of comedy are neglected ('Terentiana vero metra, quae domi tamen et in triviis inscientes ipsi canticant, Magistrorum culpa penitus ignorare'). The most charitable interpretation that one can make of Bentley's reasoning is as follows: in comedy accent and strong position generally agree; one may therefore read such verse in a scanning manner, since this is also for the most part an accentual reading.[1] Poets using other metres try to follow the same principles of composition, but with incomplete success; and when there is conflict, accent should prevail in performance. Bentley seems greatly to underestimate the degree of conflict, and presumably believed that in giving a rendering such as he advocates the metrical pattern was nevertheless recognizable; and Hermann said of him that he 'felt the rhythm of ancient verse most adequately, but did not give an explanation of his feeling' (Kapp 1941, 188).

Bentley's thinking on this matter is less clear than we might expect (cf. Beare 1957, 61); but at least his discussion shows the prevalence of a scanning reading in the schools. For the tradition of this, both in England and on the continent, as an exercise in prosody and as an aid to memorization, see Attridge 1972, 30 ff.

This two-fold tradition – pedagogical scanning and accentual reading – from the Latin grammarians to the present day, seems to have been a continuous tradition if one is to judge from the need for criticism of the scanning method by medieval writers. Around 1200 A.D. the Norman grammarian Gottfried de Vinsauf wrote: 'Generaliter sciendum est quod, qualiscumque fuerit syllaba in metro, non est aliter accentuanda in metro quam extra metrum, sed semper est accentuanda secundum hoc quod regulae docent accentuum'; and another grammarian, Aiméric, states that verse is to be recited 'non scandendo sed enuntiando' (Kabell, 25 ff; Norberg 1965, 506). For

---

[1] Bentley accepts that Latin poets were compelled by their language to have at the beginnings and ends of lines such counter-accentual forms as *omnès, malùm* – but appeals to the usage of the Greeks, who, he says, were under similar constraints; he supports this statement by such line-beginnings as Δουλὸν γενεσθαι ~, Ηκὼ νεκρων, 'ipsi enim alibi priorem acuunt, Δούλον et Ήκω' – from which it appears that Bentley's argument from the Greek is, as Kapp suggests (1941, 191 f.), based on his Henninian pronunciation of Greek (his acute accents standing for stress).

the accentual reading Kabell (30 f.) also sees evidence in the rhymes of leonine verses, as e.g. (Carmina Burana) *Feruet amore Paris, Troianis immolat aris* (with late Latin lengthening of the accented *a* of *Paris* so that it is identical with that of *aris*). At the Renaissance, Kabell points out that Erasmus (185 of the original 1528 Basle edition of his *Dialogus de recta Latini Graecique sermonis pronuntiatione*,[1] of which he himself probably read the proofs), marks the accents, and not the strong positions, in his transcription of *Georgics* iii 66 ff:

> Óptima quáêque díes míseris mortálibus áevi
> Prîma fúgit, súbeunt mórbi trîstísque senéctus,
> Et lábor, & dírae rápit inceleméntia mórtis.[2]

The same practice is revealed by the comments of Beza, who, in a discussion of accentuation appended to his *De Germana pronuntiatione Graecae linguae* (in *De vera pron. Gr. et Latinae linguae*, Stephanus 1587, 51 f.), complains of the practice in the schools whereby Latin verse is read according to the accent, and the accented vowels lengthened, with the result that in hexameters 'si duos ultimos pedes excipias, versus videri non possint'; and he illustrates the effect for iambics by marking as long the first vowels of *potest* and *pati* in Catullus xxix 1: *Quis hoc potest uidere, quis potest pati.*

That in antiquity the scanning pronunciation was the less normal way of reading seems clear from the special mention of it by the grammarians. And an interesting confirmation of the use of the accentual reading, even in schools, comes from an Egyptian papyrus containing part of seven lines from Vergil, evidently intended for Greek-speaking students, in which it is the word-accents which are marked and not the strong positions: thus[3] (*Aen.* iv 99–101):

> quin] pótius pácem aetérnam pactōs[que hymenaeos
> exerce]mus hábes tóta quót ménṭe pe[tisti
> ardet ama]ns Dído traxítque per ossa [furorem

and 66–7:

> quid delubra iuu]ant ēst móllis flámma medúllas
> interea et tacitu]m uíuit sub péctore uúlnus.

---

[1] Now available in Scolar reprint (1971).

[2] The use of acute/circumflex follows the Greek 'final trochee' rule; note also Greek enclitic accentuation in *trîstísque* (not printed, but intended to be as shown by subsequent discussion (189)).

[3] *Papiri greci e latini* (*Pubb. della Soc. ital. per la ricerca dei Papiri greci e latini in Egitto*), i (1912), 47 and Plate 21. Discussion by Moore 1924; Shipley 1938, 143 f; Kabell, 29.

An indication that the poets themselves envisaged an accentual reading is perhaps provided by the quotations by Horace, in hexameters, of phrases from senarii of Terence. Thus *Epist.* I. xix 41 *hinc illae lacrimae* ~ (from *And.* 126) and *Serm.* II. iii 264 *exclusit; reuocat: redeam?* ~ (from *Eun.* 49). In the senarii strong position and accent agree in producing stress patterns *hinc íllae lácrimae* and *exclúsit réuocat rédeam*, whereas a hexameter reading by metrical ictus would require a distortion of these rhythms to *hínc illáe lacrimáe* and *éxclusít reuocát redeám* (cf. Beare 1957, 175; Wilkinson 1963, 95).

If, then, an accentual reading was normal, we come back again to the problems of the less educated hearer, untaught in matters of quantitative metrics. What sort of idea, if any, of the underlying structure could he have derived from hearing or reading Latin hexameters? Certainly he would hear the clearly defined dynamic pattern in the last two feet; and this might give a hint, but little more in the absence of specific instruction, of the patterns underlying the rest of the line. That such may indeed have been the situation is suggested by the evidence of certain of the *Carmina Epigraphica* (= *Anthologia Latina* II, i–ii ed. Buecheler 1895–6, iii ed. Lommatzsch 1926). Some of these are superior to others, presumably reflecting higher levels of education; but some of the less good productions are chaotic, and show little understanding of pattern in the first part of the line, whether quantitative or dynamic. Thus, for example:

i 579   hoc monimentum...
         Manibus addictum sacrisque priorum
         ut aeque frui liceat, qui dominus fuerit huius,
         uendere ne liceat caueo adque rogo per numina diuom.
         uendere si uelit, emptorem littera prohibet.

iii 1988, 31

         post hanc nunc idem diuersi sibi quisque senescunt –

the latter in a poem on which Lommatzsch comments, 'carmen magis affectu scribentis atque humanitate quam arte poetica et perspicuitate sermonis insigne'. The Latin hexameter perhaps reaches its nadir in the following specimen from Arles (1–2 c. A.D.: *CE* i 470; E. Diehl, *Vulgärlateinische Inschriften*, 373 – 'ab homine plebeio et inepto composita': Hirschfeld, *CIL* xii 915):

         quat ualeas abeas pascas, multos tu habebes amicos.[1]
         si haliquit casu alite[r] aduxerit aster,

---

[1] With a faint reminiscence of Ovid, *Tr.* i 9.

aut ili Romae frater es aut tu peregre heris
et uocas acliua. quo si tu non nosti amicos,
adcnoscet homines aeg(er) quos no(n) pote sanus.
porta probat homines, ibi hest trutina ultima uitai:
aspicent ex(e)quias (ali)quis, ita ut quit euitant:
et pietas hilic paret et qui sit amicus,
[b]eneficia absenti qui facet, ilic am[icu]s herit.

As Shipley says of the *Carmina Epigraphica* (1927, xxxi), 'The faults...
point to an absence of any real feeling for an ictus beat', and (1938,
137) 'The writers are lost, in the first part of the line, in a labyrinth
to which there appears to be no clue'. Only at the end of the line do
such verses tend to show a correct $\Sigma\Sigma\Sigma\Sigma$ pattern (or at least an accentual $\Sigma\Sigma\Sigma\Sigma$: cf. *Harris 1940), i.e. precisely at the point where their
literary models will have reinforced the quantitative pattern by a
regular, audible stress; in Hendrickson's words (243), 'it is often the
index of an author's intention or ambition to construct a hexameter,
when little else corresponds to the requirements of the classical verse'.

The Latin examples are in fact in marked contrast with their Greek
counterparts, which show no evidence of ignorance of metrical patterns,
and few quantitative errors: 'most are sufficiently correct in language
and versification...of metrical eccentricities the most frequent cause
is the necessity of introducing proper names unsuited to the metre'
(*Allen 1888, 38).

The above discussion involves a change of mind, after further
consideration of the evidence, from the opinions expressed in A 1964;
a similar shift of opinion may be discovered between Hendrickson
1899 and 1949 (241).

The situation regarding the Latin hexameter is also in striking and
instructive contrast, both descriptively and historically, with that of
another verse-form derived from Greek – the Sapphic stanza. The
Greek form has for its first three lines the structure $\Sigma\Sigma\Sigma\Sigma\Sigma\Sigma\Sigma\Sigma\Sigma\Sigma\Sigma$;
whether one analyses this in terms of 'elements', as e.g. $\Sigma\Sigma\Sigma\Sigma|\Sigma\Sigma\Sigma\Sigma|$
$\Sigma\Sigma\Sigma$ (cf. Raven 1962, 77), or of 'feet', as $\Sigma\Sigma|\Sigma\Sigma|\Sigma\Sigma\Sigma|\Sigma\Sigma|\Sigma\Sigma$ (cf.
Needler 1941, 13), is irrelevant. There are no rules regarding 'bridges',
and the dynamic pattern is more likely to have been set by the musical
accompaniment than by any natural speech-stresses. Latin lyric,
however, seems generally to have been recited rather than sung or
accompanied, so that any dynamic pattern, if it were to exist, could
only be set by the language; and in terms of the Latin accent a wide

variety of rhythms is possible in the Sapphic line, depending on the location of word-boundaries: thus e.g. Catullus, li (with probable stresses marked):

> Ílle mi pár esse déo uidétur,
> ílle, si fás est, superáre díuos,
> qui sédens aduérsus idéntidem te
> spéctat et aúdit.

Horace, however (for what purpose it is not clear: cf. Wilkinson 1940), introduced a restrictive innovation. This consisted in a requirement that the 4th syllable be heavy (not 'anceps' as in Greek), and that the 5th syllable normally be followed by a caesura. In terms of the Latin word-accent this had the effect of drastically reducing the number of possible stress-patterns for the line (cf. Park 1968, 3 f.): a stress-peak falls on the 4th and 10th syllables, generally also on the 1st and 6th (in some cases secondary, e.g. ínteger uítae *scĕ*lerísque púrus), and often on the 8th (commonly secondary, e.g. síue per Sýrtis íter *aĕ*stuósas). The general pattern is then $\Sigma\Sigma\Sigma\Sigma\!:\!\Sigma\Sigma\overset{(/)}{\Sigma}\Sigma\Sigma\Sigma$. Occasional variants produce stress of the second instead of the first syllable – e.g. dum méam cánto Lálagen et última. The result is a clearly apprehensible dynamic pattern; and there is evidence that this result was popularly received.

In Horace's later work the requirement of the crucial 5th-syllable caesura was relaxed, and this has been seen as a reaction by Horace against the accentual interpretation to which his innovations had led. Particularly relevant is the case of the *Carmen Saeculare*, which was, exceptionally, to be sung by a choir of boys and girls. Horace, as Wilkinson suggests (1940, 133; cf. 1963, 110) 'might well foresee the choir gaily singing the right notes to the barbarous Roman time'; and in *Ode* iv 6, which forms a kind of prelude to the *Carmen Saeculare*, he addressed his choir in the following terms:

> . . .   . . .
> uirginum primae puerique claris
> patribus orti,
>
> . . .   . . .
> *Lesbium seruate pedem meique*
> *pollicis ictum,*

and ends with

> nupta iam dices 'ego dis amicum,
> saeculo festas referente luces,
> reddidi carmen, *docilis modorum*
> *uatis Horati.*'

In other words, the choir are specifically instructed to keep to the original Greek, Aeolic pattern, the stresses being determined by the music, and to ignore the accentual stresses of the Latin words – with Horace as their leader keeping them in time. It is in this particular context that Rudmose-Brown (1939, 33) makes the point which we have already suggested in connexion with the hexameter, that 'An uneducated Roman, even as early as the Classical period,...heard only the "accentual" rhythm. The quantitative metre of Greek importation meant nothing to him.'

In spite of Horace's later change of heart, the accentual Sapphic had come to stay. On account of its dynamic patterning it survived as a popular verse-form through to the Middle Ages, when other quantitative metres had become little more than academic exercises, e.g. by Carolingian scholars (cf. Rudmose-Brown 1939, 36; Park 1968, 5). Except amongst the learned, from the 5 c. onwards the quantitative pattern came to be more and more ignored 'beneath the ever more completely dominating accentual principle' (Needler, 11; cf. Wilkinson 1963, 108). Indeed, since both the vernaculars and spoken Latin no longer had distinctions of vowel length, any purely quantitative composition must have been entirely artificial.

The metre became particularly popular as a vehicle for Christian hymns (Rudmose-Brown 1939, 36; Needler, 12 ff.); and the non-quantitative, accentual principle is clearly seen, for example, in the hymn beginning

Ó Salutáris mícans stélla máris.

Another accentual Sapphic hymn, beginning 'O Pater sancte, mitis atque pie' (10 c. French), is familiar in the English version by A. E. Alston in the same metre: 'Father most holy, merciful and loving'. Of particular interest is the hymn stanza by Paulus Diaconus (8 c.):

> *Ut* queant laxis *re*sonare fibris
> *Mi*ra gestorum *fa*muli tuorum,
> *So*lue polluti *la*bii reatum,
>   *Sancte Io*hannes.

For three centuries later Guido of Arezzo took the syllables here in italics, which had been set to successive notes of the hexachord, as names for the notes of the scale;[1] and Needler comments (12) that 'It is manifest that in doing so he read the lines accentually'; perhaps

---

[1] The $S + I = si$ of the last verse was added at a later date.

more evident is the conception of the longer lines as falling into two sections of 5 and 6 syllables respectively.

In the early 19 c. Horace's own ode i 22 ('Integer uitae scelerisque purus') was set to music as a glee by F. F. Fleming in terms of a rhythm

The tune in turn was borrowed for the German funeral hymn 'Über den Sternen wohnet Gottes Frieden' (Seel & Pöhlmann 1959, 259 ff.) and for Philip Pusey's hymn-anthem 'Lord of our Life and God of our Salvation' (arr. John Holler, *Church Music Review* 1937, No. 1434). Lay examples of the metre are less common (Needler 1941, 7, 17 ff., 45 f.); they include Southey's poem *The Widow*, parodied by Canning in such lines as

> Bleak blows the blast; – your hat has got a hole in 't,
> So have your breeches!

Even less common are accentual imitations in modern languages of the original quantitative pattern (with accent substituting for heavy quantity). One writer of such poems was the Swiss, Heinrich Leuthold (1827–79), for example in *Die Deutsche Sprache* (Bennett 1963, 121):

> Ja, du bist der griechischen Schwester selber
> Ebenbürtig...

In English the same effect was attempted by Swinburne, e.g. (Needler, 39 f.):

> Clothed about with flame and with tears and with singing
> Songs that move the heart of the shaken heaven.

The difference between the accentual and the quantitative-imitational patterns of stress is clear: on the one hand

Σ́ΣΣ́ΣΣ́ΣΣΣ́Σ (with 'feet' or 'bars' of $3+2+4+2$)

and on the other

Σ́ΣΣ́ΣΣ́ΣΣ́ΣΣ́ ($2+2+3+2+2$): cf. Needler, 13.

An earlier attempt at the original, quantitative pattern was essayed by Sidney (in *Arcadia* 1); at least, that is the suggestion of the introduction to the poem; but when one considers such lines as 'If the mute timber when it hath the life lost', one may suspect that Sidney was at least familiar with the accentual Sapphics of the hymns (Needler, 19).

Campion's song 'Come, let us sound with melody the praises' follows the accentual Sapphic closely[1] (though this tends to be obscured by the setting).

Early German examples of the accentual Sapphic are given by Kauffmann 1907, 218 ff; cf. also Bennett, 116 ff.

The contrast between the fate of the Latin hexameter and of the Sapphic could hardly be greater, and probably reflects a difference in response on the part of the metrically untrained public in antiquity. We can perhaps find a partial parallel to the hexameter situation in more recent times if we consider the experiments in quantitative hexameters which were carried out over a brief period by some Elizabethan English writers, including notably Stanyhurst, Sidney, Harvey, and Spenser. These were based upon rules of 'quantity', derived from Latin but with some serious misconceptions (see especially Attridge 1972, chs. iv–v). Except to some extent at the end of the line, these rules tended (as in Latin) to produce conflict between the metrical pattern and the English stress-accent – the latter being in addition less simply related to quantity than in Latin. An early example (*c.* 1530–40) is cited by Roger Ascham from the pen of his friend Thomas Watson, of St John's College, Cambridge:[2]

> All travellers do gladly report great prayse of Ulysses,
>
> For that he knew many men's maners and saw many Cities;

since ideas of quantity were largely (mis)guided by spelling, Kabell (168) suggests that the original in fact had *travelers* and *manners*. As an example from Sidney, Hendrickson (247) cites

> Opprest with ruinous conceits by the helpe of an outcry

and from Gabriel Harvey

> And what so precious matter and foode for a good tongue.

As an instance of a particularly close copy of the Latin situation as regards caesura and the incidence of concord/discord, Attridge (1972, 186) cites Stanyhurst's line

> And a brace of menacing ragd rocks skymounted abydeth.

---

[1] In accordance with his view (uncommon for this time) that 'Aboue all, the accent of words is diligently to be observ'd, for chiefely by the accent in any language, the true value of the sillables is to be measured' (*Observations in the Art of English Poesie* (1602), in *Smith 1904, ii, 351).

[2] Cf. Hendrickson, 238.

Such lines are of course undescribable in terms of English prosodic principles, and can have had little rhythmical meaning to the person untaught in the strange rules upon which they were based. But this would have been considered no disadvantage by most experimenters and theorists of the time, who were obsessed with the idea of poetic language as something quite separate from other forms of language.

Sidney, however, more generally than his fellow experimenters, tends to take vowel-length into account, and mostly treats unstressed syllables as light; he tends also to favour stressed pre-caesural mono-syllables; thus, for example,

> In silence, from a man's owne selfe with company robbed.

The result is to diminish the degree of discord as displayed in the more closely Latin-based lines of Stanyhurst (Attridge 1972, 198); and it would be in accordance with Sidney's own observation on English that 'though we do not obserue quantity, yet wee obserue the accent very precisely' (*An Apologie for Poetrie*, in *Smith 1904, i, 205).

The 'quantitative experiment' was of short duration, and terminated abruptly early in the 17 c; one factor in its demise was no doubt the publication in 1603 of Samuel Daniel's *A Defence of Ryme*, of which the following comments are typical (*Smith 1904, ii, 360, 378; cf. Park 1968, 41 ff.):

As Greeke and Latine verse consists of the number and quantitie of sillables, so doth the English verse of measure and accent. And though it doth not strictly obserue long and short sillables, yet it most religiously respects the accent; and as the long and short make number, so the acute and graue accent yeelde harmonie. And harmonie is likewise number.

As for those imagined quantities of sillables, which haue bin euer held free and indifferent in our language, who can inforce vs to take knowledge of them, being *in nullius verba iurati*, and owing fealty to no forraine inuention?

Other expressions of opposition to the foreign, quantitative forms came from Alexander Gil's *Logonomia Anglica* (1621), ed. Jiriczek, *Quellen u. Forschungen* xc (1903), 142:

In carminum generibus, nihil nostris intentatum relinquitur: res tamen melius successit illis qui rythmo poesin scripserunt, quam qui numeris Latinorum. Et quamvis eo acriter docti contenderint, ut Graecorum et Latinorum numeros assequerentur, eventus tamen optatis non respondit, and from Bacon, in his *Advancement of Learning* (11.16.5 in the Latin version of 1623: cf. Hendrickson, 238):

Illud reprehendendum quod quidam antiquitatis nimium studiosi linguas modernas ad mensuras...antiquas traducere conati sunt, quas ipsarum linguarum fabrica respuit, nec minus aures exhorrent.

Similar experiments in other languages mostly fared little better; Kabell (144) cites a French poem in elegiac couplets by E. Jodelle, *A Mme Marguerite de France* (1559):

> Vierge, ta France te veut par ces vers sacrer un autel,
> > Auquel nuire le feu, l'onde, ne l'age, ne peut.
> L'age superbe ne mord les vers, dont Grece se bastit
> > Vn los eternel, ny ce que Rome grava,

which in turn was rendered no more felicitously into English by an anonymous author (Kabell, 170) under the title *To the Queenes moste excellente Maiestie* (1576):

> England with this verse doth dresse you virgin an altar
> > Whom not water, nor ayre, Iron or age can anoy.
> Age volative eates not such verse as did to the Greekes build
> > Lasting praise, nor that Rome ever engraved earst.

Amongst languages in which quantitative verse has been written in imitation of Latin models may also be mentioned Finnish, in spite of the fact that this language has a stress-accent falling on initial syllables of words: to take an example of a hexameter line cited by Collinder (1937, 162 ff.):

> altaaseen hyvälaitteiseen apesilppuja ahtaa.

With regard to the similar case of the related Hungarian, however, Kerek (1968, 23) points out that quantity is relevant in the language in determining the placement of non-accentual stresses; so that the acceptance of such verses is due to 'the *stress* assigned to them (sc. the syllables) due to their length, rather than because of their values as time units' (cf. also Kerek, 37 ff., 75 ff. and pp. 274, 277).

In German, quantitative experiments were made by the humanists of the 15–16 c., but with even less understanding of the principles involved than in the case of the English experiments; thus, for example, Conrad Gesner's line (Bennett, 20 ff; cf. also Kauffmann, 196 ff; Heusler 1917, 3 ff.):

> O vatter unser, der du dyn eewige wonung

But in the 18 c. there began in Germany a new type of imitation of the Latin hexameter, which attempted to secure agreement between the German dynamic accent and the strong position (for isolated earlier examples cf. Kauffmann, 200). The first serious plea for such an imitation came from J. C. Gottsched in 1730, and the form achieved independence with the publication in 1748 of Klopstock's *Messias* (cf. Kauffmann, 202): 'with Klopstock begins a new period in German verse; it was he who deposed the Alexandrine as Ennius drove out the Saturnian from the Roman Parnassus' (Bennett, 45; cf. Kabell, 222).

The shadow of 'quantity', however, continued for some time to bedevil the new form, and gave rise to a spate of controversy. For example, it was felt that a 3-syllable foot $\acute{\Sigma}\Sigma\Sigma$ (imitating the Latin dactyl $\underline{\Sigma}\underline{\Sigma}\underline{\Sigma}$) was unacceptable if the second syllable was 'long', or at least in some sense heavier than the third (cf. Kauffmann, 203; Heusler, 15); such feet were termed 'heavy' or 'false' dactyls. For instance, a foot such as ' ~ knechtisch ein ~ ' was preferred to ' ~ knechtisch das ~ ' on account of the 'positional length' of the second syllable in the latter; and the 'heavy' dactyl was parodied by one critic (Platen) with the word 'Holtzklotzpflock'. A particular controversy raged around the spondee, i.e. the 2-syllable foot $\acute{\Sigma}\Sigma$ imitating the quantitative $\underline{\Sigma}\underline{\Sigma}$. A disyllable in which the second syllable was in some sense 'light' was criticized as being a trochee rather than a spondee. Thus J. H. Voss, in his Odyssey translation of 1781 (Heusler, 55 f.) rendered *Od.* xv 334 (σίτου καὶ κρειῶν ἠδ' οἴνου βεβρίθασιν), with an evident attempt at the same metrical pattern,

> Sind mit Brot und Fleisch und Weine stets belastet,

but later changed the ending to ' ~ mit Wein auch stets belastet', with the 'long' *auch* replacing the 'short' ~ e of *Weine*. *Od.* xiv 1–2 was first rendered as

> Aber Odysseus ging den rauhen Pfad von dem Hafen
> Über die waldbewachsnen Gebirge, hin wo Athene,

but later amended with replacement of the 'trochee' *rauhen* by the 'dactyl' *steinigen*, of *Hafen* by the 'spondee' *Meerbucht*, and *Gebirge* by *Gebirghöhn*. Discussing Schlegel, Heusler (52) notes that in order to avoid the 'trochaic' sequences in words like *siebenhäuptigen* or *sechzigjährigen* he invents words 'which have parallels neither in Adelung nor Grimm', as *siebengehaupteten, sechzigbejahrten*. One is reminded of the artificialities of Latin dactylic verse, confronted with the impossibility of using such forms as *Scipiones, imperator,* and the introduction of such forms as *Scipiadae, induperator* (cf. Maguinness 1963, 209: 'Ce mot romain par excellence, *imperator,* était donc interdit à presque tout poète latin'); and indeed the question was seriously raised in the German debate whether a metre should be adopted which would not admit the word *Vaterland* (envisaged as a cretic ΣΣ̱Σ; cf. Heusler, 50); and one argument for the acceptance of the trochee was the patriotic one that this word could then be admitted (Minor 1893, 296, citing Paul Heyse).

One outcome of the controversy was the doctrine of 'false spondees', namely that the second syllable also must be a stressed syllable, leading to such verse-endings as (Schlegel: cf. Heusler, 60) ' ~ Doch bleibst du meinem *Gehéiss tréu*', and even, most perversely of all, to *reversed* stresses; so that Humboldt held that a line beginning 'Wenn Krankheit mich befällt' was better than 'Wenn mir die Krankheit naht' because it placed the 'strong' *Krank-* in the second part of a spondee – even though it thereby placed the weak *-heit* in strong position (Heusler, 64; cf. Bennett, 31 ff.). And, reminding one of the views of the Elizabethan quantifiers, such reversals of rhythm were actually preferred by Voss as being less 'naturalistic' and more 'artistic' (Heusler, 66). Voss in fact supported his preference by appeal to the conflicts of such Vergilian lines as 'Illi inter sese magna ui bracchia tollunt' (*Geo.* iv 174; cf. *Aen.* viii 452), whilst at the same time suggesting that simple people in Rome may well have found this too awkward, and would have preferred e.g. 'omnes inter se ui magna bracchia tollunt'. It was this 'problem' of the spondee that led some critics to reject any large-scale imitation of the Latin model; thus Platen (Köster 1902, 126; Kauffmann, 205):

> Weil der Hexameter episches Maass den Hellenen gewesen,
> Glaubst du, er sei deshalb Deutschen ein episches Maass?
> Nicht doch! folge des Wissenden Rat: zu geringen Gedichten
> Wend' ihn an! Klopstock irrte, wie viele mit ihm.

Subsequently R. Assmus (1882) condemned the spondee as a mongrel, which illustrated best of all 'how the rhythmical principles of Greek versification cannot be reconciled to the German language and versification' (Bennett, 26).

However, another result of the controversy was that by 1756 Klopstock had accepted the need to admit the trochee. The accentual basis of the German hexameter was now established, and quantity survived only as a stylistically available factor (cf. V. Hehn ap. Heusler, 15). In the hands of such poets as Goethe, Schiller, and Hölderlin it became a real vehicle for poetry (cf. Köster 1902, 125; Kauffmann, 203; Bennett, 52); and Goethe himself (cf. Minor 1893, 295) recognizes the emancipation of the trochee as a prime ingredient of its success:

> Allerlieblichste Trochäen aus der Zeile zu vertreiben,
> Und schwerfälligste Spondäen an die Stelle zu verleiben,
> ...wird mich immerfort verdriessen.

The new German model spread to other countries also. It was, however, ill suited to French, as may be seen from the verses of A. R. Turgot (Kabell, 223):

> Déjà du rythme antique ôsant reproduire l'énergie,
> L'immortel Klopstock sur tes pas vient de s'élancer.

And when Turgot offered his own hexameter translation of Vergil to Voltaire, the latter replied in praise of it as a prose rendering (cf. de Thomasson 1937, 53 f.).

In England by the late 18 c. the recognition of accent as the basis of native verse had been generally accepted in theory (as it had been for centuries in practice: cf. p. 275). The new, accentual hexameter was thus adopted without difficulty, though not with conspicuous success. It was first introduced to English readers by William Taylor of Norwich in the *Monthly Magazine* and *Monthly Review* in the period 1796–1800 (Hendrickson, 239; Park 1968, 41 ff.), and wider publicity was achieved for it by Southey's use of it in his *Vision of Judgment* (1820). In the U.S.A. it received a particular welcome from Longfellow, notoriously as the metre for *Evangeline*:

> This is the forest primeval. The murmuring pines and the hemlocks,
> Bearded with moss, and in garments green, indistinct in the twilight,
> Stand like Druids of eld, with voices sad and prophetic.

But it is generally agreed that the strict correspondence of stress and metre thus displayed results in a very monotonous effect (cf. Gross 1964, 35, 208).

It has been suggested that the introduction of the accentual English hexameter may have been responsible for a 'scanning' reading of Latin itself, that it 'produced that cheerful gallop which many of us will associate with our introduction to Virgil' (Hendrickson, 260). It was in fact advocated by J. Warner in his *Metronariston* of 1797 and by Sir Uvedale Price in his *Essay on the modern pronunciation of the Greek and Latin languages* in 1827 (Park 1968, 9 n.). But, as we have already noted, scanning of classical poetry was probably an established pedagogical practice long before this.

In spite of such statements as that 'English can offer no natural spondees except the word "amen"' (cf. Fussell 1954, 154), the German battle of the spondee and the trochee did not have to be refought in England. But one finds occasional reversions in the direction of the purely quantitative model, as e.g. in A. H. Clough's elegiacs (cf. Kabell, 223):

> Trunks the forest yielded with gums ambrosial oozing.
> Boughs with apples laden beautiful, Hesperian.

Tennyson's *Experiments in Quantity* (1863) show a mixture of accentual and quantitative criteria (cf. Kabell, 239), as in

> These lame hexameters the strong wing'd music of Homer!
> . . .
> Hexameters no worse than daring Germany gave us,
> Barbarous experiment, barbarous hexameters.

In more serious vein Robert Bridges 'relies for a large number of his long syllables on the exotic "rule of position"' (Sonnenschein 1925, 197); an example may be provided by his translation of *Aen.* vi 893–6 (from '*Ibant Obscuri*' in *New Quarterly* 5 ii, Jan. 1909):

> Twin be the gates o' the house of sleep: as fable opineth
> One is of horn, and thence for a true dream outlet is easy:
> Fair the other, shining perfected of ivory carven;
> But false are the visions that thereby find passage upward.

As Gross comments (1964, 33), 'According to Bridges' rules these lines scan exactly as their originals do. But our ears hear no metrical music.' Bridges himself was too ready to equate English with Latin as regards the function of quantity, even to the extent of suggesting (in his 'remarks on Vergilian rhythms' prefaced to '*Ibant Obscuri*', 8) that English is better off than Latin in having end-stressed 'spondees' of the type *conceal*, *unseen*, etc. (which Bridges uses at the ends of lines elsewhere in his translation); and that, had Latin possessed such word-patterns, Vergil also would have located them at this point 'to avoid the normal accent'! Later, however, in the foreword to his 'Poems in Classical Prosody', even Bridges admits that 'the difficulty of adapting our English syllables to the Greek is very great, and even deterrent.'

Finally, like any other metre, the accentual hexameter can be varied to avoid monotony. The interplay of metre and language in Vergil was of course well known to T. S. Eliot – though he is careful to suggest that its full appreciation was limited to the 'cultivated' audience (cf. p. 111). In this connexion it is of some interest to consider the opening lines of *The Dry Salvages* (one of Eliot's *Four Quartets*); these run as follows, with main stresses marked in accordance with the poet's own recorded reading:

> I dó not know múch about góds; but I thínk that the ríver
> Is a stróng brówn gód – súllen, untámed and intráctable,
> Pátient to sóme degreé, at fírst recognízed as a fróntier;
> Úseful, untrústworthy, as a convéyor of cómmerce;
> Thén only a próblem confrónting the buílder of brídges.
> The próblem once sólved, the brówn gód is álmost forgótten
> By the dwéllers in cíties – éver, howéver, implácable,
> Keéping his seásons and ráges, destróyer, remínder
> Of what men choóse to forgét...

To Gardner (1949, 34) these lines 'immediately recall the rhythm of the accentual "hexameter"'; the endings are highly suggestive, and where the natural accents do not produce a regular rhythm in the rest of the line, the number of syllables is such that varying degrees of displacement would make them do so, and would result moreover in the caesurae falling in their correct Latin positions: for example,

> Í do nót know múch about góds; but I thínk that the ríver

or, with rather more distortion,

> Úseful, úntrustwórthy, as á convéyor of cómmerce.

Gross, however, whilst recognizing (1964, 34) that 'Eliot's absorption of Virgil's hexameter is apparent in these lines', elsewhere (208) describes the metre as 'anapaestic pentameter with dactylic and spondaic substitutions' – which is also true, though hardly a useful metrical description in itself. What Eliot has clearly achieved here is, for those aware of the background, a striking interplay of different rhythms – with just enough agreement between the metrical pattern and the linguistic accent for the former not to be entirely obscured. But the reader who is not thus prepared might well experience a state of metrical bewilderment similar to that which we have suggested for the unsophisticated Roman hearer when confronted with the quantitative hexameter.

Viewed from a linguistic rather than a literary standpoint, the history of the hexameter from Homer to Eliot, through Ennius and Vergil, the Elizabethans, Klopstock and Longfellow, provides a succession of metrical mirrors in which the accentual and rhythmical characteristics of the language at any given time and place are reflected with lesser or greater degrees of distortion.

Editions of ancient Western grammatical and technical works

C   M. Consbruch (Hephaestion, *Enchiridion, cum commentariis veteribus*: Teubner, 1906).

GG   *Grammatici Graeci* (Teubner, 1867–1910: repr. 1965).

GL   *Grammatici Latini* (Teubner, 1857–1880).

H   A. Hilgard (*Scholia in Dionysii Thracis Artem Grammaticam = GG*, I.iii);

      (Choeroboscus, *Scholia in Theodosii Canones = GG*, IV.i–ii).

K   H. Keil (*GL*, i–vii).

L   A. Lentz (Herodianus Technicus = *GG*, III.i–ii).

S   R. Schneider (Apollonius Dyscolus, *Scripta minora = GG*, II.i).

U   G. Uhlig (Dionysius Thrax, *Ars Grammatica; Supplementa Artis Dionysianae vetusta = GG*, I.i);

      (Apollonius Dyscolus, *De Constructione = GG*, II.ii).

UR   H. Usener & L. Radermacher (Dionysius of Halicarnassus, *Opuscula*, ii: Teubner, 1904–29).

W   R. Westphal (Aristoxenus: Leipzig 1893: repr. Hildesheim 1965).

W-I   R. P. Winnington-Ingram (Aristides Quintilianus, *De Musica*: Teubner, 1963).

List of modern works cited

Major abbreviations of journal titles are those of *L'Année Philologique* (Paris) and the *Linguistic Bibliography* of the Permanent International Committee of Linguists (Utrecht/Antwerp).

Location of articles in journals is by first page only.

Dates in bold-face indicate that the work in question has been cited frequently in a chapter and so with date omitted after first citation.

An asterisk preceding an author's name indicates that, of two authors with the same surname, this is the one cited with an asterisk in the text. Allen, W. S. appears in the text as A.

Abdo, D. A. (1969) *Stress and Arabic Phonology*: Dissertation Ph.D. Illinois (Published as *On Stress and Arabic Phonology: a generative approach*: Beirut 1969).

Abercrombie, D. (1964a) 'A phonetician's view of verse structure': *Linguistics* 6, 5 (Reprinted in Abercrombie 1965).

(1964b) 'Syllable quantity and enclitics in English': *In Honour of Daniel Jones*, 216 (Reprinted in Abercrombie 1965).

(1965) *Studies in Phonetics and Linguistics*: London.

(1967) *Elements of General Phonetics*: Edinburgh.

Ahlberg, A. W. (1900) *De proceleusmaticis iamborum trochaeorumque antiquae scaenicae poesis latinae. Studia metrica et prosodiaca I, II*: Lund.

*Allen, F. D. (1888) 'On Greek versification in inscriptions': *Papers of the Amer. Sch. of Cl. St. at Athens* 4, 35.

Allen, W. S. (1951) 'Some prosodic aspects of retroflexion and aspiration in Sanskrit': *BSOAS* 13, 939 (Reprinted in *Palmer 1970).

(1953) *Phonetics in Ancient India*: London.

(1956) 'Structure and system in the Abaza verbal complex': *TPhS*, 127.

(1957) 'Aspiration in the Hāṛautī nominal': *Studies in Linguistic Analysis* (Special vol. of The Philological Soc.): Oxford, 68.

(1958) 'Some problems of palatalization in Greek': *Lingua* 7, 113.

(1959) 'Some remarks on the structure of Greek vowel-systems': *Word* 15, 240.

(1960) 'A note on "instability"': *Le Maître Phonétique*, 27.

(1962) *Sandhi*: The Hague.

(1964) 'On quantity and quantitative verse': *In Honour of Daniel Jones*, 3.

[361]

Allen, W. S. (1965) *Vox Latina*: Cambridge.
  (1966a) 'Prosody and prosodies in Greek': *TPhS*, 107.
  (1966b) 'A problem of Greek accentuation': *In Memory of J. R. Firth*, 8.
  (1967a) 'Correlations of tone and stress in ancient Greek': *To Honor Roman Jakobson*, 46.
  (1967b) 'The oral accentuation of Greek': *Didaskalos* 2.2, 90.
  (1968a) *Vox Graeca*: Cambridge.
  (1968b) Comment on Stanford 1968: *Didaskalos* 2.3, 152.
  (1969) 'The Latin accent: a restatement': *JL* 5, 193.
Anderson, J. (1969) 'Syllabic or non-syllabic phonology': *JL* 5, 136.
*Anderson, S. R. (1970) 'On Grassmann's Law in Sanskrit': *Linguistic Inquiry* 1, 387.
André, J. (1958) 'Accent, timbre et quantité dans les emprunts du latin au grec postérieurs au IIIe s. après J.C.': *BSL* 53, 138.
*Arnold, E. V. (1905) *Vedic Metre*: Cambridge.
Arnold, G. F. (1956) 'A phonological approach to vowel, consonant and syllable in modern French': *Lingua* 5, 253.
  (1957) 'Stress in English words': *Lingua* 6, 221, 397.
Attridge, D. (1972) *The Elizabethan experiments in English quantitative verse*: Dissertation Ph.D. Cambridge.
Axelson, B. (1958) 'Der Mechanismus des Ovidischen Pentameterschlusses: eine mikrophilologische Causerie': *Ovidiana* (ed. N. I. Herescu): Paris, 121.
Bailey, J. (1968) 'The basic structural characteristics of Russian literary meters': in Gribble (ed.) 1968, 17.
Bally, C. (1945) *Manuel d'accentuation grecque*: Berne.
Barkas, P. (1934) *A Critique of Modern English Prosody*: Halle.
Barrett, W. S. (ed.) (1964) *Euripides: Hippolytos*: Oxford.
Bauernschmidt, A. (1965) 'Amuzgo syllable dynamics': *Language* 41, 471.
Bazell, C. E. (1953) *Linguistic Form*: Istanbul.
Beardsley, M. C. See Wimsatt, W. K.
Beare, W. (1957) *Latin Verse and European Song*: London.
Beaver, J. C. (1968) 'A grammar of prosody': *CE* 29, 310 (Reprinted in Freeman (ed.) 1970).
  (1971) 'The rules of stress in English verse': *Language* 47, 586.
Beekes, R. S. P. (1971) 'The writing of consonant groups in Mycenaean': *Mnemosyne* 24, 338.
Behaghel, O. (1909) 'Beziehungen zwischen Umfang und Reihenfolge von Satzgliedern': *IF* 25, 110.
Bell, A. E. (1970a) 'Syllabic consonants': *Working Papers on Language Universals* (Stanford) 4, B1.

(1970b) *A state-process approach to syllabicity and syllable structure*: Dissertation Ph.D. Stanford.

(1971) 'Some patterns of occurrence and formation of syllabic structures': *Working Papers on Language Universals* 6, 23.

Bellermann, J. F. (1840) *Fragmentum Graecae scriptionis de musica*: Berlin.

*Bennett, C. E. (1898) 'What was ictus in Latin prosody?': *AJPh* 19, 361.

Bennett, W. (**1963**) *German Verse in Classical Metres*: The Hague.

Bentley, R. (1726) 'De Metris Terentianis ΣΧΕΔΙΑΣΜΑ': in *P. Terentii Afri Comoediae*: Cambridge, i.

Benveniste, E. (1951) 'La notion de "rythme" dans son expression linguistique': *JPsych* 44, 401 (Reprinted in Benveniste, *Problèmes de linguistique générale*: Paris 1966).

Bill, F. X. (1932) *Beiträge zur Lex Porsoniana*: Emsdetten.

Birkeland, H. (1954) *Stress Patterns in Arabic (Avh. Norske Videnskaps-Ak. i Oslo, II. Hist.-Fil. Kl.*, 1954 no. 3).

Blass, F. (1890) *Pronunciation of Ancient Greek*: Cambridge (Trsl. by W. J. Purton from *Über die Aussprache des Altgriechischen*[3]).

Bliss, A. J. (1953) 'Vowel-quantity in Middle English borrowings from Anglo-Norman': *ALing* 4, 121; 5, 22.

Bloch, B. (1950) 'Studies in colloquial Japanese IV. Phonemics': *Language* 26, 86.

Bloch, B. & G. L. Trager (1942) *Outline of Linguistic Analysis*: Baltimore.

Bloch, B. See also Trager, G. L.

Boer, R. C. (1918) 'Syncope en Consonantengeminatie': *TsNTL* 37, 161.

Bolinger, D. L. (1958a) 'A theory of pitch accent in English': *Word* 14, 109.

(1958b) 'On intensity as a qualitative improvement of pitch accent': *Lingua* 7, 175.

Bolling, G. M. (1913) 'Contributions to the study of Homeric metre. II: Length by position' (cont.): *AJPh* 34, 153.

Bolton, T. L. (1894) 'Rhythm': *AJPsych* 6, 145.

Bondarko, L. V. (1969) 'The syllable structure of speech and distinctive features of phonemes': *Phonetica* 20, 1.

Boomer, D. S. & J. D. M. Laver (1968) 'Slips of the tongue': *Brit. J. of Disorders of Comn.* 3, 2.

Borgstrøm, C. (1938) 'Zur Phonologie der norwegischen Schriftsprache', *NTS* 9: 250.

Borthwick, E. K. (1962) Review of Pöhlmann 1960: *CR* 12, 159.

Brenot, A. (1923) *Les mots et groupes iambiques réduits dans le théâtre latin*: Paris.

Broch, O. (1911) *Slavische Phonetik*: Heidelberg.

(1935) 'Rhythm in the spoken Norwegian language': *TPhS*, 80.

Brown, G. (1970) 'Syllables and redundancy rules in generative phonology': *JL* 6, 1.

(1972) *Phonological Rules and Dialect Variation: a Study of the Phonology of Lumasaaba*: Cambridge (*Studies in Linguistics*, vol. 7).

Brożek, M. (1949) 'De trimetrorum iambicorum apud tragicos Graecos exitu atque confinio observationes': *Eos* 43, 97.

Brücke, E. W. von (1871) *Die physiologischen Grundlagen der neuhochdeutschen Verkunst*: Vienna.

Brunner, L. (1956) 'Zur Elision langer Vokale im lateinischen Vers': *MH* 13, 185.

Buck, C. D. (1948) *Comparative Grammar of Greek and Latin* (rev. repr.): Chicago.

Bulloch, A. W. (1970) 'A Callimachean refinement of the Greek hexameter: a new "law" and some observations on Greek proclitics': *CQ* 20, 258.

Burger, A. (1928) *Études de phonétique et de morphologie latines* (*Recueil de Trav., Fac. des Lettres de l'Univ. de Neuchâtel*, 13).

*Burger, M. (1957) *Recherches sur la structure et l'origine des vers romans*: Geneva.

Burrow, T. (1955) *The Sanskrit Language*: London.

Campbell, A. (1953) 'Some linguistic features of early Anglo-Latin verse and its use of classical models': *TPhS*, 1.

*Campbell, L. (1971) Review of King 1969: *Language* 47, 191.

Cardona, G. (1968) 'Pāṇini's definition, description, and use of *svarita*': *Pratidānam*, 448.

Castillo, C. (1968) '"Numerus", qui graece "ῥυθμός" dicitur': *Emerita* 36, 279.

Cataudella, Q. (1968) 'Spondei in II e in IV sede nel trimetro della commedia': *SIFC* 40, 61.

Ceadel, E. B. (1941) 'Resolved feet in the trimeters of Euripides': *CQ* 35, 66.

Chaignet, A. E. (1887) *Essais de métrique grecque*: Paris.

Chandler, H. W. (1881) *A Practical Introduction to Greek Accentuation*[2]: Oxford.

Chantraine, P. (1958) *Grammaire Homérique. I: Phonétique et morphologie* (3rd imp.): Paris.

Chatman, S. (1960) 'Comparing metrical styles': in Sebeok (ed.) 1960, 149.

(1965) *A Theory of Meter*: The Hague.

Chen, M. (1970) 'Vowel length variation as a function of the voicing of the consonant environment': *Phonetica* 22, 129.

Cheng, R. L. (1966) 'Mandarin phonological structure': *JL* 2, 135.

Chlumský, J. (1928) *Česká kvantita, melodie a přízvuk* (Rés. in French): Prague.

(1935) 'Analyse de *Traité de Phonétique* de M. Grammont': *ANPE* 11, 73.

Chomsky, N. (1964) *Current Issues in Linguistic Theory*: The Hague.

(1967) 'Some general properties of phonological rules': *Language* 47, 102.

Chomsky, N. & M. Halle (1965) 'Some controversial questions in phonological theory': *JL* 1, 97.

(1968) *The Sound Pattern of English*: New York.

Christ, W. (1879) *Metrik der Griechen und Römer*²: Leipzig.

Classe, A. (1939) *The Rhythm of English Prose*: Oxford.

Cole, T. (1969) 'The Saturnian verse': *YClS* 21, 1.

Collinder, B. (1937) 'Über Quantität und Intensität': *NPhM* 38, 97.

Collinge, N. E. (1970) 'Computation and Latin consonants': in Collinge, *Collectanea Linguistica*: The Hague, 192.

(1971) Review of King 1969: *JL* 7, 253.

Conrad, C. (1965) 'Traditional patterns of word-order in Latin epic from Ennius to Vergil': *HSPh* 69, 195.

Cook, E.-D. (1972) 'On the relativity of tones': *Lingua* 29, 30.

*Cook, M. J. (1961) *Phonetic and phonemic properties of stress in English*: Dissertation Ph.D. Texas.

Cooper, F. S. See Liberman, A. M.

Cooper, G. W. & L. B. Meyer (1960) *The Rhythmic Structure of Music*: Chicago.

Crusius, O. (1892) *Untersuchungen zu den Mimiamben des Herondas*: Leipzig.

(1894a) 'Zu neuentdeckten antiken Musikresten': *Philologus* 52, 160.

(1894b) 'Die Betonung des Choliambus. 11': *Philologus* 53, 216.

Crystal, D. (1969) *Prosodic Systems and Intonation in English*: Cambridge (*Studies in Linguistics*, vol. 1).

Cunningham, I. C. (ed.) (1971) *Herodas: Mimiambi*: Oxford.

Dalbor, J. B. (1969) *Spanish Pronunciation: Theory and Practice*: New York.

Dale, A. M. (1957) 'Greek Metric 1936–57': *Lustrum* 2, 5.

(1958) 'Resolutions in the trochaic tetrameter': *Glotta* 37, 102 (Reprinted in Dale 1969b).

(1964) 'Observations on Dactylic': *WS* 77, 15 (Reprinted in Dale 1969b).

(1968) *The Lyric Metres of Greek Drama*²: Cambridge.

(1969a) 'Expressive rhythm in the lyrics of Greek drama': in Dale 1969b, 248.

(1969b) *Collected Papers*: Cambridge.

Darden, B. J. (1971) 'A note on Sommer's claim that there exist languages without CV syllables': *IJAL* 37, 126.

Davis, R. C. See Eliason, N. E.

Debrunner, A. (1930) Review of Laum 1928: *ByzZ* 29, 50.

DeClerk, J. L. See MacNeilage, P. F.

de Groot, A. W. (1927) 'La syllabe: Essai de synthèse': *BSL* 27, 1.

(1930) 'La métrique générale et le rythme': *BSL* 30, 202.

(1931) 'Phonologie und Phonetik als Funktionswissenschaften': *TCLP* 4, 116.

(1932) 'Der Rhythmus': *NPh* 17, 81.

(1935) 'Wesen und Gesetze der Caesur': *Mnemosyne* 3 ser. 2, 81.

(1968) 'Phonetics in its relation to aesthetics': in Malmberg (ed.) 1968, 533.

Delattre, P. (1944) 'L'aperture et la syllabation phonétique': *FR* 17, 281.

Delgado, J. J. (1963) 'El hexámetro virgiliano': *EClás* 7, 146.

Denniston, J. D. (1936) 'Pauses in the tragic senarius': *CQ* 30, 73.

de Saussure, F. (1889) Paper reported in *BSL* 7 (1892), xvi.

(1916/1960) *Course in General Linguistics*: London (Trsl. by W. Baskin from *Cours de Linguistique Générale*: Lausanne/Paris).

Descroix, J. (**1931**) *Le trimètre iambique*: Mâcon.

de Thomasson, Lt.-Col. (1937) 'La poésie métrique française aux xvie–xviiie siècles': *FM* 5, 41.

Dietrich, A. (1852) 'Zur Geschichte des Accents im Lateinischen': *ZVS* 1, 543.

Dihle, A. (1954) 'Die Anfänge der griechischen akzentuierenden Verskunst': *Hermes* 82, 182.

Dixon, R. M. W. (1970) 'Olgolo syllable structure and what they are doing about it': *Linguistic Inquiry* 1, 273.

Doke, C. M. (1954) *The Southern Bantu Languages*: London.

Dottin, G. (1901) 'Les composés syntactiques et la loi de Porson': *RPh* 25, 197.

Draper, M. H., P. Ladefoged & D. Whitteridge (1960) 'Expiratory pressures and air-flow during speech': *BMJ*, 1837.

Draper, M. H. See also Ladefoged, P.

Drerup, E. (1930–32) *Die Schulaussprache des Griechischen von der Renaissance bis zur Gegenwart* (= *St. z. Gesch. u. Kultur des Altertums*, Ergänzungsb. 6, 7): Paderborn.

Drewitt, J. A. J. (1908) 'Some differences between speech-scansion and narrative-scansion in Homeric verse': *CQ* 2, 94.

Drexler, H. (1933) *Plautinische Akzentstudien, I, II* (1932), *Index* (1933) (= *Abh. d. schles. Ges. f. vaterländ. Cultur*, vi, vii, ix).

(1965) '*Lizenzen*' *am Versanfang bei Plautus*: München.

(1967) *Einführung in die römische Metrik*: Darmstadt.

(1969a) *Die Iambenkürzung. Kürzung der zweiten Silbe eines iambischen Wortes, eines iambischen Wortanfangs*: Hildesheim.

(1969b) 'Arcana der Iambenkürzung': *Festschr. f. Franz Altheim. I* (Berlin), 346.

Duckworth, G. E. (1969) *Vergil and classical hexameter poetry. A study in metrical variety*: Ann Arbor.

Durand, M. (1955) 'La notion de syllabe': *Orbis* 4, 230.

Ebeling, C. L. (1960) *Linguistic Units*: The Hague.

(1968) 'On accent in Dutch and the phoneme /ə/': *Lingua* 21, 135.

Ehrlich, H. (1912) *Untersuchungen über die Natur der griechischen Betonung*: Berlin.

Einarsson, S. (1945) *Icelandic: Grammar, Texts, Glossary*: Baltimore.

Eliason, N. E. (1939) 'The short vowels in French loan words like *city*, etc.': *Anglia* 63, 73.

(1942) 'On syllable division in phonemics': *Language* 18, 144.

Eliason, N. E. & R. C. Davis (1939) *The effect of stress upon quantity in dissyllables: An experimental and historical study* (Indiana Univ. Publs., Science Ser. No. 8): Bloomington.

Eliot, T. S. (1917) 'Reflexions on *Vers Libre*': *New Statesman* viii, 204 (March 3, 1917), 518.

(1942) *The Music of Poetry*: Glasgow.

Emeneau, M. B. (1944) *Kota Texts, Part I* (U.Cal. Pubns. in Linguistics 2: 1): Berkeley/Los Angeles.

Enk, P. J. (1953) 'The Latin accent': *Mnemosyne* 4 ser. vi, 93.

Enríquez, J. A. (1968) 'Apunte sobre el problema de la apofonía vocálica en latín'; *Actas del III Cong. Español de Estudios Clásicos* (1966), III: *Coloquio de estudios estructurales sobre las lenguas clásicas*: Madrid, 85.

Epstein, E. L. & T. Hawkes (1959) *Linguistics and English Prosody* (= *SiL* Occasional Papers, 7): Buffalo.

Errandonea, I. (1945) '¿Erasmo o Nebrija?': *Emerita* 13, 65.

Exon, C. (1906) 'The relation of the resolved arsis and resolved thesis in Plautus to the prose accent': *CR* 20, 31.

(1907) 'The secondary accentuation of Latin words of the type of *consuluisti*': *CPh* 2, 341.

Fant, C. G. M. (1957) *Modern instruments and methods for acoustic studies of speech* (Report no. 8 of the Speech Transmission Lab., R.Inst. of Technology: Divn. of Telegraphy-Telephony, Stockholm).

Fant, C. G. M. See also Jakobson, R.

Faure, G. (1970) *Les éléments du rythme poétique en anglais moderne*: The Hague.

Fehling, D. (1967) Review of Allen 1965: *Gymnasium* 74, 179.

Ferguson, C. A. (1956) Review of Birkeland 1954: *Language* 32, 384.

Fink, R. O. (1969) 'A long vowel before final *m* in Latin?': *AJPh* 90, 444.

Firth, J. R. (1948) 'Sounds and prosodies': *TPhS*, 127.

(1950) Introd. to T. Grahame Bailey, *Teach Yourself Hindustani*: London.

Firth, J. R. *In Memory of J. R. Firth*, ed. C. E. Bazell et al., 1966: London.

Fischer, I. (1961) 'Phonèmes et graphèmes vocaliques dans l'orthographe ionicnne-attique classique': *StudClas* 3, 29.

Fischer-Jørgensen, E. (1941) 'Neuere Beiträge zum Quantitätsproblem': *AL* 2, 175.

(1967) 'Phonetic analysis of breathy (murmured) vowels in Gujarati': *IL* 28, 71.

Fitzhugh, T. (1923) 'The pyrrhic accent and rhythm of Latin and Keltic' (repr. from *Alumni Bulletin* Apr. 1923, Univ. of Virginia).

Fleisch, H. (1950) *Études de phonétique arabe* (= *Mél. de l'univ. St Joseph* xxviii, 6): Beirut.

Fliflet, A. L. (1963) 'Syllable type and syllable perception': *Phonetica* 10, 187.

Fónagy, I. (1958) 'Elektrophysiologische Beiträge zur Akzentfrage': *Phonetica* 2, 12.

Fouché, P. (1927) *Études de phonétique générale*, Paris (Publ. de la fac. des lettres de l'Univ. de Strasbourg, 39).

Fowler, R. (1966) '"Prose Rhythm" and Meter': in *Essays on Style and Language* (ed. R. Fowler: New York), 82 (Reprinted in Freeman (ed.) 1970).

Fraenkel, E. (1928) *Iktus und Akzent im lateinischen Sprechvers*: Berlin.

(1932) 'Kolon und Satz. Beobachtungen zur Gliederung des antiken Satzes': *NAWG*, 197.

Fränkel, H. F. (1960) *Wege und Formen frühgriechischen Denkens*[2]: München.

Frank, T. (1924) 'Latin quantitative speech as affected by immigration': *AJPh* 45, 161.

Freeman, D. C. (1968) 'On the primes of metrical style': *Language & style* 1, 63 (Reprinted in Freeman (ed.) 1970).

Freeman, D. C. (ed.) (1970) *Linguistics and Literary Style*: New York.

Fromkin, V. A. (1966) 'Neuro-muscular specification of linguistic units': *Language & Speech* 9, 170.

(1968) 'Speculations on performance models': *JL* 4, 47.

Fry, D. B. (1958) 'Experiments in the perception of stress': *Language & Speech* 1, 126.

(1964) 'The function of the syllable': *ZPhon* 17, 215.

(1968) 'Prosodic phenomena': in Malmberg (ed.) 1968, 365.

Fudge, E. C. (1969) 'Syllables': *JL* 5, 253.

Fussell, P. (1954) *Theory of Prosody in Eighteenth-century England*: New London, Conn.

(1965) *Poetic Meter and Poetic Form*: New York.

Gairdner, W. H. T. (1925) *The Phonetics of Arabic*: London.

Galton, H. (1962) 'The fixation of the accent in Latin and Greek': *ZPhon* 15, 273.

Garde, P. (**1968**) *L'Accent*: Paris.

Gardiner, P. (1952) *The Nature of Historical Explanation*: London.

Gardner, H. (1949) *The Art of T. S. Eliot*: London.

Gauthiot, R. (1913) *La fin de mot en indo-européen*: Paris.

Gay, T. See Lieberman, P.

Getty, R. J. (1963) 'Classical Latin metre and prosody 1935–1962': *Lustrum* 8, 103.

Gimson, A. C. (1956) 'The linguistic relevance of stress in English': *ZPhon* 9, 143.

(1970) *An Introduction to the Pronunciation of English*[2]: London.

Gimson, A. C. See also Jones 1967.

Goodell, T. D. (1885) 'Quantity in English verse': *TAPhA* 16, 78.

(1901) *Chapters on Greek Metric*: New York/London.

(1906) 'Bisected trimeters in Attic tragedy': *CPh* 1, 145.

Gordon, I. A. (1966) *The Movement of English Prose*: London.

Grammont, M. (1946) *Traité de phonétique*[3]: Paris.

(1948) *Phonétique du grec ancien*: Lyon.

Graur, A. (1939) 'La quatrième conjugaison latine': *BSL* 40, 127.

Gray, J. E. B. (1959) 'An analysis of Ṛgvedic recitation': *BSOAS* 22, 86.

Greenberg, J. (1965) 'Some generalizations concerning initial and final consonant sequences': *Linguistics* 18, 5.

*Greenberg, N. A. (1967) 'Vergil and the computer. Fourth foot texture in Aeneid I': *RELO* 1, 1.

Greene, W. C. (1951) 'The spoken and the written word': *HSPh* 60, 23.

Gribble, C. E. (ed.) (1968) *Studies presented to Professor Roman Jakobson by his students*: Cambridge, Mass.

Gross, H. (1964) *Sound and Form in Modern Poetry*: Ann Arbor.

Gudschinsky, S. C. & H. & F. Popovich (1970) 'Native reaction and phonetic similarity in Maxakalí phonology': *Language* 46, 77.

Hála, B. (1961) 'La syllabe, sa nature, son origine et ses transformations': *Orbis* 10, 69.

Hall, R. A. (1964) 'Initial consonants and syntactic doubling in West Romance': *Language* 40, 551.

(1971) 'The syllable in Italian phonology': *Linguistics* 67, 26.

Halle, M. (1970) 'On meter and prosody': in M. Bierwisch & K. E. Heidolph (ed.), *Progress in Linguistics*: The Hague, 64.

(1971) 'Remarks on Slavic accentology': *Linguistic Inquiry* 2, 1.

Halle, M. & S. J. Keyser (1966) 'Chaucer and the study of prosody': *CE* 28, 187 (Reprinted in Freeman (ed.) 1970).

Halle, M. & S. J. Keyser (**1971**) *English Stress: Its form, its growth, and its role in verse*: NewYork.

Halle, M. See also Chomsky, N.; Jakobson, R.

Halliday, M. A. K. (1963) 'The tones of English': *ALing* 15, 1.

Halporn, J. W. (1967) 'Nietzsche: On the theory of quantitative rhythm': *Arion* 6, 233.

Hamp, E. P. (1957) *A Glossary of American Technical Linguistic Usage*: Utrecht/Antwerp.

(1958) 'Prosodic notes': *IJAL* 24, 321.

Hanssen, F. (1882) 'Ueber den griechischen Wortiktus': *RhM* 37, 252.

(1883) 'Ein musikalisches Accentgesetz in der quantitirenden Poesie der Griechen': *RhM* 38, 222.

Hardie, W. R. (1920) *Res Metrica*: Oxford.

Harms, R. T. (1968) *Introduction to Phonological Theory*: Englewood Cliffs, N.J.

Harrell, R. S. (1957) *The Phonology of Colloquial Egyptian Arabic* (ACLS Program in Oriental Languages, Publ., B, 9): New York.

(1962) 'Consonant, vowel and syllable in Moroccan Arabic': *PICPhSc IV*: The Hague, 643.

*Harris, J. M. (1940) 'The hexameters of the Carmina Epigraphica': *PAPhA* 71, xl.

Harris, K. S. See Liberman, A. M.; Lieberman, P.

Harris, Z. S. (1944) 'Simultaneous components in phonology': *Language* 20, 181.

(1951) *Methods in Structural Linguistics*: Chicago.

Harsh, P. W. (1949) *Iambic words and regard for accent in Plautus*: Stanford.

Haugen, E. (1949) 'Phoneme or prosodeme?': *Language* 25, 278.

(1956) 'The syllable in linguistic description': *For Roman Jakobson*, 213.

(1958) 'The phonemics of modern Icelandic': *Language* 34, 55.

Haugen, E. & M. Joos (1952) 'Tone and intonation in East Norwegian': *APhS* 22, 41.

Hawkes, T. See Epstein, E. L.

Heffner, R.-M. S. (1950) *General Phonetics*: Madison, Wis.

Heike, G. (1969) *Sprachliche Kommunikation und linguistische Analyse*: Heidelberg.

Hellegouarc'h, J. (1969) 'La ponctuation bucolique dans les Satires de Juvénal. Étude métrique et stylistique': *Mélanges de linguistique...* *offerts à M. René Fohalle* (ed. C. Hyart): Gembloux, 173.

Hendrickson, G. L. (1899) Review of *Bennett 1898: *AJPh* 20, 198.

(**1949**) 'Elizabethan quantitative hexameters': *PhQ* 28, 237.

Herescu, N. I. (1960) *La Poésie Latine*: Paris.

(1963) *Style et hasard* (= *Langue et Parole*, iv): München.

*Hermann, E. (1923) *Silbenbildung im Griechischen und in den andern indogermanischen Sprachen*: Göttingen.

Hermann, J. G. J. (1800) *Euripidis Hecuba: G. Hermanni ad eam et ad R. Porsoni notas animadversiones*: Leipzig.

(1818) *Epitome doctrinae metricae*: Leipzig.

Herzog, M. I. See Weinreich, U.

Heubeck, A. (1972) 'Syllabic ṛ in Mycenaean Greek?': *Acta Mycenaea* (= *Proc. V Int. Colloq. on Myc. St.* (1970)), ii (= *Minos* 12), 55.

Heusler, A. (1917) *Deutscher und antiker Vers*: Strassburg.

Hiersche, R. (1957) 'Herkunft und Sinn des Terminus "positione longa"': *F & F* 31, 280.

Higginbottom, E. (1964) 'Glottal reinforcement in English': *TPhS*, 129.

Hilberg, I. (1879) *Das Princip der Silbenwaegung und die daraus entspringenden Gesetze der Endsilben in der griechischen Poesie*: Vienna.

Hirt, H. (1927) *Indogermanische Grammatik. I*: Heidelberg.

Hjelmslev, L. (1938) 'The syllable as a structural unit': *PICPhSc III*: Ghent, 266.

Hoard, J. E. (1966) 'Juncture and syllable structure in English': *Phonetica* 15, 96.

(1971) 'Aspiration, tenseness and syllabication in English': *Language* 47, 133.

Hockett, C. F. (1955) *A Manual of Phonology* (Mem. 11 of *IJAL* (*IJAL* 21.4, Pt. 1)): Baltimore.

Hoenigswald, H. M. (1949a) 'A note on Latin prosody: Initial *s* impure after short vowel': *TAPhA* 80, 271.

(1949b) 'Antevocalic u-diphthongs in Latin': *Language* 25, 392.

(1954) 'Media, Neutrum und Zirkumflex': *Festschr. A. Debrunner*: Berne, 209.

(1968) 'Certain semivowel sequences in Greek': *Pratidānam*, 20.

Hoerschelmann, W. (1894) '*Die Betonung des Choliambus. I*': *Philologus* 53, 214.

Hofmann, J. B. (rev. A. Szantyr) (1965) *Lateinische Syntax und Stilistik* (= I. von Müller, *Hb. d. Altertumsw.* 11.2.ii): München.

Hollander, J. (1959) 'The metrical emblem': *Kenyon Review* 21, 279.

Holmer, N. M. (1966) 'Notes on the system of stress in Maori': *AL* 9, 163.

Householder, F. W. (1964) 'A morphophonemic question and a spelling rule': *Mycenaean Studies* (= *Proc. III Int. Coll. for Myc. Studies*, 1961): Madison, Wis., 71.

Housman, A. E. (1928) 'Prosody and method II: the metrical properties of *gn*': *CQ* 22, 1.

Hrushovski, B. (1960) 'On free rhythms in modern poetry': in Sebeok (ed.) 1960, 173.

Huffman, F. E. (1972) 'The boundary between the monosyllable and the disyllable in Cambodian': *Lingua* 29, 54.

Irigoin, J. (1959) 'Lois et règles dans le trimètre iambique et le tétramètre trochaïque: *REG* 72, 67.

(1965) Review of Rossi 1963a: *GGA* 217, 224.

(1967) 'Colon, vers et période': Κωμῳδοτραγήματα: *Studia Aristophanea, viri Aristophanei W. J. W. Koster in honorem*: Amsterdam, 65.

Jachmann, G. (1916) 'Zur altlateinischen Prosodie': *Glotta* 7, 39.

Jaina, B. D. (1926) 'Stress-accent in Indo-Aryan': *BSOS* 4, 315.

Jakobi, H. (1899) 'Der Accent im Mittelindischen': *ZVS* 35, 563.

(1913) 'Über eine neue Sandhiregel im Pāli und im Prakrit der Jainas und über die Betonung in diesen Sprachen': *IF* 31, 220.

Jakobson, R. (1926/1962) 'Contributions to the study of Czech accent': in Jakobson 1962, 614 (From *Slavia* 4).

(1931/1962) 'Die Betonung und ihre Rolle in der Wort- und Syntagma-phonologie': in Jakobson 1962, 117 (From *TCLP* 4).

(1933) 'Über den Versbau der Serbokroatischen Volksepen': *PICPhSc I* (= *ANPE* 8–9), 135.

(1937a/1962) 'Über die Beschaffenheit der prosodischen Gegensätze': in Jakobson 1962, 254 (From *Mél. de linguistique...J. van Ginneken*: Paris).

(1937b/1962) 'On ancient Greek prosody': in Jakobson 1962, 262 (From *Z zagadnień poetyki: Prace ofiarowane K. Wóycickiemu*: Wilno).

(1941/1968) *Child Language, Aphasia and Phonological Universals*: The Hague (Trsl. by A. R. Keiler from *Kindersprache, Aphasie und allgemeine Lautgesetze* = *UUA* 1942: 9).

(1952) 'Studies in comparative Slavic metrics': *OSlP* 3, 21.

(1958/1962) 'Typological studies and their contribution to historical comparative linguistics': in Jakobson 1962, 523 (From *PICL VIII*: Oslo).

(1960) 'Linguistics and Poetics': in Sebeok (ed.) 1960, 350.

(1962) *Selected Writings. I. Phonological Studies*: The Hague.

Jakobson, R. *For Roman Jakobson; essays on the occasion of his sixtieth birthday*, ed. M. Halle et al., 1956: The Hague.

To Honor Roman Jakobson; essays on the occasion of his seventieth birthday, 1967: The Hague.

Studies presented to Professor Roman Jakobson by his students, ed. C. E. Gribble, 1968: Cambridge, Mass.

Jakobson, R. & M. Halle (1956) *Fundamentals of Language*: The Hague.

(1964) 'Tenseness and laxness': *In Honour of Daniel Jones*, 96.

(1968) 'Phonology in relation to phonetics': in Malmberg (ed.) 1968, 411.

Jakobson, R., C. G. M. Fant & M. Halle (1952) *Preliminaries to Speech Analysis* (MIT Acoustics Lab., Tech. Rep. No. 13): Cambridge, Mass.

Jan, C. (ed.) (1895) *Musici scriptores Graeci*: Leipzig.

Jassem, W. (1959) 'The phonology of Polish stress': *Word* 15, 252.

Jensen, M. K. (1958) 'Recognition of word tones in whispered speech': *Word* 14, 187.

(1961) *Tonemicity: Årbok for Univ. i Bergen, Hum. ser.* 1961.

Jespersen, O. (1900/1933) 'Notes on Metre': in Jespersen 1933, 249 (From *Oversigt* 1900).

(1913) *Lehrbuch der Phonetik*²: Leipzig/Berlin.

(1933) *Linguistica: Selected papers in English, French & German*: Copenhagen/London.

Jones, D. (1950) *The Phoneme*: Cambridge.

(1954) 'Falling and rising diphthongs in Southern English': *Misc. Phon. II*: London, 1.

(1962) *An Outline of English Phonetics*⁹: Cambridge.

Jones, D. (ed. A. C. Gimson) (1967) *An English Pronouncing Dictionary*¹³: London.

Jones, D. *In Honour of Daniel Jones: Papers contributed on the occasion of his eightieth birthday*, ed. D. Abercrombie et al., 1964: London.

*Jones, D. M. (1971) Review of Allen 1968a: *CR* 21, 295.

Jongen, R. (1969) 'Intonation de phrase, accent de phrase, accent de mot et accentuation rhénane': *Lingua* 23, 315.

Joos, M. (1948) *Acoustic Phonetics* (*Language* Monograph No. 23): Baltimore.

Joos, M. See also Haugen, E.

Juilland, A. (1948) Report of paper in *BSL* 43, lv.

Kabell, A. (1960) *Metrische Studien II: Antiker Form sich nähernd*: *UUA* 1960: 6.

Kalinka, E. (1935) 'Griechisch-römische Metrik und Rhythmik im letzten Vierteljahrhundert': *JAW* Supplementband 250, 290.

Kapp, E. (1941) 'Bentley's Schediasma "De metris Terentianis" and the modern doctrine of ictus in classical verse': *Mnemosyne* 3 ser. 9, 187.

Kauffmann, F. (1907) *Deutsche Metrik nach ihrer geschichtlichen Entwicklung*: Marburg.

Keith, A. B. (1928) *A History of Sanskrit Literature*: London.

Kent, R. G. (1920) 'The alleged conflict of the accents in Latin verse': *TAPhA* 51, 19.

(1922) 'The educated Roman and his accent': *TAPhA* 53, 63.

(1932) *The Sounds of Latin* (*Language* Monograph No. 12): Baltimore (Reprinted 1966: New York).

(1946) *The Forms of Latin* (Spec. Publ. of the LSA): Baltimore.

Kent, R. G. (1948) 'A problem of Latin prosody': *Mél. de philologie...* *J. Marouzeau*: Paris, 303.

Kent, R. G. See also Sturtevant, E. H.

Kenyon, J. S. & T. A. Knott (1953) *A pronouncing dictionary of American English*: Springfield, Mass.

Kerek, A. (1968) *Stress, Length and Prominence: Linguistic aspects of prosody in Hungarian quantitative-iambic verse*: Dissertation Ph.D. Indiana.

Keyser, S. J. (1969) 'The linguistic basis of English prosody': in Schane & Reibel (ed.) 1969, 379.

Keyser, S. J. See also Halle, M.

Kindberg, W. See Pike, K. L.

King, R. D. (1969) *Historical Linguistics and Generative Grammar*: Englewood Cliffs, N.J.

Kiparsky, P. (1965) *Phonological Change*: Dissertation Ph.D. MIT.

(1967a) 'À propos de l'histoire de l'accentuation grecque': *Langages* 8, 73.

(1967b) 'A phonological rule of Greek': *Glotta* 44, 109.

(1967c) 'Sonorant clusters in Greek': *Language* 43, 619.

(1968) 'Metrics and morphophonemics in the Kalevala': in Gribble (ed.) 1968, 137 (Reprinted in Freeman (ed.) 1970).

Kirk, G. S. (1962) *The Songs of Homer*: Cambridge.

(1966) 'Studies in some technical aspects of Homeric style': *YClS* 20, 73.

Klingenheben, A. (1928) 'Die Silbenauslautgesetze des Hausa': *Z. f. eingeb. Spr.* 18, 272.

Knight, W. F. J. (1950) *Accentual Symmetry in Vergil²*: Oxford.

Knott, T. A. See Kenyon, J. S.

Knox, A. D. (1932) 'The early iambus': *Philologus* 87, 18.

Körte, A. (1912) 'Die Episynaloiphe': *Glotta* 3, 153.

Köster, A. (1902) 'Deutsche Daktylen': *Z. f. deutsches Altertum* 46, 113.

Kohler, K. J. (1966) 'Is the syllable a phonological universal?': *JL* 2, 207.

Kollmann, E. D. (1968) 'Remarks on the structure of the Latin hexameter': *Glotta* 96, 293.

Koster, W. J. W. (1953) *Traité de métrique grecque suivi d'un précis de métrique latine²*: Leiden.

Krámský, J. (1966) 'On the phonological law of incompatibility of free quantity and free stress': *TLP* 2, 133.

(1969) *The Word as a Linguistic Unit*: The Hague.

Kretschmer, P. (1938) 'Der Ursprung des Fragetons und Fragesatzes': *Scritti...Trombetti*, 27.

Kuipers, A. H. (1960) *Phoneme and Morpheme in Kabardian*: The Hague.

Kurath, H. (1964) *A Phonology and Prosody of Modern English*: Heidelberg.

Kuryłowicz, J. (1948/1960) 'Contribution à la théorie de la syllabe': in Kuryłowicz 1960, 193 (From *BPTJ* 8).

(1949/1960) 'Latin and Germanic metre': in Kuryłowicz 1960, 294 (From *English & Germanic Studies* 2).

(1958) *L'accentuation des langues indo-européennes*[2]: Wrocław.

(1960) *Esquisses Linguistiques*: Wrocław/Kraków.

(1966) 'Accent and quantity as elements of rhythm': *Poetics II*: Warsaw, 163.

(1968a) 'A remark on Lachmann's Law': *HSPh* 72, 295.

(1968b) 'Hindī accentuation as a historical problem': in *Studies in Indian Linguistics* (*Vol. presented to Prof. M. B. Emeneau on his 60th birthday year*) (ed. Bh. Krishnamurti): Poona, 208.

(1968c) *Indogermanische Grammatik. II* (*Akzent: Ablaut*): Heidelberg.

(1970) 'The quantitative meter of Indo-European': in *Indo-European and Indo-Europeans* (= *Proc. III I.-E. Conf.*, 1966): Philadelphia, 421.

Labov, W. See Weinreich, U.

Ladefoged, P. (1958) (with the assistance of M. H. Draper & D. Whitteridge) 'Syllables and stress': *Misc. Phon. III*: London, 1.

(1967) *Three Areas of Experimental Phonetics*: London.

Ladefoged, P. See also Draper, M. H.

Laidlaw, W. A. (1938) *The Prosody of Terence*: London.

Langen, P. (1888) 'Bemerkungen über die Beobachtung des Wortaccentes im älteren lateinischen Drama': *Philologus* 46, 401.

Langendoen, D. T. (1968) *The London School of Linguistics* (MIT Research Monograph No. 46): Cambridge, Mass.

Lanz, H. (1931) *The Physical Basis of Rime*: Stanford.

Laum, B. (1928) *Das Alexandrinische Akzentuationssystem* (= *St. z. Gesch. u. Kultur des Altertums*, Ergänzungsb. 4): Paderborn.

Laver, J. D. M. See Boomer, D. S.

Laziczius, G. (1961/1966) 'Geschichte der Silbenfrage': in Sebeok (ed.) 1966, 171 (From *Lehrbuch der Phonetik*: Berlin, 156).

Lebrun, Y. (1966a) 'Sur la syllabe, sommet de sonorité': *Phonetica* 14, 1.

(1966b) 'Sur l'activité du diaphragme au cours de la phonation': *La Linguistique* 1966.2, 71.

(1966c) 'Is stress essentially a thoracic or an abdominal pulse? A finding of "Not Proven"': in Lebrun (ed.) 1966, 69.

(1970) 'On tension': *Linguistique contemporaine: Hommage à Éric Buyssens* (ed. J. Dierickx & Y. Lebrun): Brussels, 115.

Lebrun, Y. (ed.) (1966) *Linguistic Research in Belgium*: Wetteren.

Lecerf, J. (1969) 'Structure syllabique en arabe de Bagdad et accent de mot en arabe oriental': *Word* 25, 160.

Leech, G. N. (1969) *A linguistic guide to English poetry*: London.

Lehiste, I. (1970) *Suprasegmentals*: Cambridge, Mass.

Lehmann, W. P. (1956) *The Development of Germanic Verse Form*: Austin.
(1967) *A Reader in nineteenth-century Indo-European Linguistics*: Blooming-
ton/London.

Lehto, L. (1969) *English stress and its modification by intonation*: Ann.
Acad. Sc. Fenn., ser. B, vol. 164.

Lejeune, M. (1955) *Traité de phonétique grecque*[2]: Paris.

Lenneberg, E. H. (1967) *Biological Foundations of Language*: New York.

Léon, R., G. Faure & A. Rigault (ed.) (1970) *Prosodic Feature Analysis*
(= *Studia Phonetica* 3): Montreal/Paris/Brussels.

Lepscky, G. C. (1962) 'Il problema dell'accento latino': *ASNP* ser. ii, 31,
199.

Leumann, M. (1928) *Lateinische Laut- und Formenlehre* (= I. von Müller,
Hb. d. Altertumsw. 11.2.i): München (Repr. 1963).

Liberman, A. M., F. S. Cooper, M. Studdert-Kennedy, K. S. Harris &
D. P. Shankweiler (1968): 'On the efficiency of speech sounds':
ZPhon 21, 21.

Liberman, A. M. See also Lisker, L.

Lieberman, P. (1967) *Intonation, Perception and Language*: Cambridge,
Mass.
(1968) 'On the structure of prosody': *ZPhon* 21, 157.

Lieberman, P., M. Sawashima, K. S. Harris & T. Gay (1970) 'The articulatory implementation of the breath-group and prominence: crico-
thyroid muscular activity in intonation': *Language* 46, 312.

Lieger, P. (1926): *Der Akzent in der Verskunst der Griechen und Römer*:
Progr. Wien, Schottengymn.

Liénard, E. (1969) 'Réflexions sur l'accent latin': *Mél. M. Renard* (= *Coll.
Latomus* 101), 551.

Lightner, T. M. (1971) 'On Swadesh & Voegelin's "A problem in phonological alternation"': *IJAL* 37, 227.

Lindholm, E. (1931) *Stilistische Studien zur Erweiterung der Satzglieder im
Lateinischen*: Lund.

Lindsay, W. M. (1894) 'The accentual element in early Latin verse':
TPhS 1891–4, 405.
(1922) *Early Latin Verse*: Oxford.

Lisker, L., F. S. Cooper & A. M. Liberman (1962) 'The uses of experiment
in language description': *Word* 18, 82.

Lloyd, R. J. (1906) 'Glides between consonants in English: § 12: Syllables,
syllabification and syllabic stress': *NS* 13, 82; 160.

Lord, A. B. (1960) *The Singer of Tales*: Cambridge, Mass.

Lotz, J. (1960) 'Metric typology': in Sebeok (ed.) 1960, 135.

Lucot, R. (1969) 'Sur l'accent de mot dans l'hexamètre latin': *Pallas* 16, 79.

Ludwich, A. (1885) *Aristarchs Homerische Textkritik nach den Fragmenten des Didymos. II*: Leipzig.

Luick, K. (1897) Review of L. Morsbach, *Mittelenglische Grammatik. I* (Halle 1896): *ASNS* 98, 425.

(1898) 'Die Quantitätsveränderungen im Laufe der englischen Sprachentwicklung': *Anglia* 20, 335.

Lupaş, L. (1967) 'L'interprétation phonologique de l'accentuation attique': *StudClas* 9, 7.

Lyons, J. (1968) *Introduction to Theoretical Linguistics*: Cambridge.

Maas, P. (1957) 'Ciris 434': *Maia* 9, 223.

(1966) *Greek Metre*[2]: Oxford (Trsl. by H. Lloyd-Jones from *Griechische Metrik* (= *Einl. in die Altertumsw.*, ed. A. Gercke & E. Norden, 1.7): Leipzig/Berlin 1923).

McKinney, N. P. See Peterson, G. E.

MacNeilage, P. F. & J. L. DeClerk (1969) 'On the motor control of co-articulation in CVC monosyllables': *JAcS* 45, 1217.

Maguinness, W. S. (1963) 'Petit plaidoyer pour la poésie trochaïque': *RCCM* 5, 209.

(1971) 'De numero dactylico quaestiunculae': *Romanitas* 9, 161.

Malmberg, B. (1955) 'The phonetic basis for syllable division': *SL* 9, 80 (Reprinted in Malmberg 1971).

(1971) *Phonétique générale et romane*: The Hague.

Malmberg, B. (ed.) (1968) *Manual of Phonetics*[2]: Amsterdam.

Malof, J. (1970) *A Manual of English Meters*: Bloomington.

Mańczak, W. (1968) 'Iambenkürzung im Lateinischen': *Glotta* 46, 137.

Margoliouth, D. S. (1911) *The Poetics of Aristotle*: London.

Marouzeau, J. (1954) 'Qu'est-ce que l'allongement "par position"?': *REL* 32, 100.

(1955) 'L'allongement dit "par position" dans la métrique latine': *REL* 33, 344.

Marouzeau, J. *Mélanges de philologie, littérature, et d'histoire anciennes offerts à J. Marouzeau*, 1948: Paris.

Martin, E. (1953) *Essai sur les rythmes de la chanson grecque antique*: Paris.

Martinet, A. (1948) 'Où en est la phonologie?': *Lingua* 1, 34.

(1952) 'Celtic lenition and Western Romance consonants': *Language* 28, 192.

(1954) 'Accents et tons': *Misc. Phon. II*: London, 13.

(1955) *Économie des changements phonétiques*: Berne.

(1960) *Éléments de linguistique générale*: Paris.

Master, A. (1925) 'Stress accent in modern Gujarati': *J. Bombay Br. RAS*, n.s. 1, 76.

Maurenbrecher, B. (1899) *Hiatus und Verschleifung im alten Latein*: Leipzig.

Mehrotra, R. C. (1965) 'Stress in Hindi': *IL* 26, 96.

Meillet, A. (1900) 'La déclinaison et l'accent d'intensité en perse': *JA*, 9 ser. 16, 254.

(1905) 'Sur l'accentuation grecque': *MSL* 13, 245.

(1923) *Les origines indo-européennes des mètres grecs*: Paris.

Merrifield, W. R. (1963) 'Palantla Chinantec syllable types': *Anthr. Ling.* 5.5, 1.

Mette, H. J. (1956) 'Die Struktur des ältesten daktylischen Hexameters': *Glotta* 35, 1.

Middleton, C. (1967) 'Nietzsche on Music and Metre': *Arion* 6, 58.

Miller, C. W. E. (1902) 'The relation of the rhythm of poetry to that of the spoken language with special reference to ancient Greek': *Studies in Honor of Basil L. Gildersleeve*: Baltimore, 497.

(1922) 'The pronunciation of Greek and Latin prose, or ictus, accent, and quantity in Greek and Latin prose and poetry': *TAPhA* 53, 169.

Minor, J. (1893) *Neuhochdeutsche Metrik*: Strassburg.

Mitchell, T. F. (1956) *An introduction to Egyptian colloquial Arabic*: London.

(1957) 'Long consonants in phonology and phonetics': *Studies in Linguistic Analysis* (Special vol. of The Philological Soc.): Oxford, 182.

(1960) 'Prominence and syllabication in Arabic': *BSOAS* 23, 369.

Miyaoka, O. (1971) 'On syllable modification and quantity in Yuk phonology': *IJAL* 37, 219.

Moore, C. H. (1924) 'Latin exercises from a Greek schoolroom': *CPh* 19, 322.

Mountford, J. F. (1929) 'Greek music in the papyri and inscriptions': in *New Chapters in Greek Literature*, 2nd ser., ed. J. U. Powell & E. A. Barber: Oxford, 146.

Mouraviev, S. N. (1972) 'The position of the accent in Greek words: a new statement': *CQ* 22, 113.

Murray, G. (1927) *The Classical Tradition in Poetry*: London.

Nagy, G. (1970a) *Greek Dialects and the transformation of an Indo-European process*: Cambridge, Mass.

(1970b) Monograph (unpub.) on Indo-European metrics.

Needler, G. H. (**1941**) *The Lone Shieling: Origin and authorship of the Blackwood 'Canadian Boat-Song'*: Toronto.

*Newman, P. (1972) 'Syllable weight as a phonological variable': mimeog. (To appear in *Studies in African Linguistics*: UCLA).

Newman, S. S. (1946) 'On the stress system of English': *Word* 2, 171.

Newton, B. E. (1969) 'Metre and stress in Greek': *Phoenix* 23, 359.

(1971) 'Ordering paradoxes in phonology': *JL* 7, 31.

(1972) *The Generative Interpretation of Dialect; A Study of Modern Greek Phonology*: Cambridge (*Studies in Linguistics*, vol. 8).

Nicholson, J. G. (1968) *Russian Normative Stress Notation*: Montreal.
  (1970) 'Problems of accent in the Eastern Slavic languages': in Léon,
  Faure & Rigault (ed.) 1970, 13.
Niedermann, M. (1908) 'Une loi rythmique en latin': *Mél. de linguistique
  offerts à F. de Saussure*: Paris, 43.
Nietzsche, F. W. (1912) *Philologica. II* (= *Werke*, Bd. xviii): *Unveröffent-
  lichtes zur Litteraturgeschichte, Rhetorik und Rhythmik*, ed. O. Crusius:
  Leipzig.
Nooteboom, S. G. (1971) Review of Heike 1969: *Lingua* 27, 282.
Norberg, D. (1965) 'La récitation du vers latin': *NPhM* 66, 496.
O'Connor, J. D. & J. L. M. Trim (1953) 'Vowel, consonant and syllable – a
  phonological definition': *Word* 9, 103.
O'Neill, E. G. (1939) 'The importance of final syllables in Greek verse':
  TAPhA 70, 256.
  (1942) 'The localization of metrical word-types in the Greek hexameter':
  YClS 8, 105.
Pace, G. B. (1961) 'The two domains: meter and rhythm': *PMLA* 76, 413.
Page, D. L. (1951) *A new chapter in the history of Greek tragedy*: Cambridge.
*Palmer, F. R. (ed.) (1970) *Prosodic Analysis*: London.
Palmer, L. R. (1957) 'Some observations on the language of linguistics':
  Studies presented to Joshua Whatmough on his 60th birthday (ed. E.
  Pulgram): The Hague, 187.
Park, B. A. (1968) *The quantitative experiments of the Renaissance and after
  as a problem in comparative metrics*: Dissertation Ph.D. Oklahoma.
Parker, L. P. E. (1958) 'Incidence of word-end in anapaestic paroemiacs':
  CQ 8, 82.
  (1965) 'A metrical problem' (review of Rossi 1963a): *CR* 15, 317.
  (1966) 'Porson's Law extended': *CQ* 16, 1.
  (1968) 'Split resolution in Greek dramatic lyric': *CQ* 18, 241.
  (1970) 'Greek Metric 1957–1970': *Lustrum* 15 (publ. 1972), 37.
Parry, M. (1930; 1932) 'Studies in the Epic technique of oral verse-making:
  I. Homer and Homeric style; II. The Homeric language as the language
  of an oral poetry': *HSPh* 41, 73; 43, 1 (Reprinted in Parry 1971, 266; 325).
  (1971) *The Making of Homeric Verse. The collected papers of Milman Parry*,
  ed. A. Parry: Oxford.
Pearl, O. M. & R. P. Winnington-Ingram (1965) 'A Michigan papyrus with
  musical notation': *JEA* 51, 179.
Perret, J. (1960) 'Un équivalent latin de la loi de Porson': *Hommage à
  Léon Hermann* (= *Coll. Latomus* 44): Brussels, 589.
  (1966) 'Au service des métriciens un nouvel instrument scientifique
  (À propos de: L. Nougaret, *Prosodie, métrique et vocabulaire. Analyse
  verbale comparée du De Signis et des Bucoliques*. 1966)': *REL* 44, 117.

Perusino, F. (1962) 'Tecnica e stile nel tetrametro trocaico di Menandro':
    RCCM 4, 45.

Peterson, G. E. & N. P. McKinney (1961) 'The measurement of speech
    power': *Phonetica* 7, 65.

Pickett, V. (1951) 'Nonphonemic stress: a problem in stress placement in
    Isthmus Zapotec': *Word* 7, 60.

Pighi, G. B. (1950) 'Lunghe irrazionali e abbreviazione giambica in latino':
    Rendiconti...Bologna, ser. 5, vol. iii, 133 (Reprinted in Pighi 1970).

    (1966) 'Inter legere et scandere plurimum interesse': *Latinitas* 14, 87
    (Reprinted in Pighi 1970).

    (1970) *Studi di ritmica e metrica*: Turin.

Pike, K. L. (1943) *Phonetics*: Ann Arbor.

    (1947) 'Grammatical prerequistes to phonemic analysis': *Word* 3, 155.

    (1948) *Tone Languages*: Ann Arbor.

    (1957) 'Abdominal pulse-types': *Language* 33, 30.

    (1967) *Language in relation to a unified theory of the structure of human
    behavior*[2]: The Hague.

    (1970) 'The role of nuclei of feet in the analysis of tone in Tibeto-Burman
    languages of Nepal': in Léon, Faure & Rigault (ed.) 1970, 153.

Pike, K. L. & W. Kindberg (1956) 'A problem in multiple stresses': *Word* 12,
    415.

Pipping, H. (1937) 'Zur homerischen Metrik: eine statistische Untersu-
    chung': *CHL* 9, 6.

Platnauer, M. (1951) *Latin Elegiac Verse*: Cambridge.

    (1960) 'Prodelision in Greek drama': *CQ* 10, 140.

Platt, A. (1899) 'Sophoclea': *CR* 13, 147.

Pöhlmann, E. (1960) *Griechische Musikfragmente*: Nürnberg.

    (1966) 'Der Peripatetiker Athenodor über Wortakzent und Melodiebildung
    im Hellenismus': *WS* 79, 201.

Pöhlmann, E. See also Seel, O.

Poetics. I/II (1961/1966) *Articles and Studies presented at the 1st/3rd Int.
    Conf. of work-in-progress devoted to problems of Poetics*, 1960/1964:
    Warsaw.

Pohlsander, H. A. (1964) *Metrical studies in the lyrics of Sophocles*: Leiden.

Poirot, J. (1906) 'Quantité et accent dynamique': *MSNH* 4, 363.

Polivanov, E. (1936) 'Zur Frage der Betonungsfunktionen': *TCLP* 6,
    75.

Popovich, H. & F. See Gudschinsky, S. C.

Popperwell, R. G. (1963) *The Pronunciation of Norwegian*: Cambridge.

Porson, R. (1802) *Euripidis Hecuba*[2]: Cambridge/London.

Porter, H. N. (1951) 'The early Greek hexameter': *YClS* 12, 1.

Postal, P. M. (1968) *Aspects of Phonological Theory*: New York.

Postgate, J. P. (1923) *Prosodia Latina: an introduction to classical Latin verse*: Oxford.

(1924) *A short guide to the accentuation of ancient Greek*: London.

Pound, E. (1951) *ABC of Reading*: London.

Pratidānam (1968) *Indian, Iranian and Indo-European studies presented to F. B. J. Kuiper on his 60th birthday*, ed. J. C. Heesterman et al: The Hague.

Prescott, H. W. (1907) 'Some phases of the relation of thought to verse in Plautus': *UCal Publs. in Cl. Phil.* 1, 205.

Pulgram, E. (1954) 'Accent and ictus in spoken and written Latin': *ZVS* 71, 218.

(1965) 'The accentuation of Greek loans in spoken and written Latin': *AJPh* 86, 138.

(1969) Review of Garde 1968: *Lingua* 23, 372.

(1970) *Syllable, Word, Nexus, Cursus*: The Hague.

Raven, D. S. (1962) *Greek Metre*: London.

(1965) *Latin Metre*: London.

Reese, G. (1941) *Music in the Middle Ages*: London.

Reibel, D. A. See Schane, S. A.

Reichling, A. J. B. N. (1935) *Het Woord*: Nijmegen.

Rheinach, T. (1894) 'La musique du nouvel hymne de Delphes': *BCH* 18, 363.

Rigault, A. (1962) 'Rôle de la fréquence, de l'intensité et de la durée vocaliques dans la perception de l'accent en français': *PICPhSc IV* (1961): The Hague, 735.

Ringgaard, K. (1963) 'The apocope of dissyllables', *Phonetica* 10, 222.

Rischel, J. (1964) 'Stress, juncture and syllabification in phonemic description': *PICL IX* (1962): The Hague, 85.

Robbins, F. E. (1961) 'Quiotepec Chinantec syllable patterning': *IJAL* 27, 237.

Roberts, E. W. (1968) *A theory of phonology and phonetics applied to the word in Welsh and English*: Dissertation Ph.D. Cambridge.

Robins, R. H. (1957) 'Aspects of prosodic analysis': *Proc. Univ. of Durham Philos. Soc.* 1, ser. B (Arts) i.

(1967) *A Short History of Linguistics*: London.

(1969) Review of Langendoen 1968: *Language* 45, 109.

Robinson, I. (1971) *Chaucer's Prosody*: Cambridge.

Rosetti, A. (1959) *Sur la théorie de la syllabe*: The Hague.

Rossi, L. E. (1963a) *Metrica e critica stilistica: Il termino 'ciclico' e l' ἀγωγή ritmica*: Rome.

(1963b) 'Anceps: vocale, sillaba, elemento': *RFIC* 91, 52.

(1968) 'La *pronuntiatio plena*: sinalefe in luogo d'elisione': *Omaggio a Eduard Fraenkel per i suoi ottant'anni*: Rome, 229.

Roussel, L. (1954) *Le vers grec ancien. Son harmonie, ses moyens d'expression*: Montpellier.

Rudmose-Brown, T. B. (1939) 'Some medieval Latin metres, their ancestry and progeny': *Hermathena* 53, 29.

Ruijgh, C. J. (1970) Review of P. Chantraine, *Dictionnaire étymologique de la langue grecque. I* (Paris 1968): *Lingua* 25, 302.

Ruipérez, M. S. (1955) 'Cantidad silábica y métrica estructural en griego antiguo': *Emerita* 23, 79.

(1956) 'Esquisse d'une histoire du vocalisme grec': *Word* 12, 67.

Rupprecht, K. (1949) *Abriss der griechischen Verslehre*: München.

Sachs, C. (1953) *Rhythm and Tempo*: London.

Sadeniemi, M. (1951) *Die Metrik des Kalevala-Verses* (= *Folklore Fellows Comns.* 139): Helsinki.

Safarewicz, J. (1936) *Études de phonétique et de métrique latines*: Wilno.

St. Clair, R. N. (1972) 'Compound phonological segments': *Lingua* 29, 120.

Sampson, G. (1970) 'On the need for a phonological base': *Language* 46, 586.

Samuels, M. L. (1972) *Linguistic Evolution, with special reference to English*: Cambridge (*Studies in Linguistics*, vol. 5).

Sauvegeot, A. (1951) *Esquisse de la langue hongroise*: Paris.

Sawashima, M. See Lieberman, P.

Schade, J. (1908) *De correptione Attica*: Greifswald.

Schane, S. A. & D. A. Reibel (ed.) (1969) *Modern studies in English*: Englewood Cliffs, N.J.

Schein, S. L. (1967) *The iambic trimeter in Aeschylus and Sophocles*: Dissertation Ph.D. Columbia.

Schmidt, J. H. H. (1872) *Griechische Metrik*: Leipzig.

Schmiel, R. C. (1968) *Rhythm and accent in Homer*: Dissertation Ph.D. Washington.

Schmitt, A. (1924) *Untersuchungen zur allgemeinen Akzentlehre*: Heidelberg.

(1953) *Musikalischer Akzent und antike Metrik*: Münster.

Schoell, F. (1876) 'De accentu linguae latinae: veterum grammaticorum testimonia': *Acta Soc. Philol. Lipsiensis* 6, 1.

Scholes, P. A. (1970) *The Oxford Companion to Music*[10]: London.

Schroeder, O. (1918) 'ΡΥΘΜΟΣ': *Hermes* 53, 324.

Schwyzer, E. (1931) 'Griechische Interjektionen und griechische Buchstabennamen auf -α': *ZVS* 58, 170.

Sebeok, T. A. (ed.) (1960) *Style in Language*: Cambridge, Mass.

(ed.) (1963) *Current Trends in Linguistics. I* (*Soviet & East European*): The Hague.

(ed.) (1966) *Selected writings of Gyula Laziczius*: The Hague.

Sedgwick, W. B. (1924) 'The origin of rhyme': *RBen* 36, 330.

Seel, O. & E. Pöhlmann (1959) 'Quantität und Wortakzent im Horazischen Sapphiker': *Philologus* 103, 237.

Seidler, A. (1812) Excursus: 'De dactylo et tribracho in quinta senarii iambici sede', in *De versibus dochmiacis tragicorum graecorum. II*: Leipzig.

Setti, A. (1963) 'Ictus e verso antico': *AMAT* 27, 133.

Shankweiler, D. P. See Liberman, A. M.

Sharma, D. D. (1971) *Syllabic structure of Hindi and Panjabi*: Chandigarh.

Sharp, A. E. (1954) 'A tonal analysis of the disyllabic noun in the Machame dialect of Chaga': *BSOAS* 16, 157.

(1960) 'The analysis of stress and juncture in English': *TPhS*, 104.

Shewring, W. H. (1933) 'Prose-rhythm: an apologia': *CQ* 27, 46.

Shipley, F. W. (1924) 'Hiatus, elision, caesura, in Virgil's hexameter': *TAPhA* 55, 137.

(1927) 'Carmina Epigraphica and some problems of the Latin hexameter': *PAPhA* 58, xxx.

(1938) 'Problems of the Latin hexameter': *TAPhA* 59, 134.

Shipp, G. P. (1972) *Studies in the language of Homer*[2]: Cambridge.

Siedow, G. A. (1911) *De elisionis aphaeresis hiatus usu in hexametris Latinis*: Greifswald.

Sievers, E. (1901) *Grundzüge der Phonetik*[5]: Leipzig.

Sigurd, B. (1955) 'Rank order of consonants established by distributional criteria': *SL* 9, 8.

Sivertsen, E. (1960) *Cockney Phonology*: Oslo.

Skimina, S. (1930) *État actuel des études sur le rythme de la prose grecque. II* (= *Eus* suppl. vol. ii): Lwów.

*Skutsch, F. (1913) 'Der lateinische Accent': *Glotta* 4, 187.

Skutsch, O. (1934) *Prosodische und metrische Gesetze der Iambenkürzung* (= *Forsch. z. gr. u. lat. Gramm.* 10): Göttingen.

(1964) 'Enniana VI': *CQ* 58, 85.

Smith, B. H. (1968) *Poetic Closure. A study of how poems end*: Chicago.

*Smith, G. G. (ed.) (1904) *Elizabethan Critical Essays*: Oxford.

Snell, B. (1962) *Griechische Metrik*[3]: Göttingen.

Sobolevskij, S. L. (1956) 'Заметки о греческом произношении на основании наблюдений над строением стиха в комедиях Аристофана и в трагедиях': *Академику В. В. Виноградову LX*: Moscow, 225.

(1964) 'Ad locutionem graecam cognoscendam quid conferat versuum structura?': *Eirene* 2, 43.

Soderberg, G. C. (1959) 'A typological study on the phonetic structure of English words with an instrumental-phonetic excursus on English stress': *Trav. de l'Inst. de Phon. de Lund* 1, 1.

384   *List of modern works cited*

*Sommer, B. A. (1970) 'An Australian language without CV syllables': *IJAL* 36, 57.

Sommer, F. (1909) 'Zur griechischen Poesie. 1: Die Positionsbildung bei Homer': *Glotta* 1, 145.

(1913) *Handbuch der lateinischen Laut- und Formenlehre²ᐟ³*: Heidelberg.

(1914) *Kritische Erläuterungen zur lateinischen Laut- und Formenlehre*: Heidelberg.

Sommerfelt, A. (1931) 'Sur l'importance générale de la syllabe': *TCLP* 4, 156.

(1933) 'Sur le rôle des éléments moteurs dans les changements phonétiques': *JPsych* 30, 321.

Sommerstein, A. H. (1971) *Phonological theory and ancient Greek*: Dissertation Ph.D. Cambridge (To appear as *The Sound Pattern of Greek*: Publ. of the Philological Society: Oxford).

Sonnenschein, E. A. (1911) 'The law of Breves Breviantes in the light of phonetics': *CPh* 6, 1.

(1925) *What is Rhythm?*: Oxford.

Soubiran, J. (1959) '*Intremere omnem* et *si bona norint*: Recherches sur l'accent de mot dans la clausule de l'hexamètre latin': *Pallas* 8, 23.

(1966a) *L'élision dans la poésie latine*: Paris.

(1966b) 'Ponctuation bucolique et liaison syllabique en grec et en latin': *Pallas* 13, 21.

(1969a) 'Les hexamètres spondaïques à quadrisyllabe final': *GIF* 21, 329.

(1969b) 'Pauses de sens et cohésion métrique entre les pieds médians de l'hexamètre latin': *Pallas* 16, 107.

(1971) Review of Drexler 1969: *Gnomon* 43, 408.

Sovijärvi, A. (1958) 'Vorläufige Messungsbetrachtungen über den Wortakzent der finnischen Hochsprache' (in Finnish with German summary): *Vir* 62, 351.

Spence, N. C. W. (1965) 'Quantity and quality in the vowel-system of vulgar Latin': *Word* 21, 1.

Spier, L. et al. (ed.) (1941) *Language, Culture and Personality: Essays in memory of Edward Sapir*: Menasha, Wis.

Stanford, W. B. (1968) 'On the pronunciation of the ancient Greek accents': *Didaskalos* 2.3, 148.

Stankiewicz, E. (**1960**) 'Linguistics and the study of poetic language': in Sebeok (ed.) 1960, 69.

Steblin-Kamenskij, M. I. (1960) 'The vowel system of modern Icelandic': *SL* 14, 35.

Stetson, R. H. (1945) *Bases of Phonology*: Oberlin, Ohio.

(**1951**) *Motor Phonetics*: Amsterdam.

Stevens, K. N. (1968) 'Speech movements and speech perception': *ZPhon* 21, 102.

Stifler, T. (**1924**) 'Das Wernickesche Gesetz und die bukolische Dihärese': *Philologus* 79, 323.

Strzelecki, L. (1938) *De Senecae trimetro iambico quaestiones selectae*: Kraków.

(1948) *De litterarum Romanorum nominibus*: Bratislava.

(1965) 'Über den Gebrauch des Daktylus im trochäischen Tetrameter bei Menander': in *Menanders Dyskolos als Zeugnis seiner Epoche* ed. F. Zucker (= Deut. Ak. d. Wiss. zu Berlin: *Schr. d. Sektion f. Altertumsw.* 50), 61.

Studdert-Kennedy, M. See Liberman, A. M.

Sturtevant, E. H. (1919) 'The coincidence of accent and ictus in Plautus and Terence': *CPh* 14, 234.

(1922) 'Syllabification and syllabic quantity in Greek and Latin': *TAPhA* 53, 35.

(1923) 'The ictus of classical verse': *AJPh* 44, 319.

(1924a) 'The doctrine of the caesura, a philological ghost': *AJPh* 45, 329.

(1924b) 'Accent and ictus in the Latin elegiac distich': *TAPhA* 55, 73.

(1940) *The Pronunciation of Greek and Latin*[2]: Philadelphia.

Sturtevant, E. H. & R. G. Kent (1915) 'Elision and hiatus in Latin prose and verse': *TAPhA* 46, 129.

Stutterheim, C. F. P. (1961) 'Poetry and prose, their interrelations and transitional forms': *Poetics I*: Warsaw, 225.

Sweet, H. (1891) *A New English Grammar. I*: Oxford.

(1906) *A Primer of Phonetics*[3]: Oxford.

Szemerényi, O. (1964) *Syncope in Greek and Indo-European and the nature of the Indo-European accent*: Naples.

Tamerle, E. (1936) *Der lateinische Vers ein akzentuierender Vers. I*: Innsbruck.

Taranovski, K. (1963) 'Metrics': in Sebeok (ed.) 1963, 192.

Tarnóczy, T. (1948) 'Resonance data concerning nasals, laterals and trills': *Word* 4, 71.

Thierfelder, A. (1928) 'Iktierung des Typus *facilius*': in Fraenkel 1928, 357.

Thompson, J. (1961) 'Linguistic structure and the poetic line': *Poetics I*: Warsaw, 167 (Reprinted in Freeman (ed.) 1970).

Thomson, W. (1923) *The Rhythm of Speech*: Glasgow.

(1926) *The Rhythm of Greek Verse*: Glasgow.

Thumb, A. (1912) *Handbook of the Modern Greek Vernacular*: Edinburgh. (Trsl. by S. Angus from *Hb. d. neugr. Volkssprache*[2]: Strassburg, 1910) (Also reprinted, with '*Language*' for '*Vernacular*': Chicago, 1964).

Timpanaro, S. (1965) '*Muta cum liquida* in poesia latina e nel latino volgare':
   RCCM 7, 1075.

Todd, O. J. (1942) 'Caesura rediviva': *CPh* 37, 22.

Tomás, N. (1963) *Manual de pronunciación española*[11]: Madrid.

Torresin, G. (1966) 'Non legge di Havet ma legge di Porson': *RFIC* 94, 184.

Trager, G. L. (1941) 'The theory of accentual systems': in Spier (ed.)
   1941, 131.

Trager, G. L. & B. Bloch (1941) 'The syllabic phonemes of English':
   Language 17, 223.

Trager, G. L. See also Bloch, B.

Trim, J. L. M. See O'Connor, J. D.

Trnka, B. (1966) *A phonological analysis of present-day standard English*[2]:
   Tokyo.

Trombetti, A. *Scritti in onore di Alfredo Trombetti*, 1966: Milan.

Tronskij, I. M. (1962) Древнегреческое Ударение: Moscow/Leningrad.

Trost, P. (1964) 'Funktion des Wortakzents': *TLP* 1, 125.

Trubetzkoy, N. S. (1926) 'Die "Kurzen" und "Geminierten" Konsonanten
   der awaroandischen Sprachen': *Caucasica* 3, 7.

   (1931) 'Die Konsonantensysteme der ostkaukasischen Sprachen': *Caucasica* 8, 1.

   (1935/1968) *Introduction to the principles of phonological descriptions*:
   The Hague (ed. H. Bluhme, trsl. by L. A. Murray from *Anleitung zu
   phonologischen Beschreibungen*: Prague).

   (1938) 'Die phonologischen Grundlagen der sogenannten Quantität in
   den verschiedenen Sprachen': *Scritti...Trombetti*, 155.

   (1939/1969) *Principles of Phonology*: Berkeley (Trsl. by C. A. M. Baltaxe
   from *Grundzüge der Phonologie = TCLP* 7).

Truby, H. M. (1964) 'Pleniphonetic transcription in phonetic analysis':
   PICL IX (1962): The Hague, 101.

*Tucker, A. N. (1962) 'The syllable in Luganda: a prosodic approach':
   JAfrL 1, 122.

Tucker, R. W. (1965) 'Accentuation before enclitics in Latin': *TAPhA* 96,
   449.

Turner, R. L. (1915) 'A note on the word-accent in Greek music': *CR* 29,
   195.

   (1921) 'Gujarati phonology': *JRAS*, 329; 505.

   (1970) 'Early shortening of geminates with compensatory lengthening in
   Indo-Aryan': *BSOAS* 33, 171.

Twaddell, W. F. (1953) 'Stetson's model and the "supra-segmental"
   phonemes': *Language* 29, 415.

Uhlig, G. (ed.) (1883) *Dionysius Thrax, Ars Grammatica; Supplementa Artis
   Dionysianae vetusta* (= *GG* 1.i): Leipzig (Reprinted Hildesheim, 1965).

Ultan, R. (1969) 'Some general characteristics of interrogative systems': *Working Papers on Language Universals* (Stanford) 1, 41.

Väänänen, V. (1959) *Le latin vulgaire des inscriptions pompéiennes* (= *ADAW* 1958.3): Berlin.

Vachek, J. (1966) *The Linguistic School of Prague*: Bloomington.

(1968) *Dynamika fonologického systému současné spisovné češtiny* (English summary 'The dynamism of the phonological system of present-day standard Czech'): Prague.

Vandvik, E. (1937) *Rhythmus und Metrum: Akzent und Iktus: SO* Supp. viii.

Vanvik, A. (1961) *On stress in present-day English* (Univ. i Bergen: *Årbok* 1960 iii, Hum. Ser. 3): Bergen.

Varma, S. (1929) *Critical studies in the phonetic observations of Indian grammarians*: London.

Vendryes, J. (1902) *Recherches sur l'histoire et les effets de l'intensité initiale en latin*: Paris.

(1929) *Traité d'accentuation grecque*²: Paris.

(1936) 'Phonologie et langue poétique'; *PICPhSc II* (1935), 105: Cambridge.

Veremans, J. (1969) 'Évolution historique de la structure verbale du deuxième hémistiche du pentamètre latin': *Hommages à M. Renard. I* (= *Coll. Latomus* 101): Brussels, 758.

Vietor, W. (1894) *Elemente der Phonetik*³: Leipzig.

Voegelin, C. F. (1935) *Tübatulabal Grammar: UCal Publs. in Amer. Arch. & Ethn.* 34.2.

Vogt, H. (1958) 'Structure phonémique du géorgien': *NTS* 18, 5.

Vollmer, F. (1917a) 'Iambenkürzung in Hexametern': *Glotta* 8, 130.

(1917b) 'Kürzung durch Tonanschluss im alten Latein': *SBAW* 1917, 9 Abh.

Wackernagel, J. (1925) Review of Postgate 1924: *IF* 43 Anz., 48.

Wagener, C. (1904) 'Betonung der mit que, ve, ne zusammengesetzten Wörter im Lateinischen': *Neue Philol. Rundschau*, 505.

Wahlström, E. (1970) *Accentual responsion in Greek strophic poetry: CHL* 47.

Waldo, G. S. (1968) *Stress the right syllable: The accentuation of English words with special reference to their structure (morphology)*: prelim. edn (mimeog.): Edmonton, Alb.

Waltz, R. (1948) ''Ρυθμός et numerus': *REL* 26, 109.

Wang, W. S.-Y. (1962) 'Stress in English': *LL* 12, 69.

(1967) 'Phonological features of tone': *IJAL* 33, 93.

Warburton, I. P. (1970a) 'Rules of accentuation in classical and modern Greek': *Glotta* 48, 107.

(1970b) *On the Verb in Modern Greek* (Indiana Univ. Publs: Language Science Monogs., vol. 4): Bloomington/The Hague.

Ward, I. C. See Westermann.

Ward, R. L. (1946) 'The loss of final consonants in Greek': *Language* 22, 102.

Warren, A. See Wellek, R.

Waterson, N. (1956) 'Some aspects of the phonology of the nominal forms of the Turkish word': *BSOAS* 18, 578.

Wathelet, P. (1966) 'La coupe syllabique et les liquides voyelles dans la tradition formulaire de l'épopée grecque': in Lebrun (ed.) 1966, 145.

Watkins, C. (1963) 'Indo-European metrics and archaic Irish verse': *Celtica* 6, 194.

(1970) 'A further remark on Lachmann's Law': *HSPh* 74, 55.

Watson, J. S. (1861) *The Life of Richard Porson, M.A.*: London.

Weil, G. (1960) '*Arūḍ*': in *The Encyclopaedia of Islam*, new edn, ed. H. A. R. Gibb et al: Leiden/London, vol. i, 667.

Weinreich, U., W. Labov & M. I. Herzog (1968) 'Empirical foundations for a theory of language change': in *Directions for Historical Linguistics*, ed. W. P. Lehmann & Y. Malkiel: Austin, 95.

Weinrich, H. (1958) *Phonologische Studien zur romanischen Sprachgeschichte* (= *Forsch. z. Rom. Philol.* 6): Münster.

Wellek, R. & A. Warren (1966) *Theory of Literature*[3]: London.

Wellesz, E. J. (1961) *A History of Byzantine Music and Hymnography*[2]: Oxford.

Werner, J. (1892) *Quaestiones Babrianae* (= *Berl. St. f. cl. Phil. und Arch.* xiv.2).

West, M. L. (1970) 'A new approach to Greek prosody': *Glotta* 48, 185.

Westermann, D. & I. C. Ward (1949) *Practical phonetics for students of African languages*: London.

Westphal, R. (1883) *Aristoxenus von Tarent: Melik und Rhythmik des classischen Hellenentums. I*: Leipzig (Reprinted Hildesheim, 1965).

Wheeler, B. I. (1885) *Der griechische Nominalakzent*: Strassburg.

White, J. W. (1912) *The Verse of Greek Comedy*: London.

Whitteridge, D. See Draper, M. H.; Ladefoged, P.

Wilamowitz-Moellendorff, U. von (1924) *Hellenistische Dichtung in der Zeit des Kallimachos*: Berlin.

*Wilkinson, G. A. (1948) 'The trisyllabic ending of the pentameter: its treatment by Tibullus, Propertius, and Martial': *CQ* 42, 68.

Wilkinson, L. P. (1940) 'The Augustan rules for dactylic verse': *CQ* 34, 30.

(1963) *Golden Latin Artistry*: Cambridge.

*Williams, C. F. A. (1911) *The Aristoxenian theory of musical rhythm*: Cambridge.

**Williams, G. (1970) 'Eduard Fraenkel 1888–1970': *PBA* 56, 415.

Williams, R. D. (1950) 'The effect of elided -*que* on word accent in the hexameter': *PCA* 47, 31 (summary).

Wilson, K. M. (1929) *The real rhythm in English poetry*: Aberdeen.

Wimsatt, W. K. & M. C. Beardsley (1959) 'The concept of meter: an exercise in abstraction': *PMLA* 74.2, 585.

Winnington-Ingram, R. P. (1955) 'Fragments of unknown Greek tragic texts with musical notation. II: The music': *SO* 31, 29.

  (1958) 'Ancient Greek music. 1932–1957': *Lustrum* 3, 5.

Winnington-Ingram, R. P. See also Pearl, O. M.

Witkowski, S. (1893) 'Observationes metricae ad Herodam': in *Analecta Graeco-Latina philologis Vindobonae congregatis*: Kraków, 1.

Witte, K. (1914) 'Porsons Gesetz': *Hermes* 49, 229.

Woo, N. H. (1969) *Prosody and Phonology*: Dissertation Ph.D. MIT.

Worth, D. S. (1968) 'Grammatical function and Russian stress': *Language* 44, 784.

Wyatt, W. F. (1966) Review of Allen 1965: *Language* 42, 664.

  (1969) *Metrical lengthening in Homer*: Rome.

  (1970) *Indo-European /a/*: Philadelphia.

Young, D. (1967) 'Never blotted a line? Formula and premeditation in Homer and Hesiod': *Arion* 6, 279 (Reprinted in *Essays on Classical Literature*, ed. N. Rudd: Cambridge, 1972).

Zander, K. M. (1910) *Eurythmia vel compositio rythmica prosae antiquae. I: Eurythmia Demosthenis*: Leipzig.

Zieliński, T. (1925) *Tragodoumenon libri tres*: Kraków.

Zirin, R. A. (1970) *The phonological basis of Latin prosody*: The Hague.

Žirmunskij, V. (1966) *Introduction to Metrics* (Trsl. by C. F. Brown): The Hague.

Index

accent, 3, 11, 20, 57, 86–95 (*see also* Greek accent; Latin accent)
  dynamic, 81, 86 (*see also* stress)
  melodic, 3–5, 84–6 (*see also* pitch)
  secondary, 89–90
  Arabic, 156–8, 165
  English, 51, 57–8, 155–6, 191–9 (*see also* stress)
  Indo-Aryan, 52, 75, 93, 157–8, 270
  Norwegian, 233, 247–8, 251–2
  Serbo-Croat, 247
  Vedic, 230–1, 239–40, 243, 245–7, 252; *svarita*, 233–4
accentual verse, 102, 188
  and Latin Sapphic, 348–51
affricates (English), 193
amplitude: *see* stress
anaclasis, 109
anapaest
  'cyclic', 255
  in resolution, 330–2
anapaestics, 299, 316, 332–3
aperture, 38–40, 43, 69, 71, 135–8, 209–10
aphaeresis: *see* prodelision
apocope: *see* elision
appositive, 114, 287–8, 331–2 (*see also* enclitic; proclitic; prepositive; post-positive)
arrest (of syllable), 42–4, 62–8, 71–2, 79–80, chs 10, 13 *passim*
arsis/thesis, 100, 122–3, 275, 278–9, 342 (*see also* strong/weak position)
article, 23–5
aspiration, 3–5, 9–11
  Latin *h*, 148
  Greek ', 229

Babrius: *see* choliambic
Behaghel's Law, 119
breathing: *see* aspiration
brevis brevians: *see* iambic shortening
brevis in longo: *see* indifference
bridge, 108, 307 (*see also* Porson's Law)
  Hermann's, 118

caesura, 26, 108, 114–22, 313, 319–21

catalexis, 298–9, 301–3
chest-pulse, 12, 41–5, 78 (*see also* syllable, phonetic definition, motor)
choliambic, 206, 267, 299–301
clause, 20
climax, 119
clitic, 87, 114 (*see also* enclitic; proclitic)
clusters (strong/weak), 51
cohesion (of verse), 25, 113, 116
colon, 13, 116–20
compensatory lengthening, 52–3
competence: *see* performance
concord (vs discord, in poetry), 111, 261, 351–2
  in Latin hexameter, 138–9, 154, 190, 337–8
  in Latin pentameter, 186–7
  in Latin scenic verse, 153–4, 166–8, 190
consonant sequences, 28–30, 43–4
  in Greek, 208–22
  in Latin, 135–41
consonant/vowel dichotomy, 32–6, 42
contoid, 33, 35
contonation, 234 (*see also* Greek accent, rules of incidence)
contraction
  junctural, 143–8, 228
  metrical, 60–1, 162–4, 166, 255–8
contrast, 6, 89 (*see also* accent)
correptio Attica, 211–13, 217–19 (*see also* plosive + liquid/nasal)
correptio epica, 224–5, 290
counterpoint, 111–12, 338–9
crasis, 228
culmination, 86–7 (*see also* accent)
cursus, 116

dactylo-epitrites, 314–15
demarcation, 87 (*see also* accent)
deviation, 108–9, 110–12 (*see also* poetry, norm vs variant)
diaeresis, 114, 121 (*see also* caesura)
  bucolic, 116, 224, 287, 291, 336–7
diectasis, 258
digamma, 208, 214–15, 220–2, 224

diphthongs, 49, 134, 185, 207, 238
distinctiveness, 4, 6, 10, 87–9, 92 (*see also* accent)
disyllables, 178–88
duration, 6, 12, 46–50, 55–61, 63–4, 72, 74, 97–9 (*see also* length)

elision, 4, 113, 116, 121–2, 314
    in Greek, 226–7; and Porson's Law, 311
    in Latin, 142–50
emphasis, 95 (*see also* stress)
enclitic, 24–6, 87, 310 (*see also* Greek accent; Latin accent)
enjambment, 113–15, 120–1
episynaloephe, 121, 297
explanation (vs formulation), 18–19

ƒ + liquid, 137, 141
foot
    metrical, 61, 122–5
    phonetic, 41, 78
formulae (in poetry), 13–14, 257–8
fortis/lenis vowels, 192–7
frequency, 74, 83 (*see also* pitch)

gemination: *see* length, of consonants
gesture, 77–8, 100
glides, 224–6
glottal
    constriction, 91
    plosion, 79
    reinforcement, 58
grammar
    relevance to phonology, 17–26, 82, 89, 92
    transformational-generative, 17–19, 196
Grassmann's Law, 9
Greek accent (*see also* accent, melodic; intonation; pitch)
    Aeolic, 238–9, 256
    change to dynamic, 268–70
    circumflex, 234–5
    correlations in verse, 261–8
    diphthongs (final), 238
    enclitics, 240–4, 246, 249–51, 271
    epectasis, 240–1, 250
    'final trochee', 237, 240, 263
    grave, 244–8, 269–70
    Henninism, 271–4, 281–2, 344
    Homeric, 242–3
    interrogatives, 251–3
    loan-words to and from Latin, 260–1, 264–5
    'middle', 253–4
    musical evidence, 231–4, 247, 270–1
    negatives, 253

proclitics, 249–51
rules of incidence, 18–20, 236–53
synenclisis, 244
typology, 91–3, 230–6
vocatives, 252–3

h: *see* aspiration
heavy/light syllables, 53–65 (*see also* quantity)
heterodyne/homodyne, 261
hexameter
    English: Elizabethan, 351–2; later, 356–9
    German, 353–6
    Greek, 113, 116, 255–8, 286–92, 301–4
    Latin, 111–12, 116–17, 335–59; *carmina epigraphica*, 346–7
hiatus, 68–9, 113, 117, 142, 224–5
'hidden quantity', 141 (*see also* hyper-characterization)
hypercharacterization, 66–7, 117
    in Greek, 217, 222–3, 290
    in Latin, 141, 157–8, 176–7, 183

iambic shortening, 113, 179–85, 191–9
iambic trimeter, 304–14 (*see also* Porson's Law)
    bisected, 121, 311
ictus, 99, 153, 276–9, 341–6
    Bentley on, 342–4
indifference
    at end of line, 56, 115, 130–1, 205–7, 217, 283, 296–304, 336
    at caesura ?, 313
intonation, 3, 6, 12, 20, 85, 94
    Greek, 248–9, 251–3
isochrony, 99, 124 (*see also* duration)

juncture, 4, 6, 11, 20, 22–3, 32, 58, 71, 113, 115–17 (*see also* morph(eme); word)
    and quantity: in Greek, 209, 216–22; in Latin, 139–41
    of vowels: in Greek, 224–9; in Latin, 142–50

kinaesthetic perception, 37, 76–8, 100, 191–2

Lachmann's Law, 18–19
Latin accent, 51, 57, 93, 111, 151–91 (*see also* accent, dynamic; stress)
    in elision, 159–61
    enclitics, 158–61, 178
    fácilius, 188–90
    final, 186–8

parallels with English, 51, 57–8, 155–6, 191–9
rules of incidence, 155–61; reformulations, 161–91
secondary, 154, 181, 188–91
syntactical, 154, 160, 168–9
laxing, 66, 173–4, 256
length
of vowels, 3–5, 46–9; in Greek, 207; in Latin, 131–4; in motor terms, 62–6; under stress, 80–2, 169, 171, 174, 345
of consonants, 49–50; under stress, 80–1, 169, 269
lexeme, 24 (*see also* word)
line, 113–14, 120
end of, 106, 110, 120 (*see also* indifference)
liquids and nasals, 33, 35, 43, 69, 84, 211, 242, 317, 323–4, 326, 331 (*see also* plosive + liquid/nasal)
syllabic, 215, 218, 242
long components, 7–9 (*see also* prosody, in phonology)
long diphthongs, 67, 223–5, 290
loudness, 6, 74, 76 (*see also* stress)

marginal (vs nuclear) function, 33, 35, 38–9, 44
mātrā, 48–9, 59, 61
matrix (of stress), 163–70, 191–9, 318–34
metre; metrical pattern, 12–16, 103–25
metrics: relation to linguistics/phonetics, 15–16
modulation, 74, 91 (*see also* pitch; stress)
monosyllables, 50–1, 129–31, 177–8, 203, 283, 289, 294, 305, 307
mora, 19, 59, 92–3, 122–3, 153, 161–3, 235, 256–7 (*see also* Greek accent, rules of incidence)
morph(eme), 20, 22–3, 32, 71
motor control, 72 (*see also* syllable)

Naeke's Law, 109, 291
and Latin, 336
nasals, 69, 84 (*see also* liquids and nasals; plosive + liquid/nasal)
nasalized vowels (in juncture), 142, 147, 149
nexus, 24
Nonnus, 268, 291
nuclear: *see* marginal

oral composition, 13–14
orthography, 17, 29–30
Osthoff's Law, 66–7, 222–3

overlong syllables: *see* hypercharacterization

pattern, 101–2
pause, 55–6, 67–8, 115–17, 121, 130–1, 135, 186, 204–8, 227–8, 248–9, 297
and Porson's Law, 305, 310
pentameter, 120, 186–8, 205, 298–9
performance
vs competence, 19–20, 44, 73
of poetry, 105, 109–10, 112, 115, 150
phoneme; phonematic element, 8
phrase, 20
pitch, 3, 12, 74–6, 83–5, 94–5 (*see also* accent, melodic; Greek accent)
plosive + liquid/nasal, 57–8, 69–71, 137–41, 210–13, 217–19
poetry
levels of description, 104–5
norm vs variant, 106–12
relation to language, 12–16
Porson's Law, 26, 108, 226, 304–12, 314
and comedy, 311–12
and Latin, 335–6
position, length by, 53–4
postpositive, 120, 289, 310 (*see also* enclitic)
preposition; prepositive, 25–6, 120, 289 (*see also* proclitic)
proclitic, 24–6, 87, 120, 287–8, 307
prodelision, 148–9, 227–8
pronouns, 287
prosody
in metrics, 5–6, 12–16
in phonology, 3–12

quality (of vowels as feature of length), 46–7, 63, 132–3
quantitative verse, 100–1, 183–4, 276, 304, 339–40
quantity (of syllables), 5, 11, 20, 50–62, 64–73
in motor terms, 64–8, 71–2
$\Sigma = \Sigma\Sigma$, 162–9, 171, 235–6, 255–9 (*see also* contraction; resolution)
in Greek, 203–22
in Latin, 129–31, 135–41

recession: *see* Greek accent, rules of incidence
release (of syllable), 42–4, 62, 68–72, chs 10, 13 *passim*
resolution, 60–1
in Greek: anapaestics, 333; comedy, 329–30; dactylics, 332; Euripides,

325–7; first foot, 327–9; iambics and trochaics, 205, 316–32
in Latin, 166–9, 199
retroflexion, 9, 11, 25
rhyme, 188, 345
rhythm, xii, 96–102

s + plosive, 137, 139–40, 216
sandhi: *see* juncture
Sapphic, 109, 347–51
and Horace, 348–9
Saturnian, 113
scanning, 112, 125, 340–6
scazon: *see* choliambic
Schallfülle: *see* sonority
semivowels, 33–5, 70 (*see also* digamma)
sentence, 20
sonants, 222–3
sonority, 38–9
'split anapaest' rule, 167–9, 331–2
spondee, 123, 278
Stetson: *see* syllable, phonetic definition, motor
stress, 6, 12, 17, 74–82, 94–5, 99–101 (*see also* accent, dynamic; Greek accent, change to dynamic; Latin accent; matrix)
disyllabic, 170–86, 188–99
motor definition, 76–80
'staccato' mode, 80–1, 169–70, 185, 191–9
in Greek, 260–334
as element of melodic accent, 260–8
as accentual basis, 268–71
as non-accentual feature, 217, 274–334; metrical evidence, 279–334; musical evidence, 278–9, 294–5
disyllabic, 316–33 (*see also* resolution)
secondary, 293, 321–5
of molossi, 284–5, 289–92
of spondaic(-ending) words, 284–92
summary of rules, 333–4
strong/weak position (in foot), 60–1, 277 (*see also* arsis/thesis)
stylization, 12–13, 103–4

suprasegmental, xii, 7–8 (*see also* prosody, in phonology)
svarita: *see* accent, Vedic
syllabification, 20–1, 28–32, 43–4, 68 (*see also* syllable)
in English, 193, 196–7
in Greek, 203–22
in Latin, 129–30, 135–41
syllable, 8, 12, 27, 78
phonetic definition, 31–45; acoustic, 38–9; articulatory, 39–40; motor, 40–5; 72–3; respiratory, 38
phonological (phonotactic) definition, 27–31, 35
synaeresis, 228
synaloephe, 143, 150
synaphea, 113, 116, 206
syncopation, 111
synizesis, 146–7, 227–8

tenseness/laxness, 47–8, 50, 57–8, 63–4, 82 (*see also* length)
tension (in poetry), 110–12, 338
tone, 84, 92, 94 (*see also* pitch)
transitions, 21, 49, 81, 197
trochaic tetrameter, 314, 327–8

Vendryes' Law, 204, 211, 239, 263
verse: *see* line; poetry
versification, 5, 12 (*see also* prosody, in metrics)
vocalis ante vocalem corripitur, 142–3 (*see also* correptio epica*)
vocoid, 33, 35
vowel/consonant: *see* consonant/vowel dichotomy
vowel harmony, 7–8

weakening (of vowels), 51–2, 93, 133–4, 194 (*see also* laxing)
Wernicke's Law, 289–90
Wheeler's Law, 204, 239
word, 4–5, 8, 10–11, 20, 22–6
writing, 13–14

zeugma: *see* bridge